Facing the Limits of the Law

Erik Claes · Wouter Devroe
Bert Keirsbilck (Eds.)

Facing the Limits of the Law

Springer

Professor Erik Claes
Professor Wouter Devroe
Bert Keirsbilck
Katholieke Universiteit Leuven
Faculty of Law
Tiensestraat 41
3000 Leuven
Belgium
erik.claes@law.kuleuven.be
wouter.devroe@law.kuleuven.be
bert.keirsbilck@law.kuleuven.be

ISBN 978-3-540-79855-2 e-ISBN 978-3-540-79856-9

DOI 10.1007/978-3-540-79856-9

Library of Congress Control Number: 2008942778

Printed on acid-free paper

9 8 7 6 5 4 3 2 1

springer.com

Preface

Facing the Limits of the Law is the outcome of a research project that we launched in Spring 2005 at the Faculty of Law of the University of Leuven. We invited legal researchers and criminologists, trained in a diversity of (legal) disciplines, to share their respective research interests, to discuss their research topics, hypotheses, and results. Time, openness, and a change towards a more discursive research culture was needed, in order to break down the disciplinary walls that often separate legal researchers from each other and from criminologists.

Because common research involving a variety of legal fields and disciplines requires a common language and a common lens from which legal reality in all its diversity can be interpreted, we first developed a substantial working paper, subsequently commented on by the different contributors during a number of research seminars held in Leuven in 2005, and ultimately published (in Dutch, in *Rechtskundig Weekblad* 2005-2006, 1201-1217). "The Limits of the Law (Introduction)" presents a non-exhaustive typology of the limits of the law 'from the inside out', that is, starting from a broad understanding of the main functions and characteristics of late–modern law in the tradition of the rule of law. It offers a conceptual 'umbrella' and a common frame of reference from which the participants could borrow concepts and methodology, allowing them to compose a first abstract focusing on the types of limits of the law in their research field.

Subsequently, we organised a series of seminars during which the abstracts were collectively discussed by all the participants. The discussions helped participants in refining their research questions and methodology, but also in discovering that they were engaged in a common research enterprise. Then, during a research weekend in September 2006, all participants presented and discussed their draft papers on the limits of the law in their respective research fields. Afterwards, we summarised the comments and recommendations and communicated them to the contributors in order to finalise their individual papers.

It is important to stress that most of the chapters of *Facing the Limits of the Law* result from these series of intense closed and open research seminars held in Leuven, thereby guaranteeing integrated and peer–reviewed research. A few experts joined the project at a later stage.

Finally, we tried to do justice to the added value of each contribution to the project as a whole. When reading "Facing the Limits of the Law (Conclusion)", the reader will discover how the separate chapters contributed impressively to refining and improving the conceptual framework within which the project was started.

Leuven, September 2008

Erik Claes
Bert Keirsbilck
Wouter Devroe

Acknowledgements

We would like to thank the contributors of this volume, especially those who challenged our ideas in the first hours of the 'limits of the law' project: Dr. Tom Daems, Professor René Foqué, Dr. David Haljan, Professor Walter van Gerven, Professor Geertrui Van Overwalle, and Drs. Mathieu van Putten. We would also like to thank Professor John Bell (Cambridge) for commenting on an early draft of the introductory chapter. And finally, editing a book of this length was not possible without the language review by Dr. David Haljan and the valuable editing support of Mrs Betty Vanden Bavière.

Table of Contents

List of Tables and Figures

Tables

Figures

Chapter 1 – The Limits of the Law (Introduction)

Erik Claes, Wouter Devroe and Bert Keirsbilck

1 Introduction

At the beginning of his well–known book, *Law's Empire*, Ronald Dworkin writes: "We live in and by the law. It makes us what we are: citizens and employees and doctors and spouses and people who own things."[1] Dworkin still appears to believe in the all–embracing power of law to rule human behaviour and affairs in the greatest of detail. *Law's Empire* is a vigorous plea in favour of the potential of law, regulation, and adjudication to govern institutional behaviour and the lives of so many people according to the principles of justice and fairness. Dworkin's legal optimism, notwithstanding its argumentative strength, undoubtedly runs counter to a widespread awareness of many contemporary lawyers that law often falls short in meeting the societal expectations which are projected on it. Although it still seems as if society reposes confidence in lawyers' and judges' skills to solve through law the problems of the world, many lawyers, judges, legal scholars and citizens often no longer have an unbounded trust in the potential of law to govern society in a just and fair way. They often experience the 'limits of the law', as they are confronted with striking inadequacies in their legal toolbox, with inner inconsistencies of the law, with problems of enforcement and obedience, with undesired side–effects, and so on.

Preoccupation with legal shortcomings and with issues of adequate implementation of existing legal frameworks has of course always been the core business of legal practice and doctrine. But the contemporary experience of law's limits seems to be of another, more complex nature, which raises more fundamental questions relating the role of the law in contemporary societies. One of the basic intuitions underpinning *Facing the Limits of the Law*, is that a piece–meal improvement of the relevant legislation and case–law will not in itself be able to restore trust in the potential of the law. Our unease with law's limits surely calls for appropriate remedies. Yet such strategies cannot be found, as long as there is no clear insight into what kinds of fundamental shortcomings legal practitioners face throughout their areas of law. Put differently, we need to spell out more analytically different types of limits of the law, through a variety of legal disciplines, before we can justifiably deal with the limits of the law.

The second intuition underpinning the following chapters of *Facing the Limits of the Law* is of a more sociological kind. It comes down to the idea that our con-

---

1 R. Dworkin, *Law's Empire* (London: Fontana Press, 1986) vii.

temporary preoccupation with law's limits is not an isolated phenomenon, as it is embedded in broader cultural transformations characteristic for late–modern societies. By the term 'late–modern', reference is made to the predicament of our contemporary world in which the key–ideas of the Enlightenment (such as the belief in individual fulfilment, in the progress of science and technology, or in the regulatory capacities of bureaucratic institutions), though still informing the design of our public and private daily lives, are experienced as deeply problematic. Hence, a better understanding of the late–modern context promises to give us a more profound understanding of our unease with contemporary law.

Given the foregoing intuitions underpinning *Facing the Limits of the Law*, three research questions determine the content of this book.

- What types of limits of the law can be mapped throughout a variety of legal disciplines? How to provide in a conceptual framework that enables and structures such a mapping?
- What are the important social and cultural transformations responsible for our preoccupation with the limits of the law? And how might a better understanding of these broader trends help elucidating this experience of limits in distinct areas of the law?
- How can we deal with those limits of the law in a justifiable way?

While the second and the third research question are addressed more systematically in the final chapter of this book, this introductory chapter focuses on the first research question. The reader will discover a broad conceptual framework for mapping types of limits of the law[2], which are used and refined in the subsequent chapters throughout an extensive range of areas of law.[3] The introductory chapter, and with it the whole volume, assumes that the analysis of law's functions will help to map (types of) limits of the law (section 2)[4] which, in a further phase, can be further developed through an analysis of the characteristics of the law

---

2 In this respect *Facing the Limits of the Law* differs from comparable literature that often uses 'limits of the law' as a suggestive metaphor. See *e.g.*, H. Zeisel and E.H. Levi (eds.), *The Limits of Law Enforcement* (Chicago: University of Chicago Press, 1982).

3 Compare, existing literature on limits of law which mostly deals with limits of one particular area of the law. See *e.g.*, P.C. Yeager, *The Limits of Law: the Public Regulation of Private Pollution* (Cambridge: Cambridge University Press, 1991); B. Hepple and E. M. Szyszczak (eds.), *Discrimination: the Limits of the Law* (London: Mansell, 1992); M. King and J. Trowell, *Children's Welfare and the Law: the Limits of Legal Intervention* (Beverly Hills, Calif.: Sage, 1992); T.T. Ziamou, *Rulemaking, Participation and the Limits of Public Law in the USA and Europe* (Aldershot: Ashgate, 2001).

4 It is fair to say that most books on 'limits of the law' hitherto published deal predominantly – though not explicitly – with limits of law's function of regulation and/or dispute resolution. A popular topic is *e.g.* the limited capacity of law to respond effectively to mass crimes, whereas other publications concern the structural limits of law in efficiently regulating micro relationships, *e.g.* the behaviour of neighbours over a nuisance (see *e.g.*, R.C. Ellickson, *Order Without Law: How Neighbors Settle Disputes* (Cambridge: Harvard University Press, 1991), or land rights (*e.g.* P.C. Yeager, *l.c.*) or the allocation of resources (see *e.g.*, N.K. Komesar, *Law's Limits: The Rule of Law and the Supply and Demand of Rights* (Cambridge: Cambridge University Press, 2001)). Publications dealing with limits to law's *symbolic* capacity or to law's function of *providing for legal protection* are far less common.

(section 3). Accordingly, the first research question can be reformulated as follows: what characteristics of the law restrain law's ability to perform its most basic functions?

Before fleshing out the conceptual framework underlying the enterprise of *Facing the Limits of the Law*, it is important to note that the whole project is undertaken from a participant's perspective on the law, and not from an external point of view.[5] *Facing the Limits of the Law* identifies the limits of the law which legal experts and practitioners experience in their daily legal practice. Thus, our understanding of the law and its limits will not be purely neutral: "it tries to grasp the [...] character of our legal practice by joining that practice and struggling with the issues of soundness participants face."[6] Moreover, *Facing the Limits of the Law* departs from lawyers and citizens' acquaintance with the law as it is embedded in the tradition of the *Rechtsstaat* and the rule of law. This is not to say that our analysis of the limits of the law is only restricted to (branches of) national State law. It also addresses issues in European and international law against the general background of general principles, core values, and aspirations underpinning the traditions of *Rechtsstaat* and the rule of law.

In this respect, *Facing the Limits of the Law* largely diverges from existing literature on this topic. It does not focus solely on 'edgy' topics like the law's relationship to acts of terror[7], states of emergency, gestures of surrender, payments of reparations, and offers of amnesty.[8] On the contrary, it primarily deals with the limits of the law experienced by legal practitioners in daily legal practice. Moreover, while previous literature is mostly based on a neutral and external account of law's functions, and focuses on descriptive "limits of law imposed by the nature of and changes in the societies in which law operates"[9], *Facing the Limits of the Law* is much more engaged in its outset. It aims to understand law's functions and characteristics in light of the values and normative aspirations of the rule of law. It

---

5 See R. Janda, "Law's Limits", *S. Cal. L. Rev.* 1989–1990, 727–775, in particular 728–729.

6 R. Dworkin, *l.c.*, 14.

7 See P. Schuck, *Limits of Law: Essays on Democratic Governance*, in *New Perspectives on Law, Culture & Society* (New York: The Perseus Books Group, 2000); M. Glennon, *Limits of Law, Prerogatives of Power: Intervention after Kosovo* (New York: Palgrave, 2001); J.L. Goldsmith and E.A. Posner, *The Limits of International Law* (Oxford: Oxford University Press, 2005). See also A.B. Bali, "Stretching the Limits of International Law: the Challenge of Terrorism", *ILSA J. Int'l & Comp. L.* 2002, 403–417; M. Glennon, "Terrorism and the Limits of Law", *Wilson Quarterly* 2001, 12–18; S.L. Wells, "Crimes against Child Soldiers in Armed Conflict Situations: Application and Limits of International Humanitarian Law", *Tul. J. Int'l & Comp. L.* 2004, 287–306; D. Wippman, "Kosovo and the Limits of International Law", *Fordham Int'l L. J.* 2001, 129–147.

8 See T. Teitel, *Transitional Justice* (New York: Oxford University Press, 2000); S.R. Ratner and J.S. Abrams, *Accountability for Human Rights Atrocities in International Law* (New York: Oxford University Press, 2001).

9 See *e.g.*, A. Allot, *The Limits of Law* (London: Butterworths, 1980) ix.
See R.M. Unger, *The Critical Legal Studies Movement* (Cambridge: Harvard University Press, 1986).

therefore does not distinguish between 'descriptive' and 'normative' limits of the law.[10]

2 Functions and Limits of the Law

2.1 Introduction

In the following, an attempt will be made to sketch a broad picture of the law's functions in contemporary, late–modern society. Four functions will be dealt with. In a complex late–modern society law plays a far–reaching regulatory role, consisting of co–ordinating human behaviour and societal relations. Notwithstanding the dominance of instrumental reason in contemporary society, law also serves a symbolic function. Legal concepts, rules and principles, but also legal arguments and decisions carry and express broader cultural meanings. In addition, law serves a role in resolving inter–personal and social conflicts in a peaceful way. Finally, law safeguards basic political values such as democratic participation and provides protection from arbitrary or oppressive power exerted by public entities, private groups, or individual citizens (which can be summarised in the term 'protective legality').

In the following paragraphs these functions will be explored in order to get a first grip on different types of limits legal practitioners and citizens are confronted with.

2.2 The Regulatory Function of Law

For lawyers, judges, but also for policy–makers and citizens, it should come as no surprise to say that contemporary law plays an important regulatory role.[11] We all know that legal norms and standards govern or seek to govern our social interactions in the many fields of our daily, public, and professional lives. Law aims at setting standards for social behaviour, while at the same time providing further rules for monitoring compliance with these standards. These regulatory strategies take different shapes in different areas of law. Whereas in large swaths of private and criminal law, regulative strategies seem to be developed and managed to a large extent by sovereign State power, strategies of compliance in international law are mainly worked out by specialised international institutions.

---

10 See A. Sarat, L.L. Douglas, and M.M. Umphrey (eds.), *The Limits of the Law* (Stanford: Stanford University Press, 2005) 6–9. See also A. Gunnarsson, E.–M. Svensson, and M. Davies, *Exploiting the Limits of the Law* (Aldershot: Ashgate, 2007).

11 For a fascinating analysis of the law through the lens of regulation, see C. Parker, C. Scott, N. Lacey, and J. Braithwaite (eds.), *Regulating Law* (Oxford: Oxford University Press, 2004).

> Today international regulatory regimes for inter alia the environment, the control of disease, disarmament and weapon control, human rights, aviation and maritime pollution all operate within and are developed under the supervisory mechanisms of specialised international institutions.[12]

This prominent role of regulation in law, which manifests itself in various shapes and in a variety of areas, is evidenced by the massive production of legal rules, by an increase in regulatory authorities, and by strategies of monitoring and enforcement. Law's regulatory complexity somehow mirrors the complexity of our late–modern societies, the regulation of which proves to be extremely difficult. Eminent sociologists such as Zygmunt Bauman teach us that technological progress and global capitalism have created unlimited freedom and flexibility, while producing at the same time huge risks for personal and societal development.[13] Socio–economic instability due to a globalised economy generating overwhelming feelings of individual insecurity, the creation of ever larger groups of impoverished and alienated individuals, terrorism, extreme intolerance, worrying ecological problems such as global warming, all these phenomena reveal the darker side of our late–modern condition.[14] As a response to these paradoxical developments, contemporary societies are in a need of both flexible and far–reaching regulation. Indeed, whereas globalisation and technological progress continue to change our societies and to create ever new possibilities, the drawbacks of these rapid changes and the huge risks and complex social problems that stem from them, need to be addressed. This complex need for regulation gives birth to huge societal expectations of the law and legal practitioners.

Legal practitioners are still taught to believe that law can efficiently serve the regulatory need and thus solve the legal problems of the world, but in reality they are often confronted with the law's vulnerability on this point. They face limits in the law to the extent that they encounter the law's limited capacity to monitor effectively and enforce its normative standards. For reasons that need to be further explored, the far–reaching regulatory expectations regarding law cannot be fully met.

2.3 The Symbolic Function of Law

Contemporary law also serves a symbolic function. Indeed, as cultural anthropologists have pointed out, the emergence of modern, highly specialised systems of legal norms produced by a complex bureaucratic apparatus did not erase the

---

[12] H. Charlesworth and C. Chinkin, "Regulatory Frameworks in International Law", in C. Parker, C. Scott, N. Lacey, and J. Braithwaite (eds.), *Regulating Law* (Oxford: Oxford University Press, 2004) 247.

[13] Z. Bauman, *Globalisation. The Human Consequences* (Cambridge: Polity Press, 1998).

[14] For a splendid analysis of the malaise of modernity, see C. Taylor, *The Ethics of Authenticity* (Cambridge Mass.: Harvard University Press, 1991). See also Z. Bauman, *Human Waste. Modernity and its Outcasts* (Cambridge: Polity Press, 2004).

need of modern societies to 're–present' (as did their pre–modern predecessors) their collective identity through symbols and ritual practices. Despite its technicality, modern law reflects, to cite the French philosopher Paul Ricoeur, "la nécessité pour un groupe quelconque de se donner une image de lui–même, de 'se représenter', au sens théatral du mot, de se mettre en jeu et en scène."[15]

This symbolic dimension of the law has regained weight in contemporary societies where weakened Nation–States are trying to reaffirm their legitimacy and where new political entities, such as the European Union, are being forged. National governments are using legislation (often penal) to reaffirm symbolically the authority of the State.[16] State punishment and penal institutions are being reconsidered for their capacity to express collective emotions, values, and meanings, but also to establish and legitimise new cultural transformations.[17]

The idea that law, legal language, institutions, and practices can serve as a medium for shaping and giving voice to collective meanings is also being rediscovered in the constitutionalising process of the European Union. The project of a Constitutional Treaty clearly reflects the need of the European Union to understand itself as a political community. Especially the language of its preamble speaks volumes:

> Drawing inspiration from the cultural, religious and humanist inheritance of Europe, the values of which, still present in its heritage, have embedded within the life of society the central role of the human person and his or her inviolable and inalienable rights, and respect for law.

Notwithstanding its undeniable symbolic dimension, late–modern law reveals to a considerable extent its limited ability to serve this function appropriately. Law falls short of its function of giving voice to collective meanings, because legal concepts, principles, and procedures often are too vague and abstract to serve as a carrier of these meanings and values. This deficit is echoed in the debate around the creation of a European identity, which is often regarded as the vain endeavour of European intellectuals to construct a kind of European identity through numerous recitals full of vague and solemn words and concepts in which members of the EU Member States hardly feel recognised as European citizens.[18] Walter van Gerven remarks:

---

15 P. Ricœur, "L'imagination dans le discours et dans l'action", in P. Ricœur, *Du texte à l'action. Essais d'herméneutique II* (Paris: Éditions Esprit, 1986) 230. On the symbolic function of criminal law and punishment, see D. Garland, *Punishment and Modern Society. A Study in Social Theory* (Oxford: Oxford University Press, 1990).

16 D. Garland, "The Limits of the Sovereign State", *British Journal of Criminology* 1996, 445–471, 445. "Punishment may pose as a symbol of strength, but it should be interpreted as a symptom of weak authority and inadequate controls."

17 For criminal law and punishment as a symbolic practice through which broader cultural transformations can take place, see F. Zimring, *The Contradictions of American Capital Punishment,* in *Studies in Crime and Public Policy* (Oxford: Oxford University Press, 2003). See also E. Claes and T. Daems, "De doodstraf: Amerika versus Europa", *Karakter* 2005, issue 9, 25–29.

18 See D. Curtin, *Mind the Gap? The Evolving EU Executive and the Constitution. Third Walter van Gerven Lecture* (Groningen: Europa Law Publishing, 2004).

> All in all, the long enumeration in the preamble, and in Articles I–2 and I–3 of the Draft Constitutional Treaty, are not very appealing, and they are not of a nature to arouse feelings of attachment to the Union. The values and objectives are too general and too hollow, giving the impression that all of the representatives of the national governments and the various institutions composing the Convention that prepared the draft Constitution wanted to have their own imprint by adding one or another sentence.[19]

The referenda in France and the Netherlands seem to confirm the frail symbolic power of abstract constitutional language, as it falls short of evoking European political unity and social cohesion.

2.4 Dispute Resolution

Another important function of law relates to society's need for peaceful settlement of disputes.[20] Law is expected to:

- be able to decide cases and to bring clarity and certainty in the relations between parties;
- create peace in society which enables parties to behave in the future in a peaceful way.

In private and public law affairs, both at the national and international level, judges are expected to settle disputes in the short term and to bring social peace in the long run.[21]

In light of these high expectations, law appears to be a fragile enterprise. Legal practitioners are well aware of the limited capacities of law duly to fulfil the function of dispute resolution and pacification. The formality and adversarial nature of the judicial process is regarded by its critics to be unsatisfactory for the parties because it often obstructs the possibilities of real dialogue, and deprives the parties of the capacity to sort things out for themselves and come to a genuine reconciliation.[22] Many legal sociologists and anthropologists provide support for the view that law polarises rather than reconciles.[23] Moreover, complex and long courtroom proceedings 'mystify'[24] the process, and 'alienate' disputants from the courts, the

---

19 W. van Gerven, *The European Union. A Polity of States and Peoples* (Oxford and Portland: Hart Publishing, 2005) 56.

20 Law itself implicitly distinguishes between 'disputes' and 'conflicts'. Conflicts are those issues which lack legally recognised forums for their expression and resolution that meet the criteria of legitimacy, reliability, transparency, and non–arbitrariness. See R. Shonholtz, "A General Theory on Disputes and Conflicts", *J. Disp. Resol.* 2003, 403.

21 P. Ricœur, "L'acte de juger", in P. Ricœur, *Le Juste* (Paris: Éditions Esprit, 1995) 185: "Je distinguerai une finalité courte, en vertu de laquelle juger signifie trancher, en vue de mettre un terme à l'incertitude; à quoi j'opposerai une finalité longue, plus dissimulée sans doute, à savoir la contribution à la paix publique."

22 N. Christie, "Conflicts as Property", *British Journal of Criminology* 1997, 1–15.

23 See *e.g.*, J.S. Auerbach, *Justice Without Law?* (Oxford: Oxford University Press, 1983).

24 See J. Jacobs, "Justice Between Man and Man Towards a Code of Civil Procedure", *C.L.P.* 1985.

law, and the decision ultimately reached. 'Alternative Dispute Resolution' (ADR) and 'Restorative Justice' practices have received enthusiastic support from a wide array of proponents in response to the limits of law and, more in particular, the traditional judicial process. Referring to a variety of different techniques and programs, these practices share a common goal in that they aim to increase the satisfaction of the parties while resolving conflicts more informally but no less effectively than in traditional legal systems. Despite the success of ADR and Restorative Justice, it still remains unclear what the added value of these initiatives amounts to and which types of limits to formal law they are supposed to remedy.[25] This question risks being left unanswered since ADR and Restorative Justice have become rapidly institutionalised within established legal systems. A full analysis of the limits of law seems therefore extremely relevant in this respect.[26]

2.5 Protective Legality

Apart from its regulatory and symbolic function and its role in dispute resolution, contemporary legal systems are expected to provide for legal guarantees, for instruments of legal protection. This last function of protective legality (or legal protection) is closely related to the traditions of the *Rechtsstaat* and of the rule of law: society demands that law (in all its forms) protects citizens against the unlawful action of government, public entities, and other citizens.

Given the variety of legal systems and legal cultures that share the idea of *Rechtsstaat* or the rule of law tradition, it is a daunting task to spell out what precisely these instruments of legal protection are and what values and interests they are supposed to protect. Moreover, these values are subjected to unceasing interpretation and discussion. The legal cultures in which they are embedded are part of a complex interpretative construction which is in need of constant refinement in the light of changing societal circumstances (a 'working history'), especially in an era of globalisation and of evolving political entities such as the European Union.[27]

However, the ever changing conceptions of the *Rechtsstaat* and the rule of law do not prevent us from trying to uncover a scheme of values and aspirations that the law, in all its manifestations, purports to protect through a tight web of legal principles and fundamental rights.[28] In order to allow the authors in the following chapters to spell out (some) of these values, a robust idea of the scheme of values

[25] See A. Von Hirsch, J. Roberts, and A. Bottoms (eds.), *Restorative Justice and Criminal Justice. Competing or Reconcilable Paradigms?* (Oxford: Hart Publishing, 2003).

[26] Presumably, what is needed in the first place is a set of jurisdictional principles that delimit those areas in which informal dispute resolution techniques are both workable and permissible.

[27] For an elegant attempt to reconstruct and assess the EU in the light of the concepts and instruments of *Rechtsstaat* and the rule of law, see W. van Gerven, *l.c.*, 110 e.s.

[28] On protective legality, see also R. Foqué and A.C. 't Hart, *Instrumentaliteit en rechtsbescherming* (Arnhem: Gouda Quint, 1990).

underpinning the *Rechtsstaat* and the rule of law will be given below. To that end, a distinction will be made between the core values and the aspirations underlying protective legality.

If we concentrate on the *core* protection offered by democratic procedures, by principles of good governance, by the requirements of legality, by respect for human rights and fundamental freedoms, as well as by a system of checks and balances and judicial review, we could say that the essentials of the idea of *Rechtsstaat* and a rule of law consist, firstly, of setting minimal conditions for the control and critique of power. Law provides legal protection to the extent that it guarantees citizens minimal protection to:

- call on government and public entities to answer for their conduct;
- challenge government acts as unlawful; and
- defy critically and reasonably any government order as unlawful.

Closely linked with this idea of control and critique of power, is, secondly, the requirement that citizens, government, and public entities should act in accordance with legal standards established in advance. In this respect the traditions of the *Rechtsstaat* and the rule of law refer to the value of 'legality' which in its essence aims at protecting citizens in their capacity as responsible agents to engage in rule–guided behaviour and in their corresponding capacity to trust the rule–guided behaviour of public officials and fellow–citizens.[29] Indeed, as expressed by Lon Fuller:

> To embark on the enterprise of subjecting human conduct to the governance of rules involves of necessity a commitment to the view that man is, or can become, a responsible agent, capable of understanding and following rules, and answerable for his defaults.[30]

Finally, citizens expect law to protect them against an intrusive display of power. Here legal protection implies the recognition of citizens in their capacity to have private thoughts, motivations, and attitudes for which they need not be called to answer. A display of power is intrusive to the extent that it focuses on citizens in the way they reveal themselves in intimate and close relationships, as private identities withdrawn from the range of public power play. In other words, the protective legality role of contemporary law presupposes a basic recognition of the private autonomy and the privacy of each citizen.

Protective legality seeks to establish not only the minimal conditions for control, rule–guided behaviour, and privacy. According to Dworkin and Fuller they can also be reconstructed as honouring *ideals* and *aspirations*.[31] Accordingly, participants in these legal traditions expect law to promote these ideals of the rule of law as much as possible.

---

29 Of course different interpretations and conceptions exist as to the questions what kind of standards constrain coercive power and in what way they should be established, see R. Dworkin, *Justice in Robes* (Cambridge, Mass: The Belknap Press of Harvard University Press, 2006) 172.

30 L. Fuller, *The Morality of Law* (London: Yale University Press, 1994) 162.

31 L. Fuller, *l.c.*, 42: "The inner morality of law ... embraces a morality of duty and a morality of aspiration."

At least two important normative ideals and aspirations come to the fore when examining *Rechtsstaat* and rule of law cultures: the political ideal of 'law as integrity' and the ideal of participative citizenship. As will be noted, both ideals are intrinsically linked to each other, expressive as they are of equal respect of each citizen's human dignity.

Paraphrasing Dworkin's idea of 'law as integrity', relations between government and citizens and between citizens themselves should be shaped in accordance with the most well–balanced and coherent interpretation of those legal principles and fundamental rights underlying the legal order as a whole. "Integrity assumes that each person is as worthy as any other, that each must be treated with equal concern according to some coherent conception of what that means."[32]

Another ideal of the rule of law concerns the display of and struggle for power by government, public entities, private enterprises, and interests groups: law governed by the principles of the *Rechtsstaat* or the rule of law tries to set standards for transforming raw political power into the capacity of citizens to deliberate and act in concert, and to cooperate mutually in the public interest.[33] Acting in the public interest assumes the collective responsibility of each citizen to give the best possible expression to the political values and principles that ground its legal order as a whole. This ideal is closely intertwined with equal respect for everyone's human dignity. Following Arendt, "Respect for human dignity implies the recognition of my fellow–men (...) as builders of worlds or co–builders of a common world."[34]

The ideals of law as integrity and of participative citizenship imply each other. Indeed, mutually cooperating in the public interest, requires observing and furthering a coherent interpretation of the legal principles and fundamental rights underlying the legal order, as this is the interpretation which most honours equal respect for everyone's human dignity.

Against this rough scheme of basic values and aspirations underpinning the role of contemporary law in providing legal guarantees, a corresponding set of limits of law can be framed, enabling the contributors to this volume to examine more closely their experience of the fragility of contemporary law.

Law risks drifting away from its core values of the *Rechtsstaat*, of the rule of law, if it does not provide minimal protection to (a group of) citizens to call government and public entities to account for their acts, to question the lawfulness of government action, and to contest critically and reasonably the lawfulness of government acts. The law would fail to provide this minimum core, if it allows gross disrespect of the values of privacy, private autonomy, and legality. In such a scenario legal norms and standards fall short of protecting citizens in their rule–guided behaviour and their corresponding trust in the equally rule–guided behaviour of public officials, or in their claim for respect of their private identity.

---

32 R. Dworkin, *l.c.*, 213 and 224–275.

33 H. Arendt, *The Human Condition* (Chicago: Chicago University Press, 1958) 202; H. Arendt, *The Promise of Politics* (New York: Schocken Books, 2005) 127.

34 H. Arendt, *Origins of Totalitarianism* (San Diego, Calif.: Harcourt, 1951) 458.

The following paragraphs will further question to what extent the law, due to its basic characteristics, might be vulnerable of tumbling into such a scenario. Presumably, much has to do with the law's dependency on other societal spheres.

Sketching the aspirations underpinning protective legality might also help better assess whether and how far contemporary law has become distanced from the ideals of law as integrity, of participative citizenship and equal respect for human dignity. Law reaches its limits of legal protection

- if it insufficiently enables citizens, lawyers, judges, and politicians to engage in a process of legislation, rule–following, and adjudication according to the most coherent interpretation of legal principles and fundamental rights;
- if it does not establish optimal conditions for mutual cooperation among and recognition of citizens in their ability to cooperate mutually in the public interest.

In the following we will try to answer the question *why* law sometimes fails to realise the above–mentioned ideals of the rule of law. This too will lead to an analysis of the characteristics of law.

3 Characteristics of the Law and Refining the Law's Limits

A number of features of the law will be distinguished and discussed hereafter: law as a specific societal sphere; the open texture of law; law as a 'scientific' enterprise; law as an argumentative practice, steered by debate and resulting in decisions; law as an institutionalised practice, and, finally, law as an interplay of rules, principles, and fundamental rights.

3.1 Law as a Societal Sphere

Law presents itself as a distinct sphere, surrounded by and to be distinguished from other societal spheres, such as ethics, economy, culture, technology, and religion. It is of course not within the reach of our investigation to offer a clear view of the complex interaction between these different societal spheres. In the following chapters the reader will discover an abundance of issues in which this complex relation will be fleshed out. Nevertheless, some general remarks in this respect might prove fruitful for a further elaboration of our typology of the limits of law.

Firstly, the legal sphere is surely distinct from, but not completely separate from, other societal spheres. The general look of a legal system and its division into legal disciplines, the nature of its concepts and distinctions, the shape of its rules, principles, and procedures, and so on, all these elements to a large extent reflect other societal spheres, such as ethics, politics, economy, culture, technology, and religion. "Law", to quote Wolfgang Friedmann's well–known *Law in a*

Changing Society, "is still an instrument of order, bearing the imprint of the forces that shape our society."[35]

Numerous examples of the law's dependence on other societal spheres can be listed. We will limit ourselves here to the issue of the death penalty. Sociologists have shown convincingly that shifts in legal argument in US federal case–law mirror important symbolic transformations within American culture. Similarly, the opposite consensus in the European law of human rights on the worldwide abolition of the death penalty is to a large extent modulated by important cultural transformations, such as the evolving political will to construct a European identity.[36]

Secondly, law itself is constantly nurturing and shaping other societal spheres such as ethics and politics. It transforms everyday ethical life and political practice by means of the law's concepts, institutional structures and procedures.

In constitutional democracies, for example, politics are to a large extent shaped by the very framework of the Constitution. It would be misleading to say, as social scientists often do, that the scope, interpretation, and evolution of the Constitution is the outcome of contingent power relations, for these very power relations are organised and structured themselves by constitutional rules and principles.

Preliminary as they may be, the aforementioned remarks should suffice to sketch an answer to the question why the law risks falling short in regulating social life, in expressing common goods and the concerns of a political community, in resolving conflicts peacefully, and finally in providing citizens and political actors with legal guarantees. Two types of limits in the law seem to be relevant here. They will be spelled out here as working hypotheses, and will still need to be further qualified in the chapters following.

Firstly, law is limited in its capacity to offer guarantees against oppression and arbitrary power, as well as in its regulatory, symbolic, and peace–making role for the more fundamental reason that its practices are to a large extent dependent upon the broader dynamics generated by other societal spheres.[37]

For example, late–modern culture affixes its imprint on criminal law and on criminal justice systems. One of the characteristics of our present culture is undeniably the growing collective attention for safety and risk control.[38] The obsession for controlling deviant and high risk behaviour which in contemporary penal culture is accompanied by a collective will to discipline individuals in their deepest desires and motivations, risks eroding the law's commitment to providing each

---

35 W. Friedmann, *Law in a Changing Society* (Middlesex: Penguin Books, 2nd ed., 1972) 498.

36 See F. Zimring, *l.c.*, 16–41.

37 For this topic, see *e.g.*, R.J. Krotoszynski, "Building Bridges and Overcoming Barricades: Exploring the Limits of Law as an Agent of Transformational Social Change", *Case W. Res. L. Rev.* 1996–1997, 423–444; L. Lustgarten, "Racial Inequality and the Limits of Law", *Mod. L. Rev.* 1986, 68–85.

38 D. Garland, *The Culture of Control. Crime and Social Order in Contemporary Society* (Oxford: Oxford University Press, 2001); B. Hudson, *Justice in the Risk Society* (London: Sage, 2003) 40–77.

citizen with minimal guarantees to ensure the protection of his privacy and private identity.[39]

Society's desire to establish safety and security, and the dangers of intrusive State power such a desire involves, manifest themselves in other areas of the law as well, such as in social security law. Rules that allow public services to inquire into the means of existence of the social beneficiary often give rise to "a paternalistic 'tutelage' and authoritarian oppression of the citizens by an omnipresent, yet distant and anything but service–oriented, administrative apparatus."[40]

Secondly, framed as a societal sphere surrounded by other spheres, law falls short in accomplishing its functions to the extent that it is shown to be structurally inadequate to permeate and guide other societal spheres. These spheres often have a distinct logic, and entail concepts and structures which often resist being shaped by legal rules, principles, and procedures. As a result, attempts to regulate these spheres by law are often seen to be ineffective, producing disorder instead of generating order.

This awareness of the law's limited ability to regulate other societal spheres surely has motivated, for instance, political debate around the desirability of legalising solidarity within the family (e.g. by demanding that financially better off family members compensate social security payments to less resourceful family members). Opponents argue that it is not the law's business to frame these bounds of solidarity into the language of enforceable rights. Such a language sits ill with the delicate, affective nature of family relations.

3.2 Law as a Social Practice: The Open Texture of Law

Although law is distinct from other societal spheres and practices, it undeniably shares some characteristics with these practices. Seen as a social practice, law can be understood as a succession of actions and interactions which social actors are engaged in by following rules and by projecting normative expectations on each other. Being engaged in a social practice implies having an intuitive grasp of that practice, its (inter)actions, underlying rules, and expectations. If a person lacks affinity with that practice, inevitably he will be unable to grasp its point.[41] Applied to the law, this means that law–abiding citizens, legal actors, and legal practitioners only grasp the point of the law, its rules and principles, to the extent that they are somehow participating in the law (as social practice) and have interiorised its

39 B. Hudson, "Secrets of the Self: Punishment and the Right to Privacy", in E. Claes, A. Duff, and S. Gutwirth, *Privacy and the Criminal Law* (Antwerp and Oxford: Intersentia, 2006) 137–162.

40 See M. Cappelletti, "The Law–Making Power of the Judge and its Limits: A Comparative Analysis", *Monash U. L. Rev.* 1981–1982, 29. Compare also: R. Kaufman, "Protecting the Rights of Minors; On Juvenile Autonomy and the Limits of Law", *N.Y.U.L. Rev.* 1977, 1015–1032.

41 For this kind of analysis drawn from Wittgenstein, see extensively, C. Taylor, *Philosophical Arguments* (Cambridge, Mass.: Harvard University Press, 1995), Chs. 1, 2, 3.

rules and principles.[42] Law appears then not only as a system of written laws, but as a kind of know–how, a tacit knowledge which forms the background against which citizens and officials know how to engage in the law's business. This also implies that the meaning of legal norms is not exhausted by their semantic scope. Legal norms are but an abbreviated text of inarticulate expectations which reveal their meaning in the use of law. As with rules in other social practices, the meaning of legal norms is wholly dependent on their use.

These observations bring us to an essential feature of law, which H.L.A. Hart famously called the 'open texture' of law.[43] If legal norms are the written expression of a practice which resists complete articulation, their meaning can never be fixed. Like all other social norms, legal norms have an open texture: their meaning is not encapsulated in the words, but reveals itself in the way the rule is used, followed, interpreted, enforced, and so on.

The open texture of the law surely produces some important social benefits. It makes the law dynamic and flexible, so that public officials, legal practitioners, and law–abiding citizens can adjust the legal norms, adopted at a specific time and under specific circumstances, to new social situations and challenges. Law's open texture allows it to respond to the many societal functions it is supposed to serve. However, the open texture of law has also its drawbacks. A number of implications result from it, which will lead us eventually to distinguishing the limits of the law. In what follows, attention will be drawn to four implications of the law's open texture.

Firstly, in order to understand legal norms as meaningful, normative standards, legal practitioners and law–abiding subjects must be able to grasp the point of these norms, which presupposes an implicit know–how in dealing with these norms. This process of internalisation is vulnerable to all sorts of disturbing elements, both external (inflation of legal norms caused by the welfare State, absence of basic social trust due to extreme ethnic violence,...) and internal (abstract nature or highly technical nature of legal concepts) to the law.

Secondly, if the meaning of legal norms is dependent on their use, then it stands as an unfortunate consequence that uncertainty and doubt can always occur as to their use (and meaning) in unforeseen circumstances. As lawyers and citizens, we all have an intuitive sense of the meaning and point of criminal offences such as rape or assault and battery. But what happens when we are faced with a case in which a man is forced by another to penetrate him? Does it count as rape? Or what of the case in which two people engage by mutual consent in a repulsive sado–masochist game? Is the 'master' committing an offence of assault and battery upon the 'slave'? In such (often controversial) cases legal practitioners and citizens may fail to revert to their common sense understanding of the legal norm. The facts of the case will have cut them off from their implicit know–how of how to apply the legal norm at issue.

---

42 H.L.A. Hart initiated this line of thought in *The Concept of Law* (Oxford: Clarendon Press, 2nd ed., 1994) 128–136.

43 *Ibid.*

Thirdly, this feeling of alienation can also take massive proportions, especially in late–modern societies which are steered by far–reaching transformations and radical changes (terrorism, globalisation, environmental issues). Such transformations provoke a massive loss of meaning and have the potential of making pointless key concepts in our legal practice. A well–known example of such cultural processes in 20th century was the rise of totalitarianism and the tragedy of the Holocaust which led to a profound crisis in moral, political, and legal thinking. How to think of individual criminal responsibility in a totalitarian context in which victims as well as offenders were subjected to an all–embracing dynamic of terror? How to judge those who, through their acts, were answerable for the Holocaust if new legal concepts still had to be invented to define and understand the normative point to the atrocities they committed? According to Hannah Arendt,

> What is frightening in the rise of totalitarianism, is not that it is something new, but that it has brought to light the ruin of our categories of thought and standards of judgment.[44]

A fourth and last implication of the open texture of law comes down to the fact that legal norms and legal decisions can never fully determine their application. If their meaning lies in their use, then the effect of legal interventions and the way these legal norms are administered, are to a certain extent always unpredictable. Moreover, creating legal norms always entails the possibility of an instrumentalist use that has lost any ambition to give a justified ground to such use. Politicians and citizens might for instance fully embrace anti–racism legislation that prohibits incitement to hate, violence, segregation, and discrimination on grounds of racial origins or colour. However, such legislation, which implies a limitation on freedom of speech, can always be deployed as a tool in favour of the particular interests of political parties or social pressure groups, without bothering to ascertain whether these interests meet the standards of public reason.

As already suggested, the aforementioned implications of the law's open texture help us articulate new types of limits of the law. They partly explain why law is, to a certain extent, ill–equipped to serve its societal functions.

A first type of constraint relates to the fact that the efficient regulation of social behaviour requires an interiorisation of legal norms. This capacity for interiorisation is limited for a variety of reasons, such as the sociological fact of over–regulation in welfare States, an absence of basic trust in post–conflict societies, or given the high technical and abstract nature of the law, combined with the complex interplay of its norms. For these reasons, citizens are easily discouraged from a fully engaged understanding of the practice of the law. The lack of interiorisation inevitably restrains the law's ability to regulate social life.

A second type of limit regards the issue of hard cases and partly explains why to some extent the law is not completely adjusted to fulfil its pacificatory role. In hard cases the parties involved are disconnected from the meaning of a given legal norm (e.g. prohibition on rape) in light of certain circumstances (e.g. a man forces

---

[44] H. Arendt, "Understanding and Politics (The Difficulties of Understanding)", in H. Arendt (ed. J. Kohn), *Essays in Understanding 1930–1954. Uncollected and unpublished work* (New York: Harcourt, 1993) 318.

another man to penetrate him), and consequently lack any clear framework to come to some resolution to their dispute.

A third type of limit concerns the unforeseeability in the use of legal norms. This type of limit restrains the law's ability to regulate efficiently and to provide for legal guarantees. One of the core aspects of a legal system governed by the rule of law is that it protects citizens in their capability to engage in social interactions according to rules and normative expectations. These guarantees, which are legally articulated in terms of 'legality' and 'legal certainty', necessitate the ability of each citizen to adjust his actions subject to intervention by public officials, which in turn demands that these interventions are governed by pre–existing legal norms. But this ability is to some extent always flawed, given the fact that the meaning and scope of these norms are never totally foreseeable in the possible range of their use.

The unforeseeability in the use of legal norms is also detrimental to another fundamental value which is linked to protective legality, the value of 'law as integrity'. If the point of law depends on its use, and if the law can never determine fully how it will be applied, then it is always possible in the future that public officials and citizens interpret the norms and rules of their legal system in line with some currently favoured political and cultural trends, but yet completely at odds with a well–balanced and coherent interplay of fundamental rights, values, and principles underlying the legal system as a whole.

A fourth and last type of limit to the law concerns the issue of a massive loss of meaning, due to radical socio–political changes or far–reaching events, and leading to the erosion of our fundamental legal categories and concepts. Again this implication of the law's open texture helps cast a brighter light on the limits of protective legality, and the ability of the law to ensure a protection of basic values. Take, for example, the ideal of democracy, defined as the capacity of citizens to enter in a public space of appearance, to engage therein in mutual cooperation with fellow–citizens, and to deliberate on shared issues in the public interest. Numerous contemporary developments, such as the erosion of civil society, the growing power of media, and the rise of political populism, easily give birth to political decisions which, from a formalistic point of view, appear to be perfectly democratic. In their outcomes and in the policies they facilitate, these decisions are, however, expressive of brute power. They deny the spirit of a State purporting to be democratic and hold in contempt each citizen's ability to enter the political space in order to engage in mutual cooperation with his fellow–citizens. Criminal legislation and 'tough on crime' policies in the US and in the UK which aim simultaneously at tempering popular feeling of insecurity and at reaffirming the legitimacy of weakened Nation–States, may be called 'democratic' in that these policies are backed by massive popular support. But in doing so, they tend to compromise a deeper understanding of one of the basic categories by which the law can be conceived as aspiring to mutual cooperation among citizens in the public interest.

3.3 Law as a 'Scientific' Enterprise

Law also shares with many other social practices the ambition to be scientific. The functioning of law is guided and informed by a body of knowledge that systematises the facts of the positive law of a given legal system. From this body of knowledge, which is often called 'legal doctrine', legal practitioners also borrow new concepts and principles to apply them in their practice. In this respect law appears as a kind of intellectual game wherein concepts and principles are introduced by legal scholars, are then used and refined in practice, and are subsequently reintroduced in legal science (or vice versa, introduced by practice, and refined by legal scholars).

Another feature of law which reveals its affinity with science, is that those engaged in the practice of the law are inclined to understand the law *more geometrico*, in terms of a transparent, coherent, and rational model. Especially continental legal practitioners have been taught to understand their law as a hierarchical, linear system of clear–cut rules, the application of which in concrete circumstances is often seen in terms of simple syllogistic reasoning.

In light of this affinity between law and science, those engaged with the law encounter at least two types of limits in the law.

A first type of limit relates to the observation that, through radical changes, law has taken new shapes and structures which resist being represented *more geometrico*. One of the most far–reaching changes within the law concerns the relation between the three bodies of power: legislative, executive, and judicial. Given the loss of legislative power in many contemporary societies, in favour of executive and judicial power, it becomes misleading to represent the *trias politica* in the image of a pyramid with legislative power at the apex.[45] Moreover, in the late–modern context, law–making is no longer the exclusive prerogative of the classic *trias*.[46] Finally, it would also be misleading to grasp the complex relation between the legislator and the judge in terms of simple syllogistic reasoning, since judges increasingly spell out explicitly and even reaffirm a *law–making* competence. To sum up, contemporary law is running up against the limits of its rationalistic self–understanding.

This incongruity between the law's rationalistic self–understanding, on the one hand, and legal reality, on the other hand, partly explains why contemporary law struggles to fulfil its role of protective legality. Classic principles like the separation of powers, the principle of legality and of democratic participation (which aim to protect the citizen's ability to engage in rule–guided actions, to take part in and to challenge the legitimacy of legal norms and public decisions) become extremely vulnerable because they are in their structure far too much dependent upon and derivative of the *more geometrico* model.

---

45 See F. Ost and M. van de Kerchove, *De la pyramide au réseau? Pour une théorie dialectique du droit* (Brussels: Publications des Facultés universitaires Saint–Louis, 2002).

46 See J. Black, "Decentring Regulation: Understanding the Role of Regulation and Self–Regulation in a 'Post–Regulatory' World", *C.L.P.* 2001, 102.

A second type of limit to the law springs from the tension between the aspirations of science, on the one hand, and the very nature of law, seen as a social practice, on the other. As already argued, normative standards in law borrow their legitimacy from their being internalised by those who are subject to the law. Without any intuitive access to the foundation of these legal norms, the law's subjects are left with an understanding of legal norms seen as "orders backed by threats".[47] One of the problems with the affinity between law and science is that the abstract, conceptual language resulting from it undermines to a large extent the potential for internalisation inherent in the law itself.

This tension between the need for interiorising the meaning of legal norms and the ambition of the law to take the shapes, methods, and structures of science explains to a large extent why the law encounters so many difficulties in regulating social behaviour, in restoring social peace, in expressing cultural meanings, and in protecting basic values and fundamental rights. The highly abstract language and hermetic concepts makes it difficult for social actors to guide by law their interactions in an efficient and effective way. The scientific aspirations of the law also undermine the law's potential to figure as a framework that opens a common public space of mutual cooperation among citizens, one that facilitates conflict resolution and peace–making and that is expressive of shared values and meanings.[48]

3.4 Law as an Argumentative Practice

It is a common feature of all social practices, including law, that the actions through which they are constituted involve a degree of decision–making and of articulation of reasons and arguments which claim to inform and justify these decisions.[49]

This process of deliberation on and justification of choices and actions manifests itself in a particular way in the practice of law. Law–abiding subjects are under an obligation to account for their actions in the light of a framework of coercive legal norms. They have to give reasons why, in the circumstances of their case, they were justified in or excused from doing what the norm prohibited or obliged them to do in the first place. Alternatively, they are under an obligation to argue why they are in fact entitled to the claims implied in the legal norms they draw on. These obligations are closely related to the protective legality role of the

---

[47] See H.L.A. Hart, *l.c.*, 6, 16, 19 and 20–25.

[48] In order to remedy this type of limits in the criminal law, A. Duff argues that "[t]here must be a bridge, a bridge which is neither too long nor too far, which can take ordinary citizens from ordinary language into enough of the language of the law for them to be able to speak the relevant parts of that language in the first person." See A. Duff, "Law, Language and Community: Some Preconditions of Criminal Liability", *O.J.L.S.* 1998, 200.

[49] *Cf.* R. Dworkin, *l.c.*, 13. "Every actor in the practice understands that what it permits or requires depends on the truth of certain propositions that are given sense only by and within the practice; the practice consists in large part in deploying and arguing about these propositions."

law. If protective legality finds its normative origins in the law's recognition of each legal subject through its responsiveness to reasons and to public reason, then this recognition implies a responsibility for each legal subject to determine his stance towards the law.[50] While deliberating upon and justifying his decisions and actions, he is expected actively to define his position within a complex web of legal obligations and claims that are relevant for the case at hand.

To sum up: in matters of law, deliberation and argumentation are not really an option, the choice of which presents itself as free. This observation concerns not only law–abiding citizens; it also concerns public officials. Although they often have a considerable margin of discretion, their decisions, at least in the tradition of the *Rechtsstaat* and the rule of law, are also bound by the law. Public officials are under an obligation to justify their decisions and actions in order to guarantee respect for their legal citizens as subjects endowed with a capacity for public reasoning. An important difference, however, which marks off public officials from law–abiding citizens is that the former are, given their public function, always obliged to give reasons for their decisions. Moreover, in matters of legal adjudication, a judge is not freely able to disclaim his duty as a decision–maker, or to change his decisions endlessly.

The inescapable duty of public officials to decide upon legal matters manifests itself clearly in hard cases. In these cases, the process of complex and refined argumentation does not relieve the necessary burden of ending deliberation and of making a decision, even when after substantial deliberation no determinative argument can be found to steer judgment in one direction or another.

The identification of the law as an argumentative practice, involving a deeper political obligation to engage in a process of deliberation and argumentation, as well as an unavoidable duty to make decisions, allows us to distinguish at least two types of limits in the law.

The first type of limit flows from the observation that, although it invites and stimulates argument, the deliberative and argumentative nature of the law at the same time raises doubts as to the accuracy and legitimacy of those arguments made. As already stated, the meaning of legal norms reveals itself in their use, which by definition is never stable and remains inarticulate to a certain degree. Arguments made in support of a certain interpretation of a legal norm or concept are therefore always open to further refinement and revision.

The open–ended nature of argumentation explains in part why the law is limited in its capacity to assure the protection of basic values such as autonomy or privacy. Legal arguments on the basis of which citizens can defend these values can easily lose their ground because of rapid changes in society. They are intrinsically affected by a risk of loss of legitimacy.

The second type of limit concerns the incongruity between the obligation to provide legal argument and the inescapable duty to decide a case. On the one hand, this duty, which is necessary for law to serve its functions of regulation and

---

50 For this line of reasoning in the context of the criminal law, compare A. Duff, *l.c.*, 189–206, who links responsible citizenship to answerability and the capacity to be responsive to reasons.

dispute resolution, is hampered by the endless refinement and revision of arguments and interpretations of legal norms and concepts ("une délibération virtuellement indéfinie").[51] How to regulate human interactions efficiently, if legal arguments and the decisions they advocate, reflect constant amendment? How to contribute to the resolution of conflicts and peace in society in circumstances where reasons of argumentative refinement continually require public officials to postpone or overrule their decisions? On the other hand, the social need to decide cases, expressing itself in the practice of law itself, often appears as a limit to the law if one takes the perspective of protective legality. Committed to seeking the best arguments for their case, lawyers and legal practitioners are often aware that the nature of their decisions are rendered contingent by the limits of time and resources.

3.5 Law as an Institutionalised Practice

One of the most striking characteristics of law as a social practice is that it relates to a highly institutionalised structure in which human interactions take place.

Law refers, first, to a set of standards of behaviour regulating interactions and distributing rights and obligations among citizens and government (e.g. the rule that murder is illegal). These primary rules (to use the term coined by H.L.A. Hart) borrow their legitimacy and their binding character from the fact that they are made, administered, interpreted, and enforced by competent actors. These actors operate within an institutional structure which confers on them that power to make, administer, interpret, and enforce the law. Consequently, law also refers to secondary rules giving a stamp of authority to primary rules and establishing an institutional framework in which primary rules acquire their legal validity (e.g. the rules on the legislative process have to be followed for the rule on the illegality of murder to be valid and legitimate).[52] Consequently, the practice of the law not only takes place within a complex institutional structure, it is also the driving force behind the development of such a structure.

The origins of law, seen as a complex institutionalised practice, are surely attached to the rise of modern State power and the need for a complex bureaucratic apparatus, but that practice is also shaped by a strong concern for legal guarantees against arbitrary State power. In a legal tradition governed by the rule of law, complex institutional structures are needed in order to create and ensure a system of checks and balances between different powers, which would also allow citizens to call public officials to account for their actions and decisions. Processes of institutionalisation and processes of the empowerment of citizens are two sides of the same coin.

---

51 P. Ricœur, "L'acte de juger", in P. Ricœur, *Le Juste* (Paris: Éditions Esprit, 1995) 187.

52 H.L.A. Hart, *l.c.*, 77 e.s.

Unfortunately, this process of institutionalisation, intrinsically linked to a commitment for legal protections, risks undermining law's capacity to serve its peace–making and symbolic functions. Two types of limits of the law can be distinguished in this respect.

First, law as an institutionalised practice explains a great deal of the law's limited ability to express and represent collective values and shared meanings. While initiated by political institutions and at the same time giving shape to our political institutions, legal norms and their interplay risk becoming too complex to convey collective meanings successfully and efficiently: these norms can hardly function as the mirror in which citizens see their shared beliefs and convictions reflected.

Second, law as an institutionalised practice explains in part the limited capacity of the law to resolve disputes and restore social peace. A complex web of institutionalised actors are in part responsible for a common feeling of alienation among the disputants: they feel cut off from their own ability to resolve disputes given the intervention of a complex institutional apparatus.

Important to note here is that these types of limits of the law not only flow from a particular feature of the law (complex institutionalised structure), but, on a deeper level, from a tension between different functions of the law: its symbolic and pacifying role on the one hand, and its protective legality role on the other hand.

3.6 Law as an Interplay of Legal Rules, Legal Principles, and Fundamental Rights

A last feature of the law that holds our attention, relates to the complexity of the law's normative structure. Within the tradition of the rule of law, legal systems are to be understood in terms of a complex interplay of legal rules, legal principles, and fundamental rights. Legal rules are adopted by public officials on whom a law–making power is conferred. Whereas the standards of behaviour implied in these legal rules are written more or less precisely and are applicable in an all–or–nothing fashion, legal principles and fundamental rights, by contrast, are abstract, expressing general standards of behaviour.[53] These principles and fundamental rights express the fundamentals of each legal order and their meaning is not exhausted by a specific articulation at a given moment and in a given context. They are not applicable in an all–or–nothing fashion, but have a relative weight according to the circumstances in which they factor. On each occasion they demand careful deliberation in order to reinvent and delimit, as it were, their content in a particular case. Legal principles and fundamental rights are often in conflict with each other and, accordingly, require to be balanced against each other.

---

53 For an extensive analysis, R. Dworkin, *Taking Rights Seriously* (London: Duckworth, 19th ed., 2002).

This complex interaction between legal principles and fundamental rights brings legal practitioners and citizens often to the limits of their legal system. For the exercise of balancing shows itself to be extremely difficult, resulting in a perception that no ultimate, reasonable measure exists such as to create an equilibrium in one fashion or another.[54] In such circumstances the margin of discretion becomes an unavoidable burden. The term 'limits of the law' stands then for the limits of legal reasoning or legal rationality, revealing in the law and legal decisions zones of inescapable arbitrariness.

These zones of arbitrariness shed an interesting light on the law's limited ability to resolve conflicts and provide legal guarantees. They explain why legal decisions, when running up against the limits of legal reasoning, are facing a limited ability to restore convincingly social peace. These zones of arbitrariness also affect the law's ability to respect and protect citizens in their legitimate desire for predictable, stable governance, in their ability to question political decisions in the light of public reason. The tragic dimension to these types of restrictions in the law is that they can not be overcome by standards of reason, because they point out the very limits of these same standards.[55]

4 Conclusion

The point of departure of *Facing the Limits of the Law* is the idea that in late–modern societies, lawyers and legal practitioners are often faced with limits in the law. To allow them to deal with these limits requires a further examination of different kinds of constraints and restraints implied in the practice of law. Our introductory analysis has resulted in, admittedly, a complex typology which can be summarised as follows.

Law disposes of a limited capacity to regulate social behaviour. Constraints and restraints are in part produced by the incongruity between the law and other societal spheres, as well as by the open texture of legal norms, which, along with the scientific aspirations of the law, make the internalisation of these norms (at least potentially) problematic. The law's limited capacity to serve its regulatory role also flows from the endless and time–consuming drive for argumentative refinement in the law, which puts at risk an efficient regulation of social behaviour.

---

54 See R. Dworkin, "Natural Law Revisited", *University of Florida Review* 1982, 174.

55 Compare, N. MacCormick, "Limits of Rationality in Legal Reasoning", in N. MacCormick and O. Weinberger, *An Institutional Theory of Law. New Approaches to Legal Positivism* (Dordrecht: D. Reidl Publishing Company, 1986) 205. While the author states that we "should not overrate the extensiveness of the scope of rationality in legal reasoning", "we should recognise that even here there are limits where the judgment of experience goes beyond any reason that can be constructed within the logic of law."

The law's capacity to actualise its symbolic potential is confined by the abstract, scientific character of the law and by its institutionalised nature. The characteristics of legal practice prevent the law from representing and giving expression to shared understandings.

The law is limited in its capacity to safeguard basic political values and fundamental rights. These constraints find their origin in the dependence of law on other societal spheres which can possibly lead to the erosion of the rule of law in its very essentials. In such a bleak scenario the term 'limits of the law' comes down to *the end* of the rule of law. Moreover, constrictions on legal guarantees issue from the open texture of the law: the unforeseeable application of legal norms due to far–reaching social changes can always produce a situation in which legal norms in practice drift away from the underlying ideal of 'law as integrity'. In addition, protective legality is limited by the duty of judges to decide cases and by the abstract – often inadequate – scientific frameworks in which these decisions and underlying arguments are made. Finally, the law is limited in its capacity to provide safeguards because legal principles and fundamental rights can always give rise to mutual conflict, without there being a final, reasonable basis to find a balance in one way or another. Citizens here are delivered over to a degree of inescapable, arbitrary public power.

The law's capacity to serve its function of conflict resolution and ensuring social peace reveals itself to be limited in several respects. In this respect, the limits of the law relate to the possibility of hard cases, which deprive the disputing parties from a common normative framework in which they can engage in problem–solving. Another type of limit is connected to the strongly institutionalised character of the law. Finally, the law is restricted in its role of conflict resolution because of the dynamics of endless argumentative refinement which risk undermining the possibility of deciding a case and of bringing to term the process of conflict resolution.

In the following chapters, we will discover how these types of limits of the law, and the corresponding conceptual framework, will bear upon distinct areas of law, and how these limits can be further tested and refined throughout an extensive range of legal disciplines. In doing so, the authors of these chapters address more substantially the first research question (What types of limits of the law can be mapped throughout a variety of legal disciplines?). It will therefore be important to examine in "Facing the Limits of the Law (Conclusion)" how each of them contributed to a further elaboration of the conceptual framework around law's limits.

As to second research question, the following chapters will also help in deepening our understanding of our preoccupation with law's limits by highlighting different aspects of late–modernity. It will be a challenging task to bring these pieces of the puzzle together in the concluding chapter.

Finally, as to the third research question, the coming chapters will also contain strategies to deal responsibly with the limits of the law. Its authors will take effort in drawing on the broader normative aspirations of the rule of law, to present their strategies in their best light. We will systematise them in the concluding chapter, hoping thereby that our leading theme of law's limits does not simply reveal a bleak story, but one which might ultimately strengthen the authority of legal practice and lead to better insight into the potentials of the law. Perhaps then, new opportunities and avenues may open up.

Chapter 2 – Private Law and the Limits of Legal Dogmatics[1]

Marc A. Loth

1 Introduction: A Legal Problem

1.1 Wrongful Life

In 2005 the Dutch *Hoge Raad* (the Supreme Court) decided a wrongful life case.[2] This case concerned a woman who consulted her midwife during her pregnancy because there had been two instances of handicaps in her husband's family due to chromosomal disorder. The midwife did not think it necessary to investigate the matter any further. This was later considered a professional mistake, one with dramatic effects. When born, *baby Kelly* turned out to have serious mental and physical handicaps from which she suffered severely. The parents claimed damages – both on their own account and in Kelly's name – and their claims were upheld by both the Court of Appeal and the Supreme Court. The Supreme Court not only considered the strictly legal issues but also considered moral and pragmatic arguments which had been put forward against such so–called 'wrongful life claims'. First, there was the moral contention that sustaining these claims violated the principle regarding the dignity of human life, since it acknowledged that not being born is preferable to living in a condition like hers. Secondly, there was the pragmatic argument that sustaining claims like this would tempt doctors to practice 'defensive medicine' to avoid serious risk. Both arguments were carefully examined by the court and subsequently rejected. What does the Supreme Court in fact do here? Does it call out or explain the law to us? Or does it exceed its limits by elaborating on principles and policies, taking into account the moral grounds and the possible consequences of the ruling itself? In both directions the question arises: what constitutes the limits of private law?

1.2 Law without Limits?

The reasoning of the Supreme Court in this case exemplifies a pattern that is not uncommon in hard cases, at least not in our part of the world. In first instance it

---

1 This chapter is (in a modified version) published in *Hofstra Law Review* 2007, 1725–1752, and as *Erasmus Hofstra Law Lecture* (Den Haag: Boom Juridische Uitgevers, 2007).

2 HR 18 March 2005, LJN AR5213 (*baby Kelly*).

reasons within the context of the accepted sources of law – in this case the relevant provisions of the Civil Code in an accepted interpretation. In hard cases though, the result of this approach is not completely satisfactory, since the decision is underdetermined by the law. On the one hand, the relevant rules and precedents do not offer sufficient guidance for a decision; while on the other hand, the decision reached cannot be sufficiently justified by the relevant rules and precedents. In the light of the relevant facts the law reveals certain 'gaps', as it were, which have to be filled by factors other than the accepted sources of law. Thus the Supreme Court appeals, in second instance, to principles and policies to fill these gaps in making and justifying its decision in the case at hand. Its reasoning can therefore be considered as a two–step line of reasoning, although the steps cannot always be clearly identified or separated.

This two–step line of reasoning, however, displays some specific characteristics about the limits of law. First, it shows us that the law has what, since H.L.A. Hart, has been referred to as an 'open texture', which means that its rules, precedents, or whatever standards of behaviour will always, in the end, prove to be indeterminate. This is the result of the general nature of the language used and the unpredictability of the social reality in which legal rules, principles, and precedents are applied.[3] Rules are not self–applying, as Wittgenstein noted, and their application is therefore intrinsically mixed with the facts of the case or, in other words, its context.[4] This is the meaning of the old Roman adagium *ius in causa positum* (the law is, in the end, given with the facts). The two–step line of reasoning displays the open texture of law, but it also shows us something of the more fundamental nature of law. The contextual gaps of the law are often filled by principles and policies, by values and practices, by idealistic and pragmatic notions.

This leads to an important distinction among three different dimensions of law, namely the positivistic dimension ('law as it is', accepted sources of law), the idealistic dimension (*de lege ferenda*, 'law as it ought to be') and the pragmatic dimension ('law in action', 'law as it turns out to be'). In a perfect world perhaps, these dimensions would coincide. We do not live in a perfect world, however, and we are brought up with the tensions between 'law as it is' and 'law as it ought to be', on the one hand, and between 'law in the books' and 'law in action' on the other. Moralists and realists have made a business of exploiting these tensions as a domain of research. Lawyers, judges, and courts tend to exploit them in finding an acceptable solution for a specific case. First, they appeal to the positivistic dimension to decide a case, but in hard cases they often appeal to the other dimensions as well (as they did in the *baby Kelly wrongful life* case). Law, then, seems to encompass more than we are inclined to think at first sight. What, then, are its limits? And how are we to find them?

These are highly disputed questions in legal theory. Three Grand Old Theories of law have haunted us for many centuries now. Legal positivism acknowledges the existence of idealistic and pragmatic dimensions, but considers those to be be-

---

3 H.L.A. Hart, *The Concept of Law* (Oxford: Oxford University Press, 1961) 124.

4 L. Wittgenstein, *Philosophical Investigations* (Oxford: Basil Blackwell 1978) par. 84–87.

yond the limits of the law. It defines law by its positivistic dimension, the black letter law of our first intuition. Natural law theory, on the contrary, takes the idealistic dimension to be the defining characteristic element of law, whereas the positive norms are only shadows of these real norms, which lead a somewhat undetermined life "in the omnipresent brooding of the sky" (paraphrasing Oliver Wendell Holmes). Legal realism, lastly, considers the law to be the facts and practices that constitute legal norms and that precede and follow from black letter law. These three Grand Old Theories each take different characteristics of law to be defining: the positivistic, the idealistic, and the pragmatic dimension, respectively. As the German post–war legal philosopher Gustav Radbruch has shown convincingly, these dimensions are not to be considered as different conceptions of law but are inherent tensions *within* the concept of law. The different dimensions of law serve different values, that is, legal certainty, justice, and purpose respectively. The values can never be realised completely at the same time. In law, as elsewhere, inherent values rarely coincide, and mostly conflict with each other. The best one can do in legal practice is to look for and find an equilibrium which exemplifies an optimal combination of these values.[5]

What the Grand Old Theories share, in all their differences, is the mistaken view that the concept of law, and thus its limits, is the result of definition. In my view, instead of defining the concept of law we could do better to investigate the phenomena that present themselves as law (for example in the *baby Kelly* case). Paraphrasing Wittgenstein, one could say,

> Consider the phenomena we call 'law'. ...What is common to them all? Don't say: 'There *must* be something common, or they would not be called 'law'' – but *look and see* whether there is anything common to all. – For if you look at them you will not see something that is common to *all*, but similarities, relationships, and of whole series of them at that. ... I can think of no better expression to characterise these similarities than 'family resemblances': ...law forms a family.[6]

If we follow Wittgenstein's suggestion – don't define the law, but look at it and investigate it – what do we see and find? Is the law demarcated along tight and neat boundaries, reflecting ontological differences, as the Grand Old Theories picture it? Or does it resemble a patchwork of family resemblances of positivistic, idealistic, and realistic dimensions, as the Wrongful life case suggests? Or is law without any limits whatsoever? What does the *baby Kelly* case actually show us, what can we learn from it?

Before we address these questions, a conceptual remark about the notion of the 'limits of law' merits attention. In this chapter we use the notion of the 'limits of law' in the sense of its boundaries, especially in relation to morals and politics. The question into the limits of law then is a question of demarcation: how do we, or how should we, demarcate law from those other domains of practical rationality? As the Grand Old Theories illustrate, this is the core question of legal philosophy into the very nature of the concept of law, which – of course – is also

---

5 G. Radbruch, *Rechtsphilosophie* (Stuttgart: K.F. Koehler Verlag, 1975) 164–170.

6 L. Wittgenstein, *l.c.*, par. 66, 67.

relevant for private law. In this chapter, however, we also touch upon another dimension of the limits of law. As the *baby Kelly* case shows, the question of the boundaries of law is intrinsically connected to the limitations of law, in the sense of its shortcomings. One of the central aims of this book is to shed light on the ability of law to fulfil its basic societal functions, such as legal protection, regulation, dispute resolution, and pacification. One of the obstacles to fulfilling these functions is that private law is unable to draw its boundaries in a neat and predictable way. This, however, is not just a contingent fact. The issue is that private law, by its very nature, is unable to demarcate its domain once and for all in a definable way. Indeed this can be regarded as a limitation, as mentioned before. From another standpoint, however, it can also be regarded as a blessing since it ensures that private law is informed by moral norms and political goals. Whatever standpoint one prefers, it is one of the limits of private law that has to be taken into account in one's professional activities. Since the central aim of this book is not only to display the limits of law, but also to answer the question how to deal with them, we cannot ignore this dimension of our problem. We will return to this issue in the conclusion (section 5). Now let us try to look at our problem from a new, and hopefully unexpected, angle.

2 Solutions from Legal Theory

2.1 Law in Context

In his study *Law in Context,* William Twining gives us an anecdote from the days he lectured in private law at the University of Khartoum in Sudan. In his lecture he discussed a case in which a visitor at a zoo had been feeding a camel and had been bitten by the camel. The question of law was, of course, whether the zoo was liable for the injury caused. At the time a student raised his hand. The lecturer, happy with a question, interrupted his lecture to experience the following anti–climax. "Please, sir," the student asked, "why was the camel in the zoo?" This question puts everything into perspective. Why was the camel in the zoo, while they freely walk around in Sudan? What is the use of lecturing on the common law to an audience to whom the facts of the case are beyond comprehension? That law cannot be properly understood outside the context in which it is developed and learned, is Twining's conclusion, and he therefore pleads for an approach in law "to broaden the study of law from within."[7] In such a contextual approach there are no standard recipes in law. Lawyers should attend to the demands of the circumstances of the case – *pros ton kairon,* in the words of Aristotle[8] – and adjust their responses accordingly.

---

7 W. Twining, *Law in Context. Enlarging a Discipline* (Oxford: Clarendon Press, 1997) 13.

8 Aristotle, *Ethica Nicomachea* (Amsterdam: Kalias, 1997) 106 (bk. II, par. 2, 4).

In my opinion Twining has a strong case, because the suggested approach is not one that is arbitrarily chosen, but is itself the result of relevant developments in law and its study. Let me try to explain this, starting with the contextualisation of law *itself*. Posner has named this phenomenon "the decline of law as an autonomous discipline", by which he refers to the blurring of the sharp boundaries between law, politics, and morality. Let me illustrate this development with examples from the European context, starting with the demarcation between law and politics. Influenced by the doctrine of the separation of powers, this demarcation was rather strict until the end of the 19th century. The content of law was determined by politics, while its shape and enforcement were by and large considered to be the result of doctrinal law. With the emerging welfare State this clear division blurred, because the law became an instrument of politics to change society, while at the same time the judiciary developed new legal standards for politics. As a result of both tendencies the domain of public law has grown, while its content became more and more subject of political controversy. The best example from the Dutch context is offered by the emerging principles of good governance in administrative law, such as the prohibition of the misuse of power and of *détournement de pouvoir*. Though these principles supply additional legal standards for government, their content is seriously disputed. Only recently, politicians complained that government is hindered by the fact that these principles of good governance bring the administrative judiciary too close to the business of politics.

The relation between private law and morality shows similar developments. Until the late 19th century, law and morality were strictly separated, the law enforcing minimal standards of behaviour, leaving the aspirations and ideals to critical morality. From the 20th century onwards, the boundaries were blurred in two opposite directions: the moralisation of private law, and the legalisation of morality. On the one hand, unwritten norms of a moral character got hold of the central doctrines of tort, contract, and property. Most of the classic decisions of the Dutch Supreme Court of the 20th century belong to this category. On the other hand, more and more social relationships were brought under the influence of the law, such as those between teacher and student, parents and children, and doctors and patients ('wrongful life' is an example). Again, the domain of private law has grown, but its norms are increasingly of a social *cum* moral nature and are therefore more disputed.

A telling case from recent years suggests that this development has come to an end. The case concerned an accident in which a boy named Jeffrey drowned in unexplained circumstances after his swimming therapy in a hospital pool. At the time he was under the supervision of his mother and a hospital therapist, but neither was at the poolside in time. The parents did not claim any monetary damages, but rather asked the court for a declaration that the hospital was liable, because that would help them cope with their loss. Should a court give such a moral declaratory ruling, even if it has been conceded that the hospital is liable for the accident? Should the judge become a psychological therapist, instead of the priest or the psychiatrist? The Dutch Supreme Court denied the claim because of a lack of a legitimate interest of the claimants.[9] And that was the end of it.

These examples – however roughly sketched – show that there is every reason "to broaden the study of law from within" (as Twining has referred to it). Law cannot be understood properly – as perhaps in the late 19th century – without reference to politics and morals. Legal discourse has been extended far beyond the traditional boundaries and overlaps with political and moral discourse. As a matter of fact, in legal discourse we regularly appeal to moral principles and pragmatic arguments, besides traditional legal sources. In that sense, law is a meta–discourse, a discourse on other discourses. We could introduce the metaphor of demarcation by saying that the traditional legal sources constitute the inner limits of legal discourse, while principles and policies mark the outer limits. Most lawyers stay within the inner limits most of the time, appealing to statutes, precedents, or customary law. In hard cases, however, when the traditional sources are exhausted, we do in fact appeal to moral and political arguments, not *per se* however, but *as* legal arguments. Although we regularly appeal to other discourses than law, in law we do subject them to the limitations of legal discourse. After all, legal concepts determine what can be said (and thought) in law.

As a result, we have to be aware of two possible risks in this regard. On the one hand there is the risk of losing sight of these limitations. This is the pitfall of those lawyers who tend to forget the limitations of legal discourse, who trespass the boundaries of legal discourse unknowingly, and commit the sins of activism or moralism. They do speak in law, not as lawyers though, but as activists or moralists. On the other hand, however, we run the risk of not exhausting the possibilities because we tend to stay within the inner limits of legal discourse. This is the pitfall of the lawyers we tend to accuse of legalism, formalism, or black–letter law. Again, they do speak in law, and they even speak as lawyers, but they do not speak as open–minded lawyers. I will return to some examples of these pitfalls later on. For now, it suffices to conclude that the contextual approach of law holds between these two opposites. What, then, are the consequences for the study of law? This question will be addressed in the next section.

2.2 The Interdisciplinary Study of Law

One of the reasons "to broaden the study of law from within", as Twining has suggested and we have investigated, is the contextualisation of law itself. There is, nonetheless another good reason for this approach, and that is the contextualisation of *the study of* law (not of law itself). There are, of course, several ways to illustrate this. In legal theory it is an accepted proposition that the application of law, or the identification of a legal proposition, presupposes an interpretation of law. Apart from the facts, legal disputes are mostly disputes on different interpre-

9 HR 9 October 1998, NJ 1998, 853 (*Jeffrey*).

tations of the relevant law.[10] In hard cases different interpretations of law are supported by both parties, each struggling for recognition as the authoritative interpretation. These diverging interpretations are not always the result of mistake or bad faith (although they sometimes are), but of the different interests and perspectives of the parties, lawyers, and judges involved. Interpretation is therefore intrinsically interwoven with the argumentation of different positions.[11] Legal reasoning is essentially a practical syllogism, in which a case is confronted with arguments deduced from experience, and which results in a provisional solution. As Stephen Toulmin has shown us, this line of reasoning is always defeasible, that is, it can always be annulled by adding new information.[12] In this sense it differs from theoretical reasoning, which indeed has the potential to lead to certain and objective conclusions (given the premises). As a domain of practical reason, law lacks this comfortable certainty, leaving its practitioners to find their way in daily practice with no other means than experience and practical wisdom.

As we saw in the *baby Kelly* case, judges may appeal to those principles and policies in their reasoning beyond the more traditional legal sources. And as we argued above, this appeal is subject to the possibilities and limitations of legal discourse. If these observations hold, then this has implications for the nature of legal knowledge. We tend to consider 'thinking like a lawyer' as deliberating on positive law, that is, on the traditional legal sources. If we take the suggestion 'to broaden the study of law from within' seriously, however, then this is not enough and the legal student should learn to think like a sociologist, an economist, or a psychologist as well (recall the Jeffrey case). Or, perhaps, we should say that 'thinking like a lawyer' includes thinking like all these other professionals. A lawyer who understands law in its context will never restrict herself to the strictly legal domain, but will integrate sociological, economic, or psychological expertise. The professional knowledge of a lawyer extends beyond the strictly legal and will overlap with other disciplines. Also in this epistemological sense, law is a discourse on other discourses. In her day–to–day work a lawyer is, at the same time, to some extent an engineer, or an accountant, and such like. Not in the sense that she can replace their expertise, for example as an expert witness, but in the sense that she is capable of analysing the problem into its different aspects and addressing them on their own merits. Again, just like in speaking the legal language, we should realise that this knowledge is applied in a legal context and is therefore subject to the limitations of law and legal discourse. At the end of the day, these elements have to be integrated in one legal judgment. One could even say, perhaps, that it is the particular expertise of the lawyer to integrate all these different kinds of knowledge in a legal judgment. Similarly, a legal scholar who understands law in its context will not restrict herself to legal dogmatics in the strict sense, but will include history, literature, anthropology, and so on. A contextual

---

10 R. Dworkin, *Law's Empire* (Harvard and Cambridge, Mass.: Harvard University Press, 1986) 1–30.

11 P. Ricœur, *The Just* (Chicago and London: The University of Chicago Press, 2000) 109–127.

12 S. Toulmin, *The Uses of Argument* (Cambridge: Cambridge University Press, 1958) 107–113, 118–122, 141–145.

approach is necessarily an inclusive one, resulting in the interdisciplinary study of law.

In a similar tone of voice, James Boyd White has discussed the nature of the interdisciplinary study of law when he combatted 'doctrine in a vacuum' in legal education and pleaded for an interdisciplinary training. Such a training is not one of 'law *and* sociology', 'law *and* economy', or 'law *and* psychology', White argues, but one of 'law *as* (all these other things)'.

> This is a different view of interdisciplinary work from the usual models, for we are not interested in translating findings or even methods from one field to another; rather, in this kind of work each of the disciplines would be looked at as I suggest law should be looked at: as a language, an activity, and with an eye both to its special resources and to its limits.[13]

Put differently, 'thinking like a lawyer' implies thinking like all the others and training in the first should therefore encompass the latter. Not by imitating the sociologist, economist, or psychologist, but by being aware of the sociologist, economist and psychologist elements *in law*. After all, Twining wanted "to broaden the study of law *from within*" (not from the outside). A contextualist approach in law, therefore, implies more than just adding some social circumstances to our thinking and acting in law. It presupposes the capacity to switch perspectives, in the full awareness of the possibilities and limitations of each of the positions chosen (first and foremost the legal one). Contextualism is necessarily connected with perspectivism. There is no such thing as a "view from nowhere" (in the words of Thomas Nagel[14]), but only an observation from the viewpoint of the observer. Every observation presupposes a blind spot, which is the context that cannot be observed from the standpoint taken. One has to step aside to observe the blind spot, thus creating a new one.

2.3 Alternative Theories of Private Law

In this contextualist approach to private law, its limits then are fluid and constantly changing, depending on context and perspective. Are any alternatives available? There are two I can think of, and I call them 'back to dogmatics' and 'forward to policies' respectively. I hope to show that they represent extremes that should be avoided, since they commit the sins of respectively underexploiting legal discourse and trespassing the boundaries of legal discourse that we discussed above. The position taken here represents a middle position that, at least in my view, avoids the pitfalls of the alternatives while combining their advantages.

First, then, the programme of 'back to dogmatics', for which I take Weinrib's views to be exemplary. Weinrib is concerned with an understanding of private

---

13 J. Boyd White, *From Expectation to Experience, Essays on Law and Legal Education* (Ann Arbor: University of Michigan Press, 1999) 22.

14 T. Nagel, *The View from Nowhere* (New York, and Oxford, England: Oxford University Press, 1986).

law, his claim being that private law is to be understood in its own terms (and not in terms of its purpose). In Weinrib's view, private law is a self–understanding enterprise, that is, it is simultaneously *explanandum* and *explanans*, both an object and a mode of understanding. Thus understood, the idea of private law is considered to be a synthesis of three theses, namely formalism (the understanding of private law through its structure), corrective justice (the specification of this structure), and a Kantian notion of rights (the moral standpoint immanent in this structure).[15] In Weinrib's view, private law is autonomous, and he rejects any "law and ..." approach as resulting in either reductionism or an infinite regress. Though he acknowledges that law can be understood in terms of its history, sociology, or economy, the understanding of law in its own terms – namely legal dogmatics in its purest form – is the only legitimate approach of law.

On the other hand, there is the 'forward to policies' program, for which I take Richard Posner's ideas to be exemplary. Posner offers a pragmatist program that is practical, instrumental, forward–looking, activist, empirical, skeptical and anti–dogmatic and experimental.[16] Posner's pragmatism is quite the opposite of Weinrib's formalism. For Posner, his law–and–economics program introduces in law the ethics of scientific inquiry, because economics is the instrumental science *par excellence*. Modern economics offers the theoretical framework for the empirical research in law. The economic analysis of law therefore denies law's autonomy; legal rules are viewed in instrumental terms. Both law and legal rules are analysed in terms of means to achieve certain ends, be it wealth maximisation or something else. Its moral concern is to serve the welfare of the non–legal community. Law itself is considered to be a mechanism for social control, to be replaced by more effective ones as soon as they are available. Legal dogmatics in its current form is pretentious, prejudiced, and uninformed, Posner concludes, and should be replaced by a more pragmatic program.

This is not the time and place to address both programs on their own merits, but I do want to make the point that the proposed 'law in context' approach holds the middle ground between both poles. In more abstract terms, the comparison can be framed as follows. Like Weinrib's program, the 'law in context' approach acknowledges a certain autonomy for law and legal dogmatics, though it does take into account the increasing importance of mutual influences between law and its contexts. There is no reason whatsoever to ban approaches that focus on law in context, though we should not forget that external influences are integrated into law. That is why we preferred the expression 'law *as* ...' over 'law *and* ...', since the former expresses this need for integration in law better than the latter. Like Posner's program, ours acknowledges that law cannot be understood properly without taking its context into account (economics included), though we should not reduce law to economics. Not only because there are other legitimate perspectives, but also because law cannot be understood properly in purely instrumental

15 E.J. Weinrib, *The Idea of Private Law* (Cambridge, Mass. and London: Harvard University Press, 1995), 11–19.

16 R.A. Posner, *Overcoming Law* (Cambridge, Mass. and London: Harvard University Press, 1995), 11–15.

terms since it has and expresses values of its own. For that reason law cannot be made instrumental to any political purpose whatsoever; some purposes are simply contradictory to law's own values, such as the principles of legal certainty, justice, and purpose, distinguished by Radbruch.

'Law in context' then is preferable to 'back to dogmatics' and 'forward to policies'. In the first place, it holds the promise of better law than the alternatives. It is my conviction that contextualists do better as lawyers than formalists and activists, both with respect to the development of law and the deciding of cases. Secondly, and more importantly in this context, it provides us with a better understanding of law than the accounts of Weinrib and Posner do. Law is neither a mere instrument for policy, nor an island in itself. It is a social practice with a semi–autonomous language, methods, and values. The understanding of law then should not be merely reductionist or self–referential – as in the accounts of Posner and Weinrib – but should give insight into its relations with the different contexts in which it is developed and applied. 'Law in context' offers just that.

3 Philosophical Foundations

3.1 Private Law as a Battlefield

Private law belongs – along with medicine and theology – to the eldest of disciplines. In fact, the history of the university started in the 11th century in Bologna with the rediscovery and the study of the *Codex Iuris Civilis* of Justinian. From then onwards private law has always been – with variations in focus and method – the study of authoritative texts to solve cases. Private lawyers pretty much stuck to their methods, when science and technology emerged in the 17th century. Since the 18th century the study of society began to evolve and resulted in a process of *Ausdifferenzierung* of the various social sciences out of the shadow of the law. Economics emerged from the administration of government, political economy, and a new focus on the empirical effects of the law (Marx). Anthropology took its starting point in the study of law and legal practice in newly discovered cultures (Maine). The founding fathers of sociology took an interest in the process of modernisation in which law (like religion) played an important role (Durkheim, Weber). It is noteworthy that all the pioneers mentioned were lawyers by education: it was a new way of looking at law and society that started these new disciplines. Next, it was a process of specialisation – stimulated by external factors – that facilitated the development into separate, autonomous disciplines. This process of specialisation has, of course, advantages and disadvantages. On the one hand it focuses the necessary attention to make any progress whatsoever; while on the other hand it forces one to bracket off different procedures, methods, or perspectives, thus stimulating selective blindness. "Selective attention is one thing," Toulmin writes, but "blinders are another".[17] I will try to illustrate this later on. For now, it suffices to conclude that the demarcation between legal dogmatics and the other social sciences is a contingent matter.

As a result of these developments, the study of private law is a battlefield. On the surface it has developed rather quietly since the days of its birth, the main development being the transition from a *Ius Commune* to national codified private law in the early 19th century with the emergence of Nation–States, and now with their erosion back into a European private law. Beneath the surface however, there is a lot more going on. First, the separation between the Natural Sciences and the Humanities – "The Two Cultures", as C.P. Snow put it[18]– has left its traces in private law too. Not only in topics of substantive law (like causation), but also in method. Traditional legal dogmatics has found its home in the humanities, but from time to time ideals and devices are borrowed from the sciences. Let me mention a few examples without pretending to be complete: Langdell's legal formalism, Von Savigny's *Begriffsjurisprudenz*, Kelsen's *Reine Rechtslehre*, and Hart's analytical jurisprudence. These and other movements in (private) law shared an inspiration in science, which manifested itself in the ideals of objective knowledge, a rational method, order and system in law, and a strict separation between law and politics/law and morals.[19] As such they were nearly always followed by a reaction in the form of a turn to society: legal formalism by Holmes's legal realism, *Begriffsjurisprudenz* by *Interessenjurisprudenz*, the analytical movement by the critical legal studies, and so on.[20] We find a pendulum located in private law going back and forth between system and society, logic and experience, technique and policy. This movement had a large impact, not only on the study of private law, but also on the practice and content of private law itself.

Next, there is the differentiation in different disciplines which has not left the study of private law untouched. Paradoxically, the early differentiation of the social sciences from law confirmed the core of the study of private law in its dogmatic, practice–oriented approach. It stimulated a professional ideology that legal dogmatics sticks to positive law and its application in cases, leaving out the rest. Let me try to explain this, explicating some of the 'blinders' I mentioned before. With regard to its subject matter from the start, legal dogmatics has been a study of authoritative texts, taking these texts as the sources of positive law. In limiting itself to texts, legal dogmatics has left practice to the social sciences. To fill the gap between the study of law and the social sciences in the late 20th century bridging (sub–) disciplines emerged, such as sociology of law, anthropology of law, psychology of law, and so on. A peculiar development, if one realises that sociology, anthropology, psychology and the others emerged from the study of law in

17 S. Toulmin, *Return to Reason* (Cambridge, Mass. and London: Harvard University Press, 2001) 42, 43.

18 C.P. Snow, "The Two Cultures and the Scientific Revolution", in *Public Affairs* (New York: Charles Scribner's Sons, 1971) 13–47.

19 K. Larenz, *Methodenlehre der Rechtswissenschaft* (Berlin: Springer Verlag, 1979) 1–165.

20 A. Hunt, *The Sociological Movement in Law* (London and Basingstoke: The Macmillan Press, 1978).

the first place. This restriction to texts is one blinder of legal dogmatics, but not the only one. With regard to the purpose of the study of law, I have already mentioned that it has always been dedicated to cases, using authoritative texts as the *loci* for arguments in legal dispute. As such it operates between law and case, text and context, logic and experience. Legal dogmatics has thus always played an important social role, though at the expense of the formation of theory, which was left to other disciplines. With regard to the method legal dogmatics has always stayed close to text–analytical methods – whether the scholastic method, philology, or hermeneutics – thus leaving the use of empirical methods to other disciplines. These limitations make us aware that legal dogmatics has always been a limited enterprise: it restricted itself to positive law for pleading and solving cases by using analytical methods on authoritative texts. This is legal dogmatics in the proper sense.[21] As such, it has left empirical research into legal practice and the formation of theory to other social (sub–) sciences. Legal dogmatics has thus both defined law and its context, restricting itself to the former, and leaving the latter to other disciplines. Again, the study of law and thereby the definition of law itself appear to be a contingent matter.

Legal dogmatics has its own reasons, of course, to suggest otherwise. The authority of its expertise is underlined by the suggestion that its subject matter, purpose, and method are somehow 'given', thus resulting in the exclusion of different approaches to the study of law. As mentioned before, this focus is beneficial for the growth of knowledge within the given paradigm, but this is achieved at the cost of bracketing off different approaches and perspectives. In their day–to–day work however, legal scholars find themselves often referring to the demands of 'practice', which is an often used, and sometimes misused, expression. Sometimes it refers to the principles or policies involved, at other times to (aspects) of the context of the case, and again at other times to the particular preferences of the scholar. At this point my plea for a 'law in context' approach comes in, not as a radical alternative for the existing practice of legal dogmatics, but as a way of conceptualising the appeal to 'practice'. Does it refer to a calculation of consequences, to the social circumstances of parties involved, to the principles and policies lurking in the background of positive law, or to some other relevant context? This question can only be answered by changing perspective – from legal dogmatics to the economics, sociology, psychology, or history of law – not to end up finding ourselves in a different discipline, but to integrate this perspective in our own legal discourse. In its daily life, law *is* – besides everything else – economics, sociology, psychology, history, literature, and so on. Why then do we not integrate these perspectives in the study of law? The interdisciplinary study of law – properly understood – is meant to improve the study of law and thus to enhance our understanding of the law, no more, no less. What does that mean for the private lawyer's expertise? We will address this question in the next section.

---

[21] Larenz, *l.c.*, 204.

3.2 The Private Lawyer's Expertise

In private law, as in other disciplines, our picture of professional knowledge has long been dictated by the model of technical rationality. According to this model professional knowledge is nothing more, or less for that matter, than the application of scientific knowledge, like a kind of technology. This model fits positivistic premises, of course, since it rests on the characteristic positivist separation of means and ends, facts and values. In law, it served the purpose of the separation of 'law as it is' and 'law as it ought to be', the latter being the domain of the politician or the moralist, and the former being that of the lawyer. In legal theory, it has found expression in the movements of legalism, formalism, the case method of Langdell, and Von Savigny's *Begriffsjurisprudenz*. In practice however, the model of technical rationality served a specific need for the justification of professional practice. The rise of positivism in the 19th century demarcated a shift from a 'legitimacy of character' to a 'legitimacy of technique': the privileges of the profession were no longer justified by the social position, honour, and the authority and character of its practitioners (their courage, wisdom, responsibility), but by the application of objective and rational scientific techniques.[22] Weber has framed this shift in the social domain as one from charismatic authority (depending on the person of the authority) to authority on legal and rational grounds (depending on the methods used).[23]

Since the decline of positivism however, this model of professional practice has been discredited, both for intellectual and social reasons. Socially, we have lost our appreciation for technocrats who instrumentally apply their scientific expertise for whatever purposes. The 20th century offers plenty of examples to justify this discontent. Intellectually, we have come to a different and more complex understanding of what it takes to participate in professional practice. Let me try to express that understanding by comparing the expertise of a private lawyer with that of a private legal scholar. Three differences come into view. The first is that the body of professional knowledge of lawyers practising in the field of private law is organised differently, not according to the principle of logical coherence, but according to that of practical utility. They are not so much interested in the system of private law, of course, as in its use–based organisation. Secondly, the professional knowledge of the private lawyer has a larger component of practical knowledge than that of the private law scholar, while the latter has a larger component of theoretical knowledge. On the difference between theoretical and practical knowledge, 'knowing that' and 'knowing how', *epistèmè* and *phronèsis* (as Aristotle would say), there is such a vast amount of literature that I will not discuss here.[24] For now, it suffices to say that the first is conceptual, propositional

---

22 A. Abbott, *The System of Professions: An Essay on the Division of Expert Labor* (Chicago and London: Chicago University Press, 1988) 184–195.

23 M. Weber, *The Theory of Social and Economic Organization* (New York: the Free Press, 1964) 328.

24 G. Ryle, *The Concept of Mind* (New York: Penguin Books, 1980) 28–32.

knowledge, while the latter is of a perceptual and dispositional nature. For that reason, practical knowledge is partly "personal knowledge", as Michael Polanyi would have it, or "tacit knowledge".[25] A practitioner usually knows more than she can tell. From both the first and the second difference, it follows that the professional knowledge of the private lawyer has a larger moral component than that of the private legal scholar. The practitioner knows better what to do under what circumstances, not only from a legal point of view but also from a moral point of view. In fact, it is part of her expertise to know in private law what to do and when, as it is the scholar's expertise to fit and explain this solution in terms of the system of private law. These differences are there not to be neglected, though they do not deny the connections between both types of expertise, as both the private lawyer and the private legal scholar would confirm. What they deny, though, is that the relation between both types of knowing is simply one of application, as the model of technical rationality would have it.

The private lawyer's expertise, then, is far more inclusive than we are inclined to think. It encompasses knowledge and competences, of a legal, moral, or some other kind, both explicitly and implicitly belonging to the lawyers' repertoire. In a case like the *baby Kelly wrongful life* case, for example, the Dutch Supreme Court considered not only the legal issues, but also the moral grounds for the different options, as well as their expected consequences. This includes moral wisdom, legal interpretation, financial calculation of the consequences, and a feeling of empathy with the parties, especially *baby Kelly*'s parents. In doing so, the judges appeal to different contexts of the case, bringing to bear their moral, economic, psychological, and other experiences. To get these different contexts into view the judge has to change perspective, subsequently taking a legal, moral, economic, or other perspective, and eventually integrating them into one decision that fits and justifies the law at stake.

Now compare this way of proceeding with the alternatives: excluding non–legal elements from the decision, and following policies of one's own preference. In my view, the contextualist approach promises more informed, and therefore better law. Now let us switch to the legal scholar. For the private law scholar who is trying to make sense of the ruling, there is not much difference. When she tries to understand the ruling, she can of course neglect all the expertise that does not fit into the model of legal dogmatics as a self–sufficient enterprise (as Weinrib's scholar would do). In my view, she would thus make poor sense of the ruling and she would not do justice to the court. On the other hand, she can try to reconstruct the ruling as an attempt to realise some predetermined extra–legal policy or goal (as Posner's legal scholar would do). Again, I think she would misunderstand the ruling and would not do justice to the court. In lieu of these options, she could also try to review the ruling from different perspectives, alternatively taking the moral, financial, psychological, and legal aspects into account. In other words, she could try to study the ruling in different contexts, thus bringing different kinds of expertise to bear. At the end of the day she will attempt to integrate these different kinds

25 M. Polanyi, *Personal Knowledge: Towards a Post–Critical Philosophy* (Chicago and London: University of Chicago Press, 1958) 1962.

of expertise in a coherent understanding of the case, expressing her views on what the court has ruled and what this ruling attributes to the law. Of course, she may fail in doing so, but at least she has tried to come to a better understanding of the law than the available alternatives can provide.

4 Back to Law

4.1 Integrity in Law, and in Lawyers Too

So far we have argued the need for switching perspectives by taking different contexts into account, both in the practice and in the study of law. This approach holds the promise of better informed law as well as a more comprehensive understanding of legal practice. To fulfill this promise it is not enough to compare these different perspectives, we mentioned in passing, we really have to integrate them into our practice or understanding of the law. For James Boyd White this means that we have to put them together in something new that changes our understanding of the composite parts. "As lawyers we cannot simply accept the conclusions of others; we must make them our own, and to do that we must move out of the legal culture and into the other one."[26] For White, this process is very similar to that of the translation of texts, not as a simple substitution of words, but in the sense of creating a new discourse of meaning. In law itself this process is exemplified by the way the expertise of expert witnesses is integrated in legal deliberation and judgment. Forensic and psychiatric expertise is transformed into a legal judgment, but not without mutual influence and transformation. In the study of law, bridge–disciplines like the sociology or psychology of law illustrate the same point: their best practices are not to be considered as an application of sociological or psychological theory to law, nor as mere examples of legal imperialism, but as a contribution to new ways of looking, talking, and knowing.

In cases of the integration of non–legal knowledge, it is of course harder to pass Ronald Dworkin's integrity test than when we integrate just another legal case. Law as integrity requires an interpretive attitude: a specific case is interpreted as the best possible continuation of legal practice, thus fitting as well as justifying the practice as a whole. For legal cases this means that they are interpreted as an exemplification of the principles and values lurking behind legal rules and precedents. The question is then: what is the best realisation of these principles and values in this case? The answer to this question may, as we know, even contradict accepted interpretations of legal rules and precedents (*contra legem*).[27] Now, what happens if we try to integrate originally 'non–legal' knowledge in the body of legal knowledge, as in the examples given? The metaphor of translation

---

[26] J. Boyd White, *Justice as Translation: An Essay in Cultural and Legal Criticism* (Chicago and London, University of Chicago Press, 1990) 14.

[27] R. Dworkin, *l.c.*, 225–276.

sets us on the right track, since it makes us aware that intellectual integration is a matter of bridging cultures, that is, of languages, methods, and values. Take the example of a legal scholar and a scientist engaging in interdisciplinary research. They may be tempted to conceptualise the obstacles they encounter as differences in idiom, method, and values. The gap between their cultures almost seems unbridgeable then. Idioms cannot be translated without loss of meaning; different methods determine a different outlook, and both are in the end reducible to diverging beliefs and attitudes. Is there no way, then, to escape this fragmentation in our disciplines?

There is, and in my view it can be phrased like this. The crucial step is getting to learn to recognise the foreign elements in our own culture and thus (reciprocally) the characteristic elements in our own culture. What does the law do with forensic or scientific evidence? And what does that teach us about the legal outlook itself? How does the law conceptualise human relations, and what can we conclude about legal concepts? How do we strike the balance between the demands of safety and traditional liberty rights, and what does it tell us about these rights? How does the Dutch Supreme Court in its ruling in the *baby Kelly* case appeal to the moral principle of the dignity of human life? And what does that tell us about the relationship between law and morality? Such questions really draw our attention to interdisciplinary research, since they address the foundations of our own discipline as well. In law and its study, as in daily life, the communication with other practices cannot but influence our own practices. This is what intellectual integration is all about: a slow and difficult development of our own culture in the continuous contact with others, thereby opening new horizons, at the same time closing others.

The attempt to remedy fragmentation can be taken one step further, as a struggle against the fragmentation in ourselves. For this, we should start to consider diverging bodies of knowledge or conceptual frameworks as different communities thinking and talking. In the words of James Boyd White,

> We should conceive of the relevant world as a world of people talking to each other across their discourses, out of their languages, out of their communities of knowledge and expertise, and speaking as people seeking to be whole. We should try to write that way ourselves.[28]

Engaging in interdisciplinary research entails communication with representatives of other disciplines, getting to know their way of speaking and thinking, and thus (again, reciprocally) getting to know ourselves, as lawyers. As such it exemplifies the old Socratic wisdom in modern disguise: know thyself, as a lawyer. Self–knowledge cannot but serve a therapeutic purpose as well. The interdisciplinary study of law is not only a remedy for the fragmentation in law and our understanding of it, it is also a remedy for the fragmentation in ourselves. Changing perspective draws from different sources in us, restoring our blinders, fighting professional deformation, and leaving us as richer and more competent lawyers – not only and perhaps not even primarily because of our expertise, but at least as much

---

[28] *Ibid.*, 20.

because of our imagination. The continuous contact with different perspectives and other disciplines therefore not only makes us better lawyers, but perhaps even better persons. After all, integrity not only characterises legal systems, but people as well.

4.2 Wrongful Life Readdressed

Let us, finally, readdress the wrongful life case with which we started. In the light of what has been said thus far it can be considered to be a serious attempt to integrate a moral perspective into the legal one, since it explicitly appeals to the principle of the dignity of human life. As such it deserves our praise. Faced with the moral nature of the issue at stake, the Dutch Supreme Court was not satisfied with taking the safe road, that is, an appeal to legal sources. The Court apparently also wanted to judge the issue on its own merits, thus trying to contribute to a public debate about a controversial matter. The Court chose for itself a specific ethos, as a moral guide in a pluralistic society. Of course the members of the Court would never admit to this, but it suggests the ambition to play a social role like a "philosopher–king" as identified by Plato. The question is whether the judiciary is equipped to fulfil the function of a moral compass in matters of substantial justice in a morally divided society. It may well be, as Sunstein remarks, that, "Like all of us, judges have limited time and capacities, and like almost all of us, judges are not trained as philosophers."[29]

Has the attempt of the Supreme Court to integrate a moral perspective into its ruling in the case of *baby Kelly* been successful then? In my opinion, the answer is negative. The Supreme Court undertook to investigate whether or not sustaining the claim for compensation of the parents of *baby Kelly* (both on their own account and in the name of Kelly) would constitute a violation of the principle of the dignity of human life. The Supreme Court addresses this question no less than three times – in the context of its quashing several arguments of the defendants/appellants – showing a gradual integration of this argument in the reasons of its decision. Let us analyse the argument closer. First, the Court states that the implicit recognition of the birth of a handicapped child as 'injury' – in establishing a causal relation between the midwife's fault and the damage to the plaintiffs – does not imply any judgment whatsoever on the value of that child as a person or its existence (consideration 4.4). The argument is not yet integrated in the final reasons here; it is more or less added as a side comment, an *obiter dictum*. Second, the Court states that sustaining the parents' claim for non–material damages – which is the decision of the Court in this context – does not imply that the child is a source of grief to them, but rests exclusively on the judgment that the midwife's fault infringes the fundamental rights of the parents (consideration 4.10). The Court seems to suggest a specific reading of its own decision here: we should see

[29] C.R. Sunstein, *One Case at a Time: Judicial Minimalism on the Supreme Court* (Cambridge, Mass. and London: Harvard University Press 1999) 249.

it as a consequence of the fault, not as a judgment on the meaning of the life of the child. The argument is therefore better integrated here than in its first use. Even more integrated is the third occasion of use, when the Supreme Court deals with the defence that the damages cannot be determined, since if the fault would not have been committed, *baby Kelly* would not have been born at all. The Court rejects this defence on the legal ground that the damages should be estimated in a case like this. Sustaining this claim does not in any way imply that the existence of Kelly should be valued lower than her non–existence, the Court argues, but rests on the recognition of the unlawfulness of the acts by the midwife and the hospital. Holding them liable does not infringe Kelly's dignity, the Court concludes, but, on the contrary, facilitates her – as far as money ever can – to lead a human life (consideration 4.15). Here the argument is most fully integrated, because the Court finally provides a reason why the principle of human dignity is not infringed. But is it a good reason?

I do not think so. Although it looks plausible enough – at first sight it even looks like a truism – it changes the nature of the argument it seeks to refute. First, it addresses not so much human dignity in an abstract sense – as it was put forward by the defendants – but the dignity of this specific existence, the life of *baby Kelly*. Next, human dignity does not function as a ground for the judgment – as it was used by the German *Bundesverfassungsgericht* ("Die Verpflichtung aller staatlichen Gewalt, jedem Menschen in seinem Dasein um seiner selbst willen zu achten ..., verbietet es, die Unterhaltsplicht für ein Kind als Schaden zu begreifen") – but as a goal of the ruling (the possibilities for Kelly to lead a human life). As a result, the appeal to human dignity has been transformed from an argument of principle to a pragmatic argument.[30] In short, the Supreme Court did succeed in integrating this moral argument into its ruling, but not without a fundamental transformation of its nature. Is this a serious flaw? I think it is, for two reasons. First, it misses the point of the argument of the opponents. Nobody in his right mind will deny that compensation for damage will put *baby Kelly* in a better position to lead a human life, but that was not the argument of the plaintiffs. Their argument was that doing this will infringe the principle of the dignity of human life, and this still holds true. Besides, the argument of the Supreme Court justifies too much. The proposition that compensation for damage will put the victim in a better position to lead a human life is valid for almost any medical liability claim. In fact, the Court confines itself to a policy of victim protection.[31]

---

30 P.S. Attiyah, *From Principles to Pragmatism: Changes in the Function of the Judicial Process and the Law* (Inaugural lecture, delivered before the University of Oxford on 17th February 1978) (Oxford: Oxford University Press, 1978).

31 The line of reasoning followed here is borrowed from an earlier publication: M.A. Loth, "Engaged in a search for justice: over grenzeloze aansprakelijkheid en de moeizame integratie van een moreel principe", in M. Buijsen (ed.), *Onrechtmatig leven? Opstellen naar aanleiding van baby Kelly* (Nijmegen: Valkhof Pers, 2006) 40–47.

5 Conclusion

Starting with the ruling of the Dutch Supreme Court in the *baby Kelly wrongful life* case we asked ourselves: what constitutes the limits of private law? The Grand Old Theories defined fixed limits, as we mentioned, but they do not fit the growing complexity of legal practice today. So we changed our strategy and asked ourselves what law actually shows us. At closer inspection we found that it shows a patchwork of characteristics or family resemblances, in different combinations in changing circumstances. The *baby Kelly* case is just one example of a hard case in which the Dutch Supreme Court explicitly appeals to a moral principle and empirical effects to justify its ruling (besides the traditional appeal to legal sources). As such, it is a perfect illustration of the way the positivistic, idealistic, and pragmatic dimensions of private law interrelate.

What specific legal theory then offers the best account of the current practice of private law? In this chapter it is argued that the 'law in context' approach offers the best possible theory, both in terms of fit and in terms of justification of current legal practice. First, it does justice to the most prominent developments in law itself in the 20th century, which can be characterised as a 'contextualisation' of the legal system (by which we refer to the blurring distinctions between law, politics, and morality). Second, it seems a perfectly natural consequence of the developments in the study of law, which have resulted in a prominent position for the interdisciplinary study of law. In all respects, 'law in context' seems preferable to the most likely alternatives 'back to dogmatics' and 'forward to policies'. I have tried to present 'law in context' as middle ground between both alternatives, combining their virtues while avoiding their vices. Perhaps both alternatives can be considered as reminiscents of a surpassed positivistic ideology, but the argumentation of that hypothesis would need more attention.

The question, then, is how legal dogmatics – itself the product of contingent developments – can be enriched by the 'law in context' approach. In the most general terms, the recipe is twofold. First, we must keep an open eye for the contextuality of law and legal phenomena and be ready to give the contextual dimension of law its due. In legal practice this is stimulated by the prominence of the facts and the training of legal practitioners in their dealing with them. Their expertise contains a good deal of practical wisdom and a strong hold on moral attitudes, which is constantly triggered and strengthened. No practitioner in her right mind would deny – in principle or in practice – the contextuality of law, unless she is misled by some legal theory like Langdell's legal formalism, Von Savigny's *Begriffsjurisprudenz*, or Kelsen's *Reine Rechtslehre*. In legal dogmatics, however, it is much harder to keep an eye open for the contextuality of law. Legal scholars deal differently with law and are more subject to methodological schools and convictions. Here my second device applies. Legal scholars should do better in interdisciplinary research, not as an escape from the application of the results or methods of other disciplines in the domain of law, but as a way of changing perspective to grasp otherwise unnoticed aspects of the practice under research. This is not the "law *and* ..." approach that is viewed critically by so many, but a "law *as* ..." approach that James Boyd White has addressed.

Interdisciplinary research entails both a broadening of the horizon as well as an intellectual integration of the results. From this perspective we have readdressed the ruling of the Dutch Supreme Court in the case of *baby Kelly*. The integration of a moral argumentation – though most promising at first sight – turned out to be less than a success at closer analysis. The Court ended up surrendering to a policy of victim protection (a perfect exemplification of the 'forward to policies' approach). The reason is that it unconditionally placed the decision in the service of the humanity of the life to be lived by Kelly. There are other techniques for the integration of moral and pragmatic arguments, however, that can avoid this pitfall. The Court could have, for example, restricted its ruling to this specific case, or it could have used specific legal concepts as an intermediary for moral considerations. These techniques of integration deserve more attention than received in this chapter. The same goes for the techniques of interdisciplinary research in legal dogmatics, as a way of enriching the study of law. There is gold in those hills, but we have not yet sufficiently explored them.[32]

Let us, finally, return to the twofold problem of the limits of private law from which we started. As we noted from the start, the problem of the boundaries of private law is intrinsically connected to that of its limitations, in the sense of its shortcomings. What, then, are the consequences of the conclusions drawn for the way we should deal with private law and its inherent limitations? Three consequences can be stated explicitly. First, we must be cured of our obsession with neat and timeless boundaries between private law on the one hand, and morals and politics on the other. This obsession is a residue from legal thinking of a different age, and rests on a picture of private law that is less accurate than it ever was. The 'law in context' approach is presented as a remedy for this obsession that reminds us that private law is in constant interaction with morals and politics through the intellectual and moral operation of integration. Next, however, we must be aware that this does not mean that private law loses its own specific characteristics. On the contrary, it is on the basis of continuing reflection on legal concepts and legal argumentation in the context of their use that we constantly renew and reinvent our legal repertoire. For that reason the ideal of 'law as integrity' is constantly challenged through the comparison and confrontation of our legal perspective with other than strictly legal ways of seeing and speaking. Finally, we have argued that if we succeed in achieving some success in this renewed way of dealing with private law, this has unavoidable consequences for legal dogmatics as well. We concluded, paradoxically, that we will reach a better insight into the specific nature of private law if we integrate different perspectives and viewpoints, that is, if we open up legal dogmatics to the interdisciplinary study of law. Only then, we will be able to face the limits of private law.

---

32 This seems to be the attitude of prominent legal scholars in the Netherlands as well, such as J.B.M. Vranken, *Algemeen Deel* (vervolg) (Deventer: Kluwer, 2005) and H. Nieuwenhuis, *Waartoe is het recht op aarde?* (Den Haag: Boom Juridische Uitgevers, 2006) 1–32.

Chapter 3 – The Limits of the Law of Obligations

Kurt Willems

1 Introduction: Limits of the Law of Obligations

When examining the limits of the law of obligations, especially with regard to its regulatory and pacifying function, one notices certain domains and social spheres where legally enforceable obligations seem out of place. One can hardly imagine a social engagement between two friends ("I'll meet you at 12 o'clock for dinner") being legally enforceable. Nor the invitation to a dinner party (whether the invitation is accepted or not) or nor a father's promise to pay for his son's vacation if he obtains his university degree.[1] These agreements are part of the domain of 'non–droit'.[2]

Agreements between close relatives are often placed outside the scope op the law of obligations: "the courts must be careful when family arrangements are entered into not to try and force those arrangements into an unfitting legal straitjacket."[3] Agreements concerning one's religious conviction or religious life are usually disregarded by law. Arrangements in the domain of non–professional sports are often not legally enforceable. An agreement can also be null and void in the eyes of the law because its object or its purpose violates the public order or offends against moral standards. Contracts contrary to physical integrity, fundamental rights, or human dignity may unilaterally be revoked whenever a party deems the agreement to have become irreconcilable with his conscience.[4] Parties may also explicitly decide to keep their agreement outside the scope of the law.[5]

---

1 E. Dirix, "Le 'Gentlemen's agreement' dans la théorie du droit et la pratique contemporaine", *Rev. Dr. Int. Comp.* 1999, 223, 225 e.s.

2 J. Carbonnier, *Flexible droit* (Paris: LGDJ, 1991) 20 e.s. See also *Balfour v Balfour* [1919] 2 KB 571.

3 *Hardwick v Johnson*, (1978) 2 All ER 935.

4 *E.g.* a contract between a stripper and a nightclub, the promise to subject oneself to medical experiments, etc.

5 'Gentlemen's agreements' or 'agreements binding in honour only'. In Belgian law, parties to an agreement are allowed to keep their agreement outside the scope of the law, on the condition that they do not violate the regulations which are part of the public order or moral standards, nor the regulations which are established to protect the weaker party to a contract (E. Dirix, *l.c.*, 234–237). See also on the subject F.W. Grosheide, "The Gentlemen's Agreement in Legal Theory and in Modern Practice – The Dutch Civil Law Perspective", in *International Contract Law. Articles on Various Aspects of Transnational Contract Law* (Antwerp: Intersentia, 2004) and B. Rudden, "The Gentleman's Agreement in Legal Theory and in Modern Practice", *European Review of Private Law* 1999, 199.

The law of obligations is ever broadening its scope and covering more and more relationships. Since many of the new statutory regulations are designed to protect weaker parties to an agreement (employees, consumers, and so on) against unlawful provisions, citizens generally accept this broadening intrusion of the law into their lives. However, one argument remains particularly resilient, that is, the argument that things should be left to someone's conscience, rather than imposed by law. Indeed, the domain of morality and ethics has always had an ambiguous relationship with the law. Often they overlap; but at least as often, statutory intervention is deemed unsuited and inappropriate to regulate the moral issue at play.

2 Limits of the Law of Obligations with Regard to Morality

In the domain of morals and ethics, many values are at stake which are essential to the workings of the constitutional State. Often, it is vital that a system of law can intervene in the domain of morality and fulfill a regulatory function, in order to make sure that a certain degree of moral consciousness is always maintained within society, regardless of the cultural background, education, religious views, or moral beliefs of a particular individual. Moreover, a body of positive law, as a matter of empirical social psychology, often comes to have the content that it has because the legislator seeks to have the content of law tracking morality. In the field of obligations, there is considerable correspondence between the circumstances under which morality acknowledges a promise to be binding or justifiably broken, and those under which the law will enforce or release a contractual obligation. Provisions in the law of negligence mirror moral norms about the moral culpability to neglectful behaviour.[6] However, intervention by the law of obligations is often described as intrusive, sometimes even as disordering the internal dynamics of morality, as some situations are deemed too delicate for government regulation. A promise is quickly made; a reproach easily given between members of the same family. Utilising contract or tort law to attach legal consequences to such an action would make family life virtually impossible.[7] In other instances, the law of obligations is inapt, as in the moral duty to be generous in charity. The obligation to give to charity is a universal duty imposed upon the prosperous part of the population. On its own, it does not constitute a specific relationship between two parties which can be regulated by contract or tort law. In those cases, a regulatory function is left to the normative system of morality instead of law.

When someone does not keep his word or does not behave as might be expected of a normal, careful person, the law fulfills a pacifying function and settles the dispute. However, the law of obligations is unable to achieve its full effect

---

6 R. A. Shiner, "Law and Morality", in D. Patterson (ed.), *A Companion to Philosophy of Law and Legal Theory* (Cambridge, Mass.: Blackwell Publishing 1999) 436–437.

7 See on the rights and minors R. Kaufman, "Protecting the Rights of Minors; On Juvenile Autonomy and the Limits of the Law", *N.Y.U.L. Rev.* 1977, 1015, 1016 and B. Beignier, *L'honneur et le droit*, in *Bibliothèque de droit privé* (Paris: L.G.D.J., 1995).

whenever society deems it improper to position two persons against each other in a court of law because of the nature of their relationship, as with members of the same family, good friends, or close neighbours. The judicial procedure in its essence sets two persons against each other so that an independent public body can decide on the dispute. It therefore constitutes a hazard to reciprocal dialogue and risks polarising persons rather than pacifying them. The danger exists that the bounds of trust and goodwill are broken and irreparable damage is caused to the future relationship. Once again, it is felt within society that the normative system of morality should have been sufficient to pacify the quarrelling parties and that the law of obligations is not the proper tool for dispute settlement in those circumstances.

3 The Notion of *Obligatio Naturalis* in the Law of Obligations

3.1 About the Obligatio Naturalis

The connection between the law of obligations and morality reveals itself most clearly in the concept of the *obligatio naturalis*, which (literally translated) means *natural obligation.*[8] In Roman times,[9] the notion of *obligatio naturalis* was mostly used as a means to deal with the many incapacities in Roman law, such as slaves, married wives and children under *potestate* of the *pater familias*, and persons who had lost their legal capacity because of *capitis deminutio minima.* Another major group of situations covered by the *obligatio naturalis* were the *pacta nuda*, contracts which did not fulfill the strict requirements of *ius civile* with regard to their due form and which were not recognised as valid by the *ius gentium.* As is clear from this, in Roman times the concept of *obligatio naturalis* was mostly used to compensate for the strict regulations in the Roman law of obligations. The function and scope of the natural obligation has shifted in more recent times, however.[10] Various reasons can be cited: Canon Law with its emphasis on morality had its influence on civil law; strict formalism disappeared and the 'closed system' of contract law was replaced by an open system. The outcome of all of this was that the natural obligation lost a great deal of its importance. It has adapted itself, however. Rather than being an inherent safety net for rigorous regulation in the law of obligations, it has become a bridge between law and morality.

A natural obligation can come into play whenever a legal obligation is lacking, but the moral consciousness within society nonetheless imposes a moral imperative to act. From the moment that someone executes the moral obligation (wholly

---

[8] Except for Roman Law, the name *natural obligation* shall be used henceforth.

[9] On the *obligatio naturalis* in Roman Law: P. Cornioley, *Naturalis obligatio: essai sur l'origine et l'évolution de la notion en droit romain* (Geneva: Impr. de Journal de Genève, 1964).

[10] On the history of the *obligatio naturalis* throughout the ages: J.E. Scholtens, *De geschiedenis der natuurlijke verbintenis sinds het romeinsche recht* (Groningen: Wolters, 1931).

or partly) or when someone promises to do so, the system of law intervenes and transforms the moral imperative into a legal obligation. The law will view performance as if it were the payment of an existing legal debt. Performance can therefore not be undone on the grounds that it constitutes an undue payment. And what is more, when a moral imperative continues to exist after voluntary performance (as where the moral duty to pay for the upbringing of a child does not end after a single payment when parenthood is not legally established), a judge may decide that a legal obligation has been taken on to continue the payments for the duration of the moral imperative (in the aforementioned example, till the child reaches the age of majority, or perhaps even longer). The same principle applies with regard to the promise to execute a natural obligation, as opposed to an actual payment. The law creates a legal obligation which prevents the promisor from revoking his decision. The proverb 'promise is debt' was never more appropriate than in this particular situation.

Nowadays, many cases cover the payment of an allowance in the nature of maintenance in situations where a legal duty does not exist, or insofar as payment thereof exceeds the actual legal obligation.

The existence of a natural obligation was recognised in court between a cohabiting couple (without a cohabitation agreement), even for a determined period of time after the rupture of their relationship; between a father and his biological children when parenthood was not established; from a child towards his/her parents when performance exceeds the legal obligation; between brothers and sisters; between aunts/uncles and their nephews/nieces; between a mother/father–in–law and their son/daughter–in–law; between grandparents and their grandchildren (to the extent that they are not legally obliged to contribute to maintenance), and between ex–partners after their divorce (to pay more alimony than was granted by the judge or agreed on by the partners during the divorce).

The concept of natural obligation is also often applied to validate the payment of an extra–legal pension to ex–employees (or their widows) by an employer. Likewise, it is used when a company grants an extra–legal pension to an ex–member of the executive committee. Also recognised as falling within the scope of the natural obligation are the following: payments by a debtor after prescription of his debt or after a full discharge from personal bankruptcy proceedings; compensation from harm outside a duty to compensate in tort law; the execution of an invalid testament or the execution of a contract which has been declared null and void (except when the nullity is due to a breach of public order or moral standards), money or the pension given to a religious in return for their work after leaving the monastic or convent community; the payment of funeral costs by someone other than the legal heir; the gift of a dowry; in some cases, payment by an insurance company when the company pays before having checked that it was in fact required; the payment of gambling debts (although heavily contested in recent doctrinal writings[11]), and finally, compensation for services received, such as remunerating someone who has taken care of a person in need.

The list of situations cited in the previous paragraph is far from exhaustive. Since neither the scope of the natural obligation nor the criteria for its application are defined by law, virtually all moral duties qualify for recognition as natural obligation. For this reason, commentators have set up their own criteria which have to be fulfilled for a natural obligation to exist and to be validly executed. Not only is it necessary for the moral debtor to recognise the duty to act, but a shared moral consciousness within a certain society must also agree that a moral imperative exists. The scope of the natural obligation is therefore not completely dependent on the moral awareness of one person, which would make its application entirely subjective. Its content is somewhat objectified by the requirement of an *opinio iuris* on the existence of a natural obligation. In order to make that assessment, a judge must pay attention "aux usages et convenances généralement admis dans une civilisation donnée, aux liens qui unissent les personnes en présence, au degré de formation intellectuelle et morale de l'agent, enfin, aux circonstances".[12] In brief, when a judge deems that the attendant circumstances justify a characterisation of natural obligation, he may lawfully employ the concept.

When it comes to the execution of a natural obligation, it is a requisite that the payment is performed voluntarily, and in full awareness of the fact that one is not performing a legal duty.

3.2 The Natural Obligation as a Method to Deal with the Limits of the Law of Obligations

The greater part of the examples cited above deal with the payment of alimony and maintenance, more specifically in the situations where legally enforceable obligations are considered to be intrusive. For example, between unmarried partners, forcing their relationship into the framework of marital–like obligations would disturb the process of two persons developing a relationship and distort the complexity of human relations.[13] More or less falling within the same category is providing a dowry. Article 204 of the Belgian Civil Code stipulates explicitly that a child has no right to a dowry. The reasoning of the legislator was based on the view that these kinds of internal family matters were better left to the family themselves to decide upon. But most of these objections lapse when someone in one of

11 Gambling debts are *immoral*, rather that moral obligations. For this reason, they cannot possibly be natural obligations. If a payment cannot be recovered on the claim that it constituted an undue payment, this is because of *in pari causa turpitudinis, cessat repetitio.*

12 H. De Page, *Traité élémentaire de droit civil belge: principes, doctrine, jurisprudence*, III, *Les obligations* (Brussels: Bruylant, 1967) 77–78.

13 See on this K. Raes (ed.) *Liefdes onrecht. Het onmogelijke huwelijk tussen liefde en recht*, in *Tegenspraak Cahiers* (Ghent: Mys en Breesch, 1998) and especially the contribution by H. Willekens, "De liefde, het kind en de institutionalisering van persoonlijke relaties", 1–37.

those situations voluntarily takes upon himself an enforceable duty. Once a person, deliberately and out of his free will, executes the obligations which the law was not eager to impose, there is no reason not to ratify his actions and not to acknowledge his decision that a duty did (and perhaps still does) exist.

A payment made on a debt after the expiry of a limitation period ('prescription of a debt') is considered to be a natural obligation for yet another reason. The concept of prescription (both acquisitive and liberating) is necessary in any society because of reasons of legal certainty. After a determined amount of time, a citizen may have just cause to believe that a certain situation which has lasted for quite some time, will no longer be subject to change. Therefore, the law of obligations has to face the fact that its regulatory function is limited in time and that the liberating prescription will extinguish a creditor's right to claim on the obligation. But when a debtor, in full knowledge of the fact that he can no longer be legally forced to perform, chooses to fulfil the agreement nonetheless, the law acknowledges this to be a valid payment. *Pacta sunt servanda*, and the moral duty to stand by an agreement has the best of a technical regulation establishing the margins of a legal obligation. Likewise, when a debtor has been granted full discharge in a bankruptcy proceeding but chooses not to take advantage of this benefit and to comply with all of his previously made agreements, the law will characterise the payments as valid even though the creditor's rights to demand execution had been removed by the law. In a similar fashion, when the existence of an obligation is obstructed by other technical regulations (*e.g.* when a contract or a testament is null and void because it was not formulated in the legally prescribed form) a legal obligation is barred from arising, at least if the person benefiting from the nullity decides to invoke his right to have the contract declared null. But this does not prevent the law of obligations from recognising the contract or testament as being lawfully executed via the fulfillment of a natural obligation.

Another domain where the law of obligations was reluctant to enter, was that of the religious agreements. The promise to enter a religious community or to live one's life serving God, is not a promise the law of obligations can validate just like that.

> In the spiritual sense, the minister sets out to serve God and his master; I do not think that it is right to say that in the legal sense he is at the point of ordination undertaking by contract to serve the Church or the Conference as his master throughout the years of his ministry.[14]

As a result, no legal obligation exists for the religious community to compensate for the lack of pension rights. But where the law of obligations is reluctant to enter, the natural obligation has no difficulties to step in. Religious communities who voluntarily donate money or grant a pension are complying with their natural obligation to do so.[15]

---

14 *President of the Methodic Conference v Parfitt* (1983) 3 All ER 747.

15 R. Verstegen, "Over kloostergemeenschappen en natuurlijke verbintenissen" (note under Ghent 7th May 1997), *A.J.T.* 1997–1998, 128.

Another example of the natural obligation was the duty to compensate for services which one has received, if a legal duty to do so does not otherwise exist. When a person is gravely ill or has difficulties to walk or move around, a neighbour or a family member might come to their aid. The law of obligations chooses largely to leave these matters to friends and family. The dynamics of strong affectionate relationships should be sufficient to assure that help is found when needed and that a reward is given when appropriate. But once again, the law has no problems in accepting an obligation once someone has voluntarily indicated that he or she has a duty to help or a duty to compensate for services received. With regard to the grant of extra–legal pensions, a similar analysis can be made. The amount of money employers are obliged to contribute to social security is considered by the legislator to be a fair amount. However, if an employer feels towards one of his ex–employees that the pension which is given to the employee after his retirement is insufficient to compensate for the amount of work he did, there is no reason why the law should not validate this decision and treat the extra–legal pension as the execution of an existing obligation.

3.3 Functions of the Natural Obligation

As is clearly shown in the paragraphs above, the natural obligation does not retreat where a legal obligation would. It intervenes in religious matters and in internal family and social affairs; it is not pushed back when the validity of a legal obligation is affected or when its compulsory performance has evaporated; it does not flinch when imposing a larger duty other than the one which is imposed by black–letter law. Its recognition by a judge means that a majority within a certain legal community feel that there is a duty to perform. A moral duty, it is true – if not, one might start to wonder about the application of customary law – but nonetheless a duty. Two conclusions can be drawn from this with regard to the function of the natural obligation in the law of obligations.

On the one hand, via the concept of the natural obligation, a civil obligation is able to follow in its footsteps and to enter the domains where it was previously not applied. Not only is the law's regulatory function greatly expanded by this, it manages to do so without generating much disapproving social response, even in these 'sensitive' domains, since an *opinio iuris* exists. In other words, through the natural obligation, the law of obligations is able to transcend its own limits and to create legally binding obligations in situations where legal enforceability was initially considered to be intrusive and disordering, or at least not appropriate.

On the other hand, the natural obligation functions as a beacon for the legislator. It is a signal that society might be ready to accept an expansion of the scope of the law of obligations and that the limits of the law of obligations might have retreated. The application of natural obligations in the courts of law is therefore an important indication of society's view on morality and might be a useful tool to solve the age–old mystery of 'What is morality?'.[16]

For example: at a time when the recognition of adulterous children was still unlawful, a natural obligation to pay for their education and maintenance 'as if they were lawful children' was accepted in society. Over time, the legislator followed the changed moral views and legitimised recognition. For a more recent example, in the second half of the 1990s, judicial decisions multiplied granting alimony payments (on the basis of a natural obligation) in cases where a cohabiting couple split up. As a result, in 2003, Flanders' Catholic political party launched the idea of creating a legal maintenance obligation after the break–up of a cohabiting couple.

4 Transcending the Boundary between Law and Morality

4.1 Generalising the Analysis of the Natural Obligation

Natural obligation is a method of dealing with the limits of the law of obligation, which is intrinsic to the law of obligations itself. The law of obligations comprises *in se* a way to handle its own delimitation. Most interesting is the question to which extent all or some of the characteristics of the natural obligation can be generalised, in order to find similar means of dealing with the boundaries between law and morality, which are inherent in the law of obligations. Three main observations can be made. Firstly, the law of obligations positions itself in the background and functions as a safety net for individual initiative, rather than enforcing it. Secondly, the range of actions a legal system can undertake to connect with the moral domain is much wider than either transforming its imperatives into law, or merely standing aloof. The many subtle ways in which both social spheres are interwoven blur their boundaries to great extent and allow them to respond to any situation in the most appropriate manner. Thirdly, the use of undefined 'open norms' enables the law of obligations to adapt itself in a flexible way along with morality, without endangering the need for legal certainty.

---

[16] On the different views on 'what is morality', see P.B. Cliteur, *Rechtsfilosofie, een thematische benadering* (Nijmegen: Ars Aequi Libri, 2002) 101–110 and 141–142; W.G. Summer, *Folkways* (New York: Ginn and Company, 1907); R. Benedict, "Anthropology and the Abnormal", *Journ. of Gen. Psychol.* 1934, 59–88, also published under the title of "A Defense of Ethical Relativism", in L. Pojman (ed.), *Moral Philosophy: A Reader* (Indianapolis/Cambridge: Hacket Publishing, 1998) 33–37 and in J.A. Gould (ed.), *Classic Philosophical Questions* (New York: McMillan Publishing, 1992) 95–101; E. Westermarck, *Ethical Relativity* (London: Kegan Paul, Trench, Trubner & Co., 1932); P. Devlin, *The Enforcement of Morals* (London: Oxford University Press, 1965); H.L.A. Hart, *Law, Liberty and Morality* (Oxford: Oxford University Press, 1963) 17–24; R.A. Shiner, *l.c.*, 436 e.s.; R. Dworkin, "Lord Devlin and the Enforcement of Morals", *Yale L.J.* 1966, 986–1005 and *Taking Rights Seriously* (Cambridge, Mass.: Harvard University Press, 1966) 248.

4.2 Law of Obligations is a Safety Net

When transforming a natural obligation into a legal one, the law awaits individual action from one of its citizens and then ratifies *a posteriori* that performance. This is not as surprising as might seem at first sight. In fact, a background position is inherent to the nature of the law of obligations. In contractual matters, the *animus contrahendae obligationis* is a necessary requisite for the law to be able to play a regulatory role. Those who do not intend to enter into a contract will in principle not fall under the scope of contract law.[17] But even in situations where parties did enter into a contract or in any other situation (*e.g.* tort law) where legally binding obligations are at play, only few legal regulations are part of imperative law. The greater part of the regulations can be set aside if the parties involved agree to it.[18] The law of obligations thus leaves a great deal of freedom to the parties and limits itself mostly to the creation of a legal framework against which individual choices and agreements can take place.[19] As a result of this, legal intervention regarding obligations will more readily be accepted and less easily be seen as intruding into the private sphere than legal intervention in public law which cannot as easily be set aside. The domains where the law of obligations can fulfil its (background) regulatory and pacifying function can therefore be rather extensive, without endangering the judicial protection function of a system of law.

---

17 Cass. 2 December 1875, *Pas.* 1876, I, 37. The same principle applies in European contract law (Article 2: 101 PECL: "A contract is concluded if: (a) the parties intend to be legally bound, and (b) they reach a sufficient agreement").

18 And even in situations where imperative regulations are at play, judicial decisions have shown an increasing tendency to take the arrangement into account *as if it were* a legal contract, though at any time revocable and always limited in time (*e.g.* the arrangement between two ex–partners after their divorce that one of them is no longer legally held to pay for his/her child). So even in these instances, the law might take a (temporary) step backwards in favour of the individual choice to be legally bound by an obligation. See the overview given in E. Dirix, *l.c.*, 223.

19 With regard to the resilience of the law of obligations to impose legal obligations in the field of morality, this safety net approach bears great resemblance to the modern liberalist view of law and morality, the law creating only a minimum level of ethics and leaving people a moral space where they can make autonomous, individual choices. The law does not interfere directly with a person's private sphere and leaves each citizen the freedom for his own development and moral choices. But it keeps up in reserve the possibility to assert itself and to fulfil its regulatory and pacifying function. Intrusive penetration of the private sphere is thus prevented and the judicial protection function of the law is not put at risk. See on liberalism J.S. Mill, *On Liberty (1859)* (New Haven, Conn.: Yale University Press, 2003). See C.L. Ten, *Mill on Liberty* (Oxford: Oxford University Press, 1980). See also R. Hardin, *Liberalism, Constitutionalism, and Democracy* (Oxford: Oxford University Press, 1999) and M. Adams, "Het hemels baldakijn van recht en moraal", *R.W.* 2000–2001, 1401.

4.3 Law of Obligations Interacts with Morality in Many Subtle Ways

The interaction between law and morality can be very subtle, as the concept of natural obligation indicates. In between the positive view of law, where law and morality belong to totally different domains, and the adherents of the natural law theory who go so far as to claim that positive rules contradictory to natural law cannot be acknowledged as law, lies a large grey area which belongs neither completely to the social sphere of the law, nor completely to the social sphere of morality. The many subtle ways in which the law interacts with the domain of morality can help reduce the field of tension between the different characteristics and functions of the law, such as the tension between the abstract, technical and scientific nature of the law on the one hand, and the process of internalising the law because one is able to recognise a moral imperative in its content, on the other.[20] The various recommendations issued by government by means of soft law and the systems of disciplinary regulations for example, make the distinction between enforceable legal regulations and unenforceable moral imperatives much more vague. The concept of natural obligation even makes one domain fade into the other. Furthermore, the use of open norms with a moral connotation (*e.g.* ‘good faith’) allows the judge (and obligates him) to take into account moral rules, shared values, and existing patterns of behaviour when examining the scope of a legal rule.[21] This cross–over between law and morality acknowledges the concept of law as comprehending a combined play of legal rules, constitutional rights, and principles of justice against a background of common morals and ethics. They allow an interaction between law and morality which should comfort citizens that a legal rule or a judicial decision will not be an unworldly abstract something, but will lean very much towards the social feeling of what is ‘right’ and ‘wrong’ in a given situation. A connection is thus kept between law and morality which should reduce the alienation between citizens and the law, therefore enhancing its regulatory and pacifying function, as well as its symbolic function.

---

[20] This jeopardises the law’s regulatory function (citizens will be less willing to follow the law), its pacifying function (the law is less easily seen as a context for dispute settlement), its function of judicial protection (the law will more easily be seen as an intrusion towards an individual moral belief or value), and finally also its symbolic function (because shared values and moral views are not recognised in the law). See on this R. Foqué, “De noodzakelijke verwevenheid van recht en ethiek”, *A.A.* 1998, 6–15 and E. Claes, W. Devroe, and B. Keirsbilck, “The Limits of the Law (Introduction)”.

[21] See also the next subsection.

4.4 Law of Obligations Uses 'Open Norms'

The use of 'open norms' in the law of obligations is perhaps the most interesting technique used to connect with the moral domain.[22] This method is however not confined to the law of obligations. Legal systems in different ways leave quite explicitly places where the details of the legal substance need to be filled out by an appeal to moral notions:

> The best examples might be documents such as Constitutions, Charters and Bills of Rights. The full extent of the legal guarantee of freedom of expression, for instance, of a right to life, liberty and security of the person, or the equal treatment under the law, will need to be filled out by reference of the moral concepts themselves which such provisions seek to translate into legal rights and liberties, powers and immunities. Administrative tribunals may be called upon to act, or to judge whether others acted, 'fairly', to say whether a procedure or distribution was 'fair'. Here, too, it is natural to construe the term as referring to background moral notions of fairness.[23]

The same technique is used in the law of obligations. Apart from the concept of natural obligation, several other open norms can be found in the Civil Code and legal doctrine, such as 'good faith'[24], 'bonus pater familias', 'equity', 'abuse of the law', and so on. They represent open categories: their content has to be empirically concretised in case–law. But the result of this process is not entirely undetermined. All of them refer to an underlying moral rule or concept, which has to be used as a guideline when applying and interpreting the open norm.[25] Obviously the technique of open norms bears great risks, many of which are not limited to the use of open norms itself but intrinsic to the open texture of the law: the application of the norm can be unpredictable; its interpretation can be purely instrumental; citizens may get a feeling of legal uncertainty; no guarantee exists that an equilibrium between the legal regulations, basic rights and general principles of justice will be taken into account, and so forth. This jeopardises the regulatory and pacifying function of the law, as well as its function of providing judicial protec-

---

22 See on this H.C.F. Schoordijk, "Het gebruik van open normen naar Belgisch en Nederlands privaatrecht", in *Liber Amicorum Jacques Herbots* (Deurne: Kluwer, 2002) 325–350 and also G. Pignarre, "Que reste-t-il des bonnes mœurs en droit des contrats? 'Presque rien ou presque tout?'", *Revue des Contrats* 2005, 1290.

23 R. A. Shiner, *l.c.*, 438.

24 Due to the rule that all contracts have to be executed in good faith, one might even argue that any stipulation in contract law, no matter how clearly defined, is in fact an open norm. The notion of good faith imposes the obligation to interpret the legal norms of contract law taking into consideration all circumstances of the regulated relationship, even when those circumstances are not yet recorded in a legal regulation. M. Storme, *De invloed van de goede trouw op de kontraktuele schuldvorderingen: een onderzoek betreffende rechtsgrondslag, tekortkoming en rechtsverwerking bij overeenkomsten* (Brussels: Story–Scientia, 1990) 13 e.s., 465.

25 The existence of open norms based on morality is even accepted in some forms of legal positivism, as can be seen in the writings of Wil Waluchow. According to his theory of 'inclusive legal positivism', courts are allowed to take morality into account whenever the legal system gives the permission to do so: W. Waluchow, *Inclusive Legal Positivism* (Oxford: Clarendon Press, 1994).

tion. But many of these perils can be put into perspective when holding in mind that, in this case, the open texture is not merely a characteristic of the law; it is the consequence of the legislator's deliberate choice to rely on a moral consensus. The judicial activism which is created by their interpretation circumvents to a large extent the difficulties and limits caused by the open texture of law, because decisions are deliberately made against a background of shared moral values. Their content is determined by an internalised imperative, so citizens should generally be able to grasp the meaning of the open norm. Likewise, a judicial decision should not come as a complete surprise. This way, the law is able to adapt itself alongside with the changing moral views without causing insurmountable doubts about the content and interpretation of a legal rule. The application of shared moral values when interpreting the open norms of the civil code should also ensure that pure instrumentalism is prevented, for neither the parties nor the judge are completely free to interpret to their liking.

5 Conclusion

One can conclude that many solutions to deal with the limits of the law of obligations are intrinsic to the law of obligations itself. Notably the natural obligation and other open norms are active tools of legal expansion. Whenever a situation is at play where the law cannot perform its regulatory function, it can limit itself to *a posteriori* ratification via the notion of the natural obligation. Furthermore, the interpretation and concretisation of open norms allows the law of obligations to shift constantly its own boundaries and to create new legal duties. The overlap with morality justifies the increased scope of the law, since the duties which are derived from an open norm should already have been internalised by citizens. Finally, in situations where judicial intervention in a dispute can distort relationships or when the law is ill–adapted to the dynamics of other societal spheres, the possibility of taking morality into account and giving the most equitable judgment via the use of these open norms, should ensure that the law can fulfill its pacifying function to the best possible extent.

Chapter 4 – Labour Law and the Limits of Dogmatic Legal Thinking

Mathieu van Putten

1 Introduction

In "The Limits of the Law (Introduction)", Claes, Devroe, and Keirsbilck construct a taxonomy of the limits of the law by identifying the functions and characteristics of the rule of law. This chapter has a different approach to limits of the law. It sets out from the idea that limits of the law are limits of mankind. It is the human condition that generates the need for law. It is that same human condition that explains why law is necessarily positively and negatively limited.

Though this perspective requires an elaboration on the condition of man, it is neither possible nor the ambition to develop comprehensively such a conception within the scope of this chapter. It is only possible here to indicate some minimum requirements for a realistic conception of the condition of man. Presupposing (self–)consciousness, these can be depicted using six concepts: individual freedom, unicity, scarcity, bounded rationality, interdependency and opportunism.

Individual freedom indicates that man has the need to be able freely to determine how he acts in the private and public spheres: Man needs individual freedom to be able to convert his individuality into personality. A society that deprives most or some men of the freedom to become a person neglects this need of man. Personality makes every human unique. The exercise of freedom requires resources. Given scarcity, resources are limited and so too are the facilities to develop personality every man disposes of. The concept of bounded rationality indicates that an individual has limited theoretical and practical knowledge and a limited ability of communicating this limited knowledge to others. Thus, he is at the same time always to a certain extent incomprehensible to others and dependent on them: freedom is a necessary but insufficient condition for man to develop his personality. Bounded rationality implies that man must be embedded in a society – he is interdependent. Opportunism indicates that man will not necessarily take the common good into account when using his freedom.[1] Opportunism allows man to gloss over treating others worse than he would like to be treated himself.

In the absence of a mechanism ensuring a just distribution of freedom for all, in the end, none or only few will enjoy the freedom they need and deserve.

Law is precisely the mechanism devised to guarantee that the ability to exercise freedom is distributed in a just way, that is, in accordance with the principles of

---

1 On 'bounded rationality' and 'opportunism': O.E. Williamson, *The Economic Institutions of Capitalism. Firms, Markets, Relational Contracting* (New York: The Free Press, 1985) 30–32 and 43–52.

equality and solidarity. Given the human condition, bringing about and maintaining law is accompanied by many obstacles.

First of all, one must avoid a too reductionist view on the condition of man when developing legal norms. The various aspects of the human condition must be taken into account. Secondly, given his bounded rationality, man *qua* law–maker may adopt a wrong analysis of the problems at hand and hence develop the wrong remedies. Yet when he correctly analyses the problem, his opportunism may prevent him from developing a proper remedy. And even when he develops a right remedy for a certain problem, yet more problems may arise than the one solved, simply due to his bounded rationality and the concomitant non–ergodicity of legal norms. The non–ergodicity of legal norms is extended by the fact that man's bounded rationality requires that the law uses simple concepts to structure the complex chaos within human life. The generality of legal concepts and the fact that law must maintain order and security inevitably causes the risk of the law not bringing about the just distribution of freedom it postulated. This is all the more the case since man's unicity brings about different interpretations of legal concepts. Only when this weakness of law is taken into account in the daily application of the law can this limit of the law be remedied. Finally, opportunism implies that man does not necessarily spontaneously abide by the law. This generates the need for a system of enforcing the law. Scarcity and bounded rationality make it impossible to enforce the law fully. This can be remedied by devising techniques that reduce the need for law enforcement.

The outline above clarifies in what way some limits of the law are positive, and others, negative. Positive limits of the law correspond to the idea that the law does not limit individual freedom any more than necessary to ensure a just distribution of individual freedom. The law ends where a just distribution of freedom begins. Negative limits correspond to the idea that, because of various obstacles, the law does not always succeed in ensuring a just distribution of freedom.

Against this perspective on the limits of the law, this chapter will concisely demonstrate how modern labour law and scholarship has been and remains an attempt to remedy legal conceptions that did or do not sufficiently take man's condition into account, nor were or are able to reduce optimally the obstacles to the good functioning of a legal system.

Given the limited scope of this chapter, the approach will be illustrative. First, the origins of modern (Belgian) labour law will be briefly sketched. This will allow a quick demonstration that modern labour law in general remedies a negative limit of the law resulting from the way in which Napoleonic civil law put the principles of freedom, equality and fraternity into operation (section 2). Second, the chapter will focus on the legal conception of collective labour agreements ('CLAs') in Belgium. This will enable an illustration of how the Napoleonic civil law concepts and the all too simple strict divide between public and private law have produced a negative limit of the law. It will be shown how the legal *institutionalisation* of CLAs overcomes this negative limit (section 3). Third, it will be suggested that the legal institutionalisation of CLAs does not suffice to remedy the negative limits of the law. Their status can be – and is still – challenged from *inter alia* a constitutional and economic law perspective. The principles of any branch of the law serve to ensure a just distribution of freedom. However, when applied unlimitedly and dogmatically, the principles which protect a just distribution of freedom in one matter can disturb the balance when applied to other matters (sections 4 and 5). It will be shown how legal theory can provide the meta–juridical criteria to determine the right balance between the principles of different branches of the law, thus remedying negative limits of the law and enforcing positive limits of the law.

2 The Origins of Modern Labour Law

The ideas of freedom and equality that actuated the French Revolution were developed by Rousseau on a political level, by Quesnay and Smith on an economical level, and by the existence of guilds and corporations on a social level. On a legal level, this resulted in (i) the Decree d'Allarde of 2–17 March 1791[2], which acknowledged the freedom of labour and enterprise by abolishing any limitation on the ability to exercise a profession, (ii) the Decree Le Chapelier of 14–17 June 1791[3], which forbade unions between citizens of the same state of profession, and (iii) the constitutional recognition of absolute property rights.[4]

The Napoleonic Codes carried the project forward. The Civil Code of 1804 established property principally as the right to enjoy a good in the most absolute way and to dispose of the good (Article 544) and it consolidated the individual freedom of contract (Article 1134). The Penal Code of 1810 forbade any coalition of employees (Article 415). The fact that formal equality in the enjoyment of the freedom of contract and property could bring about substantial inequality did not find any legal consolidation. For example, in the context of labour relations, only two Articles of the Civil Code regulated labour contracts. One consolidated the principle of individual freedom, by forbidding a contract of services for life (Article 1780). The other had to do with evidence: the employer was to be believed on his word in wage cases (Article 1781).

Given the way the need for individual freedom was legally constructed in the Civil Code, "on avait organisé, sans le savoir et sans le vouloir le Code de la bourgeoisie".[5] One could say that, due to man's bounded rationality, the Civil Code did not sufficiently take the opportunistic nature of man and his unicity into account. With the Industrial Revolution, the consequences of this surfaced quickly. In fact,

---

2 Loi 2–17 maart 1791 portant suppression de tous les droits d'aides, suppression de toutes les maîtrises et jurandes et établissement de patentes.

3 Décret 14–17 juin 1791 relatif aux assemblées de citoyens d'un même état ou profession. Both statutes were applicable in Belgium after its annexation by France in 1795.

4 See Article 16 of the Constitution of 1793 and the Decree of 18 March 1793 (both cited by O. Vanachter, *Arbeidsrecht en vrijheid van ondernemen*, Ph.D. thesis K.U.Leuven, 1975, 23).

5 R. Saleilles, *De la personnalité juridique. Histoire et théorie: vingt–cinq leçons* (Paris: Rousseau, 1910) 115.

it is on the matter of labour law that the tardiness of legal thinking *vis–à–vis* the facts was first assessed.[6] Labour conditions in the 19th century, and the correlate tragic wrongs, clearly indicate the limits of the ability of the Napoleonic legal construction to distribute freedom in a just way in a liberal, capitalist, industrial society. An adjustment of the legal system forced itself on the situation.

Two main channels to procure this adjustment presented themselves. Either the State would adopt protective legislation or individual employees would form unions and use their collectivity to force employers to accept more just labour conditions. Since then both channels have been put extensively into operation. They are the core of labour law, which can in its totality be considered as an attempt to cope with the negative limits of Napoleonic civil and commercial law. Initially, however, it was not obvious how to put any of the two branches into operation.

On the one hand, the legislature was elected by a tax voting system. Thus only the wealthy were represented. Given bounded rationality and the opportunism of man, it was difficult to convince the majority of the necessity to adopt statutes dealing with the labour problem.

On the other hand, even though the Belgian Constitution contained provisions guaranteeing the right to peaceful assembly and to association, the cited rigid provisions remained applicable, thereby excluding any development of the autonomous channel. Article 415 of the Penal Code was abolished in 1866. Thus, while any coalition was no longer a felony, a new Article 310 still penalised any infringement of the freedom of labour or enterprise. Consequently, it was still very difficult to organise a strike.[7] Given the fact that the possibility of striking was the only way truly to develop the autonomous channel[8], its full exercise was still very much impeded. Only after the adoption of the universal franchise[9] in 1919, Article 310 of the Penal Code was abolished by a statute of 24 May 1921. By a statute of that same day, the freedom of association and the possibility to form labour unions was formally proclaimed.[10] The stage was set to develop a mature labour relations system with a decent collective bargaining platform.

---

6 P. Cuche, "La législation du travail et les transformations du droit", in X (ed.), *La cité moderne et les transformations du droit* (Cahiers de la Nouvelle Journée, 4) (Paris: Librairie Bloud & Gay, 1925) 166.

7 This could not impede *inter alia* the general strikes of 1886, which in itself points to a limit of the law: if the legal system manifestly does not succeed in distributing freedom in a just way, then man will disobey the rules of the system in order to adjust or overthrow that system.

8 *Cf.* L. François, *Théorie des relations collectives du travail en droit belge*, in M. Patte and M. Sojcher–Rousselle (eds.), *Collection Droit Social* (Brussel: Bruylant 1980).

9 It took until 1948 for women to acquire the right to vote in Belgium.

10 Wet 24 mei 1921 tot waarborging der vrijheid van vereeniging, *B.S.* 28 mei 1921.

3 The Legal Conception of Collective Labour Agreements in Belgium

The stage being set for a collective bargaining system, much work was still to be done on the legal conception of the CLA, the logical result of collective bargaining between employers and labour unions.

Many fundamental legal questions surround the CLA. The most relevant question in this chapter is the question of the binding force of the normative part[11] of the CLA.[12] An abundant legal literature exists around this question. This is not surprising. Answering it requires questioning the limits of the ability of legal concepts to guarantee a just distribution of freedom.

State legislation poses no problem as far as binding force is concerned. It is a characteristic of State legislation that it is applicable to all entering its range of application. This is not so however for CLAs in classical legal doctrine. Since private parties operate in the collective bargaining situation, the principles of private law prevail. That means that to the extent the normative part of the CLA is considered to be legally binding between employers and employees, it is liable to the principle of the relativity of contract laid down in Article 1165 of the Civil Code. Yet this implies that the normative part of the CLA is not applicable *inter alia.*

This is problematic for CLAs. The problem of social competition is at the origin of the need of CLAs. Consequently, it is easy to see how, given its aim of limiting social competition and, in doing so, guaranteeing social peace, the CLA has a claim to a binding force that is not reconcilable with the principle of the relativity of contract. As long as only those who have directly or indirectly consented to the CLA are bound by it, the road to downward social competition is open. This is especially problematic given the varying living conditions of the working population. For example, a 25 year old healthy single male can do with a much lower wage than a 35 year old married female providing for not only herself, but also for her three children and her husband. That is why some scholars argue that, lest the purpose of the CLA be illusory, the suggestion of an individual labour contract being inconsistent with the normative provisions of a CLA has to be invalid.[13]

Historically, many valuable attempts have been undertaken to try to explain an effective binding force for the CLA using private law concepts such as 'caretaking'/'management' (*'zaakwaarneming'/'gérance'*; Article 1372–1375 Civil Code), (tacit) mandate (Article 1984 Civil Code), third party provisions (Article 1121 Civil Code) and unnamed contracts. However, according to the predominant doctrine, it was judged that none of these legal categories allowed extending the binding force of the normative provisions of CLAs to all employees. The tenet of care-

---

11 As opposed to the obligatory part of the CLA. The normative part concerns the conditions of employment regulated in the CLA. The obligatory part concerns the obligations of the contracting parties.

12 And are considered to be the core issue of the CLA. *Cf.* A. Mazy, "Commentaar op de Wet van 5 december 1968 betreffende de collectieve arbeidsovereenkomsten en de paritaire comités", *Arbbl.* 1969, 1270.

13 A. Mazy, *l.c.*, 249.

taking/management was rejected among other reasons because it can only be applied when the person subject to the 'caretaking' does not resist. (Tacit) mandate, when accepted, only allows extending the force of the CLA to labour union and employers' organisation members. Moreover, it presupposes that the workers themselves are party to the CLA, while in general, it is asserted that only the unions are party to the CLA. Third party provisions are rejected because one can only stipulate in favour of a third party, whereas the CLA entails not only rights but also duties for the employers and employees. Moreover, a third party is not obliged to accept the provisions in its favour.[14] In cases where it was not possible to ground the binding force of the CLA in contract law, other sources of law, in particular custom ('*gebruik*'), were used to give binding force to the content of the CLA.[15] Given the restrictive conditions attached to custom as a source of law, this was not very satisfactory either.

The difficulties experienced in trying to construct the binding force of the normative provisions of the CLA using classical civil law tenets is not surprising given the fact that traditional private law concepts were not devised for remedying asymmetric power relations.[16] It is clear that the problem of the binding force of the CLA traverses the traditional public–private law divide, which has caused elaborate debates on the nature of the CLA as contract or regulation. This problem is not merely academic. Every so often, it emerges in the centre of the legal system. For instance, it did so in the late 1980s before the Belgian Council of State.[17] More recently, it was of importance in determining the constitutionality of the Flemish Decree of 29 November 2002 concerning the extension of the binding force of agreements between employee and employer organisations concerning Community and Region matters.[18] As mentioned above, the inadequacy of the traditional concepts has brought about a legal regulation: the CLA Statute.[19]

---

14 See C. De Visscher, *Le contrat collectif de travail: théories juridiques et projets législatifs* (Gent: Siffer, 1911) 69–94; R. Blanpain, *De collectieve arbeidsovereenkomst in de bedrijfstak naar Belgisch recht* (Leuven: Universitaire Boekhandel Uystpruyst, 1961) 143–149 and the references there.

15 *Cf.* M. Laloire, "Du contrat de travail au statut de l'entreprise", *Revue du Travail* 1940, 121, 126; G. Magrez–Song, "Un siècle de relations collectives de travail: du non–droit collectif à la 'dérégulation' collective", in P. Van Der Vorst (ed.), *100 ans de droit social Belge 1886/1986 – Honderd jaar Belgisch sociaal recht 1886/1986* (Bruxelles: Éditions Bruylant, 1986) 295.

16 *Cf.* A. Mazy, *l.c.*, 1270.

17 Raad van State nr. 32.348, 12 April 1989, *R.C.J.B.* 1991, 651; Raad van State 13 December 1991, *J.T.T.* 1992, 93.

18 Vlaams decreet van 29 november 2002 houdende de algemeen verbindend verklaring van akkoorden tussen werknemers- en werkgeversorganisaties betreffende gemeenschaps- en gewestaangelegenheden, *B.S.* 17 december 2002. On the constitutionality of this Decree: Arbitragehof nr. 145/2004, 15 September 2004, www.arbitrage.be. See also on this decree: O. Vanachter, "Een decreet over Vlaamse C.A.O.'s?", *Personeelszaken* 2001, 7; O. Vanachter, "Is er nood aan decreten over regionale CAO's? De collectieve arbeidsovereenkomst en de bevoegdheidsverdeling tussen de federale Staat, de Gemeenschappen en de Gewesten", *Soc. Kron.* 2001, 449; P. Popelier, "Vlaamse C.A.O.'s", *l.c.*, 154; J. Peeters, "Vlaamse C.A.O.'s: The Sequel", *A.V.I. Overlegorganen* 2003, 10; O. Vanachter, "Het Arbitragehof en het algemeen verbindend verklaren van C.A.O.'s", *Or.* 2004, 208; J. Vanthournout, "De

From a labour law perspective, the CLA Statute has given a satisfying solution to the problem of the binding force of the normative part of the CLA. The normative provisions of any CLA in the sense of the CLA Statute are applicable to employers bound by the CLA and all their employees, regardless of whether or not they are member of a trade union. Employers bound by the CLA are the employers who were either party to the agreement or acceded to it, or are members of an employer organisation which signed the agreement or acceded to it.[20] Moreover, the individual normative provisions of a CLA which was concluded within the National Labour Council (NLC) or a joint industrial committee are supplementarily applicable to all employers within the jurisdiction of the NLC or the joint industrial committee.[21] The binding force can be extended by a Royal Decree in which all normative provisions of the CLA are mandatorily applicable to all employers within the jurisdiction of the NLC or the joint industrial committee, and their employees.[22] Thus, the CLA Statute conceives the CLA as a contract with regulatory effects.[23]

By regulating the binding force of CLAs between representative employer organisations (or individual or several employers) on the one hand and representative employee organisations on the other, the limits of the Napoleonic law system which surfaced during the 1800s have been to a great extent dealt with, be it only very late in the 20th century. The result is that, by overcoming dogmatic legal distinctions between private and public law, the current legal system is much more able to fulfil its regulatory, pacifying, and protective functions. Consequently, it is more successful in guaranteeing a just distribution of freedom.

Some current doctrine asserts that the deviation from civil law of any binding force for the normative provisions of the CLA should not be exaggerated. The binding force, it is said, can to a large extent be explained by civil law tenets, in particular the tenets of party decision (*'partijbeslissing'*) by which an employer is bound, and binding third party decision (*'bindende derdenbeslissing'*) for the sup-

---

Vlaamse CAO's: het deksel op de neus van Pandora?", *T.S.R.* 2005, 125; P. Popelier, "Geen Vlaamse C.A.O.'s" (commenting Arbitragehof nr. 145/2004), *R.W.* 2004-05, 1020; B. Nyssen, "Un décret flamand sur l'extension de la force obligatoire de certaines conventions collectives de travail: un texte inutile, des libertés dangereuses prises avec le droit", *Ann. dr. Louvain* 2003, 95.

19 A first summary and incomplete regulation of just those collective agreements agreed within the joint industrial committees came about only in 1945. Some of the interpretation problems of this regulation were solved by amending the statutes of 1900 en 1922 on labour agreements for workmen and employees in 1954. However, it was only with the adoption of the Statute of 5 December 1968 on collective labour agreements and joint industrial committees (*B.S.* 15 January 1969) (hereafter the CLA Statute) that the CLA as such was legally embedded in the Belgian legal order.

20 Article 19 of the CLA Statute.

21 Article 26 of the CLA Statute.

22 Article 31 of the CLA Statute.

23 Ontwerp van wet betreffende de collectieve arbeidsovereenkomsten en de paritaire comités, (1966–67) *Parl. St. Senaat*, nr. 148, in particular 88 and 89 (advise of the Council of State). See also *e.g.*, Arbitragehof nr. 37/1993, 19 May 1993, www.arbitrage.be (in particular B.7.1); Council of State nr. 53.714, 14 June 1995, www.raadvst-consetat.be/

plementary binding force of individual normative provisions of a CLA agreed to within a joint industrial committee.[24] It is correct to assert that the legislature has created exceptions to the principle of relativity of contracts, and it is an interesting exercise to try to explain these exceptions by contractual tenets. However, one can not use these same tenets to construct binding force in the absence of a legal exception to the principle of relativity of contract, since that would lead to a disproportional hollowing out of the principle of autonomy and concomitantly of contracts as a legal basis for the development of personality. Therefore, the Belgian Constitutional Court has correctly stated that the automatic binding force, as well as the binding force which results from a Royal Decree extending it, differ from the binding force of contracts.[25]

The CLA Statute may remedy the shortcomings of civil law, quite naturally given ever–evolving material and intellectual conditions. It has not definitively consolidated the binding force of the normative provisions of the CLA. CLAs and the regulation of them are put into question from a constitutional perspective, as well as from an economic law – in particular competition law – perspective.[26] This risks reinstating a negative limit of the law. The questions and the way of dealing with them will be treated in the next section.

4 The Legal Status of the CLA vis–à–vis Constitutional Law

According to Article 33 of the Belgian 1994 Constitution, all powers issue from the Nation.[27] They are exercisable as determined in the Constitution. As indicated above, the CLA Statute allows private parties to elaborate norms which imperatively apply to persons who did not consent. The question is raised whether this is not in violation of Article 33 of the Constitution. François brought this question to the fore in 1980. The author suggested that up until that time, attention was diverted from this constitutional problem by talking of "the autonomy of modern social law". Moreover, he stated, an appeal to the notion of representativity is irrelevant for solving the constitutional problem.[28]

In 1994 the right to collective bargaining was inserted in the Belgian Constitution (Article 23). Though some suggest otherwise[29], the mere – even constitutional

---

24 W. Rauws, "De juridische aard van de collectieve arbeidsovereenkomst", in P. Humblet, B. Mergits, M. Rigaux *et al.* (eds.), *C.A.O.–Recht* (Diegem: H. van Zaaijen, losbl., september 1994) 1.3/4-1.3/6.

25 See in the aforementioned judgment of the Arbitragehof (footnote 18) section B.7.2 *in fine*.

26 Of course, there have also been serious challenges from a discrimination law perspective. This will not be elaborated on in this chapter.

27 Formerly Article 25.

28 L. François, *l.c.*, 355.

29 M. Jamoulle, "Conclusions", in M. Stroobant, M. Samblanx and P. Van Geyt (eds.), *Bedrijfsorganisatie aan de vooravond van de 21ste eeuw* (Antwerpen – Groningen: Intersentia Rechtswetenschappen, 2000) 292, fn. 28.

– recognition of the right to bargain collectively does not imply a normative power for the parties to the collective negotiation.[30]

One way to solve the problem of the alleged unconstitutionality of the CLA Statute, is to change the Constitution.[31] However, this takes time and as long as the Constitution has not been changed, the possible unconstitutionality of the CLA Statute threatens it like the sword of Damocles. In order to limit the possible negative effects of this, the question arises whether any unconstitutionality can be circumvented through a different interpretation of Article 33 of the Constitution. François himself pointed out a relevant line of argumentation for answering this question, namely defending the constitutionality of the CLA Statute by indicating that the never–ending debate on the contractual or regulatory nature of the CLA was due to a legal monistic perspective, which resulted in searching for an "introuvable nature juridique unique" of the CLA.[32] Indeed, as he indicated and referring to Santi Romano's *Ordre juridique*[33], it is only by realising that one and the same collective agreement can be looked upon differently from the State legal order and from a non–State legal order, that the nature of the CLA can be understood.

The importance of this pluralist conception of the law lies in the point that, in answering the question whether the State creates or recognises the binding force of the CLA, the pluralist conception allows explicating to what extent the State creates it: the State does not delegate a power to the social partners, but it receives this power within its legal order.[34] This is not necessarily in violation of Article 33 of the Constitution: a pluralist legal conception clearly shows that this Article only applies to the powers within the State legal order. Dorssemont has argued that such interpretation of Article 33 of the Constitution is in line with preparatory works of the Constituent Assembly.[35] It is an expression of the idea of subsidiarity.[36]

This line of reasoning of course requires a sound pluralist legal conception. Reference was already made to Romano's *Ordre juridique*. Notwithstanding the great contribution of this work to pluralist doctrine, this work appears to need further elaboration. Romano equates law, legal order, and institution.[37] In answering the question when a legal order exists, he briefly states it exists in every being or

---

30 H. Dumont, "Droit public, droit négocié et para–légalité", in G. Gérard, F. Ost and M. Van De Kerckhove (eds.), *Droit négocié, droit imposé?* (Brussel: Publications universitaires Saint Louis, 1996) 474–475; I. Kovalovszky, "À propos du pouvoir réglementaire", *Adm. Publ. (T.)* 1996, 304–306; P. Popelier, *Democratisch regelgeven* (Antwerpen: Intersentia, 2001) 292–294; P. Popelier, "Vlaamse C.A.O.'s", *l.c.*, 154–156.

31 H. Dumont, *l.c.*, 481; P. Popelier, "Vlaamse C.A.O.'s", *l.c.*, 157.

32 L. François, *l.c.*, 358.

33 S. Romano, *L'ordre juridique* (traduction française de la 2e éd. de *Ordinamento giuridico* par L. François et P. Gothot), in *Collection "Philosophie du droit"*, 15 (Paris: Dalloz 1975) xxiii+175.

34 See S. Romano, *l.c.*, 93–94.

35 *Cf.* F. Dorssemont, "De natuur van de collectieve arbeidsovereenkomst: een poging tot juridisch–pluralistische herbronning", *T.v.W.* 2001, 107, 124.

36 *Ibid.*

37 S. Romano, *l.c.*, 17 and 29.

social body with an objective and concrete existence and a visible individuality.[38] An important question then, given the existence of multiple legal orders, is the relation among them, and more specifically, the question how the legal order of the State relates to the various legal orders. In terms of Romano, this is the question of the *rilevanza* (relevance) of one legal order vis–à–vis another.

For Romano, the mere recognition of a social body being a legal order does not have any meaning towards the *relevance* of that legal order for the State legal order. It does not even matter that, from the viewpoint of the State, a certain legal order is *antijuridique.* Romano would merely accept a rejection of the legal character of a reprehensible institution when one could demonstrate that positive law is absolutely and necessarily dependent on ethics. According to the author, such a demonstration is naïve and non–existent. For a jurist, the criteria the State adopts to decide on the permissibility of certain entities should be completely indifferent.[39]

At this point, it is clear why some consider Romano's conception of the legal order as sociological, and why Romano does not provide any normative criteria for determining the *relevance* the State should recognise in a certain legal order. His notion of legal order makes an abstraction from a 'rule of law' legal order in equating a judgment based upon justice to an ethical judgment. But justice and ethics can not be equated. Justice is an intermediate concept between moral ideals, which is a harmonious synthesis between personal and transpersonal moral values – otherwise said between individualism and universalism – and which only exists in the world of ideas and the logical categories. In real life, due to man's condition, there is a constant battle between individualism and universalism. Justice enables reconciling the conflicts between personal and transpersonal norms. It replaces the individual instructions of the moral ideal by general rules, incomparable subjects by comparable categories, constant change by a certain stability. Given these logical characteristics, justice can be the basis of the law, rather than its ideal. A rule of law concept of law is then necessarily an attempt to bring about justice within a given social order.[40]

Realising this enables a devising of normative criteria to determine relations between different legal orders, even when accepting that the concept of justice varies through time and that, due to the human condition, not all positive law manages to achieve just solutions at all times. This can not be explained in any detail in this chapter. But it should be clear that this generally amounts to asserting that in accordance with the principle of subsidiarity, which is undoubtedly one of the most direct legal translations of the positive limits of the law, the legal order of the State should leave as much freedom as possible in those legal orders which are in concordance with the contextualised basic principles of rule of law legal orders and which bring about a just distribution of freedom.

---

38 S. Romano, *l.c.,* 25.

39 S. Romano, *l.c.,* 89–91.

40 G. Gurvitch, *L'idée du droit social. Notion et système du droit social. Histoire doctrinale depuis le 17e siècle jusqu'à la fin du 19e siècle* (Aalen: Scientia Verlag, Réimpression de l'édition Paris 1932, 1972) 95–113.

Relating this to the issue of the constitutionality of the current regulation of the CLA in the Belgian State legal order, it is clear that a normative pluralist theory offers a powerful argument for an interpretation of Article 33 of the Belgian Constitution that accepts the constitutionality of the current binding force of the CLA. The socio–professional legal order is a legal order that is different from the State legal order. Under Napoleonic legislation, this socio–professional legal order was not at all relevant to the State legal order and thus freedom within the order was abolished. The legislature was convinced that the application of its individual liberal principles would suffice for the law to distribute freedom justly amongst men. As indicated, it turned out otherwise. Mechanisms were developed within the socio–professional legal order that converted this legal order – despite the failing individualist liberal principles – into an order that brought about a more just distribution of freedom. By receiving the binding force that the CLA naturally has in the socio–professional legal order in the State legal order, the State legal order has recognised this to be relevant.

Interpreting the ascribed relevance to be *per se* unconstitutional in terms of Article 33 of the Belgian Constitution amounts to accepting that the Constitution honours a monistic legal conception. Not only do all powers within the State issue from the Nation, but all powers *tout court* are within the State. This is not only counterfactual, but also results *per se* in extending the task of the State legal order in socio–professional matters, thereby unnecessarily limiting the freedom of its citizens. Indeed, an omnipresent State transgresses the positive limits of the law in limiting the fundamental freedom man needs, beyond the requirements of a just distribution of freedom. In the proposed interpretation of Article 33, the reception of normative power exercised within non–State legal orders by the State is not *per se* unconstitutional. It is acceptable to the extent that the State receives normative power exercised within legal orders that enhance a just distribution of freedom and are in concordance with the basic principles of rule of law legal orders.

5 The Legal Status of the CLA vis–à–vis Economic Law

The critique of CLAs from a competition law perspective does not only bring up the extension of the binding effect of the CLA, but possibly also the CLA as such, at least at the (inter–) sectoral level. Therefore, the effects of an economic law critique on the CLA can be far more sweeping than a public law critique.

From a labour law perspective, as has been indicated above, CLAs protect a just distribution of freedom by excluding downward social competition. From a competition law perspective, CLAs limit and exclude the just distribution of freedom by restricting competition. Given such apparently contradictory interpretations of guaranteeing a just distribution of freedom, an important question is whether labour law can and should be valued against the background of competition law and vice–versa.

The Belgian CLA Statute does not contain any specific provisions on the relation between CLAs and competition law.[41] However, in 1999 the question received active consideration before the European Court of Justice.

The way the Court of Justice has dealt with the question amounts to accepting that the labour law logic supporting CLAs could – but should not – entirely be appreciated against the background of a competition law logic, at least the cartel provisions. In its jurisprudence, the Court of Justice recognises the importance of the competition law clauses in the EC Treaty.[42] However, it adds that it is important to bear in mind that the Community also develops policy in the social sphere.[43] It considers that it is beyond question that certain restrictions of competition are inherent in collective agreements between organisations representing employers and workers. Yet the social policy objectives pursued by such agreements would be seriously undermined if management and labour were subject to Article 81 of the EC Treaty when seeking jointly to adopt measures to improve conditions of work and employment. It therefore follows from a both effective and consistent interpretation of the provisions of the Treaty as a whole that agreements concluded in the context of collective negotiations between management and labour in pursuit of such objectives must, by virtue of their nature and purpose, be regarded as falling outside Article 81 of the EC Treaty.[44]

The European Court of Justice stance has been (heavily) criticised. Van den Bossche wonders whether the orthodox approach that departs from the applicability of the competition law provisions would lead to undesirable results, not because she has a an unbridled obsession with competition law, but because this would prevent endless specificity discussions.[45] Van den Bergh and Camesasca indicate that a general antitrust exemption *per se* can only be justified in the presence of substantial economies of scale, surpassing the firm level. As those are lacking, collective bargaining should be submitted to a competitive assessment. Nevertheless, they stress that collective bargaining's anticompetitive effects

---

41 Neither the Belgian 1999 Statute on the protection of economic competition (Wet 1 juli 1999 tot bescherming van de economische mededinging (Gecoördineerde vorm van de wet van 5 augustus 1991), *B.S.* 1 september 1999), nor its 2006 successor (Wet 10 juni 2006 tot bescherming van de economische mededinging, *B.S.* 29 juni 2006) which entered into force on 1 October 2006, contain any specific provisions on the issue. The issue did receive not much, if any, attention, during the parliamentary hearings on these statutes. Also, the question has not received much attention in traditional Belgian labour law doctrine (P. Humblet and M. Rigaux, "Collective agreements and competition law in Belgium", in N. Bruun and J. Helsten (eds.), *Collective Agreement and Competition Law in the EU: The Report of the COLCOM–Project* (Kopenhagen: Djof, 2001) 95–106).

42 ECJ 21 September 1999, Albany International BV/Stichting Bedrijfspensioenfonds Textielindustrie, C–67/96 at [53]. For an extensive analysis of Albany and related cases, see M. Wirtz, *Collisie tussen CAO's en mededingingsrecht* (Deventer: Kluwer, 2006). A. M. Van den Bossche, "CAO's en mededingingsrecht", in M. Rigaux and P. Humblet (eds.), *Actuele problemen van het arbeidsrecht 6* (Antwerpen – Groningen: Intersentia Rechtswetenschappen, 2001).

43 Albany at [54–58].

44 Albany at [59–60].

45 A. M. Van den Bossche, *l.c.*, 706.

should be neutralised without impairing the union's possibilities for defending the benefits to employees already achieved and for gaining further efficiencies.[46] De Vos interprets the European Court of Justice approach as the establishment of a factual supremacy of social dialogue over free competition.[47] He states CLAs could not only, but also should be evaluated from a competition law perspective.[48] To a certain extent, this amounts to the same result as an *a priori* exemption since the author argues that, once the applicability of the prohibition of cartel agreements is accepted, in case of a conflict, the next step is to fathom a special nature of aim which could help to accommodate the contested labour provision.[49] However, thereupon, De Vos takes into account the abuse of dominant position, State support provisions and the State's loyalty duty and suggestively advances that the competition law test amounts to questioning the State's acceptation of leaving it to private organisations to collectively settle labour issues in their interest and the acceptability of CLAs with extended binding force.[50]

Consequently, much debate is still to be expected on the issue. It is of course impossible to discuss thoroughly the question within the scope of this chapter. Some considerations should however illustrate that the principles of competition law and labour law only appear to be contradictory.

In an article on individual and social law, Radbruch indicates that the idea of social law has a fourfold significance:

(i) behind the equalising abstraction of the concept 'legal person', appears the concrete individuality, the status of power or of social weakness;
(ii) the possibility to protect the weak and limit the excesses of social power appears;
(iii) the idea of equality is the basis of individual law; social law is based upon the idea of comparison. The first is dominated by commutative justice; the second, by distributive justice;
(iv) the conformity between legal form and legal reality is taken to the next level.[51]

After finding that remedying asymmetrical relations can be done either by protecting the weaker party or by combating the excesses of the powerful party, Radbruch states:

---

46 R. Van den Bergh and P. Camesasca, "Irreconcilable principles? The Court of Justice Exempts CLA's from the Wrath of Antitrust", *E.L.Rev.* 2000, 503, 506–507.

47 M. De Vos, "CLA's and European competition law: an inherent contradiction?", in M. De Vos (ed.), *A Decade Beyond Maastricht: The European Social Dialogue Revisited* (The Hague/London/New York: Kluwer Law International, 2003) 71.

48 M. De Vos, *l.c.*, 66.

49 M. De Vos, *l.c.*, 73.

50 M. De Vos, *l.c.*, 86.

51 G. Radbruch, "Du droit individualiste au droit social", *Arch. de Philosophie de Droit et de Sociologie Juridique* 1931, 387, 390.

> On peut schématiquement trouver la différence de ces deux domaines juridiques [le droit ouvrier et le droit économique] dans ce fait que le droit ouvrier est fait pour protéger les individus socialement faibles et le droit économique pour combattre les excès des personnes socialement puissantes.[52]

From this perspective, the principles of labour law and economic law are not irreconcilable at all. On the contrary, they both serve the purpose of limiting the negative effects of power on a just distribution of freedom.

Competition law prevents power accumulation/creation and the abuse of power that distort the market. In doing so, it guarantees free and fair competition, which in turn guarantees reasonable prices for consumers. Thus, in guaranteeing protection against excess power by market actors or enterprises, first it guarantees market freedom (namely, freedom of enterprise), and second, it guarantees freedom by providing for just prices for goods and services.

Given market forces in a free market, however, any market actor or enterprise is still a weak actor even in the absence of individual dominant enterprises. Given opportunism of man, there is always at least one person who may compete by discarding other persons' need for freedom, thus in the end obliging other market actors to do the same.[53] This is particularly problematic in the labour market: social competition prevents individual law from establishing a just distribution of freedom between men. Guaranteeing freedom in the market does not guarantee a just distribution of freedom in the labour market. CLAs are the legal mechanism that have spontaneously emerged in the socio–professional legal order to remedy this.

Given these two fundamentally different and necessary accents on power relations, it appears that there is no conceptual reason for subsuming CLAs under competition law principles or vice–versa. Though from a technical perspective, not subsuming social law under competition law leads to the same result as first subsuming it and then excepting it, the first solution is theoretically sounder. From this perspective, the aforementioned judgments of the European Court of Justice appear as preferable to the alternative of subsumption and exception.

If labour law mechanisms are inappropriately used to create and maintain power relations that prevent a just distribution of freedom, or if economic law mechanisms are inappropriately used in creating or maintaining suppressed social actors, the legal system must provide techniques to proceed against these measures. Two ways are then possible: either the abusive social or economic measures are eliminated because they conflict with/surpass the principles of labour and economic law respectively, or they are evaluated against the background of economic law and labour law respectively. In only exempting CLAs between social partners seeking jointly to adopt measures to improve conditions of work and employment from the cartel provisions, the Court of Justice has taken the last approach in case of CLAs surpassing their social law function.

---

52 G. Radbruch, *l.c.*, 392.

53 This insight appears very early in Belgian labour law, *e.g.* Helleputte's suggestion in 1895 in proposed legislation on labour time: Proposition de loi sur la limitation de la durée du travail et sur le travail de dimanche, (1895) *Parl. St. Kamer*, nr. 90, 5–6.

6 Conclusion

The above briefly illustrates how legal pluralism and the notion of social law can be put into operation to provide a legal conceptual framework that supports the reception of the CLA as laid down in the CLA Statute and allows locating it within the legal system as a whole. It illustrates how legal theory is a tool for overcoming problems in the conception of the CLA due to dogmatic legal thinking from a civil, economic, or constitutional law perspective.

Separating the development and application of law from the condition of man leads to an instrumentalisation of law, which in turn dangerously increases the occurrence of negative limits of the law. Legal theory helps to *understand* law. Understanding law prevents the separation of law and the condition of man, thus remedying negative limits of the law and enforcing positive limits of the law.

Conclusion

Chapter 5 – The Limits of Consumer Law in Europe

Bert Keirsbilck

1 Introduction

The tension between central steering and decentralised action which is common to most contemporary States[1], is a central feature of the European Community ('EC') system too.[2] Centralisation and decentralisation forces, though acting in opposite directions, fundamentally have the same target: increasing the effectiveness of the legal system.[3]

This chapter begins by showing how EC consumer law is undergoing the opposing trend of centralisation and decentralisation.[4] Whereas the maximum harmonisation character of recent consumer protection directives points to a direction of ever more centralised and open–textured rule–making, decentralisation is at play as far as enforcement is concerned (section 2). Subsequently, it will argued that, especially in a system of decentralised enforcement, the characteristic open–texture of EC (consumer) law sets limits to some of its most basic functions (section 3). Finally, the difficult question how to deal with these limits of the law will be addressed (section 4). It will be argued that a constructive attitude towards law's open texture, promoting the political virtue of 'integrity of law' in Europe, is the right way to face these limits of the law. If legal practitioners consider law as integrity, the gap between the law and the use of law may be bridged. In addition, it will be shown how bridging the institutional gap between the upper, supranational level and the lower, national level might stimulate such integration of the day–to–day management of centralised regulation and decentralised enforcement of EC law.

---

1 See G. Teubner, "Substantive and Reflexive Elements in Modern Law", *Law and Society Review* 1983, 239.

2 See R. Van den Bergh, "The Subsidiarity Principle in European Community Law Some Insights from Law & Economics", *Maastricht Journal of European and Comparative Law* 1994, 337–366.

3 F. Snyder, "The Effectiveness of European Community Law: Institutions, Processes, Tools and Techniques", *Modern Law Review* 1993, 19–54. According to Snyder "'effectiveness' is taken to mean the fact that law matters: it has effect on political, economic and social law outside the law – that is, apart from simply the elaboration of legal doctrine."

4 See J.–P. Schneider, "Vollzug des Europäischen Wirtschaftsrechts zwischen Zentralisierung und Dezentralisierung – Bilanz und Ausblick", *Europarecht* 2005, Beih. 2, 146.

2 Centralisation and Decentralisation Forces in the Field of Consumer Protection

2.1 Centralisation of Rule–Making

Most EC consumer protection directives are based on minimum harmonisation[5], but more recent ones, such as Directive 2005/29/EC concerning unfair commercial practices[6], are based on maximum harmonisation[7] – the strongest instance of centralisation of rule–making.[8] In the Explanatory Memorandum to its 2003 Proposal, the Commission provided extensive concrete data to illustrate the existence of barriers and distortions stemming from the fragmentation of the rules on unfair commercial practices, and to demonstrate that only a maximum harmonisation measure could contribute effectively to the abolition of these barriers, both by eliminating transactions costs and increasing consumer confidence. The Unfair Commercial Practices Directive as finally adopted aims to encourage consumers and businesses to engage in cross–border trade and to stimulate the advantageous circular effects of increased cross–border demand and increased competitive pressure within the internal market. Importantly, in its 2007 Green Paper on the Review of the Consumer Acquis, the Commission proposed to revise the consumer *acquis*[9] with a view to achieving maximum harmonisation.[10]

---

5 For example, Council Directive 93/13/EEC of 5 April 1993 on unfair terms in consumer contracts, O.J. L 95/29, 21.04.1993.

6 Directive 2005/29/EC of the European Parliament and of the Council of 11 May 2005 concerning unfair business–to–consumer commercial practices in the internal market and amending Council Directive 84/450/EEC, Directives 97/7/EC, 98/27/EC and 2002/65/EC of the European Parliament and of the Council and Regulation (EC) No 2006/2004 of the European Parliament and of the Council ("Unfair Commercial Practices Directive"), O.J. L 149/22, 11.06.2005.

7 See S. Grundmann and W. Kerber, "European System of Contract Laws – A Map Combining the Advantages of Centralised and Decentralised Rule–Making", in S. Grundmann and J. Stuyck (eds.), *An Academic Green Paper on European Contract Law* (The Hague: Kluwer Law International, 2002) 295–342.

8 See, for example, Directive 2000/31/EC of the European Parliament and of the Council of 8 June 2000 on certain legal aspects of information society services, in particular electronic commerce, in the Internal Market, O.J. L 178/1, 17.06.2000.

9 Council Directive 85/577/EEC of 20 December 1985 to protect the consumer in respect of contracts negotiated away from business premises, O.J. L 372/31, 31.12.1985; Council Directive 90/314/EEC of 13 June 1990 on package travel, package holidays and package tours, O.J. L 158/59, 23.06.1990; Council Directive 93/13/EEC of 5 April 1993 on unfair terms in consumer contracts, O.J. L 95/29, 21.04.1993; Directive 97/7/EC of the European Parliament and of the Council of 20 May 1997 on the protection of consumers in respect of distance contracts, O.J. L 144/19, 04.06.1997, as amended by Directive 2002/65/EC of the European Parliament and of the Council of 23 September 2002, O.J. L 271/16, 09.10.2002 and by Directive 2005/29/EC of the European Parliament and of the Council of 11 May 2005, O.J. L 149/22, 11.06.2005; Directive 98/6/EC of the European Parliament and of the Council of 16 February 1998 on consumer protection in the indication of the prices of products offered to consumers, O.J. L 80/27, 18.03.1998; Directive 98/27/EC of the European Parliament and of the Council 19 May 1998 on injunctions for the protection of consumer's interests, O.J. L

Most EC consumer protection directives are based on a vertical approach (intended to provide specific solutions to particular problems[11]) and most of them are prescriptive rather than principle–based.[12] This approach has given rise to a fragmented regulatory environment that is considered no longer capable of fully meeting the requirements of today's rapidly evolving society and markets. The European legislator seems to be increasingly aware that the late–modern regulatory need, in this field and elsewhere, is much more complex. On the one hand, centralised rules regulating economic life are crucial both to contribute to the proper functioning of a competitive internal market and to protect the economic interests of market participants and the general interest in undistorted competition. On the other hand, the regulation of economic life must not unnecessarily restrict innovation and paralyse the progressive dynamics of the internal market. The European legislator tries to achieve this ambivalent regulatory ambition by adopting horizontal framework directives including remarkably open–textured[13] provisions. This more integrated, horizontal approach (combined, where necessary, with vertical action) has begun with the Unfair Commercial Practices Directive.[14] This Directive is a "technology–neutral EC framework directive"[15]: it functions as a safety net to cover practices which fall outside the coordinated fields of the sector–specific fair trading Directives. The open–textured definition of 'commercial practice'[16] is clearly intended to be future–proof and to cover newly occurring

---

166/51, 16.06.1998, as amended by Directive 1999/44/EC of the European Parliament and of the Council of 25 May 1999, O.J. L 171/12, 07.07.1999, by Directive 2000/31/EC of the European Parliament and of the Council of 8 June 2000, O.J. L 178/1, 17.07.2000, by Directive 2002/65/EC of the European Parliament and of the Council of 23 September 2002, O.J. L 271/16, 09.10.2002 and by Directive 2005/29/EG of the European Parliament and of the Council of 11 May 2005, O.J. L 149/22, 11.06.2005; Directive 1999/44/EC of the European Parliament and of the Council of 25 May 1999 on certain aspects of the sale of consumer goods and associated guarantees, O.J. L 171/12, 07.07.1999; Directive 94/47/EC of the European Parliament and of the Council of 26 October 1994 on the protection of purchasers in respect of certain aspects of contracts relating to the purchase of the right to use immovable properties on a timeshare basis, O.J. L 280/83, 29.10.1994.

10 See Green Paper on the Review of the Consumer Acquis, COM (2006) 744 final, 08.02.2007, 10. See also the Consumer Policy Strategy 2002–2006, COM (2002) 208, 7.5.2002 and Consumer Policy Strategy 2007– 2012, COM (2007) 99 final, 13.3.2007.

11 Green Paper on the Review of the Consumer Acquis, COM (2006) 744 final, 08.02.2007, 6–7.

12 *Idem*, 6.

13 See H.L.A. Hart, *The Concept of Law* (Oxford: Oxford University Press, 2nd ed., 1994) 128–136. See also E. Claes, W. Devroe, and B. Keirsbilck, "The Limits of the Law (Introduction)".

14 Unfair commercial practices generate a market failure by impairing the autonomous determination of the demand side of the market. The distortion of consumers' decision–making also gives rise to distortions of competition on the supply side of the market in that traders acting unfairly win business away from competitors who play by the rules.

15 Green Paper on European Union Consumer Protection, 2 October 2001, COM (2001) 531 final, 11.

16 Article 2(d) Unfair Commercial Practices Directive: "any act, omission, course of conduct or representation, commercial communication including advertising and marketing, by a trader, directly connected with the promotion, sale or supply of a product to consumers". Pursuant

practices.[17] The Directive's general prohibition[18] is elaborated on by two further provisions concerning the two types of commercial practices which are by far the most common, namely misleading and aggressive commercial practices.[19] The open texture of these general provisions creates a huge regulatory potential; it enables public officials, legal practitioners, and law–abiding citizens throughout Europe to adjust those provisions to new evolutions and challenges in Europe. Interestingly, in its 2007 Green Paper on the Review of the Consumer Acquis, the Commission proposed to adopt a new horizontal instrument[20], which would regulate in a systematic fashion issues relevant in the context of several consumer protection directives.[21] In addition, it would include the Unfair Contract Terms Directive[22] and the Consumer Sales Directive[23]. The Commission also consulted on the issue whether the new horizontal instrument should include an overarching duty for professionals to act in accordance with the principles of good faith and fair dealing in the context of consumer contracts (from the negotiation phase to the execution of the contract).[24]

---

to Article 3(1), "this Directive shall apply to unfair business-to-consumer commercial practices, as laid down in Article 5, before, during and after a commercial transaction in relation to a product."

17 Green Paper on European Union Consumer Protection, 2 October 2001, COM (2001) 531 final, 8: 'new economy' commercial practices, new advertising practices which challenge traditional print media distinctions between media content and advertising (*e.g.*, website sponsorship, affiliation, remunerated search tools, use of meta–data and links, referrals and reviews), new marketing methods such as cookies, 'spidering', co–shopping and power shopping, online gambling and gaming, internet currencies, internet auctions, …

18 Article 5(2) Unfair Commercial Practices Directive: "A commercial practice shall be unfair if: (a) it is contrary to the requirements of professional diligence, and (b) it materially distorts or is likely to materially distort the economic behaviour with regard to the product of the average consumer whom it reaches or to whom it is addressed".

19 Article 6 and 7; Article 8 and 9 Unfair Commercial Practices Directive. Unlike the grand general clause, the small general clauses do not require it to be established that a particular practice is contrary to the requirements of professional diligence, because this will be automatically presumed.

20 Green Paper on the Review of the Consumer Acquis, COM (2006) 744 final, 08.02.2007, 8–9.

21 For example, definitions of basic notions such as 'consumer' and 'professional', the length of cooling–off periods and the modalities for the exercise of the right of withdrawal.

22 See *inter alia* Article 3(1) Council Directive 93/995/EEC of 5 April 1993 on unfair terms in consumer contracts, O.J. L 95/29, 21.4.1993: "A contractual term which has not been individually negotiated shall be regarded as unfair, if, contrary to the requirement of good faith, it causes a significant imbalance in the parties' rights and obligations arising under the contract, to the detriment of the consumer."

23 Directive 1999/44/EC of the European Parliament and of the Council of 25 May 1999 on certain aspects of the sale of consumer goods and associated guarantees, O.J. L 171/12, 07.07.1999.

24 Green Paper on the Review of the Consumer Acquis, COM (2006) 744 final, 08.02.2007, 17. See also S. Grundmann, "The General Clause or Standard in EC Contract Law Directives – A Survey on Some Important Legal Measures and Aspects in EC Law", in S. Grundmann and D. Mazeaud (eds.), *General Clauses and Standards in European Contract Law* (The Hague: Kluwer Law International, 2006) 141–161; K. Calais–Auloy, "Le devoir de se comporter de bonne foi dans les contrats de consommation", in S. Grundmann and D. Mazeaud

2.2 Decentralisation of Enforcement

In the 2001 Green Paper on European Union Consumer Protection, the Commission stated that any regulatory measure must be linked to adequate enforcement structures that ensure an effective application. Markets need clear and certain rules but they also require that such rules are effectively enforced.[25] Effective enforcement of consumer protection laws – wherever the consumer or business are located – is essential to the good functioning of the internal market, the elimination of distortions of competition, and the protection of consumers. Therefore, Regulation (EC) No 2006/2004 of 27 October 2004 on cooperation between national authorities responsible for the enforcement of consumer protection laws[26] established a public enforcement regime, as a complement to the existing private enforcement mechanisms.[27]

In addition, the Commission argued that enforcement should be more or less equally effective in all Member States.[28] Some legal scholars have wondered whether there should not be some sort of European public enforcement of EC consumer law or EC unfair commercial practices law in particular (the Commission, a European Agency of Fair Trading or a European Fair Trade Commission).[29] The European legislator, however, estimated the potential efficiency benefits achieved through centralised enforcement to be quite small compared to the benefits of a policy of closeness to national businesses and consumers.[30] In contrast to the Regulation (EC) No 1/2003 of 16 December 2002 on the implementation of the

---

(eds.), *General Clauses and Standards in European Contract Law* (The Hague: Kluwer Law International, 2006) 189–195.

25 Green Paper on European Union Consumer Protection, 2 October 2001, COM (2001) 531 final, 16.

26 Regulation (EC) No 2006/2004 of the European Parliament and of the Council of 27 October 2004 on cooperation between national authorities responsible for the enforcement of consumer protection laws, O.J. L 364/1, 9.12.2004.

27 See Directive 98/27/EC of the European Parliament and of the Council of 19 May 1998 on injunctions for the protection of consumer's interests, O.J. L 166/51, 16.06.1998, as amended by Directive 1999/44/EC of the European Parliament and of the Council of 25 May 1999, O.J. L 171/12, 07.07.1999, by Directive 2000/31/EC of the European Parliament and of the Council of 8 June 2000, O.J. L 178/1, 17.07.2000, by Directive 2002/65/EC of the European Parliament and of the Council of 23 September 2002, O.J. L 271/16, 09.10.2002, and by Directive 2005/29/EG of the European Parliament and of the Council of 11 May 2005, O.J. L 149/22, 11.06.2005.

28 Green Paper on European Union Consumer Protection, 2 October 2001, COM (2001) 531 final, 18.

29 Institut für Europäisches Wirtschafts- und Verbraucherrecht, *Study on the Feasibility of a General Legislative Framework on Fair Trading*, November 2000, Vol. 2, 115–117.

30 Traditionally, decentralised enforcement of EC law is argued for on the basis of the political principle of subsidiarity. The implementation and the enforcement of EC law are carried out partly by the Commission, the Court of Justice and the Court of First Instance, but – according to the political principle of subsidiarity – it is done primarily by the Member States through national administrations and national legal systems. See K. Lenaerts and P. Van Nuffel, *Constitutional Law of the European Union* (London: Sweet & Maxwell) 2005, 103.

rules on competition laid down in Articles 81 and 82 of the Treaty[31], the 2004 Regulation on Consumer Protection Cooperation grants the Commission no enforcement rights or responsibilities.[32] The Regulation opts for a system of decentralised enforcement of consumer protection laws by national public enforcement authorities with a minimum of common investigatory and enforcement powers.[33]

3 Limits of Open–Textured EC (Consumer) Law in a System of Decentralised Enforcement

The above described *Flucht in Generalklauseln* sets limits to some of the law's most basic functions, in particular in combination within the current system of decentralised enforcement.

First, the open texture of EC general clauses risks restraining the ability to regulate economic life effectively (limits to the regulatory function of law in Europe). Understanding the law presupposes a kind of know–how, a tacit knowledge about the point of legal rules and principles. We only grasp the point of a legal rule and feel obliged to follow a rule, to the extent that we have internalised its normative underpinnings. The process of internalisation of new legal rules takes time and can easily be distorted by elements internal or external to the law. This holds *a fortiori* for newly enacted general clauses. Therefore, it is likely that, for example, the open–textured rules of the maximum harmonisation Unfair Commercial Practices Directive will dramatically restrain the Directive's ability to regulate fairness in economic life effectively. These rules will receive a concrete content only incrementally, through the slow and difficult internalisation by consumers and businesses and through the accumulation of case–law and administrative practice. In the meantime nobody really knows how the general duty not to act unfairly must be understood.

Second, the use of EC general clauses increases the probability of hard cases in which the law falls short of its dispute resolution function. A time–consuming and burdensome process of internalisation of EC general clauses in the Member States increases the likelihood of hard cases. It is likely that in the near future national courts and enforcement authorities will often not know how to apply the general prohibitions of the Unfair Commercial Practices Directive to real–life cases. Consequently, the difficulties in applying the open–textured rules of this Directive will

---

[31] See Regulation (EC) No 1/2003 of 16 December 2002 on the implementation of the rules on competition laid down in Articles 81 and 82 of the Treaty, O.J. L 1/1, 4.1.2003.

[32] See *inter alia* H.–W. Micklitz, "Transborder Law Enforcement – Does it Exist?", in S. Weatherill and U. Bernitz (eds.), *The Regulation of Unfair Commercial Practices under EC Directive 2005/29* (Oxford and Portland: Hart Publishing, 2007) 235–254 and S. Kaye, "Regulation EC 2006/2004 on Consumer Protection Co–operation", in G. Howells *et al.* (eds.), *The Yearbook of Consumer Law 2007* (Aldershot: Ashgate, 2007) 417–423.

[33] The Annex contains a list with 16 directives and regulations that protect consumers' interests. For example, the 2005 Unfair Commercial Practices Directive and the 1993 Unfair Contract Terms Directive are included in this list.

in many cases end up before the European Court of Justice, which may be asked to steer rather than to control how the fairness test is to be applied.[34]

Third, the use of EC general clauses may inhibit the symbolic role of EC law and prevent the expression and representation of implied common values and shared understandings in Europe. Maximum harmonisation measures are not just technical solutions to a problem of barriers to a fully functioning internal market. They are also designed to bind European citizens to a shared European identity.[35] For example, the Unfair Commercial Practices Directive seems to promulgate a particular scheme of principles, based on a strong belief that transparency is the main method of consumer protection and that only informed choices lead to efficient choices ensuring maximisation of consumer's collective interests.[36] The Directive has a symbolic potential "to bring the EU closer to its citizens, by dispelling the myth that the internal market is a corporate business project and delivering tangible economic benefits to their daily life."[37] However, it is uncertain to what extent the open–textured rules of the Unfair Commercial Practices Directive, when applied to real–life cases within different jurisdictions often embracing different cultural standards of social justice, will actually reflect the market–oriented approach which the Directive's drafters had in mind. Hence, the relative 'under–determination' of the Directive's provisions seems to limit the Directive's symbolic capacity of representing and expressing a European scheme of principles.[38] Likewise, it is uncertain to what extent an open–textured horizontal instrument in the field of (consumer) contract law would be able to reflect its implied philosophy – a particular balance between, on the one hand, the weight attached to individual private autonomy as expressed in the principle of freedom of contract and, on the other hand, other equally important demands for solidarity and equality as expressed in the principle of good faith.[39]

Fourth, the use of EC general clauses poses an intrinsic limit to the protective function of the law. The ways in which citizens in Europe rely on EC general

---

34 See, with respect to the Unfair Contract Terms Directive, ECJ Joint Cases C-240/98 – C-244/98 of 27 June 2000, *Océano Grupo*, [2000] ECR I-4941; ECJ Case C-478/99 of 7 May 2002, *Commission v. Sweden*, [2002] ECR I-4147; ECJ Case C-237/02 of 1 April 2004, *Hofstetter*, [2004] ECR I-3403; ECJ Case C-70/03 of 9 September 2004, *Commission v. Spain*, [2004] ECR I-7999.

35 See Study Group on Social Justice in European Private Law, "Social Justice in European Contract Law", *European Law Review* 2004, 635–674. See also T. Wilhelmsson, "The Legal, the Cultural and the Political – Conclusions from Different Perspectives on Harmonisation of European Contract Law", *European Business Law Review* 2002, 542–546.

36 See J. Drexl, *Die wirtschaftliche Selbstbestimmung des Verbrauchers* (Tübingen: Mohr Siebeck, 1998).

37 Green Paper on European Union Consumer Protection, 2 October 2001, COM (2001) 531 final, 10.

38 Compare G. Teubner, "Legal Irritants: Good Faith in British Law or How Unifying Law Ends Up in New Divergences", *Modern Law Review* 1998, 23. See also G. Howells, "Aggressive Commercial Practices", in G. Howells, H.–W. Micklitz and T. Wilhelmsson (eds.), *European Fair Trading Law* (Aldershot: Ashgate, 2007) 170.

39 See also T. Wilhelmsson, "Varieties of Welfarism in European Contract Law", *European Law Journal* 2004, 712–733.

clauses and the ways in which national public officials administer them are to a certain extent always unpredictable.[40] Decentralised application of EC general clauses is inevitably influenced by the diverging legal traditions of the Member States. Uniform application of open–textured EC law by the Member States, in the absence of autonomous Community interpretation, seems to be an unattainable ideal. For example, it is likely that the general clauses of the Unfair Commercial Practices Directive will lead to incoherent case–law across the 27 Member States. Hence, traders will not be protected adequately in their ability to engage in economic interactions on the basis of preexisting legal rules, principles and decisions (legitimate expectations).[41] In addition, no cross–border trader seems to enjoy "compliance certainty".[42] The Unfair Commercial Practices Directive does not prohibit the situation that a Member State, whose national consumers are affected by a commercial practice used by a trader in different Member States, would decide that a commercial practice is unfair under the Directive, even if the Member State in which this trader is established has already decided that this practice is not unfair (or *vice versa*).[43] Accordingly, decisions in other Member States (*e.g.,* the Member State where the trader is established) seems to be mere facts, which can be considered or neglected by a national court to reach its own judgment.[44]

---

[40] See D. Edward, "Shifting Power from Legislation to Judges and from the Central to the National Level", in S. Grundmann and D. Mazeaud (eds.), *General Clauses and Standards in European Contract Law* (The Hague: Kluwer Law International, 2006) 79–84.

[41] See J. Temple Lang, "Legal Certainty and Legitimate Expectations as General Principles of Law", in U. Bernitz and J. Nergelius, *General Principles of European Community Law* (The Hague: Kluwer Law International, 2000) 163–184. Already in the Green Paper on European Union Consumer Protection, the Commission pointed out that the major problem connected to EC general clauses was that "a certain risk of divergence in interpretation by national courts [and enforcement authorities] would always be present." See Green Paper on European Union Consumer Protection, 2 October 2001, COM (2001) 531 final, 15. In the 2001 Communication on European Contract Law, the Commission also observed that using abstract terms in EC law may considerably hamper uniform application throughout Europe. See Communication from the Commission to the Council and the European Parliament on European Contract Law, 11 July 2001, COM(2001) 398 final, 10. See also Green Paper on the review of the Consumer Acquis, 8 February 2007, COM (2006) 744 final, 17.

[42] See J. Stuyck, E. Terryn, and T. Van Dyck, "Confidence through Fairness? The New Directive on Unfair Business–to–Consumer Commercial Practices in the Internal Market", *Common Market Law Review* 2006, 117.

[43] The Unfair Commercial Practices Directive does not establish the principle of home country control and does not prohibit host State authorities to check the fairness of the practice checked by the Member State of establishment. Article 4 provides: "Member States shall neither restrict the freedom to provide services nor restrict the free movement of goods for reasons falling within the field approximated by this Directive." Compare Article 4 of the Commission Proposal for a Directive of the European Parliament and of the Council concerning unfair business-to-consumer commercial practices in the Internal Market and amending directives 84/450/EEC, 97/7/EC and 98/27/EC, 18 June 2003, COM (2003) 356 final, 41 p.). See J. Stuyck, E. Terryn, and T. Van Dyck, *l.c.*, 117.

[44] See J. Stuyck, E. Terryn, and T. Van Dyck, *l.c.*, 117.

4 How to Deal with these Limits?

4.1 Integrity in Law in Europe

Within the boundaries of the current institutional setup of decentralised EC law enforcement, a constructive attitude towards law's open texture, promoting the ideal of 'integrity in law' in Europe, seems to be a first strategy to deal with the above identified limits of EC general clauses. The ideal of 'integrity in law' entails the collective responsibility of a political community to give the most well–balanced and coherent interpretation of the legal principles and fundamental rights underlying the legal order as a whole.[45] According to 'integrity in law' in Europe, each court or enforcement authority, be it European or national, should not be satisfied with speaking with one voice in its own legal order ('horizontal coherence'[46]), but should also try to speak in a way that is representative of the legally expressed views in the entire European political community, whether by EC or national authorities (vertical coherence).[47] National courts and enforcement authorities should ensure transnational integrity among national interpretations of law of a common European origin.[48] This means, for example, that national decisions applying the Unfair Commercial Practices Directive should cohere with each other across the 27 Member States.[49] In addition, once the Member State of the trader's establishment has conducted a compliance check of a particular commercial practice, and has concluded that it is not unfair under the Directive, the trader should benefit from a *de facto* presumption that he is acting in compliance with the Directive.[50]

---

45 R. Dworkin, *l.c.*

46 See D. Curtin and E. Dekker, "The EU as a 'Layered' International Organisation: Institutional Unity in Disguise", in P. Craig and G. De Burca (eds.), *The Evolution of EU Law* (Oxford: Oxford University Press, 1999) 83 and 103.

47 S. Besson, "From European Integration to European Integrity: Should European Law Speak With Just One Voice?", *European Law Journal* 2004, 262. Arguably, vertical coherence is a *conditio sine qua non* for the law in Europe to be the law of the European political and legal community as a whole.

48 S. Besson, *l.c.*, 263. Vertical coherence means transnational integrity between national courts and authorities on the one hand and supranational coherence between European and national courts and authorities on the other. It is important to note that supranational integrity could indeed tip the balance simultaneously in the national direction on the part of European courts and authorities, and in the European direction on the part of national courts and authorities.

49 J. Drexl, "Community Legislation Continued: Complete Harmonisation, Framework Legislation or Non–Binding Measures – Alternative Approaches to European Contract Law, Consumer Protection and Unfair Trade Practices?", *European Business Law Review* 2002, 557–582.

50 See "I/A" Item Note, Interinstitutional File 2003/0134 (COD), 7860/05, 11 April 2005, 2 p. and Addendum 1 to "I/A" Item Note, Statement by the United Kingdom, the Netherlands, Luxembourg and Estonia, Interinstitutional File 2003/0134 (COD), 7860/05, 11 April 2005, 2 p.: "Since this is a maximum harmonisation directive which Member States will transpose to give equivalent effect to its principles, it should therefore ordinarily be presumed that traders who conform with the laws in the Member State where they are established will not

From the perspective of 'integrity in law' in Europe, the fact that the meaning of a general clause is dependent on its use, must be considered as an opportunity and a challenge (especially in hard cases) to interpret a general clause in a way that suits the particular case and gives a sound expression of the principles underlying law in Europe as a whole. In addition, the use of EC general clauses must be considered as allowing for a more gradual replacement of the divergent sets of values represented by the existing national rules by a common European set. It enhances a more gradual internalisation of the new European set of values and the new scheme of principles.[51]

What remains difficult to assess, however, is whether the legal principle of coherence as it currently exists in the European legal order requires this kind of (morally desirable) transnational integrity between national courts and authorities on matters of European competence.[52] Furthermore, it could be objected that it is virtually impossible to create the required willingness and readiness on the part of all parties to further the normative ideal of integrity in law in Europe. However, it must be noted that integrity is an optimisation principle (a regulative ideal). As such it should be implemented to the highest degree possible given the circumstances.[53] Moreover, integrity is a path–dependent virtue and, as such, it will gradually increase through being respected.[54]

4.2 Reform of the Regulatory and Institutional Structure

Of course, the gap between the law (regulation) and the use of law (application and enforcement) is also an institutional gap, resulting from the opposite forces of centralisation and decentralisation. It seems that the willingness to further European integrity on the part of all parties could be stimulated by bridging the institutional gap between the upper level (EC framework principles and implementing measures) and the lower level (national enforcement authorities and courts), and by improving the regulatory structure. A more close integration of the day–to–day

---

be in breach of the laws in other Member States. This *de facto* principle should be communicated to economic operators to provide them with the legal certainty and confidence needed to fully realise the potential of the internal market…" See J. Stuyck, E. Terryn, and T. Van Dyck, *l.c.*, 119–120.

51 H. Collins, "European Private Law and the Cultural Identity of States", *European Review of Private Law* 1995, 359.

52 S. Besson, *l.c.*, 263 and 264, who argues that the legal principle of coherence as it currently exists in the European legal order (Article 3 EU Treaty) may be regarded as more precise and incisive than the existing European principle of loyalty (Article 10 EC Treaty). See also J. Stuyck, E. Terryn, and T. Van Dyck, *l.c.*, note 64, who argue that transnational integrity among national interpretations of the Unfair Commercial Practices Directive "can be derived from Article 10 EC Treaty (duty of loyal cooperation)" and that, furthermore, "this would seem to be […] consistent with the ambit and rationale of the Unfair Commercial Practices Directive and its total harmonisation objective."

53 S. Besson, *l.c.*, 266.

54 S. Besson, *l.c.*, 265–266.

management of centralised regulation and decentralised enforcement of EC law could be achieved by improving the regulatory structure and by institutionalising the co–operation between the supranational level and national level. It seems that EC consumer law can draw lessons from the four–level regulatory and institutional structure in other fields of EC law, especially in EC financial law[55], but also in EC competition law.

In the field of EC financial law, the Council and the European Parliament, adopt framework directives. Such level 1 measures are of a legislative nature: they have their legal basis directly in the Treaties and decide the essential elements in the area concerned.[56] In the field EC competition law, Article 81 and 82 EC Treaty and the EC Merger Regulation[57] *mutatis mutandis* can be considered as providing for framework principles and general clauses.

In the field of EC consumer law, the Unfair Commercial Practices Directive essentially is a framework directive, setting out an over–arching general clause, elaborated further in two secondary general clauses. A forthcoming horizontal instrument in the field of consumer contract law would also be designed as a framework directive.

In the field of EC financial law, the European Commission takes measures implementing the level 1 framework directives, after consultation with the Committee of European Securities Regulators, in which the supervising authorities of all Member States are represented. These level 2 measures are of a non–legislative nature: they are not directly adopted on the basis of the Treaties and do not express the essential policy options in the area concerned.[58] In the field of EC competition law, the sole power to take level 2 implementing measures for the development of competition policy is centralised in the Commission. These measures especially consist of block exemption regulations, which the Commission can adopt solely after consultation of the Advisory Committee on Restrictive Practices and Dominant Positions, composed of representatives of the national competition authorities.

---

55 See also J. Stuyck, E. Terryn, and T. Van Dyck, *l.c.*, 146–147.
See Final Report of the Committee of Wise Men on the Regulation of European Securities Markets, Brussels, 15 February 2001, 117 p., available at http://ec.europa.eu/internal_market/securities/docs/lamfalussy/wisemen/final-report-wise-men_en.pdf. See *inter alia* Directive 2004/39/EC of the European Parliament and of the Council of 21 April 2004 on markets in financial instruments amending Council Directives 85/611/EEC and 93/6/EEC and Directive 2000/12/EC of the European Parliament and of the Council and repealing Council Directive 93/22/EEC, O.J. L 145/1, 30.04.2004, as amended by Directive 2006/31/EC of the European Parliament and of the Council of 5 April 2006, O.J. L 114/60, 27.4.2006, Directive 2007/44/EC of the European Parliament and of the Council of 5 September 2007, O.J. L 247/1, 21.9.2007.

56 K. Lenaerts and M. Desomer, "Towards a Hierarchy of Legal Acts in the European Union? Simplification of Legal Instruments and Procedures", *European Law Journal* 2005, 751–752.

57 Council Regulation (EC) No 139/2004 of 20 January 2004 on the control of concentrations between undertakings, O.J. L 24/1, 29.01.2004.

58 K. Lenaerts and M. Desomer, *l.c.*, 753.

In the field of EC consumer law, level 2 measures could include, for example, an exhaustive, legally binding 'black list' of commercial practices which shall always be considered unfair – without a case–by–case assessment against the Directive's general clauses (irrefutable presumption of unfairness). If the current black list (annexed to the Unfair Commercial Practices Directive) were to be adopted as a separate level 2 instrument by the Commission (preferably after consultation of an Advisory Committee on Consumer Protection representing all 27 national enforcement authorities), it would be more easily adaptable in view of new economic or technological developments.[59] Yet since the current black list "may only be modified by revision of the Directive"[60], any alteration, refinement, or correction necessitated by changing market circumstances needs a burdensome revision of the Directive. Obviously, a black list should not eliminate commercial practices which cannot be regarded unfair under all circumstances under the general clauses. A black list should contain only those commercial practices which in any case would meet all the conditions for application of the Directive's general clause. Unfortunately, the current black list prohibits various commercial practices which *in casu* may not be likely to materially distort the economic behaviour of the average consumer.[61] Since it must be possible to apply the *per se* rules implementing the Directive's principles in an all–or–nothing and uniform fashion throughout Europe, the rules of the black list should be crystal–clear specifications of the framework principles. However, the current black list contains various vague and ambiguous concepts[62] and, consequently, it is likely to be unclear how the black list must be handled to many real–life cases.

Level 2 measures could also include a black list of unfair contract terms. Interestingly, in its 2007 Green Paper on the Review of the Consumer Acquis, the Commission suggested to adopt "a blacklist of unfair contract terms, presumably much shorter than the existing list".[63] However, this blacklist would not be adopted as a separate level 2 measure but would be annexed to the horizontal consumer contract law instrument.

---

59 See J. Stuyck, E. Terryn, and T. Van Dyck, *l.c.*, 147.

60 Article 5(5) Unfair Commercial Practices Directive.

61 The regulatory race between national governments about the prohibitions to be listed in the black list amounted not only to a more deliberate expression and representation of the Commission's market–oriented approach, but also to unforeseen and hardly justifiable priorities of concretisation (dominated by multiple one–dimensional ideologies which are detrimental to this core market–oriented approach). This partial 'over–determination' which results from the attempt to diminish the 'under–determination' of the general clauses may stifle the development and representation of a common conception of fair commercial practices throughout the European Union.

62 See *inter alia* No. 5 ("reasonable grounds", "quantities that are reasonable"); No. 6 ("within a reasonable time"); No. 8 ("for a very limited time"); No. 9, 17, 22, 23, 24 and 31 ("falsely claiming", "creating the impression", "creating the false impression"); No. 18 ("conditions less favourable than normal market conditions"); No. 26 ("persistent and unwanted"); No. 26 ("documents which could not reasonably be considered relevant", "failing systematically to respond to pertinent correspondence"); No. 31 ("equivalent benefit").

63 Green Paper on the Review of the Consumer Acquis, COM (2006) 744 final, 08.02.2007, 18–19. These two options could also be combined (*i.e.*, some contract terms considered unfair in all circumstances while other terms presumed to be unfair).

In the field of EC financial law, the Committee of European Securities Regulators issues level 3 recommendations and guidelines, in order to ensure more uniform implementation and application of the level 1 and level 2 'hard law' measures. In the field of EC competition law, undertakings seeking legal certainty now more than ever depend on such level 3 'soft law' instruments, because of the decentralised enforcement of EC competition law and the abolishment of the notification procedure.[64] The Commission is the most prominent institution issuing such measures, giving practical guidance on how the hard law instruments must be applied to real–life cases. The Commission adopts 'steering instruments' (recommendations, opinions, resolutions, and so on) on the one hand, and 'interpretative instruments' (notices and guidelines) on the other.[65] The Commission must consult the Advisory Committee on Restrictive Practices and Dominant Positions before adopting such instruments.[66] The Advisory Committee may also discuss general issues of EC competition law.[67]

In the field of EC consumer law, a genuine Advisory Committee on Consumer Protection should be competent to discuss at regular times such general issues of EC consumer law as new commercial practices, new contract terms, changing consumer behaviour and technological innovations, and so forth, and to adopt level 3 measures.[68] Consumer and trade organisations could be granted a specific role within the Advisory Committee on Consumer Protection.[69] In the absence of a genuine Advisory Committee, it is to be hoped that the Commission itself will give this kind of practical guidance on how the fairness tests of the general clauses are to be applied to real–life cases.[70] Level 3 measures could include an indicative,

---

64 Regulation (EC) No 1/2003 of 16 December 2002 on the implementation of the rules on competition laid down in Articles 81 and 82 of the Treaty, O.J. L 1/1, 4.1.2003.

65 See H.A. Cosma and R. Whish, "Soft Law in the Field of EU Competition Policy", *European Business Law Review* 2003, 25–56. 'Steering instruments' establish new rules not inherent in the existing legal framework and can be distinguished from 'interpretative instruments', which merely clarify the existing legal framework.

66 Article 33 Modernisation Regulation.

67 Article 14(7)(3) Modernisation Regulation. The Advisory Committee shall not issue opinions on cases dealt with by national competition authorities.

68 See J. Stuyck, E. Terryn and T. Van Dyck, *l.c.*, 147.

69 The idea of stakeholder participation in the elaboration the framework principles is of course most prominent in the option of co–regulation which was considered in the 2001 Green Paper on EU Consumer Protection. The 2005 Unfair Commercial Practices Directive pays only little attention to the role which 'European codes of conduct' could play to flesh out the provisions of the Directive.

70 In the 2001 Green Paper on EU Consumer Protection, the Commission envisaged that "provision could be made for non–binding practical guidance to be developed in user–friendly language for the benefit of consumers or business, judges and enforcement officials" and suggested the adoption of Commission 'recommendations' and 'interpretative communications'. See Green Paper on European Union Consumer Protection, 2 October 2001, COM (2001) 531 final, 15. See already G. Howells, "'Soft law' in EC consumer law", in P. Craig and C. Harlow (eds.), *Lawmaking in the European Union* (The Hague: Kluwer Law International, 1998), Ch. 15.

non–binding list of unfair contract terms and unfair commercial practices.[71] Inclusion in a grey list leads to a refutable presumption of unfairness within the meaning of the general clauses. Grey lists effectively structure the use of discretion by national courts and enforcement authorities in highly disputed and practically important areas. They help enforcers and market participants understand the point of the EC general clauses. *Regelbeispiele* with 'exemplary validity' enhance the degree of legal certainty and simultaneously leave enough flexibility to handle unusual cases under the general clause.[72] If, for example, the grey list annexed to the Unfair Contract Terms Directive[73] were to be issued as a separate level 3 measure, it would become much easier to adapt this list to changing economic or technological circumstances.

Level 4 is the level of decentralised application and enforcement of EC law by national courts, supervisors, and enforcement authorities. It is up to the Commission as the guardian of the uniform application of EC law to check Member States' compliance with EC law and to take legal action against Member States suspected of breach of EC law. In the field of EC competition law[74], Regulation (EC) No 1/2003 of 16 December 2002 on the implementation of the rules on competition laid down in Articles 81 and 82 of the Treaty sets up system of supervision and control by the Commission to ensure uniform effectiveness of the decentralised application of the open–textured EC competition law provisions by national courts and competition authorities.[75]

In the field of EC consumer law, Regulation (EC) No 2006/2004 of the European Parliament and of the Council of 27 October 2004 on cooperation between national authorities responsible for the enforcement of consumer protection laws contributes to improving the quality and consistency of enforcement of consumer protection laws (mainly by removing barriers to the exchange of confidential information between the national enforcement authorities and by establishing mutual assistance rights and obligations), and, importantly, strengthens the role of the

---

71 It should be recalled that the 2001 Green Paper on EU Consumer Protection suggested that "practical guidance could be expressed through an indicative list of general and sector–specific examples of commercial practices." According to the Commission, "such a list, similar to that used in the Unfair Contract Terms Directive, would have the advantage of being more formally linked to the underlying legislation." See Green Paper on European Union Consumer Protection, 2 October 2001, COM (2001) 531 final, 15. As shown above, the European legislator eventually adopted an exhaustive black list.

72 See S. Whittaker, "Theory and Practice of the 'General Clause' in English Law: General Norms and the Structuring of Judicial Discretion", in S. Grundmann and D. Mazeaud (eds.), *General Clauses and Standards in European Contract Law* (The Hague: Kluwer Law International, 2006) 57–76 and S. Grundmann, "The General Clause or Standard in EC Contract Law Directives – A Survey on Some Important Legal Measures and Aspects in EC Law", in *idem*, 141–161.

73 Council Directive 93/995/EEC of 5 April 1993 on unfair terms in consumer contracts, O.J. L 95/29, 21.4.1993.

74 The Commission actually remains just one of the enforcers of EC competition law. The Commission can take individual decisions in cases involving Community interests or having effect on intra–Community trade.

75 M. Senn, "Decentralisation of Economic Law – An Oxymoron", ESRC Centre for Analysis of Risk and Regulation, LSE, Discussion Paper No 25, March 2005.

Commission in monitoring the protection of consumer economic interests in Europe. Within and beyond the framework of this Regulation, the Commission has to take its role as a supervisor of the decentralised enforcement of EC consumer law seriously, maintaining regulatory oversight. The need for the Commission to play this role vis–à–vis national enforcement authorities and courts has increased dramatically with the accession of countries without a long history of consumer protection enforcement.[76]

5 Conclusion

This chapter showed how the field of consumer protection is undergoing the opposing trends of centralisation and decentralisation. Furthermore, it identified distinctive limits of open–textured EC law in a system of decentralised enforcement and explained how the characteristic open texture of EC law results in unpredictable and incoherent use of EC general clauses throughout Europe, 'under–determination' of EC general clauses, and a likely incidence of hard cases. The open texture of centralised EC law in a system of sheer and unchecked decentralised enforcement restrains the extent to which the functions of law can be performed. Facing these limits of the law, the chapter argued in essence for a much closer integration of the day–to–day management of regulation and enforcement in Europe by improving the regulatory structure and by institutionalising the co–operation between the supranational level and national level. It is contended that the willingness to further the ideal of integrity in law in Europe on part of all parties might be stimulated by filling the institutional vacuum between the supranational and the national level and by improving the regulatory structure. The chapter argues that it seems preferable to adopt short, crystal–clear blacklists as separate level 2 measures, implementing the open–textured concepts, rules and principles of consumer protection directives. Furthermore, level 3 soft law measures should be adopted by an Advisory Committee on Consumer Protection or by the Commission. Such measures (including *e.g.*, grey lists) could have a crucial role in explaining businesses, consumers, national courts, and enforcement authorities how the EC general clauses are to be applied to real–life cases; in reducing the likely higher incidence of hard cases before national courts and enforcement authorities; in expressing and representing a set of values underpinning EC consumer law and shared in all Member States; and in ensuring effective and coherent application and enforcement of EC consumer protection directives throughout Europe. Finally, it is argued that, within the different functional networks of national enforcement authorities, which institutionalise the readiness of

---

[76] Green Paper on European Union Consumer Protection, 2 October 2001, COM (2001) 531 final, 18. See also A.B. Engelbrekt, "An End to Fragmentation? The Unfair Commercial Practices Directive from the Perspective of the New Member States from Central and Eastern Europe", in S. Weatherill and U. Bernitz (eds.), *The Regulation of Unfair Commercial Practices under EC Directive 2005/29* (Oxford and Portland: Hart, 2007) 47–90.

national authorities to co–operate with each other and with the Commission, the European Commission has the ultimate – but not the sole – responsibility for developing policy and safeguarding coherent application and enforcement of EC law.

Chapter 6 – The Limits of Legality in the Criminal Law

Erik Claes and Michal Krolikowski

1 Introduction

The principle of legality has been considered for long as one of the cornerstones of western criminal justice systems.[1] It appears to play an important role in legal systems both of the civil law and the common law traditions. Continental lawyers often embrace legality as one of the pillars of the *Rechtsstaat*. Common law countries, from their side, connect this principle to the essence of the rule of law.[2] The authority of the principle of legality has been made clearly visible in many constitutional democracies, where it is enshrined in written constitutional provisions.[3] Its importance also echoes in the many corollaries which are linked with legality: the prohibition of retroactive legislation (*lex praevia*), the obligation clearly and precisely to define criminal offences (*lex certa*), the obligation of strict interpretation (*lex stricta*), and the prohibition against analogous reasoning.[4] And, last but not least, the principle of legality has acquired a human rights status, since it is listed in many human rights treaties.[5]

Albeit explained differently throughout civil and common law traditions, legality revolves around the idea that public officials derive their power to prosecute, to convict, and to punish only on the basis of previously defined crimes and criminal sanctions. Moreover, according to classic continental legal doctrine, it belongs (and should belong) to the exclusive competence of the legislator to provide for such basis: *nullum crimen, nulla poene sine lege.* A weaker version of this division of roles regarding criminalisation also recurs in the common law tradition.

---

1 For the civil law tradition, *e.g.*, F. Tulkens and M. van de Kerchove, *Introduction au droit pénal. Aspects juridiques et criminologiques* (Diegem: Story Scientia, 1998) 184; A. Varinard and J. Pradel, *Les grands arrêts du droit criminel, tome I* (Paris: Dalloz, 1995) 25. For the common law tradition: see A. Ashworth, *Principles of Criminal Law* (Oxford: Oxford University Press, 2006) 68 e.s.

2 See A. Ashworth, *l.c.*, 68. According to P. Westen 'legality' is a specific form of the 'rule of law' that is distinctive to the criminal law, see P. Westen, "Two Rules of Legality in Criminal Law", *Law and Philosophy* 2007, 229–305.

3 For countries of the civil law tradition, *e.g.*, Article 12 and 14 of the Belgian Constitution, Article 16 of The Constitution of the Kingdom of the Netherlands, Article 103 III of the German Constitution, Article 24 II of the Constitution of Italy. For the countries of the common law tradition, *e.g.*, Article 1 of the United States Constitution, section 35(3)(1) of the South African Constitution.

4 These corollaries derive from legal doctrine in the continental tradition, for an equivalent in common law doctrine, see A. Ashworth, *l.c.*, 68.

5 *E.g.*, Article 7 European Convention on Human Rights.

Though the common law recognises the jurisdiction of the criminal courts to extend existing, or create new, criminal offences, a certain consensus seems to exist in many common law countries as to the idea that it is in principle the legislature which bears the major responsibility for law reform.[6]

The main reason for its apparent pivotal role in continental criminal law is that legality is supposed to shield citizens against the dangers of arbitrary application of public power, and unlawful restriction of their rights and liberties.[7] These dangers are all the more pressing when a State is granted the power to impose and administer criminal punishments. Legality serves an important guarantee–providing function in this regard. To impose on public officials the obligation to intervene in criminal law matters within the limits of clear, general, previously defined crimes and sanctions, would restrict their scope of intervention.

Despite the obviousness of its rightness, it is now a common experience among lawyers and legal practitioners that legality has encountered important limits with regard to its guarantee–providing role.[8] One could notice the recent internationalisation of many criminal legal systems which deprive the national parliaments of their monopoly on defining crimes and penal sanctions.[9] This trend affects especially the criminal justice systems of EU countries whose criminal laws are also designed by European institutions. But even more impressive is the growth in social welfare States of criminal statutes many of which contain vaguely defined crimes.[10] As a result of these developments, criminal justice systems seem to be drifting away from citizens' legitimate claim of clear, accessible, and predictable definitions of criminal wrongs. Another important point of observation relates to the judiciary. Whereas the principle of legality, at least in theory, commands

---

6 Compare A. Ashworth who prudently states that, "It appears that the English Courts no longer claim the power to create new criminal offences": A. Ashworth, *l.c.*, 70. Compare also Constitutional Court of South Africa, *Masiya v Director of Public Prosections et al.*, 10 May 2007, Case CCT 54/06, par. 27, available at http://www.constitutionalcourt.org.za/site/masiya.htm. Similar ideas of legislative priority surface also in American case–law, see F.A. Allen, "The Erosion of Legality in American Criminal Justice. Some Latter–Day Adventures of the Nulla Poena Principle", *Arizona Law Review* 1987, 396.

7 See Y. Cartuyvels, "Droits de l'homme et droit pénal, un retournement?", in Y. Cartuyvels, H. Dumont *et al.* (eds.), *Les droits de l'homme. Bouclier ou épée du droit pénal?* (Brussels: Facultés Universitaires Saint Louis, 2007) 27. Compare A. Ashworth using J. Raz's definition of the 'rule of law' as "being governed by rules which are fixed, knowable and certain – thereby enhancing liberty and reducing arbitrariness by the State's organs". A. Ashworth, *l.c.*, 68.

8 For an analysis of this phenomenon in the common law tradition, see F.A. Allen, *l.c.*, 392 e.s.

9 See M. van de Kerchove, "Développements récents et paradoxaux de la légalité criminelle et de ses corrolaires essentiels", in *Liber Amicorum Jean du Jardin* (Deurne: Kluwer, 2001) 299–320.

10 For the impact of this trend on French criminal law, see M. Delmas–Marty, "L'enjeu du code pénal, réflexions sur l'inflation des lois pénales en France", in *Mélanges offerts à Robert Legros* (Brussels: Éd. de l'Université de Bruxelles, 1985) 168. According to F.A. Allen this emergence of open norms and ambiguous statutory language in the criminal law was re–enforced by a rehabilitative ideology, since "conceiving of criminal sanctions as a form of social service moves toward enlargement of official interventions". F.A. Allen, *l.c.*, 399.

judges to interpret strictly criminal provisions, wide acceptance of teleological and evolutive methods of interpretation permits them in practice to play an important role in the process of criminalisation.[11] Some authors deeply regret this evolution, since courts tend to absorb too strongly their role as 'agencies of crime control'. As a result, the courts lose sight of their role as "intermediaries between the individual and the coercive power of the State."[12]

In this chapter three issues are addressed relating to the limits of legality in the criminal law. First, the chapter explores further to what extent larger legal and cultural transformations might be responsible for eroding the protective role or guarantee–providing function of the principle of legality (section 3). Second, the chapter examines further to what extent the limited ability of legality to play its guarantee–providing role can be imputed to some characteristics of contemporary criminal law (section 4). Thirdly and finally, the chapter suggests a strategy to respond appropriately to the limits of legality (section 5). This strategy will consist of refining more explicitly and appropriately legality's underlying values.

2 Legality and its Underlying Values

The idea that legality plays a prominent role in the protection of the interests and rights of citizens against the use of arbitrary State power embodies a complex set of interests and values. The constitutional privilege of Parliament to define criminal offences (legality in its *formal* dimension) is often grounded in the principle of the separation of powers, combined with values such as 'democratic participation' and 'public autonomy'. Each citizen should, at least in principle, have his say in what counts as criminal behaviour and what not. He has the right to influence the political powers in order to bring them in line with his private interests, in order to protect his needs and fundamental rights. This right is at stake, even more dramatically, in the criminal law where criminalisation of certain behaviour gives public authorities a warrant to interfere extensively with the liberty rights of citizens. Therefore, the process of criminalisation should be as democratic as possible in order to guarantee that the State displays its power to punish as a last resort.[13]

According to established continental legal doctrine, democratic control on a sparing use of criminal punishment is only adequately provided for in criminal affairs inasmuch as absolute priority is accorded to the parliamentary legislator in matters of criminalisation, and insofar as a strict separation of powers is re-

11 F. Ost and M. van de Kerchove, *Entre la lettre et l'esprit. Les directives d'interprétation en droit* (Brussels: Bruylant, 1989). Compare also F. A. Allen, *l.c.*, 398.

12 See A.T.H. Smith, "Judicial Law Making in the Criminal Law", *Law Quarterly Review* 1984, 50.

13 *Ibid.*, 58.

spected.[14] A similar, but weaker, version of this priority thesis can also be retraced in the doctrine and case–law of some common law countries. According to A.T.H. Smith, the judicial process and the remedy of defence are not adequate tools for democratic deliberation on the necessity of criminalisation and the imposing of a criminal punishment. Due to systemic pressures of criminalisation in the trial stage, the defendant and the judge do not occupy an ideal position for raising and discussing the issue of sparing use and subsidiarity regarding criminalisation and criminal punishment. Only in the early, legislative stage, is democratic deliberation on the necessity of criminalisation more likely to take place on a more power–free basis.[15]

But legality also reflects some crucial values with respect to its more *substantial* dimension.[16] It implies also a complex set of substantive lines of conduct, addressed to the legislature, the executive, and the judiciary in order to restrain their arbitrary use of State power. The prohibition on retrospective legislation (*lex praevia*), the obligation to define crimes precisely and clearly (*lex certa*), as well as the obligation to interpret the statutory offence strictly (*lex stricta*): all these corollaries of legality are somehow designed to protect citizens against arbitrary government.[17] Continental lawyers tend to translate this protective role of legality in terms of 'legal certainty'. Although they consider in general the rightness of legality so obvious that they do not bother too much as to articulating the content of legal certainty, standard formulations of legal certainty are widespread throughout civil and common law. In continental legal systems, legal certainty is defined in terms of a maximum predictability of officials' behaviour. Making the scope of a criminal offence as precise as possible (*lex certa*), and restricting the discretionary power of a judge to its strictest minimum, would accord citizens the power to know precisely in advance which types of behaviour would lead to criminal liability, and which not. Anglo–American scholars often explain the relation between legal certainty and legality in terms of a citizen's ability "to organise his affairs in such a way that he does not infringe the law"[18], or of having the right to an adequate warning from public officials that engaging in certain types of behaviour will result in criminal liability. When criminal offences are drafted in vague and ambiguous ways, or when they have a retroactive effect, citizens are not only faced with unpredictable behaviour by enforcement officials, they are also denied

---

14 See R. Koering–Joulin, "Pour un retour à une interprétation stricte du principe de légalité criminelle (A propos de l'article 7, 1° de la Convention européenne des droits de l'homme)", in V. Berger, *Liber Amicorum M.A. Eisen* (Brussels/Paris: Bruylant, 1995) 247 e.s.

15 A.T.H. Smith, *l.c.*, 67 e.s.

16 For the distinction, between formal dimension and substantial dimension of legality, see M. van de Kerchove, "Développements récents et paradoxaux du principe de la légalité", *l.c.*, 299–320.

17 Compare T.O. Endicott, "The Impossibility of the Rule of Law", *Oxford Journal of Legal Studies*, 1999, 2–3.

18 See A.T.H. Smith, *l.c.*, 72.

a fair opportunity to avoid punishment.[19] Such a denial flouts, in the words of Ashworth, "an incontrovertible minimum of respect for the principle of autonomy."

Besides reference to legal certainty, other political principles such as equality and neutrality, could be listed as grounding values of legality. As to equality, T.O. Endicott reminds us that we tend to relate arbitrary government with treating people inconsistently. Vague and ambiguous statutory offences would violate legality, because public prosecutors and judges would then be allowed to criminalise and punish at random, failing thereby to treat like cases alike.[20] As to neutrality, the requirement for clear scope to criminal offences (*lex certa*), and the requirement of strict interpretation of criminal statutes (*lex stricta*), also seem to play an important role. They express the concern of preventing the police, public prosecutors – and not in the least the judge – from expanding interference with the individual rights and liberties of citizens. Corollaries such as *lex certa* and *lex stricta* contribute to the realisation of the neutrality of the State, to the extent that they prevent public officials from bringing in their own value judgements with regard to the punishability of certain actions and omissions.[21]

3 Contemporary Society and the Limits of Legality

3.1 Erosion of Legality? Two Working Hypotheses

In his "Erosion of Legality in American Criminal Justice" F.A. Allen argues that in contemporary societies the protective qualities of legality are vulnerable to erosion. "Achievement of the values of legality today, can be gained only by struggle." Allen is not so optimistic for the prospects of legality, not so much because of conceptual failings, but more because of changing mentalities and practices. Applied to American social and institutional life, the author points to the extraordinary fragmentation of criminal justice administration, the absence of centralised administrative supervision, the overwhelming case–load which criminal justice agencies are faced with, and the impact of the rehabilitative era on adjudication. Similar pessimism can be found in other common law and civil law cultures, where several authors identify a considerable weakening of legality.[22]

---

19 F.A. Allen, *l.c.*, 387. In States US law this idea is phrased as the 'fair warning' and 'void for vagueness' principles. For this reference, see A. Ashworth, *Principles of Criminal Law* (Oxford: Oxford University Press, 2006) 74.

20 T.O. Endicott, *l.c.*, 3.

21 Compare A.T.H. Smith, *l.c.*, 72 e.s. See also S. Van Drooghenbroeck, "Interprétation jurisprudentielle et non–rétroactivité de la loi pénale, note sous Cour.eur. D.H. 22 novembre 1995, S.W. c. Royaume Uni", *Revue trimestrielle des droits de l'homme* 1996, 463 e.s.

22 For such a criticism in French doctrine, see J. Pradel, *Manuel de droit pénal général* (Paris: Éditions Cujas, 2004) 130.

In the following sections, we will examine two working hypotheses which support the idea that contemporary developments do indeed put pressure on legality and its underlying values. The first working hypothesis reveals a broad, detached perspective and boils down to the idea that the collective obsession for risk and safety, and the corresponding emergence of a 'culture of control', are rendering fragile legality and its underlying values in both common law and civil law cultures. The second working hypothesis entails a more engaged point of view expressing strong attachment to the civil law tradition. It suggests that convergence of civil law and common law traditions, accelerated through European integration and human rights law, is in part responsible for the weakening of legality in the civil law countries.

As will be further argued, these working hypotheses require further elaboration, and lead to the idea that processes of convergence and focus on risk not only produce limits, but also uncover deeper conceptual shortcomings relating legality and the predominant conceptions of the criminal law itself.

3.2 Risk, Safety and the Limits of Legality in the Criminal Law

In his influential but very contested book *The Culture of Control*, D. Garland attempts to make sense of important penal transformations in the UK and the US at the end of the 20th and beginning of the 21st centuries.[23] These transformations are penetrating the contemporary mind bit by bit: the reemergence of punitive sanctions and expressive justice, changes in the emotional tone of crime policy, the return of the victim, politicisation and a new populism, the reinvention of the prison, expansion of informal forms of crime control in civil society, and new management styles and working practices.[24] In order to understand these phenomena better, Garland tries to uncover the underlying patterns that tie these "indices of change" together.[25] To that end the author paints a broad picture of the social and cultural conditions of late–modern societies and gives an account of how these conditions changed the practices and mentalities of penal institutions (police, prosecution, judiciary, prison, probation service); how they changed criminological thought; and how they affected and still affect our informal ways of crime control. Garland calls the underlying pattern of these new habits and ways of thinking and responding to crime, a 'culture of control': a variety of practices and patterns of social and official behaviour that aim to respond to and control risks that pose a threat to safety.[26]

---

[23] D. Garland, *The Culture of Control. Crime and Social Order in Contemporary Society* (Oxford: Oxford University Press, 2001).

[24] *Ibid.*, Chapter 1, 1–25.

[25] *Ibid.*, 7.

[26] *Ibid.*, 163.

According to Garland, this collective obsession with risk not only flows from objective phenomena, such as the rise of crime, or the massive increase of social risks due to a highly technological, post–industrial organisation of our societies. It is also connected to deep existential feelings of insecurity which are rooted in an unstable, fluid, globalised capitalist world that glorifies a society of consumers presumed to be capable of endless reshaping and recreating their individual selves.

> More and more of the population were encouraged to pursue the goals of individual expression, self–fashioning, and gratification that the consumer society held out to everyone.[27]

Garland's analysis comes here close to the observations of Z. Bauman. According to the latter, both global capitalism (which on a local level is responsible for the permanent risk of massive unemployment) and individualisation (which pushes consumers constantly to change their life–styles, possessions, and attachments) are leaving the late–modern individual alone with his own personal strengths and weaknesses to survive. Late–modern selves tend to become locked up in the shell of individualism, and this condition provokes uncontrollable anxieties "emanating from the experiences of uncertain future and insecure present".[28] These feelings, because of their undetermined and uncontrollable nature, are easily transformed into more palpable and controllable fears, fears related to the safety of one's own body, family, home, and possessions. A 'culture of control' is not just a series of practices that try to respond to the insecurities of contemporary life, it is also a complex of collective strategies through which original, existential anxieties are "recycled into panic–arousing threats to safety" and are subsequently managed through a broad range of social and political habits.[29]

Garland's broad picture of contemporary penal change is, of course, vulnerable to criticism that it is too vague and that it does not accommodate enough the particularities of complex social realities. But the advantage of his generalisations is that they provide us a explanatory framework to give a deeper sense of the changes regarding legality, in both civil law and common law traditions. As a working hypothesis, we could state that the emergence of a culture of control seems to cut off many legislators from their sense of legality and its guarantee–providing role. A culture of control and its late–modern predicament would then be partly responsible for producing limits to legality and its underlying values. This hypothesis gains credence in at least three respects.

One can, firstly, raise serious question with regard to the deliberative quality of parliamentary legislation. In a society that cries for more safety and for protecting its citizens against potential victimisation, one can doubt whether politicians are still able to balance carefully conflicting rights and interests in the process of defining and interpreting criminal law provisions. In other words, the pressure on

---

27 *Ibid.*, 89. See also Z. Bauman, *Liquid Modernity* (Cambridge: Polity Press, 2000) 31.

28 Z. Bauman, "Violence in an Age of Uncertainty", in A. Crawford, *Crime and Insecurity: The Governance of Safety in Europe* (Cullompton: Willan Publishing, 2002) 19.

29 *Ibid.*, 60.

politicians to respond quickly to popular fears seems to run counter to the value of neutrality that underpins the principle of legality.

Remarkable is, secondly, the proliferation of new criminal offences relating capacities (instead of actions), or relating actions creating a risk of harm. All these inchoate offences broaden the scope of their applicability quite extensively, raising thereby serious question as to the predictability of official behaviour, which is supposed to be protected by legality.

Thirdly, this pressure on legislation to perceive crime more and more as a risk imposes yet another limit on the guarantee–providing role of legality. A tendency to relax the requirement of precisely formulating a criminal action or omission also affects the requirement of *mens rea* as a condition for criminal responsibility. Imposing on the legislator the duty to define precisely such actions and the degree of *mens rea*, legality assures defendants the opportunity to account reasonably for a specific realm of behaviour, to argue that they acted according to a mental state that falls beyond the scope of the criminal law, that there were justifying reasons or that they are excused in doing what they did. However, the urge of late–modern individuals to distance themselves from sources of danger prompts contemporary criminalisation to lose interest in the person of the offender *qua* responsible agent, in his legitimate rights and needs. In a culture of control, crime easily becomes depersonalised. Seen as a risk, crime is not necessarily conceived of anymore as a specific act motivated by a guilty mind. Conceptual distinctions such as purposeful, knowledgeable, reckless, and negligent acts become more and more irrelevant to the degree of criminality of certain behaviour, and criminality in general. In other words, criminalisation is drifting away from legality and its guarantee–providing role with regard to securing respect for responsible agency.[30]

While the foregoing hypothesis seems to be confirmed in many criminal justice systems, some prudence is in order once we acknowledge the simple empirical fact that German constitutional case–law has established since the early 1950s – long before the emergence of a culture of control – a tradition in relaxing legality and *lex certa*.[31] The Court acknowledged the necessity of general terms in criminalisation due to the complexities in and permanent change to contemporary life, and the constant need to respond appropriately to each case. The Court also denied the existence of the obligation to define precisely and perfectly predictably all the elements of a criminal offence. The requirement of *lex certa* is not violated if the interpretation by the judge is needed to clarify general clauses and uncertain terms.

---

[30] Compare A. Ashworth's objections against the "thin ice principle" stated in the famous *Knuller* case.

[31] German Constitutional Court, 1 BvL 120/53, decision of 30 November 1953, BVerfGE 4, 352, 358. See also German Constitutional Court, 2 BvR 308/77, decision of 21 June 1977, BVerfGE 45, 363, 372. German Constitutional Court, 2 BvR 927/76, decision of 15 March 1978, BVerfGE 48, 48, 56. My thanks to Andreas Herzog for drawing my attention to this case–law.

Besides undertaking an attempt to give another, more plausible, sociological explanation, we might also carry forward the idea that the German Constitutional Court did not simply succumb to the pressures of contemporary life. One could also say that the Court attempted to respond to the deeper problem that the requirement of a precise definition of criminal offences sits ill with the unavoidable vagueness of legal terms. Or, put in a more general way, the emergence of a culture of control does not only touch upon the realisation of legality, it also helps us to rediscover what the jurisprudential wisdom of the German Constitutional Court has revealed for a long time: in its conventional conception, legality suffers from conceptual shortcomings.[32] Before examining these conceptual limits further, we first focus on the second working hypothesis relating the erosion of legality. We will see that, despite its plausibility, this hypothesis raises even more doubts and hesitations.

3.3 Convergence of Legal Traditions and the Limits of Legality

Should traditions, and legal traditions in particular, be conceived of as a static form of social order? In his brilliant *Legal Traditions of the World*, P. Glenn argues that linking tradition with stability becomes less obvious "once tradition is seen as transmitting information."[33] Traditions are then an important resource from which reasons for change, and even disruption of tradition itself, may be derived. So, despite its power to generate cohesion, traditions are internally unstable. According to Glenn, this "problem of stability is magnified by a tradition's relation with other traditions."[34] Once traditions come in contact with other traditions, the exchange of information which results from that renders the identity of each non–exclusive. "Each contains elements of the other."[35] New elements may disrupt the continuity of, or may find support in, the recipient tradition, or hidden tensions and contradictions within this recipient tradition may be exposed.

Within the political process of European integration, all these types of exchange take place between the civil law tradition and the common law tradition. Many interesting observations and comments have been made in this regard, and there is no need to rehearse them within this chapter.[36] More relevant with regard

32 See also P. Westen who contents that we should distance ourselves from a classic dogmatic understanding of legality and its corollaries, and reconceptualise legality by deriving it from principles regarding culpability. P. Westen, "Two Rules of Legality in Criminal Law", *Law and Philosophy* 2007, 233.

33 P. Glenn, *Legal Traditions of the World. Sustainable Diversity in Law* (2nd ed.) (Oxford: Oxford University Press, 2004) 23.

34 *Ibid.*, 32.

35 *Ibid.*, 33.

36 For an extensive reference to this literature, see *ibid.*, 159, note 128. See also W. van Gerven, "Bringing (Private) Laws Closer to Each Other at the European Level", in F. Cafaggi, *The Institutional Framework of European Private Law* (Oxford: Oxford University Press, 2006) 37–77; "W. van Gerven, A Common Law for Europe: The Future Meeting the Past?",

to legality, however, is to examine what kind of exchange between common law and civil law traditions has resulted from the creation and implementation of European human rights standards in both legal cultures. Particularly interesting in this regard is Article 7 of the European Convention on Human Rights (ECHR), and the attendant case–law of the European Court for Human Rights (ECtHR). According to Article 7(1) of the Convention,

> No one shall be held guilty of any criminal offence on account of any act or omission which did not constitute a criminal offence under national or international law at the time when it was committed. Nor shall a heavier penalty be imposed than the one that was applicable at the time the criminal offence was committed.

One of the particularities of this provision is that it articulates legality in such a way that it tries to reconcile the distance between the civil law and common law traditions. Whereas in the former, a strong importance has been traditionally attached to the formal dimension of legality, to the strict separation of powers, and to the dominance of parliamentary power, legality in the latter does not exclude the judiciary from being actively involved in creating criminal offences. These differences are sought to be evened out by the authors of Article 7 of the ECHR by diplomatic use of the term "law", in stead of "written, statutory law". A similar attempt at reconciliation between both traditions is made by the ECtHR which, in *S.W. v. United Kingdom*, explicitly recognised the undeniable role of judges in the process of making criminal law.[37]

How to understand this encounter between two major legal traditions through the gateway of Article 7? One obvious way of understanding it, from a civil law perspective, would be that human rights law paved the way for a disruption of civilian fidelity to legality by a much less developed common law attachment to legality.[38] This position has been strongly defended by R. Koering–Joulin, who argues that mixing both legal traditions can only produce results that weaken the democratic quality of civil law systems. The author concludes his article with the idea that this "brassage", which issued from giving legality a human rights status, eventually results in a weakening of legality's protective function.[39] Koering–Joulin also seems to suggest that the processes of convergence should be seen in terms of an ongoing struggle, striving to extend their influence beyond the limits of their respective Nation–States. Either they expand into other domestic legal orders. Or they lose importance due to other competing legal cultures.

European Review of Private Law 2001, 485. See also R. Foqué and J. Steenbergen, "The Limits of the Law and the Development of the European Union".

37 ECtHR 22 November 1995, *S.W. v United Kingdom*, § 36. All judgments of the ECtHR can be found under HUDOC on www.echr.coe.int.

38 From a common law perspective, another view might consist in seeing the exchange as an expansion of civil law concepts through the language of human rights. See C. McCrudder, "Common Law of Human Rights", *Oxford Journal of Legal Studies* 2000, vol. 20, 491–532.

39 R. Koering–Joulin, *l.c.*, 247 e.s. See also S. Van Drooghenbroeck, *l.c.*, 63 e.s.

Taken as an interesting working hypothesis, Koering–Joulin's position gains in plausibility when applied to the Belgian constitutional context. In its judgment of 11 May 2005, the Belgian Constitutional Court fully recognised the law–making power of the judiciary, and softened its conception of legality. It referred explicitly to the case–law of the ECtHR.[40] From *Müller v. Switzerland* the Court borrowed the idea that, in some circumstances, the legislator is obliged to create vague norms in making possible adjustment to changing circumstances and in order to avoid excessive rigidity.[41] The Court also found inspiration in *Kokkinakis v. Greece*, from which it adopted the argument that the wording of a criminal offence is sufficiently clear and precise,

> … when an individual, on the basis of these wordings of the provision, and, if necessary, with the help of the interpretation by the courts, can know in advance which actions and omissions are conducive of criminal responsibility.[42]

Despite its attractiveness, the hypothesis that the common law produces limits to legality's protective role in civil law countries raises several doubts that should be taken seriously.

Firstly, whereas the influence of the common law through Strasbourg case–law is clearly traceable in the Belgian context, such an influence was absent in the early 1950s, when the German Constitutional Court held that, given the complexities of social life, the criminal law cannot do without using general terms which have to be interpreted to a large extent by the judge.[43] Again it seems as if the German Constitutional Court draws on a practical wisdom regarding legality and *lex certa*, which somehow cuts across the common law and civil law divide.

Secondly, Koering–Joulin's position seems to assume that the common law and the civil law are incommensurable traditions with exclusionary identities: the first, marked by judge–made law; the second, by the dominance of written statutory law and a firm tradition of a strict separation of powers. But this picture grossly misrepresents the complexities of both traditions. According to Glenn, the common law and the civil law are major legal traditions because of their complexities. Through their respective histories, they bare the traces of each other's influence; share important lateral sub–traditions (such as the impact of precedent); and contain each in themselves different conflicting tendencies which are in constant need of reconciliation.[44]

---

40 Belgian Constitutional Court, 11 May 2005, nr. 92/2005, B.3.3. The case–law of the Court can be consulted on: www.arbitrage.be.

41 ECtHR, 24 May 1988, *Müller and others v Switzerland*, § 29.

42 ECtHR, 25 May 1993, *Kokkinakis v Greece*, §§ 40 and 52.

43 German Constitutional Court, 1 BvL 120/53, decision of 30 November 1953, BVerfGE 4, 352, 358.

44 P. Glenn, *Legal Traditions of the World* (Oxford: Oxford University Press, 2nd ed., 2004) 354–359.

4 Legality and the Limits of the Criminal Law

The foregoing suggests that the limits of legality not only stem from broader social and cultural developments, but also result from deeper conceptual insufficiencies with regard to our established conceptions of the criminal law and of criminal justice. The limited ability of legality to provide adequately for guarantees can be imputed to at least three features which are bound up with established conceptions of the criminal law (namely, deeply entrenched positivistic instincts and a syllogistic conception of legal reasoning), and with the inevitable open texture of the criminal law.

4.1 Legal Positivism

One of the reasons why legality is so vulnerable to forces of erosion can be attributed arguably to legal positivism and its impact on the criminal law.[45] With 'legal positivism' we refer to a conception of law that in the end reduces questions of law to empirical issues.[46] Legal positivism, to quote M. Zirk–Zadowski, "treats the law as a kind of an object totally external to and independent of judges, and studied, in fact, like other natural objects."[47] What the law is in a specific case depends upon what is recognised within the legal system as the valid, applicable legal norm. If we know the rules of recognition, determining the validity and hierarchy of the sources of the norm, and determining also the period and space of applicability of the norm, then we can easily identify what the valid, posited law of a certain legal order is.[48]

From the point of view of legal protection, legal positivism promises to be an attractive conception of the criminal law. If the rules of recognition permit citizens and public officials to identify the content of the criminal law, then it would be easy for citizens to demarcate clearly in advance the boundaries of criminal behaviour. Legal positivism seems, then, the best conceptual framework for the penal apparatus to maintain fidelity to legality and its value of legal certainty.[49]

---

45 Legal positivism is not only a feature of civil law traditions. It has also emerged in common law countries: see P. Glenn, *l.c.*, 151.

46 See R. Dworkin, *Law's Empire* (London: Fontana Press, 1991) 31. "The only disagreement about law is empirical disagreement about what legal institutions have actually decided in the past."

47 M. Zirk–Zadowski, "Legal Epistemology and the Transformation of Legal Cultures", in M. Van Hoecke (ed.), *Legal Epistemology and Transformation of Legal Cultures* (Oxford: Hart Publishing, 2004) 23.

48 See H.L.A. Hart, *The Concept of Law* (Oxford: Clarendon Press, 1990) chp. VI.

49 Compare H.L.A. Hart, "Positivism and the Separation of Law and Morals", *Harvard Law Review* 1958, 606–12.

But there are also good reasons to think in an opposite direction. One could reasonably argue that legal positivism is, to a certain extent, also responsible for the decline of legal certainty and, correspondingly, for the weakening of legality. Imagine that our rule of recognition prescribes that parliament has the last word in deciding what counts as criminal and what does not, or that the rule of recognition regards a constitutional court as the final authority in defining legality and determining its weight. Or, imagine even that the rule of recognition happens to indicate that the ECtHR has its final say on the content of legality. In none of these cases there is a compelling, stable force present within the law which can ensure the enactment of clear–cut, predictable criminal provisions. The degree of precision and predictability depends on what that final authority wants as the substance of the criminal law, or on how this final authority happens to conceive the (content of the) principle of legality. Put differently, when informed by legal positivism, the criminal law can not in itself stop legality from being eroded in its content and underlying values.

4.2 Open Texture

What also stands in the way of an efficient guarantee–providing conception of legality, is the undeniable open texture of legal norms and thus of criminal offences. The term 'open texture', which was introduced into legal theory by H.L.A. Hart, refers to the fact that the meaning and scope of a legal norm – and, in our case, a norm which defines a crime – is never completely and clearly demarcated. There are always 'zones of penumbra' around such norms, which require interpretation, discussion, refining, and restating of the underlying policies and principles.[50] The clarity of a criminal offence and the borders of its scope are somehow always blurred because there are no perfectly reliable criteria that govern the use and application of the norms. The rule cannot "itself step forward to claim its own instances."[51] The meaning of a criminal offence and the scope of its reach lies in its application in specific circumstances and in the light of a concrete case. It is the perceptive acknowledgement of this phenomenon, and not the pressures of a culture of control, that was part of the practical wisdom of the German Constitutional Court. It led the Court to the conclusion that the generality and abstractness of criminal statutes render both zones of doubt as to the subsumption of cases under the terms of the norm, and judicial interpretation, inevitable.

Admitting the 'open texture' of legal norms deepens our insight into the very nature of the criminal law, but it also makes us aware of the conceptual limits to legality. Indeed, legal norms in general, and those pertaining to criminal offences

---

50 H.L.A. Hart (1990), *l.c.*, 124. "Whichever device, precedents or legislation, is chosen for the communication of standards of behaviour, these, however smoothly they work over the great mass of ordinary cases, will at some point where the application is in question, prove indeterminate; they will have what has been termed an *open texture*."

51 *Ibid.*, 123.

in particular, are inevitably on poor terms with many interests and values which legality purports to secure. Indeed, it involves implications which, if taken seriously, seem to undermine the very point of these concerns. The value of a strict separation of powers, and of the constitutional prohibition to delegate law–making power to the judge, conflicts with the inescapable margin of judicial discretion which necessarily issues from the open texture of criminal offences. And the values of legal certainty stand in contrast to that inevitable element of unpredictability regarding criminal offences.[52]

4.3 Syllogistic Reasoning

If we examine further the exchange between the common law tradition and the civil law tradition, and the implications of legality, we discover how these implications also reflect more structural limits which can be traced back to some features of the classic continental understanding of adjudication and judicial interpretation. The process of bringing cases under the (criminal) law and of interpreting legal statutes has for long been understood in terms of simple syllogistic reasoning. Under such a view, the judge performs a simple syllogism by deducing a criminal sanction from the rule (the criminal offence and the criminal sanction) and from the facts falling within the scope of the rule. The activity of interpreting rules is considered to be a clarification of the scope of the rule, and this, by exploring its literal meaning or by retrieving its original intent. New insights in post–World War II legal theory, however, have unmasked this reductionism regarding adjudication, revealing a far more complex process.

First, there is no such thing as a meaning to words *in se*, fixing the scope of a legal norm. The meaning and scope of a criminal offence are contingent upon particular situations in which the rule is used and in which its underlying expectations are expressed.[53] Therefore, interpreting criminal offences is inescapably context–dependent.

Second, the meaning and scope of a rule is not fixed before the cases is brought under its scope. It is by the occurrence of new cases after the enactment of the criminal statute, as well as through the very confrontation of these cases with the norm, that the scope and meaning of a criminal offence is adjusted and refined. In other words, the interpretation of a criminal offence, when applied to the case at hand, is inescapably retrospective.

Thirdly, interpreting criminal offences is inevitably value–oriented. Whether in clear cases, or more difficult ones, judges implicitly or explicitly assess whether

---

52 N. MacCormick comes to a similar tension between the open, arguable character of the law, on the one hand, and the ideology of the rule of law, on the other hand. See N. MacCormick, *Rhetoric and the Rule of Law. A Theory of Legal Reasoning* (Oxford: Oxford University Press, 2005) chp. 2.

53 This implies, according to R. Dworkin, that "the description 'unclear' is the result rather than the occasion of … interpreting statutory texts": R. Dworkin, *l.c.*, 352.

there are good reasons to bring the particular case under the norm. In easy cases, it would be highly reasonable to apply the criminal provisions to the concrete case. In difficult cases, however, judges will often need to strike a balance between reasons that argue against, and reasons for, the application of the criminal statute.[54] Such a balancing of the relative weight of these reasons inevitably requires a normative stance from the judge.

Like the open texture of legal norms, the complex nature of adjudication sits ill with the very values of legality. How can legality ensure neutrality of the judge, if his judicial activity is value–based from the start? And how to make the judge's interpretation predictable, if it is the confrontation with the facts which establishes, case by case, the meaning and scope of a criminal offence? And how to guarantee that equal cases will be treated equally, if judges change their habits of interpretation through various cases and under the influence of newer changes in society? If contemporary insights of legal theory prove to be correct, then protection of the values of equality, legal certainty, and neutrality through legality has not only become ineffective through broader historical and legal developments. Our syllogistic conception of legal reasoning is then also responsible for overseeing the many insufficiencies of legality. Legality, in its guarantee–providing function, would have encountered its limits already from the start, by not being in line with the context–dependent, value–oriented, and retrospective nature of adjudication. Whereas syllogistic reasoning can be blamed for having obscured the tension between legality and adjudication, contemporary culture and the convergence of different legal traditions have the merit of pushing this tension sharply to the surface.

5 How to Respond to the Limits of Legality?

5.1 Agenda

While having brought a few limits of the criminal law to the fore, at least three remarks can be made which could help us constructively respond to these limits, and thus, to the limits of legality.

The first remark concerns legal positivism and relates to the question of what conception of law and legal thinking promises to be a more adequate candidate for strengthening legality and its underlying values. What we need, is to reflect upon an alternative account of the criminal law, one which shows more resistance to these broader social dynamics. In order to remedy the limits of legality, we will propose and unfold a hermeneutic conception of the criminal law. This conception revolves around the idea that law is an interpretive practice.[55] All participants who

---

54 Compare H.L.A. Hart (1990), *l.c.*, 132. "There are reasons both for and against our use of a general term, and no form of convention or general agreement dictates its use."

55 For such an approach, see R. Dworkin, *l.c.*, chp. 2.

have a stake in the business of law are engaged in a practice of interpreting the normative point of criminal law, and its underlying values and the principles of justice.[56] New social circumstances and intensified interactions between legal cultures and traditions are seen as challenges for better articulating and reconstructing the set of principles, values which underpin the legal order as a whole.

The second remark pertains to the open texture of legal norms. Things become more complicated here. Whereas altering our positivistic way of understanding the law presents itself as a real option, liberating the criminal law from its open texture does not. On the contrary, the inevitable nature of open texture of the (criminal) law compels us to move the issue of the limits of legality in another direction. The question is not in the first place how to safeguard better legality's underpinning values. Rather the question is how to change our ideas concerning these values in order to reconcile them with the open texture of the criminal law. We have to ask ourselves, first, how to make sense of the strict separation between legislative power and judicial power, without naively denying the open texture of criminal statutes. To respond to the phenomenon of open texture appropriately, implies trying to reconsider these values so that they are capable of distinguishing justifiable open norms from unjustifiable ones. In this respect, a hermeneutic conception of the criminal law presents itself as an attractive option. Indeed, what is needed is a refinement of the legality and its underlying values in order to inform, to guide, and to restrain such practices as legislative delegation, and adjudicative value–judgments.

The aforementioned conclusions impose an alternative style of approaching the theory and practice of the criminal law. It brings to the fore a vast programme of conceptual and hermeneutic refinement of legality and its underlying values. Given the limited length of this chapter it cannot be our ambition to develop such a broad, encompassing normative theory. Coming to the end, we will engage in a more modest approach. Some intuitions regarding human dignity will be explored in order better to articulate the normative point of legality.

5.2 Legality, Legal Certainty, Human Dignity

In his *Rhetoric and the Rule of Law* N. MacCormick states that, without the rule of law, "there is no prospect of realising the dignity of human beings as independent though interdependent participants in public and private activities in a society."[57] A few paragraphs before, he contends that "legal certainty and legal security en-

[56] Compare A. Ashworth's 'fidelity to legal values' by which he means "the importance of recognizing that the criminal justice system ought to welcome conduct that promotes its integrity and ought to refuse to act upon conduct that undermines its integrity": A. Ashworth, "Testing Fidelity to Legal Values: Official Involvement and Criminal Justice", in S. Shute (ed.), *Action and Value in Criminal Law* (Oxford: Clarendon Press, 1993) 301.

[57] N. MacCormick, *l.c.*, 16.

ables citizens to live autonomous lives in circumstances of mutual trust."[58] Applied to the criminal law, MacCormick invites us to ground legality and legal certainty in human dignity and autonomy, and to connect it with conditions of mutual trust. This link is not completely surprising since human dignity figures among the core values and aims of human rights standards in general, and the ECHR in particular.[59] It is less clear, however, how to understand this vague and general notion of human dignity, in particular in connection with autonomy and mutual trust. But, even more importantly, a better understanding is needed as to how legality and legal certainty might be expressive of respect for human dignity.

Three intuitions with regard to human dignity could be helpful here. They bear heavily on H. Arendt's elucidation of totalitarianism and of the human condition.

Firstly, the experience of totalitarianism (with the holocaust as the paradigm of its dynamics) invites us to understand respect for human dignity and humanity, in terms of respecting the condition of human plurality. We, as human beings, live among other human beings whose lives are as distinct as ours is distinct from theirs. The human condition of plurality refers to the fact "that men, not Man, live on the earth and inhabit the world."[60] Characteristic for our condition is that human plurality implies and depends on our ability to express our distinctness from each other in speech and action, which explains, to refer again to MacCormick, why human independency necessarily implies human interdependency. According to Arendt, the experience of totalitarianism, the dynamics of which consisted of annihilating human plurality, taught us that the challenge of democratic societies lies in preserving the collective awareness that we as humans are equal in our distinctness and in our capacity to express our distinctness through speech and action.[61]

This first intuition enables us to understand respect for human dignity in terms of basic and equal respect for the distinct humanity of each person. Respect for human dignity also entails equal respect for the capacity of each human being to express its distinctness through speech of action. According to Arendt, the legal language of human rights, and the institutions that recognition of rights necessarily involve, are essential for democratic societies in order to allow a stable, identifiable position from which each human being can express its distinctness and can be heard in the expression of his distinctness.[62] Human rights such as the freedom for

---

58 *Ibid.*, 16.

59 This is, for example, explicitly stated in ECtHR, 22 November 1995, *S.W. v United Kingdom*.

60 H. Arendt, *The Human Condition* (Chicago: Chicago University Press, 1958) 7.

61 See H. Arendt, *l.c.*, 8, "Plurality is the condition of human action because we are all the same, that is, human, in such a way that nobody is ever the same as anyone else who ever lived, lives, or will live."

62 H. Arendt, *The Promise of Politics* (New York: Schocken Books, 2005) 94. "Man ... exists – or is realized – in politics only in the equal rights that those who are most different guarantee for each other. This voluntary guarantee of, and concession to, a claim of legal equality recognizes the plurality of men... ." Compare also H. Arendt, *The Origins of Totalitarianism* (San Diego/New York,/London: A Harvest Book, 1976) 287.

each to express his opinion and his religious beliefs become meaningless, if such a stable, public position fails to be guaranteed. According to Arendt,

> the fundamental deprivation of human rights is manifested first and above all in the deprivation of a place in the world which makes opinions significant and actions effective.[63]

Secondly, the human condition of plurality involves the capacity of human beings mutually to enter a space of appearances, and create a common world through speech and action. This capability to act together and to build a common world of understanding comes down to the capacity for each to express his own voice and standing in public and to make a claim for its justification that can be acceptable to all. The challenge of democratic societies consists then in organising political power in such a way that each person's capability to act in mutual concert is preserved. In this regard, respect for the distinct humanity of each, and thus respect for human dignity, necessarily implies participatory citizenship, which makes equal respect for participatory rights the 'badge' of human dignity. Without this badge, each of us loses his distinct humanity to reinvent and deliberate on the reasons for which we act and engage in speech.

The third intuition is closely linked with the foregoing. According to Arendt, preserving human plurality does not only depend on participative citizenship and the capacity to reinvent constantly a common world, it also depends on the continuing existence of such a common space of understanding. Of course this space of understanding has to be open for change, if we want to respect human distinctness and man's ability to add new things to the world. But this space should also maintain sufficient guidance for mutual understanding. Without such guidance, it becomes impossible to make sense of the other's words and deeds as well as to make the other answerable for it. Further, without such a common framework of understanding, we also lose the opportunity to make sense of our own distinct position, and to convince others of the sense and legitimacy of our distinct view. And finally, a common space of understanding is necessary in order to convey a climate of trust in which we can submit our words and deeds for understanding and assessment by others. Only under these conditions can we gain confidence in the legitimacy of our talk and action.

From this follows that respect for the equal distinctness of each human person, and thus for human dignity, not only requires a society of deliberative citizenship and equal respect for political rights, but also the governance of human interactions and display of State power by legal standards. Setting and following legal standards, or to use Fuller's beautiful expression, 'fidelity to law' serves as a condition for making sense of each other's distinct speech and conduct. It relates to establishing minimum conditions of mutual trust in the legitimacy of one's own words and acts, and last not but least, as a common ground for controlling the reasons by which we are judged.[64] Without such mutual trust, and without such a control, respect for the human distinctness of each person becomes impossible. The

---

[63] H. Arendt (1976), *l.c.*, 296.

[64] We draw on an expression used in M. Hildebrandt, "Technology and the End of Law".

foregoing thoughts help us also to understand an essential dimension of arbitrary State power. A State deploys its power arbitrarily, when its public officials do not guide their actions by a common framework of reasons, and, consequently, insulate themselves from the responsibility to account for the reasons they might have for these actions.[65] Arbitrary government disrespects the plural humanity, or the human dignity of each citizen, because it does not allow him to make public officials answerable for the reasons on which they act, and, consequently, to contest these reasons from his distinct view on the world.

By grasping the point of arbitrary government as a denial of human dignity, we come very close to explaining MacCormick's connection between the living of an autonomous life in mutual trust, and the principle of legality. What makes the obligation to define crimes in a clear and precise way (*lex certa*) for example an issue of human dignity, is that it confers to the legislator the following responsibility. When defining crimes, the legislator is to set legal standards of behaviour that ensure a shared framework of understanding. Such criminal offences should contain *normative guidance* for the judge and for citizens, not primarily as a response to each citizen's interest in predictable behaviour and a right to a fair warning, but as a response to each citizen's need to reveal himself in action in a climate of mutual trust. Normative guidance in criminal provisions is necessary for each citizen's need for trusting the legitimacy of his actions. If a criminal offence does not extend such guidance to citizens, then respect for human dignity risks becoming utterly fragile. Citizens are then deprived (to quote Bauman) of the "conditions of self–confidence and self–reliance on which the ability to think and to act rationally depends."[66]

---

65 Compare T.O. Endicott, *l.c.*, 18.

66 Z. Bauman, *In Search of Politics* (Cambridge: Polity Press, 1999) 17.

Chapter 7 – Corporate Wrongdoing and the Limits of the Criminal Law

Mark Fenwick

1 Introduction

Public perceptions of crime are no longer exclusively dominated by images of an urban underclass and so–called 'street crime', but increasingly involve the illegal activities of corporate executives and managers. The collapse of Enron provided a compelling narrative of managerial greed and injurious loss that captivated global public attention and came to symbolise the problem of corporate crime in the United States. High profile corporate crime cases have also occurred in many other countries, for example, the Livedoor securities fraud case in Japan, the Lee Ming Tee case in Hong Kong, and the Vodafone–Mannesmann affair in Germany. This wave of corporate scandals has prompted policy–makers around the world into a systematic reevaluation of regulatory strategies that, in many cases, has resulted in a significantly expanded role for the criminal law in regulating the organisation, financing, and activities of corporations.[1]

In spite of these reforms, however, many questions remain unanswered about what constitutes an appropriate response to corporate wrongdoing. In particular, several critics have questioned the expanded role of the criminal law in this area and have suggested that the deterrent effects of the criminal sanction have been greatly exaggerated.[2] This chapter will offer a brief introduction to some of the limits of the criminal sanction as a response to corporate wrongdoing. The chapter is not suggesting that the criminal law has no role to play in the regulation of corporations. Such an argument would be absurd. However, it is argued that the political desire to take a strong stance on corporate wrongdoing means that a large number of difficult questions about the limits of a criminal justice–based approach are being obscured and, in some cases, neglected. Consequently, alternatives to the criminal law – such as efforts to promote socially responsible forms of corporate culture – are not receiving adequate attention from politicians, the mass media or the public in general.

---

1 The most obvious example of law–making in the wake of recent scandals is the US Sarbanes–Oxley Act of 2002.

2 See, for example, W. Laufer, *Corporate Bodies and Guilty Minds: The Failure of Corporate Criminal Liability* (Chicago: University of Chicago Press, 2006) and H. Pontell and G. Geis (eds.), *International Handbook of White–Collar and Corporate Crime* (New York: Springer, 2007).

This chapter will not attempt to be comprehensive in its examination of these issues but will instead focus on two examples of the limits of existing models of criminal law in regulating corporate wrongdoing. Section 2 will examine the normative limits of the criminal sanction via a discussion of the difficulties often associated with identifying clear moral justifications for criminalising corporate wrongdoing. Section 3 will focus on the conceptual and practical limits of the criminal sanction via a discussion of corporate criminal liability. As such, a number of important issues will not be addressed, most obviously the very real obstacles associated with investigating corporate crime, the problem of selective prosecutions, the difficulties of securing convictions in cases involving well–funded defendants, debates on sentencing (specifically alternatives to the fine), and the lack of empirical evidence supporting the positive effects of punitive approaches to corporate control.[3] Moreover, the discussion will focus primarily on developments in the Anglo–American world, although the line of argument has relevance in other jurisdictions.

Before turning to the substance of the discussion it is worth noting two preliminary, but nevertheless, important points. Firstly, within English language criminological literature there is a tendency to use the term 'corporate crime' in a non–legal sense to encompass a broad range of illegal or otherwise undesirable acts that may or may not be crimes in a strict sense. An illustration of this approach can be found in John Braithwaite's definition of corporate crime as "the conduct of a corporation, or employees acting on behalf of a corporation which is proscribed . . by law."[4] By not specifying what kind of law is involved, Braithwaite accepts that 'corporate crime' not only includes acts that violate the criminal law, but extends to civil and administrative violations as well. Other scholars go further and argue that harmful but legal acts are to be included in the category of 'corporate crime'.[5]

This approach has a number of merits and certainly represents an intentional decision on the part of the authors. Most importantly, it draws on an argument first made by Edwin Sutherland in his landmark paper on 'white collar crime' that it is precisely because of their high social status that the undesirable acts of corporate officers escape the reach of the criminal law in spite of the fact the amount of damage caused may exceed that associated with so–called 'street crime'.[6] By des-

---

3 The classic empirical study on the 'practical' difficulties associated with the investigation and prosecution of corporate crime remains K. Mann, *Defending White Collar Crime* (New Haven: Yale University Press, 1985). On deterrence, see J. Braithwaite, *To Punish or Persuade* (Albany: SUNY Press, 1985) and C. Moore, "Taming the Giant Corporation? Some Cautionary Remarks on the Deterrability of Corporate Crime", *Crime & Delinquency* 1987, *33*, 388.

4 J. Braithwaite, *Corporate Crime in the Pharmaceutical Industry* (London: Routledge, 1986) 6.

5 See, for example, S. Simpson, *Corporate Crime, Law, & Social Control* (Cambridge: CUP, 2002).

6 E. Sutherland, *White Collar Crime* (New York: Dryden, 1949). Detailed discussion on the differences between 'white collar' and 'corporate crime' will not be explored here, however, the former term is often regarded as encompassing both *occupational* crime (*i.e.*, purely self–interested crime committed in the work place) and *organisational* crimes (crimes committed

ignating such harmful acts 'crimes', the severity of corporate wrongdoing can be emphasised and the bias of the criminal law exposed. However, by potentially blurring the distinction between positive analysis (what is a crime?) and normative analysis (what should be a crime?) this type of definition can be the source of confusion, especially in a contemporary context where the scope of the criminal law is far wider than when Sutherland first considered these issues in the 1940s.[7]

In this chapter, therefore, a distinction will thus be made between 'corporate crime' (corporate acts or acts on behalf of the corporation that violate the criminal law), 'corporate illegality' (corporate acts or acts on behalf of the corporation that are unlawful in the broad sense encompassing criminal, civil, and administrative illegality), and 'corporate wrongdoing' (acts which although harmful in some undefined sense are nonetheless not necessarily illegal). Although not without difficulties, this distinction at least retains a certain legal precision in its definition of corporate crime.[8]

The second preliminary point concerns the basic premise of this chapter, namely the rapid expansion of the scope of the criminal law in the context of corporate wrongdoing. This chapter proceeds from the assumption that this 'punitive turn' has been a general trend across multiple jurisdictions that can be traced back to the 1960s.[9] Due to limitations of space this premise will not be explored in detail.[10] However, it is worth perhaps making a few brief observations.

Although the recent spate of corporate scandals has renewed interest in the criminal sanction, this is not a new phenomenon.[11] In an influential article, Jack Katz suggested that political moves against corporate wrongs only really emerged in the 1960s in the US as a result of the Watergate scandal, the Vietnam War, student protests, and the civil rights movement, that is, at a time when political leaders had lost their moral authority and "considerable ability to protect power centers from moral attack".[12] Of course, this trend has not been limited to the United States.

---

by an organisation and its employees for the benefit of the organisation). Corporate crime can be regarded as a type of organisational crime. For more on this typology, see N. Shover and J. P. Wright (eds.), *Crimes of Privilege: Readings in White Collar Crime* (Oxford: OUP, 2001) chp. 1.

7 As evidenced by a sentence such as, "criminal law is utilized in corporate crime cases more than ever before", S. Simpson, *l.c.*, 16.

8 For more on these questions of definition, see J. Gobert and M. Punch, *Rethinking Corporate Crime* (London: Butterworths, 2006) chp. 1.

9 This kind of punitive turn is a more general phenomenon not limited to corporate wrongdoing. For a review of this trend see D. Garland, *Cultures of Control: Crime & Social Control in Contemporary Societies* (Oxford: OUP, 2002) and J. Pratt, D. Brown, M. Brown, S. Hallsworth and W. Morrison (eds.), *The New Punitiveness: Trends, Theories, Perspectives* (London: Willan).

10 For an earlier work highlighting the limits of the criminal law in the context of corporate wrongdoing see C. Stone, *Where the Law Ends* (New York: Harper & Row, 1975).

11 For a review of the 'fact of criminalisation', see S. Simpson, *l.c.*, chp. 1.

12 J. Katz, "The Social Movement Against White Collar Crime", in E. Bittner and S. Messinger (eds.), *Criminology Review Yearbook*, vol. 2 (Beverley Hills: Sage, 1980), 178. See also F. Cullen, W. Maakestad, and G. Cavender, *Corporate Crime Under Attack: The Ford Pinto Case & Beyond* (Cincinnati: Anderson, 1987). On the issue of changing patterns of trust see,

The clearest evidence of this punitive turn has been the creation of new categories of criminal offence combined with a greater willingness on the part of regulators to employ criminal sanctions against corporate wrongdoers.[13] Criminal law now applies to a wide range of corporate acts, including fraud (e.g. false advertising, consumer fraud, financial fraud, tax evasion), labour violations, manufacturing violations, environmental violations, unfair business practices, abuse of authority (i.e. corruption), and judicial and regulatory violations (including perjury and obstruction of justice). The recent wave of law–making in this area is, therefore, just another example of a broader trend in which politicians, keen to be perceived as taking a tough stance on corporate wrongs, hastily enact new criminal legislation in the wake of high profile scandals.[14]

Paralleling this expansion in the scope and use of criminal law has been a corresponding tendency to weaken the *mens rea* requirement for corporate wrongdoing in order to facilitate convictions. The emergence and rapid expansion of strict liability (i.e. no–fault or public welfare) offences is the most obvious example of this transformation. It is probably no coincidence that many strict liability offences are concerned with corporate activities, such as pollution, and health and safety, where there is a clear public interest at stake in halting the proscribed acts.[15] And yet, there has also been a more general trend on the part of legislators in the Anglo–American world, at least, to move from relatively 'high level' *mens rea* requirements, such as intent or knowledge, to relatively low level requirements, such as recklessness and negligence. As with strict liability, this general trend has also been important in the context of corporate regulation.[16]

In addition, many jurisdictions have responded to concerns about corporate wrongdoing by adopting a number of procedural reforms that greatly empower State actors in their efforts to regulate corporations. These strategies include expanding the powers of law enforcement agencies responsible for investigating and prosecuting corporate offenders, enacting whistleblower/witness protection legislation, and, reforming sentencing guidelines to allow for more severe and diverse

---

for example, F. Fukuyama, *Trust: The Social Virtues and the Creation of Prosperity* (New York: Free Press, 1995).

13 See F.T. Cullen *et al.*, *l.c.* Environmental regulation in the United States provides a good illustration of this trend to criminalise corporate wrongdoing. Prior to 1982, the Environmental Protection Agency (EPA) relied exclusively on compliance strategies and civil penalties to discipline environmental violations. In fact, the EPA did not employ criminal investigators until the early 1980s. On this issue, see F. Addison and E. Mack, "Creating an Environmental Ethic in Corporate America: The Big Stick of Jail Time", *Southwestern Law Journal* 1991, *44*, 1427.

14 On this style of law–making, see J. Simon, *Governing Through Crime: How the War on Crime Transformed American Democracy And Created a Culture of Fear* (Oxford: OUP, 2007).

15 See F. Sayre, "Public Welfare Offences" *Columbia Law Review* 1933, *33*, 55 for a perceptive early account that makes this connection between strict liability and corporate regulation.

16 Of course there are some very important exceptions to this trend, most obviously obstruction of justice laws, which require, for example, the destruction of documents to be 'corrupt'.

sanctions, including greater use of shame–based sanctions in cases involving corporations and corporate offenders.[17]

Since the 1960s, therefore, there has been a gradual widening of the criminal justice 'net' in the context of corporate regulation.[18] This chapter, although it is not systematic or comprehensive, raises in a preliminary way the question of whether this turn to the criminal law has always been appropriate.

2 The Normative Limits of the Criminal Law: Identifying Moral Fault in Cases of Corporate Wrong–Doing

The image of crime that has traditionally dominated both popular discourse, as well as the criminological literature, is one of clear wrongdoing involving manifestly harmful acts, such as murder, theft and rape. That is to say, acts which are self–evidently worthy of moral condemnation. Understandings of corporate wrongdoing, by contrast, are pervaded by various moral ambiguities. This is problematic because there exists a broad consensus within the modern literature on criminal law that what justifies the imposition of punishment by the State is the existence of moral fault.[19] Punishment without fault or, alternatively, punishment that is disproportionate to the degree of fault is correctly regarded as inappropriate and unjust. A consequence of this argument is that establishing the existence and degree of moral fault is an essential precondition of the application of the criminal sanction if the law is to retain its normative legitimacy.

And yet, in the context of corporate crime it is often difficult to identify in an analytically precise manner whether sufficient fault exists to justify criminalising the conduct (as opposed to imposing alternative forms of legal liability) and, perhaps more frequently, what degree of fault exists and what sanction should be applied. Conceptions of moral fault developed in the context of discussions of street crime may not be easily transferable to corporate wrongdoing.

This is an issue that has been largely neglected in the contemporary debate on corporate wrongdoing. Fuelled perhaps by sensationalist images in the mass media, the moral fault of such actions is often regarded as self–evident. However, Stuart Green, in his recently published *Lying, Cheating, and Stealing: A Moral Theory of White–Collar Crime*, sets out to challenge this view.[20] Although Green's intention is to develop a vocabulary for accurately assessing fault in a white collar

---

17 For recent works offering an overview of the above issues, see K. Brickley (ed.), *Corporate & White Collar Crime: Cases and Materials* (New York: Aspen, 2006); M. Clinnard & P. Yeager, *Corporate Crime* (New York: Transaction, 2005); and G. Geis, *White Collar and Corporate Crime* (New York: Prentice Hall, 2006).

18 The classic statement of 'net–widening' remains S. Cohen, *Visions of Social Control* (Cambridge: Polity, 1985).

19 See J. Cottingham, "Varieties of Retribution", *Philosophical Quarterly* 1979, *29*, 238, for an excellent review of this discussion.

20 S. Green, *Lying, Cheating & Stealing: A Moral Theory of White Collar Crime* (Oxford: OUP, 2006).

and corporate crime context, he begins his account by identifying various kinds of 'moral ambiguity' that pervade US and English corporate criminal law.[21]

Perhaps the most serious of these moral ambiguities is the so–called 'sticky norms' problem.[22] This is the idea that in many cases of corporate wrongdoing the imposition of criminal sanctions is not justified because it is unclear whether sufficient moral fault can be found. As Green puts it, much conduct that is subject to criminal sanction is regarded by 'significant sections' of the public, as "wrong, but not so wrong".[23] Green offers a number of interesting examples including bribery cases, failing to file government reports, intellectual property violations and insider trading. In each case, he does not defend the actions but rather highlights the difficulties in identifying the precise fault involved.[24] In the case of insider trading, for example, there is an extensive law and economics literature holding that such trading makes the market more efficient by causing market prices to reflect more complete and accurate information about the value of securities than would otherwise be the case.[25]

Green then introduces a second ambiguity, namely that although for many categories of corporate crime 'core cases' can be treated as unambiguously criminal, 'peripheral cases' may be more controversial.[26] To illustrate this 'core – periphery' distinction he contrasts bribery involving a 'bag of hundred dollar bills' with cases where the bribe being offered is less tangible, such as support in a political campaign. As Green puts it,

> in such cases, the line between serious criminality – here bribery or extortion – and non–criminality – mere 'log–rolling', 'horse–trading', or 'back scratching' – can be blurry indeed.[27]

Of course, the irony is that what often drives legislative efforts are the 'high profile', 'core' cases and the issue of 'periphery' cases is largely ignored.

As a final example of the ambiguous moral quality of such offences, Green points to the 'hybrid civil/criminal' quality of much US and UK law, including offences under the *Securities and Exchange Act*, the *Clean Water Act*, *Bankruptcy Code*, *Tax Code*, and the *Federal Food, Drug and Cosmetic Act* to give just a few examples. As Greene puts it "there is little or no qualitative distinction, at least not at the level of statutory definition, between what should be regarded as criminal and what should not".[28] Again this is an important point. It points to the difficulties legislators have in drawing clear distinctions between criminal and civil

---

21 *Ibid.*, chp. 2.

22 *Ibid.*, 24. See also D. Kahan, "Gentle Nudges vs. Hard Shoves; Solving the Sticky Norms Problem", *University of Chicago Law Review* 2000, *67*, 607.

23 S. Green, *l.c.*, 24.

24 *Ibid.*, 24–26.

25 See, for example, H. Manne, *Insider Trading and the Stock Market* (New York: Free Press, 1996).

26 S. Green, *l.c.*, 24.

27 *Ibid.*

28 *Ibid.*

wrongs and that there is some uncertainty in the degree of fault at stake in cases of corporate illegality.

Compounding the general issue of identifying moral fault is a number of other factors that differentiate corporate wrongdoing from 'traditional' crimes. Firstly, many cases of corporate wrongdoing involve unlawful acts committed by an individual or individuals working within complex organisational structures where the boundary between personal and collective responsibility is difficult to draw. This diffusion of responsibility complicates the assessment of moral fault because it makes it difficult to determine who is responsible for such conduct.[29] The imposition of corporate criminal liability may resolve this issue, but as we shall see in section 3 this has its own attendant difficulties.

Secondly, accurately delineating the kind and quality of harm that exists in cases of corporate wrongdoing can be difficult.[30] It is clear that the harm which occurs as a result of corporate crime tends to differ from the harm associated with 'ordinary' street crime. The harm is often incorporeal – such as financial loss or injury to an institution – and occurs in a non–specific physical location over a difficult to define period of time. In the case of tax offences, bribery, and insider trading, the identification of the exact degree of harm can also present real difficulties. Just to take bribery as an example, it obviously distorts the decision–making of those bribed but there are also indirect, diffuse and aggregate harms caused by such conduct – for example, loss of investor confidence, distrust of government, and bad decisions – whose value is hard to quantify.

Thirdly, in many cases, corporate crimes are often victimless or at least acts in which no one individual suffers substantial material harm.[31] This can also complicate the assessment of fault. How can we determine which citizens are victimised by environmental violations? Which taxpayers are the victims of the false tax returns? Which consumers are harmed by price fixing or violations of food safety laws? Many corporate crimes involve small amounts of harm to a large number of victims and are significant only in their aggregate. And some victims may not even be aware they are victims, nor may offenders be aware of the identity of all – or even any – of their victims.

Finally, corporate crimes are committed by society's 'success stories' in the context of surrounding conduct that is mostly legitimate and often desirable. This may partially mitigate the perceived harmfulness of such acts or alter how we evaluate moral fault. For instance, corporations and corporate executives who engage in illegal acts will also certainly be engaged in a range of other desirable activities. In addressing this point, Green offers the example of Kenneth Lay's $2.5

---

29 See generally, M. Tonry and A. Reiss, Jr. (eds.), *Beyond the Law: Crime in Complex Organizations* (Chicago: Chicago University Press, 1993).

30 On harm in general, see J. Feinberg, *Harm to Others* (New York: OUP, 1984). On harm in a corporate crime context, see S. Box, *Power, Crime & Mystification* (London: Routledge, 1983) chp. 3.

31 See S. Green, "Victims' Rights and the Limits of Criminal Law", *Criminal Law Forum* 2003, *14*, 335, and G. Stitt and D. Giacopassi, "Assessing Victimization from Corporate Harms", in M. Blankenship, *Understanding Corporate Criminality* (London: Routledge, 1995).

million donations to more than 250 charitable organisations and suggests that 'such socially beneficial conduct' is relevant for sentencing, but also – and this is more controversial – for an evaluation of "the way we perceive the harmfulness of their underlying acts".[32]

Again it is worth stressing that none of the above should be taken as suggesting that corporate crime does not cause serious harm or that there should be a massive program of decriminalisation. Rather the intention of this section was to highlight the genuine difficulties that arise when conventional approaches to moral fault are applied in a corporate context. This should not come as a great surprise since concepts of moral fault in criminal law (and everyday life, more generally) have developed in the context of 'street crime', and popular images of crime continue to be dominated by such acts. Consequently, a certain degree of confusion about the moral boundaries of corporate crime, and the ethical differences between behaviour that should be criminalised and other ostensibly similar acts that may, in some situations, be socially desirable within the context of a free market economy may be inevitable. In the light of this argument, a certain degree of caution is advised before criminal sanctions are adopted. At the very least, further study on the moral fault associated with specific categories of acts is required in order to craft legislative provisions that accurately reflect the degree of harm associated with specific forms of corporate wrongdoing. However, in the wake of scandals such as Enron, such a pause for reflection may be politically difficult to achieve. The danger of an over–zealous approach is that the newly enacted law is never utilised or that it is utilised and that injustices occur. Either way the effect would be that the legitimacy of the criminal law is compromised.

3 The Conceptual and Practical Limits of the Criminal Law: A Critical Examination of Corporate Criminal Liability

The second illustration of the limits of the crime control approach to corporate wrongdoing to be considered in this chapter is corporate criminal liability. The historical view of most western legal systems has been that a corporation could not be prosecuted for criminal acts, but that individual members of a company could be. Acts performed in the context of corporate activities might be subject to criminal law, but liability fell on the individuals and not the corporation itself. As such, corporations fell outside the domain of criminal responsibility.[33] Broadly speaking, the principle reason for this view was that a corporation is an incorporeal entity that cannot actually do or intend anything.[34] The eighteenth century

---

32 S. Green, *l.c.*, 39.

33 For example, in English law, *The Case of Suttons Hospital* in 1612 is often cited as an early precedent: "a corporation is incapable of an act of understanding and it has no will to exercise".

34 For a contemporary restatement of this argument, see S. Wolf, "The Legal and Moral Responsibility of Organizations", in J. Pennock (ed.), *Criminal Justice* (London: Routledge,

English lawyer, William Blackstone in his *Commentaries on the Laws of England*, regarded criminal capacity and liability as being confined to natural persons. He characterised the corporation as an 'impoverished legal subject' and focused on a number of procedural difficulties that arose in the case of corporate criminal liability: notably, a corporation cannot commit certain types of offence (sex crimes to take an obvious example); a corporation cannot appear in a criminal court 'in person' to defend itself; a corporation cannot swear an oath, nor can a corporation be arrested, imprisoned or executed.[35] For Blackstone, it was self–evident that corporations were not subject to criminal law.

From the late nineteenth century, however, and particularly over the latter half of the twentieth century, this situation has changed dramatically. Corporate criminal liability has expanded greatly, initially in common law jurisdictions, but more recently in a number of civil law countries as well.[36] This section will review this trend and suggest that it is highly problematic both on conceptual and pragmatic grounds. The first part of the discussion will focus on the various doctrines that determine when companies will be held criminally liable. The second part of the discussion will then examine whether corporate criminal liability adds anything to the 'liability mix' beyond what might be achieved by alternative forms of legal liability, most obviously corporate civil liability.

The traditional approach to corporate criminal liability has been so–called imputation doctrines. Such an approach requires the identification of a single human offender whose crime is then imputed to the company. By way of introduction, an interesting contrast can be made between the imputation approach of the US Federal Courts and that employed in English law. Since the early twentieth century, US courts have tended to adopt a broad vicarious liability standard whereby the criminal act of 'any employee' that occurs during 'the course of employment' and which intends, at least in part, to 'benefit' the company, can be ascribed to the company itself.[37] A company can be convicted for any crime – including crimes of intent – based on this standard.

The rationale for this approach is that without the threat of criminal liability there is little incentive for companies to curb illegal but profitable activities that place innocent parties at risk. However, the obvious difficulty is that it seems un-

---

1985). Wolf argues that criminal liability rests on the existence of moral fault and moral fault presupposes an emotional capacity to appreciate the harmfulness of one's actions. Since a company lacks such a capacity it should not be subject to criminal liability on the grounds of fairness.

35 W. Blackstone, *Commentaries on the Laws of England* (Boston: Beacon, 1962), Vol. I, chp. 18.

36 It is an interesting question, why common law jurisdiction were more willing to extend corporate criminal liability. Judicial activism plus a more pragmatic and less conceptual approach to criminal law are certainly part of the explanation. However, recently a number of civil law countries have adopted corporate criminal liability. Although Germany has resisted this trend (preferring administrative corporate liability), France, the Netherlands, and Italy and Lithuania, to pick just a few examples, have introduced corporate criminal liability in recent years.

37 The Supreme Court ruling in *New York Central & Hudson River Railway Company v. United States* 212 US 481 (1909).

reasonable to expect a large corporation to take responsibility for the acts of all of its employees, particularly since the consequences of a criminal conviction for the corporation may cause negative effects that extend to innocent third parties, such as other employees and their families. And even if the company adopts all reasonable measures to prevent its staff from committing an offence, it could still be subjected to criminal sanctions under the vicarious liability standard. Stated bluntly, if the company faces the risk of conviction regardless of its actions what incentive exists to invest too heavily in preventive measures?

The English approach, therefore, has been to ameliorate the extreme consequences of the vicarious liability standard by limiting the set of employees whose criminal acts can be imputed to the company.[38] This is the so–called identification doctrine. Specifically, only those actions and thought patterns of certain high–ranking individuals within the company – the so–called 'directing mind' – are regarded in law as the acts of the company itself. Criminal acts committed by those individuals are regarded as being committed by the company itself (i.e. their acts are 'identified' with the company). In the leading English case, a supermarket company was acquitted of falsely advertising prices on the grounds that the 'brain' of the company was unaware of the wrongdoing even though the store manager was.[39] Under the vicarious liability approach the company would have been convicted in such a case.

Although the rationale for this more restrictive approach is clear, it has resulted in a number of difficulties. Firstly, it has proven extremely difficult for English courts to arrive at a clear and consistent definition of who is a 'high managerial agent'. Similar difficulties have occurred in Canada, Hong Kong, and Australia in the use of identification standards.[40] Formal definitions – such as the Board of Directors – often fail to capture the power distribution in complex modern organisations. Substantive approaches have also proven too vague in a criminal law context. And yet, the strongest argument against identification is that it has been almost impossible for prosecutors to secure convictions against corporations in such cases because 'high managerial agents' are well–placed to insulate themselves against criminal investigation (*i.e.* they are 'judgment proof'). A series of high profile acquittals – most notably in the case against P&O for the sinking of the cross–Channel ferry, the Herald of Free Enterprise – due to the failure to secure a case against senior management reinforced public perceptions of injustice.[41] This is particularly so when low ranking employees are convicted for their part in similar incidents.[42] Judicial dissatisfaction with the identification standard can also

---

38 Canada, Australia, Hong Kong and several US states also adopt variations on this approach.

39 *Tesco Supermarkets Ltd. v. Natrass* [1972] AC 153.

40 For a review of the Canadian situation, see Department of Justice (Canada), *Corporate Criminal Liability Discussion Paper* (2002); and Hong Kong, M.J. Reimer Lau, "Director's Criminal Liability in Hong Kong", 12 *Corporate Practice* 1. Australia is discussed below.

41 *P&O European Ferries Ltd* [1991] 93 Cr App Rep 72.

42 *Attorney Generals Reference (No. 2 of 1999)* [2000] QB 796. In this case, a rail company and the driver were both charged for offences connected to a serious rail accident near London. The driver was convicted but the court dismissed the case against the rail company on

be seen in a 1995 case, *Meridian Global Funds Management Asia Ltd. v. Securities Commission*, when Lord Hoffman in an important and influential opinion of the Privy Council suggested that although there is a presumption in favour of identification in English law, vicarious liability may be adopted if the purpose of a statute is better achieved by adopting the broader standard.[43]

And yet, even the more flexible *Meridian* approach does not really address certain fundamental problems with both forms of imputation. Firstly, all imputation standards presume that one person has committed a criminal offence. In complex modern organisations where corporate decisions and actions are the result of a combination of individual acts this may be an unrealistic assumption. Secondly, by focusing on the criminal acts of one person, the collective nature of corporate criminal liability is not captured. Stated bluntly, there is simply no concept of organisational fault with imputation doctrines. Criminal liability is derived from the criminal acts of a certain class of employees and this seems a weak basis for the imposition of a criminal sanction against an organisation. Finally, corporate criminal liability for crimes of intent runs contrary to one of the basic principles of criminal law – punishment of the morally blameworthy – since it relies upon vicarious guilt rather than personal fault.

A number of jurisdictions have therefore attempted to develop alternatives to imputation. The necessity of these moves highlights the limited applicability of traditional criminal law model to corporations. The first alternative emerged in the US Federal Courts in the late 1980s, the so–called 'aggregation doctrine'. The need for aggregation arises when no individual has committed an offence but the combined effect of several individual actions is criminal. The classic example of this is the Bank of New England case from 1987, when a US bank was charged with knowingly violating the federal *Currency Transaction Reporting Act*.[44] This statute required financial institutions to report to the US Treasury all transactions in excess of $10,000. In this case a customer of a bank withdrew cash from the same account but from three different branches of the bank. The total sum for the three transactions was greater than $10,000. The bank failed to report the transactions and was subsequently prosecuted. Under imputation doctrines the bank would have been acquitted since no one individual employee had violated the rules. However, the court allowed the three acts to be aggregated in order to establish the corporation's guilt. The rationale behind a doctrine of this kind is clear: it prevents corporations evading criminal liability by compartmentalising their activities.

---

the grounds that there was no evidence that any corporate officers had engaged in any criminal act.

43 [1995] 3 All ER 918. *Meridian* involved the criminal acts of investment managers therefore the broader US standard was required in order to ensure a conviction against the company. The Meridian formula has been criticised on the grounds that the policy of a statute may be hard to find and it is unlikely that the words of the relevant provisions will provide a clear answer as to 'who' constitutes the company.

44 *United States v. Bank of New England* 821 F 2d 844 (1st Cir) (1987).

The principle difficulty with aggregation is that "the total seems to exceed the sum of the parts".[45] Two innocent states of mind are being added together to produce a guilty state of mind. Several non–culpable states (the acts of the individual bank tellers in the Bank of New England example) are combined to result in a culpable state. Again this seems to run against basic notions of criminal responsibility. Of course to those who favour aggregation it is precisely the fact that the conviction of a company does not carry any implication that the workers are guilty of any offence that means this approach is preferable for grounding organisation fault. However, there is something disturbing about the suggestion that the 'company' committed a crime in the absence of any single criminal act.[46] Another difficulty is deciding which individual acts should be aggregated (any employees or those identified with the company?) and justifying the distinction. As such, we arrive back at earlier debates about which employees are to be identified with the company.

One alternative to aggregation is a risk management model. This can be found in the English Law Commission's 1996 proposal for a new offence of 'corporate killing' as well as a 2001 reform in Italian law.[47] In both cases, the issue is whether the company's behaviour fell below what could be reasonably expected in the circumstances. That is to say, criminal liability is imposed on a company if there has been a failure on the part of the company to manage risk in a reasonable manner. Unlike the imputation and aggregation doctrines the company would be liable not for what its agents had done or thought, but for the organisation of its policies and practices or risk management.

The draft Involuntary Homicide Bill attached to English Law Commission on corporate criminal liability report illustrates this approach. A company would be liable for the crime of corporate killing if (i) 'management failure' by the corporation is cause of a person's death, and (ii) that 'failure constitutes conduct failing far below what can reasonably be expected of the corporation in the circumstances'. Many criticisms have been made of this proposal, but one issue is whether policy evaluation of the kind envisaged by the draft law is an appropriate task for a criminal court (especially in those jurisdictions with juries or lay–panels).

A similar, but even more radical, example is found in the Australian *Federal Criminal Code* of 1995. Under this law, liability is imposed on the corporation if "a corporate culture existed within the body corporate that directed, encouraged, or tolerated" criminal acts.[48] The law goes on to define corporate culture expansively as "an attitude, policy, rule, course of conduct, or practice existing within the body corporate".[49] Companies are thus prevented from hiding behind codes of

---

45 J. Gobert and M. Punch, *l.c.*, 84.

46 It is on this basis that aggregation was rejected by English courts, see *Attorney General's Reference (No. 2 of 1999)* [2000] QB 796, 798.

47 For an extensive discussion of the Italian Law reform, see J. Gobert and M. Punch, *l.c.*, chp. 3.

48 Australian *Federal Criminal Code 1995*, section 12(c)(2).

49 *Ibid.*, section 12(c)(3).

conduct or other policy statements if the reality of corporate practice is very different. Again, this approach is not without difficulties. At the very least one is obliged to distort language in ascribing criminal guilt to a corporate body on the grounds that it is responsible for the emergence of a morally blameworthy corporate culture.

As can be seen in these doctrinal debates on how to conceptualise corporate criminal liability, no consensus has emerged. Moreover, there are a number of arguments advanced suggesting that such liability does not add anything to extra existing liability strategies, notably corporate civil liability, and that even if a satisfactory doctrinal basis for such liability could be established it is simply unnecessary.[50] Generally speaking, the advocates of corporate criminal liability point to three distinguishing features of such an approach, but in each case there are serious questions to be addressed about whether it is really necessary.

Firstly, corporate criminal liability provides defendants – in this corporations – with greater procedural protections compared to civil liability. These protections would normally include, a higher burden of proof, the prohibition on double jeopardy, and the right to a jury trial or mixed panel trial. In general terms, the rationale for such protections is the prevention of false convictions. After all, modern criminal justice is less concerned with false acquittals. However, although there are good reasons in the case of individual criminal defendants it is not clear that corporations should receive such protections. Especially, since – as was noted above – the more common problem in corporate crime cases is the difficulty of achieving convictions.

Just to take the example of the prohibition on double jeopardy. This principle dictates that no defendant may be prosecuted for the same offence twice nor for a different offence based on the same set of facts. The rationale for this rule is the imbalance in resources between the State (which to all intents and purposes has infinite resources) and individual defendants (whose resources are obviously limited). In the absence of double jeopardy protection, the State would be free to pursue a defendant until their resources were exhausted and their ability to defend themselves significantly diminished. But the rationale for granting this procedural protection does not seems as forceful in the case of corporate defendants who are in a much better positioned to mount a sustained defence. Similar arguments can be made regarding other procedural protections afforded to criminal defendants. Such protections may not be desirable for corporate defendants. Consequently, corporate civil liability may be preferable precisely because it doe not entail these procedural protections.

Secondly, corporate criminal liability involves more powerful enforcement and investigative mechanisms compared to civil liability. Advocates of corporate liability argue that private enforcement is preferable when corporate wrongdoing has clearly identifiable victims and the victims are aware of the perpetrators identity. However, when these conditions are not met, public enforcement is preferred. And yet, as was mentioned in section 1 above, many jurisdictions allow public en-

---

50 See V. Khanna, "Corporate Criminal Liability: What Purpose Does it Serve?", *Harvard Law Review* 1997, *109*, 1477 and W. Laufer, *l.c.*

forcement in civil as well as criminal proceedings. In addition, it is often argued that public information gathering powers are more effective than cases involving private proceedings because the criminal enforcement model is more effective than civil enforcement at the pre–litigation stage. However, in many jurisdictions, the civil pre–litigation information gathering has been greatly strengthened in recent years thus negating this potential advantage. Obvious examples of this include discovery rules and civil investigative demands. Consequently, public enforcement may not have any inherent advantages. And if civil enforcement provides powers virtually identical they may prove more effective for no other reason than the lower standard of power applied in civil cases. The potential gains of criminal investigations, even if they do exist, may simply be negated by the higher burden of proof.

Finally, supporters of corporate criminal liability often suggest that such liability has more severe sanctions compared to civil liability and thus has a greater potential for deterring corporate wrongdoing and communicating moral condemnation. It is often argued that the unique sanctioning characteristic of criminal law is its stigmatising effect. And yet, criminal liability is not the only means regulators possess for communicating disapproval. Particularly, since there is little empirical evidence to suggest that criminal liability results in greater stigma that civil liability (particularly in tort regimes with punitive or exemplary damages).[51] It may even be the case that imposing sanctions on a fictional entity like a corporation is less effective than individual liability. Moreover, non–monetary sanctions, such as loss of license or community service can easily be adopted in a civil law context. Again the argument in favour of corporate criminal liability is quite controversial.

Concluding a review of the literature on this issue, Khanna writes:

> There is little understanding of what, if anything, it [*i.e.* corporate criminal liability] is designed to achieve . ... Indeed, the answer to the question the title poses – 'Corporate Criminal Liability: What Purpose Does it Serve?' – is almost none.[52]

Although this kind of blanket pessimism may be overstated it does point to the need for a serious rethinking of current approaches to corporate criminal liability.

4 Conclusion

This chapter has argued that the 'punitive turn' in the contemporary regulation of corporate wrongdoing has not been without associated difficulties and that the notion of the 'limits' of the criminal law is a helpful heuristic device for characterising these difficulties. Two examples were offered, (i) the difficulties in identifying the precise degree of moral fault in cases of corporate wrongdoing, as well as the

---

51 For empirical studies of public attitudes to corporate offenders, see D. Evans, F. Cullen and P. Dubeck, "Public Perceptions of Corporate Crime", in M. Blankenship, *Understanding Corporate Criminality* (London: Routledge, 1995).

52 V. Khanna, *l.c.*, 1534.

boundary between desirable and undesirable conduct, and (ii) the limited relevance of existing theories for making sense of corporate criminal liability. In both cases, these issues have been largely neglected in public and political debate. Rather, the current agenda is being driven by political elites keen to be seen as taking tough action in the wake of corporate scandals that may be unrepresentative of the general problem. This is not to deny the real issue that arises as a result of corporate actions, but rather to suggest that alternative models should also be explored. Interestingly, it is in those jurisdictions where regulators are more insulated from political pressures to 'act tough' against corporate offenders – most obviously in a transnational organisation such as the EU, for example – that more creative alternatives to the criminal sanction, such as efforts to promote a more socially responsible corporate culture, have been developed.[53] And of course, criminal law has an important role to play in this project. The intention of this chapter has been merely to emphasise the need to develop a new vocabulary for conceptualising both the fault associated with corporate wrongdoing and the form of corporate criminal liability in order to ensure that criminal law retains a genuine role in addressing what is, after all, a serious social issue.

---

53 See, for example, European Union, *Green Paper Promoting a European framework for Corporate Social Responsibility* (18/07/2001); and European Union, *The New Communication on Corporate Social Responsibility Implementing the Partnership for Growth and Jobs* (COM(2006) 22/03/2006), available online at http://ec.europa.eu/employment_social/soc-dial/csr/index.htm.

Chapter 8 – Regulating Prison Life: A Case Study of the Inmate Disciplinary System[1]

Luc Robert

1 Introduction

In "Limits of the Law (Introduction)", the editors identify and outline four functions of the law: the regulatory function; the symbolic representation of the norms and values of a group of people (or, broader, of society); the dispute resolution function (i.e. the law as a way to solve disputes); and the legal protection of citizens[2].

These functions are in constant interaction with each other, thereby calibrating one another and bringing forth new accentuations and shifting equilibriums. On top of that, each function is constituted of different factors and/or vectors, giving individual direction and weight to the particular function.

Amidst this complexity, I set out on the modest task of limiting the discussion to one function of the law, namely its regulatory function. This boils down to society's expectations vis–à–vis the law; that is, how the law serves to regulate social relations. In the light of a number of societal developments, the authors of the first chapter write: "[l]ate–modern societies [...] are in a need of both flexible and far–reaching regulation"; flexible, "because the progressive dynamics of our society cannot be paralysed", and far–reaching, "because at the same time the fundamental problems and challenges of our risk society have to be addressed". On this view, the law emerges as a panacea for societal problems. Although the authors immediately add that "... for one reason or another, the far–reaching regulatory expectations regarding law cannot be fully met ..."[3], what can be derived is that the law enjoys high–flung expectations. Such expectations of the law seem to flow from, or at least evidence, an *imperative* conception of law: the law as an imperative for what can and should be done, how and by whom. This understanding of the law implies a *top–down* perspective. Rules, regulations, and by extension, policies, are being voted on, enacted and implemented and social actors, be they institutions or individuals, should conform their actions to the rules, regulations, and policies put in place. A logical consequence of such a hierarchical conception

---

1 I would like to express my gratitude to Professor Liz Elliott (Simon Fraser University, Canada), who supervised the research and who commented on a draft of the paper, and to Erik Claes, with whom an earlier version of the paper was discussed.

2 E. Claes, W. Devroe and B. Keirsbilck, "The Limits of the Law (Introduction)".

3 *Ibid.*

of law is that there exists little or no leeway for those who have to enforce the law[4].

In this chapter, I will assess these high set expectations in a particular example. One aspect of the Correctional Services of Canada (CSC) will be looked at: the inmate disciplinary system in place in federal correctional institutions. In the last few years, CSC has embraced a relatively new corporate management strategy where controls on officials' actions are directed through strict adherence to policy (in a broad sense, comprising rules, regulations and organisational policy): "100 % compliance with 100 % of the policies 100 % of the time"[5]. This indicates a high belief in the rules, regulations, and policies in place, thereby offering evidence of the above mentioned high expectations. Such a position, if applied to the inmate disciplinary system, would result in a disciplinary reaction to any type of behaviour identified as constituting a disciplinary infraction. Rule–enforcers in this particular setting, in first instance correctional officers ('COs'), accordingly are expected to operate in full compliance with the laws governing the prison system.

In this chapter, I will look at the ways in which correctional officers enforce the formal disciplinary regulations. Research data collected during an exploratory study of the disciplinary process in a Canadian medium–security prison, Mission Institution, will be presented[6]. First, the formal disciplinary rules in force in federal Canadian prisons (and, more concretely, in Mission Institution) will be outlined (section 2). Subsequently, I will draw attention to prisons as a social setting with particular characteristics (section 3). In order to assess the imperative, hierarchical conception of the law, I will then introduce research data on the functioning and use of the inmate disciplinary system (section 4).

2 Prison Discipline: The 'Law in Books'

Prison law has developed considerably in the past few decades. Most Western nations have adopted sets of legal rules pertaining to the regulation of the prison. In Canada, the regulation of prison operations since the 1940s fell under the *Penitentiary Act* until repealed and replaced in 1992 by the *Corrections and Conditional Release Act* ('CCRA'). The CCRA is the main legislation governing the actions of federal[7] prison officials in carrying out the sentences imposed by the courts. According to s. 3 of the CCRA,

---

4 These characteristics would belong to what might be called an 'ideal type' of an imperative conception of law.

5 My thanks to Professor Liz Elliott for signalling this. She indicated hearing this statement repeatedly by different officials in response to queries about outstanding requests.

6 Following a question of the Deputy Warden in 2001, I looked into the functioning and use of the formal disciplinary system in place at Mission Institution (a unit–based prison located in Mission, near Vancouver, B.C., Canada).

7 In Canada, all sentences of two years or more are administered by the federal government. Sentences of less than two years are the jurisdiction of provincial and territorial governments.

> the purpose of the federal correctional system is to contribute to the maintenance of a just, peaceful and safe society by:
> (a) carrying out sentences imposed by courts through the safe and humane custody and supervision of offenders; and
> (b) assisting the rehabilitation of offenders in their reintegration into the community as law–abiding citizens through the provision of programs in penitentiaries and in the community.

The rule of law in Canadian federal prisons, then, aspires to embody the values of safety and humanity, in anticipation of the eventual release of prisoners into civil society.

Technically, the CCRA is further detailed in the *Corrections and Conditional Release Regulations* ('CCRR'). The Commissioner of Correctional Services Canada ('CSC') renders operational the CCRA and the CCRR through Commissioner's Directives ('CDs'). These set out more concrete guidelines for all federal correctional institutions. On the institutional level, both the federal regulations and the CD's form the framework for the specific Standing Orders ('SOs') and Institutional Post Orders ('IPOs'), the former describing institutional policy and practice, while the latter outline the job descriptions at Mission Institution.

As for the disciplinary system, the legal framework is constituted by ss. 38–44 of the CCRA. Its objectives are identified in the legislative instruments. The disciplinary process is supposed to promote the good order of the institution (CCRA, s. 38) and foster a positive correctional environment and contribute to the rehabilitation of the prisoners by allowing them to demonstrate their efforts to become law–abiding citizens (CCRA, s. 38; CD nr. 580, paragraph 1).

Section 40 of the CCRA identifies in nineteen subsections behaviour constituting a disciplinary infraction. Since these will be of importance further on, s. 40 of the CCRA is reproduced here. Section 40 CCRA states:

> An inmate commits a disciplinary offence who
> (a) disobeys a justifiable order of a staff member;
> (b) is, without authorization, in an area prohibited to inmates;
> (c) wilfully or recklessly damages or destroys property that is not the inmate's;
> (d) commits theft;
> (e) is in possession of stolen property;
> (f) is disrespectful or abusive toward a staff member in a manner that could undermine a staff member's authority;
> (g) is disrespectful or abusive toward any person in a manner that is likely to provoke a person to be violent;
> (h) fights with, assaults or threatens to assault another person;
> (i) is in possession of, or deals in, contraband;
> (j) without prior authorization, is in possession of, or deals in, an item that is not authorized by a Commissioner's Directive or by a written order of the institutional head;
> (k) takes an intoxicant into the inmate's body;
> (l) fails or refuses to provide a urine sample when demanded pursuant to section 54 or 55;
> (m) creates or participates in
> (i) a disturbance, or
> (ii) any other activity that is likely to jeopardize the security of the penitentiary;
> (n) does anything for the purpose of escaping or assisting another inmate to escape;

(o) offers, gives or accepts a bribe or reward;
(p) without reasonable excuse, refuses to work or leaves work;
(q) engages in gambling;
(r) wilfully disobeys a written rule governing the conduct of inmates; or
(s) attempts to do, or assists another person to do, anything referred to in paragraphs (a) to (r).

Notwithstanding these provisions, in case of problematic behaviour, s. 41(1) CCRA clearly states that a "staff member shall take all reasonable steps to resolve the matter informally, where possible". Only when informal resolution has been attempted but was not achieved, a charge is to be issued.

Every employee of CSC can charge an inmate (CD nr.580, paragraph 5), while contractors or other outsiders have to "inform a member of the Service" in case of "unacceptable behaviour" (CD nr.580, paragraph 6).

After a charge has been laid, a rather substantial process begins. After consolidation as a charge by a correctional supervisor, the charge is investigated. There are two types of charges, serious and minor disciplinary charges (s. 41 (2) CCRA). After the investigation of the charge, a unit manager designates it as a minor or serious disciplinary charge and under which of the nineteen subsections of s. 40 CCRA the charge can be identified.

If a charge is designated as minor, it will be heard by the institutional head or a staff member appointed by the institutional head (CCRR, s. 27 (1)). The Minister appoints a person, other than a staff member or an offender, who has knowledge of the administrative decision–making process for the purpose of conducting hearings of serious disciplinary offences (CCRR, s. 24(1)(a)). The hearing of serious disciplinary infractions is conducted by an Independent Chairperson ('ICP') (CCRR, s. 27(2)). In the institution which was studied, the ICP was a retired prosecutor. Two staff members, appointed by the warden, attend the hearings as advisors (SO nr.580.1, paragraph 14.b).

As far as the sanctions go, they differ depending on the seriousness of the charge. A summary of the measures with the different maximums for both minor and serious infractions may give us an understanding of the nature of the responses to infractions, responses which are deemed to be "first and foremost corrective" in nature (CD nr.580, paragraph 2.a). Sanctions include a warning or reprimand, a loss of privileges (for minor infractions, up to 7 days; for serious ones, up to 30 days), a fine (up to $25 (minor), maximum of $50 (serious)), performance of extra duties (for minor ones, up to 10 hours; for the serious, up to 30 hours) and, only for serious disciplinary breaches, segregation from other prisoners up to a period of 30 days (CCRR, ss. 35–39; CD nr.580, paragraph 40). In case the prisoner is found not guilty or if the charge is withdrawn[8], no consequences should follow. These formal rules aspire to regulate life in prison. Before looking into the functioning of the formal inmate disciplinary system, with particular attention to

[8] The two most important reasons for withdrawing a charge at the time of the research were: 1) the charging officer wants to withdraw the charge because informal resolution took place after the charge had been laid, and 2) administrative mistakes in the charge.

rule enforcement, I will first briefly touch upon a few characteristics of the prison as a social setting.

3 The Social Setting of the Prison

Prisons can be approached as part of the broader penality and, at the same time, they are also complex social settings. The prison is a social institution that performs various functions in late modern societies. It is, all at the same time, a symbol for law and order, a deprivation intended as the pain of punishment, a presumed clinic for moral rehabilitation, a reservoir of data for the production of disciplinary and regulatory knowledge, a tool for the temporal and spatial regulation of behaviour, and an institution for the instilling of discipline.

One particular challenge is the regulation of the prison as a social setting, which is comprised of particular characteristics endemic to what Goffman has termed "total institutions". Generally, a total institution is

> a place of residence and work where a large number of like–situated individuals, cut off from the wider society for an appreciable period of time, together lead an enclosed, formally administered round of life.[9]

The confinement of people in time and space produces social situations not usually encountered in open society. Especially in prison, dangerous conflicts can escalate over what would otherwise be considered minor annoyances, where the opportunities to avoid antagonists are virtually non–existent and resources are scarce. Continual surveillance and the lack of privacy generate other psychological effects in the form of adaptations to imprisonment, such as a dependence on institutional structures and contingencies; hypervigilence, interpersonal distrust and suspicion; emotional overcontrol, alienation, and psychological distancing; social withdrawal and isolation, incorporation of exploitative norms of prison culture, diminished sense of self–worth and personal values; and post–traumatic stress reactions to the pains of imprisonment.[10] These psychological adaptations affect the social life of the prison from the prisoners' perspective.

CO's also spend a great deal of time in the environment of the total institution. In a study of prison–influenced behaviour, Stanford Prison Experiment researchers noted the increased negativity of effect in student volunteers playing the roles of both prisoners *and* guards. "Since both prisoners and guards are locked into a dynamic, symbiotic relationship which is destructive to their human nature, guards

---

9 E. Goffman, *Asylums. Essays on the Social Situations of Mental Patients and Other Inmates* (New York: Anchor Books, 1961) xiii.

10 G. Haney, "The Psychological Impact of Incarceration: Implications for Postprison Adjustment", in J. Travis and M. Waul (eds.), *Prisoners Once Removed: The Impact of Incarceration and Reentry on Children, Families, and Communities* (Washington, D.C.: The Urban Institute Press, 2003).

are also society's prisoners".[11] Correctional officers are also human beings influenced by their environment, which affects the way they regulate prison life.

To sum up, the prison as a total institution is a unique social setting, where circumstances and situations unlike those in open society encounter social dynamics that are likewise unusual.

The first comprehensive research on the effects of prison on prisoners is generally dated to Clemmer's book, *The Prison Community*, in which the author examines the structure and social relationships in the prison community.[12] Almost twenty years later, Sykes examined the prison as an operating social system in *The Society of Captives.*[13] In it, he outlined a number of pains of imprisonment and looked at the flow of power in a maximum security prison. Later, the pains of imprisonment were the specific focus in Cohen and Taylor's *Psychological Survival*[14], a study of long–term incarceration and specifically the effects of social isolation. Since then there have been sporadic studies on social aspects of imprisonment dealing with, for example, race and social order[15], race and discretionary decision–making in prison[16], and social factors in institutional disciplinary processes.[17] The relative paucity of academic and political attention for the experience of incarceration is a cause of concern, particularly for countries where the 'new' phenomenon of mass incarceration is drastically changing the prison, both in qualitative and in quantitative ways.[18]

One of the more recent studies on the social aspects of imprisonment examines the effect of drug culture on prison culture.[19] This particular topic is salient in Ca-

---

11 The Stanford Prison Experiment, a simulation study conducted at Stanford University in 1971, attempted to "create a prison–like situation in which the guards and prisoners were initially comparable and characterized as being 'normal–average,' and then to observe the patterns of behaviour which resulted, as well as the cognitive, emotional and attitudinal reactions which emerged" (G. Haney, C. Banks and P. Zimbardo, "A Study of Prisoners and Guards in a Simulated Prison", in M. Balfour (ed.), *Theatre in Prison: Theory and Practice* (Bristol: Intellect Books, 2004)).

12 D. Clemmer, *The Prison Community* (Toronto: Holt, Rinehart and Winston, 1940).

13 G.M. Sykes, *The Society of Captives: A Study of a Maximum Security Prison* (Princeton, N.J.: Princeton University Press, 1958).

14 S. Cohen and L. Taylor, *Psychological Survival: The Experience of Long–Term Imprisonment* (New York: Pantheon Books, 1973).

15 L. Carroll, "Race, Ethnicity, and the Social Order of the Prison", in R. Johnson and H. Toch (eds.), *The Pains of Imprisonment* (Beverly Hills, C.A.: Sage Publications, 1982).

16 E.D. Poole and R.M. Regoli, "Race, Institutional Rule–Breaking, and Disciplinary Response: A Study of Discretionary Decision–Making in Prison", *Law and Society Review* 1980, *14*, 931–946.

17 C. Howard, L.T. Winfree Jr., G.L. Mays, M.K. Stohr and D.L. Clason, "Processing Inmate Disciplinary Infractions in a Federal Correctional Institution: Legal and Extralegal Correlates of Prison–Based Legal Decisions", *The Prison Journal* 1994, *74*, 5–31.

18 *E.g.* M. Bosworth and R. Sparks, "New Drections in Prison Studies: Some Introductory Comments", *Theoretical Criminology* 2000, *4*, 260; J. Simon, "The 'Society of Captives' in the Era of Hyper–Incarceration", *Theoretical Criminology* 2000, *4*, 285–308; L. Wacquant, "The Curious Eclipse of Prison Ethnography in the Age of Mass Incarceration", *Ethnography* 2002, *3*, 371–397.

19 B. Crewe, "Prisoner Society in the Era of Hard Drugs", *Punishment & Society* 2005, *7*, 457–481.

nadian institutions, where prisoner culture and norms have changed considerably since the early 1980s. Crewe's observations resonate with mine, in the sense that the desire for drugs and the economy expediting their supply have shifted the cultural norms of inter–prisoner conduct. This has added to the diminishment of prisoner solidarity, and has contributed to the creation of a culture of individual autonomy. Historical accounts of the prison community no longer wholly resonate with current prisoner subcultures. Similarly, officer subcultures have also changed since the early 1960s. The reflexive obedience to authority in the hierarchy of prison management, in which the officers occupy the bottom rung, that had characterised prisons has also gradually eroded so that officers' relationships with managers are often more distrustful than those with the prisoners[20].

This change can also be explained, at least in Canada, by a shift in the federal correctional agenda beginning in the late 1980s. This new era, euphemistically referred to by one author as the "medical model redux"[21], borrowed heavily from criminological research for 'efficient' treatment strategies and means of predicting which prisoners required which rehabilitative programs. This correctional strategy fit perfectly with the risk assessment and risk management framework of actuarial justice that was to emerge in the 1990s. Prisoners were now immersed in 'correctional programs' that were predicated on cognitive thinking skills deemed necessary for their moral development. The prison regime became one in which prisoners were regularly engaged with program officers and their respective assigned correctional officers, the latter of which are expected to perform social work duties with their charges. The great divide between prisoners and correctional officers narrowed further, and the cohesiveness among prisoners frayed. The 'common sense' factor articulated in this description intimates the irrepressible human factor in relationships between officers and prisons.

This tension between the spoken and unspoken expectations of the officers to maintain strict social distance from prisoners was initially explored in the first organisational prison reforms beginning in the 1960s. Research shows how officers would wrestle with the conflict between their personhood and their role.[22] Prisoners also experience the ambiguity of the roles and individual integrity.

These observations resonate with recent prison research, which has challenged the stereotypical notion that prisoners have different norms and values than do correctional officers.[23] With these comments on the social setting of prison in mind, I will now introduce research findings on the inmate disciplinary system in Mission Institution.

---

20 D. Duffee, "The Correction Officer Subculture and Organizational Change", in R.R. Ross (ed.), *Prison Guard/Correctional Officer: The Use and Abuse of the Human Resources of Prisons* (Toronto: Butterworths, 1981) 292.

21 S. Duguid, *Can Prisons Work? The Prisoner as Object and Subject in Modern Corrections* (Toronto: University of Toronto Press, 2000).

22 B.M. Cormier, *The Watcher and the Watched* (Plattsburgh, N.Y.: Tundra Books, 1975) 223.

23 C. Hemmens and J.W. Marquart, "Friend or Foe? Rage, Age, and Inmate Perceptions of Inmate–Staff Relations", in M.K. Stohr and C. Hemmens (eds.), *The Inmate Prison Experience* (Upper Saddle River, N.J.: Pearson Education Inc., 2004).

4 Prison Discipline, Discretion and Authority

The above discussion shows that laws (taken as a complex of rules and regulations) are in place to regulate the prison. Recent prison studies indicate that correctional officers can achieve regulation through relationships with prisoners. Although correctional officers can be seen as 'law enforcement' officers, a belief in a full–blown 'rule following or compliance model' would give too much importance to a rather legalistic view according to which behaviour is rule–driven.[24] The regulatory aspirations of an imperative, top–down conception of law already appear as difficult to attain. Yet let us now look at data on the inmate disciplinary system in Mission Institution. These will further support the presence of what can be called 'the human factor' in the use of inmate discipline.

4.1 Discretionary Rule–Enforcement

Mission Institution was built in the late 1970s according to the living unit model, which later on had to make place for the unit management model, still in force at the time of the study. This medium–security prison had a capacity for 230 prisoners, yet the daily average population in 2000 was 278 prisoners – an indication of overcrowding. As for the sentence profile of Mission Institution's population, according to the Offender Management System the day population on 19 February 2001 comprised 287 prisoners, 93 of them (32.4 %) serving sentences under six years; 53 (18.5%) six to ten years; 19 (6.6%) 11 to 15 years; seven (2.4%) 16 to 20 years; 12 (4.2 %) over 20 years; and 103 (35.9 %) of the prisoners were doing life.

In Mission Institution, a differential reliance on the disciplinary system could be noted. In 2000, with an average stock of 278 prisoners, a total of 638 disciplinary charges were registered.[25] After scoring the 638 charges per prisoner, I found that practically every prisoner (87.05 %) had been charged during the last year. Further specification brought some interesting discrepancies to the surface. Thirty–five prisoners (12.58 %) each had a minimum of five charges; their sum total of charges slightly surpassed 40 % of the total of charges (265 or 41.53 %). A small group of six prisoners (2.16 %) each had ten or more charges and together totalled 86 charges (13.48 %).

Similar results were found for charging staff members. Here the corrected database had to be used. The 588 disciplinary charges were laid by 130 officers. Thirteen charging officers worked in other institutions, but along with the transfer of prisoners, their disciplinary charges followed and were further dealt with in

---

24 A. Liebling and D. Price, "Prison Officers and the Use of Discretion", in L. Gelsthorpe and N. Padfield (eds.), *Exercising Discretion. Decision–making in the criminal justice system* (Cullompton: Willan Publishing, 2003) 88.

25 Due to a number of incorrect entries in the Offender Management System, it was not always possible to retrieve the charging officer's name. The complete database comprised 638 disciplinary charges, while a corrected one contained 588 charges.

Mission Institution. After correction, 117 officers (out of a total of 229 personnel, or 51.09 %) had laid a total of 558 disciplinary charges in 2000. Here even stronger discrepancies can be found than in the case of charged inmates. Forty staff members (17.90 %) laid a total of 418 charges (74.91 %). Among them, a small group of ten COs (4.37 %) had filed a disproportionate amount of 219 disciplinary charges (39.25 %).

One possible explanation for the different reliance of staff on the disciplinary process could be the intensity of contact with prisoners; that is, line staff could be expected to charge more often than administrative or other personnel. This hypothesis was explored during 19 in–depth interviews with line staff. If a differential use of the disciplinary system could be found there, it would suggest that differences in charging had little to do with the intensity of contact with prisoners. Together, the 19 interviewed COs had laid 103 charges in 2000. Seven of the 19 interviewed staff members had not charged anyone at all in 2000; another seven COs had filed between one and four disciplinary charges, and the other five had charged prisoners nine times or more in 2000, totalling 77 disciplinary charges. This already seems to suggest that the intensity of contact with prisoners hardly mattered in writing up disciplinary charges.

Another way to explain the disproportionate use of charges would be the presence of drugs and other items related to the informal economy. All staff in the interviews said that they would charge for drugs or other contraband. If that is the case, then the discrepancies in their use of charges are perhaps caused by a difference in the 'informal economy' between the different units, so that a limited number of line staff would more often come into contact with prisoners using or dealing drugs. There were no indications for this explanation. In fact, drugs were readily available in Mission Institution. This was well–known among all levels of the prison personnel. For example, during several meetings, management estimated the occasional to regular involvement of approximately 75 % of the prisoners in drug taking and dealing.

Part of the disproportionate use in charges between COs can be explained by job–related activities. The best example is provided by the urinalysis officer who has to charge every prisoner who refuses to provide a urine sample or who tests positive for drugs. He laid 55 charges in 2000. Apart from his job, there is only one other job position likely to increase the number of charges. The 'yard shack' officer, the CO who controls the movement of prisoners going to the correctional industry complex (CORCAN) or to the kitchen and back, might also, by the very nature of his job, encounter more situations where he has to lay a charge. Yet these are the only two job positions that might stand out in terms of charges. So this track also stops at a dead end in the search for an explanation.

One indication for the different charging behaviour surfaced in the interviews. COs indicated that inexperienced staff are more likely to lay a charge. Experienced staff draw more on other methods of dealing with problematic situations. An interview extract follows:

[This CO has joined CSC fairly recently. He has been a CO for approximately 1.5 years. During the interview, we were talking about how to deal with problems and disciplinary infractions. He mentioned having laid one charge for being disrespectful last year.]

> Q: In the case of the charge for being disrespectful, how did you first try to solve that problem? What did you do?
>
> A: It was my first week and I did not know how to deal with the situation. [...]

As they become socialised in the workforce of COs, most of them reduce their reliance on the formal disciplinary process. Yet this does not fully explain the differences among staff in resorting to formal disciplinary charges. In informal discussions with prisoners, staff and management, and in nine interviews with staff, the point came up that some staff are more rule–oriented than others. One interviewed staff member said some COs were being called 'Charge–X' (instead of CX or CO).[26]

The fact that officers differentially use the disciplinary process thus brings some broader considerations into the equation. Some of the early sociological studies of prisons presented the prison as a social setting torn in two parts. Erving Goffman, in his otherwise very interesting study *Asylums*, represented staff and inmates as two rather monolithic social groups.[27] It was Sykes who first identified certain "cracks in the monolith". Sykes noticed that staff power is often "corrupted": "the guard frequently shows evidence of having been 'corrupted' by the captive criminals over whom he stands in theoretical dominance".[28] Regulation, in this view, can only be achieved by sometimes looking the other way, by making "small accommodations" in order to avoid tensions and to reach a kind of equilibrium, a social stability which is constantly debated, contested, challenged, namely an equilibrium which is actively achieved.[29]

The 'defects of total power' of prison staff together with the above evidence indicate the existence of discretionary rule–enforcement. Discretion, in this contribution limited to the enforcement of formal disciplinary provisions, is "a critical element at almost every point in our criminal justice system".[30] As one commentator writes, "[f]ew terms have as important a place in legal discourse as 'discre-

---

26 In the slang of the prison personnel, a CO was called a CX.

27 E. Goffman, *l.c.*

28 G.M. Sykes, *l.c.*, 54.

29 *E.g.*, the discussion in A. Bottoms and R. Sparks, "How is Order in Prisons Maintained?", in A. Liebling (ed.), *Security, Justice and Order in Prison: Developing Perspectives* (Cambridge: University of Cambridge, 1997) 19.

30 B. Atkins and M. Pogrebin, "Introduction: Discretionary Decision–Making in the Administration of Justice", in B. Atkins and M. Pogrebin (eds.), *The Invisible Justice System. Discretion and the law* (Cincinnati: Anderson Publishing Co., 1978) 1.

tion'".[31] While some see discretion as an "unfettered choice whether to act, and often how to act, in a given case"[32], most often

> discretion refers to the freedom, power, authority, decision or leeway of an official, organisation or individual to decide, discern or determine to make a judgment, choice or decision, about alternative courses of action or inaction.[33]

Discretion always implies interpretation[34] and choice. The use of discretion is situated in the context of a power relationship in which one has the power to decide over what happens with the other.[35] That latter aspect can be seen as having the authority over somebody, which, as Paul Ricœur once outlined, carries at its heart a dissymetric or hierarchical relation and brings with it the power to command.[36]

4.2 Discretion and Authority

As prison research has evidenced, the central dynamics of the prison are those found in the relationships between the dominant players, the prisoners and the prison officers. "What 'goes on' in prison goes on primarily through relationships. [...] They frame, inform, constrain and facilitate staff and prisoner behaviour".[37] For the purposes of this specific discussion, it is the nature of this relationship that is significant:

> Living in prison means losing control over much of one's life. Personal autonomy is replaced by the requirement that the individual obey the commands of correctional staff. Inmate–staff relations thus comprise a crucial aspect of the institutional experience, and have been the subject of correctional research since the 1930s.[38]

The prescribed inequality of the relationships between prisoners and officers in this observation is one based on authority and law. In the observed discretionary rule–enforcement, the power relationships between staff and prisoners are of great importance. If "cracks in the monolith" are made *in order to* keep order and regu-

---

31 G.C. Christie, "An Essay on Discretion", *Duke Law Journal* 1986, *35*, 747.

32 A. Rosett, "Discretion, Severity and Legality in Criminal Justice", in B. Atkins and M. Pogrebin (eds.), *The Invisible Justice System. Discretion and the law* (Cincinnati: Anderson Publishing Co., 1978) 25.

33 L. Gelsthorpe and N. Padfield, "Introduction", in L. Gelsthorpe and N. Padfield (eds.), *Exercising Discretion. Decision–Making in the Criminal Justice System and Beyond* (Devon, Willan Publishing, 2003) 3.

34 Liebling and Price identify three sources of discretion: 1) the wording of rules themselves; 2) the situations to which the rules will apply; and 3) the official purposes guiding an organisation. (A. Liebling and D. Price, *The Prison Officer* (s.l.: *Prison Service Journal*, 2001) 116–118.)

35 G.C. Christie, *l.c.*, 778.

36 P. Ricœur, "Le paradoxe de l'autorité", in P. Ricœur (ed.), *Le juste 2* (Paris: Éditions Esprit, 2001) 107.

37 A. Liebling, D. Price and C. Elliott, "Appreciative Inquiry and Relationships in Prison", *Punishment & Society* 1999, *1*, 72.

38 B.M. Cormier, *l.c.*

late the prison, then this suggests that there might be different bases of power on which prison officers can draw.

According to the 'legitimate authority' accorded to COs as State functionaries, a strict adherence to the rules and regulations could be expected (although even such a strict compliance would not necessarily preclude discretionary (re)actions). The brief analysis of laying charges seems to suggest that some staff do not draw exclusively on their legitimate authority.

Some staff more often file disciplinary charges, a task for which they have legitimate authority, while most of the staff members who also share that authority, seldom rely on it. As the figures show, slightly more than half of all staff members laid a charge in 2000. Some staff with relatively long work experience had hardly ever filed a disciplinary charge.[39] Consequently, the existence of other power bases or types of authority can be presumed. This would imply that the law is not the only resort in the regulation of the prison.

One important impetus in discretionary rule–enforcement related to the official purposes guiding Mission Institution. Management at Mission Institution actively encouraged line staff to use their social skills as a means to regulate and control the prison. This was known as 'dynamic security', which is exerted through

> ongoing interaction, beyond observation, between correctional officers and inmates, working with and speaking with inmates, making suggestions, providing information, and, in general, being proactive.[40]

Most of the staff talked to during the research recognised the importance of communicating with prisoners and resolving problems at the lowest level possible. As noted, some COs at first charged prisoners out of inexperience, but once they had socialised into the workforce of prison staff, they came to identify the virtues of regulating through another means: they dealt with situations relationally. An example:

> Q: Do you think you often charge?
>
> A: I think there's a number of things that... Like, you could charge every shift if you wanted to. Certainly. There will be people here inter–unit visiting today, right. So, you know...
>
> Q: So, what makes you decide not to charge them?
>
> A: Well, you know... I believe a lot of things can be handled relationally. [...] It also depends on what you want to bring on yourself. [...] But I think that if the situation calls for one, then you write one. But with the little things, that you can handle in a different way, I don't think so. It matters what you want, right? I actually like that the guys come into the office and talk to you. That's okay. Obviously, when the rule is broken to an

---

[39] At one extreme, one interviewed staff member with 28 years working experience in corrections and related jobs said she had never filed a charge during the 13 years she was working in Mission Institution. Informal discussions with prisoners indicated that she was really appreciated, something she was well aware of. On the other hand, she had some problems with other staff, by whom she was referred to as a "con–lover".

[40] C.T. Griffiths and A. Cunningham, *Canadian Corrections* (Scarborough: Thomson Learning, 2000) 139.

> extreme point, I will write up a charge over that. But some guys are easy off the tier, just by talking to them. [...] Well, everybody has different ways of doing the job, right?

A further consideration on authority came up by looking at the nature of the disciplinary charges. The nature of charges is defined as follows: the unit manager designates the charge, both in terms of seriousness and in terms of the subsection of s. 40 CCRA. When a charge is written up, the charging officer gives his/her advice about the designation. The advice of the charging COs was (practically) always followed.

A database of 1998 and 1999 was put together, so that the designation of the charges could also be compared. Table 1 shows the number of disciplinary charges and their designation according to subsection. As can be seen in the table, the amount of charges slightly fluctuates, as does the number of charges per subsection. Some striking similarities came to the fore, particularly when looking at the categories of charges which represented 5% or more of the total of charges in a given year. Four subgroups of charges could be identified: 1) authority–related charges (subsections a, f and r); 2) charges related with the *sub rosa* economy of the prisoners (subsections i, j and k); 3) violence–related charges (subsection h); and 4) other charges. It can be observed that in Mission Institution, authority–related charges represented an important part of the total amount of disciplinary charges per year, at least for three consecutive years: authority–related charges reached a total of 201 charges (30.55 %) in 1998, 281 (38.39 %) in 1999 and 247 (38.71 %) in 2000. In 2000, charges designated under subsection (a) of s. 40 CCRA represented 15 % of the total amount of charges. An example from a charge comment:

> This inmate moved ahead of the yellow line prior to the early meal line bell. This inmate has been warned before and was given the option of returning behind the line when the direct order was given [charge designated as minor].

For an outsider, not familiar with the subtle dynamics in prison, this charge comment might have something alien to it. An adult male is being charged for, literally, crossing a line. Yet there is more to the above than first meets the eye. The charge in the example was written near noon, when all prisoners wait at the entrance of the dining hall. For the prisoner, once he crossed the line, given the symbolic side of 'giving in' to a CO in front of (almost) the entire prisoner population, he could hardly get back without losing face. The charge comment can also be seen as a discussion about (or rather, a contestation of) the rules, in which the CO first tried to deal informally with the transgression of this seemingly pitiful rule, but, after finding out he could not get the prisoner to comply, he resorted to another power base, his legitimate power to have prisoners obey. His authority was reaffirmed by charging the prisoner. Since the prisoner stood his ground until he received a disciplinary charge, he avoided a public humiliation in front of the others.

Table 8.1 Designated Charges at Mission Institution for the years 1998, 1999 and 2000

s. 40 CCRA Subsection		1998 Freq.	%	1999 Freq.	%	2000 Freq.	%
Valid	**A**	**56**	**8.510638**	**83**	**11.3388**	**96**	**15.04702**
	B	3	0.455927	6	0.819672	10	1.567398
	C	11	1.671733	2	0.273224	5	0.783699
	D	5	0.759878	2	0.273224		
	E	4	0.607903	3	0.409836	3	0.470219
	F	**44**	**6.68693**	**70**	**9.562842**	**56**	**8.777429**
	G			2	0.273224		
	H	**34**	**5.167173**	19	**2.595628**	**35**	**5.485893**
	I	**88**	**13.37386**	**116**	**15.84699**	**70**	**10.97179**
	J	**135**	**20.51672**	**130**	**17.75956**	**162**	**25.39185**
	K	**76**	**11.55015**	**85**	**11.61202**	**66**	**10.34483**
	L	**82**	**12.46201**	**76**	**10.38251**	**36**	**5.642633**
	M	9	1.367781	4	0.546448		
	N	1	0.151976				
	O	1	0.151976				
	P	3	0.455927				
	Q					1	0.15674
	R	**101**	**15.34954**	**128**	**17.48634**	**95**	**14.89028**
	S			2	0.273224	1	0.15674
	Total	653	99.24012	728	99.45355	636	99.68652
Missing	System	5	0.759878	4	0.546448	2	0.31348
Total		658	100	732	100	638	100

SPSS 10.0 (subsections: see Appendix 2)
Mission Institution 1998: n=658; 1999: n=732; 2000: n=638

As for subsection (r), close to 15 % of all charges were laid for wilfully disobeying a written rule governing the conduct of inmates. To some extent, this provision overlaps with disobeying a direct order from an officer, especially when the CO has to enforce the rules.

Further data was gathered to compare these findings with other institutions (see Table 2). All federal institutions in British Columbia with a medium or maximum security regime were contacted (four in total). Due to invalid data of the William Head Institution, a comparison could only be made with three other federal prisons of the same province. Two medium–security prisons, Matsqui and Mountain Institution, and the only maximum–security prison of B.C., Kent Institution, provided a database with all registered disciplinary charges in 2000.

Table 8.2 The Designation of Disciplinary Charges at Kent, Matsqui and Mountain Institutions

s. 40 CCRA		Kent 2000		Matsqui 2000		Mountain 2000	
		Freq.	%	Freq.	%	Freq.	%
Valid	**A**	**181**	**20.40586**	**65**	**8.004926**	**74**	**11.04477**
	C	**47**	**5.29876**	10	1.231527	8	1.194029
	F	**95**	**10.71026**	**133**	**16.37931**	**103**	**15.37313**
	H	**84**	**9.470124**	14	1.724138	10	1.492537
	I	**79**	**8.906426**	**175**	**21.55172**	**64**	**9.552238**
	J	**80**	**9.019166**	**126**	**15.51724**	**177**	**26.41791**
	K	23	2.59301	**43**	**5.295567**	**35**	**5.223881**
	L	41	4.622322	**71**	**8.743842**	**55**	**8.208955**
	M	**79**	**8.906426**	29	3.571429	4	0.597014
	R	**157**	**17.70011**	**130**	**16.00985**	**128**	**19.10447**
	Total	882	99.4363				
Missing	System	5	0.563698				
Total		**887**	**100**	**812**	**100**	**670**	**100**

SPSS 10.0

Only the subsections of groups 1, 2, and 3 are presented in the table. The totals at the bottom include the rest of the categories. (Average population: Kent Inst.: 267; Matsqui Inst.: 302; Mountain Inst.: 327)

In comparing the disciplinary charges of Mission Institution with those of the three other institutions, only slight differences can be observed. It seems as if the above identified categories are also of major importance in these three prisons. As for the authority–related charges, particularly Kent Institution scored high. Such findings corroborate intuitions on rule–enforcement and rule–compliance. In the data for 2000, authority–related disciplinary charges in the maximum–security prison represented nearly half (48.82 %) of all 887 charges. This could imply that the rules, regulations, and the authority of staff were more contested; that the 'accommodations' or 'corruptions' were not as far–reaching as in the case of Mission Institution; and that the regulation of Kent Institution was perhaps more based on a rule–enforcement model due to its population and/or regime.

The two other prisons had a relatively comparable percentage of authority–related charges, with 40.39 % of all charges in Matsqui and 45.52 % in Mountain Institution. As medium–security prisons, their percentages of authority–related charges are situated between, on the one end, those at Mission Institution, and, on the other, those at Kent Institution. Further study should provide answers as to the power bases used in these institutions, yet as a hypothesis, links between the modes of regulation by staff and the regime of these prisons could be suggested.

The above data also suggest that staff regulate the prison based on different power bases. This lines up with earlier studies, such as those of Hepburn, who concluded that "legitimate power remains as a solid basis of the guards' authority", while other power bases provide additional resources.[41] As far as the quantitative data is concerned, there is, of course, a caveat here. Authority–related charges only show one side of the coin; that is, they show that some prison officers seek to uphold the rules by (more or less) strictly enforcing them. These numbers do not give much information about the under–enforcement of the rules. This will not be elaborated on further in this chapter.

To round out this discussion, it can be concluded that, while discretion allows some COs to under–enforce the rules, the "legitimate authority" of any staff member remains present, as if a kind of substrate of power on which one can draw when other resources tend to fail. This could explain why staff, as reported in several interviews, feel as if they "lose [their] authority" whenever a prisoner is acquitted from a disciplinary charge: it might "undermine [their] authority".

5 Conclusion: The Disciplinary System as a Regulatory Resource

The above already presents a more complex picture of regulation, in which the law (the set of rules and regulations) serves as a 'resource' and provides COs a base of power on which they can rely. The least that can be said is that the high expectations vis–à–vis the law face substantial challenges and limits. Some of these have been touched upon in the above, while others remained untouched in this chapter. As was outlined in the introduction, the objective was modest: a discussion of the inmate disciplinary system, starting from the regulatory function of the law. Once the scope is broadened and other functions of the law are more explicitly taken into view, the picture becomes even more complex.

If law was a singularly sufficient tool for the regulation of the prison in Canada, the volume of prison–related jurisprudence[42] that has been generated both before and since the invocation of the CCRA would not exist. It is not uncommon that such jurisprudence follows from cases related to tensions between the legal protection of prisoners and the regulatory objectives of the prison.

There is a distance between the Correctional Service of Canada's "Mission Statement" and day–to–day life in prisons, "between the rhetoric and the reality, the ideology and the practice, the talk and the walk".[43] What emerges is a picture of how a top–down conception of the law runs amok when confronted with the sociological realities at work in a particular prison. What is illustrated is how rule–enforcement has its own dynamics, with rules and regulations imbued with meanings by concrete social actors (in this case, COs and prisoners) situated in particular social settings. The meaning of rules and regulations thus are, at least partially,

---

[41] J.R. Hepburn, "The Exercise of Power in Coercive Organizations: A Study of Prison Guards", *Criminology* 1985, *23*, 161.

[42] See, for key examples, www.canadianprisonlaw.com and www.justicebehindthewalls.net

[43] M. Jackson, *Justice Behind the Walls: Human Rights in Canadian Prison* (Vancouver, BC: Douglas & McIntyre, 2002) 43.

to be found in their use – a rather more 'open–textured' and bottom–up conception of the law.

In view of the above, CSC's corporate management strategy of "100 % compliance to 100 % of the policies 100 % of the time" then receives an awkward twist. There is a gap between the 'rule–following and compliance' model which CSC adheres to and the sociological realities of the prison. This gap lies in the regulation of the prison, where CSC adopts a legalistic stance: to regulate everything through policies and new rules. While admirable in the respect for law, this approach is compounded by the fact that every newly concerning incident that occurs in the system usually results in the generation of further policy to govern even more particular aspects of prison life. Policy and law, then, grow incrementally with each new curveball detected, until the prison officers' thresholds of policy knowledge are surpassed by the increasing volume and changes in correctional policy. The use of discretion by prison officers in regulating social life of prison, then, seems even more inevitable…

Chapter 9 – Criminal Law, Victims, and the Limits of Therapeutic Consequentialism

"By repairing the harm to victims,
we're helping the whole of society heal (...)
The betterment of victims equals
the betterment of the whole society"[1]

Tom Daems

1 Introduction

In the 1971 cult movie *A Clockwork Orange*, the main character Alexander de Large is thrown into prison after a night of excessive *ultraviolence*. In 'normal' circumstances, the regular night–outs with his buddies are limited to beating and raping helpless victims, yet this time Alex killed a woman by giving her a fatal blow to the forehead with a gigantic artificial penis. Alex is sentenced to fourteen years imprisonment. After spending two years behind bars, he hears rumours spreading in the prison about a new kind of treatment which could in a fortnight cure criminals of their criminal tendencies. Alex takes the opportunity to volunteer as a guinea pig for the new aversion therapy. An experimental substance 'No. 114' is pumped into his veins which makes him feel miserable. Next, Alex is strapped into a chair in a movie theatre and brutal scenes of violence, rape, and nazi–terror are projected on the screen. The conditioning sessions prove to be highly successful: nausea and vomiting prevent him from relapsing in his old habits.

Movies such as *A Clockwork Orange* ridicule and satirise some penal practices which prevailed at the time, namely treatment programmes which promised to 'cure' criminals and prepare them for return in due course to the majority of (presumably) law–abiding citizens. At that time, movie director Stanley Kubrick did not pay any attention to what might have happened to the relatives of the murder victim. How did they cope with the loss of somebody close to them? Were they able to resume their lives? How did they feel about the way in which they were treated by police officers, prosecutors, and judges? Were they in need of therapy to recover from trauma or to alleviate post–traumatic stress symptoms? And so on. Obviously, to give the movie a victimological touch would have resulted in less interesting cinema; it would have directed viewers' attention away from a much

---

[1] Paul McCold, director of research for the International Institute for Restorative Practices, quoted in A.J. Porter, "The Jerry Lee Program Research on Restorative Justice: Promising Results", *Restorative Practices E–Forum* 13 April 2006 (www.iirp.org, consulted 31 August 2006).

more appealing and exotic topic: the dystopia of a brain–washing State and the painful consequences of an obsession with order, conformity, and lawfulness. Yet, at that time, victims were not only of minor importance to movie–makers; also in society at large they hardly received any attention, notwithstanding some early victimological activity at the fringes of criminology. Victims, as some rare voices complained at that time, seemed largely to be forgotten.

By 2008 much has changed. Since the 1970s, victim surveys (which ask people about their victimisations and their experiences) have started to compile and map the impact of crime and the views of crime victims on a broad range of topics. This avalanche of numbers on victims has been complemented by qualitative research into their experiences and their dealings with the aftermath of crime. As such, this newly emerging focus on victims was able to provide an increasingly detailed picture of the other side of crime. Moreover, at the same time – and partly coinciding with the former – a victims' movement (or better: victim *movements*, since they draw their support from different corners of society ranging from feminist critiques of the patriarchal order to conservative preoccupations with getting tough on criminals) started to raise its voice and campaigned to turn victims' personal troubles into public issues, such as victims' rights and services.[2]

This reform movement, like any other, explores the limits of criminal law. Reformers, by definition, perceive the existing system to be inadequate: either it fails in doing the things it claims to do (and so we need to change the way it operates), or it should start doing other things (and so we need to change its ends). By looking at crime from different perspectives and the multiple reactions it provokes, reformers are able to highlight new, previously unseen, facets of the crime problem. As a result they question why and how we punish. Taken–for–granted reasons for justifying penalties may suddenly appear invalid, or other reasons, related to new aspects (such as victimisation), are added.

Sometimes this reform activity aims at the formulation of new 'good consequences'; that is, the criminal justice system needs to incorporate certain ends that are deemed to be desirable, goods it should try to achieve. This is what philosophers of punishment call 'utilitarian' or 'consequentialist' reasoning. If we punish on the basis of such good consequences, so the argument goes, we will be able to punish and go to bed without running the risk of suffering from sleepless nights: the deliberate suffering of the punishee turns out to be justified. This consequentialist type of penal thinking will be at the centre of this chapter. In the next section we step back a number of centuries in order to demonstrate how a penal reform movement started to question prevailing ways of thinking about punishment. With the help of the insights of a new scientific discipline called 'criminology', it aimed to instrumenalise late 19th century criminal law in order to make it more effective in the fight against crime, *inter alia* by trying to 'cure' criminals. In the third and fourth sections we return to the present. The plight of the crime victim poses new challenges for contemporary criminal law. It will be argued that a new

---

2 See *e.g.* R.I. Mawby and S. Walklate, *Critical Victimology: International Perspectives* (London: Sage, 1994); P. Rock, *Constructing Victims' Rights. The Home Office, New Labour, and Victims* (Oxford: Oxford University Press, 2004).

kind of consequentialism is in the making which strives towards 'healing victims' and which avails itself of a therapeutic language to describe what these desired 'good consequences' are: closure, emotional restoration, trauma recovery, reducing post–traumatic stress, and so on. The fifth section will explore the limits of this form of victim–oriented therapeutic consequentialism.

2 Curing Criminals

Contrary to some textbook histories of criminology which situate the origins of the discipline in the 18th century when influential thinkers such as Beccaria and Bentham developed their ideas on crime and criminal justice, more careful criminologists hold another opinion. The underlying assumption of offenders being rational and gifted with an untainted free will formed the main obstacle for the birth of an *empirical* science of the criminal:

> They made no general distinction between the characteristics of criminals and non–criminals, and had no conception of research on crime and criminals as a distinctive form of inquiry.[3]

In order to develop an empirical approach, our ways of framing the problem of crime had to change fundamentally. The idea that criminals were different from the law–abiding majority was crucial in this respect. Cesare Lombroso's 'born criminal' was the strongest manifestation of this difference and, importantly, provided the first building–block for a deterministic theory of crime (criminal tendencies being innate) that would run against prevailing liberal legal thinking.

The new ways of looking at crime all set themselves against (in varying degrees) the free will assumption of classical liberal thought. Notions like 'pathology' and 'cure' entered the debate on the causes of crime and how to tackle it.[4] This fuelled the hope that, with the help of the human sciences, it would be possible to arrive at a proper diagnosis which, in turn, would lead to an effective remedy of the problem at hand. This remedy would be targeted at the criminal individual and his biological, psychological, and genetic make–up. These two elements combined and added up to an optimistic belief in the possibility of changing human beings and bringing them back to norm–conforming behaviour.

What kind of benefits, what sort of 'good consequences' might all this intellectual activity bring in its wake? In fact, it informed a reform movement that aimed at instrumentalising criminal law in order to fight crime more effectively, in particular (especially in its early stages) by reducing recidivism, namely by rehabilitating or incapacitating those who transgressed the criminal law. Throughout the

---

3 D. Garland, "Of Crimes and Criminals: The Development of Criminology in Britain", in M. Maguire, R. Morgan and R. Reiner (eds.), *The Oxford Handbook of Criminology* (Oxford: Oxford University Press, 1994) 22.

4 D. Garland, *Punishment and Welfare. A History of Penal Strategies* (Aldershot: Gower, 1985); D.J. Rothman, *Conscience and Convenience. The Asylum and its Alternatives in Progressive America* (Boston: Little Brown, 1980).

20th century adaptations were made to the criminal justice system, for example for young, habitual, and mentally ill offenders. Criminologists speak of that period in terms of the 'rehabilitative era' – an epoch in the history of criminal justice and criminological thought which was preoccupied with 'rehabilitating' offenders. In the post World War Two period this approach to the problem of crime gained further impetus with the further development of the human sciences and the growth of *psy*–expertise.

From the 1970s onwards, however, a powerful critique started to gain momentum. This critique attacked the treatment model on (at least) three different levels. First, a *theoretical* critique: the assumption of crime being a symptom of an underlying deficiency in the constitution of the criminal came under attack. Second, an *empirical* critique: evaluation research into treatment programmes gave a grim picture of results with respect to recidivism. Third, a *political* critique: sacrificing due process and legal protection to the rehabilitation ideology with its preference for indeterminate sentencing (keeping offenders in, as long as needed) was vehemently contested. The critique also entered popular culture by means of movies such as *A Clockwork Orange*, and Milos Forman's *One Flew over the Cuckoo's Nest*.

The critics, however, were not able to put the rehabilitation ideology definitely to sleep.[5] In fact, some of them had to acknowledge that treatment programmes can – and do – have positive effects. Martinson, for example, who in an often quoted article published in *The Public Interest* coined the catch–phrase 'nothing works' (a phrase that would reverberate throughout the world of criminal justice)[6], revised his original judgment on the empirical merits of treatment programmes five years later.[7] Yet, the critique coincided with, and formed part of, an emerging societal context which was becoming increasingly hostile to the idea of offenders being helpless victims of influences beyond their control.[8] In aetiological reasoning rational choice models were on the rise (theories built upon the assumption that offenders make rational cost–benefit analyses with respect to their behaviour) and words like 'responsibility', 'culpability' and 'retribution' (or 'just deserts') started to re–enter the criminal justice vocabulary. In this climate, the grand expectations of earlier times were lowered to more realistic proportions, targeting specific groups (e.g. sex offenders) and were being informed by the insights provided by an evidence–based 'what works' movement.

---

5 F.T. Cullen, "The Twelve People Who Saved Rehabilitation: How the Science of Criminology Made a Difference – The American of Society of Criminology 2004 Presidential Address", *Criminology* 2005, *43*, 1–42.

6 R. Martinson, "What Works? – Questions and Answers About Prison Reform", *The Public Interest* 1974, 22–54.

7 R. Martinson, "New Findings, New Views: A Note of Caution Regarding Sentencing Reform", *Hofstra Law Review* 1979, 243–258.

8 See D. Garland, *The Culture of Control* (Oxford; Oxford University Press, 2001).

3 Birth (and Death) of a Metaphor: Healing Victims

At the time when rehabilitative ideas and practices came under increasing attack, victims and victimisation started to receive more and more attention. The first experiments with victim surveys took place in the late 1960s in the United States. In 1972 they became institutionalised in the United States and ten years later in Britain. Victim surveys quickly went beyond the mere counting of unreported offences. They were used to explore a wide range of phenomena: the fear of crime, the geography of crime, the links between 'routine activities' and crime, attitudes towards the police, and the particular victimisation of women, the young, and the elderly.

Increasingly victims were asked what they themselves expected from the criminal justice system. One of the core insights was that victims often experience 'secondary victimisation', the pain of having to deal with an unresponsive and insensitive criminal justice system. Victimologists also found out that victims favour being informed properly, participating throughout the criminal justice process, receiving respectful and just treatment, restoration, and so on.[9] Advocates for victim rights and services translated these needs into reform proposals to make the criminal justice system more victim–oriented. This concern for the plight of victims of crime is often formulated by means of metaphorical language. According to the Oxford Dictionary, the word 'metaphor' means "the application of a word or phrase to something that it does not apply to literally, in order to indicate a comparison with the literal usage".[10] One of the most common metaphors used by victimologists[11] and reformers[12] with respect to victimisation is the metaphor of 'healing victims'. Victims, in one way or another, need to be *healed*: their suffering needs to be alleviated, they need to be dealt with in such a way that their painful experiences soften, wither away, that they become whole again, are enabled to recover from trauma or transform, and such like.

[9] See *e.g.* E.A. Fattah, *Understanding Criminal Victimization* (Scarborough: Prentice–Hall, 1997); T. Peters, "Slachtofferschap: probleemanalyse, sociale en penale reacties", in J. Goethals and T. Peters (eds.), *De achterkant van criminaliteit* (Leuven: Leuven University Press, 1993) 5–90.

[10] E. Pollard (ed.), *The Oxford Paperback Dictionary* (Oxford: Oxford University Press, 4th ed., 2000) 506.

[11] *E.g.* A.J. Lurigio and P.A. Resnick, "Healing the Psychological Wounds of Criminal Victimization", in A.J. Lurigio, W.G. Skogan and R.C. Davis (eds.), *Victims of Crime: Problems, Policies and Programs* (Newbury Park: Sage Publications, 1990); E. Fattah, "Toward a Victim Policy Aimed at Healing, Not Suffering", in R. Davis, A. Lurigio and W. Skogan (eds.), *Victims of Crime* (Thousand Oaks: Sage Publications, 2nd ed., 1997) 257–272.

[12] For restorative justice (the reform movement which this chapter pays special attention to), references to the 'healing'–metaphor are countless. To get an impression, see K.M. Richards, "Unlikely Friends? Oprah Winfrey and Restorative Justice", *The Australian and New Zealand Journal of Criminology* 2005, *38*, 381–399. Richards dubs these discourses 'oprahfication', after the queen of the talkshow hosts, Oprah Winfrey.

In fact, metaphors can (and do) fulfil a critical function, for they challenge the *status quo*; in this case the *status quo* of a (perceived) offender–oriented criminal justice system. In times of crisis they stimulate the imagination. Reformers are constantly in search for an appealing and recognisable language that helps to increase public awareness of the perceived problem and that highlights the ways in which the problem needs to be solved. Metaphors offer a unified way of speaking and can be injected into easy slogans 'From X to Y', 'Not X, but Y!', 'The Road to Y!', 'Y!'.

Yet, metaphors are not always that beneficial or innocent. They also tend to oversimplify complex problems and may blind us to complex underlying issues.[13] In the remainder of this chapter, it will be argued that the 'healing'–metaphor actually is in the process of dying: the idea that 'it stands for something' has been lost. The metaphor has turned out to become something 'real', to be applied 'literally' and, therefore, stops being a metaphor. Healing victims, as I will try to demonstrate in the next section, tends to become a real objective, an emerging justification for penal intervention.

4 Strange Bed–Fellows? Restorative Justice and Capital Punishment

Restorative justice responses and capital punishment form part of two distinct families of criminal justice intervention which, when seen from a certain angle, seem to be diametrically opposed to each other. Restorative justice aims to provide a *constructive* answer to the problem of crime. By means of victim–offender mediation, family group conferencing, sentencing circles, and so on, it works towards a form of restoration, reparation, or reconciliation between victim and offender.[14] The death penalty on the other hand is, by definition, the summum of a *destructive* response to transgressions of the criminal law. The physical elimination of the offender, obviously, does not leave any room for speculations about a bright future in which society might live at peace with the reintegrated offender. Moreover, restorative justice literature often has an oppositional undertone. Advocates of restorative justice, especially in its early formative years, tended to distance their preferred criminal justice model from the reigning retributive criminal justice system. In polemical writing, the deficiencies of the latter and the advantages of the former were stressed. In other words, at first sight there seems to be a tremendous wall separating the two families – the 'constructive' and the 'destructive' – of criminal justice intervention.

Yet if we leave aside the normative optics which separate the 'good' responses to crime from the 'bad' for a moment, we might be able to probe restorative jus-

---

13 R. Foqué, "Het rechtsbedrijf. Een metafoor op drift?", *Justitiële Verkenningen* 1999, *25*, 10–25.

14 For a useful introduction, see J. Dignan, *Understanding Victims and Restorative Justice* (Maidenhead: Open University Press, 2005).

tice and capital punishment for similarities. This section will argue that both, when seen from the perspective of this chapter, are partly shaped as responses to a *similar* problem (how to provide an adequate response to the needs, desires and wishes of victims of crime) which is answered by having recourse to a *similar* vocabulary, a therapeutic vocabulary. This is not to argue that there is a kind of conspirational link or secret connection between the two. The interesting thing for the theme of this chapter, however, is how they both share a similar language when speaking about victims and when justifying their intervention. A closer look at the commonalities of the two forms of sanctioning, which in other respects are positioned at the opposite extremes of the penal continuum, might provide us with an indicator of the pervasiveness with which 'healing victims' comes to the fore in contemporary criminal justice discourse and practice.

4.1 Restorative Justice, Healing Victims

"Can Mediation Be Therapeutic for Crime Victims?": this is the title of a recent research article which was published by the *Canadian Journal of Criminology and Criminal Justice.*[15] In the paper the two authors explore to what extent restorative justice may help the 'healing process' of victims. They use 'therapeutic jurisprudence' as a framework to study a group of crime victims who participated in a victim–offender mediation programme in a large city in Quebec. The article takes an overly–empirical approach: does restorative justice help or hinder victims' recovery? The researchers explore themes such as victims' fear; whether participation in the programme helped them to put the event behind them; whether they benefited from meetings; whether they judged the process to be fair; whether they were satisfied with the procedure followed in their case. The results discussed in the article lead the authors, after considering the limitations of the study, to the conclusion that procedural justice facilitates 'healing' and that mediation has contributed to the victims' well–being.

This article is one recent example of how victims' needs start to enter the restorative justice research agenda in new – therapeutically imagined – ways. It inscribes itself in a new generation of empirical research on restorative justice where measuring positive effects on victims' well–being starts to occupy a central role. In early evaluation studies the satisfaction rate (To what extent are participants in a restorative programme satisfied with the experience?) was already a common tool to measure the success of restorative interventions which paid attention to victims' feelings. But now we seem to be witnessing a qualitative shift. Notions such as 'healing', 'closure', 'therapeutic effects', 'emotional restoration', 'reducing the sense of alienation', and such like, point to something different. Restorative justice in these recent reformulations is no longer merely about making or keeping all

---

[15] J.A. Wemmers and K. Cyr, "Can Mediation Be Therapeutic for Crime Victims? An Evaluation of Victims' Experiences in Mediation with Young Offenders", *Canadian Journal of Criminology and Criminal Justice* 2005, 527–544.

participants satisfied (a consumer logic), but also, and increasingly, about making victims feel better (a therapeutic logic).

American criminologist Lawrence Sherman, who plays a key role in these recent developments, pleaded for a new paradigm of 'emotionally intelligent justice' on the occasion of his 2002 Presidential Address to the American Society of Criminology:

> … a new window of opportunity is opening for criminology to reinvent justice, fueled by widespread dissatisfaction with current practices and their costs … . The time may be ripe for criminology to advance a new paradigm of justice, one that works far better than our muddled legacy of Bentham and Lombroso.[16]

Modern criminology needs to reinvent justice around the emotions of victims, offenders and society. The bulk of his address was devoted to restorative justice and its potential contributions to such a new paradigm. But he also suggested, *inter alia*, wider use of medical and nutritional programmes for offenders to improve their emotional state. Sherman quoted research on the successful use of Prozac for reducing violence or aggressive incidents and referred to a study which found that a daily dose of supplementary vitamins and minerals had a substantial effect on reducing disciplinary misconduct in prison.[17] "Is a world with more pharmacology and less prison better or worse than a world with more prison but less pharmacology?", he asks himself and the reader at the end of a section on "medical and nutrional programs".[18]

The interesting point in his address, when seen in light of the discussion on the historical roots of criminology in the second paragraph, is how he outlines a new mission for criminology which seems to provide ample space for victims' needs, yet which also, at the same time, redefines the ontology of the offender. The offender appears as an emotionally inadequate being. I will return to this latter point in section 5 where I discuss the limits of therapeutic consequentialism. At this point in the chapter I will further illustrate the ways in which restorative justice, in these recent reformulations, aims to address victims' needs along therapeutically imagined lines.

In her book *Repair or Revenge* Heather Strang, a close collaborator of Sherman, presents the results of her study on victim–oriented expectations and outcomes in relation to restorative justice conferencing. The study was conducted as part of a large empirical research programme on restorative justice, the so–called 'RISE project'.[19] The randomised design of RISE enabled Strang to com-

---

16 L.W. Sherman, "Reason for Emotion: Reinventing Justice with Theories, Innovations, and Research – The American Society of Criminology 2002 Presidential Address", *Criminology* 2003, *41*, 2.

17 *Ibid.*, 23.

18 *Ibid.*, 25.

19 'RISE' stands for 'Reintegrative Shaming Experiments' which started in 1995 in Canberra. It explicitly refers to the theory of reintegrative shaming of John Braithwaite. In an extremely influential book from 1989, Braithwaite argued that 'shame' is the missing element – the 'glue' – which is able to connect different criminological theories (labelling, subcultural, control, opportunity, and learning theories). In doing so, Braithwaite developed an ambitious general theory of crime with important policy implications: the key to tackle crime is

pare the experiences of 'court victims' (victims who were assigned to traditional court proceedings), with those of 'conference victims' (victims who were assigned to a restorative justice conference). In general, victims who participated in conferencing seemed to have better experiences. Conferencing turned out to be especially successful with respect to 'emotional restoration'. Levels of anger and anxiety were reduced. The fear of revictimisation was considerably lower than for court victims. Nearly four times as many conference victims received an apology.[20]

At this moment Strang is co–director of the The Jerry Lee Program on Randomized Controlled Experiments in Restorative Justice, a large–scale research programme based at the University of Pennsylvania, where Sherman is heading the Jerry Lee Center of Criminology.[21] The goal of the programme is to further develop evidence–based theory and policy on restorative justice. In a working paper the aim of the project is formulated as follows: "... to learn whether a new kind of justice can change people's lives for the better, with long–term effects."[22] Interestingly, the programme pays much attention to victims and how participating in restorative initiatives may change their lives for the better. The first research question following the above quote, goes as follows: "Can it cure the post–traumatic stress symptoms and improve the health of crime victims?" Somewhat further in the paper, in a section on 'Victim Effects', the question is further specified: "What are the long–term effects of restorative justice on crime victims' health, employment, happiness and lawfulness, and how long do these effects (if any) last?"[23]

It is not a coincidence that victims receive a good deal of attention in the programme and that measuring victim effects is mentioned first in the 'to do' list. The researchers conclude that benefits for victims are much more consistent than those related to offenders: the evidence related to reducing re–offending is found to be much less clear–cut. In a recently published paper they expressed the need to re-

---

shaming which reintegrates (as opposed to stigmatises). Braithwaite was the motivating force behind RISE and is a key figure in the international restorative justice movement. J. Braithwaite, *Crime, Shame and Reintegration* (Cambridge: Cambridge University Press, 1989).

20 H. Strang, *Repair or Revenge: Victims and Restorative Justice* (Oxford: Oxford University Press, 2002). See also H. Strang, "Justice for Victims of Young Offenders: The Centrality of Emotional Harm and Restoration", in G. Johnstone (ed.), *A Restorative Justice Reader. Texts, sources, context* (Cullompton: Willan Publishing, 2003); H. Strang and L.W. Sherman, "Repairing the Harm: Victims and Restorative Justice", *Utah Law Review* 2003, *15*, 15–42.

21 In a leaflet presenting the research programme and emphasising its scope, it is argued that "... the Jerry Lee Program has initiated a total of 12 RCTs [RCTs are randomised controlled trials] in restorative justice, and has been funded to undertake a total of 16 RCTs, making it the largest coordinated program of controlled experiments in the history of criminology", see: http://www.sas.upenn.edu/jerrylee/research/rj_jlc_rct.pdf (consulted: 31 August 2006).

22 L.W. Sherman and H. Strang (in collaboration with D.J. Woods, C.M. Angel, G.C. Barnes, N. Inkpen, D. Newbury–Birch and S. Bennett), *Restorative Justice: What We Know and How We Know It*, 2. See: http://www.sas.upenn.edu/jerrylee/research/rj_WorkingPaper.pdf (consulted: 31 August 2006).

23 *Ibid.*, 2 and 8.

spond to some scornful newspaper headlines. An Oxford University study which reported no crime–reducing effects of restorative justice (but neither any crime increase) in the Thames Valley area provoked headlines such as "Saying Sorry Does Not Work" and "Thugs Who Say Sorry Reoffend". Interestingly, the answer of the authors to these headlines was not to cite a long list of empirical studies which *do* find crime reducing effects. Instead they found it deplorable that none of those newspaper articles asked whether victims derived any benefit from the restorative process.[24] This move not only makes sense from a scientific point of view, given the benefits for victim are easier to measure and demonstrate, but also from a strategical point of view. A reform movement that aims to influence policy making needs to be able to adapt itself to changing circumstances, new research findings, and external demands. From that perspective it also makes more sense to explore further any potential benefits for victims of crime.

This exploration goes quite far. It has been suggested that the costs of crime should include emotional costs (victims' fear, anger, grievance, loss of trust) and medical costs (in part from post–traumatic stress symptoms ('PTSS') which include reduced immune function, higher rates of disease, greater use of medical services, higher mortality from cancer or cardiovascular disease).[25] These newly added dimensions to the crime cost figure refer to changing emotional states of victims and furthering trauma recovery. What is interesting for the theme of this chapter is not that new victim needs are being discovered – victimology has been mapping these for many years – but that arguments are now being put forward that formal reactions to crime *should* adequately respond to these needs. In other words, *new* elements, which are therapeutically imagined, are added to discussion of penal reform in order to argue that victims are not properly taken care of in the classical criminal justice system. That is, the limits of criminal law extend to new, formerly unimaginable, domains. For example, to argue that restorative conferencing is better at reducing PTSS[26] than the classical criminal justice system is not only an empirical statement, but also a normative one. It assumes that formal responses to crime *should* have low PTSS scores as one of their objectives – an objective they never had. This goes further than arguing that criminal justice agencies, in their dealings with crime victims, should be vigilant against causing secondary victimisation. The primary victimisation itself (the harm caused by the crime) becomes the target for remedial intervention. In fact, it is to move argu-

24 H. Strang, L. Sherman, C.M. Angel, D.J. Woods, S. Bennett, D. Newbury–Birch and N. Inkpen, "Victim Evaluations of Face–to–Face Restorative Justice Conferences: A Quasi–Experimental Analysis", *Journal of Social Issues* 2006, *62*, 282.

25 *Ibid.*, 281–282.

26 A.J. Porter, "Restorative Conferences Reduce Trauma from Crime, Study Shows", 2006, August 15th, www.iirp.org (consulted 31 August 2006). The article is devoted to a recent Ph. D. thesis by Caroline M. Angel which reports substantially lower levels of post–traumatic stress symptoms among victims who consented to participate in a restorative justice conference compared to those who did not. C. Angel, *Crime Victims Meet Their Offenders: Testing the Impact of Restorative Justice Conferences on Victims' Post–Traumatic Stress Symptoms* (University of Pennsylvania: Ph.D. Dissertation, 2005).

ments and objectives related to mental health care out of the therapist's office and into the criminal justice system.

4.2 Capital Punishment, Healing Victims

In a recent critique of restorative justice Annalise Acorn writes the following:

> No punitive system would presume to promise 'healing' to victims. Yet restorative justice entices victims with precisely such hopes. Concern for consumer protection seems to have been overlooked. There is no money–back guarantee if the healing doesn't happen.[27]

Acorn, a former restorative justice advocate who later became disenchanted with the whole movement, makes a number of interesting points in her book, even though she is not always giving a full account of the movement.[28] Yet, because her critique is exclusively directed at restorative justice, she fails to observe that, contrary to what she argues in the quote, punitive systems also promise to heal victims. In fact, the most punitive of sanctions, the death penalty, has been justified by having recourse to a similar kind of therapeutic language and a promise to 'heal victims'.

At the beginning of his book *When the State Kills*, Austin Sarat refers to a decision by US Attorney General Ashcroft to broadcast the execution of Timothy McVeigh who was found guilty of the 1995 Oklahoma City bombing which killed 168 people, by means of a CCTV network.[29] Ashcroft argued that victims and their relatives had a unique and compelling claim to witness the execution: watching him die came to be represented as a prerequisite for 'closure', a necessary condition for putting the victims' tragedy behind them.[30] In fact this way of reasoning also runs against an age–old belief that decent citizens should not be exposed to the 'spectacle of suffering', a belief that led to a gradual removal of the execution of a punishment (whether by death or imprisonment) out of the open view to behind closed doors.[31] The therapeutic imagination, however, makes it possible to invent new alleged benefits for victims to get closely involved with the ceremony of execution.

---

27 A. Acorn, *Compulsory Compassion: A Critique of Restorative Justice* (Vancouver: University of British Columbia Press, 2004) 67–68.

28 See J. Braithwaite, "Narrative and 'Compulsory Compassion'", *Law & Social Inquiry* 2006, *31*, 425–446.

29 Around 2000 victims were invited to witness the execution. In the end only 232 (or less than 12%) accepted the invitation. A journalist of the *Miami Herald* connected an interesting question to this observation: what does it say about the death penalty if more than 88% of those directly involved did not wish to witness an execution justified in their name? M.J. Castro, "We Kill for Vengeance, Not Closure and Justice", *Miami Herald*, 19 June 2001.

30 A. Sarat, *When the State Kills. Capital Punishment and the American Condition* (Princeton: Princeton University Press, 2002) xii.

31 S. Banner, *The Death Penalty: An American History* (Cambridge, Mass.: Harvard University Press, 2002); J. Pratt, *Punishment and Civilization: Penal Tolerance and Intolerance in Modern Society* (London: Sage, 2002).

Franklin Zimring argues that a kind of 'personal service symbolism' is at work in the American imagery of capital punishment:

> The death penalty ... is regarded as a policy intended to serve the interests of the victims of crime and those who love them, a personal rather than a political concern, an undertaking of government to serve the needs of individual citizens for justice and psychological healing.[32]

This emphasis on harm and victim psychology is a fairly recent phenomenon but has come to play a profound role in how capital punishment is nowadays pictured in the United States. Especially the term 'closure' has made impressive inroads in capital punishment talk. Prior to 1989 it did not appear in death penalty stories, but in 2001 more than 500 stories combined 'capital punishment' with 'closure'.[33]

According to Zimring three powerful functions are provided by the symbolic transformation of execution into a victim–service programme. First, it gives the horrifying process of human execution a positive impact that many citizens can identify with: closure, not vengeance. Second, this degovernmentalisation of the rationale for the death penalty means that citizens do not have to worry about executions as an excessive use of power by and for the government. When 'closure' is the major aim of lethal injections, the execution of criminals becomes another public service, like street cleaning or garbage removal, where the government is the servant of the community rather than its master. The third function of the transformation of execution into a victim service gesture is that it links the symbolism of execution to a long American history of community control of punishment.[34]

But victims and suffering not only appear at the end of the whole process with the execution of the culprit, they also have come to the fore during trial. In fact, a victim's suffering can be presented in different ways: psy–experts may testify in court, victims' experiences may be written down in reports which subsequently are presented in court, or victims themselves can testify orally in court about their suffering. The two latter forms are known as 'victim impact statements' ('VIS') and have a place in a range of Anglo–Saxon countries, and have recently also been introduced in the Netherlands.[35] Advocates of VIS argue that it can perform two main functions: an instrumental function, by influencing decision–making and affecting sentencing, and an expressive one, giving an opportunity for victims to express themselves regarding the impact of the crime. It is especially the latter which

---

32 F.E. Zimring, *The Contradictions of American Capital Punishment* (Oxford: Oxford University Press, 2003) 49.

33 *Ibid.*, 60.

34 *Ibid.*, 62.

35 See J.W. de Keijser and M. Malsch, "Is spreken zilver en zwijgen goud? Spreekrecht en het ontstemde slachtoffer", *Delikt en Delinkwent* 2002, *32,* 1–20; C. Kelk, "Slachtofferverklaringen in woord en geschrift", *Delikt en Delinkwent* 2003, *33*, 93–101; R. Kool and M. Moerings, "The Victim Has the Floor. The Victim's Right to Be Heard in Writing or Orally in the Dutch Courtroom", *European Journal of Crime, Criminal Law and Criminal Justice* 2004, *12*, 46–60.

is interesting here. It is argued that VIS has various 'therapeutic' benefits and helps victims' 'psychological healing' and 'reduce their trauma'.[36]

It is interesting to note that Erez, a long time advocate of VIS, explicitly refused to touch upon the link between VIS and capital punishment in a recent chapter where she discusses the advantages of VIS.[37] That link is a sensitive topic and probably makes VIS advocates a bit uncomfortable. At the penalty stage the available options are limited to death or life imprisonment, and an emotional testimony of how relatives of victims have suffered might tip the balance in favour of the first option. Legal scholars who are wary of too great a role for victims in capital cases have expressed deep worries about the implications of VIS in the wake of the US Supreme Court decision in *Payne v. Tennessee* in 1991. The case involved the killings of a young mother, Charisse Christopher, and her two–year–old daughter Lacie. Her little son Nicholas was stabbed. His grandmother testified in court about the devastating emotional impact this experience had on the little boy. In its ruling the Supreme Court allowed the admission of VIS in capital trials, thereby reversing its earlier case–law.[38] In critical commentary, that decision has variously been described as a "legitimisation of revenge"[39] and an "undifferentiated endorsement of harm as a sentencing factor."[40]

What we can observe, therefore, is how capital punishment, in the words of US Supreme Court Justice Scalia, needs to be "*responsive to suffering*".[41] It is here that, despite all the obvious differences, a parallel can be drawn with the discussion in section section 4.1. Both restorative responses (in their recent reformulations) and the death penalty (in its symbolic transformation) seem, to a certain extent, to be embodiments of a new kind of consequentialism in penal thinking. The

---

36 E. Erez, "Integrating a Victim Perspective in Criminal Justice Through Victim Impact Statements", in A. Crawford and J. Goodey (eds.), *Integrating a Victim Perspective Within Criminal Justice. International Debates* (Aldershot: Ashgate, 2000) 165–184.

37 E. Erez, "Integrating restorative justice principles in adversarial proceedings through victim impact statements", in E. Cape (ed.), *Reconcilable Rights? Analysing the Tension Between Victims and Defendants* (London: Legal Action Group Education and Service Trust Limited, 2004) 81, footnote 1. The reason she gives for not addressing the use of VIS in capital cases is a little too facile: "This article does not address the use of VIS in capital cases, which has attracted much of the opposition to the VIS in the United States. Most Western countries do not use death sentences as a penalty option." The simple fact that the death penalty is not an option in Western societies outside the US should not prevent a VIS advocate of engaging seriously with the reasons why so many scholars are sceptical of VIS *because of* its use in capital cases.

38 Four years earlier in *Booth v. Maryland* (1987) the majority of the Supreme Court found victim impact evidence to be unconstitutional under the Eighth Amendment's ban on 'cruel and unusual punishment'. Four reasons were given: (1) VIS create a substantial risk of prejudice; (2) the focus should be on the wrong, not the harm; (3) use of VIS would turn the trial into a test of the rhetorical skills of the victim's relatives; (4) VIS introduces passion and emotion and, therefore, would threaten the rational decision–making process. See A. Sarat, "Vengeance, Victims and the Identities of Law", *Social and Legal Studies* 1997, *6*, 174.

39 *Ibid.*, 165.

40 M.D. Dubber, "Regulating the Tender Heart When the Axe is Ready to Strike", *Buffalo Law Review* 1993, *41*, 124.

41 Justice Scalia in his dissenting opinion for *Booth v. Maryland* (1987): see *ibid.*, 175.

'good' consequences to be expected from certain ways of punishing have to do with the presumed benefits (capital punishment) or empirically assessed ones (restorative conferencing) for victims' well–being, which are situated in the future. In addition, these benefits are formulated by having recourse to a shared language, a therapeutic language. For that combined reason I would like to speak about 'therapeutic consequentialism'.

This is something different than the 'grievance satisfaction' theory of punishment, which forms part of the retributive family. Ted Honderich recently formulated the proposition at the heart of this theory as follows:

> The penalty satisfies grievances owed to the offence, and does neither less nor more than satisfy these grievances, and in so doing it is in accordance with a system that connects penalties with offences by way of grievances.[42]

At first sight, it might be tempting to see the concern for victims, as it has been formulated throughout this chapter, in line with this stream of penal thinking. Harmful actions give rise to 'grievances' and punishment is right because it satisfies these grievances through causing distress to offenders responsible for those actions.[43] As Honderich points out "… it satisfies desires of the person or persons he has freely offended against"[44], namely the victim. Yet, there are two crucial differences. First, grievance theory postulates that not only victims may get satisfaction out of punishment; also any others who sympathise with or understand the grievance desires of victims may join in the satisfaction. Therapeutic consequentialism, however, is exclusively concerned with those directly involved: victims and those who feel emotionally tied to them. In that sense it is somewhat similar to the rehabilitation / treatment stream in utilitarian thought, discussed above in section 2.[45] Yet a crucial difference is that it changes its target: its contribution to the 'greater good' is not achieved by 'making offenders better', but by 'healing victims'. Second, as Honderich argues in his book, grievance theory forms part of the retributive family. This means that it is a backward–looking theory which, contrary to therapeutic consequentialism, formulates no desired positive effects for the greater good. Satisfying a grievance desire is hardly the same as attempting to 'heal' the victim.

---

42 T. Honderich, *Punishment. The Supposed Justifications Revisited* (London: Pluto Press, 2006) 69.

43 *Ibid.*, 58–73.

44 *Ibid.*, 60.

45 See also Leslie Sebba's interesting observations about a contemporary 'victim rehabilitation model' corresponding to an earlier treatment model for offenders, L. Sebba, "The Individualization of the Victim: From Positivism to Postmodernism", in A. Crawford and J. Goodey (eds.), *Integrating a Victim Perspective within Criminal Justice. International Debates* (Aldershot: Ashgate, 2000) 55–76.

5 Limits of Therapeutic Consequentialism

There are, of course, remarkable differences between restorative responses and capital punishment. Moreover, readers may rightly object that while restorative justice advocates aim to probe for beneficial victim effects by means of careful research proponents of the death penalty merely resort to easy rhetoric about 'healing victims'. Indeed, Franklin Zimring argues that the term 'closure' has been "a public relations godsend", and that it defies empirical studies because it is a "belief system", "a justification built on a foundation of faith".[46] In that respect, there is a clear difference between the two. In addition, restorative justice claims to do much more than 'healing victims'. I am well aware of that.

The point of section 4, however, was not to make a caricature of either penal practice. Rather, the discussion intended to highlight how the metaphor of 'healing victims' has stopped being a metaphor: 'healing victims' comes to play a role in what is *expected* from penal practices. A new way of looking at punishment, of evaluating criminal justice responses comes to the fore. This is a normative issue. As was argued above in section 4.1, the empirical exploration of the limits of current penal practices from a victim–oriented therapeutic viewpoint *assumes* that such 'good consequences' *should* be included in our general assessment of the limits of the law. This last paragraph will explore some of the limits of therapeutic consequentialism.

First, therapeutic consequentialism does not come out of nowhere. Rehabilitation as a goal for penal practice was firmly embedded in the concept of the welfare State and its ideology of caring. The relation between the State and the offender came to be presented "... as a positive attempt to produce reform and normalisation for the benefit of the individual as well as the State."[47] In that sense this relation mirrored the general idea of the State being a benevolent 'risk manager'. The needy, the sick, the old, the unemployed, and the deviant, all could rely on the social welfare State to look after them. Therapeutic consequentialism, for its part, originated at a time when people and institutions were increasingly preoccupied with mental health problems and emotional well–being. The concerns stretched from primary schools looking after the 'self–esteem' of its pupils to foreign States claiming to help countries with their 'emotional recovery' in post–conflict areas.[48] There is now a stream of sociological literature that critically explores what is

---

[46] F.E. Zimring (2003), *l.c.*, 58 and 63.

[47] D. Garland (1985), *l.c.*, 31.

[48] For a strong critique of how post–conflict countries come to be 'pathologised' by means of international psychosocial programmes, see V. Pupavac, "Pathologizing Populations and Colonizing Minds: International Psychosocial Programs in Kosovo", *Alternatives* 2002, *27*, 489–511; V. Pupavac, "International Therapeutic Peace and Justice in Bosnia", *Social & Legal Studies* 2004, *13*, 377–401.

variously called 'therapy cultures' and 'therapeutic states'.[49] As Frank Furedi argues,

> the expanding usage of the idiom of therapeutics is not simply of linguistic interest. The changing form of language communicates new cultural attitudes and expectations.[50]

Human experiences come to be redefined in emotional terms. The assumption is made that people who are going through stressful or painful moments are deeply traumatised and scarred for life. People appear as emotionally inadequate, vulnerable, helpless, with low self–esteem:

> ... therapeutics does not simply reflect uncertainties; ...it also cultivates a distinct orientation towards the world. It sensitises people to regard a growing range of their experiences as victimising and as traumatising.[51]

Therapeutic intervention by a growing army of new experts is presented as the way out from such a personal predicament.

Therapeutic consequentialism starts from similar assumptions. To argue that criminal justice systems should 'heal victims' is to assume that there is something to heal, that they all are damaged or traumatised in one way or another. Yet such an assumption of victims being 'emotionally damaged' may be neither true, nor very appealing for the persons labelled in that way. Leslie Sebba argues that "(...) many – indeed, apparently most – victimizations are overcome within a relatively short period."[52] This implies that the 'heavy language' of trauma, recovery, closure and the like should be reserved for a small group of victims who really are in need of professional help. Moreover, to create the impression that all victims of crime are traumatised[53] is difficult to reconcile with the assumption that victims are able to participate in criminal justice processes, that they decide for themselves to get involved and speak for themselves in mediation programmes, and so on.

Second, not so long ago victim advocates were worried about the instrumentalisation of victims in restorative programmes, where victims were used in a setting which ultimately is oriented at the rehabilitation of offenders and their diversion from classical criminal justice procedures. But therapeutic consequentialism opens the door to a form of instrumentalisation that goes in the other direction, specifically the ways in which offenders are called upon to contribute to the healing process of the victim. Consider for example the following reasons that Wemmers and Cyr presented why victims felt less positive about their participation in a mediation programme:

---

49 See *e.g.* F. Furedi, *Therapy Culture. Cultivating Vulnerability in an Uncertain Age* (London: Routledge, 2004); J.L. Nolan Jr., *The Therapeutic State. Justifying Government at Century's End* (New York: New York University Press, 1998).

50 F. Furedi (2004), *l.c.*, 4.

51 *Ibid.*, 129.

52 L. Sebba (2000), *l.c.*, 60.

53 See *e.g.* "All these research findings indicate the *universality* of the trauma of victimization and the high levels of dissatisfaction regarding the usual treatment victims receive at the hands of the criminal justice system", H. Strang (2002), *l.c.*, 19 [my italics].

> One victim did report feeling more fearful, and this was because the offender did not regret his or her behaviour and the victim felt that he or she could offend again.[54]

> Most victims said that they felt better with respect to their victimisation after the meeting with the offender ..., but two said they felt worse. In both cases, the reason given by victims was the offender's refusal to take responsibility for his or her actions.[55]

> When victims suffered re–victimisation, they attributed this to the offender who had failed to take responsibility for his or her actions.[56]

The conclusion that might be drawn from this (if a therapeutic orientation to victims *should* be desirable – something both researchers seem to assume to be a settled question) is that in order to enhance the well–being of victims, offenders should regret their behaviour and take responsibility for their actions. The same holds true for the crucial importance that has been attributed to the role of apology. In *Repair or Revenge* Strang emphasised the "victims' need for apology"[57] and in one of the studies coming out of the Jerry Lee Progam, it was used as a criterion to measure the success of restorative conferencing: "The criterion here is whether RJ conferences result in more apologies."[58] This implies that victims' well–being, at least partly, comes to depend upon action taken by the offender: without an apology there is less chance of recovery. The danger, of course, is that this leads to a kind of 'emotional conformity' and fuels attempts to 'produce' a set of emotions that are assumed to be conducive to victims' healing. In his Presidential Address Lawrence Sherman speaks in positive terms about 'creating' and 'managing' emotions.[59] Moreover, while restorative conferencing rightly gives space for the expression of emotions, a therapeutic consequentialist orientation also allows for a deeper intrusion into the most personal aspects of offenders' lives. The fact that victim–related expectations towards offenders become more and more formalised and increasingly play a role in pre– and post–sentence decision–making implies that 'opting out' may not be an option for offenders.[60]

Third, the fact that something 'works' does not mean that it is 'just'. In 1953 C.S. Lewis criticised rehabilitation for not addressing the question of 'justice':

> We demand of a cure not whether it is just but whether it succeeds. Thus when we cease to consider what the criminal deserves and consider only what will cure him or deter others, we have tacitly removed him from the sphere of justice altogether; instead of a person, a subject of rights, we now have a mere object, a patient, a 'case'.[61]

---

54 J.A. Wemmers and K. Cyr (2005), *l.c.*, 537.

55 *Ibid.*, 538.

56 *Ibid.*, 540.

57 H. Strang, (2002), *l.c.*, 18–23.

58 L.W. Sherman, H. Strang, C. Angel, D. Woods, G.C. Barnes, S. Bennett and N. Inkpen (2005), *l.c.*, 373.

59 L.W. Sherman (2003), *l.c.*, 10 and 26.

60 T. Daems and L. Robert, "Victims, Knowledge(s) and Prisons: Victims Entering the Belgian Prison System", *European Journal of Crime, Criminal Law and Criminal Justice* 2006, *14*, 256–270.

61 C.S. Lewis, "The Humanitarian Theory of Punishment", *Res Judicata* 1953, (6), 224.

Lewis formulates a critique that seems to apply to all consequentialist reasoning. A 'cure' (or 'healing') is something that happens or not (an empirical question), but that does not mean that it is just. Therapeutic consequentialism is not about 'right' or 'wrong' but about whether I feel 'good' or 'bad' about something. It is the question of justice (which entails the crucial question of how to limit the power to punish properly) which slides into the background and the State's power to punish comes to be dressed up in a benevolent therapeutic strait–jacket.

6 Conclusion

For some readers this chapter might have taken a somewhat unpredictable turn. Being written by a criminologist, by someone who feels firmly committed to an approach towards crime that is open to challenging existing ways of responding to crime by new empirical evidence and innovative ways of thinking about criminal justice responses, readers may have expected to enter in on a discussion which would have been much harsher on criminal law's limits to deal with the plight of victims of crime. But the chapter has taken another approach. The limits of reformers' explorations of the limits of criminal law have been examined. Instead of joining the critique on the multiple ways in which criminal law fails to address the needs of victims of crime, it critically explored the ways in which those reformers *themselves* (that is, *their* limits) launched their attacks on the limits of criminal law.

This does not mean that I am not of the opinion that criminal law cannot do better in its dealings with victims of crime. Rather, I am wary about how this currently happens. Endorsing a form of therapeutic consequentialism certainly is not the way forward. Sociologists of punishment argue that the way we punish and how we think about punishment reveals a lot about ourselves and the societies we live in. Therapeutic consequentialism might provide us with a window onto some less appealing aspects of ourselves and our societies.

Chapter 10 – Restorative Justice, Freedom, and the Limits of the Law[1]

"... for Freedom and for Justice"
Brabançonne, Belgian National Anthem

Johan Deklerck

1 Introduction

In the first chapter, E. Claes, W. Devroe and B. Keirsbilck set out a conceptual framework in order to map different types of limits of the law. To that end, they distinguish different functions and features of the law. Their central intuition is that law's limited ability to fulfil these functions can, to a large extent, be imputed to some basic characteristics of the law.

The editors give substance to this intuition by showing how law as a societal sphere is often structurally inadequate to permeate and guide other societal spheres. These spheres have a distinct logic, and entail concepts and structures which often resist being shaped by legal rules, principles, and procedures; and further, "such a language [of enforceable rights] sits ill with the delicate, affective nature of family relations."[2]

Reflecting on the scientific aspirations of the law, the editors also argue that these aspirations tend to "undermine the law's potential to figure as a framework that opens a common public space of mutual cooperation among citizens, one that facilitates conflict resolution and peace–making and that is expressive of shared values and meanings".[3]

According to the editors, these intrinsic shortcomings are reinforced by another feature of the law: its institutional dimension. Especially formalism and institutional complexity can easily create "a common feeling of alienation among the disputants" when they feel cut off from their own ability to resolve disputes.[4]

In this chapter I largely concur in these basic insights. Moreover, I try to exemplify and refine them in the context of formal criminal justice and victim–offender mediation.

In a first step, this chapter will argue how criminal wrongdoing always entails a substantial reduction of personal freedom on behalf on the victim (and even on

1 My thanks to the editors, especially to E. Claes, for their valuable support.
2 See E. Claes, W. Devroe and B. Keirsbilck, "The Limits of the Law (Introduction)".
3 *Ibid.*
4 *Ibid.*

behalf of the offender). The more serious the offence, the more intense is the interference with the personal life–sphere (section 2).[5] A responsible answer to crime should always aim at bringing about a process of restoring and enlarging this freedom.

In a second step it will be contended that criminal law and formal justice are, to a considerable degree, ill–designed for triggering this process of recovery. Drawing on Illich's distinction between a heteronomous and autonomous life–sphere, I will argue that the language, the procedures, the institutions, and the ethics of the criminal law do not properly belong to the life–sphere as the means to produce and reinvent personal freedom. Their role in this regard should be limited to only a function as a 'guardian at the door'. Law's central aim revolves around *doing justice* by creating, interpreting, and enforcing the law, and not around enlarging freedom (sections 3 through 5).

In a third step, it will be argued that, in contrast with the criminal law, victim–offender mediation, as an instance of restorative justice practices[6], evidences all the necessary features to trigger a process of enlarging freedom. This process of dialogue between the primary stakeholders in an act of delinquency, belongs to Illich's autonomous or vernacular sphere displaying an ethical logic which is specially designed for enhancing freedom. By engaging in an authentic encounter, supported by a mediator, the victim and the offender are given full opportunity to express their emotions, pain, suffering, aggression, fear, and so on. This can be the start of a healing process, leading to regaining freedom in all its different layers (section 6).

In a fourth and last step, my strategy to remedy criminal law's limits with regard to enlarging personal freedom, consists of acknowledging more explicitly the complementarity between classic criminal law and criminal justice, on the one hand, and victim–offender mediation, on the other hand. Seen from this perspective an appropriate response to delinquency should be parsed in two branches. The criminal law is only one of these (section 7).

---

5 J. Deklerck and A. Depuydt, *'Re–ligare' als antwoord op 'de–linquentie'. Aanzet tot een ethische, contextuele en ecologische criminologie* (Ph. D. thesis, K.U.Leuven, Law Department, 2005) Part 3, 18–44.

6 The concept 'restorative justice' has emerged out of practices of confrontation between victim and offender within the mediation movement in the United States and Canada during the 1970s. The scientific work of, among others, H. Zehr (*Changing Lenses: A New Focus for Criminal Justice* (Scottsdale: Herald Press, 1982), T. Marshall (*Alternatives to Criminal Courts* (Gower: Aldershot, 1985)), M. Umbreit (*Crime and Reconciliation: Creative Options for Victims and Offenders* (Nashville, TN: Abington Press, 1985)) and J. Braithwaite (*Crime, Shame and Reintegration* (Cambridge: Cambridge University Press, 1989)) have had a sizeable influence on further developments. N. Christie's seminal paper, "Conflicts as Property" (*British Journal of Criminology* 1977, *1*, 1–15) has been an important theoretical start for the dissemination of restorative justice in Europe. T. Peters and L. Walgrave have played a significant role for the implementation of 'restorative justice' ideas in Belgium.

2 Delinquency as an Interruption in the Flow of Life

Being involved in a crime – as a victim, but also as an offender – is often an experience that causes us to come to a halt. Serious offences can, indeed, affect our lives profoundly. The extent to which an offence interferes in one's personal, existential life–sphere is a central criterion to assess its seriousness. A similar observation can be made of life–contexts other than the realm of delinquency. Major events in our lives, be they negative or positive, always interrupt our flow of life. In the case of serious traumas, it is as if time stands still. As a result, victims of serious offences no longer build further on their future, on their own (life–) story. The continuous stream of feelings[7] which accompanies life is somehow disordered, and swirling emotions of anger and fear continue to revolve into the events of the crime. Circular motion and circular thinking dominate the lives of the victims. Human freedom – freedom of choice, freedom of developing one's future and one's own life–projects – is severely restricted then by the inability to escape from such circular thinking. The flow of life is 'blocked' to a greater or lesser degree.[8]

This 'interruption in the flow of life' is represented in the diagram below. The vertical axis in the diagram depicts the level of life (the 'depth of the flow') from superficial to deep. The horizontal axis shows the individual flow of life that is expressed via a succession of daily occurrences and activities, moments of calm and effort, reflection and action. This is the axis of the process of life that manifests itself on different levels. Acts of delinquency interfere with life on these different levels, depending on the seriousness of the offences. This is the vertical axis on the diagram, which can be associated with a continuum from petty to serious delinquency that I will develop further below and for which the criterion is the level of existential intervention. An act of delinquency results in the flow of life becoming blocked on one or more levels. *Continuous existential integration* of smaller and greater life–experiences that constitute the life–history of individuals, then no longer takes place.[9] The result is a life with reduced freedom.

---

7 The Norwegian philosopher A. Naess talks in this sense about the 'self' as 'flow': "It is never the same. It seems more like a flow than anything solid." See A. Naess, *Life's philosophy. Reason and feeling in a deeper world,* (Athens and London: The University of Georgia Press, 2002) 23.

8 S. Christiaensen, I. Vandeurzen, and H. Verhoeven, *Herstelgerichte detentie. Van actie–onderzoek naar beleidsvorming* (K.U.Leuven, Law Department, 2000) appendix 2, 18–20, quoting R. Bastiaensen (referring to E. Neumann and E. Rolfe, *Depth Psychology and a New Ethic* (London: Hodder & Stoughton, 1969)): "Like a wild dog that after a number of years of imprisonment becomes a dangerous animal, so, according to Jung, it also happens with oppressed energies. Keeping blocked consciousness in check becomes virulent and destructive. It causes schizophrenia in the person."

9 Three forms are distinguished here: 'absorption' (being fully absorbed by what one does), 'depersonalisation' and 'derealisation' (the feeling that reality is not genuine, that you are not yourself) and 'amnesia' (serious memory problems). See J. Hutsebaut, *Trauma en de dissociatieve structuur: empirisch onderzoek van een integratief psychodynamisch model voor chronische interpersoonlijke traumatisering* (Ph. D. thesis, K.U.Leuven, Psychology Department, 2003).

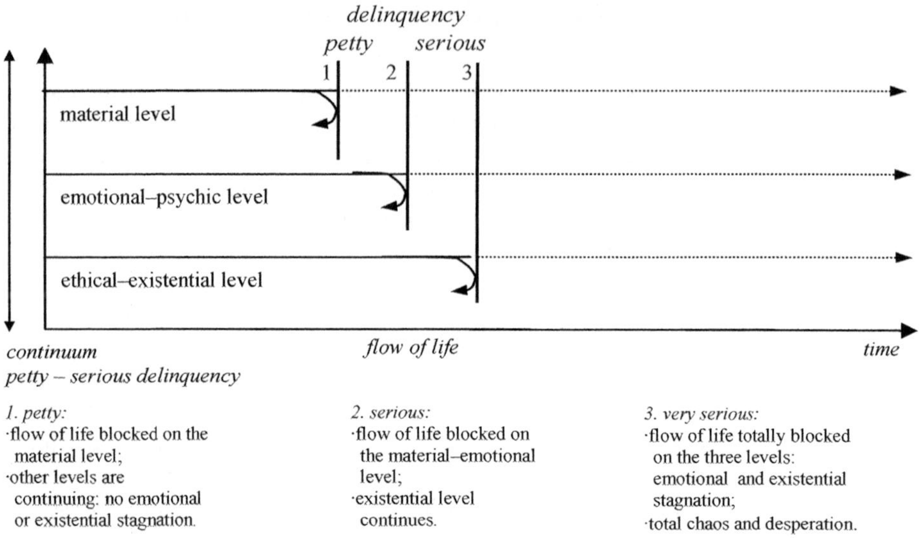

Fig. 10.1 Interruption in the flow of life

3 The Heteronomous versus the Autonomous Life–Sphere

To what extent are criminal law and formal justice able to trigger a process of enlarging freedom? In the following paragraphs it will be argued that the classic responses to crime are ill–designed for starting off such a process. In order to do so, we will take inspiration from the work of I. Illich, and from his famous distinction between the autonomous or vernacular life–sphere and the heteronomous life–sphere. These spheres are complementary to one other. In balanced societies they mutually support each other. The heteronomous life–sphere is centred on key concepts such as societal organisation, institutional frameworks, professions, administration, market economy, political institutions, productivity, financial resources, exchange values, and rights and obligations. In Western democracies these institutions and organisations are regulated by law. In contrast, the autonomous or vernacular life–sphere is organised around concepts such as personal goals and existential desires, individual flourishing, informal encounters, and networking between friends and family. In a vernacular sphere, human beings are involved in processes and practices that are not result–oriented. The vernacular sphere is the realm of human freedom and autonomy. This is depicted in the following diagram.

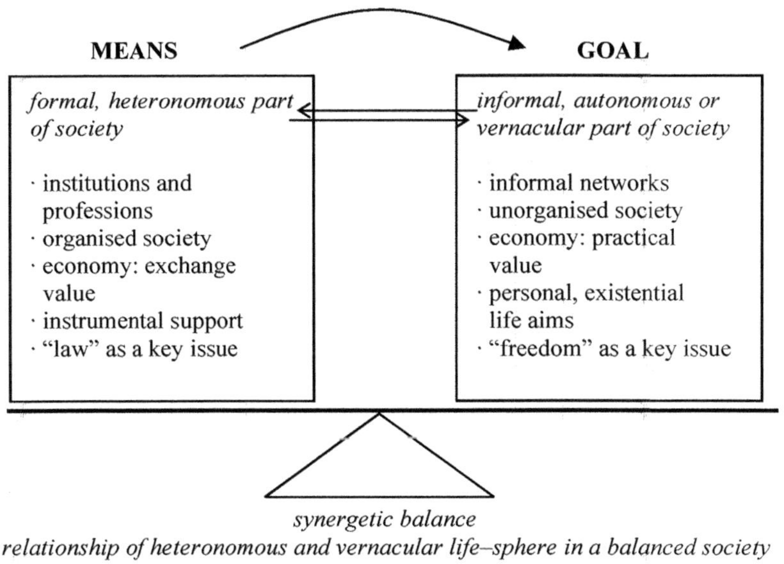

Fig. 10.2 The Heteronomous versus the Autonomous Life–Sphere

The autonomous or vernacular life–sphere and the heteronomous life–sphere feature an 'end' and 'means' relationship. But despite the fact that these networks intersect each other, there is an important differentiating element that needs to be made explicit, namely money or, to put it less bluntly, the possibility of financial representation. The question then becomes whether human interactions belong either to the exchange–value domain, or the use–value domain. Friendships and familial relationships are not for sale, and cannot be expressed in a financial unit. Human warmth or human suffering in a personal relationship has no financial value. A 'home' cannot be replaced by a more beautiful 'house'.[10] In this sense, Illich also called the autonomous life–sphere 'the vernacular life–sphere'. The Latin '*vernaculum*' means 'hearth' and everything that has to do with 'home' in the old Roman Empire.[11] It refers to those things that are not for sale, that cannot be formalised. It refers to personally lived and experienced values, pleasure and sorrow, minor and major moments together with those who are precious to you.

> The fact that there is a broad spectrum of things in human existence that have the character of a bonus, which thus cannot be produced or reproduced on demand, is … an insight that has found articulation many times in philosophy and literature. … What binds

---

10 See C.G. Jung, *Man and his Symbols* (New York: Dell Publishing, 1964).

11 I. Illich, *Gender* (New York: Pantheon Books, 1983) 68. See also: I. Illich, *La convivialité* (Paris: Seuil, 1973) 27–53. I. Illich, *The Right to Useful Unemployment and its Professional Enemies* (London: Marian Boyars, 1977).

> all of these phenomena is the fact that they belong to the order of the personal: they have an inner relationship to us, they are part of what we are.[12]

From the foregoing, it follows that the vernacular life–sphere and the heteronomous life–sphere cannot replace one another. The spheres cannot simply be interchanged. Pleasure cannot replace happiness; law cannot replace freedom; a well–organised social system cannot replace health, and consumerism does not provide a fundamental answer to existential life–questions and needs. The content of the heteronomous life–sphere cannot simply be transferred to the vernacular life–sphere, and vice versa. In the right proportions, however, they can enrich one another.

It goes without saying that these two 'worlds' must not be seen as two entities that could be strictly separated from each other. Notwithstanding current societal tendencies toward fragmentation, the vernacular life–sphere and autonomous life–sphere continually mix with one another. The heteronomous life–sphere penetrates the intimacy of our personal life, and without the presence of the basic qualities of the vernacular, the heteronomous life–sphere would be uninhabitable. They permeate each other in a very complex and refined way, just as the private life–sphere is strongly permeated by public elements, and vice versa. J. Faget, referring to the distinction between 'Gemeinschaft' and 'Gesellschaft'[13], phrases this issue as follows:

> This vision is not sufficient to describe a complex society where geographical, social, cultural, ethnic and professional communities coexist and get mixed up, and where the same person may belong to several communities and may slide from one to another.[14]

To understand better this complex interaction, it is helpful to view each individual person as a central point of intersection. Each of us carries the two 'worlds' in himself, from which follows that both spheres should be conceived more as *qualities*, than as *entities*.[15] Elements and fragments can continually be judged as belonging to one or the other side of the borderline separating both. In this complex interpenetration, we constantly deal with a 'heteronomous' or 'autonomous' valuation of the things around us in our daily life.

---

12 K. van der Wal, "De maakbaarheid der dingen", in W. Achterberg, *Natuur: uitbuiting of respect? Natuurwaarden in discussie* (Kampen: Kok Agora, 1989) 36–37. He makes a distinction between 'being' and 'making'. His concept 'bonus' largely coincides with what is intended here by the vernacular values.

13 The concepts 'Gemeinschaft' and 'Gesellschaft' were introduced in 1887 by the German sociologist Ferdinand Tönnies. 'Gemeinschaft' concerns the "community in which people are connected with each other in a natural and organic way" whereas 'Gesellschaft' serves as a model for modern society dominated by pragmatism and calculation. See F. Tönnies, *Gemeinschaft und Gesellschaft: Grundbegriffe der reinen Soziologie* (Berlin: Curtius, 1920).

14 J. Faget, "Mediation, Criminal Justice and Community Involvement: A European Perspective", in The European Forum for Victim–Offender Mediation and Restorative Justice (ed.), in *Victim–Offender Mediation in Europe. Making Restorative Justice Work* (Leuven: Leuven University Press, 2000) 40. See also A. Giddens and C. Pierson, *Conversations with Anthony Giddens: Making Sense of Modernity* (Cambridge: Polity Press, 1999) 117.

15 H. Kunneman, *Van theemutscultuur naar walkman–ego. Over de contouren van de postmoderne individualiteit* (Amsterdam: Boom, 1996).

One of the major challenges for Western societies is that the complementary relation between the autonomous and heteronomous life–spheres has grown out of balance. Human interactions are weighed down by an ever–expanding process of institutionalisation. The heteronomous life–sphere has succeeded in 'ensuring' itself a prominent place in very diverse domains: in the area of food, healthcare, safety, communication, education, emancipation, and such like. As a consequence, the heteronomous life–sphere tends to estrange us from person–related values that belong to the autonomous or vernacular life–sphere. This alienation is exemplified in the gap between political institutions and the citizen, but also in existential uprootedness and loss of self.

4 Internalist versus Externalist Ethics

Besides the possibility of financial representation, there is also another important principle of differentiation between the autonomous and heteronomous life–spheres: their *ethical structure* is fundamentally different. Referring once more to the diagram above, two kinds of ethics can be distinguished. As to the heteronomous life–sphere, human interactions are governed by a formal ethics. These guide human behaviour by rules, expressed in the law, or in other regulatory systems (religious codes or professional codes of conduct). This system embodies the ethical sensibilities of a culture and serves as a basis for developing arguments in processes of decision–making. In philosophy, this kind of ethics is called an externalist ethics, an ethics that comes from the 'outside', from external ethical codes and frameworks.[16]

As to the autonomous life–sphere, human life is governed by an internalist ethics. Research has shown that people give sense to their lives and action by drawing on their own life–experiences, instead of drawing on abstract rules and frameworks. Deep within one's self; there is a treasure of information (recall the diagram of the flow of life), built up out of what one has seen, experienced, of how one was treated as a child, of how one has been confronted with the frontier between life and death, of how one cares about his loved ones. People refer to these experiences – consciously or unconsciously – when deliberating, forging judgments, making ethical decisions, and undertaking actions. People think of their own children or the accident involving the girl next door when they are careful in traffic. The police officer, confronted with young drug dealers or burglars,

---

16 J. McDowell, "Are Moral Requirements Hypothetical Imperatives?", in *Proceedings of the Aristotelian Society,* Supplementary Volume LII, 1978. J. McDowell, "Non–Cognitivism and Rule–Following", in S.H. Holtzman and C.M. Leich (eds.), *Wittgenstein: To Follow a Rule* (London – Boston – Henley: Routledge and Kegan Paul, 1981) 141–162. J. McDowell, "Values and Secondary Qualities", in T. Honderich (ed.), *Morality and Objectivity. A Tribute to J.L. Mackie* (London: Routledge, 1985) 110–129. L. Wittgenstein, *Philosophical Investigations* (London: Macmillan) 1953. See also L. Kohlberg, *Approach to Moral Education* (New York: Columbia University Press, 1989).

thinks of his teenage son. We remember our own lost wallet that we had returned, when we find someone's. In general, when we have to make decisions, we think of how other people have acted before us, how we have been treated, and how we experienced this. This can be negative ("I don't want someone to have the same bad experience") or positive ("I also have been treated this way"). From this point of view, ethics is not something dead, purely abstract, but a living, organic process of permanently reinventing the good in concrete situations. It is a process type of ethics[17] that shows strong resemblances with an 'ethics of care'.[18]

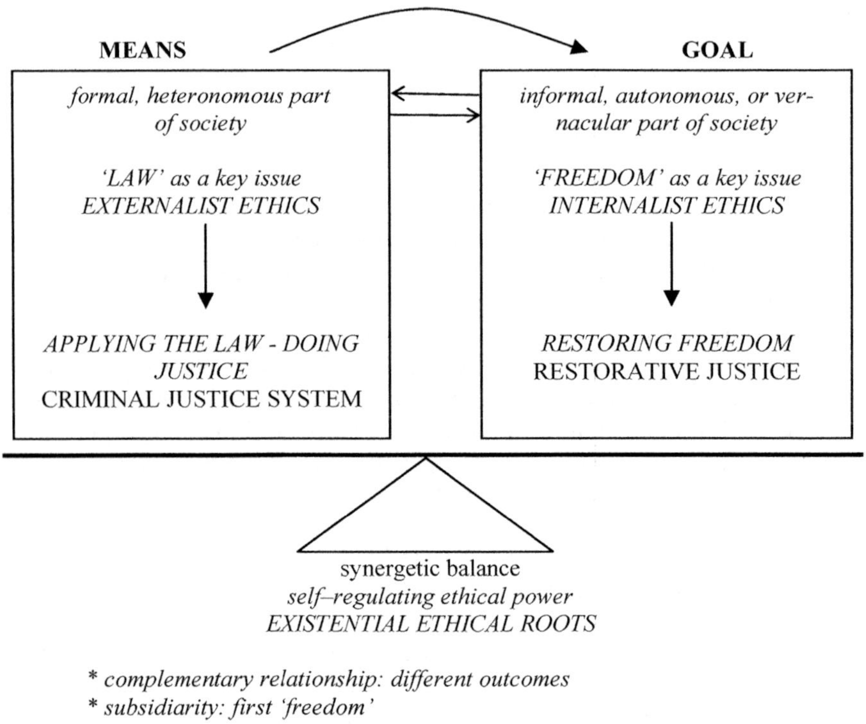

Fig. 10.3 Internalist versus Externalist Ethics

Although an internalist ethics involves a process unfolding deep within the individual, it is not purely an individual phenomenon. It is embedded in a larger whole, and flourishes within interpersonal relationships. This ethics becomes visible in the will to act against injustice, in the wish to apologise, in the openness to

17 F. Denkers, H. van Hoogen, C. Wackernagel *et al.*, *Begrepen onbehagen: politie en Rote Armee Fraktion verzoend* (Lelystad: Koninklijke Vermande, 1999).

18 See *e.g.*, C. Gilligan and B. Bardige, *Mapping the Moral Domain: A Contribution of Women's Thinking to Psychological Theory and Education* (Cambridge, Mass.: Center for the Study of Gender, Education and Human Development, 1988). N. Noddings, *Caring: A Feminine Approach to Ethics and Moral Education* (Berkeley, Calif.: University of California Press, 1986).

show regret, and in the desire to repair damage. This type of ethics goes even beyond the interaction between individuals, for it is part of the care for life itself, since it also expresses existential linkages that often have fallen asleep under the blanket of daily life.

Both ethical qualities (the internalist and externalist) have their common roots in an existential ethics that emerges from a deep level of the flow of life. Albeit in different ways, both ethics are grounded in common ethical orientations that have grown out from deep existential challenges and confrontations.

5 Enhancing Personal Freedom and the Limits of the Criminal Law

How does Illich's distinction between the heteronomous life–sphere (along with its externalist ethics) and the autonomous life–sphere (along with its internalist ethics) bear upon the criminal law and upon the importance of appropriately responding to delinquency?

When revisiting some basic functions of contemporary criminal law, a host of reasons can be listed explaining why the rules, principles and procedures of the criminal law only serve a partial and limited role in enhancing personal freedom.[19] Moreover, to a certain extent the criminal law is not well–designed for procuring such a freedom.

Firstly, seen from a regulatory perspective the value of criminal law is primarily instrumental, for it serves to influence and control risk behaviour in order to enhance overall safety in society. Safety considerations, and not enlargement of existential freedom, determines the value of criminal justice institutions. These considerations steer the criminal law, even at the cost of diminishing the freedom of the citizens in their capacity of actual or potential offenders.

Secondly, reconsidering the criminal law in its symbolic function, one could hardly state that restoring the personal freedom of victims and offender is the main objective. While the criminal law, through its process of criminalisation and punishment, is surely able publicly to recognise and reaffirm basic values in society, as well as the flouted dignity of the victim, it is much less equipped for patiently triggering a process of healing in which all the stakeholders in the conflict might overcome their loss of self. The scope of action and attention of legislators and judges is rule–based, and, therefore, inevitably makes abstraction from the complex inner life–experiences of the victims and offenders.

Thirdly, the criminal law contributes only partially to the enhancement of freedom when serving its role of protective legality. In the introductory chapter it is argued that legal guarantees enhance citizens' capabilities, to the extent that legal principles such as legality and democratic participation precondition their ability to adjust their actions to the intervention of public authorities, or to control and

---

19 Compare E. Claes, W. Devroe, and B. Keirsbilck, *l.c.*

take part in collective decisions in the public interest.[20] But these principles, which are supposed to guide the practices of the criminal law, are themselves not endowed with a power of restitution for loss of self, provoked by the traumatic experience of being involved in crime. While lack of such principles seriously diminishes our capacity to construct our lives as unfolding narrative, fidelity to criminal law and democratic procedures does not suffice in itself for putting into motion a process of enlarging personal freedom.

Given a short review of the criminal law's basic functions, one can, in sum, hardly uphold the thesis that law belongs to the autonomous life–sphere, because a central aim of enhancing personal freedom is not inscribed in the purposes of the institutional practices that define the criminal law. On top of this, reasonable, positive arguments can be proffered to defend the idea that law should be located in Illich's heteronomous life–sphere. Indeed, for reasons of legal security, equality, checks and balances, and the protection of individual rights against arbitrary State power, the criminal law is a highly formalised and institutionalised practice. The (inter)actions, decisions, and deliberations of institutional actors are narrowed down by rules and procedural patterns of actions. The professional roles and institutional powers are not dependent (and should not be) on a deep personal and existential involvement of its actors.

Being part of the heteronomous life–sphere, the criminal law falls thus short in fully accomplishing an all too neglected dimension of answering crime: the restoration of victims' and offenders' capability of seeing themselves as an unfolding narrative, integrating their life–experiences into a coherent personal identity. But this is not to say that the criminal law is completely at odds with the realm of freedom. At the end of this chapter, it will be argued that the criminal law's contribution to enhancing personal freedom can be better exploited when fully acknowledging the limits of its potential and when promoting the complementary role of restorative justice practices. But before pursuing this line of thought, an analysis of victim–offender mediation and its relation to human freedom is in order.

6 Mediation and Restoring Personal Freedom

Victim–offender mediation and other restorative justice practices such as conferencing techniques are now well–established social practices, supported by a world–wide restorative justice movement. Albeit victim–offender mediation programmes can vary in content and concept from country to country, some salient characteristics of these practices can be brought to the fore. Characteristic for these programmes is, firstly, their dialogical nature. Victims and offender are invited to enter into a communicative process in order to deal with the aftermath of crime. They are supported by a mediator who tries to facilitate the dialogue by giving each party equal space to tell his own story of the facts and of its conse-

---

20 E. Claes, W. Devroe, and B. Keirsbilck, *l.c.*

quences. Another important feature of victim–offender mediation is that the quality of the outcome (kind of restorative measures which are agreed upon) heavily depends on the quality of the dialogical process. And thirdly, almost all victim–offender mediations are steered by three guiding principles: voluntariness, neutrality, and confidentiality. Engaging in this type of restorative justice programme is *voluntary* for both parties. Each party can decide to leave the programme at any moment of the mediation process. *Neutrality* of victim–offender mediation refers to the professional ethics of the mediator whose role consists of being equally attentive to the needs and concerns of both parties. And, finally, *confidentiality* refers to the importance of keeping the exchange of feelings, stories, and experiences within the intimate space of conversation set out by the mediation process. Confidentiality serves here as a necessary condition for the building of trust between the mediator and the parties, as well as between the parties themselves.

From this short description of victim–offender mediation, a number of arguments can be developed supporting the idea that this type of social response to crime is a much better candidate for enhancing personal freedom than the criminal law and formal criminal justice. Victim–offender mediation programmes acknowledge the importance of freedom in different regards.

Firstly, given their voluntary nature, these programmes fully embrace freedom of choice for victims as well as for offenders. Both parties are thereby recognised as fully autonomous agents. Victim and offender are given the chance to take responsibility for their own stake in the process. They are free to make their own choices and to take decisions, for example, whether they will accept mediation, whether they wish to proceed together and how far, as well as what they would like to know, achieve, and what not.

Secondly, victim–offender mediation programmes undeniably generate a process of empowerment. Mediators seek to offer the greatest possible freedom for both parties to speak in their own voice and to express how they experienced their part in the story of the crime. In order to do so, mediators are trained to create a space of conversation in which the parties are capable of gradually freeing themselves from strategic interventions. These strategic elements are inevitable, since the offender is inclined 'to play along with the game' with a view toward a reduction in the sentence, or to simulate feelings of regret and remorse in order to satisfy the victim's needs. Of course, in the case of serious criminal offences, the victim will be much less likely – or even refuse – to 'play along with the game', since there is nothing in it for him, unless it be based on self–protection and avoiding the risk of being (further) victimised. With respect to less serious criminal offences, however, even victims dare to act strategically in order to obtain the greatest possible financial benefit. Damage claims, then, are often unjustly inflated with a view, for example, towards a favourable settlement with an insurer. It is up to the mediator, then, to create an environment in which these strategic acts can gradually be substituted by the common effort of both parties to engage in a relation of basic trust.

Thirdly, successful mediation requires an atmosphere of freedom from constant assessments and value–judgments of others. In other words, the mediation must take place in a 'sanctuary', a confidential, free place, safely removed from public display in which a process of healing can take place.[21]

Fourthly, the dialogical encounter of victim and offender has a strong liberating potential for both parties, containing thereby the ability to trigger a process of restoring personal freedom. Often, both parties are traumatised by the events of the offence, trapped as they are in the past, caught up in fears and circular thinking, producing thereby serious restrictions on personal freedom. It is remarkable to see that precisely through a genuine encounter between victim and offender, the systemic[22] freedom–reducing connection[23] between these parties can be broken open. This occurs when the encounter and the evolving process of communication is not conditioned anymore by the traumatic events of the crime. By taking part in the mediation process, the parties concerned are given full opportunity to connect up again with their own flow of life and, thus, to increase their own individual freedom. This requires that one overcomes one's feelings of pain, sorrow, anger, aggression, revenge, guilt, shame, and other negative feelings resulting from the offence, all of which stand in the way of a positive life–project. [24] Restoration of freedom through victim–offender mediation makes the parties then *less dependent on their environment (systemic) and at the same time more connected with their environment (existential)*. From this perspective, confrontational situations, like being involved in serious crime, can be an occasion for someone to grow existentially.

That mediation aims at enhancing personal freedom for both victims and offenders does not imply that this restoration of freedom takes the same significance for both parties. The primary goal of mediation has been achieved for the victim, when mediation enables him to liberate himself from the traumatic grip of the

---

21 Note that the concept of 'sanctuary' also has historical roots that include the Latin term '*sanctus*', or 'holy'. 'Place of salvation' or 'place of healing' thus appears to be an appropriate translation. Such a freedom–restoring place has a curative significance, and can bring about healing. H. Bianchi, *Justice as Sanctuary: Toward a New System of Crime Control* (Bloomington, Ind.: Indiana University Press, 1994).

22 L. Apostel places the concepts 'exchange–values' and 'use–values' in a *systemic* relationship: "When I (...) speak of systems and subsystems in general, and treat exchange (see Marx) as the circulation of mass and energy between subsystems, I arrive at the same duality between use–values (specific energies that allow systems to develop, further organise and perpetuate themselves) and exchange–values (masses and energies that move from system to system and connect them with each other" (author's translation). L. Apostel, J. Vanlandschoot, J. & K. Raes, *Afbraak en opbouw: dialogen met Leo Apostel* (Brussels: VUB Press, 1997) 272.

23 See also: I. Boszormenyi–Nagy and G.M. Spark, *Invisible loyalties: Reciprocity in inter–generational family therapy* (New York: Brunner–Mazel, 1984).

24 Quote from M.S. Umbreit *et al.*, "Mediating Victim Offender Conflict", Paper presented at the NATO Advanced Research Workshop Conflict, Crime and Reconciliation, Il Ciocco, Italy, 8–12 April 1991: "Consistent with prior research, crime victims who met with their offenders in the mediation program indicated that being able to meet offenders, talk about what happened, express their concerns and work out a restitution plan were more important than actually receiving compensations for their losses."

crime. Agreements at the end of mediation should provide the victim with real guarantees and opportunities for regained freedom. These guarantees can consist of reassuring the victim's feelings of safety (the offender consents in not appearing in the vicinity of the victim, or in following a therapeutic programme). Other agreements relate to paying of damages, or to contributing to the community.

For the offender, regaining personal freedom also involves leaving the past behind, albeit in a different way than experienced by victims. Giving life a new start, an existential 'blank slate', entails removing from one's self the act of crime, including the likelihood of recidivism.[25] And regaining personal freedom also involves liberating oneself from the vicious circle of feeling as both offender and victim. Mediation practices offer here more perspectives than formal justice and its fidelity to retributive punishment, since retribution more easily contributes to stigmatisation and victimisation of the offender.

DELINQUENCY AND ETHICS

	formal	*informal*
delinquency	offender–oriented definition of distance	relational, contextual definition of proximity
ethics	externalist ethics abstract ethics objective ethics	internalist ethics process type ethics experienced ethics
approach	applying rules and rights external ethical reference	repair and enlarge freedom internal ethical reference
justice	judgment, classical justice	among others, mediation process
society	institutions	informal networks

Fig. 10.4 Delinquency and Ethics

Given the pivotal role of personal freedom in victim–offender mediations, one can easily conclude that these programmes need to be located in Illich's autonomous, or vernacular, life–sphere. At the same time it can be affirmed that these practices offer the kind of freedom regaining response to crime that the criminal law undeniably fails to procure. In this respect the mediator's role differs fundamentally from a legal functionary's, who in the first place 'adds justice' to the incurred injustice. The former moves within the 'realm of freedom' and tries to restore and

[25] The results of recidivism after mediation are encouraging, certainly when compared to traditional forms of settlement. See E. Weitekamp, "Research on Victim–Offender Mediation. Findings and Needs for the Future", in The European Forum for Victim–Offender Mediation and Restorative Justice (ed.), *Victim–Offender Mediation in Europe. Making Restorative Justice Work* (Leuven: Leuven University Press, 2000) 107.

increase as much as possible the mental, emotional, and physical freedom, of the parties' concerned, all of which was conditioned by the offence.[26]

Finally, victim–offender mediation is apt to enhance personal freedom on the side of both victims and offenders, since it displays an internalist ethical structure, which is characteristic for informal practices of the autonomous life–sphere. In contrast with the criminal law whose practices draw on externalist ethics, internalist ethics functions as a kind of internal compass[27] for mediators, as well as for victims and offenders. Without recourse to coercion and enforcement of rules, this internalised ethics enables processes of auto–regulation within mediation programmes. Although this ethics can be seen as an individual quality, it also constitutes a shared language between the stakeholders in the conflict, who often come from very different social backgrounds. Indeed, internalist ethics is bound up with shared feelings of mutual recognition and respect for the vulnerability and the suffering of the other party, creating thereby a deep bond and mutual understanding between the parties involved.[28] But this kind of ethics is not only the product of the unusual relationship between victim and offender. It is based on the capacity to come into contact with the deep existential roots of life.

7 Conclusion: Seeking Complementarity between Victim–Offender Mediation and the Criminal Law

How to remedy law's limited ability to restore inner freedom? Continuous with Illich's analysis of the autonomous and heternomous life–sphere, I propose a strategy of complementarity between victim–offender mediation and formal justice. In this strategy, mediation is the primary medium that can give an impulse to fundamental restoration, because it is especially designed for enhancing material, emotional, and existential freedom. Criminal law serves here a subsidiary role in the accomplishing of personal freedom, and this in a twofold respect.

Firstly, the criminal law only needs to intervene where the informal, self–regulating power of living together in community fails to provide the necessary resources to restore this freedom. The symbolic function of the criminal law and of criminal punishment ensures that violated interests and fundamental rights are reaffirmed when legal norms are transgressed. In this subsidiary role, criminal law and criminal punishment can still play a marginal role in enhancing the personal freedom of both victims and offenders, when properly accompanied by victim–offender mediations. These programmes can help altering the sense of criminal punishment, when efforts are made to give up retributivism and to integrate criminal punishment, or therapy, into the life–story of the offender. In a complementary

---

26 J. Deklerck and A. Depuydt (2005) *l.c.*, Part 4B, 34–35.

27 J. Deklerck and A. Depuydt, "Parels Verzamelen; over de kracht van een autonome ethiek", in P. van Beers (ed.), *Frans Denkers' Moreel Kompas van de Politie* (Den Haag: Politia Nova, Ministerie van Binnenlandse Zaken en Koningsrelaties, 2001) 193–202.

28 A. Depuydt, *Re–ligie' als antwoord op 'de–linquentie'* (Diss. Lic. crim. K.U.Leuven, 1991).

relation to victim–offender mediation, criminal punishment could further guide the latter's actions in the direction of fundamental restoration.[29]

Secondly, the criminal law, its fundamental concepts and principles, plays a restricted, instrumental, and complementary role in enlarging personal freedom to the extent that legal guarantees (legal principles, procedures, respect for fundamental rights) help create the preconditions of safety, equality, and power balances between the stakeholders. Law here does have a function as 'guardian at the door'.[30] This function in itself triggers a modest dynamics of liberation: liberation of fears, of inequalities and oppression. But here again, it is important to acknowledge fully the complementary role of victim–offender mediation. Within the practice of victim–offender mediation, mediators themselves make use of informal strategies of balancing power relations which are often more effective than the purely legal ones. Within the professional ethics of mediators, special methodologies are designed for these purposes, such as appropriate communicative skills, or inviting significant third parties into the process (for example, a partner, a parent, or someone from a victim–assistance agency). This type of spontaneous correction mechanism evidences the auto–regulating forces that accompany an experience–oriented process ethics involved in victim–offender mediation.[31]

Seen from this perspective, *restoration* of criminal wrongdoing contains two different layers of meaning, each displaying a different answer to delinquency. Restoration refers, firstly, to restoring one of the highest human goods, namely human freedom. Victim–offender mediation is the process *par excellence* through which a process of enlarging personal freedom can be triggered. The criminal law's restricted ability to create preconditions for this freedom can be further reinforced by the informal strategies of victim–offender mediation.

Secondly, restoration also concentrates on reaffirming the criminal law, its flouted underlying values and civic obligations. Here again victim–offender–mediation can play an important bridging role, by trying to adjust criminal punishment more to the process of rebuilding the offender's personal freedom. Like the criminal law and victim–offender mediation, both types of restoration are complementary to each other.[32] They each have their unique place in the establishment of ethical equilibriums within society.

---

29 See the etymological origin of the the Dutch word '*straffen*' (to punish), which can be described as limiting the existentially viable parts, for example of a tree. This is fundamentally different from the retributive infliction of suffering that is generally used as the meaning of the punishment. See J. Deklerck and A. Depuydt (2005), *l.c.*, Part 4B: 222–223.

30 Here law must be given secondary priority based on a thoroughgoing principle of subsidiarity. See L. Van Garsse, "Bemiddeling als methodiek in de strafrechtelijke context", *Tijdschrift voor herstelrecht* 2003, 49–60.

31 J. Deklerck and A. Depuydt (2005), *l.c.*, Part 3, 56–58; Part 4B, 83.

32 See also C. Eliaerts and R. Bittoune, "Herstelrecht voor minderjarigen. Theorie en praktijk", in L. Dupont and F. Hutsebaut (eds.), *Herstelrecht tussen toekomst en verleden: liber amicorum Tony Peters*, in *Samenleving, criminaliteit en strafrechtspleging, 22* (Leuven: Universitaire pers Leuven) 233.

Chapter 11 – Rebuilding Trust in the Former Yugoslavia: Overcoming the Limits of the Formal Justice System

Marta Valiñas

1 Introduction

Much of the ongoing debate on how societies can and should respond to a legacy of mass abuse in the wake of large–scale conflict or of State–organised oppression deals with the question of what can be the role and contribution of law to the challenges and needs faced by these societies.

Situations in which societies find themselves devastated by heinous and widespread violence and destruction at different levels pose enormous and very real challenges to human capacity and creativity in dealing with its consequences. As the title of this chapter suggests, law – embodied in the formal justice system – encounters significant limitations in addressing mass atrocities. One can say that situations like these truly constitute a test to the potential and the limits of the law. In this chapter we will focus on the international application of criminal justice.

One of the major challenges faced in the wake of mass violence is how to rebuild trust among those who were on conflicting sides. While some claim that judicial adjudication will contribute to reconciliation between former enemies, others warn against raising unrealistic and unfounded expectations and the disillusionment that will follow thereof. We will use the notion of social trust as one of the elements of the process of social reconstruction[1] (section 2) and analyse the contribution of law to the rebuilding of that trust. This will be done through a critical assessment of how law fulfils two of its functions which are closely related to the notion of trust – the symbolic and the dispute resolution or peace–making functions (section 3).

The question of rebuilding trust among members of different ethnic groups in the former Yugoslavia is still very present. Years after the official end of the conflicts, and after a significant amount of attention and resources were drawn into the process of addressing the violations of the past, mistrust continues to play a role in the individual, social, and political spheres of these countries. Having been the stage of important advancements in the use of law to serve the interests of post–conflict justice (perhaps even at the cost of consideration of other equally

---

[1] See L.E. Fletcher and H.M. Weinstein, "Violence and Social Repair: Rethinking the Contribution of Justice to Reconciliation", *Human Rights Quarterly* 2002, *24*, 573-639.

valuable options[2]), the case of the former Yugoslavia triggers further reflection on the contribution and limits of the law. In order to benefit from hindsight analysis, we will focus only on the International Criminal Tribunal for the former Yugoslavia (ICTY or 'the Tribunal' hereafter) and not – for the moment – on the judicial mechanisms at the national level.

As the realisation of the limitations of law in rebuilding trust between opposing sides becomes more apparent in the region, there is renewed discussion on what mechanisms and approaches could assist that process. In this chapter we offer the hypothesis that a restorative approach might make a relevant contribution to the long and complex path towards social repair (section 4).

2 Trust and the Law

But, should we, and can we reasonably, expect the rebuilding of trust among former enemies to be one of the outcomes of legal mechanisms and procedures? What is, in fact, the relation between trust and law?

What we mean here by trust is what some have called 'social trust'[3], a term which evokes the interpersonal relations at the social or community level which to a great extent refer to individuals who do not already know each other. It does not, thus, refer primarily to the relations between individuals linked by family ties or close affection relations. Rebuilding social trust in the aftermath of widespread violence in this sense, is a central element of social reconstruction, defined as

> a process within a community, which returns the community's damaged social functioning to a normal level of its inhabitants' interpersonal and group relationships in a way that renews the social tissue of the community.[4]

To be sure, the concept of social trust which is being used in this chapter is closely connected to the notion of reconciliation. Albeit a constant in the literature on transitional justice, this notion remains highly controversial and is used to refer –

---

2 See, for example, Mark Drumbl citing Ruth Wedgwood: "In fact, in the deliberations leading up to the adoption of these statutes [of the ICTY, ICTR and ICC], there was essentially no discussion of alternatives to trials for human rights abusers." M. Drumbl, "Sclerosis: Retributive Justice and the Rwandan Genocide", *Punishment and Society* 2000, *2*(3), 287–308, here 297.

3 Boslego defines social trust as "an ongoing motivation or impetus for social relations that forms a basis for interaction." He adds, "Social trust can entail perceived honesty, objectivity, consistency, competence, and fairness, all of which foster relationships between individuals that must be maintained by the sustained fulfillment of these standards." J. Boslego, "Engineering Social Trust. What Can Communities and Institutions Do?", *International Health, Harvard International Review* 2005, *27*, available at http://hir.harvard.edu/articles/1319/.

4 D. Ajdukovic cited in D. Corkalo *et al.*, "Neighbors Again? Intercommunity Relations After Ethnic Cleansing", in E. Stover and H.M. Weinstein (eds.), *My Neighbor, My Enemy: Justice and Community in the Aftermath of Mass Atrocity* (Cambridge: Cambridge University Press, 2004) 143–161, here 152.

often indiscriminately – to different levels: the individual, interpersonal/community, national, and even regional level. Our understanding of social trust comes closer to the community level of reconciliation, and goes along the lines of what has been defined as a "civic trust model of reconciliation"[5]. This is not to say that reconciliation at the micro level, between individuals who shared close bonds before the conflict, often resulting from a process of individual and interpersonal healing which will normally involve a certain degree of forgiveness, is not important. However, it is not the focus of this chapter given that our purpose is to explore the role played by law in rebuilding social trust, and not in promoting individual healing and forgiveness at the micro level.

The importance of rebuilding social or civic trust among individuals who were on opposing sides during the conflict is, dare we say, self–evident. Mistrust is all too often a result of conflict, and particularly so in cases where the element of individual and group identity is politically manipulated and exploited in such a way that it becomes central in the escalation of the conflict.[6] In cases where violence and victimisation pervade every aspect of people's lives, social repair becomes a key priority in the post–conflict period. Rebuilding social trust in such contexts is essential for societies to function as such again. Robert Putnam, for example, associates social trust with "fostering tolerance and community".[7]

The notion of trust is far from being a stranger in the realm of law. Drawing on Thomas Hobbes and David Hume, Susan Dimock has argued that law should be understood as "a system of rules and principles for regulating human behaviour so as to achieve and maintain the conditions of basic trust in a community."[8] Laid against the backdrop of post–conflict justice, this idea might be more meaningful when emphasis is placed on rebuilding the conditions for basic trust rather than just on securing them. After all, those conditions have for the most part been a casualty of war.

---

5 See the International Center for Transitional Justice's understanding of reconciliation at www.ictj.org/en/tj/784.html (last retrieved 5 July 2007): "In the view of the ICTJ: Reconciliation is something that occurs in the civic or political sphere, rather than at the level of individuals. … Trust involves more than relying on a person to do or refrain from doing certain things; it also involves the expectation of a commitment to shared norms and values. The sense of trust at issue here is not the profound sense of trust characteristic of relations between intimates, but rather, 'civic' trust, which can develop among citizens who are members of the same political community but are nonetheless strangers to one another."

6 See D. Ajdukovic and D. Corkalo, "Trust and Betrayal in War", in E. Stover and H.M. Weinstein (eds.), *My Neighbor, My Enemy: Justice and Community in the Aftermath of Mass Atrocity* (Cambridge: Cambridge University Press, 2004) 287–302.

7 Cited in J. Boslego, *l.c.* The author adds that social trust has been associated with "greater levels of teamwork, knowledge–sharing, civic engagement, reciprocity, and efficiency. … [It] might signify internal peace and stability and therefore be correlated with freedom, democratization, modernization, or a number of other developmental benchmarks."

8 S. Dimok, "Retributivism and Trust", *Law and Philosophy* 1997, *16*, 37–62, 37. In the author's view, law condemns and punishes certain acts which if would not be prohibited would "undermine basic trust between members of a community". By doing so, law "secures" the "objective grounds of trust", the importance of which is that "trust is necessary to secure peace and the benefits of cooperative interaction among people."

It is our proposition that trust, understood as social trust in the way explicated above and especially when conceived in a post–conflict setting, is closely connected to two of the functions of law as developed in this book: the symbolic and the dispute resolution functions.[9]

Through its symbolic function, law is seen as a vehicle through which "values deemed important by society at large are made visible and presented by its members as shared values."[10] This corresponds to an important part of the process of truth–telling and acknowledgment held to be crucial in transitional justice, and key to the process of social repair.[11] Whereas the feasibility and even desirability of reaching a 'shared truth' about the past is more controversial[12], the importance of proclaiming loud and clear in the wake of conflict that the atrocities committed were wrong (regardless of who committed them and for which reasons) and will not be tolerated in the future is quite consensual. The fact that law in itself provides an official and authoritative type of acknowledgment that certain violations took place and that they are wrong is important, but for this to have a positive impact in social relations such acknowledgement must be internalised by individuals themselves[13] and be reflected in those relations. Only then can those values be said to be 'shared values' and only then can they contribute to laying the foundations for rebuilding trust in society. The importance of the official acknowledgment provided by law in post–conflict contexts and its interconnection with social reconstruction has been well captured by Jennifer Balint. Drawing on the "public order goals" of legal systems proposed by W. Michael Reisman, one of which is "reconstructing in a larger social sense to remove conditions that appear likely to generate public order violations", Balint suggests that law can satisfy such goals by, among others, providing official acknowledgment of what has happened and by being a "foundation moment for the society and thereby an important basis for further societal healing and reconciliation"[14]. The heart of the matter here is that, on the one hand, an acknowledgement of what happened and its wrongfulness, and on the other hand, the reaffirmation of fundamental values such as respect for human rights and the rule of law and a commitment to uphold these values in the future are essential for a society to move away from the devastation of conflict into a constructive and shared future.

This embracing of fundamental values which condemn the violence of the past and a sense of commitment to renounce similar abuses in the future is also directly connected to law's function of dispute resolution. Law is expected not only to "decide cases and to bring clarity and certainty in the relations between parties"

---

9 See E. Claes, W. Devroe, and B. Keirsbilck, "The Limits of the Law (Introduction)".

10 *Ibid.*

11 J. Halpern and H.M. Weinstein, "Empathy and Rehumanization After Mass Violence", in E. Stover and H.M. Weinstein (eds.), *My Neighbor, My Enemy: Justice and Community in the Aftermath of Mass Atrocity* (Cambridge: Cambridge University Press, 2004) 303–322, 304.

12 See for example M. Ignatieff, "Articles of Faith", *Index on Censorship* 1996.

13 P. Akhavan, "Justice in The Hague, Peace in the Former Yugoslavia? A Commentary on the United Nations War Crimes Tribunal", *Human Rights Quarterly* 1998, *20*, 737–816, 770.

14 J. Balint, "The Place of Law in Addressing International Regime Conflict", *Law and Contemporary Problems* 1996, *59*, 103–126, 116.

but also to "bring social peace which enables parties to behave in the future in a peaceful way."[15] This peace–making function of law is dependent on and at the same time reinforces the rebuilding of social trust. Social peace – and one that is sustainable – it has been argued, should not only encompass 'negative peace' (*i.e.* the absence of physical violence) but also 'positive peace' (the absence of structural violence).[16] In order to guarantee this, justice (including legal mechanisms), in the words of Wendy Lambourne, should address the needs of transformation of both structures and relationships.[17] Societal peace has also been defined as "the degree of conflict/cooperation, short of war, among groups – defined by their ethnic, religious, or other characteristics – within nations."[18] In other words, law's function of promoting social peace is related not only to a reaffirmation of the commitment to the principles of the rule of law and of peaceful resolution of disputes (through the existence of norms and institutions to that end) but it is also related to a broader goal of social pacification in the sense of contributing to the absence of feelings of revenge or renewed confrontation.

Given all that has been said on the link between social trust and the symbolic and dispute resolution functions of law, a frequently addressed topic in transitional justice discourse is unavoidable: the relation between legal responses to mass violence and reconciliation. As discussed above, here also opinions will differ according to what notion of reconciliation is being used. Martha Minow, for example, states clearly that, "Reconciliation is not the goal of criminal trials except in the most abstract sense."[19] She adds, "… reconstruction of a relationship, seeking to heal the accused, or indeed, healing the rest of the community, are not the goals [of criminal trials] in any direct sense". Here, the individual and social levels of reconciliation appear entangled. The question whether reconciliation is a goal of criminal trials or not, and whether it is in fact a result of such trials continues to spark debate.[20] It is important to note that reconciliation figures explicitly in the resolution which established the International Criminal Tribunal for Rwanda (ICTR) as one of the goals to be achieved, and although that was not the case with the resolution which created the ICTY, reconciliation has been put forward as one

---

15 See E. Claes, W. Devroe, and B. Keirsbilck, *l.c.*

16 J. Galtung cited in W. Lambourne, "Post–conflict Peacebuilding: Meeting Human Needs for Justice and Reconciliation", *Peace, Conflict and Development* 2004, Issue 4.

17 See the author's formulation of a model of 'transformative justice', in W. Lambourne, *l.c.*

18 J. Meernik, "Justice and Peace? How the International Criminal Tribunal Affects Societal Peace in Bosnia", *Journal of Peace Research* 2005, *42*, 271—289, 272.

19 M. Minow, *Between Vengeance and Forgiveness: Facing History after Genocide and Mass Violence* (Boston: Beacon Press, 1998) 26.

20 See for example, L.E. Fletcher and H.M. Weinstein, "A World Unto Itself? The Application of International Justice in the Former Yugoslavia", in E. Stover and H.M. Weinstein (eds.), *My Neighbor, My Enemy: Justice and Community in the Aftermath of Mass Atrocity* (Cambridge: Cambridge University Press, 2004) 29–48; P. Akhavan, *l.c.*; J. Meernik, *l.c.*; R. Teitel, "Bringing the Messiah Through the Law", in C. Hesse and R. Post (eds.), *Human Rights in Political Transitions: Gettysburg to Bosnia* (New York: Zone Books, 1999) 177–193; A.A. Schevey, "Striving for Accountability in the Former Yugoslavia", in J. Stromseth (ed.), *Accountability for Atrocities: National and International Responses* (New York: Transnational Publishers Inc., 2003) 39–85.

of the latter's goals or achievements by its supporters, the media, and the ICTY itself.[21] However, one must also note that with time a more humble and nuanced view on this has gained ground.[22]

The topic is bound to cause controversy at least while there is an indiscriminate use of the notion of reconciliation. In this chapter, we chose to use the notion of social trust and showed how it can be linked to functions attributed to the law, based on the belief that these apply both to law at the national level and at the international level. On the basis of this we will explore how the ICTY has fulfilled those functions, and thus, contributed to rebuilding social trust in the former Yugoslavia.

3 In Practice: How Well Can Law Serve Trust?

A great deal of hope has been placed on the potential of the ICTY to reveal the truth of what transpired during the conflicts in the former Yugoslavia and on its contribution to easing ethnic tensions by focusing on the concept of individual criminal responsibility and thus rejecting the idea of collective guilt. Both of these claims have met important challenges in practice.

In 1998 Akhavan wrote about the ICTY that "the penalization of ethnic cleansing and the exposition of the truth behind this campaign of deception will help educate and transform popular values in the former Yugoslavia" and added that "the ICTY will contribute to interethnic reconciliation by telling the truth about the underlying causes and consequences of the Yugoslav tragedy"[23]. These assertions represent well the author's and others' overt confidence in the ICTY's contribution to truth-telling, acknowledgement, and to reaffirming fundamental values in the former Yugoslavia. However, Akhavan also conceded that

> ... of course, even if the ICTY can establish a factual record of what happened, it cannot contribute to national reconciliation if this record is not recognized and internalized by the peoples of the former Yugoslavia.[24]

---

21 "Paving the Way to Reconciliation" is included on the webpage of the Tribunal under "Core Achievements", available at www.un.org/icty/glance-e/index.htm. See also L.E. Fletcher and H.M. Weinstein (2004), *l.c.,* 36 and 37.

22 It has been progressively argued that the ICTY will not be able on its own to bring about reconciliation in the Balkans. See the Address of Carla del Ponte at the Policy Briefing, European Policy Center, Brussels, 3 July 2007, available at www.un.org/icty/pressreal/2007/pr1172e-annex.htm, where the Chief Prosecutor stated that "The Tribunal alone cannot bring stability and reconciliation."

23 P. Akhavan, *l.c.*, 741 and 744.

24 *Id.* 770.

And indeed, primarily due to the distance (geographical and cultural) of the Tribunal from the people in the former Yugoslavia[25], the Tribunal's perceived lack of legitimacy in the region[26], as well as the highly problematic post–war political contexts in these countries, the record established by the ICTY met serious resistance in the region.[27] What one would have reasonably expected as a result of the judicial efforts, namely acknowledgement, was weighed against either blunt denial, or manipulative justification and counter–arguments. An important point of reflection in what concerns law's symbolic function is that those who should recognise the values affirmed by law as their own, 'shared' values are often not involved in the process of affirming those values. There is a fundamental disconnect here which may undermine well–intended efforts especially at the international level where the separation between those involved in the process of establishing what happened and its wrongfulness, and those directly affected by the events is even greater. This, in the case of the former Yugoslavia, may well have contributed to some negative perceptions of the population towards the Tribunal[28] and also to the lack of the cooperation of the authorities in the region with the Tribunal.

The extent to which the values affirmed by the Tribunal will be recognised by the population as their own, and the extent to which acknowledgment will result thereof is certainly linked to which type of truth the Tribunal is capable of producing. The limited contribution of judicial processes to unveiling the truth after mass atrocities, which was alluded to above, has been the object of many studies.[29] For what concerns us here, a limited, partial, and purely factual truth holds little chance of leading to the broad acknowledgement that post–conflict societies need

---

25 L.E. Fletcher and H.M. Weinstein (2004), *l.c.*, 31.

26 For studies and surveys on these perceptions, see for example, D. Saxon, "Exporting Justice: Perceptions of the ICTY Among the Serbian, Croatian, and Muslim Communities in the Former Yugoslavia", *Journal of Human Rights* 2005, *44*, 559–572; OSCE Serbia and Belgrade Centre For Human Rights, "Public Opinion in Serbia. Views on Domestic War Crimes Judicial Authorities and The Hague Tribunal", December 2006, available at www.osce.org/documents/srb/2007/03/23518_en.pdf; K. Cibelli and T. Guberek, "Justice Unknown, Justice Unsatisfied? Bosnian NGOs Speak About ICTY" (Tufts University, 1999); UNDP Bosnia and Herzegovina, "Justice and Truth in Bosnia and Herzegovina: Public Perceptions", 2005, available at www.undp.ba/index.aspx?PID=14.

27 According to Hodzic, "The Tribunal has without a doubt developed into a respected and powerful instrument of international justice …; in the former Yugoslavia, however, it has struggled to win the trust and full respect from the population which formed its natural constituency." R. Hodzic, "Bosnia and Herzegovina – Legitimacy in Transition", paper presented at the conference Building a Future on Peace and Justice, Nüremberg, 25–27 June 2007, available at www.peace–justice–conference.info/download/Hodzic_Expert%20Paper.pdf.

28 Surely, this aspect was exploited politically and in the media who for a long time portrayed the Tribunal as a 'political tool in the hands of the West'. See R. Hodzic, *l.c.*

29 See, for example, J. Mertus, "Truth in a Box: The Limits of Justice Through Judicial Mechanisms", in I. Amadiume and A. An–Na'im (eds.), *The Politics of Memory: Truth, Healing and Social Justice* (London/New York: Zed Books, 2000) 142–161. M. Parlevliet, "Considering Truth. Dealing with a Legacy of Gross Human Rights Violations", *Netherlands Quarterly of Human Rights* 1998, *16*(2), 141-174, 172 and 173.

in order to overcome the tensions of the past. On the contrary, as long as the 'truth' of judicial decisions continues to be challenged because of being one–sided or incomplete, tensions between the opposing sides will not be eased and may even be reinforced.[30]

Easing ethnic tensions was also an expected outcome of the Tribunal's focus on individual criminal responsibility. Individualising guilt was, in the eyes of Tribunal's advocates, necessary as a means to avoid the attribution of collective guilt among nations. The fulfilment of this peace–making function was not so obvious in reality. On the one hand, the concept of individual responsibility failed to capture the nature of the crimes being prosecuted which imply an orchestrated plan or policy and also the involvement of a considerable number of people.[31] On the other hand, this concept "bears a complex relationship to the question of identity at play in the Balkans"[32] where the "shift of identity from the individual to the collective self" during and after the war leads to strong forms of collective solidarity (or in–group favouritism) and to "delegitimisation" of the opposing group.[33] Such dynamics may account for the demonstrations of support of parts of the population for some ICTY indictees[34] as well as for the fact that, as Hodzic put it, the "'popularity' of the Tribunal was inversely proportionate to the number of those indicted coming from the ethnic community in question"[35]. The fact that, given the dynamics of the wars and the socio–political processes associated with individual and group identity, the focus on individual criminal responsibility has not brought about the expected social pacification merits further thought on how much trials can achieve in such contexts. In particular, the danger of polarisation and further social division, instead of pacification as a result of international criminal trials, should not be neglected.[36]

---

30 How the truth of the Tribunal is perceived has a major impact on its peace–making potential. See L. Aucoin and E. Babbit, "Transitional Justice: Assessment Survey of Conditions in the Former Yugoslavia", UNDP Serbia and Montenegro, June 2006, where it is stated that "the perceptions of the ICTY have sometimes actually served to heighten tensions and provoked rivalry between the different ethnic groups in the region."

31 See M. Osiel, "Why Prosecute? Critics of Punishment for Mass Atrocity", *Human Rights Quarterly* 2000, *22*, 118–147, for an interesting analysis on the objections raised to criminal prosecution to the 'large–scale, state–sponsored massacres'.

32 R. Teitel, *l.c.*, 186.

33 J. Halpern and H.M. Weinstein, *l.c.*

34 As attested by Drumbl, "simply because an act is punished after a trial does not mean that the offender or society as a whole will perceive that act as evil: often it is quite the contrary, as criminal punishment can yield sympathy, empathy or even support." M. Drumbl, *l.c.*, 300.

35 R. Hodzic, *l.c.*

36 In this respect it is worth noting Fletcher and Weinstein's statement that "international criminal trials have the effect of stigmatizing groups despite the emphasis on individualizing guilt." L.E. Fletcher and H.M. Weinstein (2004), *l.c.*, 44. See also in the conclusion of the same book, where the editors recognise that they "found criminal trials – and especially those of local perpetrators – often divided small multi–ethnic communities by causing further suspicion and fear." E. Stover and H.M. Weinstein, "Conclusion: A Common Objective, a Universe of Alternatives", in E. Stover and H.M. Weinstein (eds.), *My Neighbor, My Enemy: Justice and Community in the Aftermath of Mass Atrocity* (Cambridge: Cambridge University Press, 2004) 323–342, 323.

4 Acknowledgement and Trust: What Does a Restorative Approach Have to Offer?

Increasing attention has been drawn in recent decades to the potential contribution of restorative justice to the needs and goals of societies striving to deal with a legacy of mass atrocities. The realisation of the limits of the Western model of retributive justice[37] on the one hand, and the contemporary use of traditional mechanisms and notions of justice on the other hand, have contributed to that.

It follows from what has been said before that rebuilding trust among individuals and groups who were on opposing sides during a conflict is one of the most important and complex challenges of post–conflict societies, and that acknowledgment of harm and responsibility by all sides is crucial in that process. The question is, then, what can be the contribution of a restorative justice approach to reaching acknowledgement and to rebuilding trust?

Conceptualising restorative justice in contexts of mass (and often inter–group) violence needs further theoretical work. Here we adopt a view of restorative justice as an approach or a philosophy[38]; in other words, as a set of core values and principles which are at the foundation of the restorative justice paradigm. In this sense, we do not centre our analysis on practices or mechanisms which have been associated with restorative justice in transitional justice processes, such as truth and reconciliation commissions, particularly the one of South Africa, or the Gacaca in Rwanda, but instead we focus our attention on principles which may pervade and inform different mechanisms.

Creating a safe space for the parties to express their views, experiences and needs in the aftermath of crime has been at the centre of restorative justice, especially from the perspective of the proponents of an "encounter conception"[39] of restorative justice. Central to this conception are the principles of inclusion, active participation, and encounter.[40] The underlying idea here is that of engagement of the concerned parties in a process of dealing with the aftermath of crime. This way, the truth reached in a restorative process will not only be of a factual, but also of a dialogical nature where the narrative of one's experiences and percep-

---

37 Writing about Rwanda, Drumbl found "the ability of the genocide trials to promote social reunion, communal reconciliation and justice to be quite limited." To this he added "I also believed the trials to be hindering the development of a shared national consciousness, a sense of citizenship and political community in Rwanda." M. Drumbl, *l.c.*, 292.

38 See L. Stovel, "When the Enemy Comes Home: Restoring Justice After Mass Atrocity", paper presented at the Restorative Justice Conference "Restorative justice in post–war contexts", Vancouver, 1–4 June 2003, 10. See also H. Zehr, *The Little Book of Restorative Justice* (Intercourse, PA: Good Books, 2002) 5. The author explains, "Although the term 'restorative justice' encompasses a variety of programs and practices, at its core it is a set of principles, a philosophy, an alternate set of guiding questions".

39 G. Johnstone and D.W. Van Ness, "The Meaning of Restorative Justice", in G. Johnstone and D.W. Van Ness (eds.), *Handbook of Restorative Justice* (Devon: Willan, 2007), 5–24.

40 See, for example, D.W. Van Ness, "The Shape of Things to Come", in E.G.M. Weitekamp and H.–J. Kerner (eds.), *Restorative Justice: Theoretical Foundations* (Devon: Willan, 2002) 1–20.

tions is of key importance.[41] When transposed to the context of post–conflict societies, such a restorative approach to truth–seeking may bear great potential and overcome some of the shortcomings of judicial retributive mechanisms.[42] In fact, the restorative justice model – as embodied by truth commissions – has been presented by many authors as much better suited to perform the tasks of truth–seeking and truth–telling after large–scale conflicts.[43] The very fact that those affected participate in the process (for example by giving statements, presenting documents, and hearing others' statements) holds a greater promise that the 'truth' which will emerge will be more easily accepted and even internalised, than that emerging as a result of judicial processes. If that is the case, then acknowledgment on all sides is encouraged. Indeed, if processes such as these allow for a broader, more complete and nuanced account of what happened in the past, it will be less likely that the resulting 'truth' will be dismissed as one–sided and subject to manipulation. Acknowledgement is central to a restorative approach: it is expected that there is from the outset at least some openness by the parties to acknowledging the other's suffering and their own responsibilities; and also that as a result of these processes acknowledgment may come about more easily.[44]

It has been argued by some authors that a restorative approach also better serves societies who face social breakdown because of widespread violence and so need to restore relations and rebuild their social fabric. In the words of Laura Stovel,

> the humanizing philosophy of restorative justice makes it a natural approach for post–conflict reconciliation, where people who were once enemies need to find a way to live amongst and trust one another.[45]

Because crime, from a restorative justice perspective, is seen primarily as a violation of people and relationships, there is a central concern precisely in restoring those relationships (even if the parties did not know each other before the con-

---

41 See L. Stovel, *Long Road Home: Building Reconciliation and Trust in Post–War Sierra Leone*, Ph. D. Dissertation, 46: "Valued information may not be identical to forensic truth and it is reached discursively by humans–in–relationship."

42 See M. Valiñas and K. Vanspauwen, "The Promise of Restorative Justice in the Search for Truth After a Violent Conflict. Experiences from South Africa and Bosnia–Herzegovina", paper presented at the Fourth Conference of the European Forum for Restorative Justice "Restorative justice and beyond – An agenda for Europe", Barcelona, 14–17 June 2006.

43 J. Llewellyn, "Truth Commissions and Restorative Justice", in G. Johnstone and D.W. Van Ness (eds.), *Handbook of Restorative Justice* (Devon: Willan, 2007) 351-371.

44 See L. Stovel (Ph. D.), *l.c.*, 48: "At intergroup, national or international levels, restorative policies may require that groups in whose names crimes were committed to recognize and atone for past injustices (through compensation and symbolic acts) and acknowledge current privilege based on those crimes."

45 See L. Stovel (Ph. D.), *l.c.*, 43. Along the same lines, Jennifer Llewellyn affirms that "the need to focus on restoration of relationships in response to wrongdoing is revealed through these situations [of transitional justice] in a most compelling and urgent way." J. Llewellyn, "Truth Commission and Restorative Justice", in G. Johnstone and D.W. Van Ness (eds.), *Handbook of Restorative Justice* (Devon: Willan, 2007) 351–371, 354.

flict).[46] The "humanizing" approach of restorative justice is not only present in the answer of 'what' to restore but also 'how'. In the famed words of Van Ness and Strong, "justice requires that we work to restore victims, offenders and communities who have been injured by crime."[47] As to the how, the authors respond with the four values of encounter, reparation, reintegration and participation. While the goal is clearly stated as being that of restoration – of harm and of relations – the four values have one underlying idea, that of promoting a mutual understanding among the parties. Although it will not always be the case in practice, the idea of creating an opportunity for building empathy among the parties is at the core of the restorative philosophy.[48] Halpern and Weinstein explain that empathy "involves imagining and seeking to understand the unique perspective of another person."[49] They elaborate on how empathy between former enemies can lead to the "rehumanisation" of the other, mainly through an "individualising view of another", and how it can contribute to reconciliation.[50] Our hypothesis here is that a restorative approach to post–conflict justice, based on the ideals of restoring relations through an inclusive process of communication which aims at mutual understanding among the parties, is more likely to reach the goal of rebuilding trust among opposing sides.

The link between acknowledgement and trust – the two elements which we presented as central in dealing with a legacy of mass abuse – seems to flow easily in such a conception of a restorative approach. Acknowledgement, just like trust, requires a process of meaningful exchange between those concerned.[51] As Akhavan recognised,

> reconciliation requires a shared truth – a moral or interpretative account – that appeals to a common bond of humanity transcending ethnic affinity,

---

46 H. Zehr, *Changing Lenses: A New Focus for Crime and Justice* (Scottsdale, PA: Herald Press, 1990) 181.

47 D.W. Van Ness and K.H. Strong, *Restoring Justice* (Cincinnati: Anderson Publishing, 1997).

48 When referring to the elements of a 'restorative encounter' Van Ness states that "The purpose of the meeting is for the parties to develop understanding – of the crime, of the other parties involved, and of the steps needed to make things right. There may even be a degree of empathy that develops between them." D.W. Van Ness, "Perspectives on Achieving Satisfying Justice: Values and Principles of Restorative Justice", paper presented at Achieving Satisfying Justice Symposium, Vancouver, BC, 21 March 1997. Note that in the author's layered model, there may be situations in which "the parties do not meet directly, but communicate indirectly their stories and emotions and as a result come to understanding." D.W. Van Ness, *l.c.*, 7. This option might be more adequate to a restorative approach in cases of mass violence where a direct encounter might be unfeasible and undesirable. H. Zehr (2002), *l.c.*, 38.

49 J. Halpern and H.M. Weinstein, *l.c.*, 307.

50 *Ibid.*

51 Orentlicher, usually associated with a firm claim of the centrality of the duty to prosecute in the wake of mass abuse, has recently acknowledged the potential of "nonjudicial measures" and in particular the fact that "an effective truth commission can engage society in an inclusive process of reckoning and repair." D.F. Orentlicher, "'Settling Accounts' Revisited: Reconciling Global Norms with Local Agency", *The International Journal of Transitional Justice* 2007, *1*, 10–22.

to which he added,

> achieving a truth common to adversaries is not so much an exhaustive historical record of events as it is an empathy for human suffering that transcends the bonds of blood and soil.[52]

For such a shared truth or acknowledgment to emerge, a focus on harm and suffering (on all sides) while at the same time ensuring accountability, rather than an exclusive concern with the deeds of the accused, is crucial.[53] And here is where the restorative philosophy may provide useful insight. To be sure, the importance given to the harm suffered does not neglect, but on the contrary implies, that attention is paid to the associated responsibilities. Accountability is thus also a central part of this restorative approach. And accountability reached following such a philosophy may result in that "evil becomes acknowledged even by many of those who inflicted it in the first place."[54]

5 Conclusion

By way of conclusion let us briefly turn to the case of former Yugoslavia. While the process of truth–telling has until very recently been mostly run from the outside and has met with significant resistance in the region, genuine acknowledgement might require something more or something else than what the formal judicial system can offer. A restorative approach may offer the framework for a meaningful exchange, for an inclusive process of dialogue in which the mutual recognition of each other's suffering and an individualising view of the humanity in the other will be the cornerstones. To be sure, we are looking at a slow and long–term process. But ultimately, internalised acknowledgement, mutual understanding, and an empathic attitude toward the other will be the most powerful tools against ongoing political manipulation of the facts and political use of interpretations. And at the same time, they will be the most efficient foundations for social repair. The law has undoubtedly an important role in the long and highly complex endeavour of rebuilding social trust, but it also has significant limitations. Recognising these limitations and searching for the potential contribution of other approaches is a necessary undertaking towards which this chapter attempted at being a first step.

---

52 P. Akhavan, *l.c.*, 741 and 771.

53 Drumbl gives a powerful account of the Tadic case at the ICTY to illustrate how the concern of courts with the 'microscopic truth' overshadowed 'the most important point' which was the suffering of the victim. M. Drumbl, *l.c.*, 294.

54 M. Drumbl, *l.c.*, 300.

Chapter 12 – Legitimacy in the European Union and the Limits of the Law

"To know whereof one speaks is always beneficial; this is especially true when dealing with the problem of legitimacy..."[1]

Stefanie Dierckxsens

1 Introduction

The results of the referenda for ratifying the Treaty establishing a Constitution for Europe (Constitutional Treaty) in France and the Netherlands demonstrated with force the limits of the legitimising capacity of law. Even though the legal legitimacy of the European construction has increased considerably throughout several Treaty reviews, the European Union is confronted with a growing loss of legitimacy in the eyes of the public opinion (social legitimacy).

This contribution takes this paradox in European integration seriously. The growing gap between legal and social legitimacy will be the starting point for further investigation here. This research proposes to describe and explain the paradox from the perspective of the limits of the law.

This chapter consists of three parts. The first part aims at describing the growing gap between legal and social legitimacy, culminating in the Constitutional Treaty and its agonising ratification process (section 2). To define legal legitimacy, inspiration will be found in the classical Lincolnian triad, characterised by three dimensions of legitimacy: for, by, and of the people. These three prerequisites for law to be legitimate will be aligned with the functions of law, as set out in "The Limits of the Law (Introduction)".

The second part intends to explain the paradoxical gap by referring to the characteristics of law as enunciated in Chapter 1. Emphasis will be put on the characteristic of law as social practice and on the necessity of internalising law in order to perceive it as legitimate. Ideally, citizens should be able to perceive themselves at the same time as authors of the law and as applicants of the law. Law should reflect the identity of the community of law, brought to life in the critical discourse of autonomous citizens. Starting from this conception in which legitimacy is related to the identity of the community, the legitimacy of the European Union is considered to be problematic. In order to understand the European identity crisis

---

1 J. Habermas (translated and with an introduction by Th. McCarthy), *Communication and the Evolution of Society* (Boston: Beacon Press, 1979) 178.

better, a sociological and anthropological diagnosis of late–modern societies will be offered (section 3).

The third part seeks to bridge the gap between legal and social legitimacy. It endeavours to make suggestions how to deal with the paradox. The idea is that social legitimacy can only be realised by giving the European Union a normative appeal and by restoring the public autonomy of European citizens (section 4).

2 The Paradox in European Integration: A Growing Gap between Legal and Social Legitimacy

Without any doubt, the legal legitimacy of the European construct has increased throughout several Treaty reviews. Nevertheless, social acceptance of the European construct went through a crisis with the ratification process of the Constitutional Treaty. The citizens of France and the Netherlands rejected the text of the Constitutional Treaty on 29 May 2005 and 1 June 2005 respectively. A period of reflection was then proclaimed.

Before explaining this paradox, it is important to refine in a first step the concept of legitimacy and to evaluate in a second step the suggested increase of legal legitimacy throughout the history of European integration.

2.1 Social Legitimacy versus Legal Legitimacy

In order to analyse the European legitimacy crisis and to avoid conceptual confusion[2], the distinction between social and legal legitimacy should be clarified. Social legitimacy refers to the subjective (socio–psychological) component of legitimacy. It concerns the actual acceptance of the legal system by citizens, obedience to laws, and confidence in and allegiance to institutions. Social legitimacy is empirically measurable and manifests itself in the results of opinion polls, in the turnout at parliamentary elections, in the results of referenda, and so on. These subjective manifestations are rooted in objective legal conditions, which also can be observed empirically. In other words the objective prerequisites for law to enjoy legal legitimacy reflect the breeding ground for social legitimacy. Inspired by the classical Lincolnian triad, we can discern three prerequisites for law to be legitimate: an output–prerequisite (law for the people), an input–prerequisite

---

2 The term 'legitimacy' is used in several different ways. See amongst others D. Beetham and C. Lord, "Legitimacy and the European Union", in A. Weale and M. Nentwich (eds.), *Political Theory and the European Union* (London and New York: Routledge, 2001) 15–33; A. Føllesdal, "Democracy, Legitimacy and Majority Rule in the European Union", in A. Weale and M. Nentwich (eds.), *Political Theory and the European Union* (London and New York: Routledge, 2001) 34–48; J. Habermas (1979), *l.c.*, 178–205; J. Weiler, "Problems of Legitimacy in Post 1992 Europe", *Aussenwirtschaf* III/IV 1991, 411–437.

(law by the people), and an identity–prerequisite (law of the people). In the next subsection, these facets of legal legitimacy will be aligned with the regulatory function, with protective legality, and with the symbolic function respectively.

The relationship between social and legal legitimacy reflects no necessary link. One cannot ignore the fact that law, although it fulfils several legitimising functions, may not be accepted by citizens. On the other hand it is not unthinkable that law fails in its legitimising functions, but nevertheless generates social legitimacy. A shortage of objective legitimation factors can be the object of academic debate. However, a subjective legitimation deficit becomes a political problem since purely repressive law undermines itself. The approval of the citizens is in other words necessary for the sustainability of law. The stability of the legal order depends on its *de facto* recognition.

2.2 The Increase of Legal Legitimacy throughout the History of European Integration

As mentioned, the term 'legal legitimacy' here is not restricted to laws that are enacted and exercised in accordance with constitutional rules and appropriate procedures. Legal legitimacy is a multi–facetted concept that can be analysed by referring to the three dimensions of the Lincoln triad (for, by and of the people) and to the functions of law.

2.2.1 Regulatory Function

The output–dimension of legal legitimacy can be arranged with the regulatory function of law. Obviously the legitimacy of law is related to the efficiency of law in solving difficult societal problems. Legal rules are legitimate if and because they promote efficient outcomes. For a long time, Community law focused on the regulative dimension of legitimacy. This output–approach resulted in peace for over half a century and in the establishment of a genuine single market for goods, persons, services, and capital, with the addition of a single currency in 1999. Naturally these political and economic benefits enjoyed broad support. They reflected a win–win situation with no losers, no opposition.

However, as highlighted by Fritz W. Scharpf, this has been changing for some time now[3] and the limits of the regulative dimension of legitimacy are coming to the surface. Two reasons can be given. First of all, market–creating policy decisions nowadays are more and more controversial (e.g. liberalisation of public ser-

---

[3] F. Scharpf, *Problem–Solving Effectiveness and Democratic Accountability in the EU* (Max Planck Institut für Gesellschaftsforschung, MPIfG Working Paper 03/1, 2003) 7–8, http://www.mpi-fg-koeln.mpg.de/pu/workpap/wp03-1/wp03-1.html (Last visited 12 August 2003); F. Scharpf, *Governing in Europe. Effective and Democratic* (Oxford/New York: Oxford University Press, 1999) 45.

vices and goods, such as the liberalisation of health care). Secondly, the EU needs to take measures that correct the free operation of markets, decisions which were up until recently under the effective control of democratic accountable national governments (e.g. issues such as employment and social policy). These issues are much more contentious. National interests and political preferences tend to diverge. In other words, the controversial policy decisions imply policy choices and so–called losers opposed to the respective policy choices.

2.2.2 Protective Legality

In order to justify the controversial policy outcomes, constitutional principles (such as basic rights, the principle of division of power, principles of representative and participatory democracy, and so on) were developed in order to guarantee the protection of citizens against an invasive exercise of power. The Union's 'institutional balance' as it emerges from the current constitutional *acquis* is designed to place necessary limits on governmental power, by dividing it and subjecting it to forms of mutual control.[4] The legislative power in the Community is shared and delicately balanced between the Commission, the Council, and the European Parliament, whereas the executive power is shared, and less delicately balanced, between the Commission and the Council. The judicial power is in separate and independent hands. There exist several mechanisms of political accountability and of judicial review. In other words, the European Union is characterised by a constitutional system that complies with the rule of law concept.[5] Moreover, the emancipation of the constitutional principle of representative democracy (reflected in the revaluation of the parliamentary role in the institutional balance) throughout the history of European integration[6] not only protects citizens against intrusive exercises of power, but also tries to transform this struggle for power into another kind of power, namely the citizen's power of mutual cooperation in the public interest.

2.2.3 Symbolic Function

If Europe is characterised by its own form of constitutionalism, why bother then with a written constitutional treaty?[7] Despite the gradual development of the

---

4 See K. Lenaerts and A. Verhoeven, "Institutional Balance as a Guarantee for Democracy in EU Governance", in C. Joerges and R. Dehousse (eds.), *Good Governance in Europe's Integrated Market* (Oxford: Oxford University Press, 2002) 44 e.s.

5 See W. Van Gerven, *The European Union. A Polity of States and Peoples* (Oxford and Portland: Hart Publishing, 2005) 104–157.

6 See M. Shackleton, "The European Parliament", in J. Peterson and M. Shackleton (eds.), *The Institutions of the European Union* (Oxford: Oxford University Press, 2006) 106.

7 This question has been raised by, among others, A. Moravcsik, "If it Ain't Broke, Don't Fix it", *Newsweek International* (04.03.2002); J.H.H. Weiler, "In Defence of the Status Quo:

European constitutional system of checks and balances and the emancipation of European Parliament, the referenda on the Treaty of Maastricht and several opinion polls revealed that the European Union was desperately in need of social legitimacy. A variety of studies have been devoted to the question why Europe commands so little sympathy. In answering this question, many authors believed that a written constitution could have a catalytic effect on the European identification process[8], on the process of an ever closer Union. A European constitution could create social cohesion in the European Union that is still primarily characterised by diversity. Intergovernmental arrangements, on the contrary, lack this symbolic function of law.

2.2.4 The Constitutional Treaty

With the Treaty establishing a Constitution for Europe, a good attempt was made to improve all three legitimising functions of law. The Convention came up with solutions to make the decision–making process of the Union more efficient so that Community law would reflect better responses to practical issues. The Convention improved also the institutional balance in the European Union, for example by labelling co–decision (placing the European Parliament on an equal footing with the Council) the 'ordinary legislative procedure'.[9] Moreover, a new Title was introduced (Title VI – The Democratic Life of the Union) expressing the principles, among others, of representative and participatory democracy. Finally, with the final document drawn by the Convention reflecting a crystallisation of the constitutional *acquis*, law could play its symbolic role.

However, the ratification process revealed in a very painful way the limited capacity of law to generate social legitimacy. It is bitter irony that the Treaty establishing a Constitution for Europe, prepared by a Convention bringing together the main stakeholders in order to give the constitutional *acquis* a broader social basis of public support, was rejected implacably by the citizens of two of the Founding Fathers, while the original elitist Treaties were supported by a so–called 'permissive consensus'.[10] Undoubtedly the attempt made in the Convention was not perfect and could be improved. Certainly many other reasons could be given for the no–votes. Yet the least we can say is that the proceedings of the Convention which resulted in the Treaty establishing a Constitution for Europe did not convince or reconnect the people of Europe and did not generate social legitimacy.

Europe's Constitutional *Sonderweg*", in J.H.H. Weiler and M. Wind (eds.), *European Constitutionalism Beyond the State* (Cambridge: Cambridge University Press, 2003) 7–23.

8 See among others J. Habermas, "Why Europe Needs a Constitution", *New Left Review* 2001, *11*, 16–17.

9 On the reform of procedures and institutions in the Treaty establishing a Constitution for Europe, see K. Lenaerts and D. Gerard, "The Structure of the Union According to the Constitution for Europe: The Emperor is Getting Dressed", *European Law Review* 2004, 289–322.

10 This expression was introduced by L. Lindberg and S. Scheingold, *Europe's Would–Be Polity* (Harvard: Harvard University Press, 1970).

3 Explaining the Paradoxical Gap: The Normative Legitimacy Deficit

3.1 Empirical versus Normative Legitimacy

How can we explain that the efforts of the Convention to improve the three Lincolnian dimensions of legitimacy are in vain? This second part tries to clarify the paradoxical gap between legal and social legitimacy by referring to the characteristic of law as social practice, as enunciated in Chapter 1. In order for law to be perceived as legitimate, citizens should be able to see themselves as authors and as applicants of the law at the same time. This prerequisite implies an identification process between the rulers and the ruled. Law is legitimate then, not solely because it is *de facto* accepted by the citizens (social legitimacy), nor because it generates an efficient aggregation of private interests (regulatory dimension of legal legitimacy), nor because it is established in accordance with constitutional principles (protective dimension of legal legitimacy), nor because it is couched in a potentially symbolic document (symbolic dimension of legal legitimacy), but because it clearly reflects the normative self–understanding of the citizens in a community of law. In this way, legitimacy not only has an empirical, but also a normative component. Legitimacy means that there are good arguments for citizens to accept the law. The legitimacy of law is related to the *normative quality of law*, taking the collective identity, the foundations of the community of law as ultimate criterion.[11] To be sure, both senses of legitimacy are related: empirical legitimacy is often regarded as a necessary, though not sufficient, condition of normative legitimacy.[12]

Before examining the normative legitimacy deficit, it is important to clear up several misconceptions. First of all, the *collective identity* is not conceived as a static identity, *a priori* determined, but it is developed in the concrete political actions of autonomous citizens in the public realm. Cornelius Castoriadis refers to the collective identity of an 'autonomous society' and defines it in the following way:

> What will be the collective identity, the 'we' of an autonomous society? We are the ones who make our own laws, we are an autonomous collectivity made up of autonomous individuals. And we are able to look at ourselves, recognise ourselves, and call ourselves back into question in and through our works.[13]

The idea of *autonomous action* cannot be misinterpreted here: it does not coincide with action in accordance with one's own preferences, independent of the willing of others. Following the Kantian line, the conception of autonomy is characterised

---

11 J. Habermas (1979), *l.c.*, 182–183; R. Foqué, "De legitimatiecrisis van het publieke bestel", in L. Baljé (ed.), *Vernieuwing en Eerste Kamer. Een reflectie op het Openbaar Bestuur* ('s Gravenhage: SDU, 1994) 77–105.

12 R. Foqué (1994), *l.c.*, 80–81.

13 C. Castoriadis, cited in Z. Bauman, *In Search of Politics* (Cambridge: Polity Press, 1999) 166.

by the interplay of choice and independent validity. Self–rule is not merely a matter of prescribing one's own standards for others. It is a matter of making laws that are intersubjectively valid.[14] Gerald Dworkin's characterisation is clarifying:

> Autonomy is conceived of as a second–order capacity of persons to reflect critically upon their first–order preferences, desires, wishes, and so forth, and the capacity to accept or attempt to change these in light of higher–order preferences and values.[15]

Individuals should occupy an exocentric position in which they can make abstraction from their private interests. They should distance themselves from their 'first–order preferences' in order to reflect upon the common good and the collective identity ('higher–order preferences') they share.

Autonomous action therefore cannot be achieved in isolation. Autonomous human beings are interdependent.[16] Pursuing this idea, Hannah Arendt describes *plurality* as "*the* condition – not only the *condition sine qua non*, but the *conditio per quam* – of all political life."[17] Following the Aristotelian line, Arendt emphasises that political consciousness only comes into being when people, confronted in the public realm with human plurality, leave their familiar surroundings behind and start questioning the self–evident norms and values of the private realm in the light of the common good they share.

This is what the European legitimacy deficit is ultimately about. Dealing with the legitimacy deficiencies of the European Union, the following questions have to be taken into consideration. Does the European Union reflect an autonomous society? Does the normative self–understanding of the European citizens match with the underlying assumptions of the European Union? Does this identity (as the result of the identification process between the ruled and the rulers) serve as a frame of reference on the basis of which the normative quality of law–making can be measured? These questions have to be answered in the negative. There is no substantive frame of reference available on the basis of which the European day–to–day politics can be evaluated. European decisions do not reflect a process of self–understanding, a collective identity, as a result of which citizens alienate themselves from the European construct and from their fellow–citizens.

---

14 I. Kant (translated and analysed by H.J. Paton), *The Moral Law, Groundwork of the Metaphysic of Morals* (London: Routledge, 1948) 87–88.

15 G. Dworkin, cited in A. Ingram, *A Political Theory of Rights* (Oxford: Clarendon Press, 1994) 99.

16 A. Ingram, *l.c.*, 152–157.

17 H. Arendt, *The Human Condition* (Chigago & London: The University of Chicago Press, 1958).

3.2 The Twin Assault on Normative Legitimacy in Late–Modern Societies

3.2.1 Setting the Scene

In order to clarify the European legitimacy crisis, this subsection is going to follow an interdisciplinary approach. The sociological and anthropological diagnosis of contemporary societies that will be put forward here, aims at a better understanding of the European crisis by placing it in a broader perspective. In this diagnosis, contemporary societies are regarded as late–modern societies in a way that contemporary societies reflect a clear, but accelerated and radicalised continuation of two modern sets of forces.[18]

On the one hand, there is little in late–modern societies that was not philosophically embraced by the Enlightenment: their passion for individual freedom, their trust in reason, and (not unrelated to that trust) their fascination with control and regulation, their trust in the market, their skepticism about traditions, habits or evidences. 'Late–modernity' then, characterised by consumerism, individualism, egalitarianism, welfarism, economic and cultural globalisation, cultural relativism, is merely the agitated culmination of these essentials of Enlightenment.

On the other hand, proceeding from this insight, it comes as no surprise that the counterpoint of Enlightenment thinking, embodied in modern times by Romanticism, is also darkly reflected in late–modern societies. The vices of late–modern Romanticism are visible in the radicalisation of religions, apparent in Muslim, Christian and Jewish fundamentalism all over the world, and in the appeal of extreme–right and populist–right parties, mainly in Europe.

This subsection will show that although the tendencies of these two sets of forces appear intractably antithetical, each eschews plurality and destroys therefore any action of autonomous citizens in the public realm.

3.2.2 Neo–Liberalism

The first set of forces follows from modern Enlightenment thinking. It reflects an excessive continuation of its passion for individual freedom and its trust in reason and in the market. In our late–modern society these Enlightenment essentials are radically translated into neo–liberal thinking as imposed by the predominant global economic regime. In capitalist market ideology, social actions and interac-

---

[18] This diagnosis draws upon the work and teachings of R. Foqué, and upon the work of H. Arendt, *l.c.*, and B.R. Barber, *Jihad vs. McWorld* (New York: The Random House Publishing Group, 1995). The sociological partition is related to (though cannot be equated with) the distinction made in theories of political philosophy, such as the distinction that Kymlicka makes between utilitarianism (consequentialism) and communautarism and the distinction that Habermas makes between liberalism and republicanism (J. Habermas, "Three Normative Models of Democracy", in J. Habermas, *The Inclusion of the Other. Studies in Political Theory* (Cambridge/Oxford: Polity Press, 1999).

tions are no longer based on traditions, customs, or emotions, but on considerations of efficiency or calculation, reducing all relationships to those of means to ends. This process of *instrumental rationalisation* is provocatively described by George Ritzer. In *The McDonaldization of Society*, Ritzer describes the fast–food restaurant as having become a representative paradigm for our contemporary society.[19] He highlights four main characteristics of McDonaldisation: efficiency, calculability, predictability, and control. First of all, the fast–food restaurant is a classical example of efficiency. The hamburgers and the so–called menus are prepared in a standard way. The production process is very precisely described and determined, which saves time, energy and money. The consumer also experiences efficiency, since his loss of time is reduced to the absolute minimum, especially given the drive–through windows. Secondly, production and consumption in terms of standard units facilitate calculability. Thirdly, the standardised and uniform services also promote the predictability. Anywhere in the world, McDonalds is offering the same menus, in the same interior, with the same service. Finally, to avoid unpredictabilities, the production and consumption processes have to be controlled as much as possible.

Since the organisation of McDonalds is so efficient, so appealing, so easy to copy, there are innumerable variations. The world is becoming a 'McWorld' to use the terminology of Benjamin Barber, a global market society.[20] George Soros has labelled this process 'market fundamentalism'.[21] The whole society is conceived as a system of market–structured interactions of private persons.

In the context of economic globalisation the *role of the State* has also considerably changed. Traditionally the State symbolised societal cohesion and represented the common good. Hence, the State up until recently was best suited to counterbalance the excessive instrumental rationality of wild capitalism. The question though is whether it is any longer capable of doing so or willing to try. In our late–modern society, forces of aggressive economic and cultural globalisation provide for the privatisation of public goods and the diminishment of the State into merely one of the players in the system of market–structured interaction.[22] The predominant neo–liberal conception of the welfare State considers instrumental rationality to be the requisite tool for assessing the efficient aggregation of the private interests of citizens. The dominance of instrumental rationality reduces the common good into the general welfare, State administrators into managers and social engineers, citizens into consumers. Citizens are expected to pursue their private interests in a similar way consumers contemplate their concerns in a market. State administrators are transformed into managers and social engineers who aim at an efficient aggregation of the private interests of their voters, having elections

19 G. Ritzer, *The McDonaldization Thesis. Explorations and Extensions* (London: Sage, 1998).

20 B.R. Barber, *l.c.*

21 G. Soros, *The Crisis of Global Capitalism: Open Society Endangered* (New York: PublicAffairs, 1998).

22 R. Foqué, "De actualiteit van Montesquieu's staatkundige erfgoed", in Tweede Kamer der Staten–Generaal, *Stoelendansen met de macht, Verslag van de Conferentie over de Trias Politica op 27 januari 2006* (Den Haag, 2006) 19–23.

and power interests in the back of their minds. Whereas citizens are locked in a struggle between private interests, State administrators are involved in a competition for power. Both struggles are settled on the basis of the principles of the liberal constitution such as basic rights, free and fair elections, representative composition of parliamentary bodies, and so on.[23]

The dominance of instrumental rationality in consumer society is accompanied by the *phenomenon of conformism*. For in order to realise the four main characteristics of McDonaldisation (efficiency, calculability, predictability, and control), society expects from each of its members a certain kind of behaviour imposing innumerable rules, all of which tend to 'normalise' its members, to make them behave.[24] In other words, the fascination with optimal regulation and efficient control goes hand in hand with the passion for transparent, predictable categories. Uniform behaviour that lends itself to statistical determination and therefore to scientifically correct prediction is preferred over autonomous action.[25]

3.2.3 Neo–Romanticism

The second set of forces attempts to recapture a pre–modern, 'pre–Enlightenment' world. Here, entities lay claim to people's loyalty using pre–political identification factors such as religion, ethnicity, language, culture, and so on. Citizens are conceived as blood brothers and sisters defined by given identities. It promotes community, reinforced by the thinness and the transience of market relations, but at the expense of plurality, rendering politics into an exercise in exclusion and resentment.

As already mentioned, the increasing appeal of neo–romantic thinking can be explained by referring to the implications of neo–liberal thinking as imposed by the predominant global economic regime. First of all, the pre–political identification process, expressed in the shape of nationalism, and in religious fundamentalism, is nurtured by the neo–liberal alienation of citizens towards each other and towards the State, linked to the *erosion of social cohesion*. The appeal of the neo–romantic model is strengthened by the contemporary movement away from tradition, religion, and mystery, toward individual freedom and instrumental rationality. An evolution whose final destination could only be what Max Weber called 'the disenchantment of the world'.[26] Building a social identity has become a never–ending process of self–realisation in which individuals are no longer oriented towards the other and in which the importance of the logic of consumerism has increased. But the private choices we make as a consumer are only the identifying marks of which the significance is unsettled, as a result of which they are

---

23 J. Habermas (1999), *l.c.*

24 H. Arendt, *l.c.*, 40.

25 H. Arendt, *l.c.*, 38–58.

26 M. Weber, cited in B. R. Barber, *l.c.*

continuously exchanged.[27] Moreover, with the erosion of the role of the other, a stable benchmark has disappeared in the late–modern identification process. The resulting evanescence and thinness of late–modern social identities, linked to the rapid change of the global market society, foster an increasing feeling of uncertainty which is translated in Europe into the growing appeal of extreme–right populist parties. All these parties are offering the same recipe: nostalgia for traditions and self–evidences, obvious scapegoats and social cohesion at the expense of plurality.

Secondly, the rise of new forms of nationalism can be explained by drawing attention to another implication of the neo–liberal vision. The neo–liberal conception of the welfare State inspired by the belief in the manipulability of society (and by the trust in instrumental rationality to meet this belief) not only pulverises social cohesion, it also gives rise to *consumer dissatisfaction translated into protest votes*. Citizens have high expectations for the problem–solving capacity of State administrators. The authorities are approached in the first place, instead of in the last resort. This can be illustrated by the increased amount of lawsuits, by the rising appeal to social services, and so on. The pressure on the authorities, the so–called 'social engineers' augments, since they are blamed for any societal problem that comes to the surface. Extreme right populist parties referring to simple solutions and obvious scapegoats easily win the protest votes of the dissatisfied consumers.

3.2.4 The Impact of these Late–Modern Tendencies on Normative Legitimacy

Normative legitimacy is, as stated above, tied to respect for the public autonomy of citizens. The interpretation of autonomy defended in this chapter implies the creation of a contrafactual exocentric position: a position in the public realm in which citizens, confronted with plurality, are inclined to subject their private interests to a test of intersubjective validity. Neither the neo–liberal conception, nor the neo–romantic conception cares in the least about autonomous citizenship. In the neo–liberal conception citizens are reduced to consumers and clients whose autonomy consists of the right to pursue their private interests in a market society they cannot control. Plurality is undermined in this conception since the identity of citizens is imposed on them by a uniformising consumerism they scarcely notice.

The neo–romantic conception does little better. Reinforced by the thinness and the transience of market relations, it promotes community, but at the expense of plurality. In the neo–romantic conception citizens are conceived as blood brothers and sisters defined by given identities.

---

27 See W. Weyns, "Het 'meervoudig individu'. Een essay over zelfbeschikking in de postmoderniteit", *Tijdschrift voor sociologie* 1995, *16*(4), 364; Z. Bauman, *Liquid Modernity* (Cambridge: Polity Press, 2000) 72; E. Claes, "De duistere zijde van individualisering. Zygmunt Bauman, Paul Auster en de kracht van de literaire verbeelding", in T. Daems and L. Robert (eds.), *Zygmunt Bauman. De schaduwzijde van de vloeibare moderniteit* (Den Haag: Boom Juridische Uitgevers, 2007) 131-149.

In neo–liberal thinking, legitimacy depends on the one hand on the capacity to redeem efficiently the private expectations of the citizens, and on the other hand on the constitutional principles that regulate the process of aggregation of the individual expectations as a sort of invisible hand. Legitimacy is conceived as output–legitimacy (the effective aggregation of private interests – the regulatory function) and as input–legitimacy in a very formal way (the process of aggregation is disciplined by the principles of a liberal constitution – protective legality). The normative dimension of legitimacy is reduced to small formal constraints on the liberal constitution. But a thin layer of constitutionalism laid over a raging market society will not suffice. Nor does the neo–romantic conception of legitimacy in which the identity–prerequisite is emphasised, offer a sufficient answer to the legitimacy crisis. After all, in this conception the collective identity is considered to exist prior to the political process of collective self–understanding in which autonomous citizens are involved.

3.3 The European Legitimacy Crisis

The purpose of this subsection is to explain the normative legitimacy deficit of the EU by examining these reinforcing sets of tendencies in the European context. Although the influence of excessive Romanticism can be felt, the first tendency of accelerated Enlightenment thinking reflected in the neo–liberal model, is much more pronounced in the history of European integration.

The European Coal and Steel Community was set up as a means to prevent another bloody war on the European continent and to promote the economic interests of the Member States and their citizens. Hence, legitimacy depended solely on the capacity to redeem efficiently the private expectations of the Member States and their citizens. As mentioned above, this one–sided output–approach of legitimacy seemed to work for quite a while. After all, in the earlier European Union the aggregation of private concerns resulted in a win–win situation in which Pareto–efficiency was achieved. Since the EU succeeded in entrenching peace and a general welfare, the EU was supported by a 'permissive consensus'[28]. Nowadays, due to expanded cooperation in more controversial fields and due to further enlargement, EU policy decisions have become much more problematic. The private interests and expectations tend to diverge. A tacit consensus no longer exists and a Pareto–efficient aggregation of private interests has become an illusion. Consumer dissatisfaction has occurred, translated into a lack of social acceptance and support. Still, according to neo–liberal thinking, emphasis is put on protective legality, on the constitutional principles and procedures, such as basic rights, division of power, democratic procedures, and so on, that are believed to discipline and channel the competition of private interests as a sort of invisible hand. However, dissatisfied consumers cannot be soothed by pointing out the constitutional princi-

---

[28] As mentioned in footnote 10, this expression was introduced by L. Lindberg and S. Scheingold, *l.c.*

ples which discipline the struggle between competing interests. The formal principles are not capable of regaining the loyalty and trust of the citizens. With a provocative caricature, Joseph H.H. Weiler denounces *the neo–liberal market culture in which European citizens are converted into dissatisfied consumers who are soothed with rhetoric on citizenship and basic rights*:

> [...] the Union has become a product for which the managers, alarmed by consumer dissatisfaction, are engaged in brand development. Citizenship and the 'rights' associated with it are meant to give the product a new image (since it adds very little in substance) and make the product ever more attractive to its consumers, to re–establish their attachment to their favorite brand.[29]

On the other hand the influence of excessive Romanticism has come to the surface in the *mystification of a romantic European identity*, placing emphasis on a common conception of the European heritage. The glorification of an illusive European myth, characterised by the exclusion of 'the other', can be illustrated in the debates on the accession of Turkey to the European Union. Valéry Giscard d'Estaing, President of the Convention at that time, declared himself openly against the candidacy of Turkey in unmistakable terms:

> C'est un pays proche de l'Europe, un pays important qui a un véritable élite, mais ce n'est pas un pays européen. ... Je donne mon opinion, c'est la fin de l'Union européenne.[30]

Since Turkey is characterised by a different culture and religion, it does not matter much whether this candidate–country would fulfill the criteria of Copenhagen in order to become a Member of the European Union.

4 How to Deal with these Limits? Bridging the Gap: The EU in Search of Normative Legitimacy

Normative legitimacy seems to be undermined by the cultural monism of both the neo–liberal consumer society and the neo–romantic pre–political community. In order to establish normative legitimacy in the European Union, citizens of Member States should become autonomous citizens who are able to perceive themselves at the same time as applicants and as authors of law. Therefore they are not expected to pursue their private interests within the boundaries of law. Autonomous citizens are considered to be political responsible, willing to transform their private interests into the common good. On the other hand, the common good, the normatively defined identity of the community, does not exist prior to the democratic process. Public deliberation is the way to find out what is good in the public realm of action. So, the normative quality of the arguments is not measured against the moral content of a neo–romantic identity. The normative self–

---

29 J.H.H. Weiler, *The Constitution of Europe* (Cambridge: Cambridge University Press, 1999) 333–334.

30 A. Leparmentier and L. Zecchini, "Pour ou contre l'adhésion de la Turquie à l'Union européenne", in *Le Monde* (9 November 2002).

understanding of a community is developed in a democratic process of reason–giving in which private preferences have to be justified and transformed by making use of good arguments all affected parties can agree upon. Communicative rationality is emphasised in stead of instrumental rationality.[31]

In order to build a political union of autonomous citizens, *two suggestions* are made here. First of all, further constitutional engineering should improve the legal preconditions for a viable political union. The ambiguity of the constitutional status, the opacity of decision–making procedures and the lack of opportunity for any participation in them, make autonomous citizenship currently impossible. Further parliamentarisation should be stimulated by means of reformed decision–making procedures and clearer divisions of competences along vertical and horizontal lines, that is between the EU and the Member States and among the institutions at the EU level.

However, as stated above, the European legitimacy crisis is about more than institutions and procedural reform. Formal legal improvements do not suffice. No constitutional engineering can succeed before the content of the political project behind it becomes clearer. As long as Europe is conceived solely as a means in the system of market–structured interaction to promote the private interests, made up merely of regulations, directives, and disputes, there will be a lack of motivation for autonomous political action as described above. In other words, the overwhelming majority of the population that are currently resistant to full European unity can only be won over if the project is politicised. Autonomous citizenship can only be mobilised by giving a normative appeal to the European project.[32] In the words of Lionel Jospin:

> … il nous faut maintenant élargir la perspective, sous peine de réduire l'Europe à un marché et de la diluer dans la mondialisation. Car l'Europe est bien plus qu'un marché. Elle est porteuse d'un modèle de société …. L'Europe est d'abord un projet politique, un *contenu* avant d'être un *contenant.*[33]

As long as the normative self–understanding of the EU is depoliticised by the instrumental rationality of the neo–liberal model, European citizens will be further alienated from the European construct. The neo–romantic model cannot (from an empirical point of view) and may not (from a normative point of view) fill the gap between the citizens and the Union. After all, neither the neo–romantic model, nor the neo–liberal model now imposed by the predominant global economic regime, sits well with the kind of normative self–understanding so far prevalent across Europe as a whole. Instead, the European Union should be seen as a laboratory in which Europeans are striving to counterbalance both models.[34]

---

31 J. Habermas (1999), *l.c.*; E.O. Eriksen and J.E. Fossum, "Europe in Search for Legitimacy: Strategies of Legitimation Assessed", *International Political Science Review* 2004, *25*, 4.

32 J. Habermas (2001), *l.c.*, 11.

33 L. Jospin, Intervention de M. Lionel Jospin, Premier ministre, sur "L'avenir de l'Europe élargie", Paris, 28 mai 2001.

34 J. Habermas (2001), *l.c.*, 11; M. Telò and P. Magnette, "Justice and Solidarity", in F. Cerutti and E. Rudolph, *A Soul for Europe*, cited in J. Habermas, "Why Europe Needs a Constitution", *New Left Review* 2001, 11.

The Convention on the future of the European Union and the resulting draft Treaty establishing a Constitution for Europe made *improvements on both fronts ('le contenant' – 'le contenu')*. With the Constitutional Treaty a decisive step was taken towards a political union.

> [The Constitutional Treaty] enshrines citizens' rights by incorporating the European Charter of Fundamental Rights and turns Europe towards its citizens by holding out new opportunities for them to participate.[35]

Competences are clearer divided along vertical and horizontal lines and a further step in the emancipation of European Parliament has been taken.

Secondly, the draft Treaty establishing a Constitution for Europe reflects the crystallisation of a learning process of normative self–understanding. For a long time the political character of the European Union was strictly taboo. The political project behind the European construction was kept under wraps. The former German Minister of Foreign Affairs, Joschka Fischer, broke the political taboo by questioning the underlying *telos* of the EU and has sparked an academic and political debate on the political character of the European project. The Convention on the future of the European Union has diligently and comprehensively continued this reflection on the European polity. The Convention represented for European leaders the first occasion since the Messina Conference in 1955 to set aside the resources and time to examine in detail the question '*Quo vadis Europe*?'. The Convention–method has brought about in a unique way cross–border political discourses between multiple participants. The open communicative context created with the Convention submitted the arguments of the very heterogeneous participants to a test of intersubjective validity. In contrast to intergovernmental negotiations in which the national Heads of Government behind closed doors are assumed to represent the national interests without regard for the overall picture behind the European construct, the Convention–method forced the different participants to take an exocentric position from which they were able to reflect upon their private interests. Even when the members of the Convention had private interests in view, they were forced to defend their position with arguments that aimed at the European common good. They felt obliged to assert good intentions. Publicity forced them to hide private interests. John Elster refers here to the notion of "the civilizing force of hypocrisy".[36] The need to present arguments that show that the interests of others are served, leads to a transformation of its own preferences and puts a civilising pressure on the way in which the private interests are defined.

However, the *healing force of the Convention must be nuanced*. First of all, ambiguities in the constitutional status are kept upright.[37] Secondly, the Convention did not succeed in making the process of self–understanding manifest. The Convention failed to live up to its ambition to be socially broadly–based. In the

---

35 V. G. d'Estaing, *Rome Declaration 18 July 2003*. See http://european-convention.eu.int/docs/Treaty/Rome_EN.pdf

36 J. Elster, "Deliberation and Constitution Making", in J. Elster (ed.), *Deliberative Democracy* (Cambridge: Cambridge University Press, 1998) 109.

37 See K. Lenaerts and D. Gerard, *l.c.*, 289–322.

build–up to the referenda political leaders missed the unique opportunity of a Europe–wide debate on the political project behind the European construction. Instead the debate was polarised and with the negative results of the referenda the learning process came to a stop.

5 Conclusion

This chapter has taken the following paradox as a starting point. Although the legal legitimacy of the European Union has increased considerably throughout several Treaty reviews, the social acceptance of the European construction has reached rock bottom. Although efforts have been made to improve the regulatory function, the function of protective legality, and the symbolic function, citizens of France and the Netherlands have absolutely rejected the Constitutional Treaty. The limits of the legitimising capacity of law are becoming perceptible.

In order to explain this paradoxical gap between legal and social legitimacy, a normative conception of legitimacy was introduced. Legitimacy consists then in the worthiness to be recognised. People will obey the law because they find it worthy of respect, because of the normative quality of law. Social legitimacy will be obtained because the law reflects the normative self–understanding of the community. The normatively defined collective identity, reflected in the common good, is developed in a process of public reason–giving in which autonomous citizens are involved. In this way citizens can perceive themselves at the same time as applicants and as authors of the law.

However, in late–modern societies, normative legitimacy has become problematic due to the twin assault on autonomous citizenship. The neo–liberal model reduces citizens into consumers and the intersubjective common good into the calculable general welfare. In the neo–romantic model (reinforced by the implications of the neo–liberal vision) on the other hand the collective identity is considered to exist prior to the democratic process of will–formation of autonomous citizens. In the European context both tendencies are palpable, yet the neo–liberal vision is much more pronounced, since the European was set up as an functional organisation whose special purpose is to pursue the private concerns of the citizens of the Member States, facing an increased economic globalisation.

To conclude, in order to establish normative legitimacy in the European Union – in other words in order to fill the paradoxical gap between legal and social legitimacy – constitutional engineering will not suffice. The European Union should also be given a normative appeal. Europe should stand for a model of society that is able to counterbalance the neo–liberal and the neo–romantic vision.

Chapter 13 – The Limits of the Law and the Development of the EU

René Foqué and Jacques Steenbergen[1]

1 Introduction

In this chapter we explore the extent to which the law can be expected to enable societies and their citizens to achieve their goals in view of the challenges to representative democracies faced with a plurality of values in multicultural societies and a significant erosion of the concept of sovereignty. We will look in particular at the development of the European Union. The European integration process is partly a response to the challenges we will examine. But its multi–faceted attempts at constitutionalisation[2] also illustrate many of the paradoxes and difficulties that characterise these challenges.

In doing so we are driven by two closely related questions.[3] First, how can we structure decision–making so as to give everybody sufficient assurance that they have a reasonable degree of control over their destiny, or at least the comfort that they can identify the forces that are in control? Can we only achieve this goal by reconstructing the State at a European level, or can this goal also be achieved by pragmatic improvements to *ad hoc* structures such as the EU or the WTO, provided their place in the constitutional continuum is well–defined and transparent? Second, how far can the EU proceed as a component in the continuum between the local and the global level with pragmatic (technocratic) solutions, sometimes *à géométrie variable* (*i.e.*, with policies that do not apply equally to all Member States[4]), without being part of the problem in stead of being a key element in the regional response to global challenges?

---

1 Jacques Steenbergen only expresses his personal views.

2 This text was finalised after the IGC meeting in Lisbon on 18 October 2007 accepted the Treaty amending the Treaty on the European Union and the Treaty establishing the European Community (hereafter the Reform Treaty), but before the discussions on that treaty in the parliaments of the Member States.

3 These questions were also the outcome of an earlier study by the authors of this chapter, and to which this chapter can to some extent be seen as a sequel. See R. Foqué and J. Steenbergen, "Regionalism – A Constitutional Framework for Global Challenges?", in M. Farrell, B. Hettne and L. Van Langenhove (eds.), *Global Politics of Regionalism* (Pluto Press: London, 2004) 54–68. See along similar lines E.O. Eriksen and J.E. Fossum, "Europe in Search of Legitimacy", *International Political Science Review* 2004, 435–459.

4 See *e.g.*, the Euro zone (the EU without Denmark, Sweden and the UK) and the Schengen zone (the EU minus the UK and Ireland and plus Iceland and Norway). See further W. van Gerven, *The European Union: A Polity of States and Peoples* (Oxford and Portland, Hart Publishing, 2005) 28–34.

We start from the assumption that the law has five key functions.[5] First, the law is *an instrument to register and consolidate relations and institutions*. This is probably the primary function of the law. It has a cultural as well as a pragmatic dimension. Because of the institutional status of the law derived from the historic acceptance of the sovereign State as the ultimate source of law, and its intellectual status as the 'learned' expression of the way society is organised, the law symbolises as well as embodies the societal culture of societies.[6] In fulfilling this function, the law is as strong and effective (or as weak and irrelevant) as the underlying facts and/or the consensus between parties. It is ultimately as strong as the acceptance (legitimacy/authority) or the power of the institution applying the law. Second, the law is *an instrument for dispute resolution and management*. When legal rules were explicitly chosen by parties to register, consolidate, and rule their relations, the law is obviously (and in principle without significant controversy) the key instrument for the resolution and management of disputes. The law has a more critical role as an instrument for the resolution of disputes with or between parties who did not explicitly agree on the rules invoked to assess their behaviour or their claims. Especially when the parties did not all explicitly agree on the choice of law, the strength of the law depends as much on the acceptance (legitimacy/authority) or the power of the institution applying the law, as on the degree of acceptance (legitimacy/authority) of the rule. Third, the law is *an instrument to organise and regulate the exercise of power by public authorities in order to offer legal protection to citizens* (negative freedom). In respect of this function, the law is as strong and effective as the range of rights and enforcement mechanisms it confers on citizens and the willingness of authorities to abide by their own rules. Fourth, the law is *an instrument to organise the participation of citizens in the process of political will formation* (positive freedom). In respect of this function, the law is as strong and effective as the efficiency of its institutional model, and even more importantly, as the efficiency of the reflexive capacity of civil society. Fifth, the law is *an instrument to change relations and to create institutions or to govern their development*. In respect of change management within the context of existing institutions, the law is in the first place as strong as the willingness to change and the degree of acceptance (legitimacy/authority) of the proposed rules. A lack of enthusiasm for the proposed change can at least in part be compensated by the degree of acceptance (legitimacy/authority) and ultimately of the power of the institution introducing the new rule. In respect of the creation of new institutions, the issues are more complicated. But we can again say that the acceptance of change will depend in the first place on the willingness to change, and that a lack of enthusiasm for the proposed institutions can, but only in part, be compensated by the degree of acceptance (legitimacy/authority) of the institution(s) backing the initiative. However, once established, new institutions will live their own life and will be judged mostly on their own merits.

5 Compare E. Claes, W. Devroe, and B. Keirsbilck, "The Limits of the Law (Introduction)". We add the law as an instrument for change, and consider that the *symbolic* function is comprised in the first function.

6 *Ibid.*

We also start from the assumption that the management of issues without a significant impact on the relations between citizens and society, or the implementation of political agreements[7] of which the implementation does not require additional political decisions, can be delegated to technical (as opposed to political) organisations with a well–defined mandate that rely on the legitimacy of their founders. The governance and control structures of public technical organisations can be similar to the rules on governance that apply to private organisations.[8] Technical organisations can do without the need for consensus in implementing decisions, and they do not need to build their own *political* legitimacy. They derive their legitimacy primarily from the efficient implementation of their specific mission.

Matters are more complicated when more is needed than the implementation of an existing agreement and the management of the relevant issues requires frequent decisions with a political dimension. We assume that such decisions should either be made by a politically legitimated body or by consensus between politically legitimated bodies (*e.g.*, by institutions in which decisions are taken by consensus between politically legitimated governments).[9] The latter requires decision–making processes in the member governments that ensure that the legitimacy of governments also effectively covers the decisions of such intergovernmental organisation.

2 The Development of the EU and Globalisation

2.1 Globalisation and the Decline of the Nation–State: The EU as a Response to Globalisation

European integration in the 1950s, like the attempts to structure a world monetary system in the Bretton Woods agreements or to open markets for free trade in the GATT, was primarily a response to two factors affecting the confidence in the Nation–State. First, the trauma after two (largely European) World Wars. Nationalism was perceived by many as one of the main causes for the escalation of conflicts. The promotion of the interdependence of economies by free trade must be seen in the context of the search for a sustainable peace. This also holds true, at least in part, for the efforts to dilute both State and private power by the combined

---

7 *I.e.*, agreements on issues with a significant impact on the relations between citizens and society and which may, actually or potentially, imply a discussion on the scheme of underlying principles and value–orientations. See on the concept of the scheme of principles: R. Dworkin, *Law's Empire* (Cambridge, Mass.: Harvard University Press, 1986) 211.

8 It may be added that private corporations have sometimes a better feel for the distinction between matters requiring board decisions and management decisions, than governments for the distinction between political and regulatory issues.

9 These assumptions were developed in more detail in R. Foqué and J. Steenbergen, *l.c.*, 54–68.

promotion of free enterprise and open competition.[10] Second, the realisation that isolationism and protectionism had been inadequate responses to the economic crisis of the thirties[11], and that they would equally impede post–war reconstruction. The need to bring France and Germany closer together was widely recognised at the time of the Schuman declaration.[12]

The economic objectives and strategies were more controversial. France had opted in the post–war years for example for a rigorously planned economy on a strictly national scale.[13] It would take the convictions of a new generation of intellectuals[14] (and the end of the colonial period) before France started to embrace the idea that it needed to think in terms of a more open world in which metropolitan France should not expect to be the uncontested centre.[15] It is no coincidence that it was only at that time, during the presidency of Georges Pompidou, that France opened the door of the EC for Britain.[16] The support for free trade always remained muted. Many especially more vulnerable members of society, not only in countries with a tradition of autarky such as France, always continued to believe that protectionism was a necessary economic defence.[17] And while Britain was more inclined to see the benefits of open markets, it was even more reluctant than France to acknowledge that post–war developments significantly eroded the substance of its sovereignty.[18]

The globalisation of markets was nevertheless a virtually unavoidable consequence of technological developments. We have learned to produce services as well as industrial and agricultural products on a scale that no longer corresponds

---

10 See the introduction of competition law in Germany and Japan after the Second World War at the insistence of the US as a guarantee against the reemergence of the industrial conglomerates that had, in the opinion of the allies, greatly contributed to the war efforts of the axis powers.

11 Even the more convinced free traders had turned towards protectionism. See *e.g.,* on Lloyd George and the then UK government: Lord Home, *The Way the Wind Blows* (Glasgow: Fontana/Collins, 1979) 56.

12 The Schuman declaration constituted nevertheless in 1950 a major change in the French policy towards Germany. See *e.g.,* P.J.G. Kapteyn and P. VerLoren van Themaat, *Introduction to the Law of the European Communities* (London/the Hague/Boston: Kluwer Law International, 3rd ed., 1998) 1 e.s. It has since always been seen as one of the key objectives of European integration. References to peace did not only figure prominently in the preamble to the ECSC Treaty but also in the Preamble to the later EEC Treaty: "Resolved by thus pooling their resources to preserve and strengthen peace and liberty". It has consistently been referred to by founding fathers – see J. Monnet, *Mémoires* (Paris: Fayard, 1976) 325 and 338 e.s. – or recent commentators – see *e.g.,* N. MacCormick, "Democracy and Subsidiarity in the European Commonwealth", in N. MacCormick, *Questioning Sovereignty* (Oxford/New York Oxford: University Press, 1999) 137. See from a Belgian perspective also V. Dujardin, *Pierre Harmel* (Brussels: Le Cri, 2004) 443.

13 See *e.g.,* J. Monnet, *l.c.*, 275 e.s. The founding father of the 'common market' still refers to this period in his autobiography as "*La France se modernise*".

14 See *e.g.,* J.J. Servan Schreiber, *Le défi Américain* (Paris: Denoël, 1967).

15 See however already J. Monnet, *l.c.*, 321 e.s.

16 We may add that it was also at that time that it gave modern art from both sides of the Atlantic in Beaubourg a spectacular temple at the centre of the public forum.

17 See Z. Laïdi, *La grande perturbation* (Paris: Flammarion, 2004) 367–373.

18 See *e.g.,* C. Patten, *Not Quite the Diplomat* (London: Penguin Books, 2006) 61 e.s.

to the needs of national societies. And we have grown accustomed to a standard of living and a pattern of consumption that is sustainable only if we make use of modern technology. Disposable income and costs of consumption are thus dependent on the ability to sell goods and services beyond the borders of our domestic markets. There are therefore virtually no mainstream politicians defending a closed–society policy.[19]

Colonisation partly explains that globalisation only became a genuine challenge to the (European) Nation–States some hundred years after the industrial revolution.[20] Decolonisation and the emergence of newly industrialised countries have gradually redefined the balance of power. Thanks to half a century of efforts in GATT to liberalise world markets[21], the emergence of new markets continued to benefit to the old industrial powers after they lost the political power to impose their exports. But decolonisation implied an ever–increasing impact of reciprocity.[22] European countries can no longer hope to limit the impact of the globalisation of markets by import restrictions without losing export opportunities and causing a significant drop in the standard of living.[23] Globalisation is mostly perceived as a threat to employment by imports and dislocation, but access to markets

---

[19] See *e.g.*, Z. Laïdi (2004), *l.c.*, 343. For an example of the consequences of economic isolationism in a European environment, see the lessons from the economic history of Spain and in particular Franco's policy of autarky: *e.g.*, P. Preston, *Franco* (London: Harper Collins, 1993) 344 e.s. Franco was the last who tried to impose such policy in Western Europe.

[20] Colonies, and later the newly independent developing countries, could only satisfy their need for investment goods and consumer goods by imports from the industrialised world. Trade restrictions and the limited convertibility of currencies consolidated also in the post–colonial period traditional trade patterns with former colonial powers.

[21] It has been said that the Kennedy Round (1964–1967) led to concessions covering 70% of world trade volume, and that two–thirds of the concessions reduced tariffs by more than 50%. The parties negotiated on the basis of linear reduction coefficient. See K.W. Dam, *The GATT, Law and International Organisation* (Chicago: University of Chicago Press, 1970) 56.
In the Tokyo Round (1974–1979), the Contracting Parties aimed at a greater reduction of higher tariffs rather than setting lower tariffs. The average tariff reduction was estimated at 25.5% for the EC, 28.5% for the USA, 25% for Japan and 34% for Canada. See Director General of the GATT, *The multilateral trade negotiations of the Tokyo Round*, Geneva, 1979, 57 e.s.
See for an assessment of the results of the Uruguay Round: GATT, *Increases in Market Access Resulting from the Uruguay Round*, Genève, April 1994, 25 p.; and *European Report*, 16 April 1994, vol. 5. It has been estimated that tariffs were reduced on average by 38%, with a reduction of the average tariff between industrialised countries from 6.3% to 3.9%. 43% of trade between industrialised countries is no longer subject to tariffs, as compared to 20% before the closing of the Uruguay Round.

[22] See on the European perception of the reinterpretation of the concept of reciprocity in the Uruguay Round: H. Paemen and A. Bensch, *Du GATT à l'OMC* (Leuven: Leuven University Press, 1995) 152. UNCTAD and later the Tokyo Round also provided for "a reversed unilateral preference": the unilateral schemes of preferences to the benefit of developing countries that were "multilateralised" (or legalised) in the Tokyo Round. See *e.g.*, B. Balassa, "The Tokyo Round and the Developing Countries", *J.W.T.L.* 1980, 93 e.s.

[23] This logic convinced conservative politicians already in the early days that the UK could not afford to stay out of the EC. See *e.g.*, Lord Home, *l.c.*, 174.

abroad is also a condition for preserving employment in all sectors that can only justify present levels of activity by access to foreign markets.[24]

However, 'globalisation' only gradually became global. Just as the US market can to a significant extent sustain the economic activity in the US, the completion of the common market was for a long time all that was needed in Europe (with the possible exception of the UK). This holds true in particular for the many smaller and medium sized undertakings in Europe.[25]

It seems therefore fair to say that in the initial forty years of the European integration, the European Communities were a successful and largely adequate response to the needs and key goals of both smaller and larger Member States in post–war Western Europe, even if the EC remained well short of the political ambitions of those who strived for '*an ever closer union*'.[26]

2.2 Globalisation as a Challenge to the EU

But while globalisation initially facilitated the acceptance of European integration, globalisation has increasingly turned into a challenge to the EU institutions and their political legitimacy.

First, more than sixty years after the last war in Western Europe, the first Western European generations (for as long as we can remember) that have not seen war in their country see no risk of an armed conflict between Nation–States in Europe. And Europeans in enlargement countries, with a more vivid memory of the threats of foreign armies, tend to see NATO (and the US) as a more credible deterrent than the EU. EU citizens are therefore (rightly or wrongly) no longer motivated to accept any real or perceived price for the functioning of European institutions by their wish to preserve peace.[27]

---

24 The EU economies have traditionally been export as well as import dependent. See *e.g.*, J. Steenbergen, G. De Clercq and R. Foqué, *Change and Adjustment* (Deventer: Kluwer, 1983) 37.

25 In the early 1980s when the common market had already a significant impact and globalisation did not yet figure as prominently on the agenda, this was particularly striking in the smaller Member States. Exports represented in 1980 24% of the GDP of the Member States, but this figure was much higher in Belgium and Luxembourg (50.7%) or the Netherlands (42.7%). And while exports to third countries represented on average 46.4% of total exports, that figure was significantly lower for Belgium and Luxembourg (28.2%) or the Netherlands (27.8%): Eurostat, *Basic statistics* (1981), table 101. See for an analysis of the development in the large economies, Z. Laïdi (2004), *l.c.*, 361–363. His analysis shows that they were in 1960 on average less dependent on foreign trade than in 1890 or in 1913, but that had started to change by 1980.

26 Preambles to the EEC Treaty and the EU Treaty.

27 See G. Verhofstadt, *De Verenigde Staten van Europa* (Antwerpen/Amsterdam: Houtekiet, 2005) 53–55. See on Europe's ambiguous attitude to military power *e.g.*, Z. Laïdi, *La norme sans la force* (Paris: Presses de Sciences Po, 2005) 21 e.s., and Z. Laïdi (2004), *l.c.*, 46 and 150 e.s. The ability of European politics to confuse is illustrated by the fact that this attitude should not be read as a wish for isolationism or a rejection of any type of interventionism. Europe, both in the EU and NATO has in recent years, without apparent opposition in most

The lack of a perceived threat of armed conflicts in Europe does not imply that Europeans feel secure. But the perceived security risks are associated with terrorism, crime and immigration. They are seen as by–products of globalisation. Any institution aiming at the free movement of persons and goods tends therefore to be perceived as a contributing factor to the perceived security risks rather than as an effective remedy.

And while the European market may still be all what most European companies can be expected to explore, the pressure of imports and the risk of dislocation is now genuinely global. Enlargement has not only opened welcome new markets, it has also fuelled intra–European relocation. Enlargement has thus increased the tendency to see the European institutions as one of the driving forces of globalisation, rather than as a European response.

All who are more easily impressed by threats than motivated by opportunities can therefore be expected to see the European construction as a cause of their problems and not as a solution. They usually tend to have more vocal advocates than the optimists. And the fact that studies generally confirm that globalisation indeed increases tendencies towards inequality, is not likely to make them change their mind.[28]

The referenda on the Constitutional Treaty in France and in the Netherlands illustrate that we can no longer assume that the EU institutions are seen as the credible and adequately legitimated forum for the government of significant areas of the public domain, giving everybody sufficient assurance that they have a reasonable degree of control over their destiny, or at least the comfort that they can identify the forces that are in control. Worse, the institutions risk being perceived more as a cause of the globalisation trauma than as the key to solutions that might alleviate its impact. But this does not mean that the Member States still have the required credibility in respect of the relevant areas of policy. The crisis has two dimensions: the European polity risks losing its specific function of mediating between local, national and global perspectives, and the national States at the same time put at risk their credibility and legitimacy by losing their ability to manage effectively the interests of their citizens. In order to understand these developments we need to analyse further the significance of the modern State and its relation to civil society.

---

countries, been more active outside its borders than ever since the end of the colonial period. See for a survey J. Wouters and F. Naert, "The EU and Conflict Prevention: A Brief Historic Overview", in V. Kronenberger and J. Wouters (eds.), *The European Union and Conflict Prevention* (the Hague: T.M.C. Asser Press, 2004) 33–66.

28 See Z. Laïdi (2004), *l.c.*, 321 e.s. and 385–402.

3 The Constitutional State and the Limits of Power

The development of the modern State is a relatively recent phenomenon.[29] It can only be understood in the context the different lines of philosophical and legal thinking that have shaped western modernity. Schools of thought such as social contract thinking, the different forms republicanism of Machiavelli or Montesquieu[30], and (neo–) Kantian rights thinking provided the foundations of what we refer to as the democratic constitutional State. 'Democratic' refers to the participatory citizenship as the engine of the process of political will formation. 'Constitutional' refers to the legal structuring of the process.

The State can be seen as the format in which a political society can recognise and practice its internal cohesion and specific identity. The State also needs to be seen as the highest power in such society. The State, as a construction, is impersonal. It can not be identified with those who (contingently) have power in the State and thus exercise the power of the State. Before the building of modern States, political power in feudal Europe was fragmented. The building of the modern State was facilitated by the simultaneous development of a comprehensive theory of sovereignty in which political power was seen as unified and indivisible. In order to understand and manage today's tensions between the national and the EU levels, we need to understand the significant development of the relationship between the building of national States and the theory of sovereignty.

Various authors of the school of social contract thinking made in their diversity a decisive contribution to the clarification (in theory and practice) of both the concept of State and that of civil society. The concept of the social contract is characterised by its analytical distinction between the process of building a society (*pactum unionis*) on the one hand, and the process of structuring the exercise of power (*pactum subjectionis*) on the other.[31] The divergent interpretations of the social contract regarding the relationship between these two components of the social contract do not only show the different dimensions of the concept of State but also the deeply rooted tensions that characterise still today the notion of the State and its relations to the People, the Nation and (civil) society.[32] The modern notion of

---

29 Q. Skinner, "The State", in R.E. Goodin and Ph. Pettit (eds.), *Contemporary Political Philosophy* (Malden/Oxford/Victoria: Blackwell Publishing, 2nd rev. ed., 2006) 3–25.

30 Ph. Pettit, *Republicanism. A Theory of Freedom and Government* (Oxford/New York: Clarendon Press, 1997); Cl. Lefort, *Le travail de l'œuvre. Machiavel* (Paris: Gallimard, 1972); J. Shklar, "Montesquieu and the New Republicanism", in J. Shklar, *Political Thought and Political Thinkers* (ed. by St. Hoffmann) (Chicago/London: The University of Chicago Press, 1998) 244–261; R. Foqué, "Evenwicht van machten en rechtsstatelijke vernieuwing", in A. Alen *et al.* (eds.), *De Trias Politica ruimer bekeken* (Brussels: Larcier, 2000) 1–23.

31 W. Friedmann, *Legal Theory* (New York: Columbia University Press, 1967) 117–119.

32 See on the notion of *civil society* and its historical background in the theories of the social contract: J.L. Cohen and A. Arato, *Civil Society and Political Theory* (Cambridge, Mass./London: MIT Press, 1994) 83 e.s.

the *Nation–State* brings together the two poles of that tension and the two paths they represent: *from Nation to State* and *from State to Nation.*[33]

3.1 From Rome to Hobbes

For some, the creation and development of societies is determined by the organisation of power. This was for instance the view of the proto–liberal Thomas Hobbes (1588–1679). He saw the development of a society as a consequence of the equal and irreversible subordination of all members to a same sovereign. This line of thinking was already prepared in ancient Rome. In his view, a society finds its stability and cohesion in the recognition of a *summa potestas* in its own midst. According to Hobbes, an orderly society that organises a public space for the peaceful coexistence of citizens can only be created by the subordination to a common (State) power that allows for the development of a 'Common Wealth', defined as "a Multitude so united in one Person".[34]

Hobbes sees in the Leviathan (1651) sovereignty as a category of public law. He was the first to articulate *in juridicis* the distinction between the public and the private domain.[35] The emancipation of public law from private law meant that sovereignty was no longer seen as (private law) dominium but as (public law) representation.[36] The sovereign represents the society. Because of the irreversible nature of the delegation of power in the 'I authorise' of the *pactum subjectionis*, and of the fact that the *pactum unionis* can in this line of thinking only be understood in the context of the *pactum subjectionis*, society could not have an autonomous status in public law. It also follows from the distinction of the public and the private domain that the general interest became both a political and a legal category, and that the *raison d'état* acquired almost inevitably priority over the public forum, even though in principle it should be there that a creative citizenship can flourish.

According to social contract thinking of the Hobbesian type, the general interest is an independent category embodied and represented by the State as an expression of the contractual will of its citizens. Hobbes emphasises the asymmetry

---

33 J. Habermas, "The European Nation–State: On the Past and Future of Sovereignty and Citizenship", in J. Habermas, *The Inclusion of the Other. Studies in Political Theory* (ed. by C. Cronin and P. De Greiff) (Cambridge/Oxford: Polity Press, 1996) 105–127.

34 Th. Hobbes, *Leviathan* (ed. with an Introduction by C.B. McPherson) (Harmondsworth/London: Penguin, 1968) 223 e.s.

35 R. Foqué, "Grenzen aan de aanspreekbaarheid. Over de verhouding van de publieke en private ruimte en van het publiekrecht en het privaatrecht in de moderniteit", in R. Foqué and M. Weyembergh (eds.), *Filosofische aspecten van het privé–publiek debat* (Brussels: VUB-Press, 1997) 7–36.

36 Y.–Ch. Zarka, *Hobbes et la pensée politique moderne* (Paris: Presses Universitaires de France, 1995) 195 e.s.; L. Jaume, *Hobbes et l'état représentatif moderne* (Paris: Presses Universitaires de France, 1966).

between State and society: the State has the supreme power (and even the monopoly of force) as the representative and protector of the general interest.

3.2 Bodin

The above mentioned view is supported by the theory of sovereignty as developed already in the 16th century by Jean Bodin.[37] In his *Les six livres de la République* Bodin developed his views on sovereignty.[38] He tried to conceptualise the relations between a political society, the State, and law and power. For the purpose of this chapter, his views can be summarised in three points.

First, the State is seen as an autonomous centre of power in its relations to society. Increasing conflicts of interests in society will require a strengthening of the State's organisation and power. This means that there is a tension between the horizontal concept of society and distributive justice (conceptualised further by Rousseau) on the one hand, and the vertical concept of authority (developed by Hobbes) on the other. The management of this tension requires an appropriate normative framework and institutional structure.

Second, in the Middle Ages the highest power of the sovereign was expressed by the judicial power of his courts. Later, the centre of political power shifted to the legislator. Rule–making was no longer seen as a primarily judicial function. It developed into a State function in its own right, and we saw the development of the concept of the independent State legislator.

Third, for Bodin, State law is positive law and he sees the State as a profane State. State law is not based on natural or divine law. It derives its legitimacy from the will of the sovereign. His theory of sovereignty offers the basis for legal positivism. The positivist nature of law is intrinsically linked to the voluntarist nature of power.

3.3 Rousseau

At the other side of the spectrum of social contract thinking, the Swiss–French Jean–Jacques Rousseau (1712–1788) focussed more on society–building in the *pactum unionis* than on the organisation of power in the *pactum subjectionis*.[39] In his opinion a political society needs to be conceived as by one will, the *volonté*

37 R. Foqué, "Op de drempel van de moderniteit. De soevereiniteitsleer van Jean Bodin", *Wijsgerig Perspectief* 2000, 3–18.

38 J. Bodin, *Les six livres de la république* (facsimile of the edition Du Puys, Paris, 1683) (Aalen: Scientia, 1961).

39 On the impact of Rousseau's political philosophy on the development of modern legal thinking, see R. Foqué, "Het belang van het recht. Ontwikkelingen in de continentale rechtstheorie", in E. Brugmans *et al.* (eds.), *Recht en legitimiteit* (Zwolle: Tjeenk Willink, 1987) 35–95.

générale, which should not be confused with the *volonté de tous.*[40] Rousseau aimed at reconciling the freedom of citizens with the constraints of living together. In his views a society will be no more than a cover for conflicts between irreducible competing private interests unless that society can be seen as a moral entity, as one 'People' or as one 'Nation'. For Rousseau the social contract constitutes a People and it is the basis for its political and social freedom. The social contract is therefore more than the sum of what the contract parties wanted. It is the expression of a *volonté générale* that transcends the will of the parties. A People can only be seen as one People if it is supported by one will. And that in turn can only be workable if all can recognise themselves in that general will. This general will needs to be sufficiently strong and cohesive in order to safeguard the common interest against conflicting particular interests. The *volonté générale* is thus both the criterion for the existence of a society, or a People or a Nation and the norm governing their functioning. However, Rousseau did not see the *volonté générale* as the expression of an empirical political consensus on concrete issues, but rather as a conceptual construction.[41]

Theoretical developments that offered the basis for modern thinking about the State and State power, as we find in the writings of Hobbes and Bodin, are counter–balanced by the thinking of Rousseau on the unity of society. He does not emphasise the voluntarism of power, but the voluntarism of society itself and offers thus the basis for a philosophical analysis of civil society. In both approaches to social contract thinking, the heterogeneity of private interests gives way to the unity of the general interest. But in one school of social contract thinking, the central power of the State represses the internal disputes of civil society by an irreversible transfer of authority to the State, whereas in the other school internal conflicts concerning private interests are resolved by a restless personification of society itself.

---

40 R. Derathé, *Jean–Jacques Rousseau et la science politique de son temps* (Paris: Librairie Vrin, 1974); E. Weil, "Jean–Jacques Rousseau et sa politique", in E. Weil, *Essais et conférences,* Volume II (Paris: Librairie Vrin, 1971) 134 e.s.

41 The conceptual construction of the *volonté générale* was probably influenced by developments of modern mathematics, and more specifically by differential mathematics, which occupied philosophers like Leibniz and with which Rousseau was certainly familiar. Developments in mathematics opened new ways of thinking that made it possible to shed new light on vague notions such as 'public opinion', and that made it easier to see the people itself as free subjectivity. The *volonté générale* appears in Rousseau's reasoning as the integral in the mathematical meaning, based on the mechanism of compensated deviations. When applied to the relationship between the *volonté générale* and the *volonté de tous*, it means that differences of opinion do not jeopardise the unity of a society, provided there is consensus on the foundations of the society. However, the general will is not an empirical but a normative concept. See especially, J.–J. Rousseau, *Du contrat social*, in J.–J. Rousseau, *Œuvres Complètes* (ed. B. Gagnebin et M. Raymond), Vol. III (Paris: Éditions de la Pléade, Gallimard, 1964) 371. See on this issue A. Philonenko, *Jean–Jacques Rousseau et la pensée du malheur,* Vol. III: *Apothéoses du désespoir* (Paris: Librairie Vrin, 1984) 25 e.s., L. Ferry and A. Renaut, *Philosophie politique*, Vol. III: *Des droits de l'homme à l'idée républicaine* (Paris: Presses Universitaires de France, 1985) 76 e.s.

3.4 Machiavelli

Machiavelli would have criticised the way both schools of social contract thinking conceive the relationship between the State and the conflicting interests of its citizens. Long before Karl Marx, he described living societies as divided societies, characterised by diverging interests. Machiavelli banished the illusion that deeply rooted conflicts of interests could or should be resolved in creating an artificial contractual unity. At the same time he rejected the idea of a unified power that represents social unity.[42] For him, the State inevitably remains a heteronomous entity in its relations to society. This means that the State will develop its own interest that will be driven by a specific *raison d'état*.

3.5 Montesquieu

The realism of the Machiavellian tradition is also reflected in the frontal attack of thinkers such as Montesquieu and Kant on the theory of centralised sovereignty. In their opinion, the concept of centralised sovereignty is likely to result in abuse of power and in despotism. They consider that the State should not be conceived in terms of an indivisible sovereignty. The moderate State requires in their view a division of powers and a shared, divided sovereignty.[43]

Montesquieu developed his thinking from the philosophical background of moral scepticism.[44] Just like power should not be concentrated in one hand, truth and justice can not be the monopoly of one homogeneous concept of society. The pragmatic universality of the general principles governing the life of a society, and the way human reason functions in cultural diversity, should not be the object or result of philosophical speculation. The political approach to human reason should be defined by experience, and familiarity with diversity, and not by the assumed homogeneity of theoretical ideas.[45] The sources of truth and justice can be as diverse as the sources of power. The moderate State and the shared sovereignty are the political and legal reflection of the diversity in civil society.

---

[42] Cl. Lefort, "Repenser le politique" (1978), in Cl. Lefort, *Le temps présent. Écrits 1945–2005* (Paris: Belin, 2007) 359–367. For the actual relevance of Machiavelli's position in the context of a notion of a divided *demos*, see J. Rancière, *La mésentente. Politique et philosophie* (Paris: Éditions Galilée, 1995) 31 e.s.

[43] R. Foqué, "De actualiteit van Montesquieu's staatkundige erfgoed", in H. D. Tjeenk Willink *et al.*, *Stoelendansen met de macht* (Den Haag: Tweede Kamer der Staten–Generaal, 2006) 9–29. On the concept of *divided sovereignty* in the context of the EU, see N. MacCormick, "On Sovereignty and Post–Sovereignty", in N. McCormick, *Questioning Sovereignty. Law, State, and Nation in the European Commonwealth* (Oxford/New York: Oxford University Press, 1999) 123–136.

[44] O. Marquard, *Apologie des Zufaelligen* (Stuttgart: Reclam Verlag, 1986) 117–139.

[45] T. Todorov, "Montesquieu", in A. Renaut (dir.), *Histoire de la philosophie politique,* Vol. II: *Naissances de la modernité* (Paris: Calmann–Lévy, 1999) 384–410.

Montesquieu's arguments in favour of a moderate State are entrenched in the republican tradition.[46] In that tradition, care for the *res publica* (the general interest) is the key concern. The general interest is not perceived as being only in the care of central power of State. The care for the general interest is, on the contrary, the central issue when organising political will formation in a pluralistic and participating citizenship.

A moderate State, pluralistic civil society, and a participating citizenship should never be taken for granted. They need to be embedded and structured in legal procedures and institutions of a constitutional nature.[47] The constitutional framework should not be limited to the organisation of the division of power within the institutional structure of the State. It should also formalise the pluralism and participating citizenship by the granting of rights that should both guarantee the access of citizens to the process of political will formation (positive freedom, or the fourth function of the law referred to in the introduction to this chapter) and protect citizens against abuse of State power (negative freedom or the third function of the law referred to in the introduction).

Montesquieu developed his views of course within the context of the national State. But his analytical framework and his views on constitutionalism are also relevant for the analysis of legal and political issues in a wider context.

3.6 The Theories on State and Sovereignty and Today's Challenges

The theories on State and sovereignty that helped to shape national States thus lead to the following conclusions. First, the theories on the modern State offer, at least since the constitutionalism of Montesquieu, analytical models that can also be used in a wider context than the national State. Second, the various schools of social contract thinking all imply a high degree of social homogeneity. Third, the school of thought on the building of moderate States, represented by Montesquieu's constitutionalism, implies an explicit concern with social pluralism, but its thinking needs further refinement and adjustment in a deterritorialized perspective.

It follows that modern thinking on State and sovereignty does not offer the necessary tools to answer our present challenges, for the following reasons. First, globalisation can not be managed within the territorial boundaries of the national State. Second, a mere extrapolation of the classical concepts of the State in a deterritorialized context can only offer solutions in case the larger context is either characterised by a sufficient homogeneity or the tools and ability required for an affective management of diversity. Third, we see not only significant diversity in

---

46 J. Shklar (1998), *l.c.*; J. Shklar, *Montesquieu* (Oxford/New York: Oxford University Press, 1987) 60 e.s.

47 J. Shklar (1987), *l.c.*, 111 e.s.

the larger world, but also an implosion of heterogeneity within the national States.[48]

4 The Development of the EU and the Limits of the Law

4.1 Specific Challenges in the EU Legal Order to What the Law Can Be Expected to Achieve

4.1.1 A Very Ambitious Project

No attempt to compensate for the decline of the Nation–State and to provide a widely accepted and reasonably effective response to the challenges of globalisation in multicultural societies can be expected to be easy. Especially when the going gets rough, the European construction needs to rely more on its ability to fulfil the fifth and inherently more vulnerable function of the law as an instrument for change, than on its first and least controversial function, the consolidation of consensus.[49] Within the world of legal change management, the programme the EU institutions received from their founding fathers or defined for themselves was always most ambitious, while the support often remained ambivalent.[50]

The combination of these factors is bound to stretch to its very limits the ability of the law to deliver a setting that is able to ensure "the constant improvements of the living and working conditions of their people"[51] and "the sustainable development based on balanced economic growth".[52] As indicated in the introduction to this chapter, the establishment of new institutions with their own mechanism for the settlement of disputes (the Court of Justice) always creates a particularly demanding set of circumstances. The creation of institutions will be accepted because of the acceptance of the project or of the rules under which it was decided to create them (the pre–existent rules), but both the rules and the political environments varied significantly in the six founding Member State, and even more in the enlargement countries. And as soon as new institutions operate, they depend on the continued acceptance of their project or on the extent to which they have been

---

48 Already in the beginning of the 20th century, the American philosopher John Dewey, one of the founding fathers of American Legal Pragmatism, observed, "Inside the modern city, in spite of its nominal political unity, there are probably more communities, more differing customs, traditions, aspirations, and forms of government and control, than existed in an entire continent at an earlier epoch." See his *Democracy and Education. An Introduction to the Philosophy of Education* (New York: The Free Press, 1944, 1st ed. 1916) 21.

49 Referred to in the introduction to this chapter.

50 The opposition between the defenders of *l'Europe des Nations* and the proponents of a more supra–national construction is well–known. It should be recalled that also in countries like Belgium not everyone always shared the enthusiasm for a more supra–national Europe. See *e.g.*, on the attitude of the then Prime Minister Theo Lefèvre: V. Dujardin, *l.c.*, 449.

51 Preambles to the EEC Treaty and the EU Treaty.

52 Article 2 of the EC Treaty.

able to generate legitimacy for themselves. The latter factor defines the limits of the ability of legal rules to fulfil the essential second function of the law referred to in section 4.2 as a mechanism for dispute settlement (*i.e.*, the tool to keep in the fold those who disagree with policies and/or lose their disputes), and of their ability to continue to contribute to a process of change.

The task ahead was defined in unusually clear terms by the early decisions of the Court of Justice. The Court decided that the Treaties created a new legal order distinct from both national[53] and international law.[54] The Court has consistently chosen a pre– or quasi–constitutional approach when deciding that Community law "constitutes the constitution charter of a Community based on the rule of law".[55] But notwithstanding the distancing of the EU institutions from international organisations, no one pretends that the Union is a State.[56]

4.1.2 A Particularly Challenging Legal Environment

The Union is not striving for unity in mere diversity. Its legal environment is, since the entry of the UK, largely defined by the co–existence of three families of fundamentally different legal systems: the 'French', the 'German' and the 'British' legal system. The 'French' concept of the *État de Droit* is inherently auto–referential. The acceptability of a decision or process depends on whether they fit into the logical and interpretative model of the actual system. The system thus tends to isolate itself from the impact of any ideals and ideas that have not been converted into positive law (as illustrated by the particular sensitivities in respect of the relations between State and religion). Fact–oriented pragmatic decision–making is often difficult to fit into the system and thus jeopardises its integrity. Pragmatism thus may cause an erosion of the acceptance of the 'French' system without facilitating the acceptance of the decisions. The 'German' concept of *Rechtsstaat* remains very much influenced by *Naturrecht* concepts, notwithstanding more positivist developments. Rules derive their acceptability from their compatibility with values and norms that are external to the system and that can therefore not be changed within the system. An auto–referential logic can therefore never convey genuine legitimacy. Both pragmatic decisions and auto–referential arguments will only be accepted in so far as they happen to be reconcilable with the underlying values of the system – but the fact that they have been arrived at without taking such value–system into consideration does not inspire confidence. The 'British' *Rule of Law* concept is not a substantive but a formal concept, unlike the 'French' and the 'German' models. Pragmatic problem solving is seen as more

53 Case 6/64, *Costa/E.N.E.L.*, [1964] ECR 1199.

54 Case 270/80, *Polydor*, [1982] ECR 329.

55 Opinion 1/91, *EEA*, [1991] ECR I–6079. This Opinion was in line with a much earlier opinion of Advocate General Lagrange that Community law was the "internal law common to the Member States". See Case 8/55, *Fédération Charbonnière de Begique/High Authority*, [1954–1956] ECR 245. See further K. Lenaerts and P. Van Nuffel, *Constitutional Law of the European Union* (London: Sweet and Maxwell, 2nd ed., 2005) 11–18.

56 See further W. van Gerven, *l.c.*, 36–41.

important than logical consistency, and there is no articulated reference to an ideological or ethical dogmatic unity. The 'system' derives its legitimacy from its ability to ensure a balanced assessment of facts and interests on a case–by–case basis. Constraints caused by systems or ideologies jeopardise, in the British opinion, the quality of decision–making. These doubts about the decision–making process affect the legitimacy of the decision and the decision–making body more than the content of the decision.[57]

The legitimacy of decisions will therefore be appreciated very differently depending on the legal environment in which they are received. First, the 'French' model can only accept 'German' decisions insofar as the leading values and norms are received as positive law concepts within a legal order of the 'French' type. But by such 'absorption', they lose the quality or status that gives legitimacy to decisions in the 'German' legal order: the norms and values are reduced to 'man–made' rules that can be changed by law–makers in accordance with the rules that govern the organisation of the legal system. It can accept 'British' decisions, either because they happen to fit into the existing body of rules, or because there is a willingness to adapt the rules. In the first hypothesis, the tension between systems will not be noticed. In the second, the tension will remain unnoticed at first, but the 'received' decision will start having a life of its own that may bear little resemblance to what 'British–thinking' decision–makers had in mind. Second, the 'German' model can accept 'French' or 'British' decisions, provided they are compatible with the overriding principles on which the German legal order is based. This reference to external principles will make the decisions (and in practice any follow–up that is inspired by 'German' legal thinking) 'in principle' (*i.e.*, regardless of their content) not any easier to accept for the French and the British. Third, the British find it probably the easiest to accept foreign decisions, without an in–depth ideological or systematic assessment, provided they can be received as facts. This means that they will either have no impact beyond the immediate context in which a decision is taken, or will make their way through future decision–making according to the very factual meanderings of a system that is usually open to any better deal within the loose constraints of a legal system primarily based on the rules of due process and precedent.

We can summarise the relations between the legal families as follows, whereby 'total' refers to the possibility to accept any of the other systems as such, and 'relative' to the possibility of accepting decisions taken according to the internal logic of any of the other systems.[58]

---

57 This is a summary of the analysis in J. Steenbergen, R. Foqué and G. De Clercq, *l.c.*, 95–99.

58 *Ibid.*, 105–107 (with some amendments).

Table 13.1 Relations between the Legal Families

Conceivable *of:* ↓ *by* :→	French Type Total	French Type Relative	German Type Total	German Type Relative	British Type Total	British Type Relative
French type	–	–	No	Yes, provided the underlying values are similar	No	Yes, without guarantee for follow up decisions
German type	No	Yes, but for conflicting motives	–	–	No	Yes, without guarantee for follow up decisions
British type	No	Yes, but risk of system erosion	No	Yes, provided the underlying values are similar	–	–

The differences between concepts and expectations, if not the relative incompatibility of systems, affect constitutional models[59] and the expectations in respect of the accountability of government[60] as well as substantive law. This is aggravated by less conceptual differences which sometimes affect profoundly the attitude of Europeans to rules and policies.[61]

The above ideal–type analysis does not suggest that France, Germany and the UK are homogeneous societies in respect of their concept of law. Neither do all other Member Stares clearly belong to one of the three legal families without any qualification or divergence. But it is our view that legal systems tend to be weaker when their identity is confused or when political fractions disagree on the underlying concepts that make a legal system work. To make a system work in ideologically heterogeneous societies requires a high level of intellectual flexibility (which always risks coming at the expense of transparency, thus negatively affecting social cohesion). This is also well illustrated by the Belgian environment. The Belgian legal system is, in our opinion, a member of the 'French' family, even though its constitutional model has more in common with the British model.[62] Two of the four main political 'families' (the liberal– and the socialist families) are characterised by models of thinking that fit almost seamlessly into the French model. But Christian–democrats tend towards a more natural law oriented thinking. The same

---

59 See *e.g.,* on the British and other constitutional models: T. Koopmans, *Courts and Political Institutions* (Cambridge: Cambridge University Press, 2003) 23–26. See also W. van Gerven, *l.c.,* 105 e.s.

60 See W. van Gerven, *l.c.*, 65 e.s.

61 See *e.g.,* on the difference in attitude to rules of the French and the Italians at least partly to be explained that Italy has 90 000 laws on its books and France 7 325 (which is still a high figure if nobody is assumed to ignore the law!): see Z. Laïdi (2004), *l.c.*, 358.

62 A. V. Dicey wrote, "The Belgian constitution indeed comes very near to a written reproduction of the English constitution … ." See his *Introduction to the Study of the Law of the Constitution* (Indianapolis: Liberty Press,1982; reprint of the 8th ed., 1915) 38.

holds true for many nationalists, who moreover tend to reject the existing State. The fact that the Belgian system has survived so many crises is, in our opinion, partly due to its ability to incorporate pragmatically agreed changes, but equally by the fact that a significant number of Christian–democrats in the legal community have translated their political beliefs as expressed in Christian personalism into a positivist legal thinking in which the relationship between the church and the State is defined by the State, entirely in accordance with the French model.[63] The result is nevertheless a system that is relatively weak on inherent consistency (because the 'system' needs to be open to accept the translation of almost any compromise), without fully adopting pragmatism as its systematic justification (as in the British tradition), and with an ambiguous attitude to values that are external to the set of principles clearly expressed in positive law.

4.2 From Customs Union to Common Market and Economic Union

The approach of the Treaties and the Court of Justice proved not unduly challenging as long as the institutions' policies were not really challenged. Initial progress was even easier than expected, as illustrated by the completion of the customs union ahead of schedule.[64]

The liberalisation of non–tariff trade barriers was already more challenging, especially once the limits were reached of what a purely negative integration (abolishing rules constituting obstacles to trade)[65] could achieve, and when the legislative harmonisation process grinded to a halt because of national (often more bureaucratic than political) resistance.[66] At first 'the law' proved strong enough to deliver a solution. In its *Cassis de Dijon* judgment[67] the Court limited the consequences of the lack of harmonisation of laws and regulations by imposing the concept of mutual recognition of equivalent provisions. The solution worked, but it

---

63 See *e.g.*, V. Dujardin, *l.c.*, *e.g.*, 121 e.s. 754 and 757. The depth of the gap that long existed between Catholics and a State with a legal system of the French model is illustrated by the fact that authors like Jacques Maritain still needed to write about an obligation of Catholics to take responsibility for society in the State. See also *e.g.*, L. Tindemans, *De memoires* (Tielt: Lannoo, 2002) 556.

64 P.J.G. Kapteyn and P. VerLoren van Themaat, *l.c.*, 594 e.s.

65 See on the distinction between positive and negative integration also F. Scharpf, "Negative and Positive Integration", in F. Scharpf, *Governing in Europe. Effective and Democratic?* (Oxford/New York: Oxford University Press, 1999) 43–83.

66 By the end of 1985, the Council had adopted some 182 harmonisation directives (of which 47 amended earlier directives), but there were at the time some 23000 DIN, 18000 AFNOR, 13000 BSI norms and standards etc. See *De interne EG–markt voor industrieproducten,* WRR doc. 1985/V47, 's Gravenhage 1985, 37. See also P.J.G. Kapteyn and P. VerLoren van Themaat, *l.c.*, 578–581.

67 Case 120/78, *Rewe,* [1979] ECR, 649. See further P.J.G. Kapteyn and P. VerLoren van Themaat, *l.c.*, 642 e.s.

was far from perfect. The need to resort to a case–by–case approach inevitably implies a degree of uncertainty and a lack of transparency.

But again, the institutions responded well with the 1985 White Paper on the completion of the internal market (at the time usually referred to as the '1992 programme').[68] The degree of political acceptance of the European project has perhaps never been higher than at the time of the adoption and implementation of the 1992 programme, as is illustrated by the strong support of the Thatcher government for the completion of the common market.[69] But also then, the British support did not extent to the political reforms that were needed to facilitate the adoption of the internal market rules.[70]

4.3 Specific Challenges and Later Developments

Several developments have since raised significant challenges.

Open markets are not sustainable without a minimum degree of economic convergence, and socio–economic convergence requires a far more political–based decision–making than the harmonisation of technical standards.

Successive enlargements have significantly increased the need for (and the cost of) economic convergence in a much less homogeneous union.

A real internal market requires a common currency. Monetary integration affects the hardcore of sovereignty at the level of the Member States.[71] It also requires a significantly higher degree of *contrat social* at the level of the Union. This is well illustrated by the difficulties of Member States to meet the Maastricht criteria and to respect the constraints imposed by the Stability Pact.

All through the early years, and especially at the time of the implementation of the 1992 programme, there was increasing support for competition–based market management. This can partly be explained by the fact that Member States with more market–oriented policies had been on average more successful in coping with the economic crises between 1972 (first oil shock) and the 1990s than the Member States which had favoured a more regulatory approach.[72] However, the

---

68 *Completing the Internal Market: White Paper*, COM(85) 310 final. See further K. Lenaerts and P. Van Nuffel, *l.c.*, 141–144. See also J. Delors, *Mémoires* (Paris: Plon, 2004) 202 e.s.

69 See *e.g.*, C. Patten, *l.c.*, 67; D. Hurd, *Memoirs* (London: Little Brown, 2003) 395; J. Delors, *l.c.*, 349.

70 See *e.g.*, J. Delors, *l.c.*, 215.

71 See *e.g.*, on the relationship between the completion of the internal market and the monetary union: J. Delors, *l.c.*, 223 e.s.

72 See *e.g.*, the experiences of the UK with the policies of the Labour governments before the Thatcher period, and the experience of France with the economic policies of the socialist government in the early years of the Mitterand presidency, compared with the relatively lower inflation rates in Germany, and in the UK under the Thatcher governments.

ever–increasing pressure on companies and individuals caused by globalisation and dislocation starts eroding this consensus.[73]

The above–mentioned developments are particularly threatening to the legitimacy of the EU because the Treaty is a dangerous mix of institutional and substantive provisions. The Treaty is not policy–neutral.[74] It is based on an option in favour of an open market (*i.e.*, internal free trade[75]) and free competition[76], in which monetary policy is both made and implemented by a central bank that is largely independent from government and operating under a narrow mandate.[77] Contrary to the general perception, this has been in our opinion confirmed in the Reform Treaty. The new Article 3 stipulates:

> … the Union shall establish an internal market. It shall work for the sustainable development of Europe based on balanced economic growth and price stability, a highly competitive social market economy …)

This text is not significantly weaker than the reference to competition policy in the articles 3(g) and 4(1) of the EC Treaty. It is strengthened further by Protocol 6 to the Reform Treaty. The reference to the "*social* market economy" and "aiming at full employment and social progress" in the same provision[78], and the inclusion by the Amsterdam Treaty of Article 127(2) EC[79] have given more emphasis to social policies.[80] But the inclusion of an open–ended objective has neither put significant constraints on competition policy–makers (competition policy–makers are convinced that they ultimately act in the interest of employment), nor changed the perception of the Union. The institutions are, in other words, not exclusively empowered (and perceived as being empowered) to make policy, but established in order to pursue a specific kind of policy. This makes it easy (if not necessary) for those who dislike the policies, to reject the institutions. At a time that open market policies are often far from popular (even though the times may make them more

---

73 See for an 'early warning' from the then President of the Court of Justice: J. Mertens de Wilmars and J. Steenbergen, "The Court of Justice of the European Communities and Governance in an Economic Crisis", *Michigan Law Review* 1984, 1378. The most worrying indication of the erosion of consensus has been the opposition to the 'Bolkenstein directive' on free trade in services.

74 See for a different opinion: P.J.G. Kapteyn and P. VerLoren van Themaat, *l.c.,* 129.

75 Opinion 1/78, *Natural rubber Agreement,* [1979] ECR 2871. See also J. Mertens de Wilmars and J. Steenbergen, *l.c.,* 1379.

76 Article 3 (c) and (g) of the EC Treaty.

77 Article 2 of the Protocol on the Statute of the European System of Central Banks and of the European Central Bank.

78 Article 1(4) of the Reform Treaty.

79 "The objective of a high level of employment shall be taken into consideration in the formulation and implementation of Community policies and activities."

80 See S. Van Raepenbusch, "Les services sociaux en droit communautaire ou la recherche d'un juste équilibre entre l'économique et le social" in J.–V. Louis and S. Rodriques (eds.), *Les services d'intérêt économique général et l'Union européenne* (Brussels: Bruylant, 2006) 107 e.s. and 161.

necessary than ever), significant parts of the population will inevitably turn against the European construction as such.[81]

The fact that a competition–based open market policy and the monetary union are among the cornerstones of the EU, also makes it more difficult to manage the legitimacy of the institutions because competition and monetary policy require largely autonomous agencies.[82] Competition authorities (and other market regulators) increasingly operate in networks that bring together the European Commission and national agencies.[83] This helps to create a link between 'Brussels' and the Member States – but because the national agencies also need to be independent from national governments some may say that these influential networks only add to the democratic deficit.

The legitimacy of the institutions is increasingly compromised by the fact that the EU is still to a significant degree associated with its common agricultural policy. This policy is widely seen as having a negative impact on consumer prices, in a union with fewer farmers, and in a world were a shortage of food in industrialised countries is (rightly or wrongly) no longer perceived as a genuine risk. It is also presented in the press and in schools (with good reason) as a significant obstacle to the development of third world countries and a major contributor to pollution. With only the farmers to support it, it unites against the EU both the pro–market and the environmentalist or pro–third world factions in society. More relevant for the topic of this chapter, is the fact that such a small group of farmers is seen to have more power than the *prima facie* significantly more powerful coalition against it. This seriously erodes the extent to which the institutions of the Union can be seen as credible managers of the public domain.

Calling the institutional reform treaty a Treaty on the Constitution was ambitious. It was, at least in the mind of some, something of a gamble. They hoped to consolidate by this qualification the commitment of all who want to go forward, forcing the others to clarify their position. It was not expected that 'hardcore' Member States such as France and the Netherlands would reject the Treaty. Their rejection has significantly complicated future developments. It is inconceivable to have a hardcore (or constitutionalised) union without two key Euro–zone countries. But is equally inconceivable to ignore the public rejection. Europe seems therefore condemned to continue its path of pragmatic reforms, where necessary *à géométrie variable*. Given that we can not rule out that this pragmatic or step–by–step approach has been one of the causes of the malaise and the loss of confidence

---

81 See further J. Steenbergen, "Interpretatievragen in het Europees Gemeenschapsrecht" (preadvies voor de Nederlandse Vereniging voor de Wijsbegeerte van het Recht), 1981, 123–127 and esp. 126.

82 This is *e.g.*, clearly illustrated by the OECD criteria for the assessment of competition laws and authorities.

83 See (for the competition authorities) Article 14 of Regulation 1/2003 and Article 19 of Regulation 139/2004. See also the Commission Notice on the cooperation in the network of competition authorities, O.J. C 101/43, 27.04.2004. See, for electronic communications, Article 22 of Directive 2002/21/EC on a common regulatory framework for electronic communications networks and services, O.J. L 108/33, 24.04.2002). There are similar networks *e.g.*, for the energy sector, for financial and for postal services, etc.

in political institutions (as indicated in the introduction to this chapter), the outcome of the referenda resembles a Catch–22 situation.

Globalisation and internal diversification of societies caused by cultural change, enlargements, and large scale immigration make that the citizens of the Union find themselves in a world that is very different from the world in the 1950s and 1960s. First, we moved from a bipolar world with a well–defined security threat/enemy ('the West' versus the communist world) to a confused world where abandoned luggage may be more dangerous than foreign armies. Second, when a US led policy tends to redefine an enemy, the resulting pattern is, regardless of the official rhetoric of the US and UK governments, a dichotomy between 'us' and 'the Islam world'. But Islam is not a foreign enemy. It is a key component of almost all the big cities in a significant number of Member States (and a more significant domestic factor than communism ever was in the Union since the 1960s – with perhaps the exception of France and Italy). Third, the debate on future enlargement, and in particular with Turkey, is both revealing and confusing. It expresses the rejection in the Union of internal change that has already happened. And it may express in Turkey the wish to confirm a 'western' identity that their 'eastern component' will perhaps never allow them to have. Fourth, from a legal perspective, it is at least premature to say that we need to add Islamic legal culture to the make–up of the legal environment of the Union, but the reality may be worse than the need to include an additional type of legal culture. Significant parts of the population seem to consider it most normal to live outside our system from within. The long standing tradition of *ius personae* thinking in the Islam legal culture makes it that they are intellectually better equipped to live with this attitude than we are. If we can not cope with this issue, it will significantly constrict the limits of what the law can achieve.

Moreover, since the UK joined the EU, European institutions have mostly had a negative press, the exception being the period of the 1992 programme. This can neither be reduced to a populist expression of fear for the consequences of globalisation, nor only be blamed on a lack of transparency of the European institutions. Except for the decision–making process in the Council of Ministers, policy–making in the European institutions is probably more open than in the administrations of most Member States. But the continued complaints, in particular of Anglo–Saxons and Scandinavians, about the lack of transparency of the Council need to be taken seriously. As long as the Council is seen as the most political institution and as the centre of power in the Union, the legitimacy of policies requires that citizens can identify with the proceedings of the Council. We cannot expect the Union to be seen as a credible structure for the governance of the public domain[84], if its most political functioning is screened off.

In a highly commercialised media environment, bad news will usually sell better than good news. Politics also have more news–value than administrative technicalities. A lack of 'political content' will therefore often make it that the achievements of the institutions only receive attention from the experts. If you

---

84 See R. Foqué and J. Steenbergen, *l.c.*, 57.

deny the press a sufficient level of political drama, the general media will be even more inclined to give more coverage to problems than to achievements. These issues are exacerbated by the fact that the world at large sees Europe mostly through the eyes of the Anglo–Saxon press. In a world with dispersed sovereignty, the profound Euro–scepticism of most of the UK media has a negative impact on the limits of what can be achieved by the use of the law at the European level.

The difficulty of obtaining the type of press coverage that makes people believe in the ability of institutions to look after the latter's interests, relates to the hardcore of the issues discussed in this chapter. First, while European institutions need to position themselves as a credible centre of government in key aspects of the public domain, the fact that they are co–managed by the governments of the Member States implies that they can not do without the policy–making mechanisms and methods of inter–State diplomacy. Behind–the–screens arrangements and consensus–building are difficult to avoid. Second, the news–value of many of the decisions taken at the European level is inherently low. The consistent tendency of the press to ignore available sources must partly be explained by the fact that the content is unlikely to appeal to their audiences. It suffices to refer to a copy of the *Official Journal*, chosen at random, to see that the output of most Council meetings is hardly likely to make front–page news. But the fact that technical issues tend to look boring does not mean that a highly complex society can do without institutions that care for the technical issues.

4.4 Was the Project too Ambitious?

This raises the question whether the initial definition of the task to create a new legal order was a necessary step in order to lay the foundation for institutions and rules able to cope with the present challenges, or a bridge too far because it increased the risk that institutions and policies would both be contested, fuelling an unarticulated rejection of policies and politics and a general impression that we can at any time become the victim of developments that are beyond the control of organised society as we know it.

When accepting that Nation–States, whether acting jointly or separately, can no longer offer adequate responses to all challenges in a globalised world, major institutional developments were (and remain) necessary. And when accepting that the ability of newly created institutions to make a contribution is defined by a multi–step process in which the earlier steps define the limits of what can be achieved in the later steps[85], the Court of Justice did what needed to be done.

Given the above–mentioned incompatibilities between legal systems, the Court may not have had moreover a real choice.

---

[85] Compare J. Riley, "Constitutional Democracy as a Two–Stage Game", in J. Ferejohn, J.N. Rakove and J. Riley (eds.), *Constitutional Culture and Democratic Rule* (Cambridge/New York: Cambridge University Press, 2001) 147 e.s.

5 Have we Reached the Limits of the Law?

5.1 Can we Define the Limits?

In line with what has been said before on the functions of the law and the legal environment in the Union, and in particular of the law as an instrument for change, we need to make a distinction between the acceptance of decisions, and the acceptance of institutions (and thus of their ability to promote further change).

Rules will be accepted the easiest when they reflect consensus, namely when governments and citizens agree on change. In that hypothesis we remain fairly close to the first function of the law referred to in section 1 of this chapter.[86] There are no inherent limits on what the law can achieve within the limits of this hypothesis.

But even in respect of decisions by consensus, when taken by institutions, we already need to add a few qualifications. A decision will only be seen as the reflection of a genuine consensus if citizens have the impression that an agreement means the same for all concerned, and that the consensus was arrived at by an agreement of which they can assess its full scope. When the parties (in case of the Union, mostly the Member States) openly differ on the content and the significance of decisions, or when citizens suspect that a decision is part of a package deal whose over–all impact or content they can not assess, they will be disinclined to adhere to the 'consensus'. Or at a later stage they will conclude that the decision created an illusion of consensus. The latter attitude is for institutions more dangerous than the first. Misunderstandings on consensus are likely to undermine confidence in the institutions. This may in turn significantly affect the acceptance of the institution and impede its ability to contribute further to the settlement of disputes (the second function of the law referred to in the introduction to this chapter) or to be an instrument for further change (the fifth function of the law referred to in the introduction). This problem has haunted UK membership from the start, despite the fact that Edward Heath never pretended that membership would have no real impact on UK sovereignty.[87] More generally: over selling may occasionally create a self fulfilling prophecy, but when it undermines the credibility of law–making institutions, it significantly constricts the limits of what such institutions can achieve by law.

The requirements for the acceptance of institutions depend on the type of institution. As discussed in the introduction to this chapter, 'technical' institutions can, for their acceptance and for the acceptance of the rules they make, largely rely on the legitimacy of the constituting members and their efficiency in dealing with the issues with which they have been entrusted. But while it is arguable that the Union started at the time of the ECSC as a technical organisation (with political ambi-

86 As continental lawyers, we are inclined to add a reference to the private law function of the law, but the distinction between private and public law is already foreign to the British system.

87 See C. Patten, *l.c.,* 34–35.

tions), it has long passed that stage. When the management of the relevant issues requires decisions with a political dimension, such decisions should be made either by a politically legitimated body or by consensus between politically legitimated bodies (*i.e.*, by consensus between politically legitimated governments). Only this last aspect is still relevant when examining the limits of the law in respect of the development of the EU.

As indicated above, we believe that the European institutions can not hope to be perceived by all citizens as the politically legitimate body governing the highly sensitive aspects of the public domain that are at present within the scope of application of the Treaty by adopting the legal models of some of the constituting Members of the Union. Even worse, by doing so the Union may contribute to the erosion of the concept of law as well as of State in most of its Members. This suggests that there is not much the Union can achieve by law – but that is (fortunately) clearly contradicted by the facts (that have a general tendency to confuse theoretic analysis).

The explanation for this is, in our opinion, that while the Union has not been very successful in creating a body politic within the ambit of its powers, by stressing the fact that it created a new legal order it has succeeded in creating an environment in which its own successes and failures did not unduly impact on the concepts of law and State in Member States.

The referenda on the Constitution (and we share the view that given a vote in more Member States, France and the Netherlands would not have been the only ones to reject the Treaty on the Constitution) suggest nevertheless that the Union is reaching the limits of what it can hope to achieve by law.

But even if we in the Union have reached the limits of what the law can achieve, it is still not easy to define these limits. Based on what has been achieved successfully, we could try to define them as the possibility to create institutions entrusted with the management of trade between its Members and with third countries, as well as agriculture and competition and various other areas of competence as were be added from time to time, either by delegation (the 'first pillar', especially where decisions can be taken by qualified majority), or by consensus between its members (decisions concerning the 'first pillar' requiring unanimity and the other 'pillars'[88]). But as we see no workable criteria to distinguish between what can and what cannot be entrusted by delegation, and between what needs to be managed jointly or what should even remain strictly national (or entrusted to other fora), this definition of limits is hardly helpful!

---

[88] See on the 'pillar' structure of the EU *e.g.*, W. van Gerven, *l.c.*, 7–34.

5.2 Can we Push out the Limits?

It is (perhaps paradoxically) easier on the basis of our analysis to indicate what may push out the limits of what the law can achieve in the Union than to give a useful definition of such limits.

Compartimentalisation of the spheres of powers and differentiation of the spheres of policies[89] are preconditions for the development of an autonomous legal order – and an autonomous legal order is a prerequisite for a union governed by the rule of law (not used as a reference to the British model). Only when it is transparent whether decisions are taken at the Union or at the Member States level, will citizens not judge the legitimacy of the Union by applying domestic concepts. The more explicit articulation of powers in the new Article 4[90] and in Protocol 2 to the Reform Treaty helps to achieve this goal. It is regrettable that the more transparent description of institutions and legal instruments in Titles IV and V of Part I of the Constitutional Treaty have not been retained or lost part of the envisaged transparency.

A transparent and well–articulated compartimentalisation of spheres of powers and policies can also be positive when it reflects and helps to manage a genuinely dispersed sovereignty.[91] It is in that context very important that the Protocol 2 to the Reform Treaty clarifies the principles of subsidiarity and proportionality. The fact that the Reform Treaty is inevitably perceived as a technical formula in order to avoid a public debate in Member States that would otherwise need to organise a referendum, will on the other hand create an impression of intended non–transparency.

It also follows from the analysis that the basis for the legitimacy of the common order will be more solid if the common values in the Union are sufficiently articulated in terms of general principles of EU law. This is clearly important for the German legal family because it is for them the key to accept the delegation of power. Given the commonality of values mediated by general principles of law they are unlikely to differ substantially from the principles embodied in the French legal order. It remains, however, important to formulate such values in a way that allows them to function as legal principles in order to facilitate the acceptance of the Union's legal order by French–oriented citizens. The more explicit inclusions, be it partly by reference, in Articles I–2 and I–3 of the Constitutional Treaty were welcome, but the more succinct reference to the Charter in the new Article 6 can equally be effective.[92] We suggest using the more dynamic concept of value–

---

89 J. Steenbergen, R. Foqué and G. De Clercq, *l.c.*, 108–110.

90 Article 1(5) of the Reform Treaty; compare Article I–5 of the Constitutional Treaty.

91 See section 3 to this chapter on the constitutional State and the limits of power. See further Z. Laïdi (2004), *l.c.*, 49 e.s.; and with an explicitly positive connotation, A. Kuper, *Democracy Beyond Borders* (Oxford/New York: Oxford University Press, 2006) 197.

92 Article 1(8) of the Reform treaty. See also W. van Gerven, *l.c.*, 52–57.
We fear that the distinction in Part I of the Constitutional Treaty between objectives, values, and fundamental rights and freedoms (which moreover refer to the EC Treaty's four freedoms rather than to the rights and freedoms citizens expect to be expressed under this head-

orientation instead of differentiating between the static concept of values and the political concept of objectives while reserving the concept of objectives for the political implementation of the Union's values. The constitutional principles expressed in Title VI are, on the other hand, a most welcome expression of the Union's concept of representative democracy.

For all, and the British in particular, it is equally important to focus on decision–making procedures (including the accountability of decision–makers[93]) in order to build up the acceptability of institutions by the acceptance of the way they operate and the inclusion of potential opposition.

The focus on decision–making procedures should give special attention to the coherence of policies and the equilibrium between political and bureaucratic decision–making. In particular, the decision–making procedures should not facilitate the 'umbrella syndrome' whereby all can pretend to do well when nobody addresses the real issues.[94]

Expanding the limits of what the law can achieve requires a genuinely political interest in the process.[95] The Commission and the Parliament have made major efforts to make their decision–making more transparent and organise open consultation procedures. But, as indicated above, these efforts may fail to create an impression of open government if the press continues to believe that the genuine political decision–making is in the Council and if the Council debates remain closed (and perhaps otherwise unsuitable for public consumption).

Both a more lively political debate and a credible relationship between political and bureaucratic decision–making may also be incompatible with the exclusive right of proposal of the Commission (the least political of the non–judicial institutions of the Union).[96]

Equally challenging institutionally is the need to reflect in the organisation of the political debate the different levels of coordination and convergence required between Euro–zone Member States and between other Member States.[97]

More generally, when defining priorities in policy–making, it is obvious that the acceptance of institutions (a condition to facilitate the acceptance of their rule–making and thus for pushing the limits of the law) is helped by prioritising goals on which there is consensus, in order to build up the acceptability of institutions by the acceptance of their policies. The more we can rely on the first function of the law referred to in the introduction to this chapter, the more the law will be able to achieve. This may entail for example: more initiatives in respect of justice and security (the 'third pillar' or chapters 1–4 of Title IV of Part III of the EC Treaty as amended by the Reform Treaty[98]); perhaps more common external policy (the 'second pillar' or Articles 10a to 31 of the EU Treaty as amended by the Reform

---

ing in a constitutional document) may be more an articulation of principles for the experts than a contribution to transparency for most citizens.

93 See W. van Gerven, *l.c.*, 62 e.s.

94 See *e.g.*, A. Kuper, *l.c.*, 30 and 113 e.s.

95 See also W. van Gerven, *l.c.*, 39–44 and 238 e.s.

96 As in the EC Treaty and maintained in Article I–34 (1) of the Constitution.

97 See *e.g.*, G. Verhofstadt, *l.c.*, 88 e.s.

98 Article 1(50) and Article 2(64 e.s.) of the Reform Treaty.

Treaty[99], Title V of Part III of the Constitutional Treaty); and perhaps an accelerated reform of the common agricultural policy.[100]

For most citizens the law is in the first place a (somewhat convoluted) technique to achieve goals they do not spontaneously define as 'legal' objectives. Explaining that different rules can achieve similar purposes[101] can facilitate the acceptance of *prima facie* differences. There is, however, also a risk: it may lead to excessive legal relativism impeding the respect for rules and thus for the rule of law.

There is an urgent need to integrate the Islamic community in the local legal culture by simulating the development of an Islamic elite (in the clergy as well as in other walks of life) who can explicitly see a future for their religion within the context of a western State.

Having said that the compartimentalisation of the spheres of powers and differentiation of the spheres of policies are preconditions for the development of an autonomous legal order, the following questions inevitably raise. First, what is the model, or what can or should the model be of this (common) autonomous legal order? Second and perhaps even more importantly, will we be able to develop it in a way that helps to empower the EU institutions for an effective government of the aspects of the public domain that are within their powers? Or in other words, what type or method of development helps to extend the limits of the law by fostering the legitimacy of the institutions and the rules they produce?

It should first be said that given the need for autonomy from the national legal orders, the articulation between legal orders matters more than what the model of the common order is. Perhaps contrary to the general perception, dualist systems[102] may be better equipped to receive the development of the EU legal order than monist systems[103] – provided they fully accept the primacy of Community law.[104]

'Fair, principled and effective in addressing the real issues' seems a sound basis for the further development of a legal order with legitimacy in the opinion of most Europeans. The more difficult question is as to how systematic or coherent it should be. Legal rules clearly need to be consistent in the sense that they should not be conflicting or contradicting each other. But should we aim at more – or is a more system–oriented approach a threat to its acceptance?

All this raises the delicate issue of the relationship between institutional and substantive provisions in the Constitutional Treaty. Institutional maturity and credibility argues in favour of a separation between the genuinely constitutional

---

99 Article 1(24 e.s.) of the Reform Treaty.

100 See further *e.g.,* G. Verhofstadt, *l.c.,* 59–77.

101 See *e.g.,* the introduction to W. van Gerven et al., *Cases, Materials and Texts on National, Supranational and International Tort Law* (Oxford and Portland: Hart Publishing, 2000) 1–11.

102 See *e.g.,* Denmark, Hungary, Ireland, Malta and the UK.

103 See *e.g.,* the Baltic States, the Benelux countries, Cyprus and Poland.

104 See further on the incorporation of EU law in the legal orders of the Member States: K. Lenaerts and P. Van Nuffel, *l.c.,* 678-700. It is regrettable that the relevant provision of the Constitutional Treaty on the priority of EU law have not been retained in the Reform Treaty, even though this does as such not require the Court of Justice to change its case–law.

institutional provisions and the provisions on common policies, including the 'four freedoms'[105] and the rules of competition. But to give up part of the consolidation of what has been the hardcore of the Union, is a very high price to pay. It seems nevertheless at least advisable to have in a future draft a reviewed distribution of topics and to include former 'first pillar' issues in a different treaty, even when the rules to change that treaty are the same as the ones applying to the 'Constitution'.

The way the model should be developed in order to contribute most to empowering the EU institutions for an effective government is easier to define but difficult to pursue. One of the main criticisms of the EU construction is that it is largely a 'top–down' construction. In order to boost its legitimacy, it should be built 'bottom–up'. Again, the exclusive right of the Commission to propose legislation (the right of initiative), which is generally seen as a bureaucratic institution, does not help to create a bottom–up perception. But a right of initiative is no guarantee that the general public will identify more easily with proposals as long as large parts of public opinion fail (or even refuse) to see that Parliament as their representative in a genuine political debate that has its own place in a constitutional continuum, and that is no less legitimate than their national parliaments. The Court of Justice has shown how a bottom–up approach can work.[106] The Court also (somewhat paradoxically) seems to meet with less public resistance than the Parliament. But it is nevertheless doubtful whether a bottom–up approach by judges will also be appreciated by the general public as being genuinely 'bottom–up'. And there are inherent restrictions on what a court can achieve. We have already referred above to judge–made law, which the British are rather familiar with[107] and its inevitable lack of predictability and transparency, but which may have a more destabilising impact on lawyers more used to the 'French' legal culture. Moreover there is a thin line between creative case–law and judicial activism. And while the first has enhanced the status of the Court, the second would be likely to erode it rapidly. The Commission's efforts to publish drafts on their website and to associate interested parties in discussions on such drafts, green papers, discussion papers, and so on, followed by parliamentary consideration, is probably the best that can be achieved – provided that policies stay reasonably close to genuine concerns or that the institutions can convince their audience that it should feel concerned by the issues. It is of course also important that the development of texts shows that the Commission takes into account the input it received.

The differences in real and/or perceived relative efficiency and legitimacy of the national State and the Union in different Member States practically excludes a reconstruction of the traditional State at a European level. A significant number of

---

105 Free movement of persons, of services, of goods, and of capital.

106 See W. van Gerven, "Bringing (Private) Laws Closer to Each Other at the European Level" in F. Capaggi (ed.), *The Institutional Framework of European Private Law* (Oxford: Oxford University Press, 2006) 37–77; and W. van Gerven, "Bridging the Unbridgeable: Community and National Tort Law after 'Francovitch' and 'Brasserie', *International and Comparative Law Quarterly* 1996, 507–544.

107 The fact that the British are more used to judge–made law may explain the impression that the Court and its case–law is more easily accepted than other EU institutions, notwithstanding the fact that the British tend to be the most vocal euro–sceptics.

the present Member States will not go that far, and it may not be in their interest to do so. And it is in the interest of the others who might prefer a more ambitious integration to keep the internal market significantly larger than the domestic markets of those who might be willing to go further on the path of integration.

In order to make that internal market work and evolve, it is also in the interest of those who prefer a more political integration to operate in an environment where all feel genuinely involved in the management of the internal market regardless whether they opt for a more politically integrated Union or not. A larger market (like the EEA) effectively managed by a limited number of hardcore members linked with the other members by rather weak consultation mechanisms, is unlikely to serve the best interests of all members for long. On the contrary, the history the EEA concept and of the offers of partnership to eastern European countries has shown that offering market access without full co–government can, even if it answers the needs of its members, rarely hope to fulfil their legitimate aspirations. It may even make the loss of control over their environment more visible and destructive.

It follows that a multi–speed European construction *à géométrie variable* can only be avoided at the cost of structural stagnation or a significant threat to the future of the internal market. It seems to us that structural stagnation is at least as damaging for the vital confidence in the ability of a society to deal with its major challenges as the complexity and loss of transparency that characterise more *ad hoc* institutional constructions. But it will nevertheless be a major challenge to conceive and implement with sufficient credibility a model with clusters of competences which are: each transparent both in respect of the ambit of their powers and structure of decision–making; clearly articulated both in respect of the powers of the Member States and with regard to each other; and in conformity with the principles of subsidiarity and proportionality by organising a coherent compartmentalisation of spheres of power and policy.

6 Conclusion

When attempting to answer the question how we can give everybody sufficient assurance that they have a reasonable degree of control over their destiny, or at least the comfort that they can identify the forces that are in control, we are confronted with several problems.

First, the theories that helped to shape the modern national States offer, at least since the constitutionalism of Montesquieu, analytical models that can also be used in a wider context than the national State, but there are at least two reasons in the light of these theories why the EU as a political entity can not be conceived as a mere extrapolation of the classical State. First, because of the *intra*–State as well as *inter*–State implosion of homogeneity. Second, because the classical theories on the division of power and shared sovereignty need to be refined in the light of the factual context.

Second, we have to admit that the EU as we know it, does not give everybody sufficient assurance that they have a reasonable degree of control over their destiny. But we also have to conclude that the territorial States as we know them can no longer offer adequate responses to the challenges of globalisation.

Third, the latter conclusion leads more readily to the exploration of European solutions in a smaller and old Member State with a weak sense of national belonging, such as Belgium, than in larger Member States and/or States with a stronger sense of national identity. But the fact that it is less obvious that national States can no longer manage globalisation does not mean that it is less correct. Strong Member States (those with a strong legitimacy and effective government) that for example do not wish to have a common currency, nevertheless still have a case to argue that the EC – as it was 'pre–Maastricht' – corresponded best with their needs and aspirations, a case that many think is convincing.

Fourth, the history of the EEA concept and of the offers of partnership to eastern European countries have also taught us that offering market access without full co–government can, even if it answers the needs of its members, rarely hope to fulfil their legitimate aspirations. It may even make the loss of control over their environment more visible and destructive.

The differences in real and/or perceived relative efficiency and legitimacy of the national State and the Union in different Member States practically exclude a reconstruction of the traditional State at a European level. A significant number of the present Member States will not go that far, and it may not be in their interest to do so. It is at the same time in the interest of the others who might prefer a more ambitious integration, to keep the internal market significantly larger than the domestic markets of those who might be willing to go further on the path of integration. And in order to make that internal market work and evolve, it is also in the interest of those who prefer a more political integration to operate in an environment where all feel genuinely involved in the management of the internal market regardless whether they opt for a more politically integrated Union or not. A larger market (like the EEA) effectively managed by a limited number of hardcore members linked with the other members by rather weak consultation mechanisms, is unlikely to serve the best interests of all members for long.

The continued development of the internal market, where necessary in a context of differently structured clusters of integration *à géométrie variable*, remains therefore a valid model. But the mere layering of market thinking will not solve the present challenges. Market thinking is characterised by a reduction of civil society to the organisation of the relations between private interests. The institutional perspective on the general interest and a participating citizenship are not its central concerns. And while that may create the illusion that market thinking allows us to side–step the political pitfalls of heterogeneous societies, it becomes in reality a growing problem in a context of increasing heterogeneity. The political nature of a society is characterised by its capacity for a careful and efficient management of heterogeneity.

A well–functioning internal market based on free competition is therefore a prerequisite, but also an insufficient condition for a strong civil society, which in turn is a prerequisite for a democratic order based on the rule of law, of which the engine is a process of political will formation by a participating citizenship. And while this citizenship may be the most structured and recognisable in the national States as we know them, there will be no management of the challenges of globalisation that gives everybody sufficient assurance that they have a reasonable degree of control over their destiny without an involvement of civil society at all relevant levels.

The continued development of the internal market does not mean that Member States can not go further in political integration. But they should only do so provided they develop jointly or separately the capacity to manage the heterogeneity both within their existing national context and between them. And the coexistence of the internal market and a possible further integration between some Member States can only contribute to a better management of global issues when all Member States continue to share proportional responsibility for the management of the internal market.

Constitutionalism should therefore not be reduced to the attempts to offer the Union a 'Constitution'. It needs to offer a conceptual framework for the interface between political power (on a Member State and European or global level), a free market, and civil society that makes it possible to manage the tensions of private interests in the perspective of a shared general interest.

In doing so the law will find its limits in the ability of civil society to come to terms sufficiently with its own heterogeneity and inevitable factual challenges in order to allow for an effectively participating citizenship.

Chapter 14 – The Limits of Substantive International Economic Law: In Support of Reasonable Extraterritorial Jurisdiction

Cedric Ryngaert

1 Introduction

Ordinarily, the legislation or jurisdiction of a State stops at the State's borders. Exceptionally, the jurisdiction of a State's laws may extend beyond its borders, and apply to situations that are already regulated – or deliberately *not* regulated – by the 'territorial' State, understood here as the State on whose territory the situation arises. This is notably the case in economic law, specifically in antitrust and securities law. Jurisdiction exercised by a State over a foreign economic activity deemed harmful to that State will, in this chapter, for the sake of convenience, be referred to as 'extraterritorial' economic jurisdiction.

When exercising extraterritorial jurisdiction, a State may fail to adequately account for the interests of the territorial State, a State that presumably has a legitimate – and possibly overriding – regulatory interest in the case. Extraterritorial jurisdiction or the extraterritorial application of national laws has therefore been denounced for violating the principle of non–intervention in other States' affairs. Yet because global business–restrictive practices and securities fraud are realities which the territorial State does not face up to, States that are harmed by them are unlikely to scale down their assertions of jurisdiction. In order to accommodate foreign concerns, they may impose certain restraints on themselves, and subject their jurisdictional assertions to a reasonableness test. At bottom however, reasonableness is in the eye of the beholder, and quite frequently, the defence of national sovereignty tends to masquerade as 'reasonable jurisdiction' (section 2).

Since rational people may differ over how reasonably to exercise jurisdiction, the emphasis has recently shifted from the exercise of unilateral jurisdiction to a harmonisation of economic laws, transnational cooperation in the enforcement of these laws, and even to the establishment of international regulators and institutions (section 3). It is claimed that this 'shift to substantivism' moves beyond the fruitless debate over sovereignty – a debate in which any State somehow affected by an economic situation, either positively or negatively, brandishes 'sovereignty' to fend off the other's assertions. It is also claimed that, if internationally standardised substantive rules and procedures are increasingly used, normative competency conflicts will soon belong to the past, and the peaceful co–existence of States will be ensured.

In this chapter, it will be argued that substantivism may fail to deliver all benefits ascribed to it because of the dubious process in which substantive international law may come into being (sections 4 and 5). To put it differently, this chapter traces the *limits* of an approach that intends to supplant *procedural* international law, a law based on delimiting States' spheres of competence (the law of jurisdiction), with *substantive* international law, an international *jus commune* of substantive rules and procedures. It will be submitted that the international community, and its weaker members in particular, may, on balance, sometimes be better off with a rule–based framework of international jurisdiction than with common substantive rules and procedures saturated with the interests of the powerful. A rule–based framework may come into being if transnational judicial networks are set up, enabling frequent low–threshold contact between courts, regulators and private actors (section 6).

In terms of the perspective taken in this book, this chapter emphasises the limits of the rights–guaranteeing function of substantive international law. It is argued that, somewhat counter–intuitively perhaps, ill–conceived harmonisation–driven solutions to international (economic) problems may fail to adequately protect the rights of States and transnational economic actors. Consensual solutions are not necessarily in the best interests of those who participated in their making. Instead, this chapter will praise the unilateral exercise of extraterritorial jurisdiction by States. It does not, however, shut its eyes to problems of legitimacy and democracy that this limited concept of the role of international law embodies. It will be submitted that the law's rights–guaranteeing function could only be properly served if all the stakeholders concerned are granted sufficient procedural and participatory rights that allow them to have their voice heard, and, accordingly, to influence a State's final jurisdictional assertion touching upon their interests (section 7).

2 Extraterritorial Jurisdiction

In the field of economic law, the reach of a State's laws has been "one of the most contentious issues over the past fifty years."[1] It is not the place here to elaborate much on the intricacies of extraterritorial economic jurisdiction. It may suffice to state that the United States and Europe have not shied away from applying their economic laws, their antitrust laws in particular, to conduct occurring outside their borders but affecting their economies.

Typically, the territorial principle has been invoked so as to justify the jurisdictional assertion. Because of the indeterminacy of the territorial principle, it may however justify almost any jurisdictional assertion over foreign conduct that somehow affects a State's territory. An unrestrained application of the territorial principle in the field of international economic law ineluctably leads to upsetting

1 See S. Weber Waller, "The Twilight of Comity", *Colum. J. Transnat'l L* 2000, *38*, 563.

the foreign nations where the harmful conduct originated, and to straining the forum State's own regulatory and judicial resources. States have therefore circumscribed the territorial effects amenable to effects–based jurisdiction to direct, substantial, and reasonably foreseeable effects.

In the late 1970s, a more wide–ranging interest–balancing or reasonableness test, borrowed from the conflict of laws, was added as a restraining device.[2] Interest–balancing – weighing the different sovereign interests involved, resulting in deference to the State with the overriding sovereign interest – in effect 'multilateralises' the jurisdictional issue. In practice however, unilateralism tends to gain the upper hand, as the jurisdictional analysis suffers from a pro–forum bias: courts will apply their own, known law to a transnational situation rather than an unknown foreign law. This may be inevitable because regulatory agencies, when weighing the regulatory interest of their own State with the regulatory interest of another State, act in a double capacity. Being regulatory agencies, they are supposed to defend national regulatory interests. Yet as decentralised international arbitrators, they are also supposed to arbitrate national and foreign interests 'neutrally' and 'objectively'. Because they assume the functions of defending national *and* international interests, they may fail to deliver on either one.

3 The Substantivist Approach

Clearly, extraterritorial jurisdiction may not adequately work. Because State actors primarily defend the interests of their State of allegiance, they tend to exercise jurisdiction if such serves their narrowly–defined economic interests, regardless of global harm of the jurisdictional assertion. To justify their jurisdictional assertions, they invoke sovereignty–related links, typically based on territoriality, yet they may fail to take into account other nations' sovereignty–related links. They may either believe that public international law does not require them do so, or they may claim that, methodologically, they defer to the State with the stronger links (even if such is not always borne out in practice).

Ideally, the *better law* should be applied to a particular transnational situation, irrespective of whether that situation could be tied, almost mechanically, to a particular sovereign. Buxbaum has termed the better law approach a 'substantivist approach', because it operates on the basis of "a choice–of–law methodology whose goal is to select the better law in any given case" through an analysis of the substantive content of laws.[3] Admittedly, in disputes over the reach of a State's laws before national regulators and courts, substantive analysis may play a role, but it will typically do so within the straitjacket based on sovereignty and territori-

---

2 § 403 of the Restatement (Third) of US Foreign Relations Law (1987); *Timberlane Lumber Co. v. Bank of America, N.T. & S.A.*, 549 F.2d 597, 605–08 (9th Cir.1976); *Mannington Mills, Inc. v. Congoleum Corp.*, 595 F.2d 1287, 1292 (3d Cir.1979).

3 See in particular H.L. Buxbaum, "Conflict of Economic Laws: From Sovereignty to Substance", *Va. J. Int'l L.* 2002, *42*, 931, 957.

ality. Under traditional public international law and choice–of–law theory, a situation is indeed tied to a sovereign on the basis of formal, essentially desubstantivised connecting (territorial) factors[4], and the law of the sovereign with the strongest nexus will be applied. Substantivism however requires that 'the better law' be applied to a particular situation. The better law is not necessarily the law of the State with arguably the strongest link to the situation. It is not a particularised or *phenomenal* law, but a law which is, from an economic, social, cultural, or like perspective, the best *noumenal* law to apply. The better law may not to be found in existing legal systems, but is to be developed by concurring rational minds.

The better law approach requires policy choices for which courts are ill–equipped. For constitutional reasons (the separation of powers), they are indeed not allowed to apply what they believe is the best law for a situation. Under rules of private international law, they are only allowed to apply the law of the particular State with which the situation has the strongest – usually – territorial, nexus. In regulatory matters concerning antitrust and securities, moreover, the choice–of–law analysis typically yields only the application of forum's law, because one State does not apply another State's public laws.[5] Far from applying the best law, courts will then apply no law at all.[6] Arguably, adequate solutions to transnational regulatory problems should not be devised by courts, but by the political branches, by national regulatory agencies that have a day–to–day contact with their foreign counterparts, or by international institutions. Agencies may cooperate in the enforcement of their national laws and thus ensure that law is applied in a manner which is both effective and respectful of each of the involved State's respective substantive policy choices. In addition, if sufficient international support could be mustered, negotiations on the harmonisation of national laws could be started, either on a bilateral basis, or on a multilateral basis, possibly in the framework of an international institution (*e.g.*, OECD, WTO). In practical terms then, substantivism may be defined as a method of developing and applying the best law through harmonisation and cooperation efforts which de–emphasise rules of choice–of–law and jurisdiction informed by territorial linkage.[7]

4 Substantivism in Practice

A shift from jurisdiction to substantivism is clearly discernible in recent international practice. The doctrine also has focused more on international economic cooperation than on international economic jurisdiction.[8] At the outset, it should

4 Compare *id.*, at 956–957.

5 See *e.g.*, *The Antelope*, 23 US (10 Wheat.) 66, 123 (1825) (Marshall, C.J.), ("The Courts of no country execute the penal laws of another").

6 The court will dismiss the antitrust or securities case if it finds that another State's laws should apply, albeit without any corresponding guarantee that the case will be dealt with by the other State.

7 See H.L. Buxbaum, *l.c.*, 962–966.

8 See S. Weber Waller, *l.c.*, 579.

however be noted that a substantivist approach will appeal to national authorities only if it serves their national interests. This explains why harmonisation and co-operation have only occurred where harmonised law sufficiently resembles domestic law[9], or when the benefits obtained from harmonisation and cooperation clearly outweigh the benefits of a traditional jurisdictional approach.

Since the early 1980s, securities regulators have embarked upon a course that resolves international regulatory conflicts through cooperation and harmonisation.[10] Antitrust regulators followed suit in the 1990s.[11] Typically, States entered into bilateral memoranda of understanding providing for information–sharing and mutual assistance. While these memoranda still recognise unilateral assertions of jurisdiction by States – as they are precisely aimed at making these assertions more efficient – they are an application of substantivist theory in that the particular law of a sovereign, while still nominally applied, retreats in the face of the reciprocal international enforcement framework set forth in the memoranda.

Outside the field of antitrust and securities law, the substantivist approach has largely failed so far, because international economic transactions may be "too multifarious to be amenable to a comprehensive scheme of multilateral treaties."[12] Yet also antitrust and securities substantivism has been limited. In practice, it only governs the relations between industrialised nations, and is mainly limited to information–sharing and positive comity.[13] The outcome of bilateral cooperation between the United States and Europe, which is at an all–time high in the field of in-

---

9 See H.L. Buxbaum, *l.c.*, 964.

10 See for a detailed overview on international cooperation and assistance in the field of securities law: M.D Mann and W.P. Barry, "Developments in the Internationalisation of Securities Enforcement", Practising Law Institute, Corporate Law and Practice Handbook Series, PLI Order Number 3011, May 2004, 355, 365 e.s. The US Securities Exchange Commission (SEC) for instance partly relies on harmonised international accounting standards instead of on US standards, giving up the requirement of US GAAP reconciliation.

11 See in particular Agreement Regarding the Application of Competition Laws between the Government of the United States and the Commission of the European Communities, 4 *CMLR* 823 (1991); 30 *ILM* 1487; *O.J.* L 132, 1995; Agreement Between the European Communities and the Government of the United States of America on the Application of the Positive Comity Principles in the Enforcement of their Competition Laws, *O.J.* L 173/28, 1998; 4 *C.M.L.R.* 502 (1999).

12 X., Note, "Predictability and Comity: Toward Common Principles of Extraterritorial Jurisdiction", *Harv. L. Rev.* 1985, *98*, 1310, 1322 and 1325–26. See also A.T. Guzman, "Choice of Law: New Foundations", *Geo. L.J.*, 2002, *90,* 883, 933 ("Agreement over substantive areas of law has proven to be extremely difficult to achieve"). See also A. Bianchi, "Reply to Professor Maier", in K.M. Meessen (ed.), *Extraterritorial Jurisdiction in Theory and Practice* (London/The Hague/Boston: Kluwer, 1996) 74, 81 (holding that conflicts of jurisdiction cannot always be resolved by means of international agreements).

13 See Article III of the 1998 Comity Agreement between the US and the European Union. Whereas negative comity refers to the regulating state refraining from exercising jurisdiction because another State's interests may be more important (*i.e.*, the traditional comity concept of jurisdictional restraint), positive comity refers to the competition authorities of a requesting party "requesting the competition authorities of a requested party to investigate and, if warranted, to remedy anticompetitive activities in accordance with the requested party's competition laws". See Article III of the 1998 Comity Agreement between the US and the European Union.

ternational merger review, is not *per se* in the interests of third countries. One could imagine a situation of US and European regulators clearing a transatlantic merger in the export industry which distorts competitive conditions in developing nations, without the opinion of these nations being heard in the joint review procedure. Substantive bilateral antitrust cooperation may then reduce global welfare.[14] A global antitrust regime has been advocated[15], but has so far proved elusive because a negotiated solution possibly will only be achievable with transfer payments. The interests of developing and developed countries are indeed diametrically opposed, with developing countries having an interest in stringent antitrust regulation (having many consumers, but few producers), and developed countries having no such interest (having many consumers, but relatively few producers).[16]

International humanitarian law is probably the only branch of the law applied extraterritorially where substantivism seems to have largely succeeded. National humanitarian laws hardly differ from each other, as humanitarian law is, and has been, at least since the late 19th century, *international* humanitarian law. Codified humanitarian law was thus since its very inception *substantive* international law. A next substantivist step was undertaken when, toward the end of the 20th century, *international* repressive mechanisms, applying the same substantive international law, were set up. The establishment of the permanent International Criminal Court (ICC) in particular constitutes a major breakthrough in the international enforcement of international humanitarian law. In the wake of the adoption of the Statute of the ICC, substantivism has been taken one step further, when States overhauled their national laws concerning humanitarian law, and inserted the bulk of the Statute's criminalisations into their domestic law. This process has, however, not eased international tension regarding the extraterritorial or international application of international humanitarian law, primarily because some concepts of the law of war, such as 'necessity' and 'proportionality', are open to (possibly abusive) interpretation. The emphasis is mainly put on *economic* law here, because substantive harmonisation and coordination has not yet been fully achieved in that field of the law (because the substantive content of this law, unlike humanitarian law, dif-

---

14 See R.E. Falvey and P.J. Lloyd, "An Economic Analysis of Extraterritoriality", Centre for Research on Globalisation and Labour Markets, School of Economics, University of Nottingham (UK), Research Paper 99/3, p. 15, available at www.nottingham.ac.uk/economics/leverhulme/reserach_paper/99_3.pdf; A.T. Guzman, "The Case for International Antitrust", *Berkeley J. Int'l L.* 2004, *22*, 355, 362 (noting that "a decision on whether to bring a case in the United States or the EU may be quite different from what is in the interests of a developing country").

15 See for example P. Torremans, "Extraterritorial Application of E.C. and U.S. Competition Law", *E. L. Rev.* 1996, *21*, 280, 292; M. Matsushita, "International Cooperation in the Enforcement of Competition Policy", *Washington University Global Studies Law Review* 2002, *1*, 463; K. von Finckenstein, "International Antitrust Policy and the International Competition Network", in B. Hawk (ed.), *International Antitrust Law & Policy* (Annual Proceedings of the Fordham Corporate Law Institute, 2002) Chapter 3; M.E. Janow, "Observations on Two Multilateral Venues: The International Competition Network (ICN) and the WTO", in B. Hawk (ed.), *id.*, 2002, Chapter 4; D. Voillemot and A. Thillier, "WTO and Competition Rules", in B. Hawk (ed.), *id.*, 1999, Chapter 4.

16 See A.T. Guzman, *l.c.*, 936.

fers widely among States in the first place), and as will be argued in the next section, not necessarily regrettably so.

5 The Limits of Substantivism

If substantivism cannot be achieved, only (extraterritorial) jurisdiction will ensure that a State's interests are sufficiently accounted for. The question arises however whether even if substantivism *could* be achieved, it should be preferred over the unilateral exercise of jurisdiction. International cooperation may seem desirable because it allows all States concerned to have their voice heard. Yet in practice, the glorification of the benefits of substantivism has obscured the reality that international consultations, or the emphasis put on it, may at times produce outcomes that hardly serve the interests of justice and equity. It may be wondered aloud whether, under some circumstances, the (reasonable) exercise of (extraterritorial) jurisdiction should not be maintained.

From an economic perspective, substantive solutions have the drawback that they are expensive. The transaction costs of the unilateral exercise of jurisdiction are much lower than these of multilateral solutions, because the exercise of jurisdiction does not require cumbersome inter–State negotiations.[17] In the long run, the economic benefits of an encompassing substantive regime may possibly outweigh its initial inconveniences. Yet if a particular regulatory controversy could be isolated, such as how the international community should respond to a global price–fixing conspiracy with effects worldwide, then enforcement costs could be considerably cut if just one State is willing to shoulder the burden by establishing its jurisdiction over the conspiracy. If States were to gather around the negotiating table in search of a solution which is acceptable to all States concerned and which requires implementation and enforcement, costs would tend to soar. The cost factor of time should not be overlooked either, not only from an economic viewpoint but also from the perspective of justice. In case of private enforcement of antitrust law for instance, asking the plaintiff to wait, possibly *ad calendas graecas*, until a multilateral solution has been worked out between the various States whose interests are affected, appears unjust since this may violate the plaintiff's right to a hearing in a reasonable time, and amount to a denial of justice if a solution ultimately proves elusive. It is in this context that Professor Meessen has argued that, if negotiations fail, the courts should be able to exercise their jurisdiction.[18] It may even be submitted that, if an acceptable negotiated solution could not be reasonably expected from the outset, the courts should not stay their proceedings, but dispense justice as swiftly as possible, with due respect for foreign interests under the jurisdictional rule of reason.

---

[17] See G. Schuster, *Die internationale Anwendung des Börsenrechts* (Berlin: Springer, 1996) 683.

[18] See K.M. Meessen, "Antitrust Jurisdiction under Customary International Law", *A.J.I.L.* 1984, *78*, 783, 806.

Substantive solutions may also undercut justice at another level: at the level of fairness between States.[19] It has been argued that the exercise of extraterritorial jurisdiction may be an instrument of the powerful, because only powerful States do not have to brace themselves for retaliatory action by a foreign State upon asserting jurisdiction in a manner detrimental to that State. Powerful States also tend to ascribe their rise to power to the quality of their own laws. Viewing these laws as exceptionally good, such States may messianically apply their own laws extraterritorially, and thus impose them upon weaker, purportedly 'uncivilised' nations.[20] Reliance on harmonisation and cooperation may however be no less based on power than reliance on extraterritorial jurisdiction is. Harmonisation is not achieved nor does cooperation take place in a power–free environment. Parties to international agreements may only formally be equal.[21] In the real world, the more powerful parties will usually heavily weigh on the substantive outcome of a negotiating process. This might produce a regime that favours the interests of the powerful to the detriment of those of the weaker.[22] In the WTO for instance, conference rules provide for equal treatment of all parties, but do not apply to informal consultations.[23] In informal 'green room' consultations, the industrialised 'Quad–countries' often manage to build a consensus which they present as a 'take it or leave it' package to the other Member States.[24] As a general matter, richer and larger States have more access to information than poorer and smaller States. A large number of developing countries do also not have the necessary expertise to influence the negotiations and thus to ultimately enter into agreements that should be supposed to serve their interests.[25] It has therefore been argued, not unjustifiably,

---

19 See H.L. Buxbaum, *l.c.*, 973–976.

20 Notably in the field of securities laws the United States has behaved as a benevolent hegemon taking on a duty to stamp out the universal evil of securities fraud. See J.D. Kelly, "Let There Be Fraud (Abroad): A Proposal for a New US Jurisprudence With Regard to the Extraterritorial Application of the Anti–Fraud Provisions of the 1933 and 1934 Securities Acts", *Law & Pol'y Int'l Bus.* 1997, *28*, 477, 491.

21 Historically however, not even this formal equality was guaranteed. While nowadays all States have the right to participate in the treaty–making process, in earlier times only the great powers were invited to international conferences, the outcome of which smaller States had to abide by. See M.C.W. Pinto, "Democratisation of International Relations and its Implications for Development and Application of International Law", in N. Al–Nauimi and R. Meese (eds.), *International Legal Issues Arising under the United Nations Decade of International Law* (Den Haag: Kluwer Law International, 1995) 1260.

22 See A. Bianchi, *l.c.*, 82 (submitting that "[i]n order to attract investments or pushed by other policy reasons, weaker states may be forced to accept the impositions of more powerful states").

23 See for criticism of this method, *e.g.* WTO Watch, "NGOs Call on Trade Ministers to Reject Closed WTO Process", http://www.globalpolicy.org/ngos/int/wto/2002/1104reject.htm (last visited on 31 July 2006).

24 A breakthrough in WTO negotiations is often dependent on an initial deal brokered during quadrilateral negotiations between the United States, the European Union, Canada and Japan. See http://www.wto.org/english/thewto_e/whatis_e/tif_e/org3_e.htm (last visited on 31 July 2007).

25 See more extensively, notably in the context of WTO negotiations: J. Wouters, B. De Meester and C. Ryngaert, "Democracy and International Law", *N.Y.I.L.* 2004, 137–198.

that current substantive international law is replete with Western bias because of Western domination over the making of international law.[26]

With respect to the economic laws that have been given extraterritorial application, the antitrust and securities laws, this holds all the more true since, even as we write, quite some developing countries do not even have or enforce laws that regulate competitive conditions or punish securities fraud. Because these States are not familiar with highly specialised business regulation, they risk swallowing whatever expert nations propose to them. The proliferation of insider–trading prohibitions has for instance largely been steered by bilateral memoranda of understanding negotiated between the United States – historically the first champion of laws prohibiting insider–trading – and other (industrialised) nations that did not yet have such laws. These memoranda typically provided for cooperation in the enforcement of US securities laws, and provided for mechanisms to deal with US requests for discovery.[27] As an instrument of soft pressure, they cajoled the other party into inserting insider–trading prohibitions into their own laws, and thus harmonised insider–trading law largely on US terms.

Accordingly, in terms of their results, extraterritorial jurisdiction and substantive solutions may not differ that much. Both may coax weaker States into adapting their laws in ways desired by the powerful State. Often, extraterritorial jurisdiction and substantive solutions actually work in tandem. The initial exercise of extraterritorial jurisdiction by a State may serve as a tactical prelude to later cooperation and harmonisation agreements serving the interests of that State, especially in case foreign nations left the regulatory field fallow. The process of cooperation and harmonisation in the field of securities law may serve to illustrate this. Because of US emphasis on fair and open capital markets, tight US regulation of securities transactions has also extended to foreign transactions.[28] In a typical situation, after initially asserting its full jurisdiction over foreign transactions, the United States gradually grants exemptions in order not to cause a head–on collision with foreign nations but also, shrewdly, to win over the hearts and minds of these nations for the substance of what is not exempted. Magnanimity on the part of the hegemon may persuade States with underdeveloped regulatory frameworks to embrace readymade solutions provided by the US. This may result in organic harmonisation – States spontaneously adopting similar laws – or in organised harmonisation – States entering into international agreements dealing with the

---

26 See E. Kwakwa, "Regulating the International Economy: What Role for the State?", in M. Byers (ed.), *The Role of Law in International Politics* (Oxford/New York: Oxford University Press, 2000) 227–246.

27 See on US negotiating practice in the field of insider–trading: D.C. Langevoort, "Cross–Border Insider Trading", *Dick. J. Int'l L.* 2001–2002, *19*, 161. The first such memorandum was signed with Switzerland after conflict had arisen over the application of US discovery laws to documents located in Switzerland in the insider–trading case of *SEC* v. *Banca della Sviszera Italiana*, 92 F.R.D. 111 (1981).

28 See the seminal case of *Schoenbaum* v. *Firstbrook*, 405 F.2d 200 (2d Cir. 1968) (court applying the antifraud provisions of the US Securities Exchange Act to foreign securities transactions producing effects in the United States).

matter. Either way, the final harmonised rules will reflect US rules and their underlying values.

In the field of corporate governance, one curiously observes the US first aggressively brandishing the threat of unconditional application of the US Sarbanes–Oxley Act (2002), then European corporations and the European Commission reacting furiously[29], then the US regulatory agencies accommodating foreign concerns (2002–2005), and then finally the European Union in due course enacting its own Directive on statutory audit, with its own accommodations for foreign audit firms (2006).[30] Although the substantive provisions of the US Act and the EU Directive do not wholly coincide, it is hard to resist the conclusion that the EU was considerably influenced by the strengthening of the law in the United States. In sum, while the extraterritorial application of the Sarbanes–Oxley Act may initially have produced some resentment overseas, it may also have paved the way for a US–driven transatlantic 'convergence' of corporate governance standards.

6 Extraterritorial Jurisdiction Revisited

It has been argued that substantivism, while having theoretical appeal, may serve, like extraterritorial jurisdiction, as a transmission belt for the interests of the powerful. In the case of cooperative solutions, this happens much more implicitly than in the case of extraterritorial jurisdiction, which typically meets with stiff resistance from foreign nations. Yet once one scratches below the surface, the cooperative brilliance may fade, and substantivism turns out to be a false friend. Bereft of its illusions, States then face a choice between plague and cholera, between extraterritorial jurisdiction and international 'cooperation', between international friction and unfairness. For all the – justified – complaints about unilateral extraterritorial jurisdiction, it reemerges in the debate over just international economic regulation. It is hesitantly claimed that the exercise of extraterritorial jurisdiction may sometimes produce more equitable results than cooperative solutions.[31]

Admittedly, it has been shown how extraterritorial jurisdiction – on which substantive solutions may possibly piggyback – is as much, or even more, part of a power play as substantivism is. A system in which the US, and to a lesser extent the EU, bully developing nations by applying their laws to situations arising outside their territory but purportedly producing adverse domestic effects, is surely not attractive for this world's downtrodden. One would indeed be hard pressed to

---

29 See Letter of EU Internal Market Commissioner F. Bolkestein to W. Donaldson, Chairman of the SEC, April 24, 2003, available at http://www.iasplus.com/resource/letterfbdonaldson.pdf.

30 Directive 2006/43/EC of the European Parliament and of the Council of 17 May 2006 on statutory audits of annual accounts and consolidated accounts, *O.J.* L 157/87, 2006. See on its international aspects: Chapter XI of the directive (Articles 44–47).

31 Compare H.L. Buxbaum, *l.c.*, 975 ("[T]his process [of substantivism] may be criticised on foreign relations grounds in that it replaces "neutral" consideration of competing laws in the individual case with the application of law reflecting non–neutral values.").

advocate a system in which the European Commission would be allowed to block the merger of South African corporations, to the detriment of thousands of poor South African workers, as happened in the *Gencor* case.[32] However, if one could devise a rigorous rule–based system of international jurisdiction, modulated depending on the subject–matter to be regulated, and to which all States have to adhere, weaker countries would be more likely to go along with it. Such a system may restrict the powerful States' sphere of action and delegitimise their protest against the weaker States' own jurisdictional assertions.

For weaker States, stringent and elaborate rules of jurisdiction may not only serve as defenses against the powerful States' unwarranted assertions or as tools enabling them to actively promote their own interests by engaging in assertions of extraterritorial jurisdiction. Weaker States may also use such rules to their advantage in the course of substantive processes. As Bianchi pointed out, "[t]he bargaining position of weaker States might be stronger if it is perceived as conforming with accepted principles and rules of international law."[33] Developed jurisdictional principles may serve to pressure the powerful into drawing up an international agreement which takes the interests of the weak sufficiently into account. If the agreement were to be considered as unfair by the weak, they could leave the negotiating table and legitimately resort to exercising unilateral extraterritorial jurisdiction. Thus, the limits which substantivism faces could be overcome if substantivism were buttressed by a framework of international jurisdiction.

The question now is how such a framework of international jurisdiction should be developed. Clearly, while there may be some guiding principles applicable across–the–board, every field of the law ought to be subject to its own specific jurisdictional rules.[34] Antitrust regulators do indeed not face the same problems as securities regulators, let alone those which human rights courts do. An attractive option, which confers considerable legal certainty, is the conclusion of treaties on every subject matter.[35] These treaties could spell out the maximal reach of a State's laws. Yet because a treaty could impossibly anticipate the variety of problems arising in the real world, because exempting foreign corporations from regulation may jeopardise the principle of equality before the law[36], and because States

---

32 Commission, Case IV/M.619, decision 97/26/EC of 24 April 1996, *O.J.* L11/30, 1997 (finding that the merger would create a position of collective dominance incompatible with the common market); European Court of First Instance, *Gencor Ltd v. Commission*, Case T–102/96, [1999] ECR II–753 (approving of the Commission's assertion of jurisdiction).

33 See A. Bianchi, *l.c.*, 82.

34 See, *e.g.*, the Restatement (Third) of US Foreign Relations Law (1987), which sets forth the general principles of jurisdiction and reasonableness in §§ 402–403, and features specific sections on tax (§§ 411–413), foreign subsidiaries (§ 414), antitrust (§ 415), securities (§ 416), foreign sovereign compulsion (§ 441), and transnational discovery (§ 442).

35 It may be noted that an overarching convention on criminal jurisdiction, as proposed by the Harvard Research on International Law, "Draft Convention on Jurisdiction with Respect to Crime", 29 *A.J.I.L.* 439 (1935), has never materialised.

36 Exempting foreign conspiracies or mergers causing exactly the same effects in the regulating State as domestic restrictive practices may be a hard sell for a domestic constituency. It is unlikely that enforcement authorities will be willing to cast aside imperative domestic law in an international agreement. Compare J. Schwarze, "Die extraterritoriale Anwendbarkeit des

may be unwilling to tie their own hands too much, such a treaty – if any could be agreed upon at all – is likely to feature a flexible 'reasonableness' or 'comity' test. Comity being essentially a discretionary concept, the parties to the treaty will tend to apply the comity test in their favour[37], a deficit from which the current transatlantic antitrust Comity Agreements (1991/1998) suffer as well.[38] The role of international agreements in bringing more predictability to the exercise of jurisdiction should thus not be overestimated.

How to proceed then? As a matter of logic, before States start negotiations about an international agreement on jurisdiction, they should make sure that their regulators and courts are willing to rise above nationalist reflexes and exercise jurisdictional restraint if another State's sovereignty risks being encroached upon. It has been shown above that there is apparently not much cause for optimism given the tendency of courts and regulators 'to pull for the home crowd'. However, in an era of 'the global village' in which economic and government actors are increasingly wired, and informal transnational government networks emerge, courts and regulators are much more connected with their foreign counterparts than previously.[39] Stronger contacts and better information typically result in a greater understanding of each other's legitimate concerns. It should come then as no surprise that since the breakthrough of the Internet in the late 1990s, there have been no major conflicts over antitrust jurisdiction between US and European regulators.

At the judicial level, this process of mutual understanding has culminated, for the time being, in the 2004 antitrust decision of the US Supreme Court in the *Empagran Vitamins* case. Influenced by a number of *amicus curiae* briefs from foreign governments (namely, the United Kingdom, the Netherlands, Germany, Belgium, Canada, and Japan), the Court stated that it is to be assumed that the US Congress takes "the legitimate sovereign interests of other nations into account"[40] when assessing the reach of US law, and avoids extending its reach when such

---

EG–Wettbewerbsrechts – vom Durchführungsprinzip zum Prinzip der qualifisierten Auswirkung", in J. Schwarze (ed.), *Europäisches Wettbewerbsrecht im Zeichen der Globalisierung* (Baden–Baden: Nomos, 2002) 59–60; J.R. Atwood, "Positive Comity – Is it a Positive Step?", in B. Hawk (ed.), *International Antitrust Law & Policy* (Annual Proceedings of the Fordham Corporate Law Institute, Antitrust in a Global Economy, 1993) 79, 87 ("It is not realistic to expect one government to prosecute its citizens solely for the benefit of another. It is no accident that his has not happened in the past, and it is unlikely to happen in the future").

37 Compare M.C. Franker, "Restoration: International Merger Review in the Wake of General Electric/Honeywell and the Triumphant Return of Negative Comity", *Geo. Wash. Int'l L. Rev.* 2004, *36*, 877, 901 ("[E]ven if positive comity were extended to merger review, it would achieve only the desired effect to the extent that both parties have similar interests in the cessation of certain anticompetitive practices").

38 See D. Kukovec, "International Antitrust – What Law in Action?", *Ind. Int'l & Comp. L. Rev.* 2004, *15* (1), 20 (arguing, in the context of merger control, that regulators, applying comity, are invited to weigh unquantifiable interests of such societal subgroups as consumers, competitors, and employees).

39 See on government networks in particular A.M. Slaughter, "Governing the Global Economy through Government Networks", in M. Byers (ed.), *The Role of Law in International Politics* (Oxford: Oxford University Press, 2000) 177–205.

40 *F. Hoffman–La Roche Ltd. et al.* v. *Empagran S.A. et al.*, 124 S. Ct. 2359, 2366 (2004).

would create a "serious risk of interference with a foreign nation's ability independently to regulate its own commercial affairs."[41] In an important departure from the past, America's highest court in *Empagran* thus held that it expects courts to take foreign sovereign interests adequately into account. In 1993, the Supreme Court had been of the view in the *Hartford Fire Insurance* case that foreign policies and laws should not be heeded by US courts when giving extraterritorial application to the antitrust laws, unless the foreign State compels conduct which US law prohibits (or vice versa)[42], an approach which the European courts also take.[43] Like the fish which tends to rot from the head down, as the Russian proverb has it, the courts duly restricted the comity analysis to a "true conflict" or "foreign sovereign compulsion" analysis in the 1990s.[44] That reasonableness has now resurfaced[45] as high up in the judicial hierarchy as the US Supreme Court testifies to a belief that courts *could* and *should* take foreign sovereign interests into account, and may limit the reach of a State's laws accordingly.

Thanks to the increased transnational contacts between governments, regulators and courts, a reciprocal and principled practice of States exercising reasonable jurisdiction may emerge. From a methodological perspective, it is important in this respect that States, before asserting jurisdiction, allow or even ask other States to voice their concerns and then take them into account as being a good neighbour.[46] Obviously, this cooperative process may take place more smoothly on the basis of a facilitating transnational framework than on the basis of *ad hoc* cooperation through *amicus curiae* briefs or statements of interests. It would be useful if States were to designate official points of contact to which foreign courts could address their inquiries.

A US court, facing an antitrust problem involving a European corporation, could then inquire with an EU office in Brussels whether the EU would have qualms about a particular assertion of jurisdiction (apart from inquiring with the US executive branch whether this assertion would not raise a non–justiciable political – foreign policy – question or not). To that end, the existing Comity Agreements between the United States and the European Community could be revised. Whereas for now they only provide for cooperation between antitrust regulatory agencies, they could in future also provide for an information exchange between courts and regulatory agencies, or even between courts hearing private antitrust

---

41 *Id.*, at 2367.

42 *Hartford Fire Insurance Co.* v. *California*, 509 US 764 (1993).

43 European Court of Justice, *A. Ahlstrom Osakeyhtio and others v. Commission* (*Wood Pulp*), [1988] ECR 5244, § 20; European Court of First Instance, *Gencor* v. *Commission*, [1999] ECR, II–00753, § 103, citing ECJ, *Wood Pulp*, § 20.

44 See, *e.g.*, *United States v. Nippon Paper Industries Co.*, 109 F.3d 1 (1st Cir. 1997) (applying the *Hartford Fire* doctrine to criminal antitrust suits).

45 Interest–balancing was introduced in US antitrust law in the late 1970s in *Timberlane Lumber Co. v. Bank of America, N.T. & S.A.*, 549 F.2d 597, 605–08 (9th Cir.1976); *Mannington Mills, Inc. v. Congoleum Corp.*, 595 F.2d 1287, 1292 (3d Cir.1979).

46 In addition, courts may rely on a "transnational community of jurists" to keep unilateral assertions of jurisdiction. See D.F. Orentlicher, "Whose Justice? Reconciling Universal Jurisdiction with Democratic Principles", *Georgetown L. J.* 2004, *92*, 1057, 1133–34.

complaints.[47] At the global level, the International Competition Network could obviously play an important role in antitrust cooperation.[48] Regulatory cooperation within this network, which groups together developed and developing countries, could be enhanced[49], and membership could possibly be opened up for the courts.

By the same token, a European court that has received a complaint alleging gross human rights violations committed in a foreign country should be able to contact the territorial State, or the national State of the foreign offender if otherwise different, for more information about the facts and the investigations underway. In the situation of gross human rights violations, third–party States could also be contacted, where, for various reasons (such as prosecutorial capacity and expertise, cultural affinity, availability of witnesses, and so on), these States may have a stronger prosecutorial interest and provide a better adjudicatory forum. They may also have information that could be useful for the prosecuting State, for instance because witnesses or co–suspects have fled to their territory. Encouragingly, in the European Union, a special network of contact points regarding persons responsible for genocide, crimes against humanity and war crimes has recently been put in place on the basis of a 2002 Council decision.[50]

It seems no wishful thinking to expect that the eventual decision of a court which has sought and/or received the opinion of other States concerned, through judicial networks, will echo the other States' comments. Interestingly, from a public international law perspective, that decision, if it is subsequently not criticised by other States, may instantly come to reflect customary international law in the particular field of the law where the decision is taken[51], or at least be indicative of an emerging consensus. If the same issue arises again, States may rely on that decision as constitutive of (emerging) international law – although, admittedly, fact patterns may differ considerably, and thus complicate the legal precedent value of that decision.

---

47 If courts could transnationally communicate with each other, jurisdictional deadlock stemming from parallel proceedings and reciprocal anti–suit injunctions, as arose in the infamous *Laker Airways* litigation in the 1980s in the United States and the United Kingdom, could be prevented. See *Laker Airways Ltd. v. Sabena*, 731 F.2d 909 D.C. Cir. (1984); *British Airways Board* v. *Laker Airways Ltd.*, [1984] 3 WLR 410; [1985] A.C. 58.

48 See http://www.internationalcompetitionnetwork.org. This network was established in 2001.

49 Policy Statement of the International Chamber of Commerce, "Extraterritoriality and business", 13 July 2006, Document 103–33/5, recommendation nr. 4 (on file with the author). So far, the network has mainly formulated policy proposals for its members (national enforcement agencies).

50 Council Decision of 13 June 2002 setting up a European network of contact points in respect of persons responsible for genocide, crimes against humanity and war crimes, *O.J.* L 167/1, 2002.

51 See, *e.g.*, K.M. Meessen, "Schadensersatz bei weltweiten Kartellen: Folgerungen aus dem Endurteil im Empagran–Fall", *WuW* 2005, *55*, 1115, 1118–1119 (arguing that the rule which the US Supreme Court set forth in *Empagran* (no jurisdiction for a State over foreign–based harm caused by a global cartel on the sole ground that inflated prices paid in that State were necessary for the cartel's success) represents a rule of instant customary international law, because six foreign governments were involved in the *Empagran* proceedings as *amici curiae* and advocated the sort of jurisdictional restraint espoused by the Supreme Court and the D.C. Circuit).

Minimalists might argue that law formed in this fashion would only bind the States involved in the initial court decision. This is however an overly strict view of international law formation. International law may arguably also crystallise if States do not protest against a State's jurisdictional assertion over a situation which, on its face, concerns only one or a few other States directly. If States intend to oppose the crystallisation of a norm of customary international law, they ought to object to *any* decision which might contain such a norm that might *in future* purportedly work to the detriment of their interests. Therefore, the European Commission, Australia, Switzerland, and the United Kingdom, have recently filed *amicus curiae* briefs with the US Supreme Court in the case of *Sosa* v. *Alvarez–Machain* (2004), a case concerning the exercise of universal tort jurisdiction under the US Alien Tort Statute over the arbitrary arrest of a Mexican by a US official in Mexico.[52] The *Sosa* case did in no way directly impinge on the intervening States' sovereignty interests, but because its outcome undeniably influenced the legal position of their corporations doing business in far–flung countries where human rights are routinely trampled upon, they prospectively intervened so as to deny the validity of a norm of customary international law that would authorise States to liberally exercise universal tort jurisdiction.

States might nowadays be expected to screen court decisions of which disposition might cause them concern. The recent launch of a databank on international law in domestic courts may greatly facilitate their work (presumably the work of their Foreign Ministries).[53] Ideally, States should intervene when the trial is pending so that they could still influence the outcome. A relatively brief period during which States may express their objections against the outcome may however be reserved. After that period, ignorance of that decision may no longer be an acceptable defence. Objections raised against an analogous jurisdictional assertion after this period has expired should not be taken into account by the asserting State.

---

[52] 124 S.Ct. 2739 (2004). Brief of *amicus curiae* of the European Commission in *Sosa* v. *Alvarez–Machain* in support of neither party, available at http://www.nosafehaven.org/_legal/atca_oth_EurComSupportingSosa.pdf; Brief of the Governments of the Commonwealth of Australia, the Swiss Confederation and the United Kingdom of Great Britain and Northern Ireland as *amici curiae* in support of the petitioner, US Supreme Court, *Sosa v. Alvarez–Machain*, 23 January 2004, at p. 2, available at http://www.nosafehaven.org/_legal/atca_con_AUSsupportingSosa.pdf. See also C. Ryngaert, "The European Commission's *Amicus Curiae* Brief in the Alvarez–Machain Case", *International Law Forum* 2004, nr. 6, 55–60.

[53] See Oxford Reports on International Law in Domestic Courts, available at http://www.oxfordlawreports.com.

7 Conclusion: Limits in a Communicative Setting

In this chapter, a viable system of extraterritorial jurisdiction has been devised in which the legality of every single jurisdictional assertion is a function of the level of – reasonable – foreign protest aimed against it in timely fashion. While this system should surely take note of the glass ceiling constituted by the pervasive role of political power, low–threshold contacts among courts and regulators of different States through government networks may go a long way in avoiding or raising it. Power politics can not thrive in a communicative setting which considers all participants to be equal partners and fosters mutual understanding.

Free and fair communication will however only take place if the participants are allotted legal rights. A system that condones, and even encourages, unilateral jurisdiction of single States *limits* the role of truly international law. Yet in order for this reduced role of international law not to wreak global havoc, certain legal guarantees should be provided for. This is the role of international law: offering procedures that allow international communication and cooperation to take place, while at the same time seeing to it that the participants retain the greatest possible measure of freedom of action. Guaranteeing rights indeed implies, one the hand, that participants remain free to chart their own course, and on the other, that conflicting courses of action are mediated so as to protect every single participant's rights to the greatest extent. For the law concerning jurisdiction, this requires that impediments to transnational communication be lifted, such as through the expansion of *amicus curiae* briefs in transnational judicial procedures, or through the establishment of permanent contact points among economic regulators or prosecutors. Yet at the same time, communication channels should be prevented from becoming congested with idiosyncratic views of dominant States, States should therefore be entitled to retain their discretion to exercise jurisdiction over extraterritorial actions that blatantly violate their legitimate rights.

Extraterritorial jurisdiction surely has its limits, but possibly less so than ill–conceived substantive solutions putting the weak at a systematic disadvantage. This is not to say that substantivism has *inherent* limits. This is only to invite negotiators, of weak and strong States alike, to ascertain whether a substantive solution is also a just solution. If States are able to find common ground without abrogating the legitimate rights of the weaker among them, a substantive solution may be preferable. If they are not, a system of unilateral 'rights–guaranteeing' jurisdiction is an attractive alternative.

Chapter 15 – When Law Meets Power: The Limits of Public International Law and the Recourse to Military Force

Tom Ruys

1 Introduction

In 1963 former US Secretary of State Dean Acheson addressed the annual meeting of the American Society of International Law. Commenting on the events surrounding the Cuban missile crisis, he declared to his audience that "[l]aw simply does not deal with such questions of ultimate power – power that comes close to the sources of sovereignty."[1] Acheson's bold statement illustrates the traditional scepticism among International Relations ('IR') scholars *vis–à–vis* the capability of international law to act as a restraint on governmental decision–making in foreign policy matters. Nowhere is this scepticism stronger than when it comes to decisions on inter–State recourse to force, the *domaine réservé* of the executive, which is perceived as the ultimate battleground for a trial of strength between international law and naked power – a contest law is doomed to lose.

But is it really true that public international law stops where power begins? More recently, IR scholars have apparently begun to award greater significance to international law. International lawyers, on the other hand, have gone to great lengths to demonstrate that compliance fares better than is often thought. Against this background, the present chapter aims at gaining a better understanding of the limits of public international law by putting the traditional IR scepticism into perspective while steering clear of unwarranted juridical optimism. Building upon the different views among IR scholars and international legal theorists (section 2), we will identify a number of factors inducing compliance with public international law (section 3). Subsequently, we will briefly examine to what extent these factors apply to the *Ius ad Bellum*, namely the international law on the use of force (section 4).

---

1 D. Acheson, "Remarks", *ASIL Proc.* 1963, *57*, 13, 14.

2 Theories on International Law and Power

2.1 International Relations Theories

According to the realist school, States are driven by the pursuit of the 'national interest'. As their conflicting interests are not controlled by an overarching hierarchy, anarchy prevails. Realists traditionally attest to a strong mistrust towards international law[2], which they ultimately consider epiphenomenal.[3] It rests on power, as its content is determined by dominant States and it is upheld by these States when it serves their interests. Otherwise, the normative arrangements will have to yield to the very same power. Contrary to political and economic factors, international law does not *affect* the behaviour of States. It merely serves as a tool for powerful States to use for their own ends against weaker entities. Voluntary compliance is an illusion.

Realists also refute the idea that international institutions that fall short of a true 'world government' may be capable of preventing conflict. Collective security arrangements, including the United Nations, are no more than a method of placing power in the hands of the dominant States.[4] At the best, they manage to reduce conflict somewhat by institutionalising the status quo. Contemporary neo–realists continue to stress that international institutions have very little effect on State behaviour.[5]

The latter view is exactly what distinguishes modern realism from institutionalism. Drawing upon economics and game theory, institutionalists argue that international institutions and legal regimes influence State behaviour as a result of the benefits that can be gained through cooperation.[6] Indeed, while States recognise that their interests are best achieved through mutual cooperation, such cooperation is very costly in a purely anarchical atmosphere because of problems of cheating, unrestrained free–rider behaviour, and a lack of information.[7] The value of institutions and regimes is that they establish a 'managed anarchy', where the transaction costs resulting from inter–State cooperation are much lower.

International legal regimes thus serve a State's interests and become an integral part thereof. For this reason, States will often comply with a set of rules, even if their short–term interest would dictate them otherwise. On the other hand, institu-

---

2 A.C. Arend, "Do Legal Rules Matter? International Law and International Politics", *Virginia JIL* 1997–98, *38*, 107, 110; F.A. Boyle, "The Irrelevance of International Law: The Schism Between International Law and International Politics", *Cal. Western ILJ* 1980, *10*, 193, 201.

3 See C. Reus–Smit, "The Politics of International Law", in C. Reus–Smit (ed.), *The Politics of International Law* (Cambridge: Cambridge University Press, 2004) 14–44, at 16–17.

4 See *e.g.*, H.J. Morgenthau, "Diplomacy", *Yale LJ* 1946, *55*, 1067–1080.

5 *E.g.*, J.J. Mearsheimer, "The False Promise of International Institutions", *International Security* 1994–95, *19* (5), 47.

6 On the definition of 'institutions', see R.O. Keohane, *International Institutions and State Power* (Boulder: Westview Press, 1989) 3.

7 C. Reus–Smit, *l.c.*, 18.

tionalists recognise that respect for regimes is not absolute and that States will violate the rules once they feel that participation no longer 'pays off'. Moreover, they believe that regimes are most likely to be established and complied with in those areas where cooperative behaviour outweighs the benefits of unilateral action, as is the case for economic and resource areas.[8] By contrast, in issues of 'high politics', touching upon core security concerns, compliance will depend on whether the expected 'outcome' of a rule coincides with the State's political and economic goals.[9] If so, the rule will appear to have been respected. If not, it will virtually always be violated.

In spite of their differences, (neo–)realism and institutionalism are both *rationalist* theories that consider States to be rational actors pursuing predefined interests. This approach has been challenged by the constructivist school, which stresses that the international system is in essence a *social* structure, where States' identities and interests are the product of social interaction.[10] While constructivists do not oppose the idea that States create regimes because it serves their interests, they claim that participation therein influences States' values and the respective expectations and perceptions they hold of one another, a development which may in time alter their interests.

Of the various IR schools, constructivism is the one that awards the most importance to international law. It does so by asserting that international legal rules are part of the non–material elements which make up the international social structure. This is especially true for those fundamental legal norms, such as the prohibition on the threat or use of force, which help structure the international system as we know it.[11] International legal rules are believed to shape States' identities and interests through three mechanisms: imagination, communication, and constraint.[12] 'Imagination' implies that legal norms affect how States think they should act and what the perceived limitations on their actions are. Thus, Arend advances the possibility that a State's subscribing to the UN Charter may cause the non–use of force to become a major part of its identity.[13] 'Communication' refers to the fact that the conduct of governments is subject to the collective judgment of other governments, organs of public opinion, and international lawyers. This judgment influences the relationships between States, their future cooperation, and reputation. Finally, 'communication' is linked to 'constraint' in the sense that appealing to legal norms to justify State conduct is only a viable strategy if the behaviour under consideration is in some measure consistent with the proclaimed norms. For this reason, the very language of justification provides some constraints on action, to

8 S.D. Krasner, "Structural Causes and Regime Consequences: Regimes as Intervening Variables", *IO* 1982, *36*, 185, 191–192.

9 A.C. Arend, *l.c.*, 123.

10 C. Reus–Smit, "Constructivism", in S. Burchill *et al.* (eds.), *Theories of International Relations* (New York: Palgrave, 2nd ed., 2001) 209–230, 214.

11 See S.A. Kocs, "Explaining the Strategic Behavior of States: International Law as System Structure", *International Studies Quarterly* 1994, *38*, 535, 538–539.

12 See C. Reus–Smit, *l.c.*, 218–219.

13 A.C. Arend, *l.c.*, 133.

the extent that justificatory claims cannot be based purely on idiosyncratic grounds.[14]

Each of the three approaches tells us something about the relationship between law and power. Realism reminds us that international law is created by interest–driven States engaged in a power–maximising struggle and depends on the support of dominant States for its enforcement. However, today few IR scholars would contend that international law is wholly insignificant. The realist position cannot account for the fact that law constrains the conduct of powerful States on a daily basis. This lacuna has been addressed by the institutionalist and constructivist schools. The former has demonstrated that States' long–term interest in international cooperation generally leads them to abide by legal regimes. The latter explains how legal norms help to shape States' identities and how they play an important role in the discursive process of justification of State conduct.

2.2 International Law Approaches

Legal positivists have traditionally maintained a clear partition between international law and international politics. The positivist task and method was a scientific method, which consisted primarily in determining the existing rules of international law as they were to be found in the customary practice of States or in law–making conventions.[15] While Oppenheim conceded that legal scholars could criticise existing rules and offer opinions *de lege ferenda*, he warned that one should not mix up the rules which are really in force with those rules which we would wish to be in force.

Throughout the Charter era, however, a number of scholars grew disillusioned with the rule–oriented positivist method which was seen as out of touch with reality.[16] Thus, in the 1950s and 1960s, several legal scholars began to challenge the view of law as an amalgam of static rules, leading to a gradual shift to a more process–oriented approach to international law. This shift was mainly brought about under the influence of two groups of scholars: the Yale School, and the International Legal Process School. The former group[17], inspired by various social science disciplines, defined law not as a body of largely static rules but as a process of decisions that are both 'effective', by which they meant 'controlling behaviour', and 'authoritative', meaning that they should be in conformity with community values. The Yale School thereby identified law as an ever–continuing political

---

14 F.V. Kratochwil, *Rules, Norms, and Decisions* (Cambridge: Cambridge University Press, 1989) 12.

15 L. Oppenheim, "The Science of International Law: its Task and Method", *AJIL* 1908, *2*, 313, 333–335, 353–355.

16 F.A. Boyle, *l.c.*, 207–208.

17 *E.g.*, M.S. McDougal and W.M. Reisman, *International Law in Contemporary Perspective* (New York: Foundation Press, 1981).

process steered by the permanent interaction of claims and counterclaims. However, the School's value–oriented approach was criticised for subordinating law to policy and "[opening] the way for partisan or subjective policies disguised as law".[18] This criticism eventually led to the School's abandonment, although several authors have nonetheless made direct appeal to its process methodology, albeit without adopting its policy values.

The International Legal Process School took a more pragmatic, value–neutral stance in its endeavour to establish the relevance of law to international politics.[19] The question these scholars posed themselves was, "How – and how far – do law, lawyers and legal institutions operate to affect the course of international affairs?" More specifically, they examined the role of international law *vis–à–vis* the allocation of decision–making competence in international affairs, the adoption of regulatory arrangements for particular subject–matter areas, the development of international institutions to restrain and organise national and individual behaviour, and so on. The authors concluded that while international law was not *determinative* in relation to any of these aspects, it was nonetheless *relevant* in each case.

In the wake of the International Legal Process School, several scholars began to collect empirical evidence in order to identify *how* international law shaped decision–making concerning international relations. One of the first to do so was Louis Henkin, who wrote a passionate plea for the recognition of international law as a major force in world politics.[20] Henkin claimed that international law undoubtedly affects what States say since they always feel the need to justify their conduct by reference to the rhetoric of law. It influences moreover their conduct, by deterring or at least delaying infringement, or by leading States to choose the lesser violation. Indeed, as Henkin famously states, it is probably the case that almost all nations observe almost all of their obligations under international law almost all of the time. To underpin his argument, Henkin examined how law 'operates' in the daily business of governmental decision–making by reference to a number of international crises, such as the 1956 Suez crisis. His endeavour was copied in a series of books commissioned by the American Society of International Law, again dealing with major world crises.[21] The application of the international legal process model has moreover been introduced in other domains, ranging from international trade law to human rights law.[22] Altogether, these volumes

---

18 See X, "McDougal's Jurisprudence: Utility, Influence, Controversy", *ASIL Proc.* 1985, *79*, 266, remarks of Schachter, 267 e.s.

19 See A. Chayes, T. Ehrlich and A.F. Lowenfeld, *International Legal Process* (Boston: Little, Brown & Co, 1968, vol. I).

20 L. Henkin, *How Nations Behave* (New York: Columbia University Press, 2nd ed., 1979).

21 *E.g.*, G.M. Abi–Saab, *The United Nations operation in the Congo, 1960–1964* (Oxford: Oxford University Press, 1978); A. Chayes, *The Cuban Missile Crisis* (London: Oxford University Press, 1974).

22 See *inter alia*: R.E. Hudec, *The GATT Legal System and World Trade Diplomacy* (Salem: Butterworth, 2nd ed., 1990); R.B. Lillich (ed.), *International Human Rights: Problems of Law and Policy* (Boston: Little, Brown & Co, 2nd ed., 1991).

have amassed a great deal of support as to the relevance of law in international relations.

In more recent years, numerous authors, building on the lessons of the aforementioned schools, have examined the functions of international law in order to understand better the reasons for compliance. In general terms, one can distinguish, as in IR theory, between a rationalistic/instrumentalist optic and a reflective/normative one.[23]

The rationalistic approach holds that the strength of international law flows from the fact that States generally enter into legal regimes when it serves their interests to do so. Compliance essentially depends on whether a specific rule serves the interests of a State.[24] If this is the case, the rule will be observed. If not, it may still be followed if the State considers participation in the regime in its long–term interest. The more compelling the interest to a State in behaving contrary to the rule, the more modification, reinterpretation, and breaches there will be.[25] Law is thus observed because States thrive on cooperative regimes and desire their continuance, or because they fear harm such as retaliation.[26] The instrumentalist optic is certainly valuable insofar as it reminds us of the *raison d'être* of legal regimes. At the same time, it fails to explain satisfactorily why in 95 % of cases international law is complied with, or why States voluntarily sign up to human rights treaties. Henkin and others implicitly recognise this by identifying causes that cannot simply be reduced to the national interest, such as bureaucratic inertia, concern for reputation, or support of domestic constituencies.[27]

In general, a purely instrumentalist approach ignores the fact that international legal regimes generate a dynamism of their own, which further shapes the interests and identities of States. It endows international law with too passive a role. This brings us to the reflective approach, which elaborates on the ideas of the constructivist school in IR theory. Central in this view is the idea that law induces compliance by means of a communicative process of claims and counter–claims, or what may be described as the process of 'justificatory discourse', in which legal arguments are used to explain, defend, justify, and persuade.[28] It is indeed an inherent feature of international relations that States' conduct is subject to community

---

[23] See R.O. Keohane, "International Institutions: Two Approaches", *International Studies Quarterly* 1988, *32*, 379–396.

[24] *E.g.*, J.L. Brierly, *The Law of Nations* (Oxford: Clarendon Press, 6th ed., 1963, by H. Waldock) 71–72. See also H. Morgenthau, *Politics Among Nations* (New York: Knopf, 6th ed., 1985) 312.

[25] R.O. Keohane, "International Relations and International Law: Two Optics", *HILJ* 1997, *38*, 487, 489.

[26] See *e.g.*, K.W. Abbot, "The Trading Nation's Dilemma: The Functions of the Law of International Trade", *HILJ* 1985, *26*, 501–532; J.K. Setaer, "An Iterative Perspective on Treaties: A Synthesis of International Relations Theory and International Law", *HILJ* 1996, *37*, 139–229.

[27] L. Henkin, *l.c.*, 52–68; J.K. Setaer, *l.c.*

[28] I. Johnstone, "Security Council Deliberations: The Power of the Better Argument", *EJIL* 2003, *14*, 437, 439. This approach draws on Habermas' theory of communicative action. See J. Habermas, *Between Facts and Norms* (Cambridge: Polity Press, 1996).

judgment and that States consequently feel the need to justify their actions and persuade others in relation to its permissibility. In this regard, international law offers a regular, public, and highly articulated procedure for the assertion and evaluation of specific claims. The appraisal of State conduct is guided by the interpretive community, composed not only of governmental experts responsible for the creation or implementation of a particular legal norm, but also of other individuals regarded as possessing legal expertise and/or special knowledge in the relevant field, such as judges, lawyers, scholars, and non–governmental experts.[29] The justificatory discourse brings together beliefs and expectations and marks out standards of behaviour. It has precedential value in that the outcome will affect future appraisals of State conduct. By doing so, it not only determines the arguments States will invoke to justify their acts. It also affects what they do, since States are less likely to imagine or resort to certain conduct when they know that it will be denounced by the interpretive community.

Several legal scholars have come up with different accounts of the reflective approach to compliance, each setting different points of emphasis. Abram and Antonia Chayes, for example, have claimed that obedience to legal regimes does not hinge on the threat of sanctions, but on "the iterative process of discourse among the parties, the treaty organisation, and the wider public".[30] Harold Koh supplements the element of iteration with that of domestic internalisation and identifies the "transnational legal process" as the root of compliance.[31] Another answer comes from Thomas Franck, who sees the fairness of the international rules themselves as the key to observance.[32] Franck identifies two aspects of fairness: a procedural and a substantive one. The latter stipulates that a system of rules must satisfy the participant's expectations of justifiable distribution of costs and benefits. The former aspect, labelled 'legitimacy', requires that rules are made, applied, and enforced in accordance with what the participants perceive as right process.

3 Factors Inducing Compliance with International Law

Today, virtually every aspect of international life is to some extent governed by international legal norms. Whether we talk about the recognition of nationality, the conduct of hostilities, or international civil aviation, a wide body of treaty and customary rules binds the behaviour of States. Nobody seriously contests that in

---

29 *Ibid.* 450.

30 A. Chayes and A.H. Chayes, *The New Sovereignty* (Cambridge: Harvard University Press, 1995) 25–26.

31 See H.H. Koh, "Why Do Nations Obey International Law?", *YLJ* 1996–97, *106*, 2599, 2646.

32 See T.M. Franck, *Fairness in International Law and Institutions* (Oxford: Clarendon Press, 1995) 7 e.s.

their daily interactions, States generally comply with these norms.[33] If we now turn to the factors inducing compliance, we may again broadly distinguish between 'rationalistic' or 'functional' factors and 'reflective' or 'normative' mainsprings. The former category concerns a cost–benefit calculus of the 'sticks' and 'carrots' of compliance when weighed against the possible benefits of a contemplated violation. The 'sticks' refer to the negative rationale for compliance, in other words the fear of sanctions. Such sanctions may involve a judgment against the State by a competent court to provide reparations, compensation, or satisfaction for the wrongful conduct. Another option is the adoption of diplomatic or economic sanctions or an authorisation to use force by the UN Security Council. Finally, States may also fear the resort to non–forceful countermeasures by other States. The 'carrots' of the cost–benefit analysis refer to the benefits a State may gain through the creation and maintenance of reciprocal entitlements. As explained, States indeed thrive by the establishment of friendly relations among each other and by regulation of these relations through cooperative legal regimes and international institutions, which lead to lower transaction costs and to a higher degree of predictability. For this reason States may feel compelled to observe the norms of a legal regime in order to prompt other participants in the legal regime to do the same or to incite other States to join the regime. In the end, the 'sticks' and 'carrots' are essentially different sides of the same coin. The two sides intersect in situations where the sanction consists in the ending of a cooperative legal regime, for example when a State terminates or suspends a treaty in response to a material breach by one of the parties.[34]

On the 'reflective' side, we can distinguish between the justificatory discourse process, on the one hand, and the process of internalisation at the domestic level, on the other. As mentioned before, the justificatory discourse process exercises a constraining function on States by influencing what options for behaviour States will contemplate and select. This process operates through the formation of community judgment and rests on the idea that as members of the international community, States generally do not want to be perceived as violating international law. It is catalysed by relevant governmental and non–governmental epistemic communities. The justificatory discourse process is closely related to the States' interest in reciprocal entitlements in that its concern for reputation is not only motivated by a 'reflective' desire to be perceived as a member of good standing of the international community, but also by the 'rational' consideration that a negative judgment may undermine the violator's participation in cooperative regimes. The process of domestic internalisation, finally, involves the social, political, or legal internalisation of international legal norms. An important aspect hereof on the executive level are the bureaucratic habits and inertia which follow from the iterative application of these norms, often resulting in a State no longer conceiving the pos-

---

33 O. Schachter, *International Law in Theory and Practice* (Dordrecht: Martinus Nijhoff, 1991) 7; J.L. Brierly, *l.c.*, 71–72; H. Morgenthau, *l.c.*, 312.

34 See Article 60 Vienna Convention on the Law of Treaties, Vienna, 23 May 1969, 1155 UNTS 331.

sibility of breaching these rules. Another option, which borders on the 'fear of sanctions' dimension, concerns the possibility that international law may be invoked before a national judge as a result of legal internalisation. This provides a highly efficient path to enforce compliance, albeit one that rarely touches upon inter–State relations.

Figure 15.1 Factors inducing compliance with international law

Figure 1 presents an attempt to map the different factors inducing compliance. This presentation must, however, be approached with considerable caution. Firstly, it is very difficult to make generalisations regarding these factors since they largely meld into one another and because there is no way to establish empirically their respective quantitative impact on governmental decision–making. Secondly, the susceptibility of States to these factors varies greatly depending on the position of the violator as well as the nature of the rule that is violated. An economically or militarily powerful State, for example, may be less fearful of sanctions than a less powerful State. A secretive and authoritarian regime, on the other hand, may be less susceptible to the justificatory discourse process as it cares little for community judgment. Furthermore, domestic internalisation is linked to the State's respect for the freedom of the press, to the strength of its civil society, to the independence of its judicial system, and such like.

The rule itself also matters. Thus, the interest in reciprocal entitlements is more decisive in relation to trade regimes than it is in relation to environmental protection. Fear of sanctions is more significant with regard to treaty regimes that provide in (quasi–) compulsory settlement of disputes, such as the WTO framework.[35] Prohibitive or prescriptive standards of behaviour lend themselves better to the impact of the justificatory discourse than norms that are somewhat technical or regulatory in nature. The efficiency of the justificatory discourse process moreover greatly depends on the determinacy of a norm, namely, the degree of precision and elaboration of a particular rule, as well as on its coherence with other overarching legal principles or substantially related norms.[36] Determinacy strengthens a rule's compliance pull by limiting the addressee's liberty to interpret and by making it harder to justify non–compliance. Incoherence, on the other hand, makes it easier to justify a violation by playing out conflicting norms against each other. Last but not least, the extent to which the rule itself actually meets the shared expectations and values of the international community obviously influences the justificatory discourse.[37] It is indeed possible that a norm which was once considered 'fair' no longer meets shared values and expectations on the grounds that the context for application or the underlying values and expectations themselves have changed. If this is the case, it may produce a more divided reaction, again making it easier to escape condemnation.

Despite these comments, the four factors allow us to sketch broadly the compliance pull emanating from international legal rules, taking account of the different views among IR scholars and international lawyers. In the following section, we will try to apply this framework to the rules on inter–State recourse to force.

4 The Relevance of the *Ius ad Bellum*

In the run–up to NATO Operation *Allied Force* in 1999, US Secretary of State Albright allegedly received a telephone call from her British colleague Robin Cook.[38] The latter informed her that he had "problems with our lawyers", as they had advised that NATO needed the approval of the UN Security Council. Secretary Albright famously responded: "Robin, get new lawyers."

It is all too easy to conclude from this and other incidents[39] (if true), that international law on the use of force is but a vain project to regulate State behaviour in an area that is the playground of power interests. Questions concerning the use of force by definition belong to the domain of 'high politics', meaning that there may be strong motives prompting States to violate the rules. Still, to discard the *Ius ad*

---

35 See K.W. Abbott, R.O. Keohane, A. Moravcsik, A.–M. Slaughter and D. Snidal, "The Concept of Legalization", *IO* 2000, *54*, 401, 415–418.

36 See for example: *Ibid.*, 412–415; T.M. Franck, *l.c.*, 30–34.

37 See T.M. Franck, *l.c.*, 8–9.

38 See *inter alia* M.J. Glennon, "The Rise and Fall of the U.N. Charter's Use of Force Rules", *Hastings Int'l & Comp. L. Rev.* 2003–04, *27*, 497.

39 See also: "Wilmshurst Resignation Letter", *BBC News* 24 March 2004; "US 'Swayed' Iraq War Law Advice", *BBC News* 25 May 2006.

Bellum as wholly powerless against the armada of national interests is to forego altogether the constraining effect of international rules. Even if inter–State use of force is driven first and foremost by power concerns, these rules nevertheless exert significant compliance pull.

4.1 States' Reciprocal Interest in a Peaceful International Order

If we first turn to the rational compliance factors, it is fair to say that in general States have a common interest in keeping international relations orderly. Through their regulatory and pacifying function, the rules regulating the inter–State use of force therefore contribute to creating an environment in which the harsh effects of the 'security dilemma' are mitigated, and where cooperative diplomatic and economic relations are fostered. Both powerful and weaker States generally benefit from this. The former do so because it contributes to the preservation of their dominant position. The latter benefit because it ensures their survival in an anarchical international system. Still, there will be situations where a violation of the rules may be tempting. By resorting to military force, a State may hope to acquire access to natural resources, to obtain military intelligence, or to prevent an adversary State from becoming more powerful. In such situations, an abstract interest in upholding the international order will not generally suffice to counterbalance the envisaged results.

4.2 Sanctioning by the UN Security Council or by Third Party States

Nevertheless, there are also more specific reasons for States to abide by the *Ius ad Bellum*. One of these is the fear of possible Chapter VII action by the Security Council, an option which has become more realistic since the end of the Cold War. Thus, the Security Council may qualify inter–State use of force as a threat to peace, a breach of the peace, or an act of aggression, thus triggering its competence to adopt enforcement action. Certain resolutions are confined to 'calling upon' the parties to cease hostilities.[40] The Council has also resorted to 'naming and shaming', and has on a number of occasions imposed sanctions, such as arms embargoes, with regard to inter–State violence.[41] The instances where the Council

40 *E.g.*, SC Res. 502 (1982) of 3 April 1982; SC Res. 1701 (2006) of 11 August 2006.

41 See SC Res. 660 (1990) of 2 August 1990; SC Res. 670 (1990) of 25 September 1990; SC Res. 418 (1977) of 4 November 1977; SC Res. 546 (1984) of 6 January 1984.

has addressed the military option are mainly confined to the 1950 Korean War and the 1990 Iraqi invasion of Kuwait.[42]

In all, Security Council sanctioning of violations of the *Ius ad Bellum* has been far from consistent. On numerous occasions, Council members have been reluctant to take sides or they have attempted to shield themselves or their allies from sanctioning. This is most blatant in the case of the P–5, whose veto power not only prevents any Council enforcement action against them, but who have also employed this power to block action against other offenders. Even though the use of the veto has diminished, the probability of enforcement action remains largely a calculus of political factors.

If the Security Council fails to respond, there may still be room for international sanctioning by States themselves. Indeed, apart from merely disapproving breaches of the *Ius ad Bellum*, States may have recourse to non–forcible countermeasures or can respond by reducing other, not–legally required, cooperative behaviour (for example Official Development Assistance). If the violation amounts to an armed attack in the sense of Article 51 of the UN Charter, this triggers moreover the right to collective self–defence, an option which has indeed been invoked on several occasions. In 1958, for example, the US and the UK provided military support to Lebanon and Jordan to thwart Syrian infiltrations.[43] More recently, following the 9/11 attacks, NATO for the first time activated the collective self–defence provision of Article 5 of the North Atlantic Treaty.[44] Non–forcible countermeasures and cutbacks in cooperative behaviour have likewise been adopted on several occasions. During the 1956 Suez crisis, for example, Jordan forbade British aircraft at two British bases in Jordan to be used against Egypt and imposed an economic boycott on France[45], while Saudi Arabia and Syria broke diplomatic relations with Britain and France.[46] In the run–up to the 2003 Iraq War, the Saudis refused to allow American planes to carry out air strikes against Iraq from the Prince Sultan Base absent an explicit authorisation by the Security Council.[47] Decisions such as these may have an important impact on the conduct of military operations. This is not to say, of course, that sanctioning by third party States has been consistent over time. To the contrary, it is often influenced by a mixture of political and economical considerations. For instance, while the official position of the Belgian government was to condemn the Iraq war in 2003, it never-

---

42 SC Res. 83 (1950) of 27 June 1950; SC Res. 84 (1950) of 7 July 1950; Res. 678 (1990) of 29 November 1990.

43 (1958) UNYB 36 e.s.

44 Secretary–General Lord Robertson, Statement of 2 October 2001, *ILM* 2001, *41*, 1267.

45 *Keesing's Contemporary Archives* (1956) 15211.

46 A.M. Weisburd, *Use of Force: The Practice of States Since World War II* (Pennsylvania: Pennsylvania State University Press, 1997) 32–33.

47 "US Pulls Out of Saudi Arabia", *BBC News*, 29 April 2003.

theless permitted the transport of US military material via the port of Antwerp and authorised military flights through its airspace.[48]

Still, it seems that concerns of (il–)legality do to some extent influence the position of third party States, including potential allies. In this regard, Weisburd finds that out of the ten cases of 'classic invasion' which took place between 1945 and 1995, six were subject to significant international sanction.[49] By contrast, in relation to more limited uses of force, States have often confined themselves to expressing concern or condemnation.[50] In several cases they did not react at all.

4.3 Sanctioning at the International Judicial Level

Alleged violations of the *Ius ad Bellum* may also be subject to adjudication by the International Court of Justice (ICJ). The Court's jurisdiction may result from a specific agreement among the parties involved, or from declarations accepting compulsory jurisdiction in accordance with Article 36(2) of the ICJ Statute, which have been made by some 66 States. The latter declarations ultimately remain voluntary, since they can be revoked or modified following the appropriate procedures. Moreover, several States have added reservations, some of which exclude jurisdiction in relation to (aspects of) the *Ius ad Bellum*.[51]

Still, the ICJ has not shied away from pronouncing on the legality of the use of force in various advisory opinions as well as contentious cases.[52] In two cases the Court explicitly held a State responsible for a breach of the principle of non–use of force.[53] States have frequently attempted to challenge jurisdiction in these matters, arguing for example that the recourse to force constitutes an inherently political problem that is not appropriate for judicial resolution.[54] Yet, the ICJ has consistently rejected these objections, making clear that the use of force raises legal questions capable of objective determination by a judicial tribunal, as well as reaffirming that there exists no doctrine of separation of powers which prevents the

48 On the weakness of Belgium's legal justification, see O. Corten, "Les arguments avancés par la Belgique pour justifier son soutien aux États–Unis dans le cadre de la guerre contre l'Irak", *RBDI* 2005, 417, 421, 433–439.

49 A.M. Weisburd, *l.c.*, 59.

50 *Ibid.*, 297–303.

51 As of January 2007. The declarations are available at http://www.icj–cij.org/icjwww/ibasicdocuments/ibasictext/ibasicdeclarations.htm. (last visited 2 July 2007).

52 See *e.g.*, *Palestinian Wall Case*, Advisory Opinion of 9 July 2004, [2004] *ICJ Rep.*136–203, § 138–139; *Oil Platforms Case* (*Islamic Republic of Iran v USA*), Judgment of 6 November 2003, [2003] *ICJ Rep.* 161–219.

53 *Nicaragua Case* (*Nicaragua v USA*), Judgment of 27 June 1986, [1986] *ICJ Rep.* 14–150; *Armed activities on the territory of the Congo* (*DRC v Uganda*), Judgment of 19 December 2005, [2005] *ICJ Rep.* 116–220.

54 See C. Gray, "The Use and Abuse of the International Court of Justice: Cases Concerning the Use of Force After *Nicaragua*", *EJIL* 2003, 867–905.

ICJ from hearing a dispute which is also before the Security Council. Even though judicial regulation of armed conflicts will remain peripheral in the future, this sends out a strong signal that the use of force is a matter of law, violations of which may give rise to State responsibility. At least for States that have accepted compulsory jurisdiction, this may provide a supplementary deterrent to abstain from recourse to force.

The disincentive for embarking upon unlawful interventions would arguably be much stronger if there existed a tangible chance for criminal prosecution of the individual decision–maker.[55] In this regard, it must be noted that while the crime of aggression is today recognised as the supreme international crime, its actual operationalisation is lacking. Indeed, whereas the jurisdiction of the Nuremberg and Tokyo Tribunals was extended to 'crimes against the peace', no such provisions were incorporated in the Charters of the International Criminal Tribunals for Rwanda and the Former Yugoslavia. More importantly, at the time of drafting of the Statute of the International Criminal Court (ICC)[56], there existed strongly diverging opinions on the competence of the Court to prosecute crimes of aggression. By way of compromise, Article 5(2) opens the door to prosecution at some future time:

> The Court shall exercise jurisdiction over the crime of aggression once a provision is adopted (…) defining the crime and setting out the conditions under which the Court shall exercise jurisdiction.

The result is that aggression remains *de facto* excluded from the ICC's jurisdiction. Thus, when the Office of the Prosecutor received some 240 communications concerning the situation in Iraq in 2003 – a number of which expressed the view that aggression had taken place – the Prosecutor concluded he did not have a mandate to address the legality of the use of force.[57]

In the meantime, negotiations are continuing in the context of the ICC's Special Working Group on the Crime of Aggression. Should a compromise solution finally be found at the 2009 Review Conference of the Rome Statute (or at some later time)[58], this would potentially strengthen the compliance pull of the *Ius ad Bellum* and serve as a deterrent against at least grave violations of the prohibition on the use of force.

---

55 *E.g.*, Y. Dinstein, *War, Aggression and Self–Defence* (Cambridge: Cambridge University Press, 4th ed., 2005) 117.

56 Statute of the International Criminal Court, Rome, 17 July 1998, reprinted in *ILM* 1998, *37*, 1002–1069.

57 Office of the Prosecutor, Response to the communications concerning the situation in Iraq, The Hague, 9 February 2006, 4, at http://www.icc–cpi.int/library/organs/otp/OTP_letter_to_senders_re_Iraq_9_February_2006.pdf (last visited 2 July 2007).

58 Note that the normal provisions on amendment, laid down in Article 121 of the Rome Statute, will be applicable, meaning that every State Party may refuse to accept the amendment.

4.4 Domestic Internalisation: The Role of National Parliaments and Courts

While we have so far concentrated on 'rationalistic' factors inducing compliance, there also exist more 'reflective' factors that pressure States to respect the *Ius ad Bellum*. Indeed, while there is no room for bureaucratic habit or inertia when it comes to governmental decisions on military intervention abroad, domestic internalisation contributes to the rules' compliance pull by urging executive organs to provide an adequate justification for their actions.

Domestic internalisation is firstly illustrated by the inclusion of substantive limitations in many national Constitutions on the recourse to force[59], which help to consolidate a general prohibition against the use of force.[60] National Constitutions may also establish procedural frameworks for governmental decision–making. The most extreme situation is arguably the one in Germany, where the *Bundesverfassungsgericht* interpreted Article 87a section 2 of the *Grundgesetz* as requiring every armed operation to be approved by the *Bundestag*.[61] In most countries, however, parliamentary approval is only needed for a formal declaration of war.[62] Procedural constraints of this type have lost most of their significance given that declarations of war have largely become obsolete. Even if no formal approval is needed, national Constitutions sometimes create an obligation to consult or inform the parliament.[63] Otherwise, governments are still generally responsible to their parliament for their policies and decisions, meaning that ministers may be interpellated or that Commissions of Inquiry may be established.

In recent years, parliamentary involvement *vis–à–vis* the deployment of military forces seems to be increasing.[64] This is illustrated by the fact that governments have on several occasions – for example in relation to the 1991 Gulf War or NATO Operation Allied Force (1999) – sought parliamentary approval or have

---

59 *E.g.*, Article 11 of the Constitution of Italy, 22 December 1947; Article 6 §1 of the Constitution of Hungary, 20 August 1949; Article 9 of the Constitution of Japan, 3 November 1946.

60 L.F. Damrosch, "The Interface of National Constitutional Systems with International Law And Institutions on Using Military Forces: Changing Trends in Executive and Legislative Powers", in C. Ku and H.K. Jacobson (eds.), *Democratic Accountability and the Use of Force in International Law* (Cambridge: Cambridge University Press, 2003) 39.

61 Judgment of the *Bundesverfassungsgericht* of 12 July 1994, translated in *I.L. Rep.* 1994, *106*, 320. Remark: consider also the chapters dealing with Japan, the Russian Federation and the US in H. Ku and H.K. Jacobson (eds.), *Democratic Accountability and the Use of Force in International Law* (Cambridge: Cambridge University Press, 2003).

62 *E.g.*, Article 35 of the Constitution of France of 28 September 1958; Article 96 of the Constitution of the Netherlands, 17 February 1983.

63 *E.g.*, Article 100 of the Constitution of the Netherlands, 17 February 1983; Article 167 §1 of the Constitution of Belgium, amended in 1993, BS 8 May 1993.

64 *E.g.*, L.F. Damrosch, "Is There a General Trend in Constitutional Democracies Toward Parliamentary Control Over War–and–Peace Decisions?", *ASIL Proc.* 1996, *90*, 36. See also M. Bothe and A. Fischer–Lescano, "The Dimensions of Domestic Constitutional and Statutory Limits on the Use of Military Force", in M. Bothe, M.E. O'Connell and N. Ronzitti (eds.), *Redefining Sovereignty* (Ardsley: Transnational Publishers, 2005) 195–208.

engaged in frequent consultations with the legislative branch, even in the absence of an express obligation therefore.[65] What is important in this context is that although the parliaments are by nature political bodies where voting behaviour is largely guided by the representatives' political affiliation, legal considerations do play an important role in debates concerning the use of force. With regard to discussions within the *Bundestag* on NATO's Operation Allied Force, for example, Simma notes that, "[T]he international legal issues involved were discussed at great length and in considerable depth. The respect for UN Charter law ... was remarkable."[66] Marrero Rocha similarly argues that international law played a major role in the debates in the Spanish *Congreso* on the interventions in Kosovo (1999) and Iraq (2003), albeit that the various political parties used different types of discourse.[67] At the same time, the use of legal arguments is no guarantee for compliance. National parliaments may support and have indeed supported interventions of dubious legality.[68]

The situation might be different if national courts were to exercise some form of judicial review over governmental decisions to resort to force. Unlike national legislative branches, they would in principle be guided by national and international law to the exclusion of political considerations. However, in this regard we stumble upon a crucial 'limit' of public international law, namely its incomplete incorporation into domestic law and the restricted scope for national law enforcement. In relation to the use of force, for example, national laws generally provide very little leeway for judicial control over executive war powers. National courts themselves have moreover been highly reluctant to enforce restraints on the use of force. Thus, the German Constitutional Court rejected motions relating to the German participation in NATO Operation Allied Force in 1999[69] and the support for Turkey in the face of the US–British intervention in Iraq.[70] Again, in the US, courts have rejected claims challenging the constitutionality of the Vietnam War[71] or disputing the legality of the resolution adopted by Congress in 2002 authorising the use of force against Iraq.[72] Likewise, the UK Divisional Court dismissed a case dealing with the legality of the 2003 intervention in Iraq.[73]

In several countries, the legality of military intervention has moreover been raised in criminal cases. For instance, some attempts have been undertaken to op-

---

65 L.F. Damrosch (1996), *l.c.*, 37–38; L.F. Damrosch (2003), *l.c.*, 55–56.

66 B. Simma, "NATO, the UN and the Use of Force: Legal Aspects", *EJIL* 1999, *10* (1), 12–13.

67 See I. Marrero Rocha, "El discurso jurídico internacional en los debates del Congreso de los Diputados: los casos de Kosovo y la guerra de Irak", *REDI* 2005, *58*, 49–87.

68 *Cf.* In October 2002 for example, the US Congress passed the Joint Resolution to authorise the use of military force against Iraq (16 October 2002, *Public Law* 107–243, 116 Stat. 1497–1502).

69 Decision of the *Bundesverfassungsgericht* of 25 March 1999, 2 BvE 5/99, 1 – 21.

70 Judgment of the *Bundesverfassungsgericht* of 25 March 2003, BVerfGE 34, 108.

71 *Massachusetts v Laird,* 451 F 2nd 26 (1971) (1st Cir.).

72 *John Doe v Bush*, 322 F 3rd 109 (2003) (1st Cir.).

73 *Campaign for Nuclear Disarmament v. The Prime Minister of the UK and Oths*, [2002] EWHC 2777 (17 December 2002, Div. Ct., Brown, Kay, & Richards LLJ)).

erationalise domestic provisions criminalising aggression by starting prosecutions against members of the government.[74] So far, however, none of these attempts have succeeded. In other cases, individuals have invoked the so–called 'Nuremberg defence' to justify acts of disobedience as necessary and proportionate actions to prevent the crime of aggression. As Cryer suggests, this defence is rarely successful, although threats to raise it can embarrass the prosecution.[75]

Interestingly, in 2005, the German *Bundesverwaltungsgericht* delivered a judgment on a German officer's freedom of conscience (Article 4 section 1 of the *Grundgesetz*), which included an elaborate *obiter dictum* addressing the legality of the 2003 Iraq war.[76] The Court thereby established that the German measures supporting the Iraq war gave rise to "grave concerns in light of public international law", triggering Germany's State responsibility. Although it stopped short of explicitly qualifying the Iraq war as outright illegal, the judgment illustrates that it may not be as unthinkable as once believed that a national court could pass judgment on the legality of a military intervention (even by a third party State!).

At any rate, the judgment hardly compensates for the generally unenthusiastic position of national courts to deal with the recourse to force. This attitude was well illustrated in a recent judgment of the UK House of Lords, which explicitly subscribed to a need to "avoid drawing the courts into an area which, in the past, they have entered, if at all, with reluctance and the utmost circumspection."[77] At least until the ICC's jurisdiction for the crime of aggression is implemented, this situation is unlikely to change, and national prosecution of elites responsible for unlawful wars will remain a chimera.

4.5 The Justificatory Discourse Process and the Ius Ad Bellum

Another 'reflective' element relates to the argumentative practice of claims and counter–claims through which State behaviour is subject to the collective judgment of the international community.

At the inter–State level, claims may firstly be made on a bilateral basis between the attacking and defending States, as is illustrated by the famous diplomatic correspondence between the UK and the US following the *Caroline* incident in 1837.[78] Appraisals are also often made by third party States as well as by a variety

---

74 Such attempts were undertaken in Germany with regard to the 2003 Iraq war and Operation Allied Force (1999), as well as in Spain with regard to the 2003 Iraq war. See M. Bothe and A. Fischer–Lescano, *l.c.*, 206–207.

75 R. Cryer, "Aggression at the Court of Appeal", *JCSL* 2005, *10*, 209, 210.

76 *Bundesverwaltungsgericht*, Judgment of 21 June 2005, BVerwG 2WD 12.04.

77 *R. v Jones*, (2006) UKHL 16, § 30.

78 R. Jennings, "The Caroline and McLeod Cases", *AJIL* 1938, *32*, 82, 85.

of regional organisations and other multilateral settings, such as the League of Arab States, the EU, or the UN General Assembly.[79]

Yet, the principal forum where inter–State violence is discussed is undoubtedly the UN Security Council. This flows in the first place from the obligation, enshrined in Article 51 of the UN Charter, that the exercise of the right of self–defense be reported immediately to the Security Council. On the whole, States seem to comply fairly well with this duty.[80] In turn, States that have been the subject of an attack may also submit a complaint to the Council.[81]

Second, inter–State use of force is frequently the subject of heated debate in the Security Council, convened at the request of a Member of the Council or of any other UN Member in accordance with Article 35 of the UN Charter. A glance at these debates makes clear that the participants generally make reference to legal concepts and standards underlying the Charter framework to give meaning to the facts surrounding the use of force.[82] This is more than rhetorical gloss: it constitutes a discursive exercise that allows a distinction between good and bad arguments. It does so because the debates are structured by a shared normative framework embodied in the Charter, and because Council deliberations on inter–State violence are relatively open.[83] As the arguments are subject to public scrutiny, Council members and other participants cannot rely (solely) on political motivations and self–interest, but must appeal to the language of (legal) reason.

Hence, the legal discourse influences State positions. On the one hand, States are concerned about setting precedents. The desire of the NATO members not to make a case for unilateral humanitarian intervention through Operation Allied Force is illustrative.[84] States are also concerned about their reputations. In order to avoid negative reaction, they are likely to invoke that justification which is considered to be the most acceptable to others.[85] Even if States will often attempt to bring their actions within the Charter framework by distorting the facts or resorting to creative lawyering, the fact that they consider it important that their actions are perceived to conform to the *Ius ad Bellum* and that they consult their legal experts implicitly affirms they regard these rules as binding and relevant.[86]

---

79 *E.g.*, "EU Presidency Statement on the recent developments in Israel and Lebanon", Brussels, 13 July 2006, Ref. PRES06–207EN.

80 See C. Gray, *International Law and the Use of Force* (Oxford: Oxford University Press, 2nd ed., 2004) 101–104.

81 *E.g.*, with regard to the US strikes against Sudan in 1998: UN Doc. S/1998/786; UN Doc. S/1998/792.

82 See *e.g.*, with regard to the Israeli intervention in Lebanon in July 2006: UN Security Council, 61st session, 5489th meeting, 14 July 2006, UN Doc. S/PV.5489; UN Security Council, 61st session, 5493rd meeting, 21 July 2006, UN Doc. S/PV.5493.

83 See I. Johnstone, *l.c.*, 456–463.

84 See M.J. Matheson, "Justification for the NATO Air Campaign in Kosovo", *ASIL Proc.* 2000, *94*, 301.

85 See for example on the Cuban missile crisis: A. Chayes, *l.c.*, 65–66.

86 *E.g.*, T.M. Franck, "The Power of Legitimacy and the Legitimacy of Power: International Law in an Age of Power Disequilibrium", *AJIL* 2006, *100*, 88, 96.

The justificatory discourse is not confined to the inter–State level, but involves a much broader audience, including, *inter alia* the "invisible college of international lawyers".[87] Inter–State use of force has inspired a vast academic literature in which legal scholars have not only reflected on the correct interpretation of the law, but have also passed judgment on specific situations. International lawyers have also expressed their opinions in more public spheres, as the numerous public *démarches* condemning the 2003 Iraq war, to which hundreds of scholars subscribed, illustrate.[88]

Finally, the justificatory discourse may to some extent shape public opinion. Indeed, as the massive protests in the run–up to the Iraq war illustrate, there seems to be a growing permeation of the public discourse by legal arguments.[89] *If* legal considerations do affect public opinion, this provides a potent way through which the *Ius ad Bellum* could exert compliance pull on States. The national electorate is the ultimate adjudicator of a government's policy and may use the ballot box to punish military escapades.[90] On the international level, public opinion also matters. For instance, in the run–up to the Iraq War, the US saw its popularity plunge by an average of 30% in most European countries.[91] This suggests that conduct which is hard to reconcile with the Charter framework may reduce a State's international legitimacy, in turn negatively affecting its "soft power".[92]

Still, caution is needed. Most incidents involving inter–State use of force provoke far less public reaction than, for instance, the widely and extensively publicised intervention in Iraq (2003). Moreover, direct empirical research on the link between compliance with international law and public support is lacking.[93] Several past interventions illustrate that domestic pressure may even act as a motor for violation rather than compliance.[94]

---

87 O. Schachter, "The Invisible College of International Lawyers", *Northwestern University L. Rev.* 1977–78, *72*, 217–226.

88 For relevant documents, see *RBDI* 2003, *36*, 266–302.

89 *Cf.* Polling reports of US public opinion in the run–up to the 2003 Iraq war indicate a clear preference for military action explicitly authorised by the Security Council. At http://www.pollingreport.com/iraq.htm (last visited 2 July 2007).

90 *Cf.* T. Gaynor, "Anger over Iraq War Fuels Anti–Aznar Vote in Regional Elections", *The Independent* 26 May 2003; "Iraq Looms over UK Election Battle", *CNN* 18 April 2005.

91 J.S. Nye Jr., *Soft Power* (New York: PublicAffairs, 2004) 35 e.s.

92 *Ibid.,* 5 e.s.

93 So far, most research has focused on the so–called 'body bag'–effect. See *e.g.,* P. Everts and P. Isernia (eds.), *Public Opinion and the International Use of Force* (London: Routledge, 2001).

94 L. Henkin, *l.c.*; "Turkey 'Determined' to Defeat PKK", *BBC News* 8 June 2007.

5 Conclusion

In order to gain a better understanding of the limits and strengths of public international law, the present chapter has attempted to identify pragmatically and non–exhaustively a number of factors inducing compliance. Building upon the various theories in IR studies and international legal theory, we have broadly distinguished between rational and reflective factors, despite the two categories strongly overlapping. In applying this framework to the international law on the use of force, we have seen that many of these factors suffer from certain shortfalls. For instance, sanctioning by the Security Council is guided by political motivations and has been far from consistent. Adjudication by the ICJ is in principle based on State consent. Yet there are also positive signs, such as the growing involvement of national parliaments or the possibility that ICC jurisdiction for crimes of aggression may be 'activated' in the years to come. In general, we may conclude that violations of public international law, even in a domain as sensitive as the inter–State recourse to force, will rarely (if ever) be cost–free, even to powerful States.[95] Of course, the susceptibility of States to the various factors may vary, depending, for example, on whether a State has accepted the compulsory jurisdiction of the ICJ, the strength of its parliamentary branch and civil society, its commercial and diplomatic relations with other States, and so on. The potential costs may not be sufficient to actually deter an unlawful intervention, but this is not the point. What is crucial here is that in the decision–making process leading up to an envisaged intervention, States must and will take account of the lawfulness of their actions. In this sense, the *Ius ad Bellum* certainly is relevant. We may thus discard the realist postulate that "law simply does not deal with questions of ultimate power".

This is not to say that international law qualifies as an *autonomous* force or *power* among nations, as some international lawyers have claimed.[96] The legal rules do not generally, by their mere existence, prevent recourse to force.[97] Rather, by providing the framework against which States' actions are evaluated, they channel the justificatory discourse process that, in turn, triggers the factors of compliance pull. In other words, it is by serving as a tool of interpretation, as yardstick, that international law catalyses these factors. In the end, restating the words of Ronald Dworkin, we might conclude that States, like individuals, live in and by the Law. Like individuals, they may from time to time violate a given rule. At the same time, international law is a force to be reckoned with. Indeed, for the foreseeable future, it is clear that merely 'getting new lawyers' will not suffice to escape to the influence of public international law.

---

95 *E.g.*, O. Schachter, *l.c.*, 7; I. Hurd, "Too Legit to Quit", *Foreign Affairs* 2003, *82*–4, 204–205; L. Henkin, *l.c.*, 45 e.s.

96 *E.g.*, D. Kritsiotis, "The Power of International Law as Language", *Cal. Western L. Rev.* 1997–1998, *34*, 397, 403.

97 J. Brunnée and S. Toope, "The Use of Force: International Law After Iraq", *ICLQ* 2004, *53*, 785, 790.

Chapter 16 – Is the Rule of Law a Limit on Popular Sovereignty?

"Yet what, in the last analysis, is law?
If we simply try to define it in terms of metaphysical ideas,
we shall go on talking without reaching any understanding;
and when we have said what natural law is,
we shall still not know what the law of the State is."[1]

David Haljan

1 Introduction

Welcome to our quaint hypothetical, democratic, and pluralist State – let us call it 'Herculeum'. The majority of the inhabitants are white and of a Christian background (whether practising actively or not), with the minority comprising a collection of other major and minor religious creeds, as well as atheists and agnostics. The full range of political views finds representation, from arch–conservatism, through liberalism, to socialism, and Marxism. It is also blessed with the standard organs of State provided for in a Constitution (legislative, executive, and judicial), a constitutionally–entrenched bill of rights, and the ordinary principles and tenets of a modern constitutional democracy, such as representative and responsible government, the separation of powers, the rule of law, and so on. Indeed, Herculeum could be any or all of the current Western democratic States.

For whatever reason, things have become unsettled of late in Herculeum. A minority have become dissatisfied with the requirement that shops and businesses must close on Sunday – statutorily prescribed as a day of rest, but seemingly without any account for the particular beliefs and interests of that minority. If these wish to observe their respective faiths, they stand at a disadvantage to the majority, having thus to close two days rather than one.[2] Others have ruffled feathers over such issues as the requirement that pharmacists cannot refuse to sell contraceptives or tie the sale to a moralising lecture or the acceptance of anti–abortion pamphlets[3], or such as the acceptance of homosexual conduct and same–sex mar-

---

1 J.–J. Rousseau, *The Social Contract* (M. Cranston trans.) (Harmondsworth: Penguin, 1968) 81.

2 See *e.g.*, *R v Big M Drug Mart* [1985] 1 Supreme Court Rep. 295, *Hy and Zel's Inc.* v *Ontario (AG)* [1993] 3 Supreme Court Rep. 675 (Canada).

3 For reports on such US cases, see: http://jurist.law.pitt.edu/paperchase/2007/10/settlement-proposed-in-illinois.php; and related lawsuits in Washington State: http://www.aclu-wa.org/detail.cfm?id=727.

riage.[4] Would it truly be surprising then to observe that a number of lawsuits have been filed to challenge the relevant laws and rules, all claiming some form of breach of some constitutionally–guaranteed rights and freedoms? Hardly. But this is not all. The Herculeum courts have also been active in responding to challenges against various governmental acts, from the delimitation of electoral constituencies[5], to committing military resources to conflicts abroad[6], to the decisions to deploy various types of weapons.[7] Judicial review of the constitutionality of laws and governments acts is alive and well in Herculeum.

To the perceptive observer, at least three critical elements underlie this idyllic picture of a democratic *Rechtsstaat*. In order of increasing significance, they are as follows. First, the courts are empowered to review some, if not all, laws and administrative acts. This refers not only to some conception of judicial independence, but also by implication to the separation of powers. Second, the standard of review – the normative metric – is one of law, and in particular constitutional law. The focal point is the Constitution. This speaks to some active conception of constitutionalism. Third, and following, it is assumed that both citizens and State will defer not merely to the decisions of the courts, and obey and implement them, but also defer to and obey thus the mandates of law and Constitution.

What makes this idyllic picture so peculiar, however, is the easy and seemingly uncontested acceptance of the third proposition in a democratic State. The fundamental characteristic of a democracy is to maximise the social freedom and equality of all its rational and autonomous participants, so that no restriction on that liberty and equality may arise except through a political process whereby those participants consent to (or participate directly in) the formulation and imposition of those restrictions upon themselves. Thus, a Kant–inspired self–government is the hallmark of a democracy. And this is frequently translated into the phrase 'popular sovereignty': the people decide for themselves what their laws shall be.

But as we know, the actual practice of the democratic form only proceeds by way of majority rule. Given the endless diversity among people and their respective desires and interests, a standard of unanimity is unattainable. So for every re-

---

4 See *e.g.*, *Reference re Same Sex Marriage* [2004] 3 Supreme Court Rep. 698; *Lawrence v Texas* 539 US 558 (2003); Constitutional Court (Belgium), 20 October 2004, n° 159/2004.

5 See *e.g.*, *Baker v Carr* 369 US 186 (1962), *Lucas v Forty Fourth Gen Ass'y* 377 US 173, but see *Vieth v Jubilirer* 541 US 267 (gerrymandering cases non–justiciable) (US); *Reference re Prov. Electoral Boundaries (Sask.)* [1991] 1 Supreme Court Rep. 158 (Canada); Constitutional Court (Belgium), 26 February 2003, n° 30/2003.

6 For example, such US cases as *Luftig v McNamara* 373 F 2nd 664 (1967) (CA DC), *Orlando v Laird* 443 F 2nd 1039 (1971) (CA 2nd Cir.) (cert. denied), *Sarnoff v Schultz* 409 US 929 (1972), *Healy v James* 408 US 169 (1972), *Holtzman v Schlesinger* 414 US 1316 (1973), (a selection of the anti–Vietnam jurisprudence); *Campbell v Clinton* 203 F 3rd 19 (CA DC) (2000), *Mahorner v Bush* 224 F Supp 2nd 41 (DC) (2002) and *Doe v Bush* 323 F 3rd 133 (CA Mass) (2003).

7 For example, *Operation Dismantle v The Queen* (1985) 1 Supreme Court Rep. 441 (Cabinet decision to allow testing of cruise missiles in Canada not unconstitutional), *Pauling v McNamara* 331 F 2nd 796 (CA DC) (1964) (injunction against US detonating nuclear weapons refused); *Greenham Women Against Cruise Missiles v Reagan* 591 F Supp 1332 (SDNY) (1984) (injunction against US deployment of cruise missiles in England denied).

striction *cum* law, there will be a dissenting minority. Yet good democrats still consider these dissenters bound and compellable by that law. Is it then sufficient that the law merely issue from a constitutionally–prescribed process? That is, is the solution so easy as simply positing constitutional legitimacy *qua* validity?[8] Moreover, almost every modern democracy has a representative government, and citizens do not thereby have direct, active control in proposing and approving laws. A smaller group of officials, 'members of parliament' say, propose and enact legislation, and that (perhaps too cynically) with their own voters and constituencies in mind. Matched with this distancing of the author and addressee of the law is the sense that 'the problems of the modern State' are too complex and technical to allow for anything other than a managerial, technocratic approach of expert committees.[9] In the result, the system of public administration has diminished the real and effective power of the individual ruler, by separating the decisions from the decider.[10] At the same time, it has also separated the decision from the individual affected, making it the decision of an 'other' to be applied to one.

Far from the 'innocent' concept of popular sovereignty with direct and immediate effect, modern democracies exemplify a heavily institutionalised version in which the linkage between 'popular sovereignty' and 'actual power' is mediated through layers of rules and procedures. It is this constituted order, a system of rules and procedures, of institutions and organisations[11], which officials and citizens alike rely upon to justify any exercise of actual power. The actual exercise of political power in a (democratic) society must first pass through the optic of 'being constitutional' in order to be recognised as legitimate, as an authentic expression of 'popular sovereignty'.[12] In effect the Constitution symbolises popular sovereignty. And if we pursue this line of thought further, we should conclude that popular sovereignty can only find real expression in a constitutional language ('constitutional symbolisation').[13] This has the effect of limiting and qualifying it, with the result that popular sovereignty can only be articulated in and through the

8 F. Michelman, "Constitutional Legitimation for Political Acts", *Modern Law Rev.* 2003, *66*, 1, suggests persuasively that no such easy solution exists, let alone *a* solution. See also his "Ida's Way: Constructing the Respect–Worthy System of Government", *Fordham Law Rev.* 2003, *72*, 345.

9 The facts and arguments tracing the development of the bureaucratic welfare State need not be rehearsed here. See *e.g.*, G. Poggi, *The State: Its Nature, Development, and Prospects* (Polity Press, 1990), 30 e.s., 109 e.s. and M. van Creveld, *The Rise and Decline of the State* (Cambridge University Press, 1999) 128 e.s., 137, 239 e.s. (bureaucracy and welfare), 258 e.s. ("apotheosis" of the State), 354–377 (retreat of welfare).

10 G. Poggi, *l.c.*, suggests that the State is in fact a cluster of 'attributes', being a series of agencies, each having various official functions, and various degrees of coercive power (including sovereignty).

11 Drawing upon the definitions of 'organisation' and 'institution' proposed by A. Zijderveld, *The Institutional Imperative* (Amsterdam Universitaire Pers, 2000) 22, 31–39.

12 In other words, the 'principle of legality'.

13 See the analysis of H. Lindahl, "Democracy and the Symbolic Constitution of Society", *Ratio Juris* 1998, *11*, 12 to this effect, drawing upon the work of Claude Lefort (mediation between an inner reality and an external ideal) and Ernst Cassirer (symbolisation as a means of understanding and conferring meaning).

rule of law. The rule of law limits popular sovereignty in a democratic State. Or to recite the recent words of Canada's Supreme Court in its advisory opinion on the constitutionality of provincial secession:

> The consent of the governed is a value that is basic to our understanding of a free and democratic society. Yet democracy in any real sense of the word cannot exist without the rule of law. It is the law that creates the framework within which the "sovereign will" is to be ascertained and implemented. To be accorded legitimacy, democratic institutions must rest, ultimately, on a legal foundation. That is, they must allow for the participation of, and accountability to, the people, through public institutions created under the Constitution. Equally, however, a system of government cannot survive through adherence to the law alone. A political system must also possess legitimacy, and in our political culture, that requires an interaction between the rule of law and the democratic principle. The system must be capable of reflecting the aspirations of the people. But there is more. Our law's claim to legitimacy also rests on an appeal to moral values, many of which are imbedded in our constitutional structure. It would be a grave mistake to equate legitimacy with the "sovereign will" or majority rule alone, to the exclusion of other constitutional values.[14]

To sum up, the rule of law would thus seem to limit popular sovereignty, in the negative sense of containing and harnessing its exercise, and in the positive sense of delimiting or defining it. But does this quick sketch of an argument clearly and sufficiently explain the idyllic practice of Herculeum, and the peaceful co–existence of social power and individual freedom?

2 The Problem of Boundaries

Let us recast the issue into broader, conceptual terms. In the long and turbulent history of social power, a State most conducive to peace, order, and general happiness among men, is said to be one ruled by and under laws which have been authored wholly by those who are themselves subject to, and administer, those laws.[15] The expansion of peace and security over time would track the development of popular sovereignty – the will of the people. Constitutional law is the present articulation of that historical process by which a society would characterise and institutionalise the use and control of power among and against its members.[16] As such it is delimited surely by two important principles: the will of the people and the rule of law.

These are interesting precisely because at their convergence in constitutional matters they represent an antinomy. The first principle establishes in general terms that citizens are collectively the only legitimate source of all legislative power,

---

[14] *Ref. re Secession of Quebec* [1998] 2 Supreme Court Reps. 217, para. 67; see also paras. 71 and 72.

[15] J.S. Mill, "Considerations on Representative Government", in *Utilitarianism, On Liberty, and Considerations on Representative Government* (H.B. Acton ed.) (Everyman Library, 1983) 207.

[16] Traced out in G. van der Tang, *Grondwetsbegrip en grondwetsidee* (Rotterdam: Sanders Instituut/Gouda Quint, 1998).

and thus the only legitimate author of any law binding them. The second establishes broadly that the author of the laws is an addressee, and that the laws bind authors and addressees alike.[17] The piece is thus set for the question of sovereignty. For sovereignty consists in not being subject to any higher law than one's own will, which of course is mutable.[18] This would suggest that sovereignty acts outside of, or independently of, any given legal framework. Yet the rule of law would clearly reduce sovereignty to an exercise of political will inside a particular legal framework. Hence popular sovereignty would exist inside, in virtue of, a legal framework.

At one level, the traditional antimony between the rule of law and popular sovereignty poses the question of where 'politics' ends, and 'law' begins. Is any boundary between the rule of law and popular sovereignty inherent in the concept of law, or does it merely represent a functional understanding relative to historical social circumstances? When and how should the law bend to popular will, and vice versa? We might reasonably be tempted to formulate answers thereto based on a conception of law categorising in advance its principal functions and characteristics. This approach offers the safety of having limits and limitations to the law already built into our analytic efforts. But at a deeper level, the antimony between the rule of law and popular sovereignty requires an answer to what we mean in this context when we speak of a 'boundary' between law and politics. Rather than simply proceed from a pre–set category of limits and limitations, we should finish by formulating any limits and limitations afresh: why should there exist any boundary at all?[19]

So to foreshadow what will follow, a signal point of conjunction between law and power *cum* sovereignty is the question of normativity. The modern approach is of course to treat each of law and sovereignty abutting at that point as competitors. Inasmuch as the one can be reconciled to the other, it occurs through the optic and language of sovereignty, where sovereignty subsumes law as its instrument. The law 'limits' sovereignty only in terms of what the law itself can achieve. Beyond that, sovereignty must seek out other instruments, such as brute force, psychological tools, persuasion, and so on, to achieve its ends. Hence the limits here are 'functional' or 'instrumental' inhering in the *tools* used, and not 'substantive' or conceptual attaching to the nature and ends of sovereignty itself. But what should be the result – if attainable – of erasing the borders between law

---

17 See *e.g.*, T.R.S. Allan, "The Rule of Law as the Rule of Reason: Consent and Constitutionalism", *Law Quarterly Rev.* 1999, 221.

18 W. Blackstone, *Commentaries on the Laws of England* (Facsimile 1st ed.) (S. Katz intro.) (Chicago: University of Chicago Press, 1979) Vol. I, 160; Bodin, cited in G. Sabine, *History of Political Theory* (rev.) (New York: Henry Holt, 1950) 406; A.V. Dicey, *An Introduction to the Study of the Constitution* (E.C.S. Wade intro.) (London: Macmillan/St. Martin's Press, 1967) (relying on Austin's theory); see also the essays in N. MacCormick, *Questioning Sovereignty* (Oxford: Oxford University Press, 1999), esp. "The State and the Law", 18–22 and "On Sovereignty and Post–Sovereignty", 127 e.s., and W. Wade, "The Basis of Legal Sovereignty", *Cambridge LJ* 1955, 172 (restating the classical (Dicey–Austin) view).

19 Hence the descriptive jurisprudence of categorising functions and characteristics becomes the last step.

and sovereignty, by unifying both through the normativity concept? Let us reconstrue the rule of law, and then sovereignty, through the optic of normativity to assess whether such a workable conjunction might resolve the tension between law and politics.

3 The Rule of Law

The third proposition sketched out above in our picture of a *Rechtsstaat* (about obeying the law) does more than simply confirm the insight to the rule of law that it represents more than an instrumental conception of law as a tool of effective and orderly governance.[20] The standard analysis parses the idea of the rule of law into two branches: (1) that the government ought to rule by law ('ruled by laws, not by men') and (2) that to achieve this objective, laws must meet certain formal conditions relating to practicability and certainty.[21] Explicating the nature, scope, and nuances of those conditions has attracted the most attention, together with a concomitant and unexpressed premise that obedience to thereby formally valid laws follows more or less a matter of course. The principal benefit to those subject to law is thus having a clear and certain grasp of what conduct the law compels of all like subjects, so to facilitate obeying it.[22] While the former is championed as reducing desultory discretion and arbitrary rule, the latter tags unobtrusively behind.

But this governmental, top–down perspective tends to overlook a further unarticulated and signal premise. Not only does the rule of law bind addressees, but also the authors.[23] It bears constant reminder that the rule of law has the bilateral nature of relating author and addressee through the legal order.[24] Both are equally bound to the law, and to compliance therewith. At a very minimum, the rule of law certainly imposes restrictions on the purposes and procedures a public authority may impose by and through the law. By that means, the rule of law would

---

20 T.R.S. Allan, *l.c.*, 229.

21 For the bipartite *analysanda* of the rule of law, see *e.g.*, J. Raz, "The Rule of Law and its Virtue", in J. Raz, *The Authority of the Law* (Oxford: Oxford University Press, 1979) 210, 212–218 (a reprint of *Law Quarterly Rev.* 1977, *93*, 195), A. Marmor, "The Rule of Law and Its Limits", *Law and Phil.* 2004, *23*, 1, and P. Craig, "Formal and Substantial Conceptions of the Rule of Law: An Analytical Framework", *Public Law* 1997, 467. The *locus classicus* for the conditions to be met remains L. Fuller, *The Morality of the Law* (New Haven: Yale University Press, 2nd ed., 1969) Ch.2: generality of proscription, publicity – publication, no retroactivity, clarity of proscription, internal coherence, no impossible proscriptions, stability, and consistency. J. Raz reconstructs that list in his "Rule of Law", 214–218, departing in some respects from Fuller's Marmor. "Rule of Law and Its Limits" also discusses a like list.

22 A central contention in J. Raz, *l.c.*

23 While even A.V. Dicey, *l.c.*, 193–4, 202–3, speaks of officials being bound by the law as an instance of "equality under the law", he intends more to distinguish the UK from the continental situations where in the former the ordinary courts and general law have jurisdiction, rather than a specialised body of rules and courts.

24 Namely, the entirety of that system which, in its various parts, creates, administers, applies, adjudicates law, and such like.

prosecute its principal objective of minimising arbitrary applications of power.[25] By respecting the boundaries to the exercise of power created by the rule of law, the State thereby seeks the assent of its citizens to the legal and political order. That is, in consideration for the State abiding by the limitations imposed by the rule of law upon its administrative capacity, it can expect in return that its citizens will generally aide by the law. So the conditions regarding predictability and certainty must guide as much the conduct of officials as that of citizens. Hence, the bilateral nature of the rule of law does not reside in the formal effectiveness *per se* of its commands, but in a mutuality and reciprocity between the author of the law and its addressee in relation to obligation under law.

So if we ask, "Of what virtue, of what good, is the rule of law?", the above suggests our answer may be so simple as, "To facilitate our obeying the various rules of law in a coherent and regular fashion, to ensure public order and reasonable governance." This belies somewhat the social complexity underlying such a response. We could, with Raz, expand on the reply somewhat so as to read it, in addition to limiting the risk of an arbitrary application of political power, as also stabilising otherwise erratic or unpredictable social relationships, and as providing "a policy of self–restraint designed to make the law itself a stable and safe basis for individual planning".[26] The insight above concerning reciprocity and mutuality assists us here. So our good citizens of Herculeum enjoy peace and stability because the conditions of the rule of law enable them to plan and manage their affairs under the law with (relative) certainty and coherence.

But then we should also continue to follow Raz along this path to his conclusion that protecting freedom, autonomy, and dignity represents the ultimate objective of the rule of law.[27] Raz does not have to commit himself to any one particular philosophic camp with this tripartite objective. Instead, he would simply accept that the law intends to influence and affect decisions to act which presupposes that the subjects of the law are rational, deliberating upon their prospective actions, and autonomous, being free to choose or reject reasons and suggested acts.[28] A violation of the rule of law, such as in the inconsistent and desultory nature of arbitrary rule, offends against dignity and freedom by producing uncertainty and frustrated expectations. This, in turn, leads to disrespect and disregard of the law and its organs.[29] Peace and order are thereby put at risk. So the peace and order enjoyed by the good citizens of Herculeum are actually reflections of their rational, free nature. Thus it would appear (following Raz) that the rule of law – and so, obedience to law – depends upon a rationality criterion and an autonomy criterion.

Now having undertaken this line of enquiry, there is really nothing to prevent us from pushing its boundaries yet further. If the immediate purpose of the rule of

---

25 See *e.g. Roncarelli v Dupelssis* [1959] Supreme Court Rep. 121 (per Rand J).

26 J. Raz, *l.c.*, 220.

27 J. Raz, *l.c.*, 220–222.

28 J. Raz, *l.c.*, 221 ("respecting people's dignity includes respecting their autonomy"), 222 ("rational autonomous creatures"), and taken up in T.R.S. Allan's reconstruction of J. Raz along moderate substantive lines: T.R.S. Allan, *l.c.*, 235–237.

29 J. Raz, *l.c.*, 222.

law and its criteria is ensuring obedience to a rule, then we have seen that an implied condition is that the addressee of the rule has the rational capacity to understand and comply (rationality criterion) and the will and interest to comply (autonomy/free will criterion).[30] There is of course an obvious, further condition that a rule in fact exists and is binding. In particular, the rule must have a normative character commanding certain conduct and thus claiming obedience on those terms. A rational, autonomous agent, such as the good citizen of Herculeum, has no reason to obey or comply with any third party stipulation not in accord with his own interest or desire (his own 'will', most broadly put) unless it is a command. Clearly some extra attribute to a mere iteration is necessary to impress compliance and obedience upon the addressee in that case. By way of answer, it is the nature of being an imperative statement, a normative expression, that offers the necessary and sufficient reason to obey, to comply. No other reason is necessary. Normative statements, to borrow from Raz, provide exclusive reasons for action.[31]

Laws are characteristically normative, imperative, statements. Stipulations that merely state facts, or exhort and urge, or invite the auditor, are not understood to be normative because they do not mandate or command. Normative statements serve as standards by which conduct is approved or disapproved, is adjudged good or bad, conforming or non–conforming. Serving as an evaluative benchmark, they represent necessary and sufficient reasons in themselves to do or forgo certain acts. They demand or compel compliance. Legal rules and moral rules are the preeminent standard bearers for this class of expression. "Stores must close on Sundays." "Discrimination based on race, colour, ethnic identity, sexual orientation, or other personal characteristic is forbidden." These require us to behave in a certain way. Statements of fact, exhortations, or invitations may reasonably factor into such deliberations, but do not in themselves represent equally exclusive reasons for action. No demands for obedience inhere in these forms of expression. Indeed, such a demand is by definition inconsistent with an exhortation or invitation. And a statement of fact does not require us to undertake any action at all. "Shops in Herculeum are closed on Sunday." "The military arsenal of Herculeum contains horrifically destructive nuclear weapons." Obviously, the context may require us to account for the fact in our deliberations, and so, guide the latter. But no obligation is articulated therein.

The reference to the context of the expression signals a further important aspect. The above explanation clearly emphasises usage, the form of the expression. But naturally the context in which these utterances occur is relevant too. It would present a peculiar state of affairs if, "Buy now, pay later!", "Don't miss this televi-

---

30 Points to the second of the two implied conditions (rationality and autonomy criteria): *l.c.*, 221 ("respecting people's dignity includes respecting their autonomy"), 222 ("rational autonomous creatures").

31 J. Raz, "Legitimate Authority", in J. Raz, *Authority of Law*, 1, 17–20 ("exclusionary reasons"), J. Raz, *The Morality of Freedom* (Oxford: Oxford University Press, 1986) 53–62 and his *Practical Reason and Norms* (London: Hutchinson, 1976). See also S. Perry, "Second–Order Reasons, Uncertainty and Legal Theory", *Southern Cal. LR* 1989, *62*, 913 and M. Moore, "Authority, Law and Razian Reasons", *Southern Cal. LR* 1989, *62*, 827, esp. 854 e.s. for critical evaluation.

sion extravaganza!", or "Try some of the red wine!" demanded us to do what was expressed therein. Our understanding of the imperative style is not only conditioned upon the form of its expression, but also the context in which it is uttered. Indeed, it is just that juxtaposition of an imperative context with the use of inapposite or unusual styles such as invitation or exhortation, that creates humour or social tension such as a veiled threat or hidden insult, a play on words or a poetic flourish, and so on.

Part of what we understand to be 'the context' must also include the relationship between the author of the directive and its addressee. Not only must the author have or claim the capacity to command, but the addressee must recognise or acknowledge that capacity. There exists a social context in addition to the bare factual, linguistic situation, that which is perhaps best and simply expressed as the power relationship between the parties. By 'power' here, we mean at its broadest the capacity actually to alter a person's behaviour or to cause a person to do or refrain from a particular act. It seems self–evident that we do not accept just anyone ordering us about. Adults do not generally recognise the authority of children to issue binding commands. And we do not follow the orders of just anyone. So this is undoubtedly a *social* context, arising in and through socialisation, rather than through some genetic or otherwise naturally occurring human attributes. Inasmuch as the relationship depends on socialisation and reflects the relative social power between the parties concerned, it therefore must presume some social *order*: an articulated construct of existing and developing interrelationships among people which distributes in varying degrees and arranges the exercise of social power across the range of participants.

Important for the rule of law arising from this social order premise is the claim of authority and its recognition. The addressee of the order must recognise the authority issuing the order as just such an authority: the critical perspective is that of the addressee.[32] We can better understand why this is so by considering a number of interesting issues this proposition suggests. As a preliminary, we can assume without hesitation that the recognition of authority operates at two levels: content and status. That is, we evaluate an imperative statement both in terms of what it says, what it commands us to do, and in terms of who is issuing that command. So as a first question, what happens when we as addressees do not regard the content of the supposed order as authoritative? What we are ordered to do, so contradicts all that we believe and hold dear, or what we expect such an authority to command us to do. We need not search for obscure or extreme examples. Consider rather the Christian fundamentalist pharmacist who cannot fathom why the law would compel her to sell contraceptives.[33] Or the terminally ill patient who may not choose

---

32 Thus D. Hume, *Essays, Moral, Political, and Literary* (E. Miller ed.) (Indianapolis: Liberty Classics, 1987) 109 "… [F]orce is always on the side of the governed, the governors have nothing to support them but opinion." Cited with approval and developed by A.V. Dicey, *l.c.*, 77 e.s. concerning the internal and external limits on sovereignty.

33 See *e.g.*, s.4 of the *Health Care Right of Conscience Act* 745 Illinois Compiled Statutes 70 ("No physician or health care personnel shall be civilly or criminally liable to any person, estate, public or private entity or public official by reason of his or her refusal to perform, assist, counsel, suggest, recommend, refer or participate in any way in any particular form of

when and how to end his own life.[34] Indeed, we can even refer to that perennial favourite of those who consider there to be no obligation to obey the law: the disregarded stop–sign in the otherwise lifeless middle of a desert.[35] Moreover, the response under the rule of law may well differ when only one or a few dissent, or when a substantial number dissent: civil disobedience or mass protest. And we should rightly enquire why the number of dissenting voices should make any difference at all. The second question pertains to questioning the authority of the person issuing the order. What happens when we as addressees do not consider the latter as an authority? Perhaps the most cataclysmic versions of this are secession and *coup d'état* or revolution. In the one, a group would reject the continuing jurisdiction of the State over them and a defined territory.[36] In the other, the current governmental authority is replaced – usually by violent means – with another. It is also conceivable to picture rebellion on an individual, or on a much smaller scale: civil disobedience.[37] And again, we should enquire whether the response does or ought to differ depending on the number of participants. All this leads us to a third issue concerning the nature of the addressee's perspective to the binding nature of law. This probes the former's active or passive character, its durability, and such like. Is the recognition of the authority of government and its organs a daily matter for us as addressees, in the nature of Renan's "daily plebiscite"[38]? Or is its exercise valid only once? And have we ever actually and really ever been asked to give our assent and recognition to the authorities commanding us?

Now we do not have to attempt an answer to these three complex and profound issues in order to understand what the underlying issue actually is. In fact, the third question already began to lay it open. We had remarked above that if a stipulation already conforms to the addressee's will, then it will be done regardless of

---

health care service which is contrary to the conscience of such physician or health care personnel."), Illinois Governor's Emergency Rule of 1 April 2005, and details of the lawsuit (*Menges v Blagojevich*), available at
http://jurist.law.pitt.edu/paperchase/2007/10/settlement-proposed-in-illinois.php.
Related lawsuits in Washington State: http://www.aclu-wa.org/detail.cfm?id=727.

34 *Rodriguez v British Columbia (AG)* [1993] 3 Supreme Court Rep. 519; but see *Gonzales v Oregon* 546 US _ (2006); *Schiavo v Schiavo* _ F 3rd _ (11th Cir., March 2005).

35 W. Edmundson, "Legitimate Authority Without Political Obligation", *Law & Phil.* 1998, *17*, 43, 45 (and his note 4, listing others who have discussed the example); D. Lefkowitz, "Legitimate Political Authority and the Duty of those Subject to it: A Critique of Edmundson", *Law & Phil* 2004, *23*, 399, 415–416; W. Edmundson, "Sate of the Art: The Duty to Obey the Law", *Legal Theory* 2004, *10*, 215, 235.

36 See *e.g.*, S. Caney, "Self–Government and Secession: The Case of Nations", *J Pol. Phil.* 1997, *5*, 351, 353; L. Brilmayer, "Secession and Self–Determination: A Territorial Interpretation", *Yale J Int'l Law* 1991, *16*, 177; L. Buchheit, *Secession: The Legitimacy of Self–Determination* (New Haven: Yale University Press, 1978) 13; J. Crawford, *The Creation of States in International Law* (Oxford: Oxford University Press, 1979) 247.

37 See *e.g.*, M. Kadish and S. Kadish, *Discretion to Disobey: A Study of Lawful Departures from Legal Rules* (Stanford: Stanford University Press, 1973).

38 E. Renan, *Qu'est ce que c'est une nation?* (Conférence faite en Sorbonne le 11 mars 1882) "… L'existence d'une nation est (pardonnez-moi cette métaphore) un plébiscite de tous les jours, comme l'existence de l'individu est une affirmation perpétuelle de vie." Available at http://ourworld.compuserve.com/homepages/bib_lisieux/nation04.htm.

any imperative iteration. The latter adds no determinative quality to the iteration. But if that stipulation does not conform thereto, then clearly some extra attribute to the stipulation is required to impress compliance upon its addressee. Hence the binding nature of the law only really comes into play when an addressee could realistically want to act other than as mandated. Put practically, the binding nature of the law is relevant and effective only when an actual or potential conflict exists with the will or interests of the addressee. At the point of conflict, the binding nature makes itself felt by impressing its authority upon the addressee. The binding nature, the law's normativity, does not issue from its conformity to certain formalist criteria.[39] In fact, these simply reflect a deeper set of normativity criteria – equally 'law–oriented' – which ultimately ground our sense of obedience.

Thus the real nature of rule of law lies in its underpinning conception of (social) normativity. Whether we concentrate on content, or competence, or consent, we must eventually, inevitably stipulate what constitutes 'normativity'. That is the central idea common to all three. For each asks, from its own perspective, what is it that binds us? How does content, social status, or consent establish a duty or obligation to obey? Why we view certain commands, or certain commanders, as authoritative depends inherently upon some understanding – and practice – of normativity. It may be one based on the threat or application of violence, or on religious or humanistic grounds. It may ground itself in a some sort of solipsistic consequentialism or materialistic utilitarianism. We can lay out possible grounds so long as vocabulary and ideas permit. They all carry at their core a suggested answer to why we obey. And that core operates as the unarticulated, implicit premise to each and every legislative act, to each and every judicial decision.

4 Border Crossing: From Law to Sovereignty

So where do we stand now? We should conclude from this that the interest in or act of obeying the law does not derive merely from the law's formal characteristics, but also from its overall context and content. These two categories refer to how a law comes to be, what it purports to regulate and how, and the manner in which it is enforced. Both tie the law inextricably to social circumstances, politics, and morality. Together, context and content represent the substantive underlay of the rule of law. Whereas the formalistic account of the rule of law traded freely upon that unarticulated premise, the substantive account begins to unpack its manifold levels through the ideas of justice and fairness.

We have here a choice in how we understand this substantive underlay.[40] On the one hand, we may choose a fully substantive account of the rule of law, one

---

39 Acknowledged in effect even by A.V. Dicey, *l.c.*, 76–82, by virtue of his discussion on "internal" and "external" limits on sovereignty. See also J. Goldsworthy, *The Sovereignty of Parliament: History and Philosophy* (Oxford: Oxford University Press, 1999) 17–20.

40 See P. Craig, *l.c.*; T.R.S. Allan, *l.c.*

which relies on a particular model or theory of justice.[41] They turn immediately to substantive theories of normativity. Questions of legality and validity are answered in respect of the justness and moral content of the law. On the other, we may choose a substantive procedural account, one which relies on a model of such 'procedural goods' as equality, participation, fairness, and so on.[42] These do not rely on any one conception of normativity, but rather develop frameworks wherein such conceptions can produce their just results. But whichever substantive conception of the rule of law can be successfully and persuasively elaborated, our attention has certainly shifted from the formalistic, instrumental characterisation of the law, to one based on substantive, legitimacy–oriented criteria.

Returning to the examples in Herculeum, the questions before the courts are not whether the laws have been duly passed by the appropriate legislative organ, but whether their application and their content meet societal notions of justice and fairness; that is, whether those proscriptions have (normative) legitimacy. In a constitutional law context, it is legitimate law which commands respect and obedience. So the binding force of law – its normativity – arises from the criteria of social legitimacy. Put another way, the relevant conceptions of normativity apply (or we articulate them) through the language of legitimacy. What those criteria are plays into and represents the normative basis for the law and a legal order.

To understand this proposition requires an understanding of what 'legitimacy' means and how it relates to normativity. Legitimacy pertains to the source, the nature, and the application of power. Less broadly perhaps, any exercise of social power (of which the law is one instance) must issue from a source and in an manner accepted by the addressees of that power. If the former is not accepted by its addressees, then it either evaporates as ineffective or represents acts of brute force. If the citizens of Herculeum ignored the Sunday–closing laws, or if Herculeum officials simply terrorised citizens into obedience by the free and easy application of violence, we could hardly speak of 'legitimacy' in relation to the legal system and yet retain any semblance of credibility or reasonability.[43] The term would carry no meaning there, for it would not characterise nor qualify the exercise of power in any way, other than what was already represented. Hence legitimacy does indeed warrant the power and its exercise as presumptively deserving respect and obedience.

Examined this way, legitimacy obviously delimits the normative. To lay claim to our assent and obedience, whether as official or citizen, requires some idea already of what and how such obedience may be sought and maintained. That is, normativity regards the dominant power relationships in a society. And this brings us neatly to our opening statement that a State most conducive to peace, order, and

---

[41] For example, R. Dworkin, *Taking Rights Seriously* (Cambridge, Mass.: Harvard University Press, 1978) and *Law's Empire* (Cambridge, Mass.: Belknap/Harvard University Press, 1986) (to cite two prominent works) and J. Rawls, *Theory of Justice* (Cambridge, Mass.: Harvard University Press, 1971) and *Political Liberalism* (New York: Columbia University Press, 1996) (to cite two prominent works), most notably, argue that the rule of law necessarily relies on context and purpose which are dependent for content on (a theory of) justice.

[42] As does J. Raz, *l.c.*

[43] As with A.V. Dicey, given, *l.c.*, 76 e.s., 202.

general happiness among men, is said to be one ruled by and under laws which have been authored wholly by those who are themselves subject to, and administer, those laws. Normativity of law resides in popular sovereignty. Is it so, then, that law, the rule of law, cannot therefore limit popular sovereignty?

5 Popular Sovereignty and Normativity

Let us set out on our analysis of sovereignty from perspective of normativity from the classic (English) definition of sovereignty by Dicey and Wade.[44] In the context of parliamentary sovereignty, Dicey proposes that such is

> … the right to make or unmake any law whatever and further, that no person or body is recognised by the law of England as having a right to overrule or set aside the legislation of Parliament.[45]

This conception parses into three elements. The first is the holder of sovereignty. Now the holder can be a single individual (*e.g.*, a monarch) or body (*e.g.*, "we, the people", a '*pouvoir constituant*') or a number of bodies (*e.g.*, as in a federation). The second element is the scope of power exercisable. Obviously, it follows from the division of sovereignty among a number of bodies that each may exercise a co–ordinate jurisdiction but across different territory or people, or exercise separate jurisdiction across the same population or territory.[46] Again, the federation is the preeminent example of the division of powers.[47] The third element present in the Dicey conception is command and obedience: in short, power. This is, quite understandably, the core to the concept of sovereignty. It hearkens back to Bodin's first expression of the concept as, "supreme power over citizens and subjects, unrestrained by law".[48] As Blackstone has said, the sovereign Parliament can do everything that is not impossible.[49]

Sovereignty does not, however, merely stand as a synonym for "supreme power". We must also recognise two other critical elements in it. The first incor-

---

44 From the start, with the progenitor of the analytical concept of sovereignty, Bodin, the common departure point for most all such analyses: see *e.g.*, J. Goldsworthy, *l.c.*, 9, 17, W. Wade, *l.c.*, and N. MacCormick, "Sovereignty and Post–Sovereignty" in his *Questioning Sovereignty* (Oxford: Oxford University Press, 1999) 127 (though he tends more to Kelsen). For a more innovative approach, see M. Loughlin, "Ten Tenets of Sovereignty", in N. Walker (ed.), *Sovereignty in Transition* (Oxford: Hart, 2003) 53.

45 A.V. Dicey, *l.c.*, 40.

46 Delegated or overlapping powers do not qualify, because a non–exclusive attribution of power obviously subjects the one or other holder to the authority of the other.

47 A regional (sub–State) population is subject to the jurisdiction of both the federal (national) government and the relevant regional (sub–State) government. All regional governments exercise co–ordinate jurisdiction over their respective populations and territories. We leave to the side the more complex, but nonetheless consistent, example of asymmetric federalism.

48 Quoted in G. Sabine, *l.c.*, 405, and analysed there from the optic of power relations. N. MacCormick agrees: *l.c.*, 127.

49 W. Blackstone, *l.c.*, Vol. I, 160.

porates a boundary, or limiting factor: "relative to other competitors". We can only sketch supreme power against a background of other possible holders of power who represent actual or potential challengers to that supremacy. Every power inevitably delimits the extent of its authority with that boundary serving to prevent encroachment by others. That limit to sovereignty serves to identify itself and other like powers. Little wonder then that the concept of sovereignty intended to, and continues to, serve the interests of the State internally (against fragmentation of power centres) and externally (against interference by other States).[50] Let us call this the 'relativity criterion'. The second facet draws, perhaps obviously, upon "over citizens and subjects". Power is wielded in a social context by someone over another.[51] Power is a human agency that necessarily implies an intersubjective relationship, between a commander and a follower. Of importance here is the aspect of *relating*, of different individuals associating in specific and recurring ways. As we had remarked above, power relationships come about through socialisation, rather than being natural or genetic givens. The social context reflects the existing and developing interactions among people, as they co–ordinate (intentionally or not, voluntarily or not) their common and respective interests and desires. How that co–ordination proceeds and what it results in, represents the particular expressions of power. Thus the social context represents the source and fund of not merely the power relationships, but of the expressions of power themselves; that is, what counts as norms.

Sovereignty, then, should not be understood in an unqualified sense of political power, absolute or otherwise. Rather, as an attribute of power, its characterising or delimiting the nature of the political power at issue through the relativity criterion and the social context criteria, emphasises its construction in terms of normativity. Those terms outline why we treat certain utterances as authoritative, as requiring our obedience. Sovereignty adverts to the authentic and original source of binding social norms. From the relativity criterion we get the boundary between those norms originating 'inside' or 'within' a given political association, and those, 'outside'. An association generating norms internally is responsible only to itself (through its members) for maintaining and enforcing them. Thus Herculeum generates and observes its own standards of social behaviour, whether or not they accord with those of neighbouring States. From the social context criterion – inasmuch as popular sovereignty is in question – we get the boundary between norms originating from the people, and those from some other individual or entity. Only the former attract the character of binding. Hence to the extent of any conflict between the two, the latter must cede to the former. For example, pharmacists in

---

50 G. Sabine, *l.c.*, 399 e.s. And thus, as prominent examples, *Charter of the United Nation*, United Nations Treaty Series 1945, 993 and *Declaration on Principles of International Law concerning Friendly Relations and Co–operation among States in accordance with the Charter of the United Nations*, GA Res. 2625 (XXV) (24 Oct. 1970).

51 This recalls quite obviously the similar discussion above under "the Rule of Law", namely, that the capacity actually to cause a person to do or refrain from a particular act they would otherwise commit obtains necessarily in a context of extant social relationships. This presumes some social order which distributes and arranges the exercise of social power across the range of participants.

Herculeum are bound to sell contraceptives despite any serious moral objection to contraception. So a normative understanding of popular sovereignty sketches out the source of binding social norms as being the members of a political association. Whether or not we invoke Kantian notions of self–legislation, nevertheless we as members of such an association are creating our own exclusive reasons for action. And we are responsible to ourselves for maintaining and enforcing those norms. So a normative reconstruction of sovereignty does not merely stipulate one authentic source for social norms. It resets our perspective on sovereignty from one of command to one of obedience, from the author's perspective to the addressees', and emphasises the nature of power as a social practice. Put another way, the normative reconstruction of sovereignty puts us to explicating the Hart–inspired "internal point of view".[52]

6 Sovereignty and Boundaries

Simply put, popular sovereignty means that citizens determine the content of the laws which bind them. Although variously expressed by different authors, the common element to each particular iteration of the principle is that citizens are both authors and addressees of the law. They themselves, not some other person or entity, determine what the laws should be. Implied in this statement is of course the twofold condition of democratic citizenship: participatory democracy and obedience to the law. If citizens may determine what laws are passed, then they must necessarily have a determinative role in the legislative process.[53] Such a role exists in the various instantiations of democracy, such as republican, liberal, constitutional, and so on. Individuals *qua* citizens are authors of the law. Secondly, if citizens are passing laws, then presumably they are obeying those laws. We have analysed above law's normativity under the heading of the 'rule of law'. Individuals *qua* citizens are also equally addressees of the law.

It bears remark that little if anything at all is said about participation in the *adjudicatory* process. Not as parties, but as judges. While citizens are expected to undertake a legislative role in the concept of popular sovereignty, their contribution to adjudication is generally left unaddressed in modern expositions of democ-

52 The division between the internal point of view and the external point of view, first set out in H. Hart, *Concept of the Law* (Oxford: Oxford University Press, 2nd ed., 1994), and analysed further in, *e.g.*, D. Patterson, "Explicating the Internal Point of View", *Southern Methodist Univ. LR* 1999, *52*, 67 (normativity attaching only to the internal); D. Litowitz, "Internal Versus External Perspectives: Toward Mediation", *Florida State Univ. LR* 1998, *26*, 127 (thus the need for reconciliation and mediation between the two perspectives); T. Morawetz, "Law as Experience: Theory and the Internal aspect of Law", *Southern Methodist Univ. LR* 1999, *52*, 27 (a hermeneutics–inspired reconstruction, discounting the "external" as indivisible from, parasitic on, and part of the "internal"); and see B. Bix, "HLA Hart and the Hermeneutic Turn in Legal Theory", *Southern Methodist Univ. LR* 1999, *52*, 167.

53 For simplicity and convenience, we include herewith the executive function of the *trias*.

racy.[54] Lay juries, such as those chronicled in ancient Greek democracy[55], or those operating in medieval England[56] played a more sizeable part in the translation of legal norms into daily practice. This mediating function, the application of law, has largely been lost or at best subdued in current thinking on popular sovereignty, and politics more generally. In part, the juridical role has presumably become such a specialised area in a technical field that the jury no longer figures as the central pillar of adjudication. In part, it is also one by–product to the history of concentrating political power into the hands of a single person or a small number of individuals, that a concomitant centralising of juridical authority into a smaller number of easily controlled and politically sponsored agencies has occurred.[57] Likewise, the development of a professional legal class distinct from the ordinary citizenry and the transfer of any mediating function in adjudication to that class, tracks in no small degree the systematisation of political power into the exclusive bipolar relationship rule-givers and rule-followers.

Inheriting this perspective, our modern–day boundary between law and politics and between author and addressee, once blurred and smudged, has become a rather sharply defined boundary.[58] Only two sides are defined to exist: the author

---

54 See *e.g.*, S. Benhabib (ed.), *Democracy and Difference* (Princeton: Princeton University Press, 1996), J. Bohman and W. Rehg (eds.), *Deliberative Democracy: Essays on Reason and Politics* (Cambridge, Mass.: MIT Press, 1997), and D. Sciulli, *Theory of Societal Constitutionalism* (New York: Cambridge University Press, 1992).

55 See *e.g.*, C. Carey, "Legal Space in Classical Athens", *Greece & Rome*, 1994, *41*, 172; S. Smith, "The Establishment of the Public Courts at Athens", *Trans. and Proc. of the Am. Philol. Assoc.* 1925, *56*, 106; A. Lanni, "Spectator Sport of Serious Politics? *oí periestēkótes* and the Athenian Lawcourts", *J. Hellenic Studs* 1997, *117*, 183.

56 Broadly, up to the start of the Tudor dynasty (1465). See *e.g.*, G. Jacobsohn, "Citizen Participation in Policy Making: The Role of the Jury", *J. Pol.* 1972, *39*, 73, R. Goheen, "Peasant Values? Village Community and the Crown in Fifteenth Century England", *Am. Hist. Rev.* 1991, *96*, 42, P. Schofield, "Peasants and the Manor Courts: Gossip and Litigation in a Suffolk Village at the Close of the Twelfth Century", *Past & Present* 1998, *195*, 3, and R. Turner, "The Origins of the Medieval English Jury: Frankish, English or Scandinavian?", *J. Brit. Studs*. 1968, 1.

57 See *e.g.*, F. Maitland's treatment of the historical development of jury trials in England in his *The Constitutional History of England* (H. Fisher ed.) (Cambridge: Cambridge University Press, 1961) 120 e.s., and M. Loughlin, *l.c.*, 57-58.

58 The apparent lack of attention to the citizen's role in law application and enforcement no doubt reflects the deeply seated acceptance of the separation of powers doctrine: see C. Carey, *l.c.*. Montesquieu's principle that the reciprocal check and balance achieved by dividing the three fundamental elements to public power among separate agencies would minimise the risk of an abuse of power concentrated in the hands of but one. Only by barring a commingling of these functions, and hence any expansion thereof, can the general public benefit from a disinterested, even–handed application of each power function. This guarantees the full political liberty of the subject, see *e.g.*, L. Claus, "Montesquieu's Mistakes and the True Meaning of Separation", *Oxford J Leg. Studs.* 2005, *25*, 419 (an 'anti–essentialist' reading of Montesquieu, arguing in effect to the same conclusion as M. Vile, *Constitutionalism and the Separation of Powers* (Oxford: Oxford University Press, 1967)). Indeed, we might well consider the separation of powers doctrine to be a reaction to that historical process of concentrating power, particularly in the circumstances of 17th century France. Nevertheless, as a principle of general application, the boundaries separating the legislative role,

of law and its addressee. It is very much a top–down perspective. The legislator decrees the law, and the rest apply or obey it. Only the legislator may decide on content, its primary task as allocated under the separation of powers doctrine.[59] There is no room seemingly left over for a mutual sharing of the *trias* functions.[60] Popular sovereignty, like any other instantiation of power, operates in this bilateral framework of law–giver and law–follower. The compartmental model of political power (and its instrumental conception of law, as they have developed throughout our political history) is central to modern constitutional law. It arguably accounts for the development of constitutionalism.[61] Bounding and institutionalising social power through a (legal) instrument, a 'Constitution' – and requiring the organs so created to justify their exercise of power in relation thereto – offers a concrete manifestation.

This bilateral understanding of political power, with the opposing poles of author and addressee now so familiar here, reconstrues law as an instrument (one among many) of power. The consequence of this instrumental view is to establish conceptual limits or boundaries between law and sovereignty. Law and sovereignty (or 'politics', for short) separate practically and conceptually. Law now is viewed as 'falling outside' the conceptions of political power and sovereignty, and each traces out its own borders.[62] Of course, in certain matters, the one may run

---

the executive, the judicial, and the general public become certain, clear, and above all, impermeable.

59 Hence, the extensive discussions in certain jurisdictions about the legitimacy of judicial review of legislation for constitutional validity. See, among others, T. Campbell and J. Goldsworthy (eds.), *Judicial Power, Democracy and Legal Positivism* (Aldershot: Ashgate, 2000); C. Forsyth (ed.), *Judicial Review and the Constitution* (Oxford: Hart, 2000); M. Elliott, *The Constitutional Foundations of Judicial Review* (Oxford: Hart, 2001) (UK); M. Mandel, *The Charter of Rights and the Legalisation of Politics in Canada* (rev. ed.) (Toronto: Thompson Educational, 1994); F. Morton and R. Knopff, *The Charter Revolution and the Court Party* (Peterborough, Can.: Broadview, 2000); P. James, D. Abelson and M. Lusztig (eds.), *The Myth of the Sacred: The Charter, the Courts, and Politics of the Constitution in Canada* (Montreal & Kingston: McGill–Queens, 2002); R. Martin, *The Most Dangerous Branch: How the Supreme Court of Canada Has Undermined Our Law and Our Democracy* (Montreal & Kingston: McGill–Queens, Canada, 2003); and the US works listed in note 61 below.

60 M. Vile, *l.c.*, esp. 297 e.s., however, offers a persuasive argument that such a sharing does in deed exist.

61 On which, see *e.g.*, G. van der Tang, *l.c.*. The division lies at the heart of the US 'political questions' doctrine and the debates surrounding the interaction between the US Supreme Court and the US Congress (and government officials generally): see *e.g.*, the classic expositions of H. Wechsler, "Toward Neutral Principles of Constitutional Law", *Harvard LR* 1959, *73*, 1; A. Bickel, *The Least Dangerous Branch* (New Haven: Yale University Press, 2nd ed., 1986); J. Hart Ely, *Democracy and Distrust* (Cambridge, Mass.: Harvard University Press, 1980); J. Choper, *Judicial Review and the National Political Process* (Chicago: University of Chicago Press, 1980); and B. Ackerman, "A New Separation of Powers", *Harvard LR* 2000, *113*, 633.

62 Best conceptualised by, *e.g.*, the 'systems theory of law' of N. Luhmann, *Social Systems* (J. Bednarz trans.) (Stanford: Stanford University Press, 1984). From a more practical orientation, *e.g.*, this division is the primary premise to the US constitutional doctrine of 'political questions': see *e.g.*, L. Henkin, "Is There a 'Political Questions' Doctrine, *Yale LJ* 1976, *85*, 597; M. Redish, "Judicial Review and the Political Question", *Northwestern U LR* 1985, *79*, 1031; R. Nagel, "Political Law, Legalistic Politics: A Recent History of the Political Ques-

contiguously with the other, yet each remains nonetheless a separate system of meaning and action, with its own vocabulary. Contrast this with the lay juries, for example, which offered a less abrupt transition from law–giving to law–following.

Consider, for example, the two principal ways in which sovereignty becomes a live (legal) issue. First, it is used to justify parliamentary authority to legislate in certain ways and in certain fields. The law is simply one instrument of that power, having no separate status. So to return to Herculeum, the State (or more precisely, the government) will invoke its sovereignty as part of its justification for its various actions under scrutiny, to exclude the application of standards, precedents, or norms not emanating from the local parliament. Herculeum norms recognised or established by its Parliament only, have effect. This is not simply the 'dualism-monism' debate of applying international law in national legal orders again, but includes also the hobby–horses of positivism (moral content in law?), and a rights–oriented constitutionalism (is there a natural limit on the exercise of power?). Second and following, sovereignty is used to justify the primacy of parliamentary bodies over the courts and other political entities. This parses into two elements. To begin, Parliament may legislate in certain areas as it sees fit, without being limited in what and how it may regulate a matter. Again, a matter of power, the 'law' aspect being a secondary formality. Hence the Herculeum courts should have no jurisdiction to interfere with legislation or the legislative process.[63] They may not review legislation for constitutionality. The breadth of application is, however, limited where a Constitution expressly[64] or implicitly[65] allows for such judicial review. This is carried then further by a more foundational claim that Parliament, as a responsible and representative organ of State, has a privileged position relative to the executive and the courts, in its access to the ultimate normative source: the good citizens of Herculeum.

This suggests that sovereignty and 'popular' sovereignty more specifically, cover two interrelated propositions which may or may not be intentionally conflated. First there is the more common institutional claim.[66] This stipulates the supremacy of Parliament over the courts and beyond, such as over international bod-

---

tions Doctrine", *U Chicago LR* 1989, *56*, 643; L. Sandstrom Simard, "Standing Alone: Do We Still Need the Political Questions Doctrine?", *Dickinson LR* 1996, *100*, 303.

63 As was the case in the UK, until proclamation of the *Human Rights Act*. For the classic statement, see *e.g.*, W. Wade, *l.c.*.

64 As in the Constitutions of Belgium (Article 144) and of Germany (Article 93). In Canada, the *Constitution Act 1982* does not explicitly confer jurisdiction on any court. Rather, the courts have assumed jurisdiction by reference to s.25, granting aggrieved parties standing to apply for a remedy for infringement of rights, and to s.52, making all constitutional provisions the supreme law: See *e.g.*, *Re Manitoba Language Rights* [1985] 1 Supreme Court Rep. 721, *R v Big M Drug Mart* [1985] 1 Supreme Court Rep. 295, *Operation Dismantle v The Queen* [1985] 1 Supreme Court Rep. 441, and *Weber v Ont. Hydro* [1995] 2 Supreme Court Rep. 929.

65 As derived from the reasons in *Marbury v Madison* (1803) 5 US (1 Cranch) 137; and see also *Harris v Min. Interior* [1952] 2 SA 428 (AD) and *Min Interior v Harris* [1952] 4 SA 769 (AD), and the articles of D. Cowen, "Legislature and Judiciary", *MLR* 1952, *15*, 282 (Part I), *MLR*, 1953, *16*, 273 (Part II), and W. Wade, *l.c.*.

66 Characteristic of Goldsworthy's argument in *l.c.*, Ch. 10, esp. 254 e.s.

ies. As one of the three basic, constitutionally prescribed organs of government, Parliament is supposedly representative of and responsible to 'the people' who are the ultimate source of all norms. (This latter point of course foreshadows the second interconnected proposition.) Regular popular elections stamp Parliament with a democratic authenticity across party lines which a judiciary appointed by the executive cannot, it is argued, match. Accordingly, Parliament is better suited and better able to ascertain the authentic 'will of the people' and duly articulate it in legislative form. This sets Parliament at the top of the constitutional hierarchy, above the courts and the executive.

But we exhaust rather quickly the explanatory potential of the institutional conception on its own. There is no inherent reason why one official or organ should take precedence over another, by mere virtue of being a constitutional judge or parliamentary assembly. Referring to the organ's connection to an authentic democratic will underscore a particular conception of normative legitimacy. It seems self–explanatory that social, institutional structures would reflect the sources of normativity current in that social context. So the debate moves seamlessly onto normative terrain, examining which organs can deliver the more 'authentic' social norms. For example, then, the US debates surrounding *Aaron v Cooper*[67] and the constitutional powers of (elected) officials to disregard those judicial constitutional pronouncements considered misguided or wrong[68] are in fact debates on final source of normative (constitutional) authority in the US.[69] All these rely on a certain conception of what norms can and should bind. Positions taken on the institutional claim derive from the internal point of view.

7 The Normativity and Law

Now, the second proposition bearing upon sovereignty under our Herculeum example is just that normative claim. The Herculeum Parliament owes its primacy to the particular Herculeum social context, its social conventions. That in turn represents an agreement and belief that the most clear and authentic expression of its (imperative) democratic will emanates from a local, representative, parliamentary forum, rather than from executive fiat or judicial decision. Moreover, the expression of democratic will occurs in the form of public laws issuing from that forum. The forum is characterised by public participation and deliberation, which underline that norms and norm formation are deliberative, participatory, and public. The sovereignty of that forum, as a question of allegiance and obedience due thereto

---

67 358 US 1 (1958) (Arkansas State officials bound by prior US Supreme Court decision holding racial segregation unconstitutional and no legal or good faith excuse available for delays in implementing desegregation plan for schools).

68 See *e.g.*, M. Paulsen, "The Most Dangerous Branch: Executive Power to Say What Law Is", *Georgetown LJ* 1994, 83, 217 and L. Alexander and F. Schauer, "On Extrajudicial Interpretation", *Harvard LR* 1997, 110, 1359 (an attempt to keep the terms of reference within the institutional domain via the function of law in society).

69 *E.g.*, L. Alexander and F. Schauer, *l.c.*, 1374 e.s.

(and more broadly to civic institutions representative and responsible to the general body of citizens), is in effect a statement of being responsible to and for themselves. The people can decide by what rules they will live in and as a society. The addressees of laws obey those laws they issue for themselves, and not those issued by others outside that social context. Put in other terms, the normative authority of those norms arises from citizens legislating for themselves in a participatory and deliberative manner. They are each co-operating in the fashioning of norms in that process and the binding of themselves individually to their particular conception of them, and not just simply adopting 'alien' standards.

The second proposition, the normative one, accordingly bears a considerable burden, being the focus of our attention under the sovereignty and the rule of law rubrics. By 'normativity', we mean that standard by which we are judged and we judge others, and in virtue of which we would punish or reward. Normativity arises in the society of others: it is an associative phenomenon. It is also a reflective one, for an evaluative, critical, distancing obtains between us and the object of our consideration – including an image of self. As such a social phenomenon, there exists a number of different sources for the normative, each originating out of our membership, voluntary or not, in the multiple different associations making up our every–day life. Each grouping creates its own standards of behaviour by which its members are judged. Of course, not all such norms have immediate *public* effect; that is, extending beyond the immediate membership of the group.[70] And not all are enforced the same way, even though some measure and type of coercion figures in each and every instance. That coercion reflects the imposition of the standard over present interest and design to compel conformity.

But normativity would not excite such attention if conformity in belief and behaviour were easy givens. Plurality of values, and diversity of meaning and intention, render disagreement and divergence inevitable. Indeed, the very existence of normativity as an issue in itself stands as good proof of that plurality and diversity in any association. For associations to persist, there must be some co–ordination of action and coherence in value–orientations. The orchestra must play from the same score, from the same arrangement. Society requires a common iteration of the norms identifying and governing that association, controlling all like instances. The law is an easy shoe–in to provide this central reference point.[71] Its peculiar characteristics, identified closely in the first chapter[72], reflect a core idea of law being simply a norm, an imperative direction constraining or restraining certain conduct.

What this all suggests is first that the normative proposition of sovereignty focuses on the *addressees'*, and not the *author's* perspective, as the classic conception would have it. The formation of norms, their acceptance, and compliance with them all precede from the addressee's perspective. We might say that sovereignty

---

70 Although with a nod to H. Arendt, *The Human Condition* (Chicago: University of Chicago Press, 1970) esp; Ch. 2 "The Public and the Private Realm", also with a caveat that her distinction of 'public' from 'private' is not entirely adopted here.

71 In effect the foundation for the arguments in L. Alexander and F. Schauer, *l.c.*.

72 E. Claes, W. Devroe, and B. Keirsbilck, "The Limits of the Law (Introduction)".

(as a normative conception) is earned, not taken. Second, the addressee's perspective, being the critical optic for normativity, situates the conditions for normative force in the associative relationships of individuals making up (political) society. The coercive force of the normative, that characterising the internal point of view, arises in and through an ideation of self necessarily in a particular social context. It is means of 'symbolisation of self' *qua* aspirational goal, as the person we think we are and should be (in the eyes of others). Participating in the deliberative efforts to create norms, we bring our own interests and designs into public view by encouraging others to adopt them as their own. Transforming private interests into public concerns in this fashion sets them apart and idealises or standardises them: in short, creating normative symbols. To reiterate, those ideas or values which transform into external or public norms become symbols: characters having a certain assigned meaning, not otherwise naturally occurring nor internal to our consciousness. Hence the expression of power in an intersubjective relationship is in fact the projection of that public, common meaning (or 'symbols').

So our attempt to erase the boundaries between (the rule of) law and sovereignty has in fact brought us to the very point where boundaries are being drawn, between what is 'internal' to us, what is 'private', and what is 'external' or 'public'. We could even venture to add between the subjective, and the objective. This occurs through what is characterised as 'symbolisation'.

8 Symbolisation and Law's Limiting Power

The raw exercise of political power, as soon as it purports to be anything more than mere brute force or coercion of the instant, must observe some orderly process of articulation. That is, it must come into existence and be administered in some regular fashion. This regularity has two dimensions, one of extension over time, and the other of form. Raw power is the compelling at the instant itself. Unless there exists with the commander some ability and capacity to continue with further application of the threat or the promise of reward, the effect of either threat or promise should evaporate with that instant. Yet it seems obvious to assume that the holding and exercise of social power is intended to persist beyond a certain time and situation. So the enduring application of a threat or promise requires some regularity or ordering articulated in the form of the intersubjective power relationships. Even if the commander should engage others to ensure such continuing application, this merely establishes further, intermediary power relations as between commander and agent (as well as ultimately between agent and subject) where the same considerations of maintaining the promise or threat apply. That is, the agency relationship itself must rely on some ordering to maintain its own version of threat or promise. So we may safely accept that the desired recursivity and permanence of the command relationship depends upon some form of social structure and ordering. Structure and order quite simply serve to minimise the burden and costs of command, principally relieving the commander of re-establishing supremacy whenever issuing orders. It arranges the systematic application of rewards and punishments (threats). And correlated to this are furthermore those reasons cited by Raz concerning the rule of law: settling expectations and allowing a subject better to plan and mould behaviour as law–abiding.[73]

Now, perhaps not unsurprisingly, the legal form offers precisely these two dimensions in intersubjective power relationships. There is more to this proposition than simply rehearsing the formalistic criterion of the rule of law, and noting the enduring presence of some formalised legislative and adjudicative process throughout history.[74] The deeper connection allies law and power at their conceptual foundations, rather than merely at this instrumental, formal level. The latter, as we have argued herein, reflects this deeper connection rather than standing for it *simpliciter*. It begins to reveal itself in the realisation that social power, other than the actual push, blow, payment, or such like, can only manifest itself, be perceived, through the legal form. Social power expresses itself through law; the law is an expression of the political power to command.

One means to make sense of this proposition is via the symbolisation concept of Cassirer.[75] 'Symbolisation' represents 'work', human action in the world which is the quintessential or defining human characteristic.[76] The concept comprises a grasping of phenomena and a distancing from them. To understand this, we need to picture how it is that we come to know things in the world. Distancing refers to perception and perspective. When we see something, say a book, we see the physical object with all its characteristic attributes. The attributes are 'characteristic' because our rationality has us draw comparisons and distinctions with the other objects we have seen. It is also perceived as something 'outside' or 'other than' us, and as something in a surrounding, in a context – such as 'desk', 'bookshelf', or 'library'. Grasping is perhaps more usefully translated as 'comprehending'. We interiorise it, as a concept, and so understand the object. This internalisation occurs by ascribing meaning to the object. So 'book' conveys the ideas of writing, communication of ideas, those ideas themselves, the context perhaps of 'library' and so on and such like.

The ascription of meaning requires the instrumentality of language. We should understand by 'language' that broad conception adopted by Searle, who formulates a like proposition that we construct actively, not passively adopt, reality. It

---

73 J. Raz, *l.c.*, 220. See above note 26 and accompanying text.

74 By "legislative and adjudicative", we mean to avoid restricting the law–making function to some formal *parliamentary* process characteristic of more developed legal systems, per C.K. Allen, *Law in the Making* (3rd) (Oxford: Oxford University Press, 1939) 351, citing Maine. We intend to capture as broad a range of law–giving as possible: custom, precedent, and legislation (to borrow Allen's three categories).

75 See *e.g.*, H. Lindahl, *l.c.*, who draws upon E. Cassirer, *The Philosophy of Symbolic Forms* (R. Mannheim trans.) (New Haven: Yale University Press, 1953) and *The Myth of the State* (New Haven: Yale University Press, 2nd ed., 1974). See also E. Cassirer, "The Problem of the Symbol and its Place in the System of Philosophy" (1927), *Man & World* 1978, *11*, 411; L. Rosenstein, "Some Metaphysical Problems of Cassirer's Symbolic Forms", *Man & World* 1973, *6*, 304, and D. Koskum, *Law as Symbolic Form* (Berlin: Springer, 2007).

76 This tracks a like concept "agentive function" in J. Searle, *The Construction of Social Reality* (London: Penguin, 1995) 20–23.

encompasses all forms of utterance and expression, not just natural languages like Dutch, English, Esperanto, and Latin. Hence music, dance, pictures, symbols, numbers, and so on. A language is any system of conventional devices which mean or represent or express something "beyond themselves, *in a way that is publicly understandable*."[77] The meaning they bear is not intrinsic or inherent to them, but is intentionally imposed upon them by human agency. Hence, hunger itself as a natural State or 'language independent fact' represents the need of a biological entity to take nourishment, but 'hunger' or "I am hungry" is the linguistic device intended to mean that state.[78]

Law is this symbolising language of power, comprising the distancing and interiorising capacities of that symbolising process as applied to the intersubjective exercise of social power. In law, we have that system of conventional devices which represent the projection of behavioural standards, social norms. It is the language of power, of coercion, sanction, and reward, within the social framework but without the need for constant application of sanction or reward. Only the threat thereof remains, albeit implicit. At this level, the symbolic character (or function) of the law gives form to power *qua* sovereignty.

But this only gets us so far. It certainly satisfies as an explanation for popular sovereignty never existing without the legal form as its means of symbolisation. This is, nonetheless, a formal limit on popular sovereignty, rather a substantive one. In other words, the law demarcates the current reach of sovereignty, but does not restrict the content of that expression of power. Hence, as long as popular sovereignty adopts the legal form, it may express itself on any subject whatsoever without any restraint or constraint upon the substance thereof. It is unmistakeably the classical version of the rule of law, dressed up in more philosophical garb. We have not travelled very far from the central tenets of legal positivism.

9 Conclusion: The Addressee's Perspective and Substantive Limits on Sovereignty

To prise open the internal point of view, and posit the law (or the rule of law) as a substantive limit on sovereignty, we need to recognise both sides to the symbolisation concept. The one side speaks to transposing internal, private matters into external, public ones. The second aspect, prompted by the addressee's perspective, requires a reinternalisation, a reintegration of that public norm into the fund of designs, beliefs, desires, and such like – call them all 'commitments' – that each one of us holds, as a self–governing individual.

The central premise to rejecting the law's bounding of a sovereign stipulates that a power binding itself to a particular constitutional order is logically separate and prior to that legal order. Indeed, the latter is derivative upon it, and subsists at

77 J. Searle, *l.c.*, 60-61 (emphasis in the original).

78 J. Searle, *l.c.*, 61.

its pleasure. The sovereign may withdraw its consent to be bound to any degree at will, and without limitation. By way of contrast, if a power constituted itself through a Constitution, then the assumption is that the power exists only in and through that constitutional settlement.[79]

But as argued here, binding oneself engages the addressee's perspective. First, the sovereign must engage with an 'other' to found the obligation, which in the circumstances is society. For the case of popular sovereignty, the people engage themselves. Second, that engagement invokes the symbolisation stage, where traditionally the sovereign seeks the role of progenitor and protector of the constitutional settlement for the benefit and welfare of its subjects. The symbolic is that fund of externalised, ascribed meaning which will be reincorporated into the set of private commitments of sovereign and society. As such it is the reference point for an idealised conception of self. In the social, public context, we are speaking of an idealised conception of society.[80] Sovereignty, as we have suggested, is the projection of norms which in the case of popular sovereignty arise in an interactive, deliberative democracy. The projection of norms occurs in the form of laws, and lawful conduct. And laws arise through interaction, deliberation, and debate. Hence the content of the symbolic here is not merely 'supremacy', but more significantly, the idealised constitutional settlement, as well as those values and procedures necessary and sufficient for its preservation. Specifically, this means those aspects comprising what the editors termed 'protective legality'.[81] The addressee's perspective thus creates an idealised concept of sovereign as one acting in and through the law and integrates that conception into the sovereign's commitment to the constitutional order. The sovereign's concept of self becomes one of a sovereign *by* and *under* the law.

To claim that the (rule of) law may act as a substantive limit on (popular) sovereignty, then, is to posit limits of law on the scope and reach of any exercise of social power. Blackstone's apophthegm that Parliament can do anything that is not impossible deserves a significant nuance to 'impossible'. For that term is thus bounded by an understanding of obedience, reason, and a social context – all comprising the 'addressee's perspective', as used here.[82] A substantive limit on sovereignty means that sovereignty cannot exist or persist without acting in and through law, the legal form, and within the boundaries necessary and sufficient to create binding law. The 'bindingness' aspect invokes the addressee's perspective. That refers to the creation of social norms by the transformation of internal com-

79 Thus *Rediffusion (Hong Kong) Ltd v AG (HK)* [1970] AC 1136, 1154ff, 160ff (per Diplock); *Marbury v Madison* (1803) 5 US (1 Cranch) 137; and see also *Harris v Min. Interior* [1952] 2 SA 428 (AD). This reflects the like position of A.V. Dicey, *l.c.*, Chap. II "Parliament and Non–Sovereign Law–Making Bodies", 87 e.s.

80 See likewise, H. Lindahl, *l.c.* and note 13 above.

81 E. Claes, W. Devroe, and B. Keirsbilck, *l.c.*

82 A like bounding to (positive) law is also arguably developed by R. Alexy (relying on Radbruch: R. Alexy, "A Defence of Radbruch's Formula", in D. Dyzenhaus (ed.), *Recrafting the Rule of Law: The Limits of the Legal Order* (Oxford: Hart, 1999) 15) and by 'internal' legal positivists, such as W. Waluchow, *Internal Legal Positivism* (Oxford: Oxford University Press, 1994).

mitments through deliberation, debate, interaction, into external symbols, and the latter's re-integration into the private, personal domain. All this necessarily obtaining within a social context of recurring contacts with others.

It follows, of course, that inasmuch as that social context admits of a totalitarian level of control, so be it. If not so accepted, then the sovereign cannot arrogate and maintain totalitarian power on a legal basis. On a non–legal one certainly, but in those circumstances of continual brute force and fear, we can hardly contemplate or speak of "law" in any normal or ordinary sense. An entity applying its own will and desires to legal subjects irrespective of their will and desires (an absolute or totalitarian ruler) governs by force, not law. It is with considerable insight and reason that Hume wrote, "[F]orce is always on the side of the governed, the governors have nothing to support them but opinion."[83] The addressee's perspective reorients the idea of power and normativity from one of *imposing* to one of *accepting* norms. And this in turn suggests that for any workable concept of law, the participation of the addressee in the creation of law, its interpretation, and application – all elements to giving content to law – becomes irreplaceable. A concept of law is not merely a theory or model of rules. It is a concept of ruling oneself and others. As addressees of law, we must take responsibility for the law's content. We must also be able to take up that responsibility. We cannot leave or pass on that responsibility to others or to one of the four estates (legislature, executive, judiciary, people) which remains aloof or divorced from constant interaction and discussion with the others. In the end, the *end* of law is reached when the *ends* of law symbolise no longer a society worth striving for, no longer those values which we aspire to hold.

---

83 D. Hume, *l.c.*, 109.

Chapter 17 – Constitutional Ideals, National Identity, and the Limits of the Law

Bram Delbecke

1 Introduction

Since the dawn of the age of liberalism, civil liberties have formed a key element in constructing the identities of several Nation–States. As a matter of fact, the civil liberties which have been emphasised consequently by liberal discourse are often considered as the expressions of a particular national aim for individual and collective freedom. Therefore, these liberties are incorporated in constitutional texts, functioning as a fundamental right for the individual as well as an ideal of the Nation. In modernity, nationalism and liberalism go hand in hand. However, the relationship between civil liberties and modern nationalism is not always one of simple mutual reinforcement. Although the symbolic function of these civil liberties is highly important, their expressions sometimes threaten their own legitimity. Therefore, to preserve the cherished national liberal identity, these civil liberties sometimes need to be strategically limited. This is the paradox which will be examined in this chapter: the curious mechanism in which civil liberties, which are key elements of a particular national identity, are limited in order to control this national identity. It is a mutilation of one's own identity to maintain it at the same time. This chapter therefore explores the difficult relationship between the symbolic and the protective function of the law, showing that an instrumental conception of fundamental rights and freedoms tends to erode the guarantees offered by these rights and freedoms.

There are numerous ways to illustrate this somewhat paradoxical relationship. Instead of going through different aspects from a bird's eye view, a case study approach will be used. In the following sections, the history of the freedom of the press in 19th century Belgium will be examined. Choosing this particular history is not coincidental. On the one hand, the construction of the Belgian Nation–State since its independence in 1830 is one of the most typical examples of the creation of a national identity based upon civil liberties. On the other hand, the freedom of the press is perhaps the most typical of all classic civil liberties, being a guarantee against any form of governmental abuse of power. Because the liberal press regime of the young Belgian Nation–State was famous all over Europe, the way of dealing with this regime will reveal the complex and paradoxical relationship between constitutional ideals, national identity, and the limits of the rule of law at its best. After examining the history of the Belgian freedom of the press (sections 2 through 5), a brief epilogue will illustrate that the mechanisms discovered in the case study reveal a more general pattern. By quoting briefly the example of the freedom of the press in contemporary Turkey, one can assume this pattern shows up when a Nation–State needs to affirm its identity in front of the world (section 6).

2 Dealing with the Past by Ruling One's Own Identity: Freedom of the Press in the Belgian Constitution (1830–31)

In the fall of 1830, shortly after the Belgian Revolution, the National Congress gathered to give the freshly born Belgian State its own Constitution. This assembly was highly concerned with, among other interests, organising a constitutional framework that would give the press as much freedom as possible. It was a matter of confronting the recent past, because this concern with the freedom of the press should be considered a reaction against the former Dutch regime, famous for its rigid and repressive press policy.[1]

Amongst the leading men of the Belgian Revolution were numerous journalists, editors and lawyers who had been convicted by the Dutch regime for criticising its policy. Their appropriation of the revolution led to a specific concern with the freedom of expression and the freedom of the press in the future Belgian State. The desire of installing as much freedom of speech and freedom of the press as possible was indeed a typical exponent of early 19th century liberalism, but it was supported by Catholics too. Despite their ideological opposition, the majority of Catholics shared this concern, considering the freedom of speech the best way to guarantee the practice of any form of public religiosity.[2]

Eventually, when on 7 February 1831 the Congress approved the Belgian Constitution, freedom of the press was secured on a double level.[3] Fundamental guarantees were not only given concerning the freedom of the press itself, but also concerning the prosecution of any form of abuse of this freedom. On the first, material level, freedom of speech (and religion) in general[4] and the freedom of the press in particular were guaranteed and every kind of preventive measures was strictly forbidden: no censorship, no preventive detention.[5] On the other, procedural level, the Constitution stated that trials had to be public, and when it came to press crimes or political crimes, judges had to be unanimous to conduct the trial *in camera*.[6] The judgment on any press crime and political crime was for a jury.[7] No

---

1 C. de Bavay, "Du régime de la presse sous l'ancien gouvernement des Pays–Bas", *La Belgique judiciaire* 1869, *27*, 1393–1405.

2 V. Viaene, *Belgium and the Holy See. Gregory XVI to Pius IX (1831–1859): Catholic Revival, Society and Politics in 19th–Century Europe* (Leuven: University Press, 2001) 25–36.

3 A. Mast, *De vrijheid van drukpers* (Bruges: Die Keure, 1962); H. Schuermans, *Code de la presse* (Brussels: Larcier, 1881); J. Velaers, *De beperkingen van de vrijheid van meningsuiting* (Antwerp: Maklu, 1990) 90–139.

4 Article 14 Belgian Constitution (now Article 19).

5 Article 18 Belgian Constitution (now Article 25).

6 Article 96 Belgian Constitution (now Article 148).

7 Article 98 Belgian Constitution (now Article 150).

judge could say whether an author was guilty or not, only the majority of 'twelve men good and true' was allowed to. Penal responsibility was organised in a cascade–like way, making a remarkable exception to the common principles of criminal participation. The editor was held responsible only when the author was not known or not found in Belgium; the printer, only when neither the author nor the editor was known, and so on. The last Article of the Constitution was a 'to do'–list for future legislators, containing matters that had to be organised as soon as possible. Significantly, the number one and two on that list were legislation concerning the press and juries.[8]

Once the Constitution was approved, the National Congress remained concerned with the freedom of the press and its judge, the jury. Just before it was dissolved, that constitutional assembly enacted two decrees. The decree of 19 July organised the jury system[9], the decree of 20 July was the last act of the Congress before its dissolution and gave Belgium its first press legislation.[10] Once more, several measures enhanced the protection of the freedom of the press. The most important rule was the prohibition of any form of preventive detention, except for some very serious political press crimes.[11] The most symbolic rule was the seating in court for one accused of a press crime: not the dock for common criminals, but a 'distinct location'.[12]

When the constitutional assembly enacted the various rules regulating freedom of the press, these regulations had various functions. The Constitution as a whole is often considered one of the most typical modern Constitutions of the 19th century liberal era. As with most other laws and rules, the Constitution of 7 February 1831 and the later decrees given by the National Congress had a regulatory function, expressing the typical and profound modern conviction that legal rules, born out of national sovereignty, are effective and efficient tools to resolve – or at least guide – societal problems. Given the democratic basis of the institutional system, the Congress had huge confidence in its own capacities and those of the future (penal) legislator. Concerning freedom of the press, the constitutional assembly expressed this faith by emphasising that no penal law could be made which was vague, which restricted discussions about matters of public importance, or which created forbidden opinions.[13] At the dawn of the Belgian Nation–State, the constitutional assembly considered itself as the defender of freedom of the press by sketching its fundamental regulatory principles, thereby giving a specific message to future writers and journalists.

---

8 Article 139 Belgian Constitution (now abolished).

9 Decree of 19 July 1831 (better known as 'Jury Decree').

10 Decree of 20 July 1831 (better known as 'Press Decree'). This decree was considered provisory by its author, the National Congress, but is, after being renewed twice, still partly in force. A law of 19 July 1832 prolonged the validity of the Press Decree until 1 May 1833; a law of 6 July 1833 established the permanent validity of the decree.

11 Article 8 § 5 Jury Decree; Article 9 Press Decree. Preventive detention was not allowed for crimes which were penalised with imprisonment.

12 Article 8 § 3 Jury Decree.

13 J. Velaers, *l.c.*, 123–130.

The Belgian Constitution was born out of the Belgian Revolution, so concern with freedom of the press was determined by the two classical factors of any revolution: the motives of dislike and of anticipation.[14] As a whole, this constitutional system of organising Belgian freedom of the press was a reaction against the press policy as it had been functioning during the fifteen years of the United Kingdom of the Netherlands. The aversion to the Dutch system made it a model for the constitutional assembly, but in a contrary way, as an opposite model. Out of dislike for the Dutch system, anticipation evolved for better organisation of freedom of the press. However, the motives of dislike and anticipation are not sufficient answers, because they cannot explain the origin of the underlying displeasure.

Therefore, one must understand the function awarded to freedom of the press. The constitutional assembly was worried about freedom of the press because this was considered one of the most important means of governmental critique. It is often stated that in the tradition of the rule of law, citizens expect that law sets conditions for minimal control and critique of power. During the sessions of the National Congress in 1830–31, in an era of great faith in the power of the rule of law as the expression of national or popular sovereignty, this was a very prominent idea in the minds of the members of the constitutional assembly. These minimum standards of possible critique were set very high. The whole constitutional system concerning the freedom of the press proposed to have maximised the future capacity of control and critique of Belgian citizens, so the regulatory function of the constitutional regulations went hand in hand with its protective legality. One can say that regulating and guaranteeing by law the press and its freedom are two sides of the same coin.

However, while rule and guarantee are perhaps quite evident dimensions of constitutional press regulations, one has to consider it on a meta–level too. Although basic regulation of press freedom was highly important, the symbolic function of assuring it was perhaps even more crucial. The young State had to legitimate its independent existence, and therefore stressed, or constructed, its own particular identity as a Nation–State. In the era of Nation–States, self–determination was a very important goal on its own for the Belgian people. That is why the election of members of the National Congress was based on principles which were very democratic for their time: by maximising the national and popular sovereignty of the constitutional assembly, its members wanted to create the best conditions for a Constitution which was in accordance with the principles of the Belgian people. After the awkward experience with the approval of the Dutch Constitution of 1815 and the various problems of those parliamentary members representing the South in the Dutch Parliament[15], the young Nation–State wanted

---

[14] G. van der Tang, *Grondwetsbegrip en grondwetsidee* (Rotterdam: Gouda Quint/Sanders Institute, 1998) 173–174.

[15] The Dutch Constitution of 1815 was approved by using so–called 'Dutch mathematics'. An assembly of 1603 notables defeated the text, but by considering valid the votes of those who rejected the text because of religious reasons as approving votes, the text was considered approved.

to create a Constitution in which the principles of the Belgian Nation were fully reflected.

This spirit of political relativism was best shown in the fundamental theme of the constitutional discourse at that time: the restoration of what was considered Belgium's age–long tradition of civil liberties. Therefore, at the time of its enactment, the Belgian Constitution was one of the most liberal Constitutions in the world, but also a conservative one. This paradox is often ignored, for 19th century liberalism is easily equalled to progressionism and the urge for renewal.[16] Press freedom was seen as the most important of those liberties, a touchstone for measuring the freedom of a Nation: protecting it was opening the gate to a future of national wealth, joy, and happiness. To guarantee the freedom of the press was therefore not only an act of protecting a civil liberty, it was also a matter of representing and constructing the fundamental characteristic of the Belgian Nation–State and its identity.

Given the revolutionary context, another significant part of this Belgian identity was simply 'not being Dutch'. Fifteen of years of experience had shown that Dutch despotism and Belgian liberties were incompatible. When it came to freedom of the press, the new Belgian press regime was explicitly opposed to the former Dutch one, implicitly stating that press freedom was a typical Belgian liberty. To the constitutional assembly, the repressive Dutch press regime represented the ultimate antipode of the 'Belgian' way of dealing with the press. Therefore, several new press rules were the opposite of the former Dutch ones, such as the ingenious cascade–like organisation of criminal responsibility, or the prohibition on preventive detention.

In the opinion of the constitutional assembly, freedom of the press was not only legitimated in a negative way by turning upside down the Dutch heritage. In 1830–31, this freedom of the press could be defined in positive way because it had a specific content. It was conceived for a particular reason, as a guarantee against any form of governmental abuse of power, or as a protection of the journalist as a critic, a political watchdog. As a consequence of the presence of several writers, editors, and lawyers who had personal experience with the Dutch press regime, the vision on what freedom of the press meant was profoundly and exclusively influenced by the image that those politicians had of themselves. The fundamental aim of freedom of the press was protecting those heroic fighters for truth, freedom, and justice, because that was what they had done themselves in the recent past. They cherished the memory of themselves having undauntedly and consistently criticised the Dutch regime, leading to a newly born State where the members of the Belgian Nation could develop themselves in absolute freedom and prosperity. Therefore they wanted to establish a regime where future heroes like themselves could count on maximum protection.

The allocation of press crimes to a jury trial was highly significant on the level of dispute resolution. Although the jury system as a juridical representation of na-

---

16 A. De Dijn, "In overeenstemming met onze zeden en gewoonten. De intellectuele context van de eerste Belgische constitutie (1815–1830)", *Bijdragen en Mededelingen betreffende de Geschiedenis der Nederlanden* 2002, *117*, 25–45.

tional or popular sovereignty is contested nowadays,[17] it was considered a blessing in 1830–31. The jury was seen as the best possible judicial forum, where the accused could defend themselves in front of twelve representatives of the Nation. It was the perfect expression of the modern belief in the power of rational arguments and free debate. Hence, publicity of what happened in court was of great importance, and so Article 96 of the Constitution stated that judges had to be unanimous to conduct the trial behind closed doors. Profound debates in front of the touchstone of the Nation were considered one of the best ways for this Nation to deal with its political challengers. This had to lead to the resolution of the dispute by giving the Nation's representatives the opportunity to judge whether the acts of those accused of political crimes or press crimes were or were not contrary to the customs and usages of the Belgian Nation.

This great concern for the freedom of speech and the freedom of the press in particular is a perfect illustration of this early 19th century era of transition and revolution. By giving these liberties the best legal guarantees, these young intellectuals wanted to legitimise criticising traditional society structures. One has to bear in mind that this system reflects the ideals of a new, young, political elite, the middle–class bourgeoisie. The new bourgeois elite wanted to create for themselves the means to reform society and to adapt its structures. A discourse on the age–long tradition of Belgian liberties was therefore a very convenient instrument to make the conquest of these structures acceptable. However, by putting as few legal burdens as possible on the freedom of the press, this new elite did not intend the press to be democratised as much as possible. The National Congress stated several times that there could not be absolute equality at all, because society was divided into two classes: the upper class and the working class. This approach was of great importance for access to the passive form of freedom of the press, namely the possibility of reading books and newspapers. Just like absolute democracy was prohibited by basing the right to vote on certain property qualifications, access to the press was limited by maintaining the press stamp, the only preventive measure allowed by the National Congress. By keeping newspaper prices high, access to the press was a luxury, reserved for the rich and wealthy elite.

In short, the constitutional protection of the freedom of the press organised the future Belgian press legislation and set its fundamental limits and guarantees. However, at the same time, the Constitution itself was limited by its context of origin – the Belgian Revolution – its ideals and its principal authors, the young and ambitious intellectuals of the wealthy bourgeoisie. In 1831, Belgian press legislation was deeply influenced and restricted by the origins and roots of the Belgian constitutional assembly, its members, and their personal experiences. One can say that the brief words of Article 18 of the Constitution were supported by a specific mental framework, one which was directly and profoundly influenced by the recent past and the role some members of the constitutional assembly had played. But because the constitutional press law proved to be closely linked to the circumstances of 1831, this link was at the same time its most substantial limit.

---

17 W. Roumier, *L'Avenir du jury criminel* (Paris: LGDJ, 2003) 32–36.

3 Dealing with Challengers to Belgian Society: Practising Press Law in 19th Century Belgium

Despite the euphoria and the belief that the National Congress had created the possibility of a glorious future for the newly born State, reality soon set in. It became clear that the constitutional organisation of press freedom had its own particular limits which were not – or even could not have been – foreseen. The press proved to be easily abused. Several changes in 19th century society urged the legislator to impose restrictions on new forms of expression. The following will suggest that generally all changes in 19th century Belgian press law were restrictions made by a Nation–State in need of protection of its own image.

After its independence, the Belgian State had to deal with its Orangist opponents, those who still supported the Dutch regime and King William. The growing–pains of Belgium and its institutions were easy targets for the mockery of its adversaries. To prevent further Orangist agitation, the law of 25 July 1834 forbade every form of Orangist propaganda.[18] The law was abandoned when Belgium and the Netherlands were reconciled in 1839 by the Treaty of the XXIV Articles.[19]

While the Orangist protest gradually faded away in the 1840s, a satirical and republican critique of King Leopold emerged. During the fall of 1846, several publications scoffed at his luxurious way of life. All of the authors who had criticised Leopold's abuse of Belgian tax money were brought to trial, but in court they proved in a rather hilarious way that their critique was not malevolent, and therefore could not be punished.[20] They were all set free, so the Head of the Justice Department proposed avoiding future mockery of the King by amending the existing press law. By the law of 6 April 1847, the Parliament penalised every form of malevolently insulting the person of the King or the Royal family.[21]

During the 19th century, amending the press law was more a matter of strategic burdens on what expression could be tolerated within the Belgian Nation–State. The only amendment of press law which facilitated the freedom of the press was the abolition of the former mandatory and expensive press stamp by the law of 26 May 1848. While elsewhere in Europe the revolutionary spirit spread, the young Belgian Nation had to prove its right of existence in the face of the leading international powers. By taking certain strategic measures, a revolution was avoided and the existence of Belgium was legitimised on an international level.

Criticising Heads of State remained a major issue in the 1850s, when several French opponents of the new French emperor, Napoleon III, escaped to Brussels, and started a hate campaign against him. The French government then urged the Belgian government to handle these opponents with force, all the while threaten-

---

[18] T. Luykx, "Over de orangistische pers in België", in *Album Prof. Dr. K. Baschwitz* (Amsterdam, 1956) 12–25.

[19] The law is still in force.

[20] Article 3 of the Press Decree required that the insulting of the King happened malevolently.

[21] B. Delbecke, "Verlekkerd op geitenmelk en een kalkoenhoedster. Over de ontstaansgeschiedenis van de wet van 6 april 1847", *Pro Memorie. Bijdragen tot de rechtsgeschiedenis van de Nederlanden* 2005, 7, 115–131.

ing military action. The Belgian government yielded quickly by passing the law of 20 December 1852 which forbade insulting foreign Heads of State. Nevertheless, the French government still kept complaining because every time Napoleon III was insulted by the Belgian press, the French government had to lodge a complaint. This problem was resolved by the law of 21 March 1858 introducing the possibility of an *ex officio* procedure.[22]

After these amendments, Belgian press law was not varied for a time. Some proposals were introduced when the Penal Code was revised in 1867, but the chapters concerning press law were deleted and postponed until the press law as a whole could be revised – which never happened. It was the violent wave of strikes in 1886 which urged the Belgian government again to adjust its penal and press law. Based on the writings of the leaders of the socialist movement, such as Edward Anseele and Alfred Defuisseaux, the government considered public incitement a threat to Belgian society, whether it had criminal effect or not. The temporary law (valid for three years) of 23 August 1887 forbade every incitement of a list of criminal acts which were directly linked to the events of the strike of 1886, such as the destruction of steam machines or telegraph lines. Although this law was barely enforced, the Belgian government still feared public provocation and continued this statute with the law of 25 March 1891, together with an expansion of the list of crimes.[23]

These amendments are of the utmost importance for one's understanding of the role of the Belgian press and its freedom in the 19th century. But perhaps the most striking evolution in press law was jurisprudential. It soon became clear that the jury system was far more a burden than a blessing. Jury trials were long, expensive, inefficient, and their judgments were often considered highly capricious. So solutions were sought. In matters of calumny, slander, or defamation, all of which constituted the vast majority of press trials, a more flexible alternative was found in the civil action of indemnification, based on Article 1382 of the Civil Code (general tort provision). This route was finally approved by the Court of Cassation in 1863.[24] But this jurisprudence sparked profound discussion, with numerous legal scholars stating that this was contrary to the spirit of the Constitution, which had subjected every press crime to a jury. This led to a remarkable initiative in the Belgian Parliament, where some members proposed changing the procedure by requiring a preliminary judgment of the jury stating whether the text was calumnious or not. After several attempts, the proposal was eventually turned down in 1879.

As stated above, the rules of the Constitution concerning the freedom of the press were a reaction to the repressive Dutch press regime. As evidence of this re-

---

[22] T. Luykx, "Negentiende–eeuwse pers–processen en hun invloed op de Belgische perswetgeving", in *Actuele problemen rond krant, radio en T.V.* (Gent: Story–Scientia, 1967) 30–42. These laws have recently been abandoned by the law of 13 February 2005.

[23] See B. Delbecke, "Les émeutes de 1886 et la participation criminelle. La provocation publique des lois du 23 août 1887 et du 25 mars 1891", *Revue du Nord* 2007, 215–216. This law too is still in force.

[24] Cass. 24 January 1863.

pression, the 1831 partisans of press freedom often referred to the fact that of more than 50 press trials, only one trial took place in the North of the United Kingdom of the Netherlands. Although little is known about the number of press trials that were held during the 19th century, nevertheless this number still by far exceeds the number of trials during the Dutch period. To give an example: 36 press crimes were brought to the Assise Court of Brabant in the period between 1831 and 1847.[25] The limits on the freedom of the press were not only a matter of restrictive laws with a highly symbolic character, it was also a matter of effective judicial repression.

4 Liberty, Identity, and their Mutual Limits: The Discourse on the Freedom of the Press in 19th Century Belgium

As seen above, the freedom of the press was restricted several times, especially when the Belgian society or its institutional pillars were challenged or threatened. Nevertheless, during the 19th century, the debates on the freedom that dominated the discussions of the constitutional assembly was generally continued.[26]

Maintaining this discourse meant that the specific position of the freedom of the press amongst other political and civil liberties remained an extremely popular theme. The freedom of the press was considered the crowning moment of the Constitution. Together with the freedom of public worship[27], the freedom of education[28] and the freedom of public meetings[29], it was seen as one of the four elementary liberties which were necessary to give a Nation its absolute freedom. One can say that, during the 19th century, nationalist discourse paralleled the identification of the Belgian Nation with the existence of an age–long tradition of civil and political liberties. The Constitution was considered the ultimate confirmation of these Belgian customs and usages. Hence, it was called ‘august’, ‘eternal’, ‘indestructible’, ‘generous’, and so on, and was consequently stressed as the alpha and omega of the Belgian tradition of liberties. Moreover, this belief led to a cult of the Constitution and its creator, the National Congress. In discussions on the several adaptations to constitutional civil and political liberties, the Congress was constantly called the great benefactor of Belgium. 19th century Belgium was ex-

---

25 M. Debaere, *l.c.*, 109.

26 An excellent example of this discourse can be found in the speeches of public prosecutor Charles Faider. See B. Delbecke, “Gerechtelijke nationale cultuur en haar blinde vlek. De mercuriales en gelegenheidsredes van Charles Faider bij het Hof van Cassatie”, *Tijdschrift voor rechtsgeschiedenis* 2007, *75*, 363–394.

27 Article 17 Constitution (now Article 19).

28 Article 18 Constitution (now Article 24).

29 Article 19 Constitution (now Article 26).

tremely grateful to the constitutional assembly and continually praised its merits. This cult even had material exponents, such as statues and processions.[30]

Although there was a great variety of constitutional liberties, they all fit in the same framework because they were supported by the unity of the Belgian Nation. In the post–Napoleonic age of Nations, the Belgian Nation thought of itself as a Nation ahead of the other European Nations, due to the benefits of the Constitution. This opinion was considered corroborated by facts. Since 1831, the prosperity of the Belgian Nation was said to be proven by various material exponents: new monuments were raised everywhere in the country, new and modern harbours were the gates to the world, trade and industry expanded, schools, railroads, and such like were built, and so on. A perfect example is the study of the famous magistrate Charles Faider, who published his *Étude sur la statistique nationale* in 1865. In his statistics, he expressed the steadily growing degree of intellectual activity and material prosperity. His conclusions were an almost euphoric expression of his belief in Belgium's brightest future.[31]

In this discourse about liberties, the organisation and the role of the Belgian justice played a significant role. The magistracy presented itself as the true guardian of the age–long tradition of liberties. The fundamental unity of the Belgian Nation was reflected in the pyramidal structure of the Belgian justice system, with the Court of Cassation at the top. Thanks to the profound understanding of what was called 'the palladium of Belgian liberties' by the Belgian judges, these liberties were preserved. Parallel to the historical characterisation of liberties, a similar age–long tradition of 'Belgian' magistrates was cherished.[32]

The 19th century Belgian discourse on the freedom of the press was an expression of the typical liberal belief in the power of the individual to develop himself and to turn his society into a perpetually improving environment. The extension of the discourse over the freedom of the press as a pure protection of the journalist as a political watchdog was the root of this belief. By repeating that the constitutional guarantee of criticising despotism and abuse of power would lead to a better society, the political characterisation of the freedom of the press was steadily stressed. It was the elite's projection of its own image of success. Nevertheless, the discourse remarkably ignored the press as a possible threat to society. Although amendments to press law were inspired by the concern to avoid 'dangerous' opinions, these restrictions were hardly mentioned. Freedom of the press was almost exclusively approached as a pure blessing, giving the Belgian Nation the greatest splendour. The august status of Belgian liberties was repeated again and again, until the end of the 1880s. The laws restricting the freedom of the press or the high rates of press trials, however, were hardly mentioned.

How can one explain the 19th century gap between the restrictions on the freedom of the press and the discourse on this liberty? Or, why was the way of talking

---

30 J. Janssens, *De Belgische natie viert. De nationale feesten 1830–1914* (Leuven: University Press, 2001) 47–56; R. Röttger, "Capitol and capital. Het 'moment Anspach' in de Brusselse urbanisatie en liberale politieke cultuur, 1860–1880", *Stadsgeschiedenis* 2006, *1*, 27–50.

31 C. Faider, *Étude sur la statistique nationale* (Brussels, 1865).

32 B. Delbecke, "Gerechtelijke nationale cultuur en haar blinde vlek", forthcoming.

about freedom of the press not in accordance with the way of dealing with the press? In fact, the legislator could never fully regulate the press and get a grip on its different forms of expression and content. A principal clue to these limits lay in the fact that in 1830–31, freedom of the press was conceived for a particular reason, as a guarantee against any form of governmental abuse of power, or as a protection of the journalist as a critic, a political watchdog. In reality, this was only one of many types of journalism. Most writers and journalists wrote occasionally or to have a little extra income. Because maximum civil liberties, with a well–guaranteed freedom of the press amongst them, was one of the cornerstones of the Belgian identity, giving up the freedom of the press meant giving up one of its own most fundamental reasons of existence. Due to this invented tradition, the Belgian Nation had to avoid that on the international level. The image of a free and happy Nation was not spoiled by the excesses of the several civil liberties. Paradoxally, maintaining the image of a free and highly civilised Nation with maximum liberty implied compensating this discourse by limiting this liberty. This process can only be understood as a Nation's pragmatic attitude to preserve its own identity and existence.

But the problem with maintaining the freedom of the press was not only about preserving the image of Belgium on an international level. One must have a closer look at the relationship between the rules concerning the freedom of the press as they were stated in 1831, and the ideals underlying these rules. The ideals that had supported the freedom of the press as conceived by the constitutional assembly proved to be the origin of its limits at the same time. It indicates the inherent difficulties of dealing with the so–called 'open texture' of the law[33], in this case the constitutional approach to the freedom of the press. The meaning of legal rules is never fully encapsulated in the words, but reveals itself in the way the rule is used, followed, interpreted or enforced. This implies that although the exact words of a rule remain the same, the interpretation might differ in time, which is exactly what happened concerning the freedom of the press in 19th century Belgium. However, this differentiation did not manifest itself in one exclusive way. One must be aware of the socio–economical differences between the several actors dealing with the press, its freedom, and its various aspects.

The ideals behind the constitutional rules proved to be internalised by an elite which dominated the political institutions as well as the public discourse during the 19th century. If the meaning behind the norm is a constructive element of the identity of Nation or society in need of approval and acknowledgement, manipulating the norm implies therefore manipulating that identity and therefore threatening its existence. The symbolic function of constitutional press legislation was far more important, presenting Belgium as a traditional but extremely liberal Nation, crowned with maximum protection to the freedom of speech and its most effective means, the press. Stressing its own specific, age–long liberal character, the Bel-

---

33 See E. Claes, W. Devroe, and B. Keirsbilck, "The Limits of the Law (Introduction)". The concept 'open texture' is developed in H.L.A. Hart, *The Concept of Law* (Oxford: Clarendon Press, 2nd ed., 1994) 128–136.

gian Nation–State constructed and maintained its own reason of existence and legitimation.

However, the elite which approached freedom of the press in the same way as the constitutional assembly did in 1831 was powerful but small. Most other people did not share the nationalist ideals of the elite in the same enthusiastic way. Consequently, these people did not fully grasp the point of the constitutional rules as outlined by the National Congress. The fact that in matters of slander or defamation a civil action of indemnification was far more popular than the penal jury trial, proves that the political and nationalist connotations to the freedom of the press were not shared by everyone. It proves the unpredictability of the effects of law, seeing how the constitutional assembly could not foresee how this freedom of the press would be interpreted during the 19th century. The various problems of dealing with the freedom of the press as it was organised in 1831 were the consequences of a gap between the 'constitutional' and idealist approach of the elite on the one hand, and the pragmatic attitude of most other people on the other. Most people did not or even could not participate in the many exponents to the celebration of the Constitution, because these manifestations were meant for a specific audience: the intellectual, political, industrial, and judicial top layer of Belgian society. As most people were significantly less confronted with the nationalist discourse, they did not share in it. The lack of internalisation of the constitutionalist ideals was therefore perhaps the most fundamental origin of the gap between practice and discourse.

The example of the success of the civil action is at the same time an excellent example to demonstrate that the antithesis between the selective elite and most other people should not be considered in a too absolute way. The previously quoted decision of the Court of Cassation in which the possibility of a civil action was accepted, was stated in favour of Charles Rogier, a famous liberal politician and one of the former leaders of the Belgian Revolution. Given this past, one might think that he was an ardent defender of the jury system. In 1847, he admonished those who disdained the jury and criticised the rise of a civil jurisprudence in press matters.[34] Nevertheless, when it really came to his own interests, he chose not to confront a jury with his own cases, but preferred a more certain civil action. Apparently, pragmatism was preferred over idealism. The decision of the Court of Cassation on this matter is therefore a good example of a so–called 'hard case' in which the meaning behind the words of a rule – in this case the Constitution – is challenged. This case is a good example of the conflict between the ideals as they were enunciated by the discourse, and the possibilities of a pragmatic approach. It indicates that contrasting the political elite as the partisans of the nationalist approach to the freedom of the press with the pragmatic approach of other people would therefore be sketching a caricature of the 19th century approach to this freedom.

---

34 *Annales Parlementaires de Belgique* (1846–47) 1279.

5 No More Heroes: The Changes to Freedom of the Press as a Result of an Evolving Perception of World and Mankind

The glorification of the freedom of the press and the nationalist discourse gradually faded away when social pressure grew at the end of the 19th century. After the violent strike of 1886, the freedom of the press was no more one of the striking constitutive elements of the Nation, but one of its possible cunning enemies. Liberties were gradually considered as possible dangers, easily leading to several forms of abuse which could profoundly harm the Belgian society.

The previously quoted laws of 1887 and 1891 on the prohibition of public provocation marked the rise of a new discourse. It was the discourse of social defense, a discourse of a Nation in need of rigid social control. By penalising public provocation even when no one had given consequence to it, the Belgian Parliament expressed a new view on the position of the individual in society. He was no longer considered an absolutely autonomous being, in total control of himself and fully responsible for his deeds and his actions. The 19th century liberal individualism became less prominent, and social determinist theories started to flourish. Against the background of the massive protest of the working class people against their poor social conditions, the minds of politicians, legal scholars, and social scientists changed. Man was no longer considered the absolute master of his thought and actions, so he was no longer exclusively responsible for them. On the contrary, politicians and intellectuals increasingly stressed the fact that individuals were mostly determinated by their social environment. This gradual turn in the perception of world and mankind was accompanied by the rise of the new concept of degeneration, pointing out that society was organic and composed of stronger and weaker parts. The optimism of rationalist ideals at the dawn of the 19th century changed into the pessimism of the *fin–de–siècle*, as it was expressed in, for example, the naturalist literature of Zola and the criminalist theories of Lombroso.[35]

This profound change of mentality is best shown in the late 19th century political discourse on strikes.[36] It was, however, also of great importance for the freedom of press and the freedom of speech in general, because it implied a new view on social as well as on criminal responsibility. By giving up individualist ideas, one gave up the ideals of the solitary critic or journalist who was blessed with the greatest constitutional guarantees to fight against any form of abuse. Writers and journalists were more and more considered instigators and intriguers, not criticising abuse of power or governmental conduct, but abusing themselves the social situation of the masses of the poor to disrupt society. As society was considered an organic whole, there was a fundamental need for prohibiting taking advantage of

---

35 D. Weber, *Homo criminalis. Belgische parlementsleden over misdaad en strafrecht* (Brussels: VUB Press, 1996) 15–22.

36 J. Deferme, "Alles strijdt, wat naar vrijheid haakt. Theorievorming over de staking in de Belgische politiek", *Bijdragen en Mededelingen betreffende de Geschiedenis der Nederlanden* 2002, *117*, 145–167.

the awkward position of the lowest social classes. It meant giving up the profound rationalist and individualist notions that once lay at the basis of constitutional ideals.

But one might also consider the fact that at the end of the 19th century, the position of the bourgeois class of intellectuals, industrials, and professionals in society had fundamentally changed. In 1830–31, their conquest of the Belgian Nation–State by adapting its rules and legislation to their own needs was an act of challenging the old structures of power which still dominated society. Fifty years later, they were no longer the challengers of society. To them, the structures of the *Ancien Régime* were no longer a threat, but only a vague and distant memory. By fully taking advantage of the political possibilities of the liberal Constitution, this bourgeoisie had managed to conquer the key positions of modern Belgian society. From then on, it was a matter of social control to maintain this situation. Besides, the Belgian Nation–State at the end of the 19th century was no longer in desperate need of legitimation before the rest of the world. Focusing on internal social problems had become the number–one priority.

6 Conclusion and Epilogue

In short, in 19th century Belgium, liberty and national identity profoundly influenced each other, but at the same time restricted their mutual possibilities. One might conclude that the history of the freedom of the press in 19th century Belgium is a fine example to demonstrate that the instrumentality of the rule of law can be profoundly limited by the ideals and the people who support them. Generally, the approach of the constitutional assembly to freedom of the press was the same approach by the new political and intellectual elite who had conquered the key positions in modern Belgian society. The curious mechanism of interaction between the symbolic and the instrumental function of the law and their mutual limiting is not peculiar to 19th century Belgium. It is a pattern which can be discovered in various Nation–States which, in their quest for a modern and liberal national identity, always somehow seem to try to limit the freedoms and liberties used to construct and maintain these identities. These mechanisms can be found in 19th century liberal Nation–States, but are still applied nowadays. It is interesting to see how these mechanisms still function in some States who intend to join the western tradition of modernity and liberalism. The *ratio* is the same. Because they are trying to represent themselves as modern Nations guaranteeing civil liberties and freedoms, they have difficulties tolerating critical expressions who spoil this image of modernity and tolerance.

A particular example is the current way of dealing with freedom of speech and freedom of the press in Turkey. This freedom is anchored in Article 26 of the 1982 Turkish Constitution. As a member of the Council of Europe, Turkey ratified in 1954 the European Convention on Human Rights, whose Article 10 guarantees freedom of speech. Since Ataturk, Turkey has been presenting itself as a modern and liberal Nation–State. However, although Turkey has been emphasising its modern identity, the past decades have shown that the Turkish authorities did not hesitate to stop writers and journalists criticising the policy of the government. Sensitive topics include the position of the Kurdish minority or the way of dealing with the memory of the genocide against the Armenian people by the Turkish authorities in 1915. Journalists and writers, amongst whom is Nobel Prize winner Orhan Pamuk, were prosecuted for having offended the identity of Turkey. Most prosecutions were based upon Article 301 of the Turkish Criminal Code[37] that outlaws insulting the Turkish identity. Others were easily considered incitements to terrorist attacks. It seems that in the opinion of the Turkish authorities, insulting Turkishness is about everything that does not match the image they keep of themselves. Therefore, even the way of spelling a word was considered an insult.[38] One can discover the same process in the history of the freedom of the press in 19th century Belgium. Turkish identity is based on liberal premises on the one hand, but at the same time this identity is rigidly maintained by limiting the civil liberties which are fundamental part of this identity. Expression which does not match the picture of one modern and homogeneous Nation–State are not tolerated, but the discourse keeps on stressing the modern and liberal character of the Nation.

However, it is not unlikely that this process of limiting the freedom of the press will come to an end in the near future, or at least will be eased. The European Court of Human Rights (ECtHR) has stated several times that Turkey has violated freedom of speech, stressing the obligation to install a more liberal press regime. Nevertheless, this did not result in a profound change of the press regime. Despite the decisions of the ECtHR, Turkish authorities have not tolerated dissident or critical opinions. But things have changed since Turkey began negotiating with the European Union (EU) in order to be accepted as a Member State. The EU emphasises repeatedly tolerance towards dissident opinions as a necessary condition for entry into the EU. Therefore, the prospect of economic prosperity will probably force the Turkish government to liberalise its press policy. As a matter of fact, a more liberal press law is being fashioned and the rules about the freedom of speech in the anti–terrorism legislation are being liberalised too. It is rather ironic that Europe and the western world, which is in some way the addressee of the Turkish liberal discourse and one of the reasons for its repressive press policy, is compelling Turkey to cut back these limiting measures. It indicates that the limits of the (rule of) law are never fixed concepts. They are determined by the range of tension between idealism and opportunism, and evolve in accordance with the ever changing political and social context.

---

37 Article 159 of the former Criminal Code.

38 In October 2005, a procedure was started to forbid the Kurdish organisation Diyarbakir. One of the reasons for this procedure, was the 'un–Turkish' way of spelling Kurdish in the name and the statutes of the organisation.

Chapter 18 – Privacy Rights as Human Rights: No Limits?[1]

Aagje Ieven

1 Introduction

The concept of privacy has often been criticised for its vagueness. However, its notorious 'open texture'[2] is also its strength: thanks to the inherent vagueness of the concept, privacy – as a human right – has been able to maintain its capacity to remedy emerging limits to law's regulating function in response to profound political, social and economic changes, and enormous technological progress. Take for example the case–law regarding the European Convention on Human Rights (hereinafter, the ECHR or the Convention). The rise of modern technology with its sophisticated devices for surveillance and information storage urged a heightened sensitivity to intrusions upon personality rights and informational privacy. The European Court of Human Rights (hereinafter, the ECtHR or the Court) reacted by broadening its interpretation of 'private life', protected by Article 8 of the ECHR, so as to include these new forms of interference. When the secularisation of society and the ensuing increase in moral freedom of the individual encouraged claims of decisional freedom under the label of private life, these also met with success when tested before the Court. It stipulated that privacy rights protect free choice in sexual relationships[3] and ensure legal recognition of one's sex change.[4] The Court even found that the right to choose the circumstances of one's own death could be said to fall under the scope of 'private life'.[5] Open texture and the judicial interpretation necessitated by it, were indeed the driving forces behind the development of the right to be left alone into a right to control over personal information and to live life according to one's own choice.[6] Thus, privacy rights as human rights were able to fill in the gaps where national privacy laws had failed to regulate, and they stimulated new national legislation.

---

1 The author would like to express her thanks to all the participants in the seminar 'Limits of the Law' held in Leuven, 2006. She is particularly grateful to Erik Claes, René Foqué, Bert Keirsbilck and Willem Verrijdt for useful comments on the draft she presented there. Additional research and the final drafting of the chapter took place during a research visit at Columbia University's Center for the Study of Human Rights funded by the Fulbright Program.

2 See E. Claes, W. Devroe, and B. Keirsbilck, "The Limits of the Law (Introduction)".

3 ECtHR, 22 October 1981, *Dudgeon v United Kingdom*. All judgments of the ECtHR can be found under HUDOC on www.echr.coe.int.

4 ECtHR, 11 July 2002, *Christine Goodwin v United Kingdom*.

5 ECtHR, 29 April 2002, *Pretty v United Kingdom*.

6 See E. Claes, W. Devroe, and B. Keirsbilck, "The Limits of the Law (Introduction)".

This does not mean, however, that there are no limits to privacy rights as human rights. The features of open texture and the ensuing necessity of judicial interpretation can, and have in some cases, compromise(d) another function of privacy rights, their most important function as human rights: the protective, power–critical function.[7] My aim in this chapter will therefore be, first, to explore how judges' implicit views on the judicial interpretation of open textured legal concepts affect these protective limits and, second, to offer pathways for a remedy to those limits.

To begin with, a study of judicial interpretations of privacy rights under Article 8 ECHR will be undertaken, showing the limits to the Convention's protection of privacy rights. The next section will argue that the limits to Article 8's protective capacity can, at least partly, be attributed to the Court's minimalist practice of interpretation (section 2), which corresponds to a positivist perspective on human rights (section 3). Ways in which a change in philosophical perspective might be able to remedy the protective limits of human rights law will therefore be explored.[8] An alternative, constructivist perspective on human rights, in the neo–Kantian tradition of authors like Rawls, Habermas, and Dworkin, will be proposed and its general features outlined (section 4). Finally, I will try to show how the constructivist perspective allows for more generous, power–critical judicial interpretations of the privacy rights protected by the Convention and how this would influence the concrete outcome of certain cases (section 5).

2 Open Texture and Judicial Interpretation of Article 8 ECHR

2.1 The Margin of Appreciation Doctrine

Article 8 states the following:

> 1. Everyone has the right to respect for his private and family life, his home and correspondence.
>
> 2. There shall be no interference by a public authority with the exercise of this right except such as is in accordance with the law and is necessary in a democratic society in the interests of national security, public safety or the economic well–being of the country, for the prevention of disorder or crime, for the protection of health or morals, or for the protection of the rights and freedoms of others.

As shown above, the open texture and judicial interpretation of the term 'private life' in the first paragraph were key to its success in remedying the protective limits of law. The second paragraph, however, leaves room for interpretation as well. Generally, the requirements that State interference is to be in accordance with the law and in the interest of one of the public goals listed, are quite clear and not too

7 *Ibid.*

8 *Ibid.*

difficult to satisfy. Very often, then, the Court's assessment of the legitimacy of interference rests on the interpretation of what is 'necessary in a democratic society'. On the basis of this phrase, the Court developed the margin of appreciation doctrine, which holds that:

> By reason of their direct and continuous contact with the vital forces of their countries, State authorities are in principle in a better position than the international judge to give an opinion on the exact content of these requirements as well as on the 'necessity' of a 'restriction' or 'penalty' intended to meet them.[9]

Therefore States enjoy a 'margin of appreciation' in determining the necessity of certain measures and restrictions, while the Court exercises marginal control over this decision. The way in which the Court uses this control, and in which it has thus interpreted 'necessity in a democratic society', has attracted plenty of criticism: the Court applies the margin inconsistently; exercises less than rigid control, and never discusses what exactly the notion of a 'democratic society' entails.[10] That, on top of all this, the Court's interpretation of paragraph 2 limits the protective capacity of privacy rights as human rights, is what the following case studies are to illustrate.

2.2 The Margin of Appreciation and the Limits of Privacy Rights as Human Rights

2.2.1 Chapman v UK

In the case of Chapman, a Gypsy woman and her family were prohibited from living in a caravan on land she owned, because her occupation of it violated the environmental rights of others. This interfered with both her family and private life, the Court said, since it prevented her from living according to her traditional life–style. A margin of appreciation was left to local authorities in assessing the necessity of the interference, as they were "better placed ... to evaluate local needs and conditions."[11] This margin was to be wide, because planning decisions involved "a multitude of local factors" and therefore the Court would mainly examine the availability of procedural safeguards to the individual.[12] The applicant's argument

---

9 ECtHR, 7 December 1976, *Handyside v the United Kingdom.*

10 Y. Arai–Takahashi, "The Margin of Appreciation Doctrine in the Jurisprudence of Article 8 of the European Convention on Human Rights", *Netherlands Quarterly of Human Rights* 1997, *16*, 41, 61; A. McHarg, "Reconciling Human Rights and the Public Interest: Conceptual Problems and Doctrinal Uncertainty in the Jurisprudence of the European Court of Human Rights", *MLR* 1999, *62*, 671, 687; C. Ovey and R. White, *European Convention on Human Rights* (Oxford: Oxford University Press, 3rd ed., 2002) 210; P. Mahoney, "Judicial Activism and Judicial Self–Restraint in the European Court of Human Rights: Two Sides of the Same Coin", *HRLJ* 1990, *11*, 57; and D. Feldman, "The Developing Scope of Article 8" *EHRLR* 1997, *3*.

11 ECtHR, 18 January 2001, *Chapman v United Kingdom*, §§ 90–91.

12 *Ibid.*, § 92, citing ECtHR, 25 September 1996, *Buckley v United Kingdom*, § 75.

that the emerging international consensus on the need for special protection of Gypsies (embodied in the Framework Convention of the Protection of National Minorities) should narrow down the margin of appreciation, was dismissed on the ground that the consensus was not sufficiently concrete as "the signatory States were unable to agree on the means of implementation." On the basis of its examination of the decision procedure (rather than its unfortunate result) the Court determined that the authorities had not overstepped their margin of appreciation.

2.2.2 Hatton v UK

In the 2001 *Hatton* case, a Chamber of the Court extended the already recognised environmental rights under Article 8 to include the protection of citizens against noise nuisance.[13] Excessive noise from nightly flights arriving and departing from a nearby airport disturbed Mr. Hatton's sleep and interfered with his personal life in a thoroughgoing way. Despite the margin of appreciation, the Court deemed that

> in the absence of any serious attempt to evaluate the extent or impact of the interferences (…) and generally in the absence of a prior specific and complete study with the aim of finding the least onerous solution as regards human rights

it could not agree that the Government had struck the right balance between Mr Hatton's right to private life and the economic interests of the country.[14] The case was referred to the Grand Chamber, which instead found that national authorities, with direct democratic legitimation, are better placed to evaluate local needs and that in matters of general policy, the margin of appreciation available to the domestic policy–makers should be a wide one.[15] It viewed its own role as limited to "reviewing whether or not the particular solution adopted can be regarded as striking a fair balance"[16], rather than the least onerous one. No violation was found this time around.

2.3.3 Fretté v France

In the case of *Fretté v France*, the Court accepted that the French refusal to authorise adoption by a homosexual man constituted an interference with his private life.[17] Lacking a consensus between State Parties on these "delicate issues", the Court considered it "quite natural" that a wide margin of appreciation was left to local authorities.[18] It also referred to the inconclusive evidence regarding possi-

---

13 ECtHR, 9 December 1994, *López Ostra v Spain*; ECtHR, 19 February 1996, *Guerra and others v Italy*. ECtHR, 2 October 2001, *Hatton v UK*.

14 ECtHR, 2 October 2001, *Hatton v UK*, § 107.

15 ECtHR, 7 August 2003, *Hatton v UK*, § 97.

16 *Ibid.*, § 123, my emphasis.

17 ECtHR, 26 February 2002, *Fretté v France*.

18 *Ibid.*, § 41.

ble consequences of adoption by homosexuals, which, combined with the too small number of children eligible for adoption to satisfy demand, was sufficient reason to exclude homosexuals as prospective adoptive parents. The Court did not even criticise the fact that, lacking conclusive scientific evidence, the French authorities had excluded homosexuals on the basis of prejudice alone.

2.3.4 The Limits of Human Rights Law

In each of these cases, the Court's interpretation of 'necessity in a democratic society' in such a way as to leave States a wide margin of appreciation where general policy or general morality are concerned, amounts to a lack of redress for vulnerable individuals whose private lives have been disrupted quite thoroughly. It seems the Court is not keen on playing the role of pioneer in protecting the interests and rights of minority group members and vulnerable individuals against the power of numbers, economy or general morality. It hides behind the margin of appreciation so as not to make that too explicit. This constitutes a clear limit to the protective, power–critical function of privacy rights as human rights. The question is why the Court would allow this.

2.4 The Margin of Appreciation and Minimalist Judicial Interpretation

2.4.1 Arguments for the Margin of Appreciation Doctrine

One explanation is that, because of its institutional structure, the effectiveness of Convention rights depends on the voluntary subjection of the Council of Europe Member States to the legal order of the ECHR.[19] Therefore the Court must maintain their confidence, which could explain why it feels that it can only expand the protection afforded by the Convention by slow and cautious progress on a case–by–case basis, depending on consensus.[20]

At the same time, the Court's interpretation of paragraph 2 points to a deeper conviction about the limited role of a court in a democracy. The Court feels it is ill–placed to assess the complex local factors that influence policy decisions[21], but another reason why it prefers to leave these intact is that "national authorities have direct democratic legitimation"[22] whereas the Court does not. When Protocol No. 11 judicialised the Convention's international control machinery and abolished the

---

19 See P. Mahoney (1990), *l.c.*

20 This explains why it often expands its interpretation of private life under the first paragraph in cases where it will not find a violation due to a wide margin of appreciation afforded under the second paragraph. My thanks to Erik Claes for useful discussion on this point.

21 As it did in the Chapman case for example.

22 ECtHR, 7 August 2003, *Hatton v UK*, § 97.

adjudicative role of the Committee of Ministers, the President of the Court stressed how important he considered this completion of the institutional separation between democratic powers.[23]

2.4.2 Minimalism

The concerns underlying the use of the margin of appreciation are indications of the Court's implicit view on judicial interpretation, one which closely resembles judicial minimalism. In his *One Case at a Time. Judicial Minimalism on the Supreme Court*[24], Cass Sunstein describes a pervasive practice within the US Supreme Court of "doing and saying as little as is necessary in order to justify an outcome."[25] He names several justices who "embrace minimalism ... for reasons connected with their conception of the role of the Supreme Court in American government."[26]

In general, minimalist decisions are narrow rather than wide, which means they try to decide only the case at hand and avoid determining the outcome of other/future cases[27], which corresponds to the Court's reluctance to contest policy decisions. Moreover, they are shallow rather than deep: "they attempt to reach incompletely theorised agreements" whenever there is a "possibility of concrete judgments on particular cases, unaccompanied by abstract accounts about what accounts for these judgments."[28] This ties in with the Court's use of the margin of appreciation to 'hide' its real reasons for not finding a violation.

Minimalist judges favour open–ended standards over strict rules, consider the possible consequences an important factor in their decisions and prefer flexibility and effectiveness to predictability, among others. As we have seen, the ECtHR's interpretation of Article 8, paragraph 2 is also inspired by concerns about possible consequences (losing the allegiance of Member States) and the effectiveness of the protection of Convention rights.

Sunstein also argues that minimalism can promote democracy.[29] By saying no more than strictly necessary, it leaves issues open for political discussion. Moreover it can actively enhance deliberative democracy by promoting reason–giving and accountability on the legislative and executive branches, who have to answer to their electorate. Minimalist rulings, settling as little as possible, can serve as a "'remand' to the public, alerting people to the existence of hard issues of principle

---

23 Speech by Mr Luzius Wildhaber, President of the European Court of Human Rights, at the "Solemn hearing of the European Court of Human Rights on the occasion of the opening of the judicial year", held on 21 January 2005. See www.echr.coe.int (last visited 30 May 2007).

24 C. Sunstein, *One Case at a Time. Judicial Minimalism on the Supreme Court* (Cambridge, Mass.: Harvard University Press, 1999).

25 *Ibid.*, 3.

26 *Ibid.*, 9.

27 *Ibid.*, 10.

28 *Ibid.*, 11–13.

29 *Ibid.*, 5.

and policy."[30] The ECtHR shares this view on the necessity of a strict separation of powers in a democratic society and on the limited role of a Court therein.[31]

3 The Positivist Perspective

So minimalism fits the adjudication of the ECtHR much in the way it does that of the US Supreme Court. In this section, I will argue that the minimalist reasoning behind the Court's use of the margin of appreciation points to an underlying positivist perspective on law. This perspective will be contrasted with the alternative of constructivism, which holds other ideas on judicial interpretation and has different implications for the protective, power–critical function of human rights law.[32]

3.1 The Separation of Law and Morality and a New Source of Validity

For a long time now, legal positivism has been the ruling theory of law[33] and in the debate on human rights, too, it is widely considered "the only important alternative to the natural law interpretation of human rights."[34] It no longer looks for an independent, *a priori* source of validity (like a higher authority or a natural order) and rejects the idea that moral rights are 'givens' from which legal rights derive. In contrast, positivism's separation thesis holds that law and morality are logically distinct from one another and thus it must turn to a different source of validity. For a positivist, whether or not a law is valid depends upon the way it has come into existence. In early versions of legal positivism, like Bentham's and Austin's, this takes place through a command by the sovereign. More recent versions of legal positivism argue that the validity of positive law depends upon convention, on actual agreements between actual people. Positivism's most prominent advocate of late, Herbert Hart, argued that a legal norm is valid if it can be determined to have come into existence in a way that is considered and accepted to be valid within a

---

30 *Ibid.*, 135.

31 Much could be said about the Court's rather limited view of democracy and in part, the loss in the protective function could be remedied by articulating a more elaborate view of deliberative democracy – see my "Privacy Rights in Conflict", in E. Brems (ed.), *Conflicts between Fundamental Rights* (Intersentia, forthcoming). Thanks to René Foqué for useful discussion on this point. In this chapter however, I concentrate on the remedies provided by and alternative perspective on law.

32 See E. Claes, W. Devroe, and B. Keirsbilck, *l.c.*

33 R. Dworkin, *Taking Rights Seriously* (Cambridge: Harvard University Press, 1978) vii.

34 G. Ulrich, "Universal Human Rights: An Unfinished Project", in K. Hastrup (ed.), *Human Rights on Common Grounds: The Quest for Universality* (Kluwer, 2001) 195–223, 205.

certain legal system. If this is the case, the legal norm is treated as a positive, social fact, exempt from the need for on–going justification.[35]

Can human rights be treated as such? For that to be the case, there has to be an international legal system within which there is agreement on what is a valid way for international legal norms to come into existence.

The Vienna Convention on the Law of Treaties of 27 January 1980 regulates the conclusion, entry into force, observance, application, interpretation, amendment, modification, invalidity, termination, and suspension of international treaties, namely international agreements between two or more sovereign States governed by international law. This Convention consolidates the existence of an international legal system as well as the system's internal validity criteria. It lies down the rule that validity of an international legal norm rests upon a State's consent (Article 9) and identifies the persons who can legitimately act for a State in granting that consent (Article 7). The Vienna Convention thus stipulates a positivist criterion of validity as convention – and as the Vienna Convention applies to the ECHR and the Court regularly refers to it in its adjudication, positivism permeates the Court's view on law as well.

3.2 The Separation of Law and Politics: Autonomous Law

Whereas for natural law theory, positive law as well as political power originate in an independent source of natural law, positivism strictly defines and separates politics and law. The law determines form and procedure: it tells us who has the power to make law and how they should do it in order for new laws to be legitimate. The controversy over law's content, and the political power struggle relating to it, is seen as separate. The legal discipline becomes an 'objective' and specialised field of study and distinctively legal institutions (like courts) emerge which specialise in the certification of legitimisation.[36]

While on the international level a legal system is gradually emerging, the differentiation and separation between law and politics is far from complete. Especially in the area of human rights the tasks of interpretation, application and enforcement of norms remain largely with political organs. The United Nations' human rights protection system is completely informed by the balancing of political powers and depends on diplomatic pressure for its enforcement.

The separation between politics and the law has perhaps most fully taken place in the institutional structure surrounding the ECHR. The Convention system incorporates a legislative (the Council of Europe), an executive (the Committee of Ministers) as well as a judicial body (the ECtHR). The aforementioned Protocol 11 completed this separation by installing a fully judicialised protection system in the form of a permanent, professional Court which took on the sole adjudicative

---

35 *Ibid.*

36 P. Nonet and P. Selznick, *Law and Society in Transition: Toward Responsive Law* (New York: Harper Colophon, 1978) 56.

role (previously shared with the Committee of Ministers). With this new Court emerged an 'expertocracy' apt to legitimate State power.

Mr. Luzius Wildhaber, former President of the Court, has said that:

> ... the fact that the EU Constitutional Treaty provides ... for the accession of the EU to the Strasbourg Convention System powerfully demonstrates how important it has become today for the credibility of action by public authorities to allow external judicial control over their compliance with human rights standards.[37]

This illustrates, first, how the Court indeed draws a sharp line between its métier and that of politicians and, second, how important it considers this separation for its legitimising role. The fact that the doctrine of the margin of appreciation rests partly on a perceived necessity of strict separation between law–making and policy–making, as demonstrated in the previous section, also testifies of the Court's view of law as autonomous.

3.3 Statism and Sovereignty

Article 9 of the Vienna Convention points to States, or their representatives as determined by Article 7, as the endorsers of a validating convention. The bulk, if not all, existing international law has indeed come about either through States' signing, ratifying, and observing treaties and conventions, or their observing certain implicit rules of conduct which then become customary law. Thus, a positivist perspective on law will be inclined towards the doctrine of statism.[38] This doctrine holds that sovereign States are the relevant actors in the international legal field and the principal subjects of theories of international law. It builds on the notion of sovereignty, which entails that a State effectively in control of its citizens and territory can freely regulate its internal affairs and can, on its own grounds, choose to be bound by an international convention.

While statism is indeed a predominant feature of international law, in human rights it provides for a paradoxical situation. Human rights are typically accorded to individuals, but their validity rests upon agreements between States and in most human rights documents these States are still considered as the primary subjects of petition rights. This makes States at once the most important protectors and the most likely violators of individual human rights.

The 11th Protocol to the ECHR made the right to individual petition automatic and mandatory for every State Party to the Convention. This solves the lack of remedies for violations of human rights inflicted upon individuals by their own States. Nevertheless there is still a concern for State Parties' continued support for the Convention and this plays a large part in the Court's minimalist interpretation

---

37 L. Wildhaber, *l.c.*

38 For an instructive discussion of statism, sovereignty and non–intervention, see F. Tesón, *A Philosophy of International Law* (Colorado: Westview, 1998) 39. My definition of statism is based on his account.

of the rights embodied in the Convention. At the core of the margin of appreciation doctrine is the idea that States are sovereign and their allegiance and trust necessary to maintain the effectiveness of the rights protected by the Convention.

3.4 Positivism and the Protective, Power–Critical Function of Law

Now that it is clear how the Court's minimalism is inspired by a positivist perspective on human rights, the link between this perspective and the loss in protective function must be made.

First of all, it is because of the Court's adherence to the separation between law and morality and to validity as convention that a loss in the protective function of Article 8 occurs. In morally sensitive cases, like that of *Fretté v France*, it affords a wide margin of appreciation to local authorities unless there is a broad international consensus and positive law in most State Parties is in fact on the same line. In other words, the Court's adherence to validity as convention causes a loss of protection for those who go against conventional morality.

Secondly, the Court's deference to local authorities in 'policy cases', like Hatton and Chapman, flows from its positivist view on the relation between law and politics. Consistent with the idea that its role pertains to the procedural aspects of law only, the Court in these cases did not review the content of privacy–restricting measures or look for the solution least restrictive of human rights. Rather, it asked whether the applicant's views were sufficiently taken into account throughout the decision procedures and whether *a* fair balance had been struck. Obviously a loss of protection occurs between *the* fairest and *a* fair balance, as becomes very clear from the difference in outcome between the 2001 and 2003 judgments in the *Hatton* case.

A third way in which the Court's positivist perspective leads to a decrease in protection afforded by Article 8, is the statism that comes with it. As the allegiance of the Member States is needed for the effectiveness of the Convention, the Court will not easily offend States and will generally afford them a wide margin of appreciation. This reasoning probably applies to all three of the cases described above. In this way, however, privacy rights as human rights do lose their power–critical function: those in power get to decide which rights are granted and thus rights no longer set limits to what those in power can demand from or do to individual citizens or vulnerable minorities.

4 The Constructivist Perspective

All of this prompts the question of whether positivism is the only viable alternative to natural law theory for grounding human rights. I argue that there is at least one other perspective which does away with natural law theory's metaphysical assumptions and which offers better prospects for the protective function of privacy rights as human rights. This alternative view is constructivism, a perspective that is steadily gaining popularity in the human rights debate and whose principal proponents are John Rawls, Jürgen Habermas, and Ronald Dworkin.[39] This section will concern the questions of how constructivism (at least the Rawlsian version presented here) does away with natural law's metaphysical assumptions without reverting to validity as convention and of how it differs from positivism in the two other aspects which make that view vulnerable to loss in the protective function of human rights.

4.1 Validity without Metaphysical Assumptions, Validity beyond Convention

In the face of a plurality of irreconcilable religious, philosophical and moral doctrines, constructivism as a perspective on human rights does not present itself as a 'comprehensive moral doctrine' governing every aspect of human life.[40] It limits its scope of application to the question of legitimisation of political power and presents itself as a 'political conception of rights'. But despite this turn away from metaphysical foundations, and in contrast to positivism, constructivism holds that objective, universal justification of human rights norms is feasible.

To this end, it does not seek validity in actual convention, as positivism does, but, in tradition with social contract theory, in hypothetical agreements about the rules governing the political institutions which define rights and duties. If, under certain conditions, reasonable people could be expected, in all reasonableness, to agree on a set of rights they ought to grant one another, these rights can be considered objectively and universally valid.

---

39 Both Rawls and Habermas refer to Kant as their source of inspiration, while Ronald Dworkin, in turn, cites Rawls as a source for his foundation for a theory of rights. Other proponents of what I have dubbed constructivism are Ingram, Tesón, Donnelly and Scanlon, among others, J. Rawls, *A Theory of Justice* (Cambridge, Mass.: Harvard University Press, 2nd ed., 2001); *Political Liberalism* (New York: Columbia University Press, 2nd ed., 1996); J. Habermas, *Between Facts and Norms. Contributions to a Discourse Theory of Law and Democracy* (Cambridge: Polity Press, 1996); "Remarks on Legitimation Through Human Rights", *Philosophy and Social Criticism* 1998, *24*, 157; R. Dworkin (1978), *l.c.*; A. Ingram, *A Political Theory of Rights* (Oxford: Clarendon, 1994); F. Tesón, *l.c.*; J. Donnelly, *Universal Human Rights in Theory and Practice* (Ithaca: Cornell University Press, 2nd ed., 2003); T.M. Scanlon, *What We Owe to Each Other* (Cambridge, Mass.: Harvard University Press, 1998).

40 J. Rawls, *Justice as Fairness. A Restatement* (Cambridge, Mass.: Belknap Press, 2001) 14.

'Under certain conditions', because the hypothetical nature of the sought agreement or contract makes it possible for constructivism to stipulate conditions as to the situation (sometimes called the 'initial situation') in which agreement must be reached. Constructivism contends that every reasonable person who would find herself in this initial situation and repeat the procedure of reasoning according to the conditions laid out, would come to similar conclusions. Thus the initial situation produces an agreement in outcomes[41], and this unanimity creates objective, universal validity. For the constructivist, then, X is a right if all persons under the conditions of the initial situation can reasonably agree that X is a right.

4.2 The Moral Basis of Rights and Statism

In the Rawlsian version of constructivism, the conditions imposed upon the initial situation are well–known under the name of the 'original position'. In the original position, contractors have general knowledge, but they are placed under a so–called 'veil of ignorance', which obscures any knowledge about particulars, such as their place in society, class position, social status, natural assets and abilities, intelligence, strength, race or gender.[42] One is not even aware of one's own character, ideas of what is good or valuable, or life–plans. In this way, contractors are equal in their relative ignorance and in their inability to negotiate a contract that will privilege them.

These preconditions are not randomly chosen. At the basis of the construction of the legitimating procedure is the idea of our moral nature as potentially autonomous human beings. On the constructivists' view, human rights are what we owe to each other if this capacity for autonomy is to be realised.[43] It is thus both the basis for and the projected outcome of human rights and any framework for human rights must therefore be justified in relation to it. This is done by constructing the initial situation in such a way as to embody the notions of freedom and equality as the original position does through the veil of ignorance.

There is a connection between morality and human rights law then, if the moral conception of personal autonomy is at the basis of human rights and if that is what human rights are to bring about. If constructivism is serious about the rejection of moral realism, this basis of rights cannot originate from an independent moral reality or "depend on a particular comprehensive moral doctrine or philosophical

---

41 A. Ingram (1994), *l.c.*, 119.

42 J. Rawls (1999), *l.c.*, 11 and 118–123.

43 J. Donnelly (2003), *l.c.*, 14. I will not go into the specifics of the notion of autonomy or the capacity for autonomy here, as it would digress too far. For an elaborate discussion of liberal notions of autonomy as a basis for rights, see A. Ingram (1994), *l.c.*, especially Chapter 5 "The Moral Basis of Rights." Her account of autonomy includes a political component, reconcilable with Arendt's idea of citizens as co–builders of a common world, as discussed in E. Claes, W. Devroe, and B. Keirsbilck, *l.c.*

conception of human nature."[44] Within this perspective, justification takes place by reference only to values that can be understood and affirmed without presupposing any particular comprehensive doctrine.[45] Instead it turns to the socio–political and historical context which gave birth to the notion of human rights from which it reconstructs "certain fundamental ideas seen as implicit in the public political culture of a democratic society."[46] This 'public political culture' can include political institutions of a democratic constitutional regime, traditions of constitutional interpretation as well as historical documents and well–known political writings.[47] The notion of free and equal persons is indeed fundamental to human rights. It is literally mentioned in several human rights declarations[48] and implicit in most of the conventions.[49] The notion of personal autonomy, moreover, can be reconstructed as the background assumption behind the liberal democratic perspective which gave rise to human rights and which attaches so much importance to freedom, equality and tolerance.[50]

While neither positivism, nor constructivism are necessarily accompanied by statism, constructivism's moral basis in the autonomy of individuals makes it less vulnerable to statism. Despite the fact that the most prominent constructivist account of international human rights, John Rawls' *Law of Peoples*, adheres to statism, most constructivists do not. In contrast to positivism, constructivism is "conditioned, but not simply determined by objective historical processes" like those which led to our current human rights regime.[51] Moreover, as its basis lies in the autonomous individual, it will see States as instruments to realise personal autonomy and consider the promotion of individual autonomy as more important in cases where States' and individuals' interests conflict.

---

44 J. Rawls, "The Law of Peoples", in S. Shute and S. Hurley (eds.), *Human Rights: Theory and Measurement* (New York: St. Martin's Press, 1993) 68.

45 J. Rawls (2001), *l.c.*, § 57. Rawls calls this "reasonable justification", and to be sure this furthers the protective function of law – see E. Claes, W. Devroe, and B. Keirsbilck, *l.c.*

46 J. Rawls (1996), *l.c.*, 13. See also J. Rawls (2001), *l.c.*, 2.

47 J. Rawls (1996), *l.c.*, 13–14 and 376.

48 In the preamble of the Déclaration des Droits de l'Homme et du Citoyen, in the first article of the Universal Declaration of Human Rights, in the preamble of the American Declaration of the Rights and the Duties of Man.

49 The Declaration of Independence, the preamble of the UN International Covenant on Civil and Political Rights, the preamble of the UN International Covenant on Economic, Social and Cultural Rights, and the preamble of the American Convention on Human Rights, among others.

50 A. Ingram (1994), *l.c.*, 97–99.

51 J. Donnely (2003), *l.c.*, 16.

4.3 Relationship between Politics and Law

Constructivism endorses procedural rights guaranteeing representative government and electoral control, because these rights reflect and also promote individual autonomy. However, unlike positivism, it does not carve these procedural rights into stone, strictly separating the process of democratic law–making from the processes of application and interpretation. The idea of individual autonomy, present in the public political culture, is not just a source of human rights. Through the application and interpretation of human rights, this ideal also continues to shape public political culture. For constructivism, the task of justification of human rights and reshaping society through human rights is an ongoing one. This means the thought–experiment of the original position can and should be repeated over and over again. Here lie incredible advantages: it leaves room for social change and makes sure that

> [when] rights become institutionalized as a central part of political and administrative culture, they [do not] lose their transformative effect and are [not] petrified into a legalistic paradigm that marginalizes values or interests that resist translation into rights–language. [52]

This means that the task of justification is not over once rights have been institutionalised. Judges cannot remain concerned only with the question of how a law came into being or of which procedure lead to a rights–restricting measure. To justify their judgment they must also give reasons for why autonomous individuals could reasonably be expected to endorse a certain restrictive measure.[53] Constructivism does not have the problem positivism has with overriding public policy and majoritarian interests, because for the constructivist the question whether something is a right does not depend on convention but on whether reasonable persons in the original position could reasonably be expected to agree to it. Since the original position is a hypothetical viewpoint, which can be taken up by anyone at any time, and because, due to the veil of ignorance, the parties' reasoning in the original position is identical and the agreement unanimous, it does not matter who takes up this viewpoint. This means that judges as well as politicians can justify rights reasoning from the original position.

---

52 Koskenniemi expresses this fear in M. Koskenniemi, "The Effects of Rights on Political Culture", in P. Alston *et al.* (eds.), *The EU and Human Rights* (Oxford: Oxford University Press, 1999) 99.

53 See E. Claes, W. Devroe, and B. Keirsbilck, *l.c.*

5 A Remedy for the Protective Limits of Privacy Rights as Human Rights?

In this section it will be argued that a change in perspective on law on the part of the ECtHR might indeed have an impact on the way it handles open texture through judicial interpretation, and that therefore, this shift in philosophical perspective might provide for a remedy to the limits to the protective function of privacy rights as human rights. First, it is discussed whether minimalist interpretation like the ECtHR's would fit the constructivist perspective. Next, these views will be applied to the three cases discussed and it will be shown how a constructivist perspective urges for different outcomes which honours the protective, power–critical function of human rights.

5.1 Does Minimalism Fit Constructivism?

A judge's implicit views on judicial interpretation generally makes a difference in what Ronald Dworkin has dubbed 'hard cases', cases "which cannot be brought under a clear rule of law."[54] In such cases, minimalism's directions are to judge narrowly and theorise shallowly in order to maintain the proper role of judges and to promote democratic debate. This could be said to fit with constructivism for two reasons. First, constructivism stresses the importance of representative government and electoral control, in virtue of their reflection of personal autonomy. As judges are neither representatives nor the subjects of electoral control, one might argue that a constructivist would want them to judge narrowly, decide only the case at hand, and leave more far–reaching decisions up to politicians. This would further the protective function of law by ensuring the possibility of contradicting the legitimacy of State action.[55] Secondly, one might argue that, with the idea of a morally autonomous person at its basis, constructivism has an interest in promoting the accountability of the State and that it stimulates democratic by judging minimally.[56]

It is indeed the case that constructivism values democratic debate and reason giving for their autonomy–promoting character. But it would be a mistake to conclude that only politicians could and should take part in deliberations concerning rights. This would empty the constructivist notion of rights: the essence of rights, after all, is that they override public policy and majoritarian interests if these compromise individual autonomy in a way which not everyone could reasonably be expected to accept. Exactly for this reason, it is judges who decide hard cases, because, unlike politicians who have to think about their next election, they are not prone to give priority to majoritarian interests.

---

54 R. Dworkin (1978), *l.c.*, 81.

55 See E. Claes, W. Devroe, and B. Keirsbilck, *l.c.*

56 *Ibid.*

As we have seen, according to the constructivist, a judge can take up the viewpoint of the 'original position', much to the same effect as if politicians would. Moreover, as argued above, there is good reason that she should. A judge cannot escape her duty to decide the case at hand and a very good way in which to promote democratic political debate is indeed to judge narrowly, that is to decide only the case at hand. But it is hard to see how constructivism could also prescribe that a judge must refrain from offering a motivation for her decision that everyone, including those involved in the case, could reasonably be expected to accept. Thus minimalism's prescription of shallowness does not fit constructivism at all.[57]

5.2 A Constructivist Perspective on the ECtHR's Privacy Case–Law

What would a constructivist interpretation of Article 8, paragraph 2, look like then? How should the Court judge narrowly but not shallowly? Consider again the *Fretté*, *Hatton* and *Chapman* cases, discussed above.

5.2.1 Fretté v France

France refused Mr. Fretté the possibility of becoming a 'prospective' adoptive parent, his sexual orientation being the only reason. The Court accepted this interference with private life because of a lack of evidence on the effects of homosexual parenting on children and because of a lack of consensus among Member States. However, autonomous individuals in the original position, who might turn out to be homosexual themselves once the veil of ignorance is lifted, could not reasonably be expected to accept this type of discrimination on the simple grounds of bias and without any prospect of change, for consensus is, in the end, what will matter. This does not mean that the Court should have obliged France to allow adoption for homosexuals. But, from a constructivist viewpoint, both France and the ECtHR fell short of justifying their decision to exclude homosexuals from adoption. If the Court could not find more compelling reasons to deny Mr. Fretté the opportunity of adoption itself than a lack of consensus, it should at least have urged the French authorities to do so, by recommending that a decent study be ordered, or by asking that they keep their measure in review, should new evidence arise.[58] I believe this would have served the protective and power–critical function

57 Note that the court set out a judges' duty to duly motivate decisions. See, for example: ECtHR, 12 February 2004, *Pervez v France*; ECtHR, 29 September 2005, *Kurti v Greece*. Thanks to Willem Verrijdt for useful discussion on this point.

58 This could easily be done by analogy with the gender identity cases in the United Kingdom, where the Court did not declare violations in the earlier cases (ECtHR, 17 October 1986, *Rees v United Kingdom*; ECtHR, 27 September 1990, *Cossey v United Kingdom*; ECtHR, 30 July 1998, *Sheffield and Horsham v United Kingdom*) but made increasingly stronger rec-

of law by questioning a prejudice on the basis of which discrimination is now permitted to exist.

5.2.2 Hatton v United Kingdom

In the *Hatton* case, the Court left intact a policy decision which thoroughly disturbed the applicant's sleeping pattern and thus interfered with his private life, because it viewed its own role as limited to "reviewing whether or not the particular solution adopted can be regarded as striking *a* fair balance"[59], rather than *the* fairest balance that could have been struck all things considered. Despite the fact that the State had significant economic interests in upholding the existent flight schedule, a judge concerned with realising each individual's capacity for autonomy would not have been satisfied with the fact that *a* fair balance had been struck. Moreover, one could not reasonably expect parties in the original position to accept a certain measure if alternatives less restrictive to their personal autonomy existed. In other words, I doubt that a constructivist judge would have overturned the 2001 *Hatton* judgment so easily.

5.2.3 Chapman v United Kingdom

In the *Chapman* case, a member of a minority group was robbed of the possibility of shaping her life according to her traditional traveller life–style. Again, there is no question that her rights as an autonomous individual were interfered with. Did the environmental rights of others justify this interference? Would a person in an 'initial situation', possibly belonging to this minority, reasonably agree to a scheme where environmental rights are very strictly enforced so that travellers can only live on designated sites? He or she might do so on the condition that sufficient sites were provided. But in this case, the provision of designated sites was left up to local authorities, which effectively lead to scarcity of designated sites and to overpopulation, bad hygiene, and a lack of security on these designated sites. As the dissenting judges clearly state, the United Kingdom's "legislative and policy framework does not provide in practice for the needs of the Gypsy minority"[60], and therefore I do not think this framework could have been the outcome of an agreement in the original position. From a constructivist point of view, then, the margin of appreciation afforded to UK authorities would not necessarily have been very narrow, but

> where the planning authorities have not made any finding that there is available to the Gypsy any alternative, lawful site to which he or she can reasonably be expected to move, there must exist compelling reasons for the measures concerned.

---

ommendations to the UK authorities to review their system of recording the sex of postoperative transsexuals.

59 ECtHR, 7 August 2003, *Hatton v United Kingdom*, § 123, my emphasis.

60 ECtHR, 18 January 2001, *Chapman v United Kingdom*, Dissenting opinion, § 5.

Whereas the ECtHR's majority in this case only examined the procedure leading to her eviction, a constructivist Court would have examined these substantial reasons. This would most certainly have protected the Gypsy minority, in the UK and elsewhere in Europe, far better than the standing judgment does.[61]

6 Conclusion

These case studies show that a constructivist perspective on human rights offers an interpretation of paragraph 2 of Article 8 of the Convention, which is more protective of individuals and minorities whose privacy rights have been interfered with, and more critical of the reasons those in power adduce for interfering with privacy rights than the Court's current positivism–inspired minimalist interpretation.

61 *Ibid.*, § 3.

Chapter 19 – The Limits of the International Petition Right for Individuals: A Case Study of the ECtHR

Willem Verrijdt

1 Introduction

Since its founding in 1959, three procedural reforms have theoretically increased an individual's access to the European Court of Human Rights ('ECtHR'). Although this international right for an individual's petition ('IRIP') has brought the Convention system closer to its own objectives, it has, together with four other elements, created an ever–growing problem of backlog before the Court, as a consequence of the frequent use which the Member States' citizens have been making of this individual–based procedure. Thus, the theoretical increase in an individual's access to the Court goes hand in hand with a decrease in the system's effectiveness. Since the entry into force of the procedure set out by the 11th Protocol in 1998, the balance has tilted in favour of diminishing effectiveness.

Section 2 provides an overview of the goals of the European Convention for the Protection of Human Rights and Fundamental Freedoms (the 'ECHR' or 'Convention') and the ECtHR, pointing out the evolution towards a recognition of the IRIP for every alleged victim. In section 3, the conflict between two main aspects of this IRIP, leading to a limit inherent in the enforcement of human rights, is analysed. Its several interrelated causes are explained, as well as its consequences for every function of international human rights law. In section 4, the most suggested solutions to this limit are discussed, with special attention for the question concerning the ECtHR's role.

2 The International Right of Individual Petition

2.1 *Objectives and Evolution of the ECtHR–Procedure*

The main objective of the Council of Europe (COE) was to prevent States from lapsing into totalitarianism.[1] The ECHR, deriving from ideas such as the common

---

1 L.–E. Pettiti, "Réflexions sur les principes et les mécanismes de la Convention. De l'idéal de 1950 à l'humble réalité d'aujourd'hui", in L.–E. Pettiti, E. Decaux and P.–H. Imbert (eds.), *La Convention Européenne des droits de l'homme* (Paris: Economica, 1995) 27; Lord. H.

heritage of political traditions, ideals, freedom, and the rule of law, was established so as to be an effective guarantee for every individual's civil and political rights.[2]

The control machinery ensuring the effectiveness of the rights within the ECHR pursued two goals, which have until recently been considered to act as each other's complement.[3] On the one hand, the ECtHR was entrusted with the mission to ensure a correct interpretation of the ECHR and in doing so, to systematically raise human rights' standard across Europe.[4] This approach, called the *constitutional justice* model, can perfectly do without an IRIP, as long as problematic situations are brought to the ECtHR's attention in some other way. On the other hand, the ECtHR was also created to apply the ECHR in individual cases, providing *individual justice* whenever the domestic procedures failed to protect the citizens against human rights violations.[5] The 'Group of Wise Persons' has recently stressed both missions as equally important.[6]

Before the ECtHR's inauguration in 1959, the individual's possibilities were limited.[7] Once the Court was installed, its proceedings revealed features of both approaches, although the *constitutional justice* model dominated. Individuals were granted the procedural entitlement to institute international proceedings against a Member State for allegedly violating the substantive human rights set out in the ECHR. These proceedings could culminate in a binding decision by a judicial organ, the ECtHR. The alleged victims, however, did not have any individual access to the Court itself. They could only apply to the European Commission of Human Rights, a semi–judicial body, which would examine the case's admissibility.[8] If a

---

Woolf, *Review of the Working Methods of the European Court of Human Rights* (http://echr.coe.int, 2005) 8.

2 J. Vélu and R. Ergec, *La Convention Européenne des droits de l'homme* (Brussels: Bruylant, 1990) 40–43. The ECtHR describes the ECHR as "a constitutional instrument of European public order for the protection of individual human beings", and its own role, as "to ensure the observance of the engagements undertaken by the Contracting Parties": ECtHR, 12 December 2001, *Bankovic v Belgium*, § 80. All judgments of the ECtHR can be found under HUDOC on www.echr.coe.int.

3 P. Sardaro, "The Right of Individual Petition to the European Court", in P. Lemmens and W. Vandenhole (eds.), *Protocol No. 14 and the Reform of the European Court of Human Rights* (Antwerp: Intersentia, 2005) 62.

4 Former ECtHR President L. Wildhaber, "A constitutional future for the European Court of Human Rights", *HRLJ* 2002, 162.

5 F. Vanneste, "A New Admissibility Criterion", in P. Lemmens and W. Vandenhole (eds.), *Protocol No. 14 and the Reform of the European Court of Human Rights* (Antwerp: Intersentia, 2005), 72–73; F. Tulkens, M. Fischbach, J. Casadevall and W. Thomassen, "Pour le droit de recours individuel", in G. Cohen–Jonathan and C. Pettiti, *La réforme de la Cour européenne des droits de l'homme* (Brussels: Bruylant, 2003) 171–175.

6 Group of Wise Persons, *Report of the Group of Wise Persons to the Committee of Ministers*, 10 November 2006, SAGES (2006) 6, § 24.

7 Individuals could lodge complaints before the Commission, which mainly mediated between the Member State and the individual. In hard cases, the Committee of Ministers, a fully political organ, could identify violations and condemn Member States.

8 The Commission's policy in this respect was very strict, declaring *de plano* inadmissible some 86.5% of all applications lodged.

case was declared admissible, only the Commission and the other Member States could refer it to the Court. Furthermore, every Member State was free to accept the ECtHR's jurisdiction and to recognise the IRIP before the Commission.

During the following 50 years, both reforms of the control machinery and the ECtHR's jurisprudence have stressed the individual–relief–based character of these international proceedings. Following the entry into force of Protocol 9 in 1994, individuals obtained the possibility to refer their cases to the ECtHR themselves, after they had been declared admissible by the Commission. The Court could, however, still refuse to hear the case if a panel consisting of three judges unanimously decided that the case did not "reveal a relevant question of interpretation of the Convention and did not warrant consideration by the Court for any other reason".[9]

The radical reform of the control machinery which Protocol 11 contained, showed a strong emphasis on improving *individual justice*. Entering into force in 1998, it abolished the Commission and granted to every individual direct and immediate access to the ECtHR, which would examine the admissibility of every case itself. Moreover, the ECtHR's jurisdiction and the IRIP were made compulsory for every COE Member State.

The IRIP's fundamental importance was also stressed in the ECtHR's jurisprudence, stating that

> the convention right to individual application ... has over the years become of the highest importance and is now a key component of the machinery for protecting the rights and freedoms set out in the Convention.[10]

The ECtHR is the international body where the right of an individual petition at the international level has reached the highest degree of maturity,[11] guaranteeing for the 800 million inhabitants of the 47 COE Member States a (theoretically) effective control on the compliance by the Member States with the Human Rights set out in the Convention.

2.2 *Aspects of the International Right of Individual Petition*

This unique European right implies a number of features, which are mostly classified under three categories.[12] The first one comprises the direct and unrestricted access to an international judicial body. This right may be subject to some formal requirements and conditions of jurisdiction, but when these are met, any alleged victim is empowered to initiate international proceedings against a Member State, even by a simple letter and without legal assistance.

---

9 Article 48 ECHR (1994), as amended by Article 5 of Protocol 9.

10 ECtHR (GC), 4 February 2005, *Mamatkulov and Askarov v Turkey*, §§ 99–129.

11 P. Sardaro, *L.c.*, 47.

12 *Ibid.*, 49.

The second category, the judicial character of the proceedings, covers several procedural safeguards aimed at ensuring the fairness of the proceedings.[13] Every alleged victim has *locus standi* before the Court, while a number of measures guarantee the decision's impartiality and legitimacy.

The ECtHR's remedial powers, which are unique in international law, constitute the third feature.[14] Not only can the ECtHR condemn Member States violating the ECHR, it can also order them to pay damages to the victim. In some cases, it can even put an end to a violation by demanding specific measures.[15]

These three aspects of the IRIP would be merely theoretical – and therefore useless – if they were not effective, in the sense that in practice they would not succeed in restoring the *status quo ante* for every individual victim. As laid down in Article 13 ECHR and mentioned in numerous ECtHR judgments, effectiveness is a key feature in the Convention system. This effectiveness is to an important extent guaranteed by the second and third aspect described above, but these guarantees do not suffice. When an individual has his human rights violated, individual redress needs to occur as soon as possible, accounting for the time required by the judge to evaluate the sometimes complex situation and to balance individual versus public interest. If individual redress follows many years after the violation, however, this is nothing but a caricature of what individual redress should be: the aphorism 'justice delayed is justice denied' applies most strongly if human rights are at stake. Effectiveness can therefore be named the fourth aspect of the IRIP.[16]

The effectiveness of the control machinery has, however, always been one of the most important issues in European human rights law. During the last two decades, and certainly since the entry into force of Protocol 11 in 1998, this effectiveness has been stretched to its limits – and even undermined – by the enormous number of applications lodged with the ECtHR.

3 Limits of Legal Protection

Human rights law aims at accomplishing the law's functions which law can have: the regulatory function, the symbolic function, the dispute resolution, and the function of protective legality.[17] As human rights are strictly individual and often a matter of individual versus State, the protective function seems to be the most important one. It is an inherent limit within this protective function, however, that

---

13 *Ibid.*, 49–50.

14 *Ibid.*, 50.

15 ECtHR (GC), 8 April 2004, *Assanidze v Georgia*. The Court, however, only takes these measures not foreseen in the ECHR when the violation, "by its very nature, … does not leave any real choice as to the measures required to remedy it".

16 It might as well be placed under the judicial character of the proceedings, as is done for the domestic proceedings in Article 6(1) ECHR, but placing it next to the other three categories emphasises more clearly that it adds an extra dimension, the dimension of functioning in practice, to each of them.

17 See E. Claes, W. Devroe, and B. Keirsbilck, "The Limits of the Law (Introduction)".

prevents the current ECtHR procedure from being fully effective, while also causing the European human rights system to fall short in its three other functions.

3.1 Flooding in Strasbourg: Figures[18]

During the first years of its existence, the Convention system only had to deal with some 10 to 20 cases each year. This number, however, has risen each year. Already in 1980, when 404 cases were lodged before the Commission,[19] some concerned voices questioned the ability of the procedure at that time to keep up with this increasing input.[20] From 1990 on, when new States started to access the COE, the problem extended rapidly.

Under Protocol 9, the incoming case–load had risen from 10 000 cases in 1993 to 14 000 in 1997. Under Protocol 11, this number has expanded dramatically from some 18 000 in 1998 to over 50 000 in 2006. The ECtHR, which has already made enormous efforts to optimise the operation of its registry, is helpless against this flood, as this comparison between input and output shows.

Table 19.1 Flooding in Strasbourg

Year	Input	Inadmissible or struck out	Declared admissible	Judgments	Output	Backlog increase
2001	13 845	8 989	739	889	9 728	4 117
2002	28 214	17 868	578	844	18 450	9 764
2003	27 189	17 272	753	703	18 034	9 155
2004	32 512	20 350	830	718	21 181	11 331
2005	35 402	27 612	1 036	1 105	28 648	6 754
2006	39 373	28 160	1 634	1 560	31 354	8 019

Between 1997 and 2006, the number of pending cases increased by 58 443. By May 2007, a dazzling number of 95 750 cases were awaiting a decision. Some 25% of those cases had not even been assigned to the competent chamber. Considering the Court's annual output, this represents a waiting period of some four years per case. Delays of six years and more before a judgment on the merits issues, are no exception. Audits have shown that the number of pending cases will increase by 20 % per year. If no immediate action is taken, it will exceed 250 000 by 2010.[21]

---

[18] ECtHR Registry, "Survey of Activities 2006. Information Document Issued by the Registrar of the European Court of Human Rights", at www.echr.coe.int, 33.

[19] Lord H. Woolf, *l.c.*, 7.

[20] H. Schermers, "The Eleventh Protocol to the European Convention on Human Rights", *European Law Review* 1994, 368.

[21] Lord H. Woolf, *l.c.*, 4 and 8, based on the Memorandum by the Secretary General, 12 May 2005, which was based on internal and external audits.

In 2005, the core backlog, namely cases having exceeded the one year time limit allowed for each stage of processing, comprised about 27 200 cases.[22] For the moment, some 4 % of the cases pending (2 100 cases) have been so for more than five years, falling well below the standards for reasonable delay prescribed by the Court itself under Article 6(1) ECHR.[23] This percentage represents an important part of the well–founded cases, since they take most time to examine. It is estimated that some 40 % of the core backlog are Chamber cases that need examination on the merits.[24]

3.2 Analysis: Diminishing Marginal Utility

The synchronism between every reform the control machinery was subject to and the major increases in the number of individual petitions catches the eye immediately. Significant increases in the number of filings took place in 1994 and in 1999, together with the entry into force of Protocol 9 and Protocol 11 respectively. Furthermore, a connection can be noticed between the steady progression of input during the last five years and the efforts the ECtHR has made to improve its registry proceedings. The Court's output, as a consequence of these rationalisations, rose too, but at a slower rate. There seems to be a strong connection between improving the Court's accessibility on the one hand and the shocks in the ever increasing number of applications and backlog, on the other.

An important factor in the ECtHR's problem can be explained as a problem of diminishing marginal utility, inherent in the protective function of the IRIP exercised at such a large scale. A procedure's capacity, certainly when applied in such a vast jurisdiction, can encounter a point of saturation, after which every further reform becomes counterproductive, generating more disadvantages than advantages for the (potential) individual applicant. This is only one among many related causes, yet one of the most difficult to remedy. It also strengthens the effects of some other causes.

3.2.1 Diminishing Marginal Utility

The ECtHR can be considered as a production process, in which the procedure represents the assembly line; the individual applications form the raw material, and the number of judges and other staff equal the human resources. The judgments, which have to be of the highest standards both qualitatively and quantitatively, represent the output. As to the goal of the proceedings, this comparison fails, since the ECtHR does not pursue profit, but provides for a public good for some 50 000 annual applicants and some 800 million potential applicants. This

---

22 *Ibid.*, 49.

23 *Ibid.*, 8.

24 *Ibid.*, 49.

public good, guaranteeing the effectiveness of the Convention system, comes down to maximising the proceedings' utility for individual applicants. The ECtHR does not have a free choice regarding the quantity of raw material it processes, since the IRIP's features described above require every unit of raw material to lead to a qualitative final product as fast as possible.

In all production processes, the law of diminishing marginal utility sets inherent limits to growth capacity, since every subsequent expansion of one input factor in production processes tends to add less to the total productivity than the previous one. At a given moment, when the last reform's added utility equals zero, the production process reaches its saturation point, after which every further reform will prove to be counterproductive rather than to add some utility or profit. Maximising benefits implies raising the production until a level is reached where the next expansion would show no marginal utility. The ECtHR's production process is subject to high expectations, since its output is measured in terms of utility for individuals, resulting from the fundamental choice to grant to all COE citizens an effective international cause of action. In this respect, the ECtHR's *total utility* comprises all of the benefit that an individual applicant can have from the control machinery, and the *marginal utility* stands for the utility for individual applicants added by the last reform of the Strasbourg system.

3.2.2 The ECtHR's Diminishing Marginal Utility

Mainly because of its extensiveness, the ECtHR's jurisprudence production process is subject to the diminishing marginal utility pattern. Maximising the ECtHR's accessibility, which merely consists of some procedural changes granting the right to complain directly to a judicial body, would have no negative side effects if there was only one applicant in the picture. The IRIP needing to be maximised for millions of individuals, however, slows down the effects of every new reform. With every procedural change granting a more extensive IRIP, many potential applicants are turned into real applicants, for instance because they feel their winning chances have risen, or because they finally fulfil the admissibility criteria. The Court's expanded accessibility itself involves – among several other causes – the expansion of the number of complaints. When the rising number of applicants exceeds the proceedings' extended capacity to cope with all of them, a bottleneck of cases leads to an extended backlog.

Most important to notice is the ostensible inevitability of this diminishing marginal utility, since the problem consists of two input factors in the same production process conflicting in the achievement of the process' goals. When the introduction of the larger assembly line by itself attracts an additional number of raw materials exceeding the assembly line's extended capacity, an even larger assembly line would be no solution, since it would entail an even larger boom in the influx of raw material. Human resources have not risen to the same extent as the influx of raw material, partly because of practical reasons such as the building's capacity, partly because the budget falls short.[25] Moreover, some important judicial features, such as the high number of judges in each Chamber, tend to slow the process down. Throwing these features overboard would, however, harm the proceedings' judicial aspect, which was described above as another essential IRIP feature.

It is precisely the effect of this self–generating bottleneck which causes the marginal utility to diminish. The utility gained by maximising the first aspect of the IRIP, the direct access to an international court, is decreased – maybe even undone – by the loss this provokes on the fourth aspect, justice within a reasonable time. Ironically, a procedure which is designed to be actively used becomes less useful simply by the use made of it.

3.2.3 Marginal Utility Posing Limits to the International Petition Right of Individuals

Both the fundamental choice to grant an IRIP to every European citizen and its implementation in international court proceedings appear to have some inherent limits due to a diminishing marginal utility pattern. This statement necessarily raises some questions about the protective function of international human rights law. The IRIP, a key feature in the European human rights system, is unable to live up to high expectations, failing to provide for individual justice within a reasonable time. Individual redress many years after the fact is a mere theoretical redress[26], such as when an individual lodges a complaint against his Member State because of the unreasonable delay in internal proceedings, and it takes the ECtHR another five or more years to come to a decision. These long delays may keep potential claimants with well–founded cases from lodging a complaint against their Member States. The States can also make abuse of the long delays by persisting in the violations as long as no judgment has been filed, such as by maintaining the unlawful detention of political activists. They might even claim that a judgment delivered some five years after the facts does not reflect reality anymore, and therefore does not need any implementation.[27] If a well–functioning IRIP seems to be an illusion, it is unclear how individuals can be effectively protected against human rights violations committed by States unwilling to abide by the ECHR .

The described limit does not result from two functions of law contradicting one another, but it is ingrained in the IRIP itself when applied on such a large scale as the 47 COE Member States. It is therefore an inherent limit within the protective

---

[25] The Court's 2006 budget amounted to 44 189 000 euros. This covers judges' remuneration, staff salaries, and operational expenditure (information technology, official journeys, translation, interpretation, publications, representational expenditure, legal aid, fact–finding missions. etc). See www.echr.coe.int.

[26] Or, as Lord Woolf writes: "If 'justice delayed is justice denied', then a large proportion of the Court's applicants ... are effectively denied the justice they seek" (Lord H. Woolf, *l.c.*, 8).

[27] L. Wildhaber, "The Place of the European Court of Human Rights in the European Constitutional Landscape", speech given at the 12th European Constitutional Courts Conference, 2002, www.confcoconsteu.org/reports, 7.

function of international human rights law. This statement will have its consequences for possible remedies: ill–considered reforms might have an opposite effect, generating in the long run an even larger backlog. Long–term solutions will have to strengthen the output–ability, without entailing an even larger input–boom.

3.3 Other Related Causes

Diminishing marginal utility alone cannot explain all of the ECtHR's problems. Even if the individual utility of the proceedings could be maximised, the Court would not be used if there were no (alleged) human rights violations across Europe. In a thorough report published in 2005, Lord Woolf, the former UK Lord Chief Justice, distinguishes four other causes.

The first parallel cause is the counterproductivity of success: the ECtHR has always had the highest of standards, striving to give every application full consideration, and to grant every applicant assistance and satisfaction.[28] In doing so, the ECtHR has raised some very high expectations among European citizens. Evaluating their winning chances as very high, many potential applicants have thus been encouraged to lodge a complaint against their Member State. This cause is influenced by and influences the diminishing marginal utility of every proceeding's reform, since the ECtHR is currently perceived as a unique mix of accessibility and high standards. In this respect, one often hears the phrase that the ECtHR is becoming a victim of its own success.[29] Since lowering the ECtHR's adjudication standards in order to lower citizens' expectations does not improve the IRIP's utility, this factor is to be taken into account without any chance of remedying it.

The second and most important parallel cause is the COE's vastly expanded spatial jurisdiction.[30] From 1990 on, many Eastern European States, mostly new democracies, have ratified the ECHR. Since in these countries the capacity of judicial systems is still being developed[31], this factor has changed the COE's main task from fine–tuning well–established and well–functioning democracies to establishing democracy and rule of law in new and relatively fragile democracies.[32] Figures showing that in May 2007, 58% of the ECtHR's pending case–load derived from 5 Member States,[33] and that 70% of the judgments are directed against

---

28 Lord H. Woolf, *l.c.*, 7.

29 *Ibid.*, 71.

30 From 12 Member States in 1959, over 35 Member States in 1994, to 47 Member States in 2007.

31 Lord H. Woolf, *l.c.*, 9; L. Wildhaber, *l.c.*, 5.

32 P. Mahoney, "New Challenges for the European Court of Human Rights Resulting from the Expanding Case Load and Membership", *Penn State International Law Review* 2002, 21.

33 Russia (22.3%), Romania (11.7%), Turkey (9.8%), Ukraine (8.4%) and Poland (5.8%). 12 out of 47 Member States represent 81.2% of the 95 750 pending cases.

8 Member States,[34] prove that the ECtHR's architecture was not drawn for this task. Keeping in mind that the ECtHR is still relatively unknown in these countries, this vast number of applications only represents the tip of the iceberg.[35]

This second cause will be very difficult to remedy, since it derives from an enormous cultural gap between the Western European founders of the COE which lived in a long tradition of democracy and rule of law, and the Eastern European countries which did not even have this tradition when they joined the COE in the early 1990s. Internalising these values and establishing these traditions will take a good deal of time. In the meantime, throwing manifestly unwilling Member States out of the COE cannot be an option since, in that case, the citizens who need the Convention system the most would be radically cut off from its protection. On the other hand, a flood of condemnatory ECtHR judgments might even enlarge the gap between these countries and the COE, rather than make something fundamental happen.

This enormous cultural gap places the ECHR on a mission of an insurmountable ambiguity. On the one hand, its human rights provisions being used to impose a fundamental ideological shift on somewhat autocratic countries which do not fully understand these values, the ECtHR acts as the cement for pan–European regionalism. From this pan–European point of view, all governments should accept the ECtHR's decisions, also the unpopular ones, because this is an inescapable part of belonging to the community of democratic States.[36] On the other hand, the ECtHR is allocated the task to provide for individual redress for every citizen in these countries who has his fundamental rights violated, implying a deluge of condemnatory judgments aggravating the opposition between the ECtHR and its main addressees. Since the normal functioning of the mechanism providing the cement causes the two entities to drift apart, an IRIP–based regional human rights procedure can only work effectively after the cement is created in another way.

The third parallel cause is the massive influx of hopeless cases. The very broad implementation of the IRIP, the abolition of the Commission, and probably also the high expectations raised by the ECtHR's jurisprudence have lead to an enormous number of clearly inadmissible cases. Since many people appeal to Strasbourg without any legal advice or assistance, and without any knowledge of the ECtHR's competence or conditions of admissibility, often raising questions that have nothing to do with the ECHR, some 85 per cent of all cases arriving in Strasbourg are manifestly inadmissible.[37] These cases take a lot of time to process, and divert the Court's attention away from more deserving cases. Many people think

---

[34] In 2006, 334 out of 1560 judgments were in cases against Turkey (21%), 190 against Slovenia, 120 against Ukraine, 115 against Poland, 102 against Russia, 96 against France, and 73 against Romania.

[35] Lord H. Woolf, *l.c.*, 9: Alvaro Gil–Robles, Commissioner for Human Rights, states that "what is saving Strasbourg, is that people still do not know about it".

[36] L. Wildhaber, "Solemn Hearing of the ECtHR on the Occasion of the Opening of the Judicial Year", 19 January 2007, www.echr.coe.int, 3.

[37] Total inadmissibility even exceeds 95 per cent, rising to 96,4 per cent in 2005. See H. Woolf, *l.c.*, 19.

of Strasbourg as a fourth instance reexamining every single national legal aspect of their case, whereas this has never been the Court's purpose.[38]

This high percentage points out an enormous gap between the expectations of those who apply to the Court and what it can actually deliver. In a small number of cases, the underlying issue might be the proceedings' instrumentalist use,[39] such as their being (ab)used as a magnifying glass or to drag out already lost national cases, but in the vast majority of cases, the only problem is a lack of awareness and understanding of the ECtHR's real purpose and jurisdiction.[40] In those cases the rejected applicant often does not understand the reasons for dismissal, since he receives only a short letter stating that his case cannot be examined, and he might thus have the feeling that after the domestic legal system, also the international legal system has let him down.

The fourth parallel cause is made up by repetitive or 'clone' cases. While only a fraction of all admissible cases raises a new question of human rights law, other cases arrive in Strasbourg despite the ECtHR's already having settled the legal point in a prior case, and despite its already having condemned a Member State, often even the same Member State, for the same violation. Repetitive cases are estimated to represent some 60% of all potentially well–founded cases.[41] If all judgments would be properly implemented by the Member States, this problem should not occur at all. This also shows the difficulties the ECHR and ECtHR have in changing traditions within the Member States and creating the cement for pan–European regionalism. This cause thus also points out some lack of internalisation, especially in Eastern Europe, as the Polish Division analysis reveals.[42] This sometimes plain refusal to comply with the COE standards affects the Court's remedial powers, an essential aspect of the IRIP presuming the Member States' strict compliance with condemnatory judgments. Relieving the ECtHR of the burden of these repetitive cases is vital in preserving its long–term viability[43], but it should be done at the level of politics, since this cause proves the IRIP's inability to enforce human rights in manifestly unwilling States.

3.4 Other Related Consequences

As described above, this combination of problems mainly affects the human rights' protective function. The backlog and ineffectiveness problems, however, also keep international human rights law from fulfilling its other functions.

---

38 ECtHR President L. Wildhaber, "Changing Ideas About the Tasks of the European Court of Human Rights", speech cited by Lord H. Woolf, *l.c.*, 9.

39 See E. Claes, W. Devroe, and B. Keirsbilck, *l.c.*; C. Taylor, *The Ethics of Authenticity* (Cambridge, Mass.: Harvard University Press, 1991) 5.

40 Lord H. Woolf, *l.c.*, 9.

41 *Ibid.*, 38–39.

42 Of the 700 potentially admissible Polish cases allocated to a decision body in February 2005, less than 100 raised new Convention issues. The rest can be considered repetitive.

43 Group of Wise Persons, *l.c.*, § 35–36.

As to the regulatory function, the ECtHR is expected to deliver guidelines concerning the interpretation and application of the ECHR by the governments. Because of the backlog, these guidelines are delayed[44], which leads to legal uncertainty and to many individuals suffering from the same violations.

As to the function of dispute settlement, the time needed by the ECtHR to come to a judgment holds up the conflict between a citizen and his Member State concerning this citizen's most fundamental rights without any certainty regarding the outcome.

As to the symbolic function, the ECHR is the most important expression of the foundations of Europe's concepts of democracy and rule of law, being a symbol of "a common heritage of political traditions, ideals, freedom and the rule of law".[45] The ECtHR considers the democratic regime and the rule of law to be "the cornerstones of the protective mechanism instituted by the ECHR".[46] When the key institute supervising these ideals within the Member States proves to be unable to fulfil its role, the underlying values represented by this symbol also take a severe blow, not only because of their diminishing enforceability, but because this lack of enforceability makes the ECtHR's theoretical statements meaningless in practice.

Subsequently, since the described problems increase the judges' workload, the consequences for the protective function of human rights law may become even more dramatic. The ECtHR has been under considerable pressure to increase its efficiency and productivity, and very much has already been done.[47] This raises some concerns that focus on quantity will undermine the quality of the ECtHR's judgments, and thus the credibility of the Convention system itself.[48] If a gain in quantity would be to the detriment of the quality of the Court's work, it would bring no improvement for individual applicants. One danger is that the ECtHR's inability to provide justice within a reasonable time will weaken the rigor with which it examines the Member States' shortcomings in reasonable delay cases.[49] The exclusion of tax payers, aliens, and election candidates from the reasonable delay guarantee[50] and the increasing margin of appreciation granted to the Mem-

---

44 Lord H. Woolf, *l.c.*, 8.

45 Preamble of the European Convention on Human Rights. See also L. Wildhaber (speech cited by Lord H. Woolf), *l.c.*

46 ECtHR, 22 March 2001, *Streletz, Kessler and Krenz v Germany*, § 82.

47 Lord H. Woolf, *l.c.*, 10, where, among others, the Court's sophisticated IT–system is mentioned.

48 L. Wildhaber, "Address to the Liaison Committee, 20 October 2005", as cited by Lord H. Woolf, *l.c.*, 11. Contra: J.–P. Costa, "Solemn Hearing of the European Court of Human Rights on the Occasion of the Opening of the Judicial Year", 19 January 2007, www.echr.coe.int, 3.

49 J. De Meyer, "Het E.V.R.M. Vijftig jaar", in P. Lemmens (ed.), *Uitdagingen door en voor het EVRM* (Mechelen: Kluwer, 2005) 180–185.

50 ECtHR, 5 October 2000, *Maaouia v France*; 12 July 2001, *Ferrazzini v Italy*; 21 October 1997, *Pierre–Bloch v France*. The exclusion of civil servants by the Pellegrin–jurisprudence (ECtHR, 8 December 1999) was in principle undone by ECtHR, 19 April 2007, *Vilho Eskelinen v Finland*.

ber States in the application of Articles 8–11 ECHR[51] can be seen as examples of diminishing quality in order to gain time.

Adopting any type of policy which avoids examining potentially well–founded cases on the merits not only contradicts law's protective function, it also constitutes a discriminating measure rendering the range of the protective problem even larger. Furthermore, this type of jurisprudence tends to make human rights, originally conceived as a simple set of *do's* and *don'ts*, quite technical and difficult to understand[52], making their internalisation even more difficult for Member States whose human rights tradition has never been of the highest standard.

4 Solutions

4.1 The Philosophical Question: Petitioners versus Constitutionalists

The overload of cases and the backlog this causes have initiated a discussion within the ECtHR and among scholars, called 'the philosophical question'.[53] The issue of the debate is whether the ECtHR's key function is to provide individual relief for every single applicant, or whether its mission is more a constitutional one of determining issues on public policy grounds in the general interest.[54] While the so–called petitioners cling on to the established IRIP described above[55], according to former ECtHR President Luzius Wildhaber (the most important spokesperson of the constitutionalists), the place of individual relief, however important, is secondary to the primary aim of raising the general standard of human rights protection and extending human rights jurisprudence throughout the community of Convention States.[56] The system's effectiveness should then be measured in the ability to avoid repetition of the circumstances giving rise to a violation.

---

51 See A. Ieven, "Privacy Rights as Human Rights: No Limits?". See also J.A. Brauch, "The Margin of Appreciation and the Jurisprudence of the European Court of Human Rights: Threat to the Rule of Law", *Columbia Journal of European Law* 2005, *11*, 113–150.

52 This sophistication entails the dangers of law as a scientific enterprise, see E. Claes, W. Devroe, and B. Keirsbilck, *l.c.*

53 See P. Sardaro, *l.c.*, 54–56; F. Vanneste, *l.c.*, 70–73; S. Greer, "Constitutionalizing Adjudication under the European Convention on Human Rights", *Oxford Journal of Legal Studies* 2003, *23*(3), 405–433; J.–F. Flauss, "Faut–il transformer la Cour européenne des droits de l'homme en juridiction constitutionnelle?" *Recueil Dalloz* 2003, 1638.

54 L. Wildhaber (speech cited by Lord H. Woolf), *l.c.*, 4.

55 F. Tulkens, M. Fischbach, J. Casadevall, and W. Thomassen, *l.c.*, 171–175; W. Thomassen, "Het individueel klachtrecht moet behouden blijven. Over het Europees Hof voor de Rechten van de Mens en zijn toekomst", *NJCM–Bulletin* 2003, 13.

56 L. Wildhaber, *l.c.*

This philosophical question has never arisen when the backlog problems were not as insurmountable as today. Both the ECtHR's key functions, individual justice and the watchdog role, seemed to be accepted alongside one another, with an increasing emphasis on the first one, whereas today the feeling is that they contradict one another, with the IRIP restraining the Court's opportunity to concentrate effectively on raising the human rights standards across Europe. The constitutionalists' restraint towards individual justice should not be condemned, since it derives from the conviction that a single court can only improve human rights in Europe if it deals with a few leading cases only each year, focusing on the most important ones. This paradox of human rights protection is a direct consequence of the massive influx of repetitive Eastern European cases, which is to a large extent caused by the lack of internalisation by countries such as Russia of the standards described in the ECtHR's jurisprudence.

This question indeed should not be one of philosophy. If the *individual justice* system can work, it should be made to work. If individual justice on such a large scale proves to be impossible, the *constitutional justice* model is the only possible path to follow. Admitting that the ECtHR cannot retain its individual approach under these circumstances would of course set back the enforceability of human rights by some decades. It would be equal to admitting the impossibility of international individual justice and it would raise some questions as to the essence of human rights being nothing but theoretical statements lacking the ability to be effectively enforced. It would also throw overboard this unique achievement related to the traditions of individualism human rights are embedded in. Before concluding this way, every possible way to make the individual justice model work should be examined.

4.2 Solutions Upholding the International Right of Individual Petition

Several possible solutions have been proposed and implemented in order, on the one hand, to divert some cases away from the Court, and on the other hand, to improve the Court's ability to deal with the rest more effectively while still acknowledging the IRIP. Due to the limited scope of this chapter, only the most important ones will be discussed.

4.2.1 Reestablishing the Principle of Subsidiarity

Regardless whether the ECtHR's main function is an individual or a constitutional one, it has always been clear that it was a subsidiary body[57], only to be called upon when the Member State concerned was unable or unwilling to redress a human

[57] As can be shown by Article 1, 13 and 35 (1) ECHR.

rights violation.[58] It can, however, only be subsidiary if citizens can put their human rights arguments on the table in domestic proceedings.

In the *Kudla* case[59], the ECtHR stated that Article 13, which grants the right to an effective domestic remedy for every ECHR violation, implies that a citizen should have a domestic legal action to assert a breach of the right of trial within a reasonable time. If there is no domestic remedy available, the ECtHR can condemn the Member State for a breach of Article 13. In its reasons, the ECtHR explicitly mentions a point of legal policy: if the individual would have sufficient domestic causes of action at his disposal, he would not be obliged systematically to apply to the ECtHR for complaints that can be solved at national level as well, involving a large benefit for the Convention system's long–term effectiveness. Unfortunately, this often applied jurisprudence has two main limits, since the ECtHR only applies this reasoning to length of proceedings cases, and since Article 13 only asks for a remedy provided by a 'national authority', which does not necessarily imply a judicial authority.[60]

Tackling the problem of repetitive cases also requires all Member States to implement all condemnatory judgments. In the *Broniowski* case[61], introducing the 'pilot judgment procedure', the ECtHR developed an interesting tool for the monitoring of implementation. Poland was found to have breached the right of property held by a whole class of individuals. The ECtHR explicitly pointed out the violation's underlying structural causes, and made clear that general measures at a national level were needed in implementing the judgment to remedy the systemic defect underlying the Court's finding, taking into account the many people affected. It even indicated which possibilities were open for the respondent State. All similar applications were adjourned, pending the implementation of the relevant general measures.[62] When the appropriate measures were taken, all 167 similar cases were struck of the Court's list with one simple decision.[63] Although this procedure seems vital for the Court's future, one critical remark should be made: this practice distinguishes between one applicant obtaining a judgment against his Member State, and all other applicants in similar situations, whose cases are put on hold. This reduces the system's dispute settlement role for many individuals. The only

58 ECtHR, 10 May 2001, *Z and Others v United Kingdom*, § 103; L. Wildhaber, *l.c.* The Group of Wise Person's Report reiterates this principle as one of the cornerstones of the system for protecting human rights in Europe.

59 ECtHR, 26 October 2000, *Kudla v Poland*, §§ 146–160.

60 P. Frumer, "Le recours effectif devant une instance nationale pour dépassement du délai raisonnable. Un revirement dans la jurisprudence de la Cour européenne des droits de l'homme", *J.T.Dr.Eur.* 2001, 51.

61 ECtHR, 22 June 2004, *Broniowski v Poland*.

62 Decision of the Fourth Section, 6 July 2004; Press release no. 400, 31 August 2004, "Bug River cases adjourned". See Lord H. Woolf, *l.c.*, 39–40; P. Leach, "Beyond the Bug River? A New Dawn for Redress Before the European Court of Human Rights", *EHRLR* 2005, 148.

63 On 28 September 2005, the *Broniowski* case itself was struck off the list following a friendly settlement between the applicant and Poland. On 19 June 2006, the Grand Chamber delivered a new Pilot Procedure Judgment in the *Hutten–Czapska v Poland* case.

thing that can neutralise this discrimination, is the Member State's remedying the underlying systemic problem.

4.2.2 Protocol 14

Already in 2000, the COE was convinced that new procedural reforms were needed to tackle the ECtHR's ever–growing backlog. After years of preparation, Protocol 14 was opened for signature on 13 May 2004. It contained some measures guaranteeing a higher effectiveness, both in input as in output, but many analyzers have already stated that, although it will increase the ECtHR's productivity by some 20 to 25%, it will most likely be insufficient.[64] Moreover, Russia's refusal to ratify hinders its entering into force and thus delays any advantage it might have.

The first type of measures changes the ECtHR's division into committees, chambers, the grand chamber, and the newly created single–judge formations.[65] The single–judge formation consists of one judge, assisted by reporters from the Registry[66] (who will probably do most of the work, even preparing a draft decision for the judge). This formation takes over the task previously entrusted to the committee of three judges declaring inadmissible the manifestly inadmissible applications.[67]

A committee of three judges can, by unanimous vote, declare an application admissible and at the same time render a judgment on the merits if the underlying question is the subject of well–established case–law.[68] This provision implies that judgments not only end a conflict *inter partes*, but also have precedential value[69], which can be seen as a step in the evolution towards a constitutional court. This procedure will probably play an important role in tackling repetitive cases.[70]

Having created a new mechanism for manifestly inadmissible and manifestly well–founded cases, Protocol 14 leaves the chambers and the grand chamber with more time to deal with the cases raising new questions. Furthermore, it leaves them with more possibilities to guide the parties to friendly settlements.[71]

---

64 Group of Wise Persons, *l.c.*, § 32.

65 See P. Lemmens, "Single–Judge Formations, Committees, Chambers and Grand Chamber", in P. Lemmens and W. Vandenhole (eds.), *Protocol No. 14 and the Reform of the European Court of Human Rights* (Antwerp: Intersentia, 2005) 31–43.

66 New Article 24(2) ECHR.

67 New Article 27(1); Explanatory report, § 67. According to Lemmens, only the cases for which the inadmissibility results from the reading of the application itself, are aimed at (P. Lemmens, *l.c.*, 34).

68 New Article 28(1), b.

69 P. Lemmens, *l.c.*, 36.

70 Explanatory Report, § 68; P. Lemmens, *l.c.*, 37.

71 F. Ang and E. Berghmans, "Friendly Settlements and Striking out of Applications", in P. Lemmens and W. Vandenhole (eds.), *Protocol No. 14 and the Reform of the European Court of Human Rights* (Antwerp: Intersentia, 2005) 89–104.

The second type of measures aims at improving and accelerating the execution of judgments[72], a practice on which the protection system depends: full execution of judgments helps to enhance the Court's prestige and the effectiveness of its action and has the effect of limiting the number of applications submitted to it.[73] Firstly, Article 39 foresees supervision by the Committee of Ministers on the execution of friendly settlements. Secondly, the forthcoming Article 46, § 3 to 5, empowers the Committee of Ministers, when it considers a State is refusing to abide by a final judgment, to refer this question to the ECtHR. When the Court finds that the State is unwilling, the Committee of Ministers has to take appropriate measures. It can only be hoped that this type of supervision by a political body will not be subject to political reasoning rather than to concern about individual effectiveness.

The third reform which Protocol 14 contains is the most controversial one. The ECtHR has to declare inadmissible any application if the applicant has not suffered a *significant disadvantage*. There are two exceptions: if the rejected grounds have not been duly considered by a domestic tribunal, or if "respect for human rights as defined in the Convention ... requires an examination of the application on the merits", the ECtHR retains jurisdiction.[74]

This provision represents an important ideological shift. Whereas, until now, the IRIP has always gained ground, this measure is a first step in the direction of the creation of a constitutional court, taking away the IRIP for applicants for whom the human rights violations have only caused insignificant physical, moral, and pecuniary harm. This first step is not a very good one: it discriminates between human rights violations on the basis of the effect these have had on the victims, while the ECtHR has never been and should never be conceived as a court for only serious human rights violations. Moreover, it seems very difficult to determine whether a human rights violation has provoked a significant disadvantage or not.[75] The question can even be raised whether the consequences of any kind of human rights violation can ever be called 'insignificant'. The ECtHR has already stated that the criterion of significant disadvantage will be applied with the utmost reticence, affecting some 4% of all cases at most.[76] This small impact only adds to the statement that this arbitrary intrusion into the IRIP should not have occurred. It is strange that during the preparation of Protocol 14, measures such as obligatory legal assistance, the compulsory use of French or English, and the establishment of a court fee were considered a bridge too far in the light of the IRIP, but this direct hit was nevertheless accepted.

---

72 W. Vandenhole, "The Execution of Judgments", in P. Lemmens and W. Vandenhole (eds.), *Protocol No. 14 and the Reform of the European Court of Human Rights* (Antwerp: Intersentia, 2005) 105–121.

73 Group of Wise Persons, *l.c.*, § 25.

74 P. Sardaro, *l.c.*, 50–66; F. Vanneste, *l.c.*, 69–88.

75 F. Vanneste, *l.c.*, 76–78.

76 *Ibid.*, 81.

4.2.3 The Woolf Report and the Group of Wise Persons

The review by Lord Woolf of the Registry's working methods suggested some administrative steps to be taken without amending the Convention. Some suggestions aim at diverting cases away from the Court. For example, Woolf concludes that much time is lost by processing mere communications or partial applications as applications. Adopting a stricter policy concerning the nature of an application would avoid thousands of useless files each year.[77] Another possibility to divert cases away from the Court is the working out of possibilities of alternative dispute settlement such as ombudsmen[78] or friendly settlements.[79]

At several places in his review, Woolf points out the importance of information and education, both for governments and for potential applicants,[80] which would contribute to redressing the second and the third causes described above. With this purpose in mind, a pilot project for an Information Office was launched in Warsaw in 2004. One COE lawyer provides information on the requirements as to admissibility, and makes potential applicants aware of the domestic remedies which are still available. This project has already proven that there is a serious demand for such information, and that the information provided can contribute to reducing the number of applications lodged in Strasbourg.[81] Therefore, Woolf suggests the further development of this concept into Satellite Offices of the Registry, especially in the countries generating the largest volumes of applications, where they would constitute the first obligatory step towards an admissible application.

Woolf concludes that by adopting these recommendations, the Court's internal efficiency would be stretched to its limits, so that further increases in incoming cases could not be dealt with by new rationalisations. Moreover, even all of those reforms combined with an expected entry into force of Protocol 14 will, according to him, be insufficient.

In November 2006, the Group of Wise Persons issued its long–expected report, which consisted of several types of measures. The most far–reaching suggestion was to create a separate *Judicial Committee*, consisting of judges other than those of the ordinary court. This Judicial Committee would have jurisdiction to hear all cases which could be declared manifestly well–founded or manifestly ill–founded on the basis of well–established ECtHR case–law, leaving the ECtHR itself with more time to focus on the cases which deserve an examination on the merits.[82]

---

77 Lord H. Woolf, *l.c.*, 19–24.
78 *Ibid.*, 31–34.
79 *Ibid.*, 42–47.
80 *Ibid.*, 26–27.
81 *Ibid.*, 27–28.
82 Group of Wise Persons, *l.c.*, § 51–65.

4.2.4 Evaluation: Marginal Utility

Not only will all these reforms be unable to tackle the current backlog and the ever–increasing number of applications, the increase of the ECtHR's productivity they would imply, will probably be subject to the same marginal utility logic to which the Protocol 9 and Protocol 11 reforms were subject. However, the effect might not be that large as it was before, since in this reform, the IRIP as such was not extended – there has even been a step back with the new admissibility criterion described above – and only intended to augment the effectiveness. But even then, every supply of better individual justice will entail its own demand. This factor should be taken into account when evaluating the impact that all these measures might have.

Moreover the ECtHR itself, the scholars and the politicians, are all becoming aware of the fact that the Court's current structures cannot be maintained much longer. A more radical reform of the whole control mechanism, including the co-operation with other COE institutions, is needed. The concession made to the constitutionalists with the new admissibility criterion might therefore not be the last one.

4.3 The ECtHR as a Constitutional Court: Giving it All Up?

Lord Woolf's conclusion recognises that every small reform will fail, and that a fundamental reform of the Convention system implies the creation of regional courts of first instance, allowing the existing Court to play a different role, whereby it ceases to be accessible as of right, but can instead control and select its own case–load.[83] Although a huge setback, this proposal recognises the fundamental problem of the mass of non–meritous cases taking up the time the Court needs to render leading judgments of the highest quality.[84] It also seems to be the only way out of the vicious circle of marginal utility described above.

It is true that once the ECtHR has diagnosed the existence of a human rights violation, the general purpose of raising the level of human rights protection in the State concerned is not served by continuing to issue judgments establishing the same violation.[85] The next victim's stake, however, is. But should it be the task of that same Court, consisting of 47 judges for 800 million Europeans, to pass judgment in every single one of those cases, or can this task be entrusted to another body? Probably this is mainly a question of execution of prior judgments (see the *Broniowski* case described above), for which the responsibility does not lie with the ECtHR. Fully relying on national remedies to be created would be impossible

---

83 *Ibid.*, 70. Also see P. Lemmens, "Het 14de Protocol bij het E.V.R.M.: het Europees Hof tegen zijn ondergang behoed", in P. Lemmens (ed.), *Uitdagingen door en voor het EVRM* (Mechelen: Kluwer, 2005) 141–143.

84 L. Wildhaber, *l.c.*, 6.

85 *Ibid.*, 6.

as well, since not all Member States seem to have internalised the ECHR and its standards. Sovereign national human rights courts in Eastern Europe would also be under much more political pressure than their Western European counterparts. Political peer pressure will be the only factor which can force unwilling Member States to comply with the ECtHR's condemnatory judgments.

The Group of Wise Persons has taken the decision to maintain the ECtHR's individual–based procedure. Setting up a system of regional courts of first instance would entail a risk of diverging case–law, it would be very costly, and it would raise a large number of procedural issues.[86] A certiorari system, in which the ECtHR would decide whether or not to take up cases for examination, was felt to undermine the philosophy underlying the Convention.[87]

4.4 The End of Human Rights?

In *The Origins of Totalitarianism* Arendt explains how minority groups and stateless persons between the two World Wars were completely deprived of their human rights, although these rights had been described since the French Revolution as inalienable.[88] While nobody needed this individual protection more than these human beings, the minority groups and the stateless did not have any access to human rights protection, simply because they did not belong to a nation which was willing to protect and enforce them. The League of Nations was unable to fill this protective gap because Nation–States did not accept any infringement on their sovereignty. This protection problem systematically increased until it was too large for any type of solution, leading to the democratic countries' unwillingness to take up their responsibility.

Arendt concludes that human rights in fact prove to be nothing but civil rights, their protection fully depending on government and international institutions. If these governments or institutions are unwilling or unable to play their protective role, human rights are nothing but unenforceable declarations. She therefore suggests a new concept of human rights, rephrasing this concept as an underlying possibility to give meaning to one's life: every individual has the right to membership in an organised community, in which he is judged upon his thoughts and acts, and therefore has the freedom to think and to act. This right to belong to humanity is to be guaranteed by mankind itself.

The individual's inability to enforce his own human rights, although there is nothing which is more closely linked to the individuality than these rights, might well be human rights law's most fundamental weakness: in order to be fully effective, the protection of the individual against the government needs the govern-

86 Group of Wise Persons, *l.c.*, § 41. The Court's new president, Jean–Paul Costa, concurs with that view: J.–P. Costa, *l.c.*

87 *Ibid.*, § 42.

88 H. Arendt, "The Decline of the Nation–State and the End of Human Rights", in H. Arendt, *The Origins of Totalitarianism* (Harcourt: Brace, 1951) 267–302.

ment's cooperation. The ECtHR's recent history shows this weakness' consequences for human rights law's protective function: a supranational Court supervising the COE Member States' human rights practice fails to live up to the high expectations if even a small group of these Member States refuses to abide with its standards of jurisprudence. The cumulation of individual petitions this provokes paralyses the ECtHR in the fulfillment of any of its functions, while abandoning the IRIP would harm the human rights' protective function just as much. The ECtHR has insufficient tools to penetrate into the sovereignty of unwilling Member States and to make something fundamental happen. Before this situation leads to a problem so large that any hope of a solution is in vain, political pressure should provoke an ideological shift in Eastern Europe. Although this political pressure, which can be imposed by the COE or the EU, is, in the given circumstances, a necessity, admitting that only politics can make the difference equals admitting that human rights are inherently ineffective concepts.

However, adjusting the concept of human rights does not provide a way out, since there is no point in defining them without reference to their protective function. Arendt's reconstructed human rights concept lacks this protective function and effectiveness, being a mere philosophical precondition for the existence of the human rights as we know them. The inherent limits within the concept of human rights lead to nothing but an insurmountable paradox: human rights can only offer protection against the government if this government allows human rights to play this protective role, and therefore, this concept falls short precisely when it should play this role, specifically when dealing with governments not allowing this. Equally paradoxical, an individual–relief–based supranational Court can only be viable in a situation where the protection it offers is actually superfluous.

5 Conclusion

The ECtHR's task cannot be conferred on the Member States, since some of them lack the needed human rights standards to cope with it. In order to guarantee legal protection, the ECtHR should be fully competent to supervise the ECHR's application in as many States as possible, with an IRIP conceived as broadly as possible. As a consequence of an inherent limit in the protective function of human rights applied at such a large scale, enhanced by a lack of internalisation of the standards the Court employs by some Eastern European Member States, and a similar gap in the citizens' understanding in the Court's functions, this international body, however, fails to play its protective role.

Many Eastern European countries have only joined the COE and ratified the ECHR because this constitutes a necessary step towards EU membership, not because they subscribed – or even understood – the principles underlying it. These principles had, until then, always been the cement on which the COE was built. This cement has largely evaporated due to the COE's excessive growth during the 1990s. However, this cement should already be common to all participating countries before the regional organisation can function, whereas currently, the same principles are asked to act both as the cement and as the goal of the COE.

A single Court cannot be expected to uphold, let alone to create this cement if a significant number of Member States remains unwilling to subscribe and internalise the COE's basic principles. Law is unable to play such a role, since it is powerless if it is confronted with an unwilling State's sovereignty. An individual–relief–based international Court not only proves to be unable to create cement out of thin air, it also drowns in the flood caused by this combination of problems, failing to live up to the high expectations it is asked to fulfill.

The ECtHR as a constitutional court would also be unable to create this cement. It will even have fewer weapons to force unwilling Member States into the human rights way of thinking. Any type of supranational court can only work on a solid basis of, on the one hand, sufficient and effective domestic remedies and, on the other hand, a systematic execution by all Member States of all condemning judgments, which are *conditiones sine quibus non* for the effectiveness of human rights and for any kind of regionalism based upon them. These two foundations, however, are consequences of the pre–existence of sufficient cement, which means that they, or the court founded on them, are by definition unable to create this cement themselves.

Before human rights law and its enforcement can play any role in pan–European regionalism, this regionalism must first be established on a solid basis of human rights, which would imply a major ideological shift in Eastern Europe. Only sufficient political pressure, thorough human rights education and several years of patience, will be able to establish this ideological shift in the fragile Eastern European democracies. A very strong Council of Ministers will therefore be necessary in the years to come in order to provide a life–line for the ECtHR and even the COE.

Furthermore, the question needs to be answered whether it is tolerable for Western Europe to impose Western inventions called 'rule of law' and 'human rights' on other parts of the world, which are embedded in totally different cultures. This question about universality versus relativity of human rights is addressed by Vandenhole's chapter. As to law, it can only be noted that all COE Member States have, by ratifying the ECHR, taken up the obligation to fully incorporate its standards into their legal order.

Chapter 20 – The Limits of Human Rights Law in Human Development

"The more uncomprising reality is that the struggles for human rights and justice lie 'beyond law'."[1]

Wouter Vandenhole

1 Introduction

Within the human rights community, expectations about the potential of human rights law to contribute substantially to human development[2] are high. The development community tends to be sceptical, and some human rights scholars too – among which Philip Alston, the Special Adviser to the High Commissioner for Human Rights on the Millennium Development Goals and Human Rights[3] – have started to express some cautionary remarks (section 2).

It is submitted that human rights law, notwithstanding its potential to meaningfully contribute to human development, faces severe limits indeed. These limits relate partly to some of the characteristics of (human rights) law, such as its focus on the individual and on State sovereignty. Others go to the ideological heart of the liberal State (section 3). Perhaps paradoxically, as important as the limits themselves, human rights lawyers' *awareness* and acknowledgement of these limits may determine and circumscribe the developmental potential of human rights law. For the more these limits are ignored, the less likely it becomes that human rights law plays a meaningful role in bringing about human development (section 4).

There is a long–standing – albeit rather marginal – debate on the potential of law in general to contribute to development. After its demise in the mid 1970s, the belief in developmental legal engineering reemerged to a certain extent in the

---

* This chapter draws on research which was partly funded by the Netherlands Organization for Scientific Research (NWO). I would like to thank all those who have furthered my thoughts on this issue, in particular at the LSE interdisciplinary conference 'Crossing the Boundaries' on 24 March 2006, on which occasion I presented a slightly differently orientated paper. All opinions and mistakes are of course my sole responsibility.

1 R. Dhavan, "Ambedkar's Prophecy: Poverty of Human Rights in India", *Journal of the Indian Law Institute* 1994, *36*, 8, 27.

2 The adjective 'human' denotes that the emphasis is not on *economic* growth or development of a country, but rather on the improvement of the living conditions for the people.

3 See P. Alston, "Ships Passing in the Night: The Current State of the Human Rights and Development Debate Seen Through the Lens of the Millennium Development Goals", *Human Rights Quarterly* 2005, *27*, 755.

early 1990s, following the collapse of the Berlin Wall.[4] Lessons that have been drawn from this general debate may also be applied to human rights law more particularly. One is the need to avoid naïve legal instrumentalism. It seems imperative and widely recognised that sufficient attention be paid to principles like the rule of law and the independence of the judiciary. It has been pointed out however that these principles are not only legal principles, but that they are part of an ideological package which is commonly denoted as the 'liberal State'.[5] While this does not need to be problematic in itself, any absence of awareness thereof might well be, such as, when legal reform is attempted in a society in which these ideological underpinnings are not widely shared or present.

It is submitted that human rights law and litigation is confronted with at least three fundamental limits when deployed for the sake of human development: conceptual limits, limits of legitimacy and ideological limits (section 3).

Two *conceptual* limits are discussed in more detail: the concern with individual rights and the premise of sovereign equality. Traditional human rights law litigation is ill–suited to address satisfactorily issues of human development for two major reasons. First, it takes an individualised approach to fundamentally structural problems. Secondly and at a more fundamental level, both national and international efforts to mobilise human rights law for human development seem to be frustrated and inhibited by the obstacle of presumed equality. Lifting the veil of formal equality between individuals and States appears to be a common challenge at national and international level respectively in order to increase the relevance of human rights law for human development. While such an undertaking threatens one of the longstanding principles of law, it may even have a more profound implication, in that it touches upon one of the underpinning ideological values of human rights law and liberalism.

Issues of *legitimacy* too pose limits to human rights law. Considerations of legitimacy arise with regard to judicial activism and the legal conceptualisation of the right to development and third–State human rights obligations. The crucial question with the latter two conceptions is how far the human rights concept can be stretched without become self–defeating.

A major *ideological* limit of human rights law is that it can only meaningfully contribute to human development in a certain legal context, namely that of the rule of law. In light of the fragility, subversion or absence of the rule of law in a high number of third world countries, this is probably the most serious limit the human rights community has to acknowledge. Moreover, at a minimum, social justice must be accepted as a fundamental value in society.

The limits of human rights law and litigation in contributing to human development in countries in the South require first and foremost critical *awareness* about their existence (section 4). Some limits may be partly remedied through a

---

4 See *e.g.* A. Seidman, R. Seidman and T.W. Wälde (eds.), *Making Development Work. Legislative Reform for Institutional Transformation and Good Governance* (The Hague: Kluwer, 1999).

5 See *inter alia*, I. Shivji, "The Rule of Law and Ujamaa in the Ideological Formation of Tanzania", *Social and Legal Studies* 1995, *4*, 147, 150–151.

critical rethinking of certain aspects of human rights law. However, the more it is tried to reconceptualise human rights law to increase its developmental relevance, the more likely this results in a loss of legitimacy and reduced legal recognition (see for the latter our discussion on the right to development and third–State obligations). Human development requires collective and structural approaches, and the commitment of many actors. While human rights law may be amenable to partial transformation over time in order to become better equipped to confront these challenges, in the end the exigencies of a structural and multi–actor approach may expose the insurmountable limits to human rights law.

A final word of caution. The attempt undertaken in this chapter, that is to identify the multiple limits of human rights law, is not a plea for legal conservatism. It is rather intended as an awareness–raising exercise for human rights lawyers who engage in human development. While it may be possible, and should certainly be tried, to overcome to the maximum extent possible the limits exposed, human rights lawyers should keep in mind at all times that every attempt at conceptual innovation may be confronted with more fundamental limits, and will be challenged by them. A *conditio qua non* for success in innovative human rights lawyering is that the rule of law and social justice are to be referred to as basic principles of the State's set–up, *inter alia* to legitimise political power.

2 Promising Tales: Innovative Human Rights Approaches to Development

In what follows, three legal conceptions are presented in which an attempt has been undertaken to deploy innovatively human rights law for human development. The selection process has been rather random, in that these conceptions represent the issues I have been researching over the past decade. Nevertheless, more general conclusions can be drawn about the limits of human rights law to contributing to human development.

First, an example in domestic law is succinctly described. Social Action Litigation in India (SAL) has been a judicial enforcement strategy for human rights of the Indian poor. Secondly, two conceptual innovations in international law are scrutinised: the legal conceptualisation of a human right to development, and the elaboration of third–State obligations under the International Covenant on Economic, Social and Cultural Rights (ICESCR).

These three innovative legal conceptions have at least one fundamental characteristic in common. All three build on the premise that the veil of formal equality of legal subjects is to be lifted if human rights law is to be of some relevance in the context of development. SAL rebuts the fiction that parties confronting each other in human rights litigation (individuals or groups versus the State) are equal. Taking the fundamental inequality of the litigating parties as a starting point, with the State as the stronger party, the Indian Supreme Court has attempted to reconceptualise human rights litigation in order to make it more receptive to those who want to challenge structural obstacles for human development. The conceptions of the human right to development and of third–State human rights obligations challenge the international law fiction of sovereign equality of States. While SAL may represent a ground breaking departure from procedural rules as applicable in ordinary domestic litigation, many of its elements can also be found in human rights procedures before the UN quasi–judicial bodies or regional human rights courts. The attempts to lift the veil of formal equality of States are clearly more contentious and are perceived to entail a more fundamental questioning of one of the basic tenets of (international) law.

2.1 Domestic Law: Social Action Litigation in India[6]

SAL can be described as a doctrine of procedural relaxations, in order to facilitate both access to justice and the production of evidence in human rights cases. By allowing furthermore for specific and detailed remedies and for supervision of the implementation thereof, it attempts to improve human rights protection. It is a judicial response to the perceived procedural limits of human rights litigation in addressing structural issues of poverty and human development.

SAL has six main procedural characteristics. First of all, the rules of standing have been relaxed in a two–fold way. Secondly, the formalities for lodging a complaint have been eased substantially. Thirdly, evidence can be gathered by a commission of inquiry that is appointed by the court. Fourthly, the procedure purports to be not of an adversary nature. Fifthly, far–reaching remedial measures can be ordered. Sixthly and finally, the execution of the remedial orders is supervised and followed up upon. The first two innovations concern the launch of the procedure; the next two have to do with its conduct, and the last two with its outcome.

The poor and disadvantaged often do not have access to the courts because of their disadvantaged position in society. They lack the human and financial resources to take an issue to court.[7] In its landmark decision in the *Gupta* case, the Indian Supreme Court departed consciously from the traditional rules of *locus standi*. First of all, the rules of *locus standi* were relaxed in these cases in which a specific legal wrong or legal injury was caused to a person or a class or group of persons. Secondly, the rules of standing were also liberalised in cases of so–called 'public injury' or injury to the public interest, namely cases in which the State acted in violation of a fundamental right or failed to carry out an obligation ensu-

6 For an extensive discussion, see *inter alia* W. Vandenhole, "Human Rights Law, Development and Social Action Litigation in India", *Asia–Pacific Journal on Human Rights and the Law* 2002, *2*, 136.

7 Compare K. De Feyter, *Human Rights. Social Justice in the Age of the Market* (London: Zed Books, 2005) 60.

ing from a fundamental right, to the detriment of the public interest and the rule of law.[8]

Simultaneously with the liberalisation of the rules of standing, the Indian Supreme Court also relaxed the rules of procedure and the formalities for lodging a human rights complaint, so as to remove as much as possible any procedural hurdles. It accepted therefore that a complaint could be lodged with an ordinary letter, a telegram or even a post card ('epistolary jurisdiction').[9]

As to the conduct of the procedure itself, two innovations were made, which have been coined 'investigative' and 'collaborative' litigation.[10] First, the appointment of commissions of inquiry was introduced to free the poor and citizens acting *pro bono publico* from gathering the relevant evidence. The commission has to report to the court, and is often also expected to formulate suggestions and recommendations for resolving the issue. Secondly, it was attempted to introduce a form of collaborative litigation, in which the parties were not considered to be opponents, but collaborative stakeholders. The adversarial procedure is departed from in that the other party is not to be regarded as an adversary.[11] Together with the introduction of the idea of collaborative litigation, an active role for judges in the proceedings was also favoured. The judge is expected to participate actively in the case, *inter alia* by appointing (when necessary) a commission of inquiry, by ordering innovative remedies and by supervising execution of the orders given.

In light of the urgent character of many cases, and of the ongoing nature of many human rights violations, frequent use has been made of interim orders. The Supreme Court of India has also substantially broadened the scope of remedies, aiming at *restitutio in integrum*. In order to translate entitlements into concrete benefits[12], the Court's orders have been very specific and detailed. Inevitably, the Supreme Court often infringes upon the traditional division of powers between the judiciary and the executive. To a certain extent, it plays the role of a policy–maker and takes over the task of the executive. Baxi has coined the term 'creeping jurisdiction' to indicate the process by which the Court, issuing consecutive interim orders in a case, progresses from the claims in a specific case to the wider social problems involved.[13] Sometimes the Court has even granted relief beyond what had been asked by the petitioner. It has also gone beyond the concrete case by extending the remedies to the whole class of persons on whose behalf the claim was

---

8 Indian Supreme Court, *S.P. Gupta v Union of India*, [1982] *All India Reporter* (hereafter *AIR*) SC at [17–18].

9 U. Baxi, "Taking Suffering Seriously: Social Action Litigation in the Supreme Court of India", in N. Tiruchelvam and R. Coomaraswamy (eds.), *The Role of the Judiciary in Plural Societies* (New York: St. Martin's Press, 1987) 39 and P.N. Bhagwati, "Judicial Activism and Public Interest Litigation", *Columbia Journal of Transnational Law* 1985, *23*, 561, 571.

10 The terminology is borrowed from C.D. Cunningham, "Public Interest Litigation in Indian Supreme Court: A Study in the Light of American Experience", in J. Kapur (ed.), *Supreme Court on Public Interest Litigation. Cases and Materials. The Debate over Original Intent* I (New Delhi: LIPS, *s.d.*) A–74 - A–76.

11 Indian Supreme Court, *Sheela Barse v Union of India PIL–SCALE* 1511 at [8].

12 M. Gomez, *In the Public Interest* (Legal Aid Centre, University of Colombo, 1993) 79.

13 Baxi, *l.c.*, 42. See also Cunningham, *l.c.*, A–80.

made, by making the remedial orders binding for the whole class of defendants, or by offering remedies for others than strictly those on whose behalf the complaint was lodged.[14]

The execution and implementation of the Indian Supreme Court's orders and judgments have been very problematic. Therefore, a final innovation in SAL concerns the Court's supervision over the implementation of its interim orders and final judgments. Sometimes, the Court appoints a supervisory mechanism to report back to it. In a number of cases, the Court has itself supervised that implementation, and has left open the possibility for the petitioner(s) to return before it in case of non–compliance.

2.2 International Law: Right to Development and Third–State Obligations

Turning to international law, two attempts to link up conceptually human rights law and human development are shortly discussed, specifically the elaboration of a human right to development and of third–State human rights obligations.

2.2.1 The Human Right to Development

The right to development represents an attempt to link up human rights law and human development by creating a human right to development. Initially located in international development law and intended to give voice to claims for fairer international economic relations between North and South, the concept was then transferred to the realm of human rights law.

Although different approaches can be taken to the legal conceptualisation of the right to development, ranging from rejecting or questioning the (human) rights nature of the right to development[15], over a minimalist conceptualisation firmly situated within mainstream international human rights law, to a rather maximalist approach of stretching the human rights concept as far as possible[16], it seems

---

14 Cunningham, *l.c.*, A–80.

15 See for example K. De Vey Mestdagh, "The Right to Development", *Netherlands International Law Review* 1981, *25*, 30, 53; P. de Waart, "State Rights and Human Rights as Two Sides of One Principle of International Law: the Right to Development", in P. de Waart, P. Peters and E. Denters (eds.), *International Law and Development* (Dordrecht: Martinus Nijhoff, 1988) 372; M. Kenig–Witkowska, "The UN Declaration on the Right to Development in the Light of its Travaux Préparatoires", in P. de Waart, P. Peters and E. Denters (eds.), *International Law and Development* (Dordrecht: Martinus Nijhoff, 1988) 383; A. Rosas, "The Right to Development", in A. Eide, C. Krause and A. Rosas (eds.), *Economic, Social and Cultural Rights. A Textbook* (Dordrecht: Martinus Nijhoff, 1995) 254–255.

16 Examples of a maximalist approach can be found, in P. Alston, "Some Notes on the Concept of the Right to Development", in D. Prémon (ed.), *Essais sur le concept de 'droit de vivre' en mémoire de Yougindra Khushalani* (Brussels: Bruylant, 1988), 84. See also K. De Feyter,

appropriate to focus here on the 1986 UN General Assembly Declaration on the Right to Development. Notwithstanding repeated calls for a Convention on the Right to Development, the 1986 General Assembly Declaration on the Right to Development has remained so far the most authoritative statement of the human right to development.

Article 1, para. 1 of the Declaration defines the right to development as

> an inalienable human right by virtue of which every human person and all peoples are entitled to participate in, contribute to, and enjoy economic, social, cultural and political development, in which all human rights and fundamental freedoms can be fully realised.

The right implies the full realisation of the right of peoples to self–determination (Article 1, para. 2). Article 2, para. 1 emphasises that "[t]he human person is the central subject of development and should be the active participant and beneficiary of the right to development."

The right–bearers in the Declaration are "every human person and all peoples" (Article 1, para. 1). A multiplicity of duty–bearers is mentioned: all human beings, individually and collectively, and States (Article 2, paras. 2 and 3). States have however the primary responsibility for the creation of national and international conditions favourable to the realisation of the right to development (Article 3, para. 1). Article 2, para. 3 clarifies the duty of States at the national level: "States have the right and the duty to formulate appropriate national development policies." Article 8 adds that "States should undertake, at the national level, all necessary measures for the realization of the right to development [...] [and] should encourage popular participation in all spheres [...]." In Article 5 it is stipulated that "[S]tates shall take resolute steps to eliminate the massive and flagrant violations of the human rights of peoples and human beings." States should also take steps to eliminate obstacles to development resulting from failure to observe civil and political rights, as well as economic, social and cultural rights (Article 6). The other Articles contain a mixture of the duties attaching to both developing and developed States, with a strong emphasis on co–operation. States have the duty to co–operate with each other in ensuring development and eliminating obstacles to development (Article 3, para. 3). They have the duty to take steps, individually and collectively, to formulate international development policies. Complementary to the efforts of developing countries, effective international co–operation is essential to providing these countries with appropriate means and facilities (Article 4). According to Article 6, all States should co–operate with a view to promoting, encouraging and strengthening universal respect for and observance of all human rights and fundamental freedoms for all. They should also promote the establishment, maintenance and strengthening of international peace and security (Article 8).

The Human Rights Approach to Development II (Antwerp: University of Antwerp, 1992) 555–556, who defines the human right to development from a double perspective. The internal dimension implies the right of individuals and peoples (minorities and indigenous peoples) towards the domestic State to participate in the determination of the development policy and in the distribution of the benefits. The external dimension entails positive obligations for third–States and the international community.

It is fully acknowledged that the UN Declaration is only one element in the ongoing political discussion on the right to development. The work done and the progress made more recently in working groups may therefore be substantially different from the contents of the Declaration. Here, the focus is nevertheless on conceptual legal developments, not on the political bargaining process related to this legal conception, nor on pragmatic efforts to imbue the concept with practical relevance.[17]

2.2.2 Third–State Obligations under the ICESCR

The elaboration of extraterritorial human rights obligations for States parties to the ICESCR, namely obligations which arise when States act outside their territory or when their actions have extraterritorial effects, corresponds to the increasingly felt need to identify the respective responsibilities of States in the North and the South for the realisation of economic, social and cultural rights in the South. What seems plain common sense – States are not allowed to do abroad what they are not allowed to do domestically – does not necessarily make legal sense. Even more contentious is whether States are to do abroad what they are expected to do at home under human rights law. Hampered by a jurisdiction clause or even by an explicit reference to territory (as is the case with the International Covenant on Civil and Political Rights, ICCPR), supervisory bodies in the field of civil and political rights have recognised the extraterritorial application of civil and political rights provisions in limited cases only.[18] In the absence of a jurisdiction clause and in view of the multiple explicit references to international assistance and cooperation in the ICESCR, it has been argued that third–State obligations do exist under the ICESCR.

The tripartite typology of State obligations that is usually employed to clarify domestic State obligations can be equally useful for spelling out the meaning of third–State obligations.[19] The tripartite typology may also prove extremely rele-

---

[17] The current working group and its subsidiary, the task force, have decided to work on the assessment of global partnerships for development (as referred to in Millennium Development Goal No. 8) from the perspective of the right to development, in an attempt to make its deliberations more concrete and relevant (see, for a confirmation, UN Doc.E/CN.4/2006/26, *Report of the Working Group on the Right to Development on its seventh session* (Geneva, 9–13 January 2006), para. 26).

[18] The state of the art is well reflected in F. Coomans and M. T. Kamminga (eds.), *Extraterritorial Application of Human Rights Treaties* (Antwerp: Intersentia, 2004); see also S. Skogly, *Beyond National Borders: States' Human Rights Obligations in International Cooperation* (Antwerp: Intersentia, 2006).

[19] R. Künnemann, "Extraterritorial Application of the International Covenant on Economic, Social and Cultural Rights", in F. Coomans and M.T. Kamminga (eds.), *Extraterritorial Application of Human Rights Treaties* (Antwerp: Intersentia, 2004) 212–213; M. Sepúlveda, *The Nature of the Obligations under the International Covenant on Economic, Social and Cultural Rights* (Antwerp: Intersentia, 2003) 373–374; M. Craven, *The International Covenant on Economic, Social and Cultural Rights – A Perspective on its Development* (Oxford: Clarendon Press, 1995) 147–149.

vant for determining the degree of legal recognition particular third–State obligations enjoy on a scale from soft to hard law. The third–State obligation of respect, to refrain from interfering with the realisation of economic, social and cultural rights in other countries[20], has been said to be a minimum obligation[21], which moreover is easy to identify and well–documented, and which relates to the direct conduct of the third States concerned. It is a "rather strong obligation"[22] that can be argued to be "part of existing human rights law (*de lege lata*)."[23] On the other hand, the third–State obligations of protection (against third parties under their control) and of completion or fulfillment have been said to be "still part of the law 'under construction', that is the law as it ought to be (*de lege ferenda*)."[24] The obligation to fulfil clearly is the most contentious one.[25] Any suggestion of a *legal* obligation to provide development aid for example has invariably been met by fierce rejection of even the most generous donor countries.

Basically, just as in the case of the human right to development, the conceptualisation of third–State obligations under the ICESCR represents an attempt to broaden the circle of duty–bearers for development. Whereas the human right to development does this in a comprehensive way, *i.e.* for all human rights, the elaboration of third–State obligations takes a more fragmented approach, in that rather specific obligations are identified with regard to each of the economic, social or cultural rights guaranteed in the Covenant. It can, for example, be argued that the EU agricultural subsidies for structural overproduction of sugar, which is then exported to the South at dumping prices, to the detriment of local farmers, is in violation of the third–State obligation of the EU Member States, which all happen to be States parties to the ICESCR, to respect the right to an adequate standard of living.[26]

---

20 The obligation to respect corresponds to the traditional understanding of human rights (mainly civil and political rights) as entailing a negative obligation on behalf of the State.

21 UN Doc. E/CN.4/2005/47, *Report of the Special Rapporteur on the Right to Food, Jean Ziegler*, 24 January 2005, at 48; F. Coomans, "Some Remarks on the Extraterritorial Application of the International Covenant on Economic, Social and Cultural Rights", in F. Coomans and M.T. Kamminga (eds.), *Extraterritorial Application of Human Rights Treaties* (Antwerp: Intersentia, 2004) 190.

22 *Ibid.*, 193.

23 *Ibid.*, 199.

24 *Ibid.*, 199.

25 See M. Craven, *l.c.*, 148.

26 For a discussion of this issue, see W. Vandenhole, "Third State Obligations under the ICESCR: a Case Study of the EU Sugar Regime", *Nordic Journal of International Law* 2007, *76*, 73–100.

3 Limits of the Law

The limits of the law can be situated at different levels. The concern here is with more fundamental and inherent limits of (human rights) law itself, rather than with practical difficulties of the specific legal conceptions outlined. As the relationship between human rights law and human development is central to the three 'promising tales' narrated, the limits highlighted here pertain to the developmental or emancipatory potential of human rights law at the national and the international level.

Three types of limits will be distinguished: conceptual limits, limits of legitimacy and ideological limits. As pointed out in the introduction to this chapter, the exercise undertaken here of pointing out some of the limits of human rights law is not intended to criticise or weaken the law. Instead, it is thought imperative for lawyers active in the field of human development to be fully aware of these limits, so as to be able to devise legal strategies in full acknowledgement of the limits of the law.

3.1 Conceptual Limits

With 'conceptual limits' is meant these limits which operate at the level of (human rights) law itself. They relate to fundamental principles or underlying concepts of (human rights) law. Two issues are discussed in more detail: the concern with individual rights and the premise of sovereign equality.

3.1.1 Individualism

Human rights law is traditionally pictured as the relationship between the individual and the (domestic) State. The right–bearer in human rights law is the individual, the duty–bearer is the domestic State. The individual approach of human rights law sits uneasily with the structural and collective challenges which human development poses. Human development cannot be addressed adequately in a fractured and individualised manner. Therefore there seems to be a mismatch between the fundamentally individual orientation of human rights law and the fundamentally structural and collective challenges human development entails. De Feyter has well–documented for example how in the famous *Lubicon Lake Band* case the claim for recognition of an indigenous people's collective right to economic self–determination was transformed by the United Nations Human Rights

Committee[27] into the violation of "an individual cultural right of a minority member that could be remedied by adequate compensation."[28]

Individualism is central to human rights law. Apart from the right to self–determination, no other collective rights have been recognised in international human rights law. The recognition of the right to self–determination in common Article 1 of the 1966 International Covenants (ICCPR and ICESCR) has been explained as a historical accident. It is to be situated in the process of decolonisation of many third–world countries during the negotiation process. Clearly, the right to self–determination is of a different nature than human rights, not only because of its collective character, but also because its final aim is different. While self–determination aims at a *distribution* of sovereignty, human rights only purport to *confine or limit* the exercise of sovereign power.[29] Developed States therefore insisted on the separation in the Covenants of the right to self–determination in a different part. In any event, the right to self–determination cannot be invoked in the *individual* complaints procedure before the Human Rights Committee. Under the ICESCR too, it is most unlikely that the right to self–determination will be covered by any future complaints procedure, which is currently under negotiation.

SAL circumvents the issue to a large extent by introducing collectivised standing, so that individuals can complain on behalf of a group or a collectivity of individuals. There may seem to exist less of a need to elaborate and recognise collective rights when collectivised standing is guaranteed. Not all human development issues can be satisfactory settled through collectivised standing however. Hard cases may include the demands of indigenous peoples or minorities for their own development model: these demands cannot be fully accommodated for by collectivised standing, as the substantive claims cannot be subsumed under the existing list of individual human rights.[30]

One of the challenging issues in the elaboration of the human right to development is the identification of rights–holders. The Declaration on the Right to Development recognises both individuals and peoples as active subjects of the right to development, but clearly still leans towards rights of individuals ("the human person"). The United States, one of the opponents of the Declaration on the Right to Development, which has meanwhile politically recognised the existence of a human right to development at the Vienna World Conference on Human Rights, has systematically argued that it is a right inherent in the individual.[31] This considerably weakens the potential relevance of the right to development for groups such as minorities or indigenous peoples. Some have argued that (developing) States too can be active subjects of the right to development. While this may make po-

---

27 The Human Rights Committee is the monitoring body of the 1966 International Covenant on Civil and Political Rights (ICCPR).

28 K. De Feyter, *World Development Law. Sharing Responsibility for Development* (Antwerp: Intersentia, 2001) 156.

29 *Ibid.*, 45. For a historical overview of the right to self–determination, *Ibid.*, 37–46.

30 *Ibid.*, 156.

31 UN Doc A/C.3/60/SR.47, para. 16: "all individuals should be able to develop their intellectual and other capabilities to the fullest possible extent through the exercise of civil and political rights".

litical sense and be fully arguable as a matter of international development law, it dangerously blurs the distinction between human rights and inter–State law. One of the distinctive characteristics of human rights law is that it purports to protect individuals against absolute State power and that it imposes fundamental welfare obligations on the State. While the focus on the individual as the only subject in need of human rights protection, thereby neglecting groups, is to be criticised, invoking human rights language for the protection and justification of claims of weaker *States* (developing States) is flawed, for it puts into danger the fundamental function of human rights law, of protecting against abuse of power by the *State* (and, possibly, by extension, by other powerful actors).[32]

It seems to be assumed quite generally that for reasons of conceptual integrity human rights law is to keep its individualistic tenet. Collective rights may well deserve legal recognition, though not as *human* rights. However, the individualism of human rights law may conflict with the more comprehensive and collective approach human development requires. While a degree of *procedural* flexibility on this point has been shown by the Supreme Court of India, among others, it seems very unlikely for the time being that major inroads can be made in the individualism of *substantive* human rights law. This means that human rights law from a human development perspective will inevitably be experienced as fundamentally limited. The deployment of human rights law in the context of human development efforts will come at the cost of individualisation. The translation of real–life problems and complaints into human rights issues deforms them substantially, in hard cases probably even to a point at which human rights law might be rejected as useless. As was highlighted above, the only legally entrenched collective right so far in a legally binding human rights instrument, the right to self–determination, is fundamentally different from individual human rights, in that it does not seek to check, but rather to challenge sovereign power. This collective right cannot be invoked in complaints procedures.

3.2.2 Equality

In the context of human rights litigation, equality of the litigating parties is usually assumed or required. The principle of full answer and defence implies that both parties are given the opportunity to have knowledge of and comment on the observations filed and the evidence adduced by the other party.[33] In SAL, it has been recognised that parties in human rights litigation are often not equal, but to the contrary find themselves in a fundamentally uneven position whereby an economically and socially weak individual faces a powerful State, as represented by its agents. SAL has therefore reconceptualised the adversary procedure into a collaborative one. Collaborative justice is based on the fact that parties do not always

---

32 J. Donnelly, "In Search of the Unicorn: the Jurisprudence and Politics of the Right to Development", *California Western International Law Journal* 1985, *15*, 473, 508.

33 Indian Supreme Court, *Edwards and Lewis v the United Kingdom*, [2004] *ECR* at [46–48].

have the same social or economic power. As a consequence, when one of the parties belongs to a deprived section of society,

> [he or she] is bound to be at a disadvantaged [position] as against a strong and powerful opponent under the adversary system of justice, because of his difficulty in getting competent legal representation and more than anything else, his inability to produce relevant evidence before the court.[34]

The direct impact of the Supreme Court orders and judgments in SAL has been rather limited, mainly due to the uncooperative attitude of the executive. This raises fundamental questions of the factual impact of collaborative litigation, which purports to address the inequality between the litigating parties. Acknowledgement of inequality and procedural adaptations to address inequality have not been able to *change* power relations on the ground, and have therefore also been only modestly successful in contributing to better living conditions such as for bonded labourers.

Equality is without doubt one of the core substantive principles of human rights law. This has been reaffirmed time and again. Equality has been claimed to be "the most important principle imbuing and inspiring the concept of human rights", along with liberty,[35] the "dominant and recurring theme of international human rights law"[36], "one of the most frequently declared norms of international human rights law"[37], and "one of the major themes of most UN core human rights treaties".[38] Human rights treaties guarantee equality both in law and before the law. Although attention has been paid to substantive (in)equality, there is still hesitation and reluctance to accommodate substantive or *de facto* inequality through, for example, affirmative action.[39]

Not only in human rights litigation and substantive law, but more fundamentally in the concept of law itself, individuals are perceived as equals. Few lawyers will have difficulty in admitting that formal equality of individuals is a legal fiction. The challenge however is not so much to *admit* the legal fiction, but to *relinquish* it altogether. Only then would the limit that the assumption of equality poses be really superseded. The legal principle of equality is, however, unlikely to be given up easily, for it corresponds to an assumption of equality in the underlying ideology of liberalism. Formal equality, next to liberty, is a key assumption of liberalism and human rights law alike. Both take as a starting point the individual, who is assumed to be equal to all other individuals. While it was for a long time that human beings were unequal by nature, starting from the Enlightenment "the

34 Indian Supreme Court, *Bandhua Mukti Morcha v Union of India*, [1984] *AIR* at [13].

35 M. Nowak, *U.N. Covenant on Civil and Political Rights. CCPR Commentary* (Kehl: Engel, 1993) 458.

36 A. Bayefski, "The Principle of Equality or Non–Discrimination in International Law", *Human Rights Law Journal* 1990/1–2, *11*, 1, 2.

37 *Ibid.*, 1.

38 B.G. Ramcharan, "Equality and Nondiscrimination", in L. Henkin (ed.), *The International Bill of Rights. The Covenant on Civil and Political Rights* (New York: Columbia University Press, 1981) 246.

39 See W. Vandenhole, *Non–Discrimination and Equality in the View of the UN Human Rights Treaty Bodies* (Antwerp: Intersentia, 2005).

dominant idea was of natural equality in the tradition of natural law and social contract theory."[40]

The legal fiction of equality is reproduced at the level of States. Sovereign equality is one of the basic tenets of international law, including international human rights law. According to Cassese:

> Of the various fundamental principles regulating international relations, this is unquestionably the only one on which there is unqualified agreement and which has the support of all groups of States, irrespective of ideologies, political leanings, and circumstances. It is safe to conclude that sovereign equality constitutes the linchpin of the whole body of international legal standards, the fundamental premise on which all international relations rest.[41]

Constitutive of sovereignty is *inter alia* the right that no other State intrude in the State's territory. Legal equality requires that all States are treated on the same footing.[42]

The sanctity of sovereignty can be seen for example in the discussions on the right to self–determination, as exemplified in the negotiations on the UN Declaration on the rights of indigenous peoples, in which their right to self–determination is recognised. The right to self–determination lays a fundamental claim on the distribution or transfer of sovereignty. Human rights, in the mainstream understanding, do not fundamentally challenge sovereignty. They are more moderate checks against abuses in the exercise of sovereign power, which is not challenged in itself though.[43]

Reality is at odds with this fundamental tenet of international law. States are not equal at all. States in the South, with a colonial past and an economic structure that is often based on agriculture and raw materials, are structurally disadvantaged in current international economic relations. As De Feyter has pointed out:

> [D]eveloped and developing [...] States were equal in law and thus enjoyed the rights inherent in full sovereignty. The statement should not disguise, however, that in fact sovereign equality is a fiction. Even the law sometimes treats developing and developed States differently. Both in international decision–making procedures on peace and development (at the UN Security Council) and on financial and economic issues (within the Bretton Woods institutions, and informally at the WTO), developed and developing States do not carry equal weight.[44]

Framing claims for fairer international economic relations in human rights terms raises fundamental issues. Human rights law concerns the relationship between uneven actors, and purports to protect the weaker actor (the individual or group) against the absolute power of the stronger one (the State). Applying human rights terminology to the uneven global economic relations implies recognition of the

---

40 S. Gosepath, "Equality", in E.N. Zalta (ed.), *The Stanford Encyclopedia of Philosophy* (Winter 2005) at http://plato.stanford.edu/archives/win2005/entries/equality/ (last visited 28 June 2006).

41 A. Cassese, *International Law* (Oxford: Oxford University Press, 2001) 88.

42 *Ibid.*, 89–91.

43 K. De Feyter (2001), *l.c.*, 43 and 153.

44 *Ibid.*, 43.

unevenness and abridged sovereignty of some States, in contradiction with the fundamental tenet of sovereign equality. Developing States highly value sovereignty, for it confirms the political independence gained during the decolonisation struggle. It also serves the purpose of conveniently shielding dictatorial or corrupt regimes against too much external interference in their domestic affairs. Developed States insist on the equality of States for the recognition of fundamental inequality might entail obligations to rectify this inequality.

Attempts to elaborate third–State obligations under the ICESCR face the latter limit too. The recognition of obligations for States in the North to respect, protect and fulfil economic, social and cultural rights of individuals in the South would pose a basic conceptual challenge as well as represent a major factual change. Development cooperation might then no longer belong to the realm of charity and moral obligations, but become under certain circumstances a *legal* obligation with far–reaching effects. Lifting the veil of equality, as was pointed out earlier, may be undesirable for all States, both in North and South, albeit for different reasons. For it might also impact on other aspects of sovereignty, which States conveniently want to shield away from international attention and interference.

The right to development and third–State human rights obligations touch upon one of the most fundamental principles of the current international legal order. Unless there is a sincere openness to revisit the over–riding principle of sovereign equality, all attempts to elaborate a right to development or third–State obligations may well be doomed to face serious and continuous opposition in the future too, for their attempt to transcend the limits of international law represents a challenge to one of its basic and constitutive principles.

3.2 Legitimacy

It is submitted that not only conceptual challenges, but issues of legitimacy too pose limits to human rights law. Considerations of legitimacy arise both in the context of SAL (in particular on the issue of judicial activism), and with regard to the legal conceptualisation of the right to development and third–State human rights obligations. The crucial question with the latter two conceptions is how far the human rights concept can be stretched without becoming self–defeating.

It is submitted that an independent and socially activist judiciary is the absolute minimum for the effectiveness of SAL, and thus for a meaningful operational contribution of human rights law to development on the national level. Judicial activism stands for judicial law–making, which implies that the judge takes policy decisions, is a policy–maker. Harwood identifies four phenomena or practices of adjudication in his working definition of judicial activism.[45]

Judicial activism is the opposite of judicial restraint, passivism or deference, which represents a formalistic and positivistic perception of the judicial role. Judi-

---

45 S. Harwood, *Judicial Activism: A Restrained Defense* (San Francisco: Austin & Winfield, 1996) 2.

cial passivism implies limiting the role of judges to mere interpretation, and excluding any judicial value–judgment.[46] Arguments in favour of judicial restraint refer to the division of powers between the legislative and the judiciary, to the independence of the judiciary, to the lack of expertise of judges in policy issues and to the lack of effective control on and over the power of judges.[47]

For SAL to be successful, the judiciary is to be both independent and activist. Both the lack of independence (or a perception in that sense) and excessive activism (or the perception thereof) may create problems of legitimacy. Therefore, it is important to have both built–in checks and limits to judicial activism on the one hand, and entrenched guarantees for the autonomy of the judiciary on the other. The limits to judicial activism are both formal and substantive. Formally speaking, the mode or procedure of judicial law–making differs from legislative law–making in that it is characterised by a connection with the parties[48] and by the impartiality and independence of the judge.[49] From a substantive point of view, judges are bound by values; this means that judicial law–making is not an exercise of discretionary and subjective value choices of the judge concerned, but that it is fundamentally a value–judgment.[50] The judge is accountable either to universal or to constitutional values.[51]

As argued above, one of the distinctive characteristics of human rights law is that it purports to protect individuals (and, by extension, possibly groups) against State power. Invoking human rights language for the protection and justification of claims of weaker *States* (*i.e.* developing States) risks not only a flawed but also a delegitimised concept of human rights. If the concept of rights holders in human rights law is stretched to such an extent that States are included, the human rights concept may become the subject of conceptual overkill and lose the political legitimacy it enjoys from States ('legitimacy from above', the legitimacy granted or withdrawn by States as the law–makers on the international scene). Therefore, lawyers, including activist or radical ones, need to be aware of and guard the critical contours of human rights law, so as to avoid self–defeat. An unavoidable consequence seems to be that the human right to development needs to be defined within mainstream legal human rights thinking. The human right to development thus defined may have little to offer in furthering human development though, for it is unlikely to satisfactorily address fundamental structural issues. This may further challenge its legitimacy, but this time 'from below' (as granted or withdrawn by the alleged beneficiaries of human rights law), for it is unable to fulfil its emancipatory mission for the most disadvantaged. A paradox appears: in order to

---

46 *Ibid.*, 80–85.

47 *Ibid.*, 85–96.

48 Which implies *inter alia* an adversarial procedure; moreover, a judgment has to be reasoned, which is yet another safeguard against irresponsible judicial activism. See R. Dhavan, *Judge and Be Judged. India's Judiciary – An Institution of Governance*, PILSARC Working Paper no. 154 (New Delhi: PILSARC, 1997), at 18.

49 M. Cappelletti, *The Judicial Process in Comparative Perspective* (Oxford: Clarendon, 1989) 30–31.

50 S. Harwood, *l.c.*, 108–110.

51 P.N. Bhagwati, *l.c.*, 576; R. Dhavan (1997), *l.c.*, 14 and 18.

be relevant on the ground and to gain legitimacy from below, a number of conceptual innovations are required in framing the right to development. These innovations come, however, to the detriment of political legitimacy and acceptability from above. So the harder we try to conceptualise the human right to development in such a way as to gain legitimacy from below, the less acceptable it becomes politically, and the more it loses legitimacy from above.

3.3 Ideological Limits

A third set of limits are of an ideological nature. If policy–makers do not accept the rule of law and do not show the willingness to appear before an independent judge, effective human rights litigation becomes very difficult if not impossible. The relevance of human rights litigation for human development becomes equally unlikely if the value of social justice is marginalised or absent in a society. Here, the analysis of the ideological limits is limited to human rights litigation at the national level (as in the context of SAL).

3.3.1 The Rule of Law

The rule of law basically refers to the recognition of the primacy of law over politics. It holds as a basic premise that the political exercise of power is restrained and contained by law, that government is bound by the law. Both formal and substantive elements play a role. Substantially, government is bound by constitutionally entrenched fundamental rights and principles, and by pre–constitutional societal principles. Formally, institutional safeguards like the separation of powers, the supremacy of the legislature and the principle of legality, and judicial review by an independent judiciary are constituent elements of the rule of law.

An independent judiciary is a cornerstone of both the rule of law, and of SAL. This independence concerns *inter alia* an independence from the legislature and the executive, based on the division of powers in a constitutional setting. The importance of an independent judiciary in general[52], and for the protection of human rights in particular[53], goes unquestioned. However, in many countries of the South,

52 See *e.g.*, the Basic Principles on the Independence of the Judiciary, adopted by the Seventh United Nations Congress on the prevention on crime and the treatment of offenders (Milan 26 August – 6 September 1985) and endorsed by the General Assembly in two resolutions (A/RES/40/32 and A/RES/40/146); see also the regional declarations on the independence of the judiciary (*e.g.*, the "Beijing Statement of Principles of the Independence of the Judiciary in the Law Asea Region" of the Law Association of Asia and the Pacific (1995) (published in *Asia–Pacific Journal on Human Rights and the Law* 2000, 158–164) and the 'Caïro Declaration' of the Third Conference of the Francophone Ministers of Justice (1995)).

53 The UN Commission on Human Rights has pointed out the relationship between the weakening of safeguards for the judiciary and the gravity and frequency of human rights violations (see its resolutions on the independence and impartiality of the judiciary, jurrors and

the independence of the judiciary is problematic. Therefore, the improvement of the independence of the judiciary is a major challenge for the feasibility of SAL, and for a meaningful operational contribution of human rights law to human development.

The point made here is not that only in the case of a full observance of the rule of law is SAL feasible. What matters is that the rule of law is referred to as the organising principle of the State set–up, *inter alia* to legitimise political power. In other words, at a minimum, the ideological relevance of the rule of law must be recognised. As has been shown, at least in Africa, the rule of law has often been replaced by other sources of legitimacy.[54] The rule of law is absent or largely irrelevant for legitimising political power. This means that human rights law is bound to be largely irrelevant too.

Inevitably, the relevance of human rights law to human development is situated in a politically liberal setting. Rather than to deplore or to fight this particular ideological context[55], it seems necessary to fully realise the inherent ideological connotations and preconditions of human rights law when examining its potential relevance for the poor in the South. Human rights form part of a more comprehensive liberal ideological package, including the rule of law, constitutionalism, multi–party systems, and so on. Human rights law cannot be looked at in isolation from this package. Again, this is not to criticise liberal ideology, but to raise awareness about the limits this poses to the developmental potential of human rights law in the context where this liberal ideology is not embraced, not so much out of ideological resistance, but simply because it does not correspond to the world view of people.

3.3.2 Social Justice

As was put rather bluntly in one of the first SAL judgments of the Indian Supreme Court, the judges "must shed their character as upholders of the established order and the status quo."[56] Social Action Litigation or similar legal conceptions are preconditioned by the preparedness of the judiciary to opt for social justice in their activism. The adjective 'social' specifies what the purpose or rationale of judicial law–making is, namely the protection and realisation of socio–economic human

---

assessors and the independence of lawyers: *e.g.*, E/CN.4/RES/2005/33). See also the World Conference on Human Rights, "Vienna Declaration and Programme of Action", A/CONF.157/23, part I, at 27.

54 See *inter alia*, Y. Ghai, "The Rule of Law, Legitimacy and Governance", *International Journal of the Sociology of Law*, 1986, *14*, 179–210; I. Shivji, *l.c.*, 147.

55 As for example Shivji has done, see I. Shivji, *The Concept of Human Rights in Africa* (London: Codesria, 1989) and I. Shivji, *l.c.*, 147.

56 Indian Supreme Court, *People's Union for Democratic Rights v Union of India, PIL–SCALE* at [3].

rights, as opposed to conservative judicial activism aimed at the protection of the right to property and of economic interests.[57]

The Indian Supreme Court grounded its social activism in the social welfare State and social justice, as embraced in the Indian Constitution. It argued that "social and economic justice [...] is the signature tune of our Constitution"[58] and that "[i]n a welfare state [...] it is the obligation of the State to provide medical attention to every citizen."[59] The reference to social justice and the welfare State clearly implies an element of ideology. Clearly, neo–liberalism and a belief in the unchecked free market now forms a competing, and for quite some States/societies a more attractive ideology. It remains to be seen whether the change in time frame since the conceptualisation of SAL in the 1980s has been so dramatic as to question fundamentally the present–day relevance of SAL, as some have argued. In any event, for our purposes it is important to stress this ideological aspect, since different ideological options in society may determine and delimit the ideological space the judge can exploit.

One could argue that the insertion of economic, social and cultural rights in the legal order testifies in itself to an ideological choice for the social welfare State and social justice. On the other hand, the UN Committee on Economic, Social and Cultural Rights has emphasised that the ICESCR does not require a choice of a particular economic system.[60] It therefore seems safe to conclude that while the integration of economic, social and cultural rights in a legal order imposes some minimum obligations on States, it does not automatically imply an ideological choice for a social welfare State. Cutbacks in social spending and the downsizing of social provisions in many States parties to the ICESCR or the European Social Charter, without outspoken condemnation by their respective supervisory bodies, seems to support this proposition. Recognition of economic, social and cultural rights may well constitute nevertheless an acceptance of a degree of social justice as a primary value.

As explained above, the limits to judicial activism are twofold, being both formal and substantive. From a substantive point of view, judges are bound by values. Judicial law–making is not an exercise of the discretionary and subjective value–choices of the judge concerned, but is fundamentally a value–judgment.[61] The judge is accountable either to universal and inalienable or to constitutional values.[62] This brings us to the justification of the particular direction that is taken in judicial activism, namely *social* judicial activism. Social judicial activism can only be legitimate if social justice is recognised either as a universal or as a consti-

---

57 See T. Koopmans, "The roots of judicial activism", in F. Matscher and H. Petzold (eds.), *Protecting Human Rights: the European Dimension. Studies in Honour of G.J. Wiarda* (Cologne: Heymanns, 1988) 318–319 and M. Ghouse, "The Two Faces of Judicial Activism", in K.L. Bhatia (ed.), *Judicial Activism and Social Change* (New Delhi: Deep & Deep, 1990) 107–108 as far as the US is concerned.

58 Indian Supreme Court, *Bandhua Mukti Morcha v Union of India*, [1984] *AIR* at [9].

59 Indian Supreme Court, *Rakesh Chandra Narayan v State of Bihar*, *PIL–SCALE* at [29].

60 CESCR GC No 3 (1990), *The Nature of States Parties Obligations* (Article 2, para. 1) at 8.

61 S. Harwood, *l.c.*, 108–110.

62 P.N. Bhagwati, *l.c.*, 576; R. Dhavan (1997), *l.c.*, 14 and 18.

tutional value which may be grounded in pre–constitutional values. In our view, the integration of economic, social and cultural rights, either by treaty adherence or constitutionalisation, offers a sufficient basis for *social* judicial activism. The degree to which economic, social and cultural rights are legally entrenched may impose limits on the extent of social judicial activism, although this is not necessarily the case. The experience with SAL in India shows how even non–enforceable provisions can serve as a forceful base for social judicial activism. Constraints may however arise out of the need for legitimacy, both from above and below.

4 Conclusion

The human rights community, and in particular human rights lawyers, often ignore or neglect the limits of human rights law, particularly in the context of human development. The effectiveness of human rights law depends, however, largely on a proper assessment of its potential and its limits. Disciplinary modesty, as in the recognition of the limits of law, is therefore necessary. Given the fundamental and insurmountable character of some of the limits of human rights law, resort may have to be had to other disciplines in order to further explore and understand them.

The plea made in this chapter to recognise the limits of human rights law may appear to some as conceptual conservatism, and as offering a good excuse to stick to traditional human rights law. Respecting the limits of the law may seem to foreclose all conceptual innovation. This is clearly not what is intended by our insistence on the need for recognition of the limits of human rights law. The challenge rather is to try to overcome to the maximum extent possible the limits exposed, while keeping in mind at all times that every attempt at conceptual innovation may be confronted with the more fundamental limits, and will be challenged by them.

Recognition of the limits of human rights *law* is not akin to recognition of the limits of *human rights*. Other disciplines and/or human rights strategies may well be able to go beyond the inherent limits of law and/or legal strategies. With regard to SAL for instance, the need for multi–dimensional strategies has been stressed from the beginning.[63] Human rights law and litigation can and will never be an autonomous vector of structural societal change; their embeddedness in a broader strategy is crucial. This decentralisation of the law does not deprive it of all meaning and importance. To the contrary, it may well increase its importance, if deployed strategically and in full awareness of its many limits.

---

63 Indian Supreme Court, *People's Union for Democratic Rights v Union of India, PIL–SCALE* at 2.

Chapter 21 – Limits of Human Rights Protection from the Perspective of Legal Anthropology

Stijn Deklerck, Ellen Desmet, Marie–Claire Foblets, Joke Kusters and Jogchum Vrielink

1 Introduction

Aspiring to embrace the whole of a specific field of knowledge is an illusory temptation. The authors who attempt to do so are therefore few and far between. The opposite approach, which consists of defining the limits of a discipline, seems intellectually more honest. Yet here, too, there are few who are willing to take the risk. It would be hard to imagine thirty or so physicians getting together to produce a collective work focusing on the limits of their knowledge. It is certainly easier to sing the praises of the strengths of a discipline than to reveal its limitations. It is thus all the more remarkable that the venture undertaken by the initiators of *Facing the Limits of the Law* has now come to fruition. For what they have achieved is in effect a *tour de force*, gathering a large number of fellow jurists around a common project with the aim not of rehashing the law but, on the contrary, of identifying the questions, themes and aspirations that elude the field, or for which the law offers only partial solutions. The ambition represented by this work in a sense goes beyond the knowledge of the law, and aims at a better understanding of what it is that escapes its grasp and thereby challenges it. It implies calling into question the definition and the method of analysis of legal matters.

It should come as no surprise that a team of legal anthropologists has shown a keen interest in taking part in this venture. According to Norbert Rouland,

> Legal anthropology is a science that, by virtue of its position at the threefold level of established norms, practices and representations by human actors, seeks to define the general operating mechanisms of legal systems, drawing upon the experiences of western and non–western societies.[1]

It does not consider law as a coherent set of rules decreed *a priori* by the public authorities or to the respect of which the latter can at the very least compel individuals. Anthropological experience reveals a multiplicity of laws, often inconsistent among each other, regarded as rational only by the group concerned, mostly independent – at least partly – of State authorities, and which for the most part cannot be reduced entirely to a set of rules.

---

[1] N. Rouland, "Anthropologie juridique", in D. Alland and S. Rials (eds.), *Dictionnaire de la culture juridique* (Paris: Quadrige/Lamy – Presses Universitaires de France, 2003) 63.

In order to do so, legal anthropology uses an empirical method that differs significantly from that of the classic legal sciences. The anthropologist is not interested solely in norms, but ascribes at least as much importance to their effectiveness. To his end, he or she studies the law primarily via the concrete behaviours of legal actors with respect to enacted laws or judicial decisions, which these actors may implement, challenge, circumvent or simply ignore. By revealing the gaps that can exist between the legal norm and the behaviours of individuals and groups, the investigations of the anthropologist in the field indicate, specifically, that the State is not the sole producer of law, but that law is very often made by various social groups as well. The anthropologist is generally more prepared to use the concept of 'differentiated worlds' – some would refer in this regard to legal pluralism[2] – which shows more clearly what is happening in reality: rules of behaviour (laws) usually have meaning only in relation to the world of the actors to which they apply. Field research reveals numerous contradictions between State *(i.e.*, official) legislation and its effectiveness in the field. To the anthropologist, the legal phenomenon is first and foremost, regardless of the local system, a set of individual and collective struggles and consensus on their results in the areas that a community or society considers vital.

At the present time, anthropologists are called upon to address the most diverse range of questions: the struggle of indigenous communities throughout the world; the functioning of various forms of conflict resolution and/or search for conciliation; the difficult issue of addressing minority rights; the (re)definition of secularism, the reconciliation of universalism and particularism in the definition and implementation of human rights standards, etc.

---

2 J.-G. Belley, "Le droit comme 'terra incognita': Conquérir et construire le pluralisme juridique", *Canadian Journal of Law and Society* (special issue: Legal Pluralism) 1997, 1-15; M. Chiba, "Three Dichotomies of Law. An Analytical Scheme of Legal Culture", *Tokai Law Review* 1987, 279-290; B. De Sousa Santos, "Law: A Map of Misreading. Toward a Postmodern Conception of Law", *Journal of Law and Society* 1987, 3; B. Dupret, M. Berger, and L. al-Zwaini (eds.), *Legal Pluralism in the Arab World* (The Hague: Kluwer International, 1999); J. Griffiths, "What is Legal Pluralism?", *Journal of Legal Pluralism* 1986, 1-55; M.B. Hooker, *Legal Pluralism – An Introduction to Colonial and Neo-Colonial Laws* (Oxford, Oxford University Press, 1975); M.-M. Kleinhans and R.A. MacDonald, "What is 'Critical' Legal Pluralism?", *Canadian Journal of Law and Society* (special issue: Legal Pluralism) 1997, 25-46; A. Lajoie, R. McDonald, R. Janda, and G. Rocher (eds.), *Théories et émergence du droit; Pluralisme, surdétermination et effectivité* (Brussels: Bruylant/Thémis, 1998); S.E. Merry, "Legal Pluralism" (review article), *Law and Society Review* 1988, 869-896; H. Petersen and H. Zahle (eds.), *Legal Polycentricity. Consequences of Pluralism in Law* (Aldershot: Dartmouth, 1995); S. Roberts, "Anthropology and Legal Pluralism", in *Law & Society* (prov. ed., February 2000) (Onati: IISJ, 2000) 11-22; N. Rouland, "A la recherche du pluralisme juridique: Le cas français", *Droit et Cultures* 1998, 217-262; F. Strijbosch, "Het concept pluralisme in de rechtsantropologie", in N.J.A. Huls and H.D. Stout (eds.), *Recht in een multiculturele samenleving* (Zwolle: Tjeenk Willink, 1993) 69-84; B.Z. Tamanaha, "The Folly of the 'Social Scientific' Concept of Legal Pluralism", *Journal of Law and Society*, 1993, 192-218; A.C. 't Hart, "Recht en pluralisme: kwesties van begrip en principe", in N.J.A. Huls and H.D. Stout (eds.), *Recht in een multiculturele samenleving* (Zwolle: Tjeenk Willink, 1993) 85-98; J. Vanderlinden, "Return to Legal Pluralism", *Journal of Legal Pluralism* 1989, 149-157; F. von Benda-Beckmann, "Comment on Merry", *Law and Society Review* 1988, 897-902.

In what follows, we provide four illustrations of legal anthropological research. They all address – in four different contexts – the issue of the limits of human rights protection. These are research projects still in progress, conducted by researchers who, with a view to the book project *Facing the Limits of the Law*, have agreed to shed a particular light on their – still very fresh – field experience. They do so by showing how, in a particular context, that is to say starting out from the particular, the importance of human rights protection in shaping behaviours and expectations is intrinsically related to the particular culture and basic values of the actors involved and, albeit of lesser importance, to their positions with respect to State law, whether international, national or regional/local. The contexts described are very different. It is primarily the angle of approach that makes it possible to regard the four contributions as illustrations of a single intellectual process: through a concrete and varied subject matter that shows the existence of law(s) outside the State, one discovers a never–ending dialectical interaction between the formal and the informal, between State and non–State expressions of law and justice, an approach which breaks away from the vision that reifies the State and its laws as an artificial entity detached from the dynamic social context of its interpretation and application. Human rights protection is but a particular example of this phenomenon.

The illustrations draw upon (field) experiences that differ vastly from one another. The first illustration (section 2 – "Racism and the Limits of the Criminal Law") demonstrates the development by Belgian legislators over the past 25 years or so of an ever–increasing criminalisation of discriminatory acts, with a striking focus on racist speech and publications. But it also shows how restrictions on the freedom of speech that are primarily to be seen as displays of power on part of State authorities with a view to (re)affirming their primacy, but that do not address underlying problems such as fear and insecurity, may produce paradoxical outcomes. J. Vrielink, throughout his fieldwork, came across a number of such outcomes.

The second illustration (section 3 – "The Limits of Human Rights Protection for Indigenous People") addresses the limits of human rights protection for indigenous peoples. E. Desmet identifies three types of limits. A first kind of limit is conceptual: are human rights at all appropriate as an instrument for indigenous people to strengthen their claims and improve their position vis–à–vis State authorities? A second limit is based on the observation that the concrete effect of (international) human rights on the legal situation and living conditions of indigenous societies remains in many cases negligible, since their implementation depends on a number of conditions that cannot easily be satisfied: the approval of global human rights standards, control by international treaty monitoring bodies and, last but not least, the acceptance (and thus effectuation) of international norms and court decisions as well as of constitutional provisions. A third limit are the many risks of misunderstandings between State authorities and indigenous movements, as well as within these movements, as to what the people concerned expect from the human rights system.

The third illustration of anthropological expansion of the traditional field of legal research when addressing issues of human rights protection brings us to China (section 4 – "Confucian Tradition and Socio-Economic Rights Protection in Contemporary China"). Confucian values have recently been (re)introduced in the official State ideology of a 'Harmonious Society'. Field research reveals that in fact these values have never ceased to exist in Chinese society. The official revival of Confucianism in recent years only accentuates traditional practices. Human rights protection in China cannot be understood in disregard of these values and the practices they induce. S. Deklerck's short case–study of parents of autistic children serves to demonstrate this here.

The fourth and last illustration concerns the observance of Jewish religious law and more particularly of Jewish divorce law (section 5 – "Judaism between Religious Freedom and Gender Equality"). J. Kusters wonders whether freedom of religion in itself can justify gender inequalities. Ethnographic data show that the construction of gender equality that is implied within the human rights system does not necessarily correspond to the aspirations of Jewish women. State intervention in such cases offers no solution to some of the hardships of Jewish divorce law, since the women are not looking for gender equality standards to be enforced in their own situation. When religious norms prevail, human rights appear bound to remain inadequate.

The golden thread running through all four illustrations is the thesis of an incomplete State domination ('*étatisation*') of the law (section 6).

2 First Illustration: Racism and the Limits of the (Criminal) Law

J. Vrielink

2.1 Antiracism and the Law: Belgian History in a Nutshell

Over the past 25 years, legal anti–racism measures in Belgium gradually took the form of a 'tough on crime' policy. The country was a slow starter, though. In the mid 1960s the United Nations had already drawn up the International Convention on the elimination of all forms of racial discrimination (ICERD), Article 4 of which requires State parties to take (legal) action against racial discrimination and 'hate speech'. Belgium acceded to the ICERD only in 1975[3], and even then with a declaration restricting the application of Article 4 as regards the freedoms of expression, assembly and association.[4] After this rather reticent ratification, it took

---

3 By way of comparison: Belgium's neighbouring countries France, Germany and The Netherlands all ratified between 1969 and 1971. Only Luxembourg waited longer (1978).

4 When finally Belgium did ratify, it did so with a declaration regarding Article 4, the relevant part of which reads as follows: "(...) The Kingdom of Belgium (...) considers that the obli-

Belgium another six years to implement its obligations under the Convention, which it finally did by means of the Antiracism Act of 1981.[5]

This Act was initially a criminal law[6], which on the one hand prohibited certain discriminatory acts.[7] On the other hand, the Act introduced a number of restrictions on the freedom of association and the freedom of speech. More specifically, it entailed prohibitions of: incitement to racial hatred, discrimination and violence; announcing an intention to said attitudes and acts; and, finally, cooperation or association with organisations or groups that practice or advocate discrimination.

At the outset the sanctions for these infractions were intentionally kept relatively limited. This was done for several, interconnected reasons. First of all, the legislators at the time were sceptical about *effecting* societal and behavioural changes by means of the (criminal) law in matters of conscience and morality. For example, the Explanatory Memorandum to the Act stated:

> Christianity has for twenty centuries, and rationalism for two centuries, attempted to appeal to *humanity's* conscience by means of education and upbringing, without however having convinced it of their pleas and actions. Therefore the community's disapproval of acts inspired by racism or xenophobia should be expressed by means of a moderate punishment.[8]

Furthermore, the legislators considered moderation important, since they deemed excessive punishment liable to generate counterproductive results, thereby adding to the very evils the legislation was intended to counteract.[9] The example of the 'Prohibition' of the manufacture and sale of alcoholic beverages in the US – and its manifold adverse and unintended consequences – was repeatedly invoked in this regard.[10] Moreover, it was also feared that excessive punishment would result

---

gations imposed by Article 4 must be reconciled with the right to freedom of opinion and expression and the right to freedom of peaceful assembly and association."

5 30 July 1981 (Moniteur 8 August 1981). See extensively on the Antiracism Act, D. De Prins, S. Sottiaux and J. Vrielink, *Handboek Discriminatierecht* [Handbook of Discrimination Law] (Mechelen: Kluwer, 2005) 291–413.

6 In 2007 civil provisions were introduced into the Act itself. Civil antiracist provisions did exist prior to this, namely since 2003. They had previously been part of other legislation, however.

7 Initially only discrimination in the context of goods and services and discrimination by public servants was prohibited. It was not until 1994 that racial discrimination in the context of employment was outlawed. This too had to do with realism and modesty: it was believed that the burden of proof would be insurmountable in the context of employment, and that therefore the law would create false expectations and only induce frustration (*Parliamentary Documents*, Chamber of Representatives 1980–81, no. 214/9, 21). Ten years after the introduction of the provision there still has not been a single conviction on the basis of it.

8 *Parliamentary Documents*, Chamber of Representatives 1979, no. 214/1, 3.

9 *Parliamentary Documents*, Chamber of Representatives 1980–81, no. 214/9, 9; *Parliamentary Documents*, Chamber of Representatives 1979, no. 214/1, 3; *Parliamentary Acts* Senate, 18 July 1981, 2227.

10 *Ibid.* Prohibition (1920–1933) was established by means of the Eighteenth Amendment of the United States Constitution – notably the only amendment to have ever been repealed – along with the 'Volstead Act'.

in apprehension on the part of the public prosecutor, and finally the aim of the legislation was expressly seen to be communicative rather than repressive.[11]

In the initial eight or nine years, the application of the act was – largely – in line with this perspective. A change occurred, however, in the transition from the 1980s to the 1990s. The rapid rise of radical right–wing political parties at the time – especially in Flanders[12] – ushered in a shift in approach. In 1989 a Royal Commission for Migrant Policy was established, mainly in response to the first big election victory of the extremist Flemish Block.[13] The Commission put forward a number of ambitious proposals, several of which had to do with the application and scope of the Antiracism Act, which was now regarded as defective: the Act had yielded insufficient results and therefore amendments were required, the Commission argued, without however investigating the reasons for this perceived failure.[14]

The first project initiated after the Commission had submitted its final report was the creation of an institution the main assignment of which would be to make sure the Act would be more frequently and more successfully applied. This became the Centre for Equal Opportunities and Opposition to Racism (CEOOR or Centre), created in 1993. To achieve its aim, the Centre was to receive and examine complaints with regard to the Act and it was exceptionally endowed with the authority to take independent legal action. The antiracist policy of the official public prosecution office was considered deficient to such a degree that it was deemed necessary to institute a specialised body to assist it in – or even take over – its responsibilities in this domain.[15]

Subsequently, things started to move more rapidly. On the one hand, several new legislative initiatives found their origins in recommendations made by the Centre. In 1995 this led to the enactment of a Holocaust Denial Act[16]; in 1999 the Constitution was amended so that (only) 'racist' publications were thenceforth exempt from the general protection regime for 'press infractions'[17]; in that same year

---

11 *Parliamentary Documents*, Chamber of Representatives 1980–81, no. 214/9, 9.

12 The Dutch–speaking, northern part of Belgium.

13 J. Blommaert and A. Martens, *Van blok tot bouwsteen* [From Flemish Block to Building Block] (Berchem: EPO, 1999) 13.

14 J. Velaers, "Verdraagzaamheid ook t.a.v. onverdraagzamen?" [Tolerance for the Intolerant?], in X, *Recht en verdraagzaamheid in de multiculturele samenleving* (Antwerpen: Maklu, 1993) 308.

15 See critically, R. Verstraeten, *De burgerlijke partij en het gerechtelijk onderzoek. Het slachtoffer in het strafproces* [The Civil Party and the Judicial Investigation. The Victim in Criminal Proceedings] (Antwerpen: Maklu, 1990) nos. 709–710.

16 Even though it had been demonstrated in practice that Holocaust denial could be successfully tried by means of the Antiracism Act. See, Correctional Court Brussels, 11 April 1991; Court of Appeals Brussels, 8 November 1991. Compare, Correctional Court Brussels, 20 April 1993.

17 In Belgium press infractions are subject to a special protection regime that entails they can only be tried by a jury. The Belgian legal system in general combines (professional) judge trials with jury trials. As a general rule jury trials are reserved – on the one hand – for the most severe crimes (murder, rape, terrorism, etc.). On the other hand, several other infractions are referred to juries, not so much because of their 'severity', but rather due to their 'nature': political crimes, for example as well as press infractions. Due to their subversive

legislation was implemented that was to lead to a loss of State party financing of political parties "hostile to human rights", which was taken to imply: if they engaged in racist speech; and in 2003 a general Antidiscrimination Act was passed.[18]

On the other hand, the original legislation was amended repeatedly[19], in the course of which the scope was broadened, new charges were introduced, the main sanctions were reinforced and additional ones added, such as the deprivation of civil and political rights in the case of a (first) conviction.[20] The most recent amendments of the Act were particularly telling in this regard. In 2007, Belgian discrimination law in general underwent a metamorphosis. One of its aims was a so–called 'decriminalisation': the specialised architects of the amendments wanted to shift the focus from criminal law to civil law in the legal struggle against discrimination, considering this to be a more effective approach. Although the Antiracism Act too was initially included in this move, it is striking that it was eventually excluded: whereas the Antidiscrimination Act and the Gender Act now entail only two criminal provisions, the Antiracism Act comprises no less than six. Not only were the original provisions in the Act maintained, one was also replaced to include more far–reaching limitations on the freedom of expression, introducing a prohibition on the 'dissemination' of 'ideas based on racial superiority or hatred' (see further below). In order to achieve this, certain measures aimed at shifting the burden of proof in civil proceedings were sacrificed in the political bargaining.

This focus on 'speech' – as expressed by the latter example – is more generally striking. Many of the measures are first and foremost – or even exclusively – aimed at verbal and textual expressions of racism, rather than racist behaviour or

---

nature and the fact that they are often based on ideas that are virulently critical of the State, the government or generally 'the powers that be', the drafters of the Belgian Constitution had deemed it inappropriate for these criminals to be tried by a judge appointed precisely *by* 'the system'. In practice this means that press infractions are hardly ever taken to court, since generally priority is given to cases referred to jury trials due to their severity (see above). Since this system got in the way of antiracist policies, the Constitution was amended in 1999 to make a *single* exception for press infractions "motivated by racism or xenophobia" (Constitution, Article 150). These were thenceforth to be tried by professional judges, facilitating prosecution, albeit at the expense of constitutional consistency and guarantees.

18 This is merely a selection of some of the measures and legislation that passed them. Additional ones are continually being proposed, however. There have been for example: proposals to render the additional sanction of the deprivation of civil and political rights mandatory for each conviction on the basis of the Antiracism Act and the Holocaust Denial Act; proposals to introduce an 'Ethical Register', denying certain rights to companies and businesses if ever they are convicted on the basis of said acts; proposals concerning the ineligibility of politicians who (or whose parties) have been convicted of racism; proposals to refuse recognition of parties in parliament if (one of) their members or 'allied associations' has been convicted for racism; proposals to expand the Holocaust Denial Act in order to include all genocides and all crimes against humanity in its scope; proposals to expand preventive censorship by postal services of 'racist propaganda'; etc.

19 More specifically on: 15 February 1993 (Moniteur 19 February 1993), 12 April 1994 (Moniteur 14 May 1994), 7 May 1999 (Moniteur 25 June 1999), 20 January 2003 (Moniteur 12 February 2003), 23 January 2003 (Moniteur 13 March 2003), and 10 May 2007 (Moniteur 30 May 2007).

20 For the time being this additional sanction is optional. It is likely shortly to become mandatory however, since proposals to this end have been submitted (see above).

discriminatory acts. This fact is also clearly reflected in the application of the relevant acts and provisions by the Centre: over 80% of all racism cases[21] concern speech in one way or another.[22]

2.2 To the Limits ... and Beyond

In short, the history in Belgium clearly demonstrates a move away from the legislators' initial, moderate intentions and communicative approach. The development is one of increasing repression: a slide into harsher penal sanctions; the introduction of exceptional measures; the expansion of provisions and the enactment of new laws. Striking, finally, is the predominant focus on racist speech and publications, rather than on discriminatory acts.

This impressive 'demonstration of power' by means of the criminal law stands in marked contrast with ongoing racial discrimination, the continuing success of radical right–wing parties, growing multicultural tensions, and even eruptions of racist violence. Rather than leading to critical reflection on the uses and effectiveness of the criminal law in these matters, these facts appear to lead to a 'flight forward': time and again – *e.g.,* when the media or minority groups report that the problems still endure or that other ones have arisen – politicians tend to respond by announcing new criminal measures.

A recent example of this concerns a proposition to prohibit assistance to and membership of extreme right–wing and fascist groups. In a fit of 'righteous indignation' it was hastily drafted in response to a number of concerts by Nazi skinheads in the Belgian countryside.[23] The proposal was formulated so broadly however, that it not only included said groups, but also all mainstream faith–based communities and religions, as well as a number of political parties. Blatantly unconstitutional as it was, it would still probably have been passed, were it not for last minute criticisms from the (Flemish) League for Human Rights[24], a civil rights NGO, as a result of which discussions and the vote were postponed.[25]

---

[21] By way of comparison: although the legislation is more recent, it is clear that where other discrimination grounds – such as disability, sexual orientation and religion – are concerned, the types of cases that are brought to trial hardly ever have to do with speech issues.

[22] Up until 2003 a partial explanation for this 'skewed' distribution was the fact that it was also much harder to meet the burden of proof in cases of actual discrimination (*e.g.*, in employment and goods and services). I say 'partial' since the fact that something is hard(er) does not release a responsible government institution from the duty of applying these laws and provisions in a balanced manner, instead of taking the easy road. Moreover, since 2003 – with the introduction of civil provisions and a distribution of the burden of proof – little has changed. With regard to racism, it is still predominantly speech infractions that are brought before the courts by the Centre.

[23] See *Parliamentary Documents*, Chambre of Representatives 2006-07, no. 51-3140/1.

[24] The League stated amongst other things: "this is the most far–reaching limitation of the constitutional freedom of association [ever]. It is being pushed through parliament in a rush, by means of a special urgency procedure. Without any study, without any comparison with German or French legislation, without any respect for human rights and jurisprudence. As

Let us take a brief look at some of the reasons for this: what factors in present-day societies and in Belgium in particular can serve to explain the developments and tendencies described above? First of all, contemporary societies in general have increasingly become characterised by moral heterogeneity or even moral relativism.[26] At the same time, the need for a common moral code seems to be inherent in human thinking. This has 'naturally' led to a tendency to look to the law for redressing any moral and social problem, since no other (common) standards are left to govern society.[27] If something is regarded as either good or bad, the law is expected and required to direct it.

The government in turn is unwilling or at least uninclined to admit it can do little (more) to redress certain problems. Contemporary Nation–States are in decline and have in fact proven (and are proving) incapable of fully addressing the fears and insecurities of their citizens and of efficiently organising social solidarity among them.[28] For fear of a further loss of legitimacy and power, however, they tend to cling to what little they have left, in an attempt to – at least symbolically – reaffirm their primacy. As such, the State prefers to respond to citizens' requests and insecurities by undertaking 'firm' action. The criminal law, with its highly symbolic concepts of punishment and wrongdoing, and with its strong ritual dimension, is the ideal vehicle for communicating this 'firmness' and 'control', while minimising (direct) expenditure.[29] More for less, so to speak.

Now, racism occupies a special position with regard to the above. Somehow it is one of the few exceptions to society's moral relativism or lack of consensus[30]: "regarding charges of racism there is no taboo on judgmentalism – no permissive laissez–faire attitude".[31] In my understanding this is not so much in spite of, but precisely *because* of society's increased heterogeneity: in order for diverse socie-

---

such, parliament is demonstrating an extremely cavalier disregard for our rights and freedoms". D. De Prins (League of Human Rights), "Neonazi–verbod oeverloos en slordig" [Prohibition of Neo–Nazis Boundless and Careless], *De Morgen*, 17 April 2007.

25 Until after the elections of June 2007. See for the proposition: *Parliamentary Documents*, Chamber of Representatives 2006–7, no. 51–3014/1.

26 See *e.g.*, G. Himmelfarb, *The De–Moralization of Society: From Victorian Virtues to Modern Virtues* (New York: Knopf, 1995); J.W. van Deth and E. Scarbrough, *The Impact of Values* (Oxford: Oxford UP, 1995); W. Jagodzinski and K. Dobbelaere, *Religious and Moral Pluralism* (Brussel: Application to the European Science Foundation, 1996).

27 At once increasing the pressure on and further problematising the classical distinction between law and morality.

28 On the decline of the Nation–State, see, M. Mann, *The Rise and Decline of the Nation State* (Oxford: Blackwell, 1990); G. Jáuregui Bereciartu, *Decline of the Nation State* (Reno: University of Nevada, 1994).

29 Compare: E. Claes and J. Vrielink, "Cultural Defense and Societal Dynamics", in M.–C. Foblets and A.D. Renteln (eds.), *Multicultural Jurisprudence: Comparative Perspectives on the Cultural Defense* (Oxford: Hart Publishing, 2007).

30 Along with terrorism and sexual offenses.

31 Compare: P.M. Garry, "Racism Is a Sin. But Why Is it the Only One?", *American Experiment Quarterly* 2005, fall–issue, 1–14. Garry's analysis is descriptive, however, rather than explanatory, and it is also concerned mainly with the adverse effects he perceives the treatment of racism as a primary social sin having on (the moral standards applied to) minority groups.

ties to remain stable and to function, States (feel they must) attempt to avoid and suppress any sign of cultural or 'racial' clashes at all costs. As such, racism comes to be regarded as the 'primordial sin', and therefore worthy of virtually unlimited condemnation and indignation. All the more since few other things are apt to gather comparable moral accord and unity.

The power display by the criminal law, its nearly exclusive focus on speech and speech–related behaviour, and its 'flight forward' are in our view inextricably bound up with the above. The former – to begin with – is supposed to show that the threats of 'xenophobia' and the spectres of totalitarianism are taken seriously. It allows the State to at once display indignation and deep offense, and thereby 'score' on a moral and popular level, while also communicating that the issue will be forcefully tackled, thereby symbolically (re)affirming its power in the mind of the public at large. The message is that the criminal law is on the case, so we can all sleep soundly. As for the fact that mainly racist *speech* should bear the brunt of this symbolical repression: it is of course no coincidence that racist expressions are the cheapest and simplest of the racist acts to prosecute. Moreover, its (apparent) explicitly (im)moral character and easy communicability to the media and the public at large also contribute to rendering it an ideal target for the symbolic politics mentioned above.[32]

However, the problem with all this is that such politics by means of the criminal law – especially since they are geared predominantly to verbal expressions – fundamentally do little in the way of solving or preventing issues of racism. Underlying problems are not tackled, to say the least.[33] Therefore, problems are bound to resurface, and at the next sign of this happening, the State needs to go through these motions again and repeat its ritual 'exorcism': hence the 'flight forward'.

---

[32] This tendency to focus on expressions can take on remarkable forms. In 2004 a government 'Action Plan' was announced, partly in response to a number of serious racist incidents that had occurred in the course of the summer of that year. In Antwerp individuals from the Jewish community were assaulted, while in the town of Broechem an asylum seekers' centre had been the object of an attack. As a result, it would seem entirely appropriate that the government responded. However, 6 out of the 10 measures that were proposed had to do predominantly with speech and speech–related behaviour (including: increased repression of racism on the internet; screening of places where racist or anti–Semitic speech could take place; and enabling the postal services to refuse the distribution of propaganda by extremist political parties). 3 other measures were geared to facilitate co–operation between government institutions (*e.g.*, the CEOOR and the police). Only a single proposal had a direct bearing on the problem of violence (*i.e.*, the introduction of safety measures in order to better protect risk–sensitive buildings of the Jewish community and asylum seekers' centres).

[33] On the contrary, it turns out they are exacerbated by them (see further below).

2.3 Legal Issues, Side Effects and Counterproductive Tendencies

To be clear, racism in its many guises is indeed a serious threat and needs to be treated as such. Discrimination on the basis of race or ethnicity is clearly unacceptable, both morally and legally speaking. Furthermore, the adverse societal and psychological effects of 'hate speech' have also been convincingly argued and demonstrated in legal and socio–legal research.[34] As such, the processes described above might not be a problem, if it were not for the fact that they are harming the legal system, the individuals involved and society in general. Current criminal measures concerning (anti)racism in Belgium tend to lose sight of several 'limits of the law', harming both the legal system as well as the individuals involved and society in general, and to that extent are problematic.

Let us start off with some of the legal problems that the legislation gives rise to. Being perceived as a main sin or evil, racism tends to overshadow and surpass other legal concerns or considerations, leading to an erosion of a number of rights and key principles, thereby harming the legal system in general.

When we look at the Belgian practice, it becomes clear first of all that the struggle against racism tends easily to trump even constitutional safeguards and rights. Especially in the face of racist *speech*, the impossible becomes possible: restrictions based purely on content; preventive censorship; (obligatory) deprivation of civil and political rights; exceptions to constitutional regimes of protection, etc. This is not to say that these measures – considered separately – are by definition unconstitutional. Distressing, however, is on the one hand the ease and self–evidence with which they are introduced, and on the other hand their ever–growing number. Justifications that normally are stringently applied when limiting fundamental rights are no longer deemed necessary: in establishing most of the measures mentioned, the legislators merely referred to the fact that the freedom of

---

[34] See *e.g.*, L.B. Nielsen, "Situating Legal Consciousness: Experiences and Attitudes of Ordinary Citizens About Law and Street Harassment", *Law & Society Review* 2000; L. Leets, "Experiencing Hate Speech: Perceptions and Responses to Anti–Semitism and Anti–Gay Speech", *Journal of Social Issues* 2002, 341–361; G. Cowan and D. Khatchadourian, "Empathy, Ways of Knowing, and Interdependance as Mediators Of Gender Differences in Attitudes Toward Hate Speech and Freedom Of Speech", *Psychology of Women Quarterly* 2003, 300–308; L. Leets, "Subtle, Pervasive, Harmful: Racist and Sexist Remarks in Public as Hate Speech", *Journal of Social Issues* 2002, *2*, 265–280; L.B. Nielsen, *License to Harass. Law, Hierarchy, and Offensive Public Speech* (Princeton and Oxford: Princeton University Press, 2004); A.E. Brownstein, "Regulating Hate Speech at Public Universities: Are First Amendment Values Functionally Incompatible With Equal Protection Principles?", *Buff. L. Rev.* 1991, *38* (1); R. Delgado, "Campus Antiracism Rules: Constitutional Narratives in Collision", *Nw. U.L. Rev.* 1991 (5), 343; R. Delgado, "Words That Wound: A Tort Action for Racial Insults, Epithets, and Name–Calling", *Harv. C.R.–C.L. L. Rev.* 1982, *17*, 133; T.C. Grey, "Responding to Abusive Speech on Campus: A Model Statute", *Reconstruction* 1990, Winter, 50; C.R. Lawrence III, "If he Hollers Let him Go: Regulating Racist Speech on Campus", *Duke L.J.* 1990, 431; M.J. Matsuda, "Public Response to Racist Speech: Considering the Victim's Story", *Mich. L. Rev.* 1989, *87*, 2320; H.W. Saad, "The Case for Prohibitions of Racial Epithets in the University Classroom", *Wayne L. Rev.* 1991, *37*, 1351; R.A. Smolla, "Rethinking First Amendment Assumptions About Racist and Sexist Speech", *Wash. & Lee L. Rev.* 1990, *47*, 171.

expression is not absolute, and 'therefore' deemed the proposition to be not only acceptable but even indispensable. Legally speaking, however, freedom is of course the rule, the exception to which must be convincingly demonstrated to be strictly necessary and justified: the burden of proof lies with those proposing the restriction. Where racism is concerned, however, the reverse situation has come to hold true. The bromide that the 'freedom of speech is not absolute' is regularly employed as a *carte blanche* that warrants just about any restriction or limitation within the scope of antiracism. To put it bluntly: the phrase "freedom of speech is important, but ..." has become little more than the antiracist equivalent of "I'm not a racist, but ..."[35]

Furthermore, the fact that the struggle against racism, and again especially the struggle against racist speech, has been governed by the intention to obtain full control of the phenomenon, is causing key concepts and principles of the criminal law to be corroded or neglected. For years now the aim has been virtually one–sidedly to bring any and all racially offensive expressions under the application of the relevant laws. Where this turned out not yet to be the case, then the legislation had to be expanded or new provisions, measures and sanctions enacted.

A major cluster of principles that comes under strain in this process concerns criminal responsibility, *mens rea* and the principle of legality and foreseeability.[36] The 'flight forward' has broadened the relevant provisions and their applications to such an extent that they are liable to include a vast range of expressions, speech and publications, thereby both seriously reducing the foreseeability of the potential applications of the relevant provisions as well as rendering irrelevant the intentions of defendants and the context in which expressions were made.[37] To start with the last, the ever–broadening provisions facilitate an 'appropriation' of speech, implicitly infusing it – by means of the law – with a meaning beyond what was, at least demonstrably, intended. 'Racism' then becomes the result of 'legal ascription', detached from context and motivation, and based on a moral judgment that can be made by anyone against one's words and their alleged meaning: words can become 'racist' in a *legal* sense as soon as someone – not just the victim, but anybody – considers them to be so.[38] Secondly, and closely related to this problem, the developments described above impair the foreseeability of the application of the relevant provisions and prohibitions: their implications and reach become

---

[35] J. Vrielink, "Strafbare ideeën: geen goed idee" [Punishable Ideas: Not a Good Idea], *Samenleving en Politiek* 2007 (3), 9.

[36] The principle of legality entails that no conduct may be held criminal unless it is precisely described in a (previous) criminal law. In the practice of the Belgian criminal law, one of the main requirements of the principle is that the text and application of criminal provisions be sufficiently foreseeable and clearly delineated. See extensively on the principle of legality and its implications and meaning in Belgian criminal law: E. Claes, *Legaliteit en rechtsvinding in het strafrecht* [Legality and Adjudication in the Criminal Law] (Leuven: Universitaire Pers Leuven, 2003).

[37] This is not to say that this concerns all or even a majority of the applications; it merely serves to point out that there *are* some such cases.

[38] *Cf.* B. O'Neill, "After Hate Speech, the War Against 'Mate Speech'", *Spiked–Online* 13 March 2007.

subjective to the point of being wholly unpredictable, thereby impairing the capacity and rights of citizens to be able to accurately assess when and to what extent their behaviour constitutes an infraction of the criminal law and is liable to expose them to prosecution (see further below).

A final principle that is thus undercut is the principle of criminal proportionality. Its function in the (Belgian) criminal law is to relate means, particularly sanctions, to ends and to do so in a balanced manner.[39] Ends do not justify all means in a State guided by the rule of law. Antiracist policies in Belgium have tended over the years to lose sight of this fact, however, systematically increasing the main sanctions attached to the provisions in the legislation as well as adding new ones, while at the same time the provisions themselves (see above) have been broadened. Racism has become so charged with moral condemnation that it emotionally surpasses all other crimes,[40] having in effect entered a league of its own. This in turn serves to justify almost any possible sanction and leads to a neglect of the way in which these sanctions might relate to sanctions for other crimes. The reasoning boils down to this: racism is unambiguously Evil. Fighting and sanctioning racism is therefore Good; and the more of something Good, the better. Proportionality is the victim of this line of reasoning.

Aside from the legal issues, as is often the case with attempts at social engineering by means of law[41], the personal and societal effects of legal intervention in this domain are not what was hoped or expected. An in–depth qualitative, empirical study into the experiences of 38 plaintiffs and 39 defendants in cases involving racist hate speech is still underway[42], but preliminary results indicate that the effects of the application of this legislation are often counterproductive. If anything, it appears to contribute to a *widening* of social, racial and cultural divides in Bel-

---

39 For an illustration of the way in which antiracist policies erode the principle of proportionality, see, E. Claes and J. Vrielink, "Antiracisme en rechtsstatelijke strafrechtspleging" [Antiracism, Criminal Adjudication and the Rule of Law], *Nieuw Juridisch Weekblad* 2005, no. 99, 151–168.

40 Illustrative of this point is the fact that the main Belgian civil rights organisation has formally turned against much of the anti–terrorism legislation as well as its applications. The organisation also offered to provide a lawyer to one of Belgium's most notorious child abductors and rapists when it turned out it was hard for him to find someone to defend him. The same organisation, however, was the *prosecuting* party in several cases targeting racist speech, *e.g.*, in the trial against the Flemish Block and complaints against radical websites. My point is *not* that the civil rights organisation should not have positioned itself differently in the first two cases or issues, but only to contrast these previous positionings with their policy regarding racist speech.

41 Virtually the entire body of scholarship in both the anthropology and the sociology of law can serve to attest to this in one way or another. See *e.g.*, J. Griffiths, *Is Law Important?* (Deventer: Kluwer, 1978); J. Griffiths, "Legal Pluralism and the Social Working of Law", in A. Soeteman *et al.* (eds.), *Coherence and Conflicts Concerning the Law* (Zwolle: Tjeenk Willink, 1991); N. Zeegers, J. Witteveen and B. van Klink, *Social and Symbolic Effects of Legislation Under the Rule of Law* (Lewiston, N.Y.: Edwin Mellen Press, 2005).

42 J. Vrielink, *'Van haat gesproken'... Een rechtsantropologisch onderzoek naar ervaringen rond de bestrijding van groepsgerichte uitingsdelicten in België* [Speaking of Hatred... A Legal Anthropological Study Regarding Experiences in the Struggle Against Expression Crimes in Belgium], in preparation.

gium. Some of these effects appear to be inherent in any legislation targeting hate speech. However, an analysis of attitudes and experiences of other, more 'moderate' categories of perpetrators shows that a number of the negative effects of the legislation, and especially those that are liable adversely to affect wider society, are in fact inextricably bound up with the legal problems identified above.

2.4 Conclusion: Limitless Law or Self–Limiting Law?

In short then, the antiracist mindset has in Belgian criminal law policies led to a loss of perspective on several 'limits': limits posed by other rights and procedures; limits dictated by principles such as reasonableness, gravity and harm and limits as to the desired personal and societal effects of legal intervention. The moderation and realism that once were at the heart of the legal antiracist endeavour have all but disappeared due to subsequent societal developments.

Interestingly, this would *not* appear to mean that law becomes truly 'limitless', a mere instrument in the pursuit of antiracist policies. Although – for quite some time – judicial institutions appeared to go along relatively uncritically with developments in this direction, of late there have been signs of self–corrective tendencies. The most significant of these is a new stance on these issues by the Belgian Constitutional Court. Whereas this Court initially seemed to be relatively permissive of limitations of rights and principles where it concerned antiracist measures – upholding, for example, the Holocaust Denial Act – more recent rulings demonstrate a more stringent approach.[43]

In 2004 especially, the Court struck down several provisions of the Antidiscrimination Act. It was particularly strict regarding restrictions of the freedom of speech and the principle of legality. First it ordained that in order for the prohibition of 'incitement to hatred and discrimination' to be lawful, it was required to show the presence of a special, malicious intent. Secondly, the Court nullified the prohibition of 'announcing one's intention to racial hatred, discrimination and violence'. It stated that

> such a prohibition … suffocates every debate, since it precludes the possibility of the person expressing his intention to be contradicted and dissuaded from realising this intention.

The Court thereby explicitly opted for the principle of the 'marketplace of ideas': 'bad ideas' should be responded to with 'good ideas', rather than with prohibitions.[44] Censorship merely leaves bad ideas unchallenged, repressing rather than interrogating them.

---

43 See, for an analysis, S. Sottiaux and J. Vrielink, "De Negationismewet op het hellend vlak" [The Holocaust Denial Act on the Slippery Slope], *Tijdschrift voor Mensenrechten* 2005 (2), 6–13.

44 The concept is often attributed to Justice Holmes, in his dissenting opinion in *Abrams v US* (250 U.S. 616 (1919)). He stated: "Persecution for the expression of opinions seems to me perfectly logical. If you have no doubt of your premises or your power and want a certain re-

This ruling has also had significant effects on the application of the Antiracism Act and the Holocaust Denial Act. First, the requirement of a specific intent has since been taken by some lower courts to hold for the incitement provision in the Antiracism Act as well, due to its largely identical wording. It has even been applied to the Holocaust Denial Act.[45] The results are striking. The judgments that have taken the Constitutional Court's requirement seriously are characterised by a markedly higher level of analysis[46], and there is a (re)introduction of the *context* of the conflict in question as a relevant consideration. On the one hand, this approach serves to filter out cases involving futilities or unintended offences, reinserting personal responsibility into the equation. On the other hand – since the legal verification of specific intent requires more in-depth analysis of the conflict or incident at hand – it provides *all* parties involved with a greater opportunity to detail their lived experiences and considerations, thereby contributing to the ideal of a more communicative law.

Secondly, the annulment of the prohibition of 'announcing one's intention' has also had effects on the Antiracism Act, since it too had been copied from this Act. The direct result of it being struck down in the Antidiscrimination Act was that it has been used much less in the Antiracism Act since. This was in itself a positive development: there was little consistency to be discovered in the jurisprudence it had given rise to until then, and the more 'extreme' cases that were tried on the basis of it could easily have been brought under the application of the incitement provision.[47] However, the indirect results of its demise were less encouraging. When it became clear that the Antiracism Act too would have to lose the 'announcement provision' – since it could no longer reasonably be considered constitutional – the CEOOR requested a 'substitute'. In line with the processes described above, the legislators followed this request, introducing the aforementioned prohibition of the dissemination of racist ideas. Although this provision is almost literally derived from the ICERD[48], Belgium – as mentioned –

---

sult with all your heart you naturally express your wishes in law and sweep away all opposition. To allow opposition by speech seems to indicate that you think the speech impotent (...) or that you doubt either your power or your premises. But when men have realised that time has upset many fighting faiths, they may come to believe even more than they believe the very foundations of their own conduct that the ultimate good desired is better reached by free trade in ideas – that the best test of truth is the power of the thought to get itself accepted in the competition of the market, and that truth is the only ground upon which their wishes safely can be carried out. That at any rate is the theory of our Constitution." The actual term was coined in the Supreme Court decision *Keyishian v Board of Regents* (385 U.S. 589, 605–606 (1967)).

45 See *e.g.*, Correctional Court Dendermonde, 3 April 2007; Correctional Court Hasselt, 1 March 2007; Correctional Court Antwerp, 9 February 2007; Correctional Court Dendermonde, 24 October 2005.

46 If by nothing else this is already 'physically' indicated by the fact that they are by far more extensive than the average previous judgment.

47 J. Vrielink, S. Sottiaux and D. De Prins, "Het Vlaams Blok–arrest, artikel 150 van de Grondwet en de interpretatie van de antiracismewet" [The Flemish Block Judgment, Article 150 of the Constitution and the Interpretation of the Antiracism Act], *Tijdschrift voor Vreemdelingenrecht* 2004, (2), 98–99.

48 See Article 4a ICERD.

has made a restricting declaration to this Treaty precisely on this point. This is a fact that the proponents of the new provision failed to mention in the parliamentary discussions.[49] Moreover, it seems apparent that this new provision is in conflict with the principles embodied in the latest Constitutional Court ruling: if the 'marketplace of ideas' means anything, it would probably be that the dissemination of ideas cannot in itself be subject to sanctions.[50] Not only do the annulment of the announcement provision and its rationale attest to this: the Court, in its 2004 ruling, also happened to strike down a *civil* provision concerning the dissemination of 'discriminatory expressions'. It stated that

> the Act fails to point out when and to what extent these discriminatory expressions exceed the threshold permissible in a democratic society of conveying ideas liable to 'shock, disturb or offend'. Therefore, the provision does not meet the strict requirements that limitations to the freedom of expression are subject to.[51]

If this already holds for a civil provision, criminal ones with a similar basis – such as the new addition – would seem to stand little chance of surviving the Court's scrutiny.

It would appear therefore that the legislators have not fully heeded the lessons from the previous collision with the Constitutional Court.[52] However, seeing that the entire body of Belgian discrimination law was revised in 2007, the Constitutional Court will no doubt soon be presented with an opportunity to revisit this matter at greater length and pronounce itself on the constitutional limits particularly of antiracism.

Who knows: in time the outcome of the current unchecked policies and legislation in this matter could well turn out, paradoxically, to be a *greater* degree of

---

49 When the opposition drew attention to its omission, the response was that the declaration only stipulates that freedom of speech should be respected in implementing the ICERD, but that "there is no incommensurability whatsoever between the penalisation of the dissemination of ideas based on racial superiority or hatred on the one hand and the freedom of speech on the other hand" (*Parliamentary Documents*, Chamber of Representatives 2006–07, no. 51–2720/9, 40). This would *de facto* render the interpretive declaration without content: if it has no bearing on even the broadest restriction on the freedom of speech entailed by the ICERD (being the 'dissemination of racist ideas'), it follows that the declaration would be void of *any* content or implication. Such an interpretation, however, would appear far–fetched: common (legal) sense would suggest the interpretative declaration not be *entirely* without content, to say the least. It stands to reason that it would not have been made in the first place, if that were the case. Furthermore the current view is at odds with that of the original legislators of the Antiracism Act, who had explicitly rejected the penalisation of 'racist insults' (that had been part of the initial proposal of the Act), considering this amongst other things to conflict with the aforementioned interpretative declaration. See, *Parliamentary Documents*, Chamber of Representatives 1979, no. 214/1.

50 *Cf.* S. Sottiaux and J. Vrielink, *l.c.*.

51 Constitutional Court (Belgium), no. 157/2004, 6 October 2004, B.73.

52 In response to criticism by the opposition, the majority did stipulate a number of additional – and previously unmentioned – prerequisites in order for the 'dissemination of racist ideas' to be subject to punishment (*e.g.*, special intent; restrictive interpretation of 'dissemination', etc.). At the same time, however, the majority refused to explicitly include these requirements in the provision itself, leaving it to the judiciary to decide whether or not to take them into account.

constitutional protection of the rights and principles currently under pressure. It is worth remembering that current First Amendment doctrine in the United States *also* developed from past mistakes and policies that had got out of control: think – for example – of the McCarthy era.[53] The limits of the law might be best described as 'elastic' in that sense: one can stretch them quite a bit, but taken to the extreme they are liable to snap right back in your face.

3 Second Illustration: Worlds Apart Together: The Limits of Human Rights Protection for Indigenous Peoples

E. Desmet

3.1 Introduction

Recent decades bear witness to an enhanced interaction between indigenous peoples and human rights. As the national legal system is usually inclined to give preference to the interests of the dominant section of society, indigenous peoples have appealed to international human rights law in their struggles to safeguard or recover their territory and autonomy. And not without success: standard–setting initiatives such as ILO Convention 169 and the Draft UN and OAS Declarations exclusively address indigenous rights. Moreover, international judicial[54] and treaty monitoring[55] bodies have taken significant steps towards interpreting "undifferentiated"[56] human rights and minority rights in a culturally sensitive way.

In spite of these advances, there are substantial limits to the protection available and afforded by human rights. There are at least three clusters of limitations to the legal protection function of human rights law for indigenous peoples: one inherent in the notion of human rights, one arising from State conceptions and one emanating from indigenous representations.

---

53 See the extensive discussion of the historical development of First Amendment doctrine: S. Walker, *Hate Speech. The History of an American Controversy* (Lincoln and London: University of Nebraska Press, 1994). See, for an excellent analysis of the McCarthy era: M.H. Redish, *The Logic of Persecution. Free Expression and the McCarthy Era* (Stanford: Stanford University Press, 2005).

54 Landmark cases are Inter–American Court on Human Rights, 31 August 2001, *Mayagna (Sumo) Awas Tingni Community v Nicaragua*, Ser. C No. 79; African Commission on Human and Peoples' Rights, *The Social and Economic Rights Action Center for Economic and Social Rights v Nigeria*, Communication No. 155/96 (2001).

55 *E.g.*, Human Rights Committee, General Comment 23, Article 27 (Fiftieth session, 1994), UN Doc. CCPR/C/21/Rev.1/Add.5 (1994); Committee on the Elimination of Racial Discrimination, General Recommendation 23: Indigenous Peoples, UN Doc. CERD/C/51/misc13/rev4 (1997).

56 P. Thornberry, *Indigenous Peoples and Human Rights* (Manchester: Manchester University Press, 2002).

3.2 Concept of Human Rights

A preliminary question is whether human rights constitute an appropriate instrument *at all* for advancing the cause of indigenous peoples. Originating in the western hemisphere in the aftermath of the Second World War, human rights in their philosophy and formulation bear the stamp of the individualistic, western liberal ideal.[57] As Panikkar says, "the present–day formulation of Human Rights is the fruit of a very partial dialogue among the cultures of the world".[58] Consequently, there are some inherent tensions between the cosmology and claims of indigenous peoples and the logic of human rights. Indigenous demands of collective rights challenge the originally individual approach of human rights. The multi–dimensional relationship of indigenous peoples to their territories and natural resources cannot be reduced to the intrinsically economic concept of property.

With respect to the right of indigenous peoples to retain their own customs, institutions and methods for dealing with offences, human rights function as 'red lights': indigenous norms and practices are accepted only as long as they are not incompatible "with fundamental rights defined by the national legal system and with internationally recognised human rights".[59] There is an intrinsic tension: human rights are expected to ensure the well–being of indigenous persons, but simultaneously they are the ultimate touchstone for restricting indigenous peoples' rights of self–determination and autonomy. Thus, besides addressing the limits *of* human rights protection for indigenous peoples, the desirability of imposing restrictions *on* the application of human rights to indigenous societies should be reviewed.

3.3 State Conceptions

An adequate human rights protection tailored to indigenous peoples' needs also continues to be hampered by classical State conceptions. Although we have come a long way, indigenous peoples' demands are still to a greater or lesser extent regarded as shaking the foundations of the State, namely its national sovereignty and territorial integrity. Such State conceptions do not constitute limitations of human rights law *per se*, but limit the effectiveness of human rights. They impact, among others (i) on the progressive formulation and approval of global human rights standards, (ii) on the decisions of international treaty monitoring bodies, and (iii) on the implementation of international norms and judgments. These three propositions will now be illustrated.

---

57 *See* M. Mutua, *Human Rights. A Political and Cultural Critique* (Philadelphia: University of Philadelphia Press, 2002).

58 R. Panikkar, "Is the Notion of Human Rights A Western Concept?", *Interculture* 1984, *17* (1), Cahier no. 82, 43.

59 Article 8(2) Convention No. 169 concerning Indigenous and Tribal Peoples in Independent Countries (1989). See also Article 9(1) [hereinafter ILO Convention 169].

For the time being, the adoption of international human rights norms for indigenous peoples has come to a standstill. The Human Rights Council had recommended that the UN General Assembly adopt the Declaration on the Rights of Indigenous Peoples.[60] On 28 November 2006, however, the Third Committee of the General Assembly adopted a non–action motion put forward by Namibia on behalf of the African Group of States.[61] The Committee decided to defer consideration of the Declaration to allow time for further consultations and to conclude this consideration before the end of the sixty–first session of the General Assembly in September 2007.[62] The African Group is preoccupied with, among others,

a) the definition of indigenous peoples;
b) self–determination;
c) ownership of land and resources;
d) establishment of distinct political and economic institutions; and
e) national and territorial integrity.[63]

This enumeration is exemplary of States' concerns as regards indigenous peoples' rights. The core right of self–determination is especially controversial, as it is often equivocally interpreted as necessarily implying secession from the dominant State.

With regard to the decisions of international treaty monitoring bodies, Shelton concludes upon review of the decisions of the Human Rights Committee that

> despite the Committee's broad definition of cultural rights in General Comment 23, it has chosen to limit claims of autonomy by minority groups, thus upholding the sovereignty and territorial integrity of States.[64]

Traditional State conceptions also hinder an adequate implementation of international norms at the domestic level. An example here constitutes territorial rights in Peru. ILO Convention 169 includes the term "territory", which it defines as "the total environment of the areas which the peoples concerned occupy or otherwise use", thus considering it a broader concept than "land".[65] Peru abstained from voting Convention 169 in the International Labour Conference, partly because of its concern regarding the use of the term "territories".[66] According to classical conceptions of international law, the territory is one of the constitutive elements of the State, and States are entitled to exercise exclusive authority within this territory. Such an interpretation is detrimental to indigenous peoples, for whom control over their territories is a necessary condition for their spiritual and material well–

---

60 Human Rights Council, resolution 2006/2, 29 June 2006.

61 See www.un.org/News/briefings/docs/2001/afrgrouppc.doc.htm.

62 A/C.3/61/L.57/Rev.1 (2006).

63 Assembly of the African Union, Decision on the United Nations Declaration on the Rights of Indigenous Peoples, 30 January 2007, Assembly/AU/ Dec.141(VIII).

64 D. Shelton, "The UN Human Rights Committee's Decisions", *Human Rights Dialogue: "Cultural Rights"*, Spring 2005, Series 2, No. 12.

65 Article 13 ILO Convention 169.

66 J. Anaya, *Indigenous Peoples in International Law* (Oxford: Oxford University Press, 2nd ed., 2004) 85–86, notes 100 and 103.

being.[67] Peru subsequently ratified the Convention, but did not adapt its domestic legislation. The peasant and native communities can acquire rights only over limited lots of land, a situation that leads to an artificial fragmentation of their ancestral territories.[68]

Likewise, the judgments of international courts are often not satisfactorily executed by the convicted State. A remarkable example is the landmark case of *Mayagna (Sumo) Awas Tingni Community v Nicaragua* (2001) of the Inter–American Court on Human Rights, which was the first legally binding decision of an international tribunal that recognised the collective rights of indigenous peoples to their lands, territories and resources.[69] Despite their groundbreaking work on the international legal plane, the sentence of 2001 and the resolution concerning provisional measures of 2002 have still not been adequately complied with by the government of Nicaragua.[70] A key explanatory factor for this is the political conceptions based on the "traditional pretension of the Nicaraguan State to ownership of the lands and natural resources of the Atlantic Coast".[71]

The various cases above attest that international human rights law and the daily reality of many indigenous communities are still often 'worlds apart'. The UN Special Rapporteur has identified this implementation gap between law and practice as "the main problem" of the human rights situation of indigenous peoples today.[72] This deficient implementation is due not only to traditional State conceptions. Other factors also play a prominent part, such as limited economic and human resources; the historical and ongoing differential power relations between indigenous peoples and their encapsulating State; and political will, although also moulded by classical State points of view. Other societal spheres, mainly politics, thus interfere with an adequate implementation of human rights law.

---

67 M. Ludescher, "Indigenous Peoples' Territories and Natural Resources: International Standards and Peruvian Legislation", *Law and Anthropology* 2001, *11*, 156–178, 159.

68 In the words of a high civil servant of the Peruvian State: "we understand territories as lands". This contradicts the meaning attached to 'territory' in ILO Convention 169.

69 See note 54 above. For the proceedings and context, see J. Anaya and C. Grossman, "The Case of Awas Tingni v. Nicaragua: A New Step in the International Law of Indigenous Peoples", *Arizona Journal of International and Comparative Law* 2002, *19* (1), 1–15.

70 *Mayagna (Sumo) Awas Tingni Community (Provisional Measures),* Resolution of 6 September 2002, IACtHR Ser. D.

71 Translation by the author. "Observaciones sobre el cumplimiento del Pacto Internacional de los Derechos Civiles y Políticos por parte del Estado de Nicaragua, Presentadas por el Programa de Derechos y Políticas Indígenas de la Facultad de Derecho de la Universidad de Arizona en representación de la Comunidad Awas Tingni, ante el Comité de Derechos Humanos", 27 September 2005, para. 17, available at www.law.arizona.edu/depts/iplp/advocacy/awastingni/documents/CDH_report_Nicaragua92005.pdf (last visited 3 August 2007).

72 UN Commission on Human Rights, *Report of the Special Rapporteur on the situation of human rights and fundamental freedoms of indigenous people, Mr. Rodolfo Stavenhagen*, para 83, E/CN.4/2006/78 (2006) [hereinafter Report Stavenhagen].

3.4 Indigenous Representations

A third kind of limits to human rights protection derives from the fact that formulating claims in the language of human rights may have unintended or unexpected consequences. The recourse to human rights is in itself "a cultural process, which impinges on human subjects and subjectivities in multiple and contradictory ways".[73] As such, the embrace of indigenous peoples' aspirations by the human rights system has influenced the self–representation of the indigenous movement. Sieder and Witchell note that indigenous leaders often depict an "essentialised, idealised and atemporal indigenous identity" to substantiate their claims, inspired by global discourses on indigenous peoples and deemed necessary or useful to advance their demands.[74] This image of harmony denies the internal heterogeneity of indigenous communities and the dynamic character of their identity, which is constantly recreated in interaction with national and transnational processes. It may lead to the marginalisation of poorer or non–dominant sections of the indigenous population and to an isolation of indigenous peoples from wider processes.[75]

In sum, States and indigenous peoples are entangled in a web of misinterpretations (by the State) and misrepresentations (by the indigenous movement), which limits the potential of human rights protection.

3.5 Conclusion: Which Way Out?

Are there tentative ways out of these limitations? First, are human rights fundamentally appropriate means of furthering indigenous demands? Or are human rights and indigenous peoples two worlds too different to fit together? On a basic level, this contribution supports the view that we must engage in a genuine intercultural dialogue, and thus

> think in a fundamentally plural way, acknowledging that there may be fundamentally different choices that Men have made to think about their lives and to organise them.[76]

---

73 J.K. Cowan, M.–B. Dembour and R.A. Wilson, "Introduction", in J.K. Cowan, M.–B. Dembour and R.A. Wilson (eds.), *Culture and Rights. Anthropological Perspectives* (Cambridge: Cambridge University Press, 2001) 1–30, 3.

74 R. Sieder and J. Witchell, "Advancing Indigenous Claims Through the Law: Reflections on the Guatemalan Peace Process", in J.K. Cowan, M.–B. Dembour and R.A. Wilson (eds.), *Culture and Rights. Anthropological Perspectives* (Cambridge: Cambridge University Press, 2001) 201–225, 201.

75 *Ibid.*, 202.

76 C. Eberhard, "Human Rights and Intercultural Dialogue, An Anthropological Perspective", Lecture for the Summer Course "Cultural Identities and Human Rights" organised by the International Institute for the Sociology of Law in Oñati, 9–13 July 2001, 11, available at www.dhdi.org (last visited 3 August 2007).

Pending the outcome of such a dialogue, a more pragmatic and immediate stance would call for an intensification of efforts to adopt specific human rights standards for indigenous peoples, such as the UN and OAS Declarations, and to further open up the interpretation of general human rights law to indigenous viewpoints.

With respect to the 'red light' function of human rights, which restricts the indigenous administration of justice, the Colombian Constitutional Court has provided a particular interpretation. The Court stated that "in a nation where cultural diversity is recognised, no world view can prevail over the other, let alone attempt to dominate", implying that human rights cannot always automatically take precedence over indigenous decisions.[77] The Court limited the human rights against which the indigenous ways of administering justice are to be checked to a core group: the right to life, the right to be protected against slavery and torture, and the criterion of due process.[78] The jurisprudence of the Court

> seems to be the most ambitious attempt to devise norms that permit a maximisation of indigenous autonomy in the administration of justice without losing sight of fundamental human rights.[79]

However, to think in a "fundamentally plural way", as suggested above, raises the question to what extent one culture can claim to impose *any* standards on another.

Second, the reluctance of some States to recognise indigenous claims, founded on arguments of sovereignty and territorial integrity, is at least partially caused by a limited knowledge and understanding of indigenous worldviews and realities. Given that 'the law' is intrinsically dynamic, it cannot itself be blamed for the sustained rigidity towards indigenous peoples. Garcia then situates the roots of the unsatisfactory legal treatment of indigenous peoples in the realm of values: the current Latin American republics are still steeped in the colonial values inherited from their western predecessors.[80] Therefore, Nation–States and the indigenous peoples living within their borders need to enter into an intercultural dialogue. A genuine respect for the rights of indigenous peoples requires that these rights be interpreted according to their own views and cosmologies.[81] Capacity building programs would be useful in order to acquaint national civil servants with both international human rights norms and indigenous conceptions. In this sense, the sec-

---

77 T 496 (26 September 1996). See A. Hoekema, "A New Beginning Of Law Among Indigenous Peoples. Observations by a Legal Anthropologist", in F.J.M. Feldbrugge (ed.), *The Law's Beginnings* (Leiden: Martinus Nijhoff, 2003) 181–220, 188–189.

78 T 349 (8 August 1996).

79 W. Assies, "Multi–Ethnicity, The State and the Law In Latin America", *Journal of Legal Pluralism* 1999 (43), 145–158, 157. See also W. Assies, "Indian Justice in the Andes: Re–Rooting or Re–Routing", in T. Salman and A. Zoomers (eds.), *Imaging the Andes: Shifting Margins of a Marginal World* (Amsterdam: Aksant Academic Publishers, 2003), also available at www.alertanet.org (last visited 3 August 2007) and E. Sánchez Botero, "Reflexiones antropológicas en torno a la justicia y la jurisdicción especial indígenas en una nación multicultural y multiétnica", available at www.alertanet.org (last visited 3 August 2007).

80 P. García Hierro, "Territorios indígenas: Tocando a las puertas del derecho", in A. Surrallés and P. García Hierro (eds.), *Tierra adentro. Territorio indígena y percepción del entorno* (Copenhagen: IWGIA Document No. 39, 2004) 277–306, 279.

81 J.A. Fiske, "Introduction", *Law and Anthropology* 1996, *8*, X.

ond issue is to some extent similar to the first, both being instances of different 'worlds' (human rights / Nation–States on the one hand; indigenous peoples on the other hand) who need to find a way to interact respectfully .

In Peru, the fragmentation of indigenous territories is to be reversed by a consolidation, a reunification of the communal titles.[82] Ideally, a new *sui generis* legal figure reflecting the concept of indigenous territories should be established, with the full participation of indigenous peoples.[83]

The implementation gap between human rights and indigenous realities needs to be addressed at both the national and international level. Domestically, international standards are to be incorporated and implemented. When norms are inconsistent, human rights legislation should be given preference.[84] The human rights bodies at the international level should endeavour to develop ways of making their decisions binding and create a sanction apparatus for States that persevere in not complying.[85] Also, the accessibility of international mechanisms for indigenous peoples should be enhanced, as they often lack knowledge on "how to engage in the [human rights] law's business".[86]

Turning to the third issue, indigenous peoples and their representative organisations may consider nuancing their idealised representations and giving space to internal diversity and divergent voices. The romantic image that outsiders have constructed of indigenous ways of life and which to some extent still persists may be helpful in the short run, but dangerous and counterproductive in the long run.

> The challenge is how to ensure that indigenous communities govern themselves in a manner that is tolerant of difference ... without legitimising external imposition by State authorities or 'new colonialism' in the name of equality or human rights.[87]

In conclusion, international human rights law has made significant progress towards a formulation and protection tailored to the needs of indigenous peoples. Nevertheless, various limitations of diverse nature and intensity continue to obstruct the road towards a full–fledged respect for indigenous rights in a truly multicultural society. Most urgently needed are an adequate implementation and enforcement of existing international human rights standards.

---

82 F. Ballón Aguirre, *Manual del derecho de los pueblos indígenas. Doctrina, principios y normas* (Lima: Defensoría del Pueblo, 2004) 72–74.

83 See for an elaboration of this point García Hierro, *l.c.*

84 Report Stavenhagen, *l.c.*, para 100.

85 *Ibid.*, para 72.

86 E. Claes, W. Devroe, and B. Keirsbilck, "The Limits of the Law (Introduction)".

87 Sieder and Witchell, *l.c.*, 22.

4 Third Illustration: Confucian Tradition and Socio–Economic Rights Protection in Contemporary China

S. Deklerck

The 'limits of the law' form a basic part of traditional Chinese legal thought. According to Confucianism, which heavily influenced traditional Chinese legal thinking, law can only be a secondary tool to govern society. Moral precepts, or '*Li*', are the most important norms of social order. Moral education is the ultimate way to guide society towards harmony, and the role of law can only be of secondary importance. In China today, Confucianism is making a comeback. At a time when China is facing growing discrepancies between rich and poor, widening disparities between rural and urban areas, and a legal and social system unable to cope with all the inequalities, the Chinese government has started to promote Confucianism very explicitly. The official revival of Confucian values accentuates practices already existing in Chinese society – disadvantaged groups such as the disabled have mostly counted on traditional rather than legal ways to find societal acceptance and support.

What follows is an illustration of the role traditions can play in socio–economic rights protection, both on governmental level and on grass–roots level. Law and legal practice are but part of a wider culture, and attention should be paid to other cultural aspects which take up a prominent role in people's life.

The illustration largely foregoes underlying and widely debated research questions regarding the compatibility of human rights and Chinese (Confucian) tradition.[88] The purpose here is to highlight the importance of the Confucian tradition when discussing the Chinese implementation of socio–economic rights[89] as they can be found in international human rights documents[90] and in many Chinese laws.[91]

---

88 For a standard work on this question, see W.T. De Bary and Weiming Tu (eds.), *Confucianism and Human Rights* (New York: Columbia University Press, 1998).

89 This challenge has also been raised at debates concerning the universality/relativity of human rights. See E. Brems, *Human Rights: Universality and Diversity* (International Studies in Human Rights, Vol. 66) (The Hague: Martinus Nijhoff, 2001), who adopts a framework of 'inclusive universalism' to give a proper place to specificities of different cultural traditions when implementing human rights.

90 Such as the International Covenant on Social, Economic and Cultural Rights, signed and ratified by China in October 1997 and March 2001 respectively.

91 In Chapter 2 of the Constitution of the PRC, fundamental rights of Chinese citizens are mentioned. See Articles 33–56 Constitution of the PRC. Other important laws are mentioned throughout this contribution to this chapter.

4.1 Confucianism and its Influence on the Chinese Legal Tradition

> The Master said, Govern the people by regulations, keep order among them by chastisements, and they will flee from you, and lose all self–respect. Govern them by moral force, keep order among them by ritual and they will keep their self–respect and come to you of their own accord.[92]

Confucianism emerged in the 5th century B.C., and developed into "a true cultural phenomenon which became inextricably linked to the whole of Chinese civilisation."[93] Most authors cite Confucianism together with Legalism as the major schools of thought contributing to the formation of Chinese legal thought.[94]

An important aspect of Confucianism is its representation of man. According to Confucian thought, a human being only becomes human in his relations with other people. A person does not come to the world as an isolated entity – a person exists only because he is connected to others.[95]

Confucianism identifies five 'cardinal' relationships within society: the relationship between sovereign and subject, father and son, elder and younger brother, husband and wife, and friend and friend.[96] The family is the most important entity within society. Relationships within the wider society have to be modelled on the relationships within the family. The relationship between sovereign and subject, for example, is conceived of in terms of that between father and son, and the relation between friend and friend in terms of the one between elder and younger brother.[97]

The final goal of government is the correct operation of these relationships.[98] This alone can lead to a 'Harmonious Society'.

Law in this approach is seen as an inferior and flawed instrument for governing society. According to Confucianism, the primary norms in society are the '*Li*'. These are not rules issued by the State, but norms of morality and habit.[99] The Li are relational rules determined by tradition and bring harmony to society. The Li describe extensively how people should relate to each other in societal life, and the duties of all people vis–à–vis each other. The Li may differ from person to person in society, according to social status. There is therefore no concept of equality

---

92 Confucius, *The Analects* (trans. Arthur Waley) (Beijing: Waiyu jiaoxue yu yanjiu chubanshe, 1997) 12–13.

93 A. Cheng, *Histoire de la pensée chinoise* (Paris: Seuil, 1997) 55.

94 H. Piquet, *La Chine au carrefour des traditions juridiques* (Bruxelles: Bruylant, 2005) 33.

95 A. Cheng, *l.c.*, 62.

96 J. Chen, *Chinese Law, Towards an Understanding of Chinese Law, its Nature and Development* (The Hague: Kluwer Law International, 1999) 8.

97 Yu–lan Fung and D. Bodde (eds.), *A Short History of Chinese Philosophy* (New York: The Free Press, 1948) 21.

98 J. Chen, *l.c.*, 9.

99 It is hard to give an exact definition of the concept of Li. Heuser gives a number of translations: Li is rite, the sum of all sacral rules, ethics, the sum of all norms you have to obey in the social life, the relational rules determined by tradition, norms to bring order into the social life. R. Heuser, *Einführung in die Chinesische Rechtskultur* (Hamburg: IFA, 2002) 68.

when applying the Li. They describe, among many other things, the absolute respect children owe their parents, the respect subjects must show to their sovereign, etc. The Li have to be maintained primarily by society, which can enforce the Li by forms of social pressure.[100] Official State law, or '*Fa*', is merely an auxiliary instrument. Only grave infractions of the Li can be punished by the Fa.[101] Dealings in court have to be avoided as much as possible. Ideally, society should be ruled through morality. The sovereign and his officials are expected to rule through moral example.[102] Law and regulations are seen as essentially limited instruments with which to govern society – they can have only a short term effect, whereas the Li have a long term effect.

Legalism, the other main influence on China's legal tradition, emerged between the 4th and the 3rd century B.C.[103] The Legalists put law, and more specifically penal law, at the centre of their theories of government. The sovereign is the ultimate source of the law.[104] He has to govern society by issuing strict rules that must be obeyed by everyone without distinction.

Whereas Legalism did exert tremendous influence on the Chinese legal tradition, exemplified for instance in Chinese techniques of codification[105], Confucianism dominated the whole imperial era in China. From the Han dynasty (206 – 220 B.C.), where one can speak for the first time of a 'confucianisation' of law[106], until the end of the Qing dynasty (ending in 1911), the influence of Confucianism on Chinese law was immense.

4.2 The Revival of Confucianism

Mao Zedong was a fervent critic of Confucianism until his death in 1976.[107] Confucianism was something that belonged to China's feudal past, unfit for the new and Communist China. After his death, Deng Xiaoping in the 1970s started building up the current Chinese legal system. The main reason for launching reforms was economic in nature. China had to open up to the outside world, it had to develop an economy able to play a prominent role on a global level, and the legal system was regarded as a prime means of achieving these goals. Law, defined as predictability and regularity in economic transactions, was crucial to the attainment of economic ends.

---

100 H. Piquet, *l.c.*, 41.

101 The law or *Fa* was conceived by the Confucians mainly in terms of penal law. *Cf.* H. Piquet, *l.c.*, 42.

102 F.W. Mote, *Intellectual foundations of China* (New York: McGraw–Hill, 2nd ed., 1989) 43.

103 H. Piquet, *l.c.*, 43.

104 Yongping Liu, *Origins of Chinese Law. Penal and Administrative Law in its Early Development* (Hong Kong: Oxford University Press, 1998) 183.

105 H. Piquet, *l.c.*, 46.

106 J. Chen, *l.c.*, 14.

107 See for example A.J. Gregor and M. Hsia Chang, "Anti–Confucianism: Mao's Last Campaign", *Asian Survey* 1979, *19* (11), 1073–1092.

The past three decades saw considerable effort to establish a functioning legal system in China.[108] The Chinese government continuously renewed its commitment to building up a legal system able to govern all aspects of societal life. This commitment was formalised in 1999, when the goal of evolving towards a 'Socialist Rule of Law' country was written into the Constitution of the People's Republic of China.[109]

After the reforms initiated by Deng Xiaoping, Confucianism gradually rose from its ashes. During the 1990s, intense debates were held among intellectuals in mainland China as to the future of Confucianism.[110] Noteworthy are the discussions concerning Confucianism and Human Rights. In 1991, the Chinese government published its first White Paper on Human Rights, espousing a very relativistic outlook on human rights by emphasising that the Chinese situation could not be judged in total disregard of its historical and national conditions, nor could it be evaluated according to the preconceived model or standard of another country or region.[111] Not surprisingly, the ensuing worldwide debate on Human Rights and Asian Values engaged many Chinese scholars.[112]

It was only very recently, however, that Confucianism has begun its real revival. The Chinese government has started to promote Confucianism very explicitly during the last few years. It conducted huge televised and official celebrations for the birthday of Confucius.[113] The teaching curriculum for secondary schools now officially includes the Confucian classics, and some experimental schools have even been set up that focus largely on the classics.[114] Abroad, the government

---

[108] This process has been and is being extensively discussed in Western and Chinese literature. See, amongst others: R. Peerenboom, *China's Long March Toward Rule of Law* (Cambridge: Cambridge University Press, 2002); S. Lubman, *Bird in a Cage. Legal Reform in China After Mao* (California: Stanford University Press, 1999); W.P. Alford, "A Second Great Wall? China's Post–Cultural Revolution Project of Legal Construction", *Cultural Dynamics* July 1999, *11* (2), 193–213; Hongming Gui, *Fazhi Shixian Lun* [On the Realisation of the Rule of Law] (Nanjing: shifan daxue chubanshe, 2000).

[109] Article 5 Constitution of the PRC.

[110] H. Piquet, *l.c.*, 35, referring to Bing Huai (trans. Xavier Gange), "La Chine en quête d'une nouvelle morale ", *Perspectives Chinoises* 1995, (30).

[111] State Council of the People's Republic of China, *Human Rights in China* (Beijing: State Council of the People's Republic of China, 1991) ii, 85. (First white paper on human rights.)

[112] This debate started in full force after the 1993 UN Vienna World Conference on Human Rights. The Bangkok Declaration, drawn up in conclusion of a regional preparation session for the 1993 United Nations Conference on Human Rights in Vienna, clearly reflected criticism of the universality of human rights, and showed a certain consensus among several East Asian countries. China, in contrast to other countries like Singapore, was never very vocal about its Confucian heritage or the cultural aspect of the relativity claim. Chinese scholars joined however in the academic debates. See for example, Yong Xia (ed.), *Public Law*, Vol. 1 (Falu chubanshe, 1999) (Subject discussion: Chinese Culture and Human Rights); Yong Xia, *The Origin of the Concept of Human Rights – History of the Philosophy of Rights* (Zhongguo zhengfa daxue chubanshe, 1992).

[113] T. Crowell, "The Confucian Renaissance", *Asiatimes* 16/11/2005 at www.atimes.com/atimes/China/GK16Ad01.html (last consulted 14/06/2007).

[114] D.A. Bell, "China's Leaders Rediscover Confucianism", *International Herald Tribune* at www.iht.com/articles/2006/09/14/opinion/edbell.php (last consulted 14/06/2007).

has been promoting Confucianism via branches of the Confucius Institute, a Chinese language and culture centre.[115]

Confucian values also seem largely to permeate the official ideology currently used by China's Communist leaders. This was brought to the fore when in 2005 Hu Jintao introduced the construction of a 'Harmonious Society' (*hexie shehui*) as the new socio–economic ideology of the Communist Party of China: it stands for the development of democracy, the rule of law, justice, sincerity, amity and vitality, as well as a better relationship between government and people.[116] Although numerous official sources have warned of the risk that this harmony may be the equivalent of the 'utopian' ideas of sages in the past[117], the term 'Harmonious Society' contains an undeniable referral to Confucianism. Moreover, Hu's new ideology echoes Confucian themes when he says that China should promote such values as honesty and unity, as well as forge a closer relationship between the people and the government.[118]

This renewed attention to Confucianism comes at a time when China is faced with a growing gulf between rich and poor, widening disparities between rural and urban areas, and a legal and social system unable to cope with all these inequalities. That is no wonder: the conception of the Harmonious Society clearly expresses the fact that unrestrained economic growth can no longer be the main focus of China – it emphasises the need for an overall societal balance.

Confucianism can help provide the nation with a much–needed ethical anchor in times of moral void caused by the decline of Marxism and the abundance of material temptations.[119] For the government, the promotion of Confucian values offers several advantages:

> Confucianism means order, submission to one's superiors, dedication to the State, defence of the family, ... Confucian values are favourable to a harmonious development, because they can limit individual wants and desires. Indeed, Confucianism considers the interest of the group more important than those of the individual and can thus assure social order.[120]

---

115 *Ibid.*

116 "Building Harmonious Society CPC's Top Task", *China Daily* 20/02/2005 at www.chinadaily.com.cn/english/doc/2005-02/20/content_417718.htm (last consulted 14/06/2007).

117 A. Miller, "Hu Jintao and the Sixth Plenum", *China Leadership Monitor* (20) at www.media.hoover.org/documents/clm20am.pdf (last consulted 14/06/2007).

118 Another example can be found in the reemergence of the word 小康社会 (*xiaokang shehui*) or society of small peace/comfort/health. The word was first used in the Confucian Classic of Rites, where it pointed to the predecessor of a world where everything was at peace. It has recently been used by Jiang Zemin and afterwards Hu Jintao in the sense of 'relatively well–off society': a goal for China to achieve in the near future. See for a short explanation "All About Xiaokang", *People's Daily*, 10/11/2002 at www.english.people.com.cn/200211/10/eng20021110_106598.shtml (last consulted 14/06/2007).

119 T. Crowell, "The Confucian Renaissance", *Asiatimes* 16/11/2005 at www.atimes.com/atimes/China/GK16Ad01.html (last consulted 14/06/2007).

120 J.–P. Beja, "Naissance d'un national–confucianisme?", *Perspectives Chinoises* 1995, (30), 9.

The current affirmation of harmony is intended by China's leaders to reflect their concern for all classes. Threatened by the discontent of the poor, the government commits itself to do more for those bearing the brunt of China's development, and it expects obedience in return.

Moreover, by widely promoting Confucian values of solidarity and care, the Chinese government encourages its citizens to take up their share of providing for the unfortunate. Care of the elderly can serve as an example. In Confucianism, *xiao*, or filial piety is one of the most important social precepts. Children have a firm duty to take care of their parents. This duty has been inscribed in several Chinese laws dealing with the elderly[121], but the practice of family care for the elderly has been waning as modern times have put a considerable strain on family ties. Recently, when the plight of the growing elderly population in China came to the fore, the value of filial piety received nationwide attention. One recent case aptly illustrates this attention. A county in Henan province issued new rules stating that government employees must be nice to their parents as well as being good at their jobs. Special investigators will check up on the background of each official, and will assess his/her family values.[122] This practice points to imperial times: filial piety used to be one of the main criteria for the selection of officials as early as the Han Dynasty.

While the slogan of building a 'Socialist Rule of Law' country sounded loudly under Jiang, the construction of a 'Harmonious Society' gets a lot more attention under the reign of Hu. The 'Harmonious Society' does include attaining the rule of law, but the overall message being spread is one of patience while a complete legal and social system protecting the interests of everyone is being established. In the meantime, Confucian values are promoted to fill in the gaps.

4.3 Confucianism and Rights: A Case Study at the Grassroots

The official revival of Confucian values mostly accentuates practices already existing in Chinese society – disadvantaged groups such as the disabled have mostly counted on traditional rather than legal ways to find societal acceptance and support. To illustrate this point, I will describe one of my fieldwork studies in the area of disability. I base myself on interviews and observations at the organisation named XingXingYu – a social organisation that struggles for the empowerment of parents of autistic children.[123]

---

121 Article 10 Law of the People's Republic of China on Protection of the Rights and Interests of the Elderly, Standing Committee of the National People's Congress, promulgated 29/08/1996. See also Articles 21 and 28 Marriage Law of the PRC, Standing Committee of the National People's Congress, promulgated 28/04/2001 (amending the Law of 1981).

122 "Filial Piety Plays a Part in Promotions", *China Daily* 09/04/2007 at www.chinadaily.com.cn/cndy/2007-04/09/content_845788.htm (last consulted 14/06/2007).

123 Fieldwork conducted intensively from October 2003 up until January 2004. Research activities included unstructured and semi–structured interviews with staff of the organisation and

XingXingYu teaches courses to parents of autistic children aged 3–12 years.[124] During a long–term course, the parents are taught the essentials of ABA (Applied Behaviour Analysis) – an educational technique specifically aimed at developing the social and mental skills of autistic children. As specialised help or even scientific research on autism is scarce in China[125], parents are taught to become experts (or at least trained educators) themselves. Throughout the course, parents also receive guidance on how to deal with the society around them and their autistic child. XingXingYu places strong emphasis on the fact that autistic children are valid citizens of China, who have fundamental rights which deserve protection. Tian Huiping, the director of XingXingYu, considers the education of the parents to rights consciousness as one of her main tasks.[126] The idea that "people exist for the good of the society"[127] (instead of the society existing for the good of the people), is still deeply imbedded in the mind of Chinese people, she says, and she tries to convince people to see it otherwise. Speaking in a language more reminiscent of Confucian concepts of duty than of international concepts of rights, she affirms that the family has the primary duty to help disabled members of the family, but that society has a duty towards all of its members as well. Parents can help their children, especially after the courses at XingXingYu, up to a certain point. After this point is reached however, it is the duty of society to accept the child into its midst. It is not only the child who has to adapt to society, but the converse is also true. Tian Huiping stresses the fact that parents have the task of holding society to the fulfilment of its duties.[128]

A practical topic that directly illustrates the latter point, and causes stress to almost all the parents, is the search for a school for their autistic child. Parents and the organisation both see schooling as very important – even if the child may not be able to acquire academic knowledge, attending school can certainly improve the social skills necessary for daily interaction with society. None of the parents I spoke to at XingXingYu planned to take their child to a special school – they mostly said that these schools were not equipped to deal with autistic children, or simply that there were no special schools in their home district. Most of the parents planned to take their child to a normal school. 'Mainstreaming' is in fact the

students of the parental courses, participant observation in the classes of Xingxingyu, analysis of written material issued by Xingxingyu.

124 Early intervention is crucial when dealing with autism – the majority of the families at Xingxingyu have a child younger than 6 years, but in 2002 Xingxingyu also started to arrange courses for families with older kids.

125 Xingxingyu, founded in 1993 by a mother of a boy with autism, has based itself for the development of its courses on foreign materials, and is considered throughout the whole of China as the organisation with the most expertise surrounding autism.

126 Recorded Interview Tian Huiping, 31/12/2003, Beijing, Xingxingyu.

127 *Ibid.*

128 Notes on lecture of Tian Huiping to parents/students, 31/10/2003, Beijing, Xingxingyu.

most common option for disabled children in China: children with different abilities follow classes together with normally developing peers.[129]

Getting a school to agree to enrol an autistic child is a serious problem. Neither XingXingYu nor any of the parents interviewed mentioned the legal right of every Chinese child to receive education, nor did they refer to the fact that legal provisions explicitly compel ordinary schools to accept disabled persons who are able to respond to ordinary education.[130] Moreover, when I mentioned these legal provisions myself during the interview, there seemed to be a consensus among parents and XingXingYu staff not to stress these legal provisions too much when contacting the school – this could lead to an unwilling attitude on the part of the school staff. A lawsuit would almost certainly never lead to a victory, and even if parents were to win a lawsuit it would still be practically impossible to send their child to this unwilling school. Instead, success stories of parents mainstreaming their children seem to focus on the courage of the parents in standing up for their child, and on their ability to establish good and personal contacts with the school staff.[131] Many of the parents I interviewed planned to use the lectures given at XingXingYu to approach the schools, make good personal contacts with the school staff, deliver a positive report of their child's condition, stress the fact that the family is doing everything possible to improve the development of the child, and finally point to the duty of society to accept all people regardless their (different) abilities.

This short description of the plight of parents of autistic children points to the omnipresence of Confucian values in Chinese societal life. The central position occupied by the family structure and the overall importance attached to education (*cf.* the XingXingYu education concerning rights consciousness, the importance of education for the child, educating the school on the plight of autistic children, etc.) are just a few examples that point to the Confucian heritage. It is interesting to note that XingXingYu promotes rights consciousness, mitigating Confucian notions of the primacy of the collective over the individual which are still very pre-

---

129 M. Deng, K.F. Poon–McBrayer, E. Farnsworth and H. McCabe, "The Development of Special Education in China: A Sociocultural Review", *Remedial and Special Education* 2001, *22*, 288-298.

130 See the Compulsory Education Law of the PRC, Standing Committee of the National People's Congress, promulgated 29/06/2006 (replacing the law of 1986). The Law of the PRC on the Protection of Disabled Persons also explicitly mentions the right to education of disabled persons, and even provides that ordinary educational institutions shall provide education to disabled persons who are able to respond to ordinary education. Articles 18 and 21 Law of the PRC on the Protection of Disabled Persons, Standing Committee of the National People's Congress, promulgated on 28/12/1990. The use of this law is controversial however regarding autism, as it was in 2003 (and still is) debatable whether autism is in fact qualified as a disability in China according to the official standards of China. See *Canjiren shiyong pingding biaozhun* [Practical evaluation standard for disabled] at www.cdpf.org.cn/zhengce/xg-zl-006b.htm (last consulted 14/06/2007).

131 Notes on lecture of Tian Huiping to parents/students, 31/10/2003, Beijing, Xingxingyu. See also stories published in XingXingYu's magazine, for example Jing Fang, "Yiwei Qingdao muqin de qingsu" [The Tales from a Mother of Qingdao], *Xingxingyu Tongxun*, 2000, *17*, 13–17, and Yuelai Zhen, "Nü'er Li Jinglin de jiuxue licheng" [The Process of Daughter Li Jinglin Attending School], *Xingxingyu tongxun*, 2000, *18*, 16–22.

sent in the mind of the parents of autistic children. The use of the law is avoided, however, and is considered useless – rightly so in a China where specialised education for autistic children is still a distant dream. Instead, people invest in creating personal understanding among the school staff, striving at, as Hu calls it in his theory on the harmonious society, societal solidarity and amity.

4.4 Conclusion

The above illustration underlines the need for an approach to socio–economic rights protection in China which takes into account the role played by tradition. Cultural knowledge and a proper understanding of tradition are indeed essential for realistic contributions to debates on more effective (human) rights protection in China.[132]

Rights consciousness is growing in China and has been continuingly flourishing in the minds of Chinese citizens, thanks to the commitments of the Chinese government to the 'Socialist Rule of Law', the increased contact with international views on human rights, and the work of social organisations such as XingXingYu. Chinese laws formally protect the rights of weaker groups in society such as the disabled and the elderly. However, in fact they are often not implemented because of lacunae in the social system and the absence of a judiciary system that is open to claims based on these laws. But this does not mean that people stop looking for ways to access their rights. Instead, Chinese citizens look for more traditional forms of support, by making use of Confucian values which are helpful to their plight.

In light of China's legal tradition, dominated by the Confucian view that law is only a secondary governing tool and emphasising moral precepts and moral education for ruling society; and the current Confucian revival, the key question is how the Chinese government can set up a more effective system of rights protection, one that takes into consideration traditional values and ways to strive for their support.

---

[132] See D.A. Bell, *Beyond Liberal Democracy: Political Thinking for an East Asian Context* (Princeton, N.J.: Princeton University Press, 2006), who similarly argues that local (cultural) knowledge is essential for realistic and morally informed contributions to debates on political reform in the East Asian region, as well as for mutual learning and enrichment of political theories.

5 Fourth Illustration: Judaism between Religious Freedom and Gender Equality

J. Kusters

5.1 The Relationship between Human Rights and Judaism

In discussing the relationship between human rights and Judaism, it is often claimed that Judaism has always had its own conception of human rights and that human rights were embedded within the Jewish tradition long before the international community started to speak in those terms, let alone to engage in their enforcement.[133] What is more, the very concept of human rights seems to stem from religious values[134], not the least from the Judaeo–Christian tradition.[135]

Be that as it may, when it comes to gender–specific human rights[136], most of the violations are grounded in religious practices. The competition that exists between religion and human rights apparently turns into a clash when it comes to gender equality. And precisely because it involves religiously embedded practices, the clash is all the more difficult to overcome, since the violation is often argued in terms of the right to freedom of religion.[137] As yet, there exists no clear–cut hierarchy between these two norms: on the one hand gender equality and on the other the right to freedom of religion.

---

[133] *E.g.*, W.H. Brackney, *Human Rights and the World's Major Religions. I. The Jewish Tradition* (Oxford: Praeger, 2005); S.D. Breslauer, *Judaism in Human Rights in Contemporary Thought* (Oxford: Greenwood Press, 1993); M.J. Broyde and J. Witte, *Human Rights in Judaism: Cultural, Religious and Political Perspectives* (Lanham: Jason Aronson Publishers, 1998); L.E. Goodman, *Judaism, Human Rights and Human Values* (Oxford: Oxford University Press, 1996); D. Novak, *Natural Law in Judaism* (Cambridge: Cambridge University Press, 1998); D. Novak, "Religious Human Rights in Judaic Texts", in J. Van der Vijver and J. Witte (eds.), *Religious Human Rights in Global Perspective. Religious Perspectives* (The Hague: Kluwer Law International, 1996) 175–202.

[134] D. Patel, "The Religious Foundations of Human Rights. A Perspective From the Judeo–Christian Tradition and Hinduism", www.nottingham.ac.uk/shared/shared_hrlcpub/HRLC_Commentary_2005/PATEL.pdf; M.E. Marty, "Religious Dimensions of Human Rights", in J. Van der Vijver and J. Witte, *Religious Human Rights in Global Perspective. Religious Perspectives* (The Hague: Kluwer Law International, 1996) 1–16.

[135] A. Maoz, "Can Judaism Serve as a Source of Human Rights?", *Heidelberg J. Int. L.* 2004, 677–721.

[136] The prohibition of gender discrimination and the principle of gender equality are generally acknowledged as human rights: Articles 1, 13, 55, and 76 United Nations Charter; Articles 2 and 16 Universal Declaration of Human Rights; International Covenant on Economic, Social and Cultural Rights; International Covenant on Civil and Political Rights; Convention on the Elimination of all Forms of Discrimination against Women, as well as the European Convention on Human Rights, American Convention on Human Rights; the African Charter on Human and Peoples' Rights.

[137] D.J. Sullivan, "Gender Equality and Religious Freedom: Toward a Framework for Conflict Resolution", *J. Int. L. & P.* 1991–92, 795–796.

The insight that a particular conception of gender is constructed within a religious–legal practice does not, in itself, constitute an 'objective' and 'reasonable' justification for gender inequality. Not even when trying to define it as a matter of religious liberty.[138] With regard to gender equality specifically, the European Court of Human Rights has stated that "very weighty reasons would have to be advanced before a difference of treatment on the ground of sex could be regarded as compatible with the Convention".[139] Moreover in trying to assess the factors that determine equality, one has to include the social, national and historical context in which gender differentiation occurs, in order to see whether and, if so, how the combination of all these factors results in a *de facto* gender (in)equality. An accommodating policy on part of the State towards religious minorities might for instance have major repercussions on the functioning of gender differentiation within religious law.

As was mentioned before, freedom of religion in itself does not offer an objective justification for a limitation of the right to gender equality. Freedom of religion encompasses the right to observe and apply religious law and to maintain and establish religious tribunals.[140] But this freedom of religion may be conditioned by limitations. The international norms guaranteeing this freedom indeed include the possibility of restrictions, inter alia in order to protect the right of others. Again, these limitations should be proportionate to the aim they wish to achieve. Therefore, although religious law falls under the scope of the fundamental freedom of religion, and individual as well as communal religious observance is thereby entitled to protection, it cannot simply put aside women's human rights. What is more, the latter can justify a restriction of the former.

Thus, in order to balance these two rights one needs to gain insight into the religious system in question, and into its principles and applications, in order to determine whether there is an infringement of one of these two rights and whether there is a reasonable and objective justification for this limitation. As regards gender, in order to truly understand the status of women in a given situation, the concept of gender should not be examined in isolation but together with all the surrounding factors that determine her position. The same holds true for religion, since in order to assess the significance of a religious law or practice within a particular belief system, as well as its effects on women's equality, the religious law or practice must also be examined in its political, social and economic context. The question whether religion effectively poses a problem in terms of human rights, and if so, how, may depend on external factors such as class or Church–State relations.[141]

---

138 D.J. Sullivan, *l.c.*, 803–804.

139 European Court of Human Rights, 28 May 1985, *Abdulaziz Cabalis and Blandali v United Kingdom*, www.echr.coe.int.

140 F. Caportoti, *Study on the Rights of Persons belonging to Ethnic, Religious and Linguistic Minorities,* U.N. Doc. E/CN. 4/2/384/I, U.N. N° E 78 XIV.1, 1979, 70–71; Sullivan, *l.c.*, 805.

141 *Cf.* D.J. Sullivan, *l.c.*, 811.

5.2 Jewish Law

In Judaism, the observance of religious law is an integral part of religious practice. The Jewish religion, especially from the orthodox point of view, is an *orthopraxis*, meaning that one professes one's religion through legal practice; the more one adheres to the legal norms, the more pious one becomes. The corpus of Jewish law, the *Halacha*, on the one hand comprises rules that determine the relation between God and his people, but on the other hand also provides an elaborate legal framework for the relationships between members of the Jewish community themselves. This part of the *Halacha* highly resembles a traditional legal system, in that it deals with most of the subjects that a legal systems usually regulates.[142]

The rules a Jewish person has to abide by are called the *Mitsvot*; it is according to these guidelines that Jewish life is structured, in an almost all–encompassing way. One striking feature of the *Mitsvot* is that the duties of a Jewish man differ considerably from those of a Jewish woman. Whilst men are obliged to lead a life of study, women are responsible for keeping the Torah alive in a different way, namely by bringing up the children in accordance with the Jewish spirit. A key idea in Judaism is that the world is, and should be, ordered along gender lines. Looking at the role of the Jewish woman, one can see that her role is located primarily in the domestic, private sphere and that she is first and foremost a mother. Her role is nonetheless highly valued, since as a mother she is responsible for transmitting Jewish culture and identity.[143]

This particular religious status – the Jewish woman is even said to be constructed as the radical Other within Judaism – is reflected in her legal status. Normative Judaism is essentially male and the Jewish woman seems to be inscribed in the legal system as a merely passive legal subject. As a result, her legal position differs substantially as well as formally from that of a man. In court, for instance, the testimony of a woman is not accorded the same value as that of a man.[144] This obviously has repercussions on the enjoyment of her rights, not only under Jewish

---

[142] *Cf.* M. Elon, *Principles of Jewish Law* (Jerusalem: Encyclopaedia Judaica, 1990).

[143] Concerning the construction of gender within Judaism, see J.R. Baskin, "Rabbinic Judaism and the Creation of Woman", in M. Peskowitz and L. Levitt (eds.), *Judaism Since Gender* (New York: Routledge, 1997) 125–130; L.D. Gordon, "Toward a Gender–Inclusive Account of Halakhah", in T.M. Rudavsky (ed.), *Gender and Judaism. The Transformation of Tradition* (New York: New York University Press, 1995) 3–12; B. Greenberg, *On Women and Judais* (Philadelphia: The Jewish Publication Society of America, 1998); S. Grossman and R. Haut, *Daughters of the King. Women and the Synagogue* (Philadelphia: The Jewish Publication Society, 1992); P.E. Hymann, *Gender and Assimilation in Modern Jewish History: The Roles and Representation of Women* (Seattle: University of Washington Press, 1995); D.R. Kaufman, *Rachel's Daughters. Newly Orthodox Jewish Women* (New Brunswick: Rutgers University Press, 1993) 243; C. Longman, *Beyond a God's Eye View in the Study of Gender and Religion with a Case Study: Religious Practice and Identity among Strictly Orthodox Jewish Women* (Ghent, Ph. D. Thesis, 2002); M. Peskowitz and L. Levitt (eds.), *Judaism Since Gender* (New York: Routledge, 1997); T.M. Rudavsky, *Gender and Judaism. The Transformation of Tradition* (New York: New York University Press, 1995).

[144] M. Elon, *Principles of Jewish Law* (Jerusalem: Encyclopaedia Judaica, 1990).

law but also in relation to secular rights, such as her human right to equality. The Jewish divorce procedure provides a clear illustration of the latter.

5.3 Jewish Divorce Law

The basis of Jewish divorce law is to be found in Deuteronomy 24:1:

> When a man taketh his wife, and marrieth her, then it cometh to pass, if she finds no favor in his eyes, because he hath found some unseemly thing in her, that he writeth her a bill of divorcement, and giveth it in her hand, and send her out of his house.

Only the man can hand over the bill of divorce, the *Get*, only he can divorce his wife. She cannot divorce him. Many stipulations were added in rabbinic times in order to soften the discretionary and unilateral character of the husband's right to divorce.[145] Nevertheless, the right to initiate a religious divorce basically still lies in the hands of the husband and in his alone. Even the best rabbinic scholars have not been able to resolve the case of the *Agunah.* It is the case of the Jewish wife who wishes to divorce her husband religiously but cannot because her husband is unable or unwilling to give her the *Get.* As a consequence, she is 'chained' to her husband and cannot enter into a new relationship without this relationship being adulterous. Besides the fact that adultery is an utterly reprehensible act within Judaism, the children of such a union will be considered *mamzeriem*, illegitimate children, who are excluded from the Covenant with God.

More recently, however, 9/11 caused the Rabbinical Court of America to rule concerning the *World Trade Center Agunot.*[146] A lot of women were left in a doubtful situation since their husbands were missing and would therefore most probably never be able to hand over a *Get*. The fact that the corpses were missing complicated things severely, since the *Halacha* requires circumstantial evidence of the husband's death. Finally, the majority of these cases were solved based on the argument of the high degree of probability of the death of the husband. When it is a matter of unwillingness on the part of the husband to cooperate, it is much harder to come to a solution, since the *Get,* according to *Halacha*, should be given out of free will, without external pressure.

While these limitations to the right of the wife to divorce have been strongly questioned from a feminist perspective, no solution has been reached thus far. Although partial solutions have been advanced from within Reform and Conservative Judaism, the problem seems insurmountable from an Orthodox perspective. A reform from within the *Halacha* encounters a variety of objections concerning legitimacy, which is the reason why the problem lingers on. Many nevertheless urge that a reform is necessary, since there is a universal principle of gender equality at

---

145 For instance by way of implementing additional formalities and the Ketubah as a semi–marriage contract.

146 *Cf.* C. Jachter, "The Beth Din of America's Handling of the World Trade Center Agunot", www.koltorah.org/ravj/Agunot%201.htm; J. Prager, "The World Trade Center Tragedy and the Aguna Issue", *JHCS* 2002, *44*, 5–30.

stake. In order to achieve an adequate solution to the problem, a reform from within the *Halacha* seems necessary. In principle, women can claim the right to gender equality, as guaranteed in several international norms, yet hardly any amelioration has so far stemmed from these norms. Why is this so?

The primary reason is that, despite the fact that there is a Jewish feminism, gender equality is not a relevant issue to every Jewish woman, especially not to women within the Orthodox communities. Although the role of women within Judaism is primarily a male construction, this conception has become internalised and defines Jewish womanhood in a profound way.[147] As a result, the construction of gender that is implied within the human rights conception simply does not match the perception these Jewish women have of their identity as a woman, let alone the perception they have of gender equality. Therefore the relevance of human rights to the position of some ultra–orthodox Jewish women may be questioned. However, this explanation does not suffice.

Besides the particular concept of gender, the legal dimension of religious identity also plays an important role, and in a way that has more implications for the efficacy of human rights. We have mentioned the prominence of Jewish religious law as part of religious observance. In Judaism, religion, and thus law, is perceived as an internal, private matter. Historical and actual political contexts have further confirmed this perspective. Considering, then, that law marks the boundaries between the Jewish community and Gentile society, it also has an identitary function. It is possible that this identity is simply of greater relevance to Jewish women than is gender equality. When thinking of women as agents of their own struggle(s), the foregoing implies that it cannot be taken for granted that Jewish women will necessarily claim gender equality.[148] The fact that they do not claim it in this regard does not necessarily mean that they cannot, they just might not want to. The argument that State intervention may constitute an incentive and thus bring a partial solution to some of the hardships within Jewish law therefore becomes less convincing, since this would mean too much of an intrusion into their autonomy, religious as well as legal.[149]

One might then ask whether gender equality is not of such importance that States should try to enforce it regardless of whether it is claimed. And indeed, the Convention on the Elimination of All Forms of Discrimination determines that States do have the obligation to adopt legislative measures to modify or abolish customs and practices that constitute discrimination, to take appropriate measures to change patterns of stereotyped conduct, and possibly even to take special temporary measures (affirmative action measures) to accelerate the achievement of equality.[150] In relation to the *Agunah*, however, this has proved to be a very deli-

---

147 C. Longman, *l.c.*

148 The results of my own research seem to confirm this (forthcoming).

149 As such the matter is related to freedom of religion either way, be it in a collective or individual way, for the husband or the wife.

150 *Cf.* Articles 2, 5 and 16 of the Women's Convention.

cate matter. A legislative intervention of the State of New York[151], for instance, had the troublesome effect that while a husband could indeed be persuaded to hand over the *Get*, the validity of this divorce procedure was disputed within the Jewish communities; as a result, Jewish women were even worse off. An invalid *Get* equals no *Get*, and the most extreme interpretation of this situation implied that the mere existence of this *Get* legislation would preclude the possibility of ever having a valid Jewish divorce.[152] The mere existence of the law, with its financial implications for reluctant husbands, was from this perspective thought to amount to an illegitimate coercion, since the law made it impossible to ascertain whether the *Get* was given out of free will or out of fear of the repercussions. This example confirms the anxiety that, in order to gain a higher degree of gender equality, one might sacrifice the possibility of preserving the integrity of a system of religious law.

5.4 Conclusion: Which Normative System Prevails?

Like the construction of gender, the concept of law (and/or religion) implicit within a religious legal system can be constructed in such a way as to claim legal autonomy and thus withdraw from the authority of the State, and what is more, to do so in an efficient way. As we have tried to show, this becomes particularly apparent in relation to Judaism, in the context of which two normative systems co–exist. In order to try and understand which legal sphere becomes relevant in which situation and which one defines gender or gender equality, one should look as well at the mechanisms that determine which normative system legal subjects turn to in order to define their identity and/or legal status. When the religious normative system prevails, human rights appear destined to remain inadequate.

6 Conclusion: Human Rights Bound to Remain Inadequate?

The methodology of legal anthropology differs considerably from that of the traditional legal sciences. In the traditional teaching of law students, practically all attention is focused on the study of norms. Legal anthropology does not neglect these, but accords at least as much importance to two other levels: the *representations* and the *practices* of legal actors.

Representations are the totality of ideas and values that are specific to a society as a whole or to one particular social group. They therefore have a collective nature, insofar as these ideas and values are shared by a certain number of individu-

---

[151] *Equal Distribution Law,* Act of 17 July 1992, ch. 415, 1992 N.Y. Laws 1212 (codified at *New York Domestic Relations Law* § 236 B (5) (h), (6) (d) (Mc Kinney Supp. 1993)).

[152] L. Zornberg, "Beyond the Constitution: Is the New York Get legislation good law?", *Pace L. Rev.* 1995, *15*, 758.

als. We have demonstrated this to be the case in the various examples presented here, notably in China, in Peru and within the Orthodox Jewish community. Representations often form a system, and are in any case closely linked to the particular culture of a society or a group, as these evolve depending on historical circumstances.

Practices consist of concrete forms of behaviour by various actors in relation to the norms in force, norms which they may apply, challenge or avoid, under the guise of interpretation. In the teaching of law, little space is devoted to the way in which norms are in fact applied, and even less to the situations in which they are not applied at all. There remains, therefore, a field of investigation that is wide open to sociologists and anthropologists of law. The latter must necessarily incorporate a stage of field research into their work, for this is a core element of all anthropological study. By identifying the gaps that may exist between the norms and the behaviours of individuals and groups, field research often gives rise to the observation that the State is not the exclusive source of law. The law of a group can also be generated by its ancestral traditions (for instance, indigenous legal traditions), by religion (for example, Judaism) or by various representations coming from specific cultures (such as Confucianism) that have little or nothing to do with State law.[153]

Human rights offer an excellent illustration of the gap that may exist between a norm of abstract law and its concrete application in the most diverse contexts. The notion of human rights derives both from ethics – through the underlying values of justice, liberty, equality, fraternity, solidarity – and from the law, through the process of recognition, the modalities and the systems of guarantees that this implies. By their very nature, human rights are subjective rights to which the human person alone can lay claim, and which are binding on both the State (and secondarily to the international community) and on other individuals and the various groups which they form. Human rights are today entrenched in positive law and constitute grounds for sanctions.

The evidence for this insertion is called into question by the examples that we have presented in this study. The process of universalising principles and norms that underlie human rights in practice clashes with the diversity of cultural contexts. Anthropology is the applied field study that is best suited to explaining the obstacles that arise in the course of the advancement of human rights. These obstacles are numerous. Anthropology shows us in particular that the notion of human rights comes from historical circumstances that affect very specific societies (western ones) and that, as a result, their supposed universality is not obvious to everyone. In the face of this observed failure, there are two possible options. The first consists in refusing to call into question the notion of human rights, but focusing instead even more determinedly on constructing a veritable normative edifice at global and regional levels that confirms the definitive insertion of human rights into positive law around the world. This first option may be accompanied by a further extension of the list of recognised rights, in order to take into account certain

---

[153] In the same vein: M. Walzer, *Spheres of Justice. A defence of Pluralism and Equality* (Oxford, Basil Blackwell, 1983).

specific cultural aspirations. The second option is more respectful of cultural specificities and takes as its point of departure that it is up to individuals and the groups they form to make their own contribution to the development and enrichment of a concept over which no one has a monopoly.

The anthropological method follows the second option. It shows that it is not the universality of human rights that must prevail, but rather their capacity to integrate, and that what matters above all is to subject this integrative capacity to a consensus within the various groups and communities and to *their* decision to open up – or not – to the innovative potential of human rights. The widespread violation of human rights is not necessarily a legitimate interpretation of the reality of individuals and of the groups which they form. The anthropologist seeks to listen to this reality and to uncover the reasons – without judging them – that explain why the universal enshrinement of human rights is so difficult to achieve. These reasons vary in accordance with the context.

Chapter 22 – Functions and Limits of Patent Law

Geertrui Van Overwalle and Esther van Zimmeren

1 Introduction

In the past decade patent law has been in turmoil and has been seriously criticised.[1] Some observers even go as far as to call it "*eine Vertrauenskrise des Patentsystems*"[2] (a crisis of confidence of the patent system). Criticism of the operation of the patent system arose from scientists and the general public, on the one hand, and legal scholars and patent experts, on the other. The first group has expressed serious doubts on the patentability of software and human genes[3], whereas the last group has been highly concerned about patent quality and the proliferation of patents. The ongoing consultation procedures on patent reform in Europe[4], ini-

---

* The present research was supported by the Research Foundation – Flanders (Fonds voor Wetenschappelijk Onderzoek – Vlaanderen, FWO) and the Vancraesbeeck Fund. The authors would like to thank Erik Claes, Wouter Devroe, Hans Graux, Bert Keirsbilck, Wim Schols and Birgit Verbeure for their valuable comments on an earlier draft of this chapter.

1 In the context of the present chapter, the notion 'patent law' and 'patent system' has to be construed in its widest sense. It does not only refer to pre–grant, but also to post–grant issues. Furthermore, it does not only encompass legislation embedded in international treaties and in the European Patent Convention (EPC), but also rules laid down in national patent acts and stemming from judgments from national (patent) courts.

2 I. Schneider, "Die Interdependenz von Technik und Recht – eine vernachlässigte TA–Perspektive, konkretisiert am Beispiel der Transformation des Patentrechts vom technikfreisetzenden zum regulativen Recht in der Bio–Patentierung", in A. Bora, M. Decker, A. Grunwald and O. Renn (eds.), *Technik in einer fragilen Welt. Die Rolle der Technikfolgenabschätzung* (Berlin: Sigma, 2005) 409–436.

3 These doubts were especially expressed in the framework of the debates on Directive 98/44/EC of the European Parliament and the Council of 6 July 1998 on the legal protection of biotechnological inventions, O.J. L 213/13, 30.07.1998 (hereinafter EU Biotechnology Directive). For some comments, see G. Van Overwalle, "Legal and Ethical Aspects of Bio–Patenting: Critical Analysis of the EU Biotechnology Directive", in P. Drahos (ed.), *Death of Patents* (Oxon: Lawtext Publishing, 2005) 212–227. Also some doubts were raised with regard to the Proposal for a Directive of the European Parliament and the Council on the patentability of computer–implemented inventions, Brussels, 20/02/2002, COM(2002) 92 final, (hereinafter EU CII Directive).

4 The development of the European patent system is taking place at three levels: (a) the harmonisation of national patent regulations by the EU; (b) the possible creation of an EU wide Community patent (European Commission, Proposal for a Regulation of the Council on the Community Patent, 1 August 2000, COM (2000) 412 final, see also: Agreement No. 89/695/EEC of the European Commission relating to Community patents done at Luxembourg on 15 December 1989, amending the Agreement relating to Community patents done at Luxemburg on 15 December 1975, O.J. L 401/1, 1989); and (c) the application by the EPO of the European Patent (EPC) (Convention on the Grant of European Patents of 5 Oc-

tiated by both the European Union (EU) and the European Patent Office (EPO) separately, and in the US offer an excellent momentum for a more thorough examination of the problems observed in patent law.

This chapter starts by describing some major trends in patent law and practice in more depth and throws some light on the concerns to which they give rise (section 2). In aiming at a better comprehension of these trends and concerns, an analytical model has been deployed revolving around the objectives and functions of the law (section 3). Applying this analytical model to patent law demonstrates that patent law is largely unable to fulfil its major objectives and functions within the current social and political context. The objectives and functions, for which patent law appears to be inapt highlight some limits of patent law. These limits are widely illustrated with examples from the field of biotechnology and human genetics (section 4). In an effort to deal with the limits encountered, attention is paid to options for remedying problems and limits (section 5).

The present chapter has been based primarily on an analysis of Europe, but will occasionally consider US and international developments as well.

2 Current Trends in Patent Law

The present tumult around patent law may be imputed to three basic trends. A first trend, which until now has received a lot of attention in the media and academic literature, relates to the *expansion* of the patent system, both in terms of patentable subject matter and the number of patents granted, and the implications thereof. A second trend has to do with to a shift of *forum* of patent decision–making and the growing awareness of governance issues, both in terms of levels and actors. A third trend stems from an emerging role played by *ethical* considerations and human rights concerns, both with regard to the existence and the exercise of patent rights.

2.1 Expansion

Patentable subject matter. Over the past decades, patent law has expanded significantly, not least in terms of patentable subject matter. The scope of patentable subject matter has considerably been stretched by the EPO and national patent offices. Patent law has adapted itself to the new realities of ICT and genetics by extending protection to computer–related inventions and biological material. Patent offices now grant patents related to such material as a matter of routine. The patenting of genetic engineering products has often been presented as a natural and logical ap-

---

tober 1973 as revised by the Act revising Article 63 EPC of 17 December 1991 and the Act revising the EPC of 29 November 2000, available at www.epo.org/patents/law/legal-texts/epc.html). The latter remains outside the realm of the EU.

plication of the basic principles of patentability simply extended to biotechnology. In the field of biotechnology, patent protection is now available for micro-organisms, plants, animals and elements isolated from the human body, including genes. Notably in the field of genetics, the expansion of subject matter has led to wide concerns. Principal concerns relate to the further appropriation and instrumentalisation of the human body through patents.

Patent quality. Patent law has not only expanded in respect to scope, but even more so in respect to the number of patents granted. The current pace of innovation and government policies aimed at encouraging private and public entities to apply for patents[5], has led to a considerable increase of patent applications. Statistics clearly show an exponential growth in patenting over the past decades.[6] The steady increase in patenting activity has led to a widespread concern relating to the quality of patents. Some critics even seem to suggest that the explosion of patents has spurred the grant of low quality patents.[7]

Patent thickets. The raise of patents has not only led to concerns with regard to patent quality, but equally to concerns about the potential negative effects of the proliferation of patents on further innovation and commercialisation. Various scholars worry about the risk that the current intense use of the patent system will

---

5 The US Bayh Dole act is the often cited ultimate example of government initiatives ('copied' by many European governments) aimed at stimulating the ownership of IP in federally funded research. Act of 12 December 1980, Pub. L. No. 96–517, § 6(a), 94 Stat. 2311–2320 (1980) (codified as amended at 15 U.S.C. §§ 200–212 (1994). For a detailed summary of the legislative history of this Act, see R.S. Eisenberg, "Public Research and Private Development: Patents and Technology Transfer in Government–Sponsored Research", *Va. L. Rev.* 1996, *82*, 1663, 1688–1695. Furthermore, C.R. McManis and S. Noh, *The Impact of the Bayh–Dole Act on Genetic Research and Development: Evaluating the Arguments and Empirical Evidence to Date*, Paper presented at the IPSC 2006 at Berkeley (on file with the authors); D.A. Adelman, "A Fallacy of the Commons in Biotech Patent Policy", *Berkeley Tech. L. J.* 2005, *20*, 985; D.C. Mowery, R.R. Nelson, B.N. Sampat and A.A. Ziedonis, "Ivory Tower and Industrial Innovation: University–Industry Transfer Before and After the Bayh–Dole Act in the United States", 2004 (on file with the authors) and A.K. Rai and R.S. Eisenberg, "Bayh–Dole Reform and the Progress of Biomedicine", *Law & Contemp. Probs.* 2002, *66*, 289.

6 One may consult the Annual Reports of the EPO (www.epo.org/about-us/office/annual-reports.html) or look into EPO statistics (www.epo.org/about-us/office/statistics.html) (last visited 24 October 2007). Detailed graphs illustrate a clear increase in patent applications, see for example, the table representing the EPO in figures from 2002–2006 (www.documents.epo.org/projects/babylon/eponet.nsf/0/82162336C20C094BC12572F9003C3188/$File/entwicklung_zahlen.pdf, last visited 24 October 2007), or the detailed table representing European applications from 1990–2006 (www.epo.org/about-us/office/statistics/applications 1990-2006.html, last visited 24 October 2007).

7 Although, it is generally accepted that the quality of EPO patents is higher than those of the United States Patent and Trademark Office (USPO) and the Japanese Patent Office (JPO). See for instance, B. Doern, *Global Change and Intellectual Property Agencies* (London: Pinter, 1999).

create "patent thickets"[8]: dense webs of overlapping patents that a researcher or a company must hack its way through in order to actually develop and commercialise a new product.[9] It is to be feared that in some circumstances exclusive property rights can block effective economic applications of assets. This phenomenon may in turn lead to what has become known as the "tragedy of the anti–commons"[10], a situation where multiple (overlapping) private property rights prevent the efficient combination of assets.[11]

2.2 Forum Shifting

Globalisation. Apart from a clear tendency towards an expansion of the patent system, some remarkable developments can be observed with regard to the decision–making process in patent law as well. From its inception, patent law has been characterised by multi–level and multi–institutional decision–making: from the outset patent law and policy have developed at different levels, the national and the international, and at various forums within those levels. However, over the past decades, the negotiations and the decision–making process of intellectual property (IP) issues in general and patent law in particular have exponentially shifted from the national to the global level. Decision–making with regard to IP and patent law has equally moved from national governments[12] to international institutions such as the World Intellectual Property Organisation (WIPO) and the World Trade Organisation (WTO). This shift of forum raises serious concerns with regard to good governance. The current type of decision–making may result in the underrating of national and local aspirations, and untransparent and incoherent patent policies and practices. However, at the same time this creates some sound competition between the institutions involved.

---

8 C. Shapiro, "Navigating the Patent Thicket: Cross Licenses, Patent Pools and Standard Setting", in E. Jaffe, J. Lerner and S. Stern (eds.) *Innovation Policy and the Economy, Vol. I* (Cambridge: MIT Press, 2001) 119–150.

9 F.M. Scherer, "The Economics of Human Gene Patents", *Academic Medicine* 2002, *77*, 1348–1367.

10 M.A. Heller and R. Eisenberg, "Can Patents Deter Innovation? The Anticommons in Biomedical Research", *Science* 1998, *280*, 698 and M.A. Heller, "The Tragedy of the Anticommons: Property in the Transition from Marx to Markets", *Harvard Law Review* 1998, *111*, 621.

11 This situation of the anti–commons is usually contrasted with the tragedy of the commons, where too many individuals have privileges of use (or the right not to be excluded) in a scarce resource (G. Hardin, "The Tragedy of the Commons", *Science* 1968, *162*, 1243. To illustrate the tragedy, Hardin introduced an hypothetical example of a pasture shared by local shepherds. The shepherds wish to maximise their yield, and so will increase their herd size whenever possible. The pasture runs the risk of overgrazing and degradation in the long run. For more, see G. Van Overwalle, "L'intérêt général, le domaine public, les commons et le droit des brevets d'invention", in M. Buydens and S. Dussolier (eds.), *L'intérêt général et l'accès à l'information en propriété intellectuelle* (Brussels: Bruylant, 2008a) in press.

12 In Europe, it first shifted to the European level, where the EPO may grant European patents, which result in a bundle of national patents as far as exploitation of the patent is concerned.

Expertisation. The decision–making process is also influenced by the growing technological and technical nature of patent law. This complexity has led to decision–making by highly qualified technical and legal experts. IP and patent legislation increasingly emerge from so–called 'epistemic communities': "networks of professionals with recognised expertise and competence in a particular domain and an authoritative claim to policy–relevant knowledge within that domain".[13] They meet all over the world at a wide range of academic and institutional forums.[14] The dominant core of the epistemic community that has been the main influence on IP law–making consists of transnational elites with important IP portfolios to protect technically minded lawyers[15], legally trained scientific experts and legally trained officials exchanging information, ideas, and arguments and suggesting diagnoses and cures.

These groups of experts play an important role on various levels. First, they play a role in *policy*–making, both at the national and the European level. In Europe, the EPO has created some platforms where the experts gather, such as the Standing Advisory Committee before EPO (SACEPO). At SACEPO users from industry, patent attorneys and national patent offices discuss patent–related topics.[16] Specific professional organisations in the area of IP, including patent law, are actively involved in the patent law policy and decision–making process as well. Examples are the International Association for the Protection of Intellectual Property (AIPPI), the International Association for the Advancement of Teaching and Research in Intellectual Property (ATRIP), and the American Intellectual Property Association (AIPLA). All three organisations are consulted in the framework of the current patent law reforms. Second, experts are recognised in patent case–law. In the US, in particular the court system reflects the specialised nature of patent law. The US has institutionalised a 'patent court' by giving a unique role to the United States Court of Appeals for the Federal Circuit (CAFC) as an appellate body in patent matters. Even within this court, patent matters are heard by a limited number of judges.[17]

The concentration of expertise within a limited number of (advisory) bodies and courts, having great weight, raises serious concerns of democracy. Full reliance on a small group of patent law experts for worldwide patent harmonisation may lead to democratic deficits.

---

13 P.M. Haas, "Introduction: Epistemic Communities and International Policy Coordination", *International Organization* 1992, *46*, 1–35, 3.

14 F. van Waarden and M. Drahos, "Courts and (Epistemic) Communities in the Convergence of Competition Policies", *Journal of European Public Policy* 2002, *9*, 913–934.

15 S. Picciotto and D. Campbell, "Whose Molecule Is It Anyway? Private and Social Perspectives on Intellectual Property", in A. Hudson (ed.), *New Perspectives on Property Law, Obligations and Restitution* (London: Cavendish, 2003) 279–303.

16 See also S. Borràs, "The Governance of the European Patent System: Effective and Legitimate?", *Economy and Society* 2006, *35*, 594–610, 11.

17 S. Thambisetty, "Chapter 13 – The Institutional Nature of the Patent System: Implications for Bioethical Decision–Making", in C. Lenk, N. Hoppe and R. Andorno (eds.), *Ethics and the Law of Intellectual Property: Current Problems in Politics, Science and Technology* (forthcoming) (manuscript on file with the authors) 341–372, 357–359.

2.3 Ethics and Human Rights

Existence of patent rights. A third trend in the changing patent landscape stems from a growing sensitivity to ethical considerations and human rights in patent law. The relationship between ethics and patent law is by far not new. Ever since the emergence of national patent systems in the 1800s, the notion of morality was articulated by legal doctrine and has been implicitly assumed in national patent acts and daily patent practice.[18] What can be witnessed today, is a more compelling appeal to the notion of morality to stop the further widening of patent law in the field of biological material. Serious concern is voiced that, even with some guidance at hand[19], it is not clear where the border lines of patentable subject matter lie when it comes to human material; witness the current debate in both legal and societal circles on the patentability of DNA sequences and human embryonic stem cells.[20]

Unlike ethics, the relationship between human rights and IP rights has been undertheorised for a long period. IP rights have remained a "normative backwater" in the burgeoning post–World War II human rights movement.[21] Only over the past decade, human rights discourse has gained wider attention and commentators have started to explore the relation between IP and human rights in more detail.[22] The increased attention to human rights in a patent law context echoes an underlying concern, namely that patent law may be focusing too one–sidedly on trade, technological advance, economic welfare and financial gain, rather then on social welfare and the development dimension.

Exercise of patent rights. The growing sensitivity to ethics in patent law does not only come to the fore when exploring patentable subject matter and the coming into existence of patent rights. Recent events have also orientated the ethical debate towards the exercise of patent rights, especially in the field of health care. Over the last years, some biotech companies have either refused to license some inventions or have licensed them exclusively at relatively high prices. The breast

---

18 See G. Van Overwalle, "Biotechnology and Patents: Global Standards, European Approaches and National Accents", in *Genetic Engineering and the World Trade System,* D. Wüger and T. Cottier (eds.) (Cambridge: Cambridge University Press, 2008b) 77–108.

19 More in particular the EU Biotechnology Directive (see footnote 3).

20 G. Van Overwalle and N. Berthels, "Patents and Venus. About Oocytes and Human Embryonic Stem Cells", in *Stem Cells and Women's Health – Cellules souches et santé des femmes – Stamcellen en vrouwengezondheid* (Louvain–la–Neuve: Anthemis-Intersentia, 2007) 148–178; G. Van Overwalle, "Patenting Stem Cell Research in Europe and in the United States", in W. Bender, C. Hauskeller and A. Manzei (eds.), *Crossing Borders. Cultural, Religious and Political Differences Concerning Stem Cell Research* (Münster: Agenda Verlag, 2005) 519–546; G. Van Overwalle, *Study on the Patenting of Inventions Related to Human Stem Cell Research* (Luxemburg: European Communities, 2002).

21 L.R. Helfer, "Toward a Human Rights Framework for Intellectual Property", *Vanderbilt University Law School Public Law and Legal Theory. Working Paper 06–03* (available at www.ssrn.com/abstract=891303).

22 *Cf.* L.R. Helfer, "Human Rights and Intellectual Property: Conflict or Coexistence?", *Minnesota Intellectual Property Review* 2003, 5, 47–61.

cancer (BRCA) gene patents and the restrictive licensing policy of the patent holder Myriad have manifestly illustrated this tendency and have given rise to a strong and worldwide reaction amongst scientists at clinical laboratories.[23] However, also universities and public research institutes tend to license their inventions exclusively in order to safeguard optimal research funding opportunities.[24] Concerns are being expressed on how restrictive licensing practices can ultimately hinder access to health care and the supply of diagnostic testing services in particular.

3 Objectives and Functions of Patent Law

The trends observed point to some problematic areas in current patent law. A better comprehension of these trends and their implications requires a carefully thought–out methodology. The interpretative strategy applied in the present chapter to examine current patent law and practice revolves around the *objectives* and *functions* of patent law: we look at current trends through the lens of objectives and functions of the (patent) law. In doing so, we partly apply the analytical model set forth by Claes, Devroe, and Keirsbilck.[25]

3.1 Objectives and Principles of Patent Law

The major objective of IP law in general and patent law in particular is to offer protection to the inventor against free riding and to encourage the development and disclosure of knowledge and innovation with a view to fostering scientific, technical and social progress in the interest of society at large. In order to pursue this objective inventors are given the opportunity to recoup their investments by way of a patent right. Inventors[26] may file a patent application and a patent will be granted provided the invention is new, involves an inventive step and is susceptible to industrial application.[27] In order to obtain a balance between the interests of the patent holder in recovering his investments, and the public interest in access to

---

[23] G. Matthijs and D. Halley, "European–Wide Opposition Against the Breast Cancer Gene Patents", *European Journal of Human Genetics* 2002, *10*, 783–784.

[24] See, however, for instance A. Kapczynski, S. Chaifetz, Samantha, Z. Katz and Y. Benkler, "Addressing Global Health Inequities: An Open Licensing Approach for University Innovations", *Berkeley Technology Law Journal* 2005, *20*, 1031–1114 and L. Pressman, R. Burgess, R. Cook–Degan, S.J. McCormack, I. Nami–Wolk, M. Soucy and L. Walters, "The Licensing of DNA Patents by US Academic Institutions: An Empirical Survey", *Nature Biotechnology* 2007, *24*, 31–39.

[25] See E. Claes, W. Devroe, and B. Keirsbilck, "The Limits of the Law (Introduction)".

[26] *Cf.* Articles 58–62 EPC: the right to a European patent shall belong to the inventor or his successor in title (for persons entitled to apply for obtaining a European patent).

[27] Article 52(1) EPC.

knowledge incorporated in the patented invention, the exclusive right is limited to 20 years and the embedded knowledge is made available by publication in the patent register. A granted patent confers on the holder the exclusive right to prevent others from making, using, selling or importing the invention without his permission, for a period of 20 years and for a specific territory. The patent holder can decide to valorise his patent right in different ways: he can exploit the invention himself or permit others to exploit his invention and transfer the rights, for instance by way of a license agreement.[28]

Recent developments on the international and European level have triggered a debate on the rebalancing of the goals of patent law, and on giving greater weight to public interest concerns. Patent law should no longer merely grant a right providing patent protection to the private inventor as an incentive to innovate and disclose, but should equally guarantee specific fundamental personal rights[29], adopt measures necessary to protect public health and nutrition[30] and safeguard the freedom to do research more widely.

3.2 Functions of (Patent) Law

Our interpretative strategy does not only focus on the objectives of patent law, but equally revolves around the functions of the law, thereby outlining the functions of law in general and zooming in on the functions of patent law in particular. The examination of the functions is primarily aimed at translating the general theory of law into the area of patent law.

Regulatory function. The major function of the law is to regulate relations between the authorities and the citizens, and amongst citizens.[31] Legislation, provided it is dynamic and customised according to the changes within society, is regarded as a useful instrument to solve complex problems within society. By drafting, applying, interpreting and enforcing the rules, law co–ordinates the interactions between the authorities and the people (vertical relationship) and between persons (horizontal relationship).[32] In this way a framework for a co–ordinated and efficient society may be created.

Patent law institutionalises patents as an instrument for the right holder to recover his investments in research and development. The underlying idea is that

---

28 In a license agreement, the licensor will grant to the licensee the right to use the patented invention according to the conditions outlined in the agreement and for a specified period.

29 The right to informed consent (*cf.* Recital 26 of the EU Biotechnology Directive, see footnote 3) and the right to protection of traditional knowledge (*cf.* Statement 19 of the Doha Ministerial Declaration, November 2001).

30 Article 8(1) TRIPs.

31 See E. Claes, W. Devroe, and B. Keirsbilck, *l.c.*

32 This distinction between the horizontal and vertical relationship is especially common in European law, for instance with respect to the effects of different kinds of legislative instruments (Treaty provisions, regulations, directives).

without this exclusive right, inventors would not be encouraged to do such investments.[33] Patent law establishes competent authorities and prescribes patentability criteria, formal requirements and granting procedures. In doing so, patent law regulates two facets. On the one hand, patent law regulates the vertical relationship by regulating the granting procedure enabling competent patent offices (public authority) to grant patents (exclusive rights) in accordance with the criteria determined in the patent law/treaty. On the other hand, patent law governs the horizontal relationship to some extent, by defining the contours of the right in the post–grant phase between the patent holder and the potential licensees and the public at large.

Symbolic function. Law may also be regarded as a mechanism to clarify the binding values within a specific society. It is an instrument to determine, establish and publicly disseminate a statement of the norms valued highly in that society. This symbolic function should be integrated in the legislation itself, and the procedures and institutions.[34]

Patent law is a technical field of law. Many patent experts would even argue in favour of a purely technical, value–free type of (interpretation of) the law. However, the public debate surrounding the patentability of biological material and software has shown that the general public does appreciate a value–driven consideration of patent law.

Function to provide legal guarantees. Finally, today's society expects the law to protect its citizens against illegitimate action by the authorities and other citizens. A major aim of legislation is to regulate the relations between authorities and citizens and citizens amongst themselves in such a way that the most balanced, effective and defendable coherent set of legal norms is safeguarded. Such a balanced legal system should grant each citizen concerned access to an effective 'enforcement mechanism' and the capacity to act in the public interest. This includes access to the formal, legislative decision–making process (political participation) and access to the courts (judicial review).

Patent decision–making is a multi–level and multi–institutional governance field: patent law and policy is developed at different levels (the global level, the European level and the national level) and within various forums at those levels. It is questionable whether the mechanisms and procedures currently in place guarantee adequate and wide access to the formal legislative decision–making process. Patent granting procedures, in turn, mainly take place at the European and national level. European and national patent law provisions prescribe access to administrative boards (opposition and appeal) and (national) courts to enable third parties to

---

33 Economic studies on this presumption are, however, inconclusive. In fact, the effect of patents on innovation and diffusion depends on particular features of the *patent regime*. See for a brief explanation: Organisation for Economic Co–operation and Development (OECD), *Patents and Innovation: Trends and Policy Changes* (Paris: OECD, 2004) (available at www.oecd.org/dataoecd/48/12/24508541.pdf) 9–10.

34 See E. Claes, W. Devroe, and B. Keirsbilck, *l.c.*

challenge the validity of a granted patent, and patent holders to claim infringement of their proprietary right.

4 Limits of Patent Law

Close reexamination of the trends and concerns through the lens of the objectives and functions of patent law clearly reveals and uncovers a number of limits of the current patent system.[35] Patent law appears to be limited in its ability to regulate and change social and individual behaviour, to mirror and incorporate values, and to provide legal guarantees. The present chapter aims to clarify these limits in patent law and to offer a wider context for understanding the trends and concerns observed.

4.1 Regulatory Function

Patent law appears to be largely inapt in fulfilling its regulatory function with respect to both the *vertical* (patent authorities – patent applicants) and the *horizontal* relationship (patent holders – potential licensees, general public, patients).

Patent quality. Patent law's failure in the vertical relationship is illustrated by the general criticism of patent quality. High quality patents predominantly refer to patents which describe an invention that is truly new, involves a real inventive step for the 'person skilled in the art' and is industrially applicable. The grant of high quality patents thus implies a rigorous review of prior art, strict application of the patentability criteria and clear claim construction. Moreover, in order to guarantee the quality of patents, there has to be relatively little uncertainty over the breadth of the patent claims (*i.e.* over the technical features of a patent claim), as well as whether these claims are likely to be upheld in opposition or legal proceedings after the grant of the patent.[36] Low quality patents may lead to "considerable uncertainty among inventors and would–be commercialisers of inventions". They might equally slow "down either the pace of innovation or investment in the commercialisation of new technologies".[37] Hence the risk of granting low quality patents is not only alarming in the light of the vertical regulatory function of pat-

---

35 In the context of the present chapter, the notion 'limits' does not refer to *practical, concrete* limits from a technico–legal viewpoint, but rather relates to more *theoretical, abstract* limits from a philosophy of law perspective.

36 B.H. Hall, S.J.H. Graham, D. Harhoff, and D.C. Mowery, *Prospects for Improving U.S. Patent Quality via Post–grant Opposition* (UC Berkeley Working Papers, Department of Economics, Working Paper No. E03–329, 2003), 2–3.

37 B. Doern, *l.c.*, 3

ent law (legal uncertainty), but also in view of the major objective of patent law, namely encouraging research and development and promoting innovation.

Patent thickets. Patent law demonstrates an even more urgent void in the horizontal relationship. The European Patent Convention (EPC) primarily regulates the pre–grant and granting phase, and the coming into existence of patent rights.[38] After the centralised granting procedure, the European patent equals a bundle of national patents with respect to exploitation and enforcement. But national legislation does not contain overall guidelines or rules relating to the post–grant phase, and the exercise of patent rights and licensing behaviour.[39] Outside Europe, jurisdictions seem to suffer from the same lack of legal rules guiding patent holders in the exercise of their rights and their exploitation endeavours.

The phenomenon of patent thickets resulting in royalty stacking may be seen as an exponent of this vacuum. In the absence of clear guidelines on the exercise and licensing of patent rights, users may be confronted with too many patent rights (held by multiple patent owners) which would be difficult to clear as it would require too many license agreements and the related license fees may ultimately hinder potential licensees from developing and commercialising new products. The proliferation of patents and subsequent royalty stacking may thus well stifle innovation. In the area of genetics, this 'anti–commons effect' may even restrict access to and development of fundamental health care services. Even though there is no wide evidence that an anti–commons effect has indeed emerged in genetics[40], it follows from this example that in some cases patent law may have the paradoxical effect of blocking further research and development, and access to health care services. The lack of guidance and the resulting problems thus raise doubts as to whether patent law is still able to fulfil its objectives (foster innovation, public health interests) and the (horizontal) regulatory function.

Restrictive licensing. Patent law's inability to regulate the horizontal relationship has also been highlighted in the field of diagnostic testing, where some practices of restrictive licensing may be observed. Laboratories have been confronted with cease and desist letters from patent holders or exclusive licensees, which have induced some of them to cease performing specific tests and/or refrain from test development.[41] Such restrictive licensing policies may adversely affect the quality of

---

[38] Chapter IV, Articles 71–74 EPC, deals with the European patent applications as an object of property, which can be transferred, assigned and licensed.

[39] National patent acts merely offer some very specific provisions on exploitation, such as a research exemption and compulsory licensing schemes.

[40] See M.M. Hopkins, S. Mahdi, P. Patel and S.M. Thomas, *The Patenting of Human DNA: Global Trends in Public and Private Sector Activity* (The PATGEN Project) (A Report for the European Commission) (Brighton, UK: SPRU, November 2006) and US National Research Council of the National Academies–Committee on Intellectual Property Rights in Genomic and Protein Research and Innovation, *Reaping the Benefits of Genomic and Proteomic Research: Intellectual Property Rights, Innovation, and Public Health* (Washington, D.C.: The National Academies Press, 2005).

[41] *Ibid.*, 105, 111 and 112.

the care as the single provider could dictate medical practice without quality control or peer review, the capacity of the exclusive licensee/patent holder might not meet patient demands, and without price competition prices may rise and lead to a drain on funds of public health services. Ultimately this may hinder access to health care and block access to these fundamental services[42], thus putting the objectives of patent law at risk.

4.2 Symbolic Function

Patent law also seems to be rather misappropriated in performing its symbolic function. Limits may originate from both internal and external forces. On the one hand, these limits are created by internal legal principles: the most basic legal presumptions and principles of law such as legal certainty, and deeply rooted values and traditions. On the other hand, limits may equally arise from external developments on the European and international forum. The globalisation trend in patent law and the subsequent North–South divide are good examples in this regard. It is a common phenomenon that creates limits and problems on different levels and in various fields.

Existence of patent rights and ethics. The appropriateness of patenting human DNA sequences and genetic technologies has been a matter of severe debate and controversy both in academic circles and in civil society. Stretching the scope of patentable subject matter to human genes and stem cells has equally triggered the attention of people from various convictions. Although public attention for human gene patents has decreased lately, the controversy lingers on[43], especially in the field of human embryonic stem cells. The persisting debate results from the fact that the status, and thus patentability of the human body is closely intertwined with ethics, culture and religion, and that patent law and practice run into difficulties when reflecting fundamental values related hereto. Moreover, ethics, culture and religion are highly variable and dynamic disciplines. All the more reason for policy–makers to carefully weigh and reassess such considerations on a regular basis. However, legal certainty does not permit 'monthly' fundamental reappraisals of patent regulations. So, this characteristic of law in comparison to other disciplines, inherently restricts the capacity of patent law to fully comply with the symbolic function of the law.

---

42 I.R. Walpole, H.J.S. Dawkins, P.D. Sinden and P.C. O'Leary, "Human Gene Patents: The Possible Impacts on Genetic Services Healthcare", *Medical Journal of Australia* 2003, *179*, 256–283.

43 R.S. Eisenberg, "Why Gene Patenting Controversy Persists", *Academic Medicine* 2002, *77*, 1381–1387.

Exercise of patent rights and ethics and human rights. Ethics does not only challenge our views on patentable subject matter and the coming into existence of patent rights, but has equally reshaped our assessment with regard to the exercise of patent rights. The general public is very sensitive to restrictive and unreasonable licensing, especially in the field of health care. This sensitivity closely relates to underlying values and norms, such as equality (equal access to health care) and solidarity. Patent law does not always seem capable of fully integrating those values and thus stops short of its symbolic function once again.

The human rights discourse adds to the multi–faceted ethical debate in patent law by introducing yet another set of perspectives and values, such as human dignity, the right to informed consent, the right to food, the right to education and research, and the right to access to information.[44] The controversies surrounding the implementation of human rights in patent law illustrate patent law's battle to incorporate commonly accepted and shared values and rights into its policy objectives and they raise doubts as to the capacity of patent law in performing its symbolic function.

Globalisation. The current globalisation trend equally illustrates patent law's failure to achieve its symbolic function. Global negotiations make it harder on countries to tailor patent law to suit local palates[45] and to implement lower limits if it would be in their development interest to do so.[46] Developing countries which would benefit from a lower level of IP/patent protection to enable them to move on to a higher level of education and development are continually confronted with demands for strict enforcement of IP legislation by industrialised countries.[47] Paradoxically, these industrialised countries and especially the US (the most committed advocate of high IP standards nowadays) did not support the same strict observance of IP during their own technological revolution.

The Agreement on Trade–Related Aspects of Intellectual Property Rights (TRIPs)[48] is the example par excellence for illustrating the differing developmental agenda and the North–South divide in the decision–making process, and patent law's failure to accommodate diverging value sets. For a long time, international IP norm setting was dealt with in the framework of the World Intellectual Property Organisation (WIPO). The first international convention including some provi-

---

44 See G. Van Overwalle, "'Human Rights' Limitations in Patent Law", in W. Grosheide (ed.), *The Human Rights Paradox in Intellectual Property Law* (Oxford: Edward Elgar Publishing Ltd, 2008c) in press.

45 H. Laddie, in Commission on Intellectual Property Rights, *Integrating Intellectual Property Rights and Development Policy* (London: DFID, 2002) iv.

46 World Bank, *Global Economic Prospects and the Developing Countries* (Oxford: Oxford University Press, 2001) 147. Also see See G. Van Overwalle (2008b), *l.c.*, 77–108.

47 P. Drahos, "Death of a Patent System", in P. Drahos (ed.), *Death of Patents* (Oxon: Law Text Publishing, 2005) and P. Drahos and J. Braithwaite, *Information Feudalism: Who Owns the Knowledge Economy?* (London: Earthscan, 2002).

48 Trade–Related Aspects of Intellectual Property Rights, Annex 1C to the Agreement establishing the World Trade Organisation (WTO) of April 1994, Marrakesh. Entry into force: 1 January 1995, at www.wto.org/english/docs_e/legal_e/legal_e.htm#TRIPs (last visited 28 August 2007).

sions on patent law, the Paris Convention for the Protection of Industrial Property, was negotiated at WIPO in 1883.[49] During the General Agreement on Tariffs and Trade (GATT) Uruguay Round in the 1980s and 1990s, IP standard setting gradually shifted in a twofold way. Industrialised countries sought to elevate rudimentary IP standards while developing countries demanded preferential measures that would have weakened pre–existing obligations. Furthermore, industrialised countries preferred GATT as a platform for IP negotiations rather than WIPO. The simultaneous shift of focus and forum should not come as a surprise, as both are closely linked: WIPO's competence is restricted to IP, whereas within the framework of GATT there would be room for connecting IP protection to trade and investments. Technologically advanced countries, mostly developed countries, favoured GATT as it offered them an opportunity to press for high IP standards that could be used as a bargaining chip in exchange for access to the markets of industrialised countries for developing nations. The (current) WTO forum would in addition provide facilities for effective enforcement and dispute settlement. Countries in process of industrialisation, mostly developing countries, favoured WIPO, the original forum for IP (harmonisation) negotiations, but finally gave in.[50] Close observers explain this outcome by the fact that the US had set the scene for TRIPs through a series of bilateral negotiations on IP, threatening with trade retaliations. Successful negotiations on TRIPs and thus higher IP standards would equal a 'good conduct certificate' and the US would desist from using its trade enforcement tools to obtain stricter standards.[51] This later appeared to be a 'trap' because after the conclusion of TRIPs, the US actually intensified the level of bilateral activities.[52]

As the forum of decision–making has gradually shifted from the local to the global level, the scope of protection of patent law is increasingly subjected to multi–level and multi–institutional governance. Patent law appears to be less apt to represent national values and to guarantee national public interests as expressed

---

49 Paris Convention for the Protection of Industrial Property of 20 March 1883, as revised at Brussels on 14 December 1900, at Washington on 2 June 1911, at The Hague on 6 November 1925, at London on 2 June 1934, at Lisbon on 31 October 1958, and at Stockholm on 14 July 1967, and as amended on 28 September 1979,
available at www.wipo.int/treaties/en/ip/paris/trtdocs_wo020.html (last visited 24 October 2007).

50 See P. Drahos and J. Braithwaite, *l.c.*; C.M. Correa and A.A. Yusuf (eds.), *Intellectual Property and International Trade: The TRIPs Agreement* (London: Kluwer Law International, 1998) 4–6, 23.

51 P.K. Yu, "The International Enclosure Movement" (forthcoming Winter, *Indiana Law Journal* 2007, *82*), also at www.papers.ssrn.com/sol3/papers.cfm?abstract_id=896134; A.A. Yusuf, "TRIPs: Background, Principles and General Provisions", in C.M. Correa and A.A. Yusuf (eds.), *Intellectual Property and International Trade: The TRIPs Agreement* (London: Kluwer Law International, 1998) 3–20; M. Halewood, "Regulating Patent Holders: Local Working Requirements and Compulsory Licenses at International Law", *Osgood Hall L. J.* 1997, *35*, 254 and C.M. Correa, "The GATT Agreement on Trade–related Aspects of Intellectual Property Rights: New Standards for Patent Protection", *EIPR* 1994, *16*, 327–335.

52 P. Drahos, "Intellectual Property and Pharmaceutical Markets: A Nodal Governance Approach", *Temple Law Review* 2004, *77*, 406.

by developing countries. This raises the question as to what extent patent law still performs its symbolic function.

4.3 Function to Provide Legal Guarantees

It is also questionable to what extent current patent law is adequately equipped to fulfil the function to provide legal guarantees. The function to provide legal guarantees has a rather broad scope, but in the framework of the present chapter emphasis is laid on two distinct aspects. First, attention is paid to the obligation to guarantee access to and participation in the legal and the political decision–making process, the latter not being restricted to representation of citizens by parliamentarians (political participation). Second, the focus is oriented towards the obligation to guarantee effective and legitimate access of citizens to means that protect against illegitimate action by the authorities and other citizens (judicial review). The important role of experts in patent law and its institutionalisation may endanger the realisation of the first safeguard, whereas especially financial constraints may endanger the second obligation.

Expertisation. Over the past decades, IP decision–making has become the almost exclusive province of an epistemic community of IP experts.[53] This type of narrowly based decision–making seems to indicate a democratic deficit at various stages and might be defined as "the tragedy of anti–governance".[54]

When it comes to law–making, both national parliaments and the European Parliament (EP) run into tremendous difficulties with technical matters.[55] In a field of law as complex and technical as patent law, politicians often do not have the necessary specialised knowledge and leave it to their experts. Nevertheless, it is fascinating to see that members of national parliaments and of the EP have been very active in some areas of patent law over the past few years. This activity largely related to attempts of the European Union (EU) to harmonise specific areas of patent law, such as biotechnology and software. The national parliaments, as well as the EP got actively involved in detailed discussions and had briefings with well–informed stakeholders and lobbyists to feed them with technically complex data. Their active participation ultimately led to a considerable delay in the European decision–making process on the EU–Biotechnology Directive[3] and to a complete failure regarding the EU–CII Directive.

---

53 H. Somsen, *Regulating Modern Biotechnology in a Global Risk Society. Challenges for Science, Law and Society* (Inaugural Lecture delivered on the occasion of the appointment to the chair in Biotechnology and Law at the University of Amsterdam, 12 December 2004, Amsterdam: Vossiuspers, 2005); P. Drahos and J. Braithwaite, *l.c.*

54 G. Van Overwalle, "Intellectual Property Rights or Wrongs? Setting the Scene: Current Debates and Issues", paper presented at *CropLife International Annual Conference*, Brussels, 2 June 2005.

55 S.P. Turner, *Liberal Democracy 3.0: Civil Society in an Age of Experts* (London: Sage 2003) 9.

Cost. Although European and national patent law provisions prescribe access to opposition and appeal (administrative boards) or court procedures to enable third parties to challenge the validity of a granted patent, and patent holders to claim relief from infringement of their proprietary right, high patent litigation costs may block effective access to relief before the court for parties with insufficient resources. At present, especially the cost for defending a European patent may become extremely high, as singular infringement procedures have to be launched in each and every designated Member State where a patent holder seeks to protect his rights.

5 Remedies to Limits in Patent Law

As has become clear, patent law is experiencing difficulties in fulfilling its objectives and functions. The limits encountered in patent law do not always arise directly from patent law but are often a product of the political and social context in which the patent system is embedded. Consequently, remedies are not necessarily to be found *within* the patent system, but may also be situated *outside* patent law. Competition law, self–regulation, ethics and informal norms may play a complimentary role in the reform of the patent system in dealing with the limits observed. Remedies may arise from institutional or political initiatives and may be inspired by scholarly research.

5.1 Regulatory Function

In order to assist modern patent law in achieving its major objectives and coping with its regulatory function, steps may be contemplated in the area of patent quality and patent licensing behaviour.

Patent quality. To prevent a 'hold up' of the pace of innovation, only high quality patents should be granted. High quality patents imply a rigorous review of prior art, strict application of the patentability criteria and clear claim construction. As current quality assurance mechanisms[56] seem not to suffice to guarantee high quality patents, additional measures should be taken. Recent initiatives envisaging the review of the patent system in the light of patent quality may play an important role in attaining the principal objective of patent law and in strengthening the regulatory function.

---

[56] See for instance, A. Pompidou, "Recent Developments in the European Patent System", 26th Conference on Intellectual Property Rights, Patents Forum (29 November 2006) (available at www.epo.org/about-us/press/speeches/061129.html).

Indeed, the EPO and the European Commission, DG Internal Market, have separately initiated a discourse on the future patent law within Europe.[57] In its consultation procedure EPO explicitly focuses on the "future of the European patent *system*"[58], whereas the European Commission launched a public consultation on the "future patent *policy* in Europe"[59]. Both initiatives include patent quality considerations. During the Public Hearing organised by the European Commission on 12 July 2006, patent experts, multinationals and SMEs all emphasised the importance of this issue.

Also in the US[60] concrete proposals to enhance patent quality are under discussion, in particular the potential of a post–grant review process modelled after the European opposition system and peer review of the patent quality by scientists.[61] Notably the latter is interesting, as such a system may not only improve patent quality, but may also reinforce the function of patent law to provide legal guarantees, which is at present seriously hampered as well.

Patent thickets. Patent law hardly provides rules with regard to exploitation and licensing, and patent holders have a wide discretion on how to exercise their rights. Competition law equally leaves considerable freedom to the patentees to set up li-

---

57 The introduction of legal measures on the European level articulates an additional complexity: the delicate co–existence between the European Commission and the EPO and the risk of conflicting institutional competencies.

58 EPO, "The Future of the European Patent System – A Series of conferences", at www.hearings.european-patent-office.org/background/index.en.php (last visited 28 August 2006) – our italics.

59 European Commission, "Public Hearing on the Future Patent Policy in Europe", 12 July 2006, at www.ec.europa.eu/internal_market/indprop/patent/hearing_en.htm (last visited 1 August 2006); C. McCreevy, "Closing Remarks Public Discussion on Future Patent Policy in Europe" (Public hearing Future Patent Policy in Europe, Brussels, 12 July 2006, SPEECH/06/453, at www.europa.eu.int/rapid/ (last visited 1 August 2006); European Commission, Questionnaire – On the patent system in Europe (Brussels, 9 January 2006). at www.ec.europa.eu/internal_market/indprop/patent/hearing_en.htm (last visited 1 August 2006) and European Commission, "Preliminary Findings: Issues for Debate", (Public hearing Future Patent Policy in Europe, Brussels, 12 July 2006), at www.ec.europa.eu/internal_market/indprop/patent/hearing_en.htm (last visited 1 August 2006) – our italics.

60 W.H. Schacht, "Patent Reform: Issues in the Biomedical and Software Industries" (Report for Congress, Washington, D.C.: Congressional Research Service (CRS), 7 April 2006), at www.fas.org/sgp/crs/misc/RL33367.pdf (last visited 1 August 2006); Patent Reform Act of 2005, H.R. 2795, at www.thomas.loc.gov/cgi-bin/query/z?c109:H.R.2795:/ (last visited 1 August 2006); S.A. Merrill *et al.*, *A Patent System for the 21st Century* (Washington D.C: The National Academies Press, 2004), also at www.nap.edu (last visited 1 August 2006) and Federal Trade Commission, "To Promote Innovation: The Proper Balance of Competition and Patent Law and Policy" (October 2004), at www.ftc.gov/os/2003/10/innovationrpt.pdf (last visited 1 August 2006).

61 See www.peertopatent.org/ (last visited 12 September 2007). See also, B.S. Noveck, "'Peer to Patent': Collective Intelligence, Open Review, and Patent Reform", *Harv. J. L. & Tech.* 2006, *20*, 123–162; G. Brumfiell, "US Patent Office Ponders Peer Scrutiny", *News@nature.com* 2006, at www.nature.com/news/2006/060515/full/060515-4.html (last visited 7 August 2006); and J.R. Thomas, "Collusion and Collective Action in the Patent System: A Proposal for Patent Bounties", *U. Ill. L. Rev.*2002, 305–353.

censing agreements. Competition case–law, the decisions of the European Commission and the EU group exemption regulation[62] may, however, serve as a roadmap for IP licensing policies. The prospect of time and cost intensive license negotiations and subsequent royalty stacking might discourage second comers to develop new products and processes in certain areas. Various measures can be considered to optimise the negotiation of a multitude of license agreements and to improve the access and use of patents, thus contributing to both the major objective and the regulatory function of patent law.

New collaborative licensing models, which comply with the conditions set out in competition law and which may facilitate access to and use of the patented inventions, have been suggested in institutional circles (WIPO, WHO, HUGO (Human Genome Organisation), OECD (Organisation for Economic Co–operation and Development, etc.)). Recent scholarly research has taken this suggestion to heart and has further explored so–called patent pools and clearinghouses as a solution for patent thickets in the field of genetics.[63]

Restrictive licensing. As patent law and competition law leave considerable freedom to licensing partners to set up their licensing agreement, exclusive licensing is not prohibited. Nevertheless, exclusivity may lead to a seriously blocking position and may hamper access to essential public health services. At present, two measures exist which might temper cases of extreme monopolistic licensing behaviour of patent holders: the compulsory licensing scheme in patent law and the abuse of dominant position provision in European competition law. Such tools, either internal or external to patent law, might be used to meet the growing concern regarding the hindering effects of patents. However, that might not suffice and additional measures should be contemplated which safeguard access to fundamental health care services, and thus reinforce the major objectives in patent law.[64]

One such measure may be the introduction of informal norms of fair licensing behaviour. The US National Institutes of Health (NIH) and the OECD support this idea. The NIH set an example by developing ‘Best Practices for the Licensing of

---

[62] Commission Regulation (EC) No. 772/2004 of 27 April 2004 on the application of Article 81(3) of the Treaty to categories of technology transfer agreements, O.J. L 123/11, 27.04.2004. This Regulation replaces Commission Regulation (EC) No. 240/96 of 31 January 1996 on the application of Article 85(3) of the Treaty to certain categories of technology transfer agreements, O.J. L 31/2, 09.02.1996. Its is supplemented by the Commission Guidelines on the application of Article 81 of the EC Treaty to technology transfer agreements, O.J., C 101/2, 27.04.2004.

[63] *E.g.*, G. Van Overwalle, E. van Zimmeren, B. Verbeure and G. Matthijs, “Models for Facilitating Access to Patents on Genetic Inventions”, *Nature Reviews Genetics* 2006, *7*, 143–148; B. Verbeure, E. van Zimmeren, G. Matthijs and G. Van Overwalle, “Patent Pools and Diagnostic Testing”, *Trends in Biotechnology* 2006, *24*, 115–120; E. van Zimmeren, B. Verbeure, G. Matthijs and G. Van Overwalle, “A Clearinghouse for Diagnostic Testing: The Solution to Ensure Access to and Use of Patented Genetic Inventions?”, *Bulletin of the World Health Organization* 2006, 352–359.

[64] See G. Van Overwalle, “Gene Patents and Public Health. Setting the Scene”, in G. Van Overwalle (ed.), *Gene Patents and Public Health* (Brussels: Bruylant, 2007) 11–24.

Genomic Inventions'[65] for government–funded research already in 2000. The best practice guidelines were revised and finally published in 2005. Also in 2005, the OECD launched its 'Guidelines for the Licensing of Genetic Inventions'[66] setting out the principles and best practices for the licensing of genetic inventions used for human health care purposes. The Guidelines intend to assist governments both in the development of governmental policies and in their efforts to encourage appropriate behaviour in the licensing and transferring of genetic inventions. The OECD strongly advises, for instance, to encourage rights holders to agree to licensing terms and conditions that maximise the utilisation of their genetic inventions, such as setting a reasonable overall royalty burden and non–exclusivity of the license, and for private and public sector participants to develop mechanisms to decrease transaction costs in acquiring rights to use the patented inventions.[67] Furthermore, Stanford University issued a White Paper entitled "In the Public Interest: Nine Points to Consider in Licensing University Technology"[68] based on the licensing principles developed by 11 major universities and research institutes and the Association of American Medical Colleges in order to stimulate universities to adopt licensing strategies in the public interest and for society's benefit.

The NIH has proved quite effective in the enforcement of its guidelines, because of the 'carrot' it holds in the form of research funding. The OECD, although an important global actor in its relation with States, cannot promulgate rules directly binding for individuals, such as patent holders (horizontal regulatory relationship). Moreover, no legal authority is closely supervising the observance of the OECD licensing guidelines. Respect for the OECD Guidelines is thus merely a moral obligation, which cannot be imposed by any court and lacks the necessary legal certainty, and the same applies to the principles put forward in the Stanford University White Paper. Nevertheless, the institutional economics' "law and norms theory"[69] teaches us that moral persuasion may be more effective than legal au-

---

65 US Department of Health and Human Services, National Institutes of Health, Best Practices for the Licensing of Genomic Inventions: Final Notice, April 2005, Federal Register, Vol. 70, No. 68, 11 April 2005, 18413-18415, at www.ott.od.nih.gov/policy/lic_gen.html.

66 OECD, "Guidelines for the Licensing of Genetic Inventions", C(2005)149/Rev1 (2006), available at www.oecd.org/dataoecd/39/38/36198812.pdf [hereinafter OECD Guidelines].

67 OECD Guidelines, cons. 1.6, 4.1, 4.4, 5.3.

68 Stanford University, "In the Public Interest: Nine Points to Consider in Licensing University Technology" (6 March 2007), available at www.news-service.stanford.edu/news/2007/march7/gifs/whitepaper.pdf. Also see, G. Van Overwalle, "Reconciling Patent Policies and University Mission", *Ethical Perspectives* 2006, *13*, 231–247, available at www.ssrn.com; G. Van Overwalle, "Octrooien op maat? Naar een evenwicht tussen publieke opdracht en privaat goed", in B. Pattyn and G. Van Overwalle (eds.), *Tussen markt en agora. Over het statuut van universitaire kennis* (Leuven: Peeters, 2006) 181–214.

69 This theory examines formal and informal norms as part of the constraints that shape human behaviour. For more information, see *e.g.*, R.C. Ellickson, "Law and Economics Discovers Social Norms", *J. Legal. St.* 1998, *27*, 537–552.

thority, as in international law and 'cyber–governance'.[70] Informal norms are "distinct from legal rules, the violation of which is typically punished by private actors".[71] However, one should note that informal norms are in many cases ultimately embedded in the law and based on property entitlements and contractual arrangements.[72]

Self–regulation, possibly implementing the OECD Guidelines or the Stanford University White Paper, imposed by scientific and trade organisations on their members may be an alternative solution. In this respect, the initiative of the European Society for Human Genetics to set up a panel of scientific and patent experts preparing a report and recommendations on patenting and licensing in human genetics for its members is significant.[73]

5.2 Symbolic Function

In an aim to bump up the symbolic function in current patent law, initiatives to reassess the scope of patent law, taking into account ethical values and human rights, as well as measures to further governance in patent law decision–making, may be elaborated.

Patentability and ethics. Patent legislators and policy–makers have several options for overcoming the failure of patent law to adequately perform the symbolic function. First, it is essential to better inform the general public in order to overcome misunderstandings and to explain the background of the current status of patent law. In this regard, interest groups representing the wide diversity of perspectives and the media have an important responsibility.

Second, a more restrictive application of patentability criteria and scope of patent claims in relation to specific technologies might be considered.[74] Controversies, such as the ones surrounding the EU CII–Directive and the EU Biotechnol-

---

70 *E.g.*, M. Lemley, "The Law and Economics of Internet Norms", *Chicago–Kent L. Rev.* 1989, *73*, 1257–1294 and M.A. O'Rourke, "Fencing Cyberspace: Drawing Borders in a Virtual World", *Minn. L. Rev.* 1998, *82*, 609, 641–45. O'Rourke evaluates the netiquette of linking and framing on the Internet.

71 S. Thambisetty, *l.c.*, 364.

72 *E.g.*, M. Lemley. *l.c.*, 1257–1294.

73 European Society of Human Genetics, Patenting and Licensing Committee – Public and Professional Policy Committee, *Patenting and Licensing in Genetic Testing. Ethical, Legal and Social Issues* (www.eshg.org/PatentingandLicensingDraftBackgrPaper07062007.pdf (last visited 16 October 2007)). The recommendations are expected to be released mid December 2007 (www.eshg.org/ (last visited 16 October 2007)).

74 Formally, patent law operates as a 'one size fits all system'. All inventions, irrespective of the technological field must satisfy the same patentability criteria. However, patent doctrine contains different industry–specific 'sub–cultures' of interpretation, even if not explicitly acknowledged. Such 'technological exceptionalism' is basically a way to marginally modify the doctrine in order to adapt the law to new technologies. See S. Thambisetty, *l.c.*, 352.

ogy Directive could have been an opportunity to argue for a more restrictive application.[75]

Third, the 'ethical clause', excluding inventions of which the commercial exploitation is considered to run counter to 'ordre public or morality' from patentability[76], might be reassessed. This could especially be interesting in the field of genetics. In an effort to offer some concrete guidance on the exact scope of the twin concept 'ordre public and morality' in genetics, a non–exhaustive list of inventions which shall be considered unpatentable, was laid down in the EU Biotechnology Directive[77] and subsequently implemented in the EPC[78] and national legislations. Excluded from patentability are: processes for cloning human beings, processes for modifying the germ line genetic identity of human beings, uses of human embryos for industrial or commercial purposes, and processes for modifying the genetic identity of animals, which are likely to cause them suffering without any substantial medical benefit to man or animal as well as animals resulting from such processes. Although the list does provide a framework for ethical assessment, the list does not set the minds of all the critics of expanded patentability to rest. Some observers fear that this exclusionary provision does not aim at limiting the patent implications of certain biotechnological inventions, but wishes to exclude certain fields of research.[79] Patent law should indeed take into account ethical concerns and can and may act as a "moral tollbooth"[80], but patent law should only do so to the extent that it concerns matters which are directly and inextricably linked with patent law and the implications of the exercise of patent rights. Patent law should not interfere to (indirectly) regulate research. Since a direct link is missing between ethics and patents in the exclusionary provision, those commentators argue that this provision should be abolished and the exclusions should be treated in research regulations. Other observers, advocating the absolute prohibition "to patent life", will not be satisfied by the narrow wording of the ethi-

75 I. Schneider, *l.c.*, 419. Also see P. Jacobs and G. Van Overwalle, "Gene Patents: An Alternative Approach", *EIPR* 2001, *23*, 505–506.

76 See The Danish Council of Ethics, *Patenting Human Genes and Stem Cells, A Report* (Copenhagen: The Danish Council of Ethics, 2004), at www.etiskraad.dk/sw475.asp (last visited 31 August 2006); A.T. Caulfield, E.R. Gold and M.K. Cho, "Patenting Human Genetic Material: Refocusing the Debate", *Nature Reviews Genetics* 2000, *1*, 227–231; P. Drahos, "Biotechnological Patents, Markets and Morality", *EIPR* 1999, *21*, 441–449; G. Van Overwalle (ed.), *Octrooirecht, Ethiek and Biotechnologie – Patent Law, Ethics and Biotechnology – Droit des Brevets, Éthique et Biotechnologie* (Brussels: Bruylant, 1998) and S. Sterckx (ed.), *Biotechnology, Patents and Morality* (Aldershot: Ashgate, 1997).

77 More in particular in Article 6.

78 Rule 32d Implementing regulations to the EPC, at www.european-patent-office.org/legal/epc/ (last visited 28 August 2006).

79 G. Van Overwalle, "Legal and Ethical Aspects of Bio–Patenting: A Critical Analysis of the EU Biotechnology Directive", in C. Baumgartner and D. Mieth (eds.) *Patente am Leben?: ethische, rechtliche und politische Aspekte der Biopatentierung* (Paderborn: Mentis–Verlag, 2003) 145–158.

80 R.E. Gold, "The Moral Tollbooth: A Method that Makes Use of the Patent System to Address Ethical Concerns in Biotechnology", *The Lancet* 2002, *359*, 2268–2270.

cal clause. Moreover, new ethical questions will probably emerge with new technologies arriving.

Ethics and human rights. For patent law to be widely accepted and generally recognised as a regime incorporating and representing values, one may argue that patent law should be more tightly linked to the human rights discourse. Human rights might act as valuable and necessary complements of patent rights and might serve as a counterbalance of patent rights when centering too one–sidedly on trade, access to markets and economic calculus.

Overlooking the human rights catalogue, a few concepts and rights come to the fore which might play a significant role in this respect. First and foremost, the concept of human dignity may introduce certain restrictions on patentable subject matter in patent law, in order to safeguard the rights of human beings and human embryos. Next, the right to food may open an avenue to impose restrictions in patent law in the interest of consumers. Besides, the right of informed consent invites patent law to be cautious in respect of the rights of donors of human biological material, testees and patients, and the rights of traditional knowledge holders. Furthermore, the right to access to public health might safeguard the rights of patients, by limiting the rights of patentees through the introduction of a compulsory license system. Finally, the right of access might provide adequate trajectories for innovators or users, in order to have efficient access to technological innovations and improvements through the disclosure requirement.[81]

It has been argued that all these human rights can be factored into patent law, through the gateway of public interest. A contemporary interpretation of public interest will prove to offer a more then skeletal basis for taking into account human rights into patent law.[82]

Globalisation. Patent law will most probably not be able to cope with the failure to fully incorporate the symbolic function when it comes to governance, as this limit results from a general feature of the international political decision–making process: the existence of frictions between industrialised and developing countries and inequalities between big and small countries, between first inventors and second comers.

However, the upcoming 'nodal governance' theory[83] may be a useful instrument in this regard. This theory aims to examine the power differences between 'nodes', set up new 'nodes' and analyse the potential of strategic relationships. Governance today is characterised by a plurality of actors (States, companies, WTO, WIPO, institutions of civil society, etc.) forming more or less intercon-

---

81 See G. Van Overwalle (2008c), *l.c.*

82 *Ibid.*

83 S. Burris, O. Drahos and C. Shearing, "Nodal Governance", *Australian Journal of Legal Philosophy* 2005, *30*, 30–58; P. Drahos (2004), *l.c.*, 401–424; S. Burris, "Governance, Microgovernance and Health", *Temple Law Review* 2004, *77*, 335–358 and P. Drahos, "Introduction to the Nodal and the Global", *RegNet Conference The Nodal and the Global* (9–11 December, 2003).

nected governance networks, a plurality of instruments (economic pressure, norm creation, moral persuasion, etc.) and rapid developments. Nodal governance is an elaboration of contemporary network theory that explains how a variety of actors operating within social systems interact along networks to govern the systems they inhabit. Burris, Drahos and Shearing argue that governance in these social systems is substantially constituted in 'nodes': institutions with a set of technologies, mentalities and resources that mobilise the knowledge and capacity of members to manage the course of events. Nodes are in general points on networks, the sites where the curves that constitute networks intersect. Nodes may take a variety of forms: from legislators and government agencies through non–governmental organisations to firms or even gangs. Networks are the means through which nodes exert influence. 'Superstructural nodes' bring together representatives of different nodal organisations in order to concentrate the members' resources and technologies for a common purpose. However, this does not mean that the various networks will be completely integrated.

Tying together networks is one very important way in which nodes gain the capacity to govern a course of events. It creates a node with increased resources and a structure that enables the mobilisation of those resources to produce action by other nodes in the network. Superstructural nodes are the 'command centres' of networked governance.[84] They can be employed for the purpose of lobbying for instance, the United States Trade Representative (USTR) or the EP.

Therefore, developing countries and interest groups should not go at it alone. They should join their forces both in resources (including manpower) and in building a structure that can mobilise action by other nodes and thus the various networks. Such a superstructural node of developed countries and interest groups may generate more bargaining power in the present debate of so–called TRIPs^{+}–provisions (IP standards that require a higher level of protection than the safeguards prescribed by TRIPs). The superstructural node could be exploited to promote a debate sensitive to local preferences and values, and thus help to (re)establish the symbolic function of patent law.

5.3 Function to Provide Legal Guarantees

In an attempt to fortify the function of patent law to provide legal guarantees, new modes and concepts of democracy should be explored and implemented, leading to the reinforcement of the obligation to guarantee access to and participation in the legal and the political decision–making process (political participation). Moreover, the obligation to guarantee effective and legitimate access for citizens to means that protect against illegitimate action by the authorities and other citizens should be equally contemplated (judicial review).

---

[84] S. Burris, O. Drahos and C. Shearing, *l.c.*, 31–38.

Expertisation. According to 'updated' theories of democracy, democracy refers not only to the role of parliament in governing (patent) law and political accountability, but moves beyond that. Stakeholder participation and deliberative democracy complement conventional parliamentarian representation. The "activation of a critical citizenry and different layers of political sub–elites" enables them to take part in complex, technical and political deliberations and to participate actively in the different levels of political life.[85]

At the European level there are several examples of forms of institutionalised activation of a critical layer of citizens or sub–elites. Interesting examples of institutionalised access to the decision–making process in patent law are the possibility for third parties to send statements throughout the patent application procedure (so–called 'amicus curiae briefs').[86] Other examples are the consultation procedures of the European Commission and the hearings by EPO, such as the ones concerning the future of the patent system in Europe. In particular, small and medium–sized enterprises (SMEs) have a special status in these consultations.[87] Nevertheless, the legitimacy of such initiatives is sometimes criticised. Critics argue that there seems to be a very strong interface with the professional patent community and large industry and a rather weak interaction with a wider spectrum of stakeholders (in particular the opponents). This might explain the activities of the latter and lobbyists during the debates in the EP and national parliaments.[88] It is essential to provide opportunities for full stakeholder participation and to put into place the necessary channels for dialogue in order to prevent the image of a bias of the European patent system in favour of large firms and clients. Stakeholder participation is also at the core of the recent US 'peer to patent' project, where scientists are invited to provide comments on patent applications.

Participation in the patent system by a 'critical layer of citizens' will not be evident. From the perspective of the general public the patent institutions are too complex and obscure. Taking into account the opinions of well–informed interest groups with good and reliable communication channels to the general public may constitute a more effective instrument. Moreover, the nodal governance theory may assist in mobilising diffused knowledge and capacity which rests with non–governmental organisations that have been excluded from governance until now.

---

85 S. Borrás, *l.c.*, 6, who also cites J. Bohman, "International Regimes and Democratic Governance: Political Equality and Influence in Global Institutions", *International Affairs* 1999, *75*, 499–513, 513.

86 Article 115(1) EPC [Observations by third parties]: "Following the publication of the European patent application, *any person* [our italics] may present observations concerning the patentability of the invention in respect of which the application has been filed: […]" and Article 11b(1) of the Rules of Procedure of the Enlarged Board of Appeal of the EPO [Statements by third parties]: "In the course of the proceedings before the Board, any written statement concerning the points of law raised in such proceedings which is sent to this Board by a *third party* [our italics] may be dealt with as the Boards thinks fit."

87 On the importance of SMEs, see also, A. Pompidou, "Intervention of Professor Alain Pompidou, President of the European Patent Office, at the public hearing on future patent policy in Europe", Brussels, 12 July 2006.
at www.european-patent-office.org/news/pressrel/2006_07_12_e.htm.

88 S.P. Turner, *l.c.*, 11.

These means might assist patent law in helping to achieve effective access to and participation in the political decision–making process.

Cost. In turn, the fact that any person can start an opposition procedure against a granted patent[89] at a reasonable price, clearly demonstrates an effective way to guarantee access to protective measures against illegitimate action by the authorities and other citizens within current European patent law. The US is contemplating inserting a similar opposition system which mirrors a certain interest in strengthening the function of patent law to provide legal guarantees.

In Europe, on the other hand, several measures for cutting down the high overall litigation cost are still under discussion. The ongoing consultation procedures on patent reform[90], initiated by the European Commission and the EPO, have revived the debate on the proposals for a Community patent, the European Patent Litigation Agreement (EPLA) and the London Protocol, which ultimately all aim at diminishing (granting and) litigation costs. Moreover, this debate has led to interesting insights into the complex relationship between the EPO and the European Community in the area of patent litigation.

The purpose of the Regulation on the Community Patent[91] is not to replace the existing European (EPC) and national systems, but to create an additional regime, which will be integrated in the existing system. The Community patent would serve as an option for inventors to obtain a single patent which is legally valid throughout the European Union instead of a bundle of national patents. The Community patent would in particular be issued by the EPO as a European patent, specifying the territory of the Community rather than individual Member States. A Community patent would be granted in one of the official languages of the proceedings before the EPO (English, German or French) and would be published in that language with a translation of the claims into the other two languages. A translation of the Community patent into all the Community languages would not be necessary. The system also provides for the creation of a centralised Commu-

---

89 Article 99(1) EPC [Opposition]: "Within nine months from the publication of the mention of the grant of the European patent *any person* [our italics] may give notice to the European Patent Office of opposition to the European patent granted. [...]".

90 See references in footnote 4. For a critical opinion on the most recent developments, see J. Pagenberg, "Another Year of Debates on Patent Jurisdiction in Europe and No End in Sight?", *International Review of Intellectual Property and Competition Law (IIC)* 2007, 805–825.

91 Latest official document of the EU on the Community patent: Council of the European Union, Portuguese Presidency, Working Party on Intellectual Property (Patents), *Towards an EU Patent Jurisdiction – Points for discussion*, Brussels, 30 October 2007, 14492/07 PI 42, available at register.consilium.europa.eu/pdf/en/07/st14/st14492.en07.pdf. For more background information, see *e.g.*, European Commission, Communication from the Commission of 3 April 2007 to the European Parliament and the Council – Enhancing the patent system in Europe, COM (2007) 165 final; Council of the European Union, Proposal for a Council Regulation on the Community Patent, COM (2000) 421 final; European Commission, Commission Communication of 5 February 1999: Promoting innovation through patents – The follow–up to the Green Paper on the Community patent and the patent system in Europe, COM (1999) 42 final; and Green Paper of 24 June 1997 on the Community patent and the patent system in Europe, COM (97) 314 final.

nity Intellectual Property Court[92] to safeguard consistency in case–law. The Community patent regime might remedy two problems in current European patent practice with regard to cost. First, the regime might achieve a substantial reduction of the overall cost of patenting, including costs relating to translation and filing. At present the grant of a European patent is considerably more expensive than its US or Japanese counterpart: a European patent designating 13 countries is 11 times more expensive than a US patent and 13 times more expensive then a Japanese patent.[93] Second, the Community patent regime might contribute to a considerable decrease of the overall cost of litigation. The current system of patent litigation in the EU suffers from having to initiate patent litigation procedures in several countries on the same patent issue, which leads to high litigation costs, as well as cross–border litigation and forum shopping, and lack of legal certainty. However, the creation of a Community patent system remains a sensitive issue and this dossier is still deadlocked after many years of discussions between the European decision–makers. The impasse is partly due to the disagreement about the need to file translations into all Community languages. Access to translations is particularly relevant in view of all three functions of patent law described, namely the regulatory function, the symbolic function and the function to provide legal guarantees.

The discussions on the EPLA[94] remain staggered as well. This draft agreement would become an optional protocol to the EPC which would commit its signatory States to an integrated judicial system, including uniform rules of procedure and a common appeal court. The European Patent Court would have jurisdiction over infringement actions and claims or counterclaims for revocation of a European patent. It would comprise both legally and technically qualified judges. The language regime would be based on the language regime of the EPO. However, the EU Members States disagree on a couple of issues with regard to EPLA, such as the relationship between EPLA and the European Community, including the role of an eventual Community patent in EPLA, and on the qualifications of the European Patent Court judges. Some EU Members States are in favour of an active participation of the European Community (EC) in the EPLA process. Involvement of the EC would be required as the EPLA touches on subjects which are already covered by EC acquis communautaire.[95] Some other EU Member States take the view that

---

92 European Commission, Proposal of 23 December 2003 for a Council Decision conferring jurisdiction on the Court of Justice in disputes relating to the Community patent, COM (2003) 827 final; European Commission, Proposal of 2 December 2003 for a Council Decision establishing the Community Patent Court and concerning appeals before the Court of First Instance, COM (2003) 828 final.

93 European Commission, Communication from the Commission of 3 April 2007 to the European Parliament and the Council – Enhancing the patent system in Europe, COM (2007) 165 final.

94 EPO, Working Party on Litigation, Draft Agreement on the establishment of a European patent litigation system, 16 February 2004, available at www.documents.epo.org/projects/babylon/eponet.nsf/0/B3884BE403F0CD8FC125723D004ADD0A/$File/agreement_draft_en.pdf.

95 *E.g.,* Directive 2004/48/EC of the European Parliament and of the Council of 29 April 2004 on the enforcement of intellectual property rights, O.J. L 157/45, 30.04.2004; Council Regulation (EC) No. 44/2001 of 22 December 2000 on jurisdiction and the recognition and

creating a new jurisdiction parallel to the Community jurisdiction would be complicated and risks creating inconsistencies. In case the Community patent would be realised later on, it would lead to duplication of EU–wide patent courts. They prefer to set up a unified court structure which could deal with litigation both on European patents and future Community patents. As to the qualification of the judges, some people seriously doubt whether it would be possible to appoint technically educated judges with no full legal qualifications. Here, reference can be made to what already has been examined regarding expertisation and the importance of not only having technically minded patent experts involved in the patent law system.

Despite all the efforts on the European political level with regard to patent litigation, for the time being the London Agreement appears to be the only solution which will be realised in the foreseeable future. The objective of the London Agreement is to create "a cost attractive post–grant translation regime for European patents".[96] The parties to the Agreement undertake to waive the requirement for translations of European patents to be filed in their national language. In practice, the major consequence of the Agreement would be that patent owners of a European patent will no longer have to file a translation of the specification for patents having one of the three EPO languages as an official language. In October 2007, France finally voted in favour of the adoption of the London Agreement. This was essential as the Agreement must be ratified by at least eight Contracting States, including the three States where the most European patents took effect in 1999 – that is, France, Germany and the United Kingdom.[97] It is expected to come into effect in the first half of 2008.

6 Conclusion

IP rights play an important role in present day knowledge–based economies. Patent law in particular is a major legal instrument to encourage the disclosure of information and technologies, to stimulate public and private entities to invest and thereby further innovation primordial for economic and social progress. In order to deliver on the potential of new technologies and to achieve the desired benefits such technologies offer to society, a clear enabling environment and regulatory structure are essential.

Over the past decade, some remarkable trends have been observed in patent law and practice: extension of patentable subject matter, growing attention for patent quality, appearance of patent thickets and restrictive licensing practices, emer-

---

enforcement of judgments in civil and commercial matters (Brussels I), O.J. 12/01, 16.01.2001.

96 EPO, Agreement dated 17 October 2000 on the application of Article 65 EPC, OJ EPO 2001, 549, available at www.documents.epo.org/projects/babylon/eponet.nsf/0/595FE5E1FC71DD4EC12572BC0058E29D/$File/Agreement_17102000.pdf.

97 Article 6 of the Agreement.

gence of governance issues such as the North–South divide, increasing influence of 'epistemic communities', as well as an enlarged role of ethics and of human rights. Our analysis has shown that these developments, both within patent law itself and external to patent law, confront the system with its limits. The complex, dynamic, institutionalised, societal and scientific nature of patent law creates limits on how patent law may fulfil its objectives and functions, namely the regulatory function, the symbolic function and the function to provide legal guarantees. These limits require a more holistic, outward–looking perspective, as other areas of (legal) expertise such as competition law, self–regulation, ethics and human rights may assist in filling the gaps.

The trends observed and the limits encountered call for further research on the flaws and failures of today's patent law system and for reflection on how to shape the future patent regime. If a review of the system would be restricted to controlling the symptoms (concrete problems in the day–to–day practice of the patent offices) without having diagnosed the actual 'disorder' (inaptitude of patent law to fulfil its objectives and functions), it may 'steal into' the whole system despite the availability of 'modern treatments' and remedies. A sound and well–functioning patent system and an effective and legitimate patent law, accepted by a wide range of stakeholders (scientists, business people, and patients) and by the public at large, are of utmost importance in a knowledge–based economy.

Chapter 23 – Technology and the End of Law

Mireille Hildebrandt

1 Introduction

In this chapter we will argue that if we do not embody legal norms in new technological devices and infrastructures, we may reach the end of law. At the same time we will argue that if we do embody legal norms in technological devices we may still reach the end of the *rule of* law. In short, first, we argue that legal normativity in an information society needs translation into new technological devices to sustain the instrumental and protective normativity that is central to constitutional democracy, and second, we also argue that an unreflective translation of legal standards into technological artefacts is dangerous if technology is wrongly seen as only instrumental to human intention.

To argue our point, we will use the example of an emerging technological infrastructure that will probably have far–reaching implications: the so–called 'Internet of Things', or 'Ambient Intelligent Environment'. These implications concern the way we perceive things, the way we are present in this world, and the way we can live together with things and human beings (section 2). Instead of building only on schools of thought within law and legal theory, we will analyse the potential consequences with the help of the philosophy of technology. Beyond naïve optimism and ideological pessimism, the philosophy of technology has developed insightful ways to investigate the actual implications of specific technological devices and to speculate about what this means for our shared world (section 3). We will draw on, amongst others, the phenomenological inquiries of Don Ihde and the anthropological observations of Bruno Latour, and on the critical reconstruction of their work by Peter–Paul Verbeek. Verbeek provides a critical link to legal normativity, because he assesses the morality of *things*. This in itself is enough to raise the eyebrows of many a reader, since modernity has taught us that things can only be instruments, while human beings – as Kant stipulated – should never be treated as pure instruments but always be respected as autonomous creatures.

We hope that the reader will bear with us when we discuss the 'Internet of Things' in some detail, and explain how a philosophy of technology can enhance our understanding of the implications of this emerging technological infrastructure. After this exploration *beyond the limits of the law* we will return to the legal field to investigate what legal normativity amounts to and how it compares to technological normativity (section 4). We will explain how both law and technology can be constitutive or regulative of human (and non–human) interaction, seeking to discern relevant similarities and differences. Serious investigation into the normativity of modern law, however, clarifies that contemporary law in Western societies is already technologically embodied, and we will describe the material embodiment of legal norms in written language and the consequences of the use of written language and written law for legal normativity (section 5).

Finally, we will discuss the end of law from the two perspectives mentioned above (section 6). Firstly, we will argue that if we do not embody law into new technologies, the emergence of 'Ambient Intelligence' and the 'Internet of Things' will mean the end of law as an effective and legitimate instrument for constitutional democracy. Secondly, we will argue that this cannot mean that legal norms can be embodied in whatever way in any kind of technological device or infrastructure. We will relate a relational conception of law to a pluralist conception of technology and submit that both lawyers and technologists should stop taking for granted deterministic, causal conceptions of technology and voluntaristic conceptions of law. Only in that case can we continue the process of reconstituting our shared world with a technologically embodied law that adequately installs and protects constitutional democracy.

2 The 'Internet of Things'

2.1 Turning the Offline World Online

Just imagine that all *things* in your environment seem to know where you are, what you do, and – better even, or worse – what you want and arrange that you get it. Walking into your office, the lights turn on with the intensity you prefer, based on an analysis of the day's light intensity and your 'lighting' habits. Sitting down your computer screen comes alive with a customised website that has filtered today's news for your personal interests, while your personal digital assistant (incorporated into your wristwatch) has already handled three attempts to reach you, preventing you from being flooded with text messages, phone calls, and other types of communications. These attempts to reach you are neatly sorted by priority and urgency and will be brought to your attention at the right moment. The right moment is inferred from close observation of your behaviour during the past months, and constantly adjusted to the latest real–time behaviour that is recorded by your 'animated' environment. Note that the adjustments to your environment do not take place because you programmed it with your conscious preferences, but because it anticipates these preferences – mostly before you become aware of them.

This environment thrives on interconnectedness: all things (clothes, books, cups, pencils, tables, chairs) are provided with RFID ('Radio Frequency Identification') tags that communicate wirelessly with RFID readers that are connected with online databases that store and aggregate the data. At the same time the environment is equipped with sensor devices and cameras that detect movement, temperature, sound, and so on, of both things and people, while the data are again stored in online databases. With the use of data–mining techniques, a commercial enterprise can search these data to discover relevant patterns which predict the future behaviour of both things and people. On the basis of these predictions service providers cater to your thus inferred wishes, adapting the environment to your preferences. This is what the Information Society Technologies Advisory Group (ISTAG) called the 'Vision of Ambient Intelligence' (AmI)[1], describing the emergence of a user–centric intelligent environment. It is also what the International Telecommunication Union (ITU) calls the 'Internet of Things',[2] because the intelligence of this environment is located in the connection between numerous *things* in the offline world via online databases and communication. In fact this would turn the offline world online.

If all this sounds like science fiction, we should remember the radical technological developments of the last 200 years, from the invention of the steam engine, through the widespread use of electrical light, to the introduction of computers and the exponential rate of change in information technologies during the last 50 years.[3] The combination of the unprecedented increase in computing power and the concomitant reduction of its costs have facilitated the birth of a host of communication technologies that are becoming both mobile and wireless to an extent previously unthought–of. The mobile phone allows us to communicate non–stop from every corner of the world with every other corner of the world, while the laptop does the same for more regularised communication. We are, in short, flooded with information, or at least with data, and we seem to have become ever more available for contact with others, a fact which also blurs the borders between our working, social, and private lives. This presses forward the question how to cope with this new situation encroaching upon our private, social, and public habits, destabilising established checks and balances, calling for reliable techniques to assess incoming data, and to put a limit on the demands of what some call 'multi–tasking' (a phenomenon previously reserved for women combining a plurality of tasks at the nexus of work and home).

2.2 Profiling Technologies: From Data to Knowledge[4]

The 'Internet of Things' is designed to lift part of the burden of this information overdose from our shoulders, by programming the environment without disturbing us with queries about our preferences. It depends on the RFID and sensor tech-

---

1 ISTAG, *Scenarios for Ambient Intelligence in 2010* (Information Society Technology Advisory Group 2001) at http://www.cordis.lu/ist/istag–reports.htm; E. Aarts and S. Marzano (eds.), *The New Everyday. Views on Ambient Intelligence* (Rotterdam: 010 Publishers, 2003).

2 ITU, *The Internet of Things* (Geneva: International Telecommunications Union (ITU), 2005).

3 J. Garreau, *Radical Evolution. The Promise and Peril of Enhancing our Minds, our Bodies – and What it Means to be Human* (New York: Doubleday, 2005).

4 The author is co–ordinator of 'profiling' within the FIDIS (Future of Identity in Information Society) NoE (EC financed network of excellence), see www.fidis.net for a number of multidisciplinary edited reports on the subject.

nologies indicated above, but by themselves these technologies seem only to increase the overdose of proliferating data, making it impossible to discriminate even between noise and information. To discern which data may be relevant and to find out how they correlate, we need another technology, one which combines high–speed computing power with mathematical techniques to query the mass of data in search of significant patterns. This technology is called 'profiling', and it is based on a process of 'knowledge discovery in databases' (KDD).[5] Without moving into specialist discussions of algorithms that detect correlations between data in databases, one could describe profiling as the discovery of patterns that present knowledge which enables anticipation of future events based on what has happened in the past. This knowledge is mostly probabilistic but can be highly refined and can reveal patterns otherwise not detectable. For instance, the discovery of the relationship between specific genes and a specific disease is based on profiling technologies. Actually, scientists can calculate the chance that a specific disease will occur without having any insight into the complex chain of causation between genotype and phenotype. Correlations must not be conflated with causes or reasons: they do not (yet) reveal what causes or motivates them.[6] Many correlations are spurious because, for example, a correlation is caused by some third factor which influences both variables that do not have any impact on each other. In the case of genetic profiling the chance that certain genes correlate with a specific disease will usually vary, depending on other factors like other genes, epigenetics, hormonal levels within the organism, characteristics of the physical environment and/or the life–style of a person. The extent to which this possibility depends on such other factors can again be revealed by the use of profiling technologies, including behavioural profiling. From the moment that a non–spurious correlation is established, this constitutes knowledge which turns specific data into information. In other words, profiling technologies allow one to discriminate noise from information in the light of specific knowledge. This means that data can be either noise or information, depending on the knowledge inferred from them.[7] And, because different knowledge–constructs can be inferred from the same data, depending on the objective of the profiler, data can be noise for one profiler and information to another. If a real–estate agent wants to sell houses, he will be interested in behavioural patterns other than law enforcement agencies which track suspects of money laundering, yet all inferred from the same data.

---

5 B. Custers, *The Power of Knowledge. Ethical, Legal, and Technological Aspects of Data Mining and Group Profiling in Epidemiology* (Nijmegen: Wolf Legal Publishers, 2004) 35–55.

6 I. Stengers, *Sciences et pouvoirs* (Paris: La Découverte, 1997) 62–63. This is a crucial point. From 2002–2007 the author of this chapter has been collaborating with Isabelle Stengers, Bruno Latour, Serge Gutwirth and others on the subject of 'correlatable humans' in the framework of the InterUniverisity Attraction Poles project, *The Loyalties of Knowledge*, financed by the Federal Belgium Science Policy. M. Hildebrandt, "Profiles and Correlatable Humans", in Ch. Henning, N. Stehr and B. Weiler (eds.), *Knowledge and the Law* (New Brunswick N.J.: Transaction Books, 2007).

7 M. Hildebrandt, "From Data to Knowledge: The Challenges of a Crucial technology", *Datenschutz und Datensicherheit* 2006, *30*(9), 548–552.

Profiling technologies thus revolutionise the construction of knowledge in three ways. First, relevant patterns can be inferred from masses of trivial data that nobody would have thought relevant. Second, data can be collected, stored, and mined in an unobtrusive way without harassing or even disturbing people. Third, as a consequence, people may be completely unaware of the knowledge that is being constructed, having no idea why certain risks or opportunities are offered or refused.[8]

Profiling allows the selection of relevant data in the light of specific purposes. It basically amounts to pattern recognition, which is one of the crucial competences of all living beings.[9] The ultimate objective of profiling in a more general sense is to prepare an adequate 'fit' within the environment, allowing an organism to adapt itself and/or to adapt the environment in an adequate way. Technologically mediated profiling is preconditional for AmI, which aims to adapt the environment to a person's inferred wishes. To do this the process of automated knowledge discovery must be followed by a process of automated decision–making, based on what is called 'machine to machine' (M2M) communication.[10] This means that the processing of data and the subsequent adjustment of the environment take place without burdening people with any of the complexities involved. As has been said, the adaptations of the environment are meant to take place *autonomically*, in a similar way as our autonomic nervous system takes care of our vital functions without requesting our conscious consent. Human intervention mainly concerns adjustments made in the software that runs these networked environments, while in the ideal situation the programs learn to anticipate the need for change or repair.

'Ambient Intelligence' is a vision not yet realised. Whether and when (partial) realisation will occur is unclear. What is clear, however, is that the enabling technologies are being diffused as we speak, preparing a technological infrastructure which will change the way we live. To assess the consequences of widespread automated application of profiles before such application is in force, some intelligent speculation is called for. If we wait until the machines take over it may be difficult to revoke the whole process, even if we conclude that it has undesired effects on the way we organise our world. Especially when one acknowledges that technological devices and infrastructures can be designed in one way or another – with different consequences – a speculative assessment is a precondition for informed decisions about the introduction and design of emerging technologies. In the next subsection potential implications of an 'Internet of Things' will be explored for public goods like privacy, equality, fairness and due process.

---

8 L. Lessig, *Code and Other Laws of Cyberspace* (New York: Basic Books, 1999) 150–154; B. Custers, *l.c.*, 55–80.

9 M. Hildebrandt, "Defining Profiling: A New Type of Knowledge", in M. Hildebrandt and S. Gutwirth (eds.), *Profiling the European Citizen. A Cross–disciplinary Perspective* (Dordrecht: Springer, 2008) chapter 2.

10 J.O. Kephart and D.M. Chess, "The Vision of Autonomic Computing", *Computer* 2003 January.

2.3 Potential Impacts on Privacy, Equality, Fairness and Due Process

According to Agre and Rotenberg the right to privacy can be defined as "the freedom from unreasonable constraints on the construction of one's own identity".[11] By moving away from 'traditional' definitions that focus on secrecy and isolation[12], this working definition has the advantage of understanding privacy as a relational and dynamic concept that does not take one's identity for granted as a given that must be protected from outside influence. On the contrary, the default position seems to be that human identity is forever under construction since identity itself is relational: our subjectivity emerges in confrontation with other subjects, whose gaze is constitutive for our sense of self.[13] The right to privacy is not associated with freedom from constraints, because there is no freedom without constraints, but firmly rooted in the competence to ward off *unreasonable* constraints. Lawyers are familiar with vague terms like 'unreasonable' and most have little illusions about attempts to fix their meaning in advance. Nevertheless, the interpretation of what counts as unreasonable needs guidance. Privacy can be defined as a private good, something most people value for its own sake or for their own sake, and which can be exchanged for other goods. It can even be described as a consumer good to be traded for other consumer goods, provided the 'owner' gives her consent. A judge could base her judgment of what counts as 'unreasonable constraints' on such a conception of privacy, for instance demanding informed consent and the absence of duress. In a constitutional democracy, however, privacy should also be understood as a public good. In that case we take into account that privacy as we know it has been created by means of a legal framework for the sake of a viable democracy, which means that privacy cannot be taken for granted and needs to be sustained by an effective rule of law. This also implies that to sustain privacy as a public good it cannot be traded at will by individual citizens. From this perspective, privacy and identity building are preconditions for a strong civil society that depends on citizens who feel free to speak up for their own interests. To decide when constraints on identity–building become unreasonable we need to keep in mind that privacy is not just a private but also a public good.[14]

---

11 P.E. Agre, "Introduction", in P.E. Agre and M. Rotenberg (eds.), *Technology and Privacy: The New Landscape* (Cambridge, Mass.: MIT, 2001) 7.

12 D.J. Solove, "Conceptualizing Privacy", *California Law Review* 2002, *90*, 1087–1156.

13 M. Hildebrandt, "Privacy and Identity", in E. Claes, A. Duff and S. Gutwirth (eds.), *Privacy and the Criminal Law* (Antwerpen/Oxford: Intersentia, 2006) 43–58. A relational conception of human identity has been philosophically argued by: P. Ricœur, *Oneself as Another* (Chicago: The University of Chicago Press, 1992); G.H. Mead, *Mind, Self & Society. From the Standpoint of a Social Behaviorist* (Chicago: The University of Chicago Press, 1959/1934); J. De Mul, "Digitally Mediated (Dis)embodiment. Plessner's Concept of Excentric Positionality Explained for Cyborgs", *Information, Communication & Society* 2003, *6* (2), 247–266.

14 About privacy in the information age in relation to the constitutional democratic State: S. Gutwirth, *Privacy and the Information Age* (Translated by Raf Casert) (Lanham Boulder New York Oxford: Rowman & Littlefield, 2002). About the need for an adequate mix of le-

In a relational conception of identity, personhood, and privacy (understood as arising from an assessment of the other's expectations regarding oneself) mutual profiling is crucial. As mentioned, profiling is a matter of pattern recognition upon which an organism depends to achieve its goals in a particular environment. Most such profiling takes place subconsciously, as it were 'under the skin'. One's identity is continuously rebuilt in the process of profiling the expectations of others, whether we choose to meet these expectations or reject them. The confrontation with others allows us to anticipate their actions and thus allows us to tune our own actions to the patterns of interactions that constitute our shared world. An important distinction must be made between the mutual profiling activities of those that share an *Umwelt* and those of people that share a *Welt* without sharing an *Umwelt*. We should take into account that the move from mutual profiling in a face–to–face life–world, to profiling in an extended environment changes the scope of the mutuality. The mutual attunement amongst people that may never meet but nevertheless share a jurisdiction depends on an intermediate level of shared habits and beliefs. In that case mutual individual profiling is partly replaced by explicit learning processes in which the patterns are not *recognised* as a result of mutual interaction but rather *acquired* as a result of formal learning techniques (reading, writing). The emergence of large–scale societies that cannot depend on face–to–face profiling thus coincides with the appearance of written text, often implying the rise of a class of scribes who have privileged access to the sources of the tradition that constitutes the society.[15] This creates unequal access to knowledge between the literate and the illiterate, often amounting to an effective monopoly that is carefully protected by the literate class. This class may be co–opted by those in power, but they may also form a buffer zone between those in power who make use of the latter's knowledge, and those that are being ruled. A viable democracy depends on the extent to which citizens have access to the knowledge that informs the decision–making processes of those in power. This is why reading and writing are preconditional for effective citizenship in modern democracies. The process of automated profiling described above seems to introduce new inequalities of access to knowledge. Those in power are those that can afford to have others profiled, using knowledge made available by the 'new literates' of the information society: those that produce the software to mine the ever increasing mass of data, discriminating noise from information in the process of constructing new knowledge. The central questions seem to be, "Who is profiling whom?", and "How can those that are being profiled anticipate what profilers expect from them, based on the patterns their machines have detected?"

---

gal opacity tools (to protect privacy) and transparency tools (to promote fairness and due process): P. De Hert and S. Gutwirth, "Privacy, Data Protection and Law Enforcement. Opacity of the Individual and Transparency of Power", in E. Claes, A. Duff and S. Gutwirth (eds.), *Privacy and the Criminal Law* (Antwerpen/Oxford: Intersentia, 2006).

15 *Cf.* H.P. Glenn, *Legal Traditions of the World* (Oxford: Oxford University Press, 2004 2nd ed.), *e.g.* 7–13, 61–65, 127–129.

Lack of such anticipation, due to the fact that we are entirely unaware of the way we are being profiled, amounts to a major 'constraint on the construction of one's own identity'. Being profiled without having the legal or technological means to assess how those that can afford profiling will interpret our behaviour may lead us into a Kafkaesque situation.[16] This is the case when some of the risks or accusations that we confront have been attributed on the basis of knowledge which we do not have, or when benefits that we receive are beyond our control insofar as we do not know on what grounds they are provided. That others know facts about us which we do not know about ourselves can thus be a violation of our privacy caused by unequal access to knowledge and information. This inequality will have other consequences beyond privacy. Central tenets of constitutional democracy, like fairness and due process, may be at stake.[17] This not only concerns criminal procedure, but also private law in which consent plays a crucial role. If I am not aware of the type of knowledge that can be inferred from the way I surf on the internet (profiling of web users), or from my keystroke behaviour (behavioural biometric profiling), I may allow access to such data without overseeing the consequences, I may even trade access to seemingly trivial data without having a clue as to the impact this may have – in the end – on everyday risks and opportunities. As long as we cannot assess the knowledge which may be built from the data we leak, the exchange of data for whatever advantage is not fair. Due process is at stake whenever we are confronted with the negative consequences of decisions taken on the basis of automated profiling: whenever credit is refused, insurance is refused, or a premium raised; whenever a sale is cancelled or entry forbidden due to a profile that is applied to us without any chance effectively to check and understand the construction of the profile.[18] Even if Article 15 of the Data Protection Directive of the European Community declares that we have a right not to be subject to automated decisions, we may (1) not be aware of such decisions or not be aware that they were taken automatically, or it may be (2) that minimal human intervention renders the provision inapplicable without taking away the substance of automatic decision–making. In the case where Article 15 does apply and we are aware of this we may (3) not have the time or energy to exercise this right to any significant extent, thus turning it into a symbolic piece of legislation that legitimises a practice in need for more effective means for contestation.[19]

---

16 D.J. Solove, *The Digital Person. Technology and Privacy in the Information Age* (New York: New York University Press, 2004).

17 J. Bohn, V. Coroama *et al.*, "Social, Economic, and Ethical Implications of Ambient Intelligence and Ubiquitous Computing", in W. Weber, J. Rabaey and E. Aarts (eds.), *Ambient Intelligence* (Berlin: Springer, 2005) at www.vs.inf.ethz.ch/publ/papers/socialambient.pdf (last visited 23 August 2006).

18 D.J. Steinbock, "Data Matching, Data Mining and Due Process", *Georgia Law Review* 2005, *40* (1), 27.

19 L. Bygrave, "Minding the Machine. Art. 15 and the EC Data Protection Directive and Automated Profiling", *Computer Law & Security Report* 2001, *17*, 17–24.

3 Technological Normativity

3.1 Technology is neither Bad, nor Good, but never Neutral

In the preceding discussion of the 'Internet of Things' I have sketched the potential emergence of a specific technological infrastructure. For a lawyer this may be a bridge too far. I took the risk of losing my audience. However, I cannot move into the issue I want to discuss without a serious introduction to an actual technological development. The reason is that I want to avoid a general discussion about Technology, with general conclusions about the impact of technology on human society. Technological optimists and pessimists alike tend to speak about Technology without discerning the actual implications of specific technological arrangements.[20] Such generalisation also allows lawyers to base their views about technological normativity on general propositions that usually boil down to a comfortable combination of technological determinism and legal voluntarism, however untenable in theory and unfruitful in practice. Instead we hold that technology in itself is neither good nor bad, but it is never neutral (the non–neutrality thesis).[21] This means that before we can make moral assessments of a specific technology – let alone Technology in general – we should investigate the normative implications of such a technology. In fact the sketch provided in the preceding section was a first attempt in such an investigation. Claiming that technology is never neutral also implies that the fact that technology in itself has no moral value does not depend on the fact that only abuse of a technology can be qualified as bad. The non–neutrality thesis claims that every technology invites certain behaviours and inhibits others, or even enforces certain behaviours while prohibiting others. This is what we would like to call the normative impact of a technology (not of Technology in general). Normativity thus does not presume deliberation or intention on the part of a technology, nor even on the part of its designers. To clarify this point I will briefly refer to the work of Bruno Latour, Don Ihde, and the way Peter–Paul Verbeek has synthesised their insights.

3.2 Non–Human Actors and Multi–Stable Technologies

To understand the normative impact of a technology we need to understand what things do or how things act. Common sense tells us that things do not act. They can be acted upon, but the initiative will always be human. Things have no will, no intention, and no capacity for reflection. Therefore it would not make sense to speak of things that act. In his quest to disengage from our 'traditional' (modern-

20 P.–P. Verbeek, *What Things do. Philosophical Reflections on Technology, Agency and Design* (Pennsylvania State University Press, 2005).

21 M. Kranzberg, "Technology and History: 'Kranzberg's Laws'", *Technology and Culture* 1986, *27,* 544–560.

ist) common sense categorisations like subject and object, Bruno Latour proposes to think in terms of human and non–human actors.[22] This does not imply that non–humans act as subjects, that is, as agents with explicit intentions or a sense of self. Nor does is imply that humans have become objects which have no say in the matter. It does imply a symmetrical view on the relations between things and people: things are not only acted upon, they also act and these actions may impact humans. The interactions between humans and non–humans can take shape in different ways, depending on both the particular technology and the particular way in which humans associate with it. This can be termed a 'pluralist perspective' on technology. In this view it is not the case that material is merely passive, awaiting human intervention, for this would amount to a type of technological instrumentalism that considers technology to be a neutral tool. Such technological instrumentalism would locate the legal implications of new technologies in their possible abuse, without regard for their normative implications because these are non–existent according to an instrumentalist view of technology. In a pluralist perspective it is also not the case that material entirely controls human interaction, leaving no room for alternative use or design, for this would amount to a type of technological substantivism that considers technology to be determinate for human behaviour. Such technological substantivism would locate legal implications of new technologies in the unavoidable changes they evoke in order to adapt the legal system to the new situation.

A pluralist view of technologies considers both humans and non–humans as actors, capable of actions that shape our common world. The advantage of this understanding of action is that it takes the actions of technological devices seriously, without taking them for granted. If your 'Ambient Intelligent Environment' caters to your preferences before you become aware of them, this will invite or even re–enforce certain behaviours, like drinking coffee that is prepared automatically at a certain hour or going to sleep early during week days (because the central heating system has lowered the temperature). Other behaviours may be inhibited or even ruled out, because the fridge may refuse a person another beer if the caloric intake exceeds a certain point. However, the impact of 'Ambient Intelligence' cannot be taken for granted. For instance, it may be the case that the environment raises the level of comfort and ease to an extent that causes health problems due to a lack of physical movement; but – depending on design and user interactions – the environment could also raise the level of healthy movements by making certain products or services conditional upon such movements. This can depend on the design of the software, but it can also depend on the interaction between user and AmI environment. In terms of Latour, engineers can 'delegate' certain programs of action into a technology due to the fact that a technology embodies a 'script' that imposes certain behaviours on the user.[23] This script is not just the set of directions for use, it is rather the 'built–in' set of 'prescriptions' that impose themselves on

---

[22] B. Latour, *Nous n'avons jamais été modernes. Essai d'antropologie symmétrique* (Paris: La Découverte, 1991).

[23] B. Latour, *La Clef de Berlin et autres leçons d'un amateur de sciences* (Paris: La Découverte 1993).

the user: inviting one choice of action rather than another, inhibiting one choice of action in favour of another. Speed bumps, a different lay–out of the pavement, the planting of trees at the cross–roads which takes away the view of the other road, all encourage specific alternatives of action and discourages others. This can be compared to a road sign that prohibits speeding, providing another type of encouragement to slow down based on the legal competence to regulate urban traffic. However, in both cases (technological and legal inhibition of speeding) the alternative action remains open (though this may cause damage to the car, or give rise to punishment).

The actions of a technology cannot be taken for granted. Whatever 'script' is built into a device by its designer, the interactions between users and the technology most often produce many unforeseen patterns of use, revealing other 'scripts' that are also – unintentionally – built into the material. We call these 'side effects', but such a term expresses a naïve focus on the human intention of technology designers and diverts the attention from the different ways in which a specific technological design can entangle itself with human interaction. This is what the post–phenomenological philosopher of technology Don Ihde calls the "multi–stability of technologies".[24] Even though the telephone was invented and intended for the exchange of information, the script that unrolled was more focused on communication *per se*, and this holds good for both the fixed and the mobile telephone, and even for the Internet. The point is that human intention does not define the normative impact of a technology, because this will depend on the possible courses of actions that are disclosed by a new technology and the actual ways in which users attach themselves with the technology.

3.3 Understanding Technological Normativity

Building on the non–neutrality thesis, the concept of non–human actors and the multi–stability of technologies, technological normativity can now be defined as the way in which specific technologies disclose certain courses of action and foreclose others, thus inviting or enforcing certain courses of action and/or inhibiting or ruling out certain courses of action. Drawing on Searle's distinction between regulative and constitutive rules[25], we could say that technologies which invite or inhibit behaviour that is also possible without such technologies are regulative of the behaviour, while technologies which make a behaviour possible that is not (or not anymore) possible without these technologies are constitutive of the behaviour. An example of a technology that inhibits behaviour is a red light on the dashboard of a car whenever the driver does not fasten his seatbelt. In this case the technology is regulative: one can easily drive around without the seatbelt. But if a connection is made to the start–motor such that the car will not start if the seatbelt

---

24 D. Ihde, *Technology and the Lifeworld. From Garden to Earth* (Bloomington and Indianapolis: Indiana University Press 1993).

25 J.R. Searle, *Speech Acts, An Essay in the Philosophy of Language* (Cambridge, 1969).

is not fastened, the technology has become constitutive for the action of fastening one's seat belt.[26] This is an example of 'Ambient Intelligence': the car 'knows' that your seatbelt is not fastened and it adapts your environment autonomically by making it impossible to start the car. A legal rule that prohibits driving without a seatbelt will always be regulative. Thus the technology achieves something a legal rule in this particular case could not have achieved: it has made driving without the use of the seatbelt impossible.[27]

A more generic articulation of technological normativity would be 'the way specific technologies constrain human and non–human interaction'. It may be important at this point to emphasise that in our opinion these constraints comply with the non–neutrality thesis. The constraints are norms, which explains why technology is never neutral; it always has an impact on our choices of action. But such normativity also complies with the proposition that technology is neither good nor bad, because the moral evaluation of these norms cannot be detached from the context in which the technology functions. For instance, the normative impact of AmI may be that privacy as we understand it today will simply disappear because the machines that record our behaviours can store them much longer than human memory could do, and because these machines can correlate whatever they store with other data so as to arrive at conclusions not within the reach of the individual human mind.[28] Whether this is good or bad will depend on our understanding of privacy and on the emergence of newer forms of privacy. If the normativity of AmI consists in the fact that we are being watched by machines instead of humans, we may consider this to be a good thing: intimate observation by machines can take place without breaking doors or windows; and as long as humans have no access to intimate knowledge of identifiable persons – unless a legitimate suspicion arises – we may not care about the information the machines collect. Providing people with pseudonym identification may be a new type of privacy, adequately attuned to the normative implications of profiling technologies. The normativity of AmI may also consist in the fact that profiles are applied to individual persons, resulting in a benefit or exclusion from certain services (insurance, admission to a university college, recruitment, and so on), thus disclosing or foreclosing certain courses of action. Depending on the accuracy of those profiles and the justification for any resultant exclusion, we might reject such technological normativity as morally wrong if the profiles were unreliable or abused. However, we could also claim that the sheer fact that a technological infrastructure allows such refined discrimination is in itself morally wrong, because it assesses people on the basis of previous behaviour patterns, thus locking people into their past to an extent previously unthinkable.

---

[26] B. Latour (1993), *l.c.* A similar technology is already in use to prevent drunk driving, *cf.* M.L. Wald, "A New Strategy to Discourage Driving Drunk", *NYT*, 20 November 2006.

[27] Compare the example of the constitutive legal norm that has made a marriage without registration at the civil registry impossible, discussed in section 4.1 below.

[28] B.J. Koops and R. Leenes, "'Code' and the Slow Erosion of Privacy", *Michigan Telecommunications and Technology Law Review* 2005, *12* (1), 115–189.

To evaluate the moral impact of a technology we need to assess its normative impact: what does the technology do to alternative choices of action? Depending on such prospective assessment we can then evaluate the moral implications, deciding whether, and under which conditions these normative implications are good or bad.

4 A Generic Theory of Legal and Technological Normativity?

4.1 Code as Law or Law as Code

In his *Code and Other Laws of Cyberspace*, Lawrence Lessig suggests that we should acknowledge the constitutive and regulative impact of what he calls 'code' on cyberspace.[29] Code is the software and hardware that makes cyberspace what it is; it is what he calls the 'architecture' or the constitution of the Internet. He stresses the fact that this architecture has a specific design which is constitutive for the fact that we can move around in a new space (surfing, e–mail exchange, and such like) and it also regulates how we can behave (anonymously, identifiably, using specific software with specific possibilities, and so on). Other designs would have been possible, constituting a potentially very different, for instance, less public, Internet. From the fact that the designers of the Internet's code had a choice of whether and how to organise cyberspace, Lessig concludes that in cyberspace 'code is law'. It seems that because code and law produce comparable normative impacts he conflates the two. There are good arguments to stress the similarities of computer code and law. They both regulate behaviour whenever they constrain human interaction, and they are both constitutive for human interaction to the extent that they make specific actions possible, which would not be possible otherwise. Before arguing the difference between legal and technological regulation, we will first pay attention to the way they compare.

If I want to get married and I violate one of the legal rules which stipulate what counts as a valid marriage (for instance, registration at the civil registry), then I will simply not be married. Compliance with the rule is preconditional for the legal consequence of marriage. In legal theory such a rule can be called 'constitutive', again following Searle's distinction.[30] If I want to drive a car on the motorway and violate one of the rules which stipulate how to drive, then I may be subject to some punishment. But I can violate traffic rules and still drive a car: in legal theory such a rule is regulative. Some legal scholars seem to suggest that the difference between legal and technological impact is that legal norms provide a person with a choice to obey or disobey, while technological restrictions force a

---

[29] L. Lessig, *l.c.*, 6–7.

[30] M. Mittag, "A Legal Theoretical Approach to Criminal Procedure Law: The Structure of Rules in the German Code of Criminal Procedure", *German Law Journal*, 2006, 7, 637–646.

person to comply with a rule.[31] This is simply not correct. Both law and technology generate constitutive and regulative types of normativity. As the example of a smart car discussed above demonstrates, one can design a technology that invites a driver to fasten her seatbelt or one can design a technology that forces the driver to fasten her seatbelt (unless she decides to walk). The difference is that in this particular case the law does not have such a choice: it can only regulate this behaviour.[32] One of the reasons why autonomic profiling and autonomic adaptation of the environment may be considered controversial is that in certain circumstances it can achieve a measure of compliance not within the reach of the law. This could mean that its normative impact reaches beyond the limits of the law.

This by itself is a good reason not to conflate code with law. However, if we want to evaluate whether or to what extent technological enforcement of legal norms is good or bad, we will need a more precise understanding of the way modern law regulates society in comparison to emerging technologies. In the next subsection we will describe the way pre–modern laws have developed into the autonomous legal systems characteristic of modern law.

4.2 Technological Embodiment of Modern Law

Wesel made a point when he wrote, "What in fact is law? Answering this question is about as simple as nailing a pudding to the wall."[33] Yet to discuss the limits of the law in relation to technology, we need to nail down some points.

It is not surprising that legal theory developed a hermeneutical conception of law. Hermeneutics originated from the study of authoritative texts and modern law is embodied in text. Thus legal hermeneutics builds on the practice and theory of textual interpretation, starting from the premise that a text does not speak for itself: it cannot dictate its meaning since this depends on its implicit reference to other texts and on the context in which the text is read, or used. To understand the legal normativity of modern law we need to assess the impact of the fact that it is embodied in a system or network of interrelated texts. Actually the technological embodiment of modern law is the written text. With 'modern' law we mean the legal traditions which emerged in Western societies after the Middle Ages, with the rise of 'modernity' that eventually brought about the advance of unified systems of legal norms. One of the paradigmatic changes that occurred in this period

---

31 R. Brownsword, "Code, Control, and Choice: Why East is East and West is West", *Legal Studies* 2005, *25*(1), 1–22; L. Tien, "Architectural Regulation and the Evolution of Social Norms", *International Journal of Communications Law & Policy* 2004, *9*, 1-13.

32 This difference could be explained by differentiating between institutional facts and brute facts, reiterating the traditional modernist divide between a given causally determined material world (brute facts) and a constructed intentional and free mental world (institutional facts). *Cf.* J.R. Searle, *The Construction of Social Reality* (New York: The Free Press, 1995).

33 U. Wesel, *Frühformen des Rechts in vorstaatlichen Gesellschaften* (Frankfurt am Main: Suhrkamp 1985) 52: "Was ist eigentlich Recht? Eine Antwort ist ähnlich einfach wie der bekannte Versuch, einen Pudding an die Wand zu nageln." (author's translation).

of transition was the shift from local, oral traditions to trans–local written traditions.[34] To assess the fundamental changes which occurred with this shift we will follow Paul Ricœur's comparison of two types of language use ('discourse'): the use of oral language ('*parole vive*') and the use of written text ('*écriture*'). The first difference between the use of oral and language and written text concerns the aspects of time and space. Both spoken and written language unfold in time and space, they are both volatile and fleeting, having a history marked with a beginning and an end. However, written text seems to suspend this volatility by fixing the text in material signs (letters), which can be understood as the introduction of a technology.[35] The use of language is solidified, taking a more durable shape that creates a new dimension to the issuance of text, a dimension that no longer depends on physical closeness of the subject that 'speaks'. This shift is related to the second difference: while speaking is always under the custody of the speaker, who will accompany her words with non–verbal gestures to ensure correct interpretation, written text is liberated from the custody of the author. Though the text is not separated from the author, the relation between author and utterance is "stretched and complicated".[36] In the end, the meaning of the text will begin a life of its own and "escape the author's horizon".[37] The textual embodiment creates a gap between the author and the meaning of his text, extending the scope of the text because it can no longer be entirely determined by the author's intentions. This relates to the first difference: the text survives its author because he cannot supervise its interpretation. This allows continuous calibration of the meaning in new contexts. The third difference concerns the way spoken and written language refer to the world outside the text. Spoken text concerns ostentative reference and presumes a shared *Umwelt*. Written text creates a distance between writer and reader which extends the scope of reference to a world that is now basically 'opened' by the text, creating a middle ground between people who may never meet.[38] In a way this text – this technology – is constitutive for the world it discloses. The fourth difference concerns the addressee of the utterance. In the case of speaking, the other is present, being one (or more) particular person(s). Writing cannot limit itself to one or more specific persons; even if it were explicitly directed to specific individuals it cannot predict who will read it at some point in time. Written text unavoidably creates an unlimited public. Summarising the shift from oral to written discourse initiates a paradigmatic move (1) towards material fixation of mean-

---

34 H.P. Glenn, *l.c.*, especially chapters 3 (on the oral, chthonic legal traditions) and 5 (on the civil law tradition), and H.P. Glenn, *On Common Laws* (Oxford, Oxford University Press, 2005) in which he describes the emergence of trans–local common laws.

35 See on the difference between a technology (defined as having a material component) and a technique (defined as a style, mode, habit of doing things or a calculative or rational method) D. Ihde, *The Philosophy of Technology. An Introduction* (New York, Paragon House, 1993) 47–48. About the shift from the use of written language to ICT see P. Lévy, *Les technologies de l'intelligence. L'avenir de la pensée à l'ère informatique* (Paris: La Découverte, 1990).

36 P. Ricœur, *Du texte a l'action. Essais d'herméneutique II* (Paris, Éditions du Seuil, 1986) 188.

37 *Ibid.*, 187.

38 *Ibid.*, 189.

ing, (2) liberating the meaning of the text from the intentions of the author, (3) creating a shared world beyond the immediate environment, and (4) creating a fundamentally unlimited public, beyond face–to–face communities.

This analysis can be extended to the introduction of written law.[39] Oral legal traditions have developed sophisticated mnemonic techniques to (re)establish the law. The shift from such non–material techniques to the material technology of the written legal text again implies four types of differences. Firstly, written law can guide interactions beyond the local context, providing the possibility to establish jurisdiction for communities of people who may never meet in person. Secondly, this results in a situation in which the addressees of legal norms are not necessarily the same as the addressors, as was the case in a face–to–face community of peers.[40] That is, modern law does not depend on the shared *Umwelt* but can be said to create a *Welt* by means of legal texts which actually constrain the actions of humans who have never met, allowing them to attune their actions to the same written standards. Thirdly, this leads to conflicts of interpretation since a text cannot interpret itself and the author cannot control the way readers use his text. The failed attempts to restrict interpretation to 'plain meaning' or 'the framer's intention' demonstrate how the technological embodiment of modern law in written text eventually liberates the meaning of the law from the intentions of the historical legislator. This, however, does not mean that anything goes. To create legal certainty both the ruler and those who are ruled need instruments to stabilise the meaning of legal texts in order to stabilise the legitimate expectations which guide the interactions of those who share jurisdiction. This need is met by the development of legal doctrine. Legal doctrine systematises and unifies modern law, ensuring a certain measure of predictability – objectifying the construction of a system of interrelated legal norms, resembling Kelsen's legal system. In the end, the complexity of such legal systems demands highly specialised legal professionals to maintain their coherence. It becomes virtually impossible for governments to rule *by* law, because the lawyers are the only ones who can effectively keep the whole body of law together. This initiates the rule *of* law, meaning that law reaches a certain degree of autonomy. Fourthly, the extension of the scope of the law beyond the local context implies that the scope of the legal community is in principle unlimited: the reach of a written legal norm is no longer restricted to those who share an *Umwelt*.

---

39 As elaborated more extensively in M. Hildebrandt, *Straf(begrip) en procesbeginsel. Een onderzoek naar de betekenis van straf en strafbegrip en naar de waarde van het procesbeginsel* (Deventer/Rotterdam: Kluwer/Sanders Instituut, 2002), section 1.4.

40 On the shift from a society of peers to one of subjects to one of citizens: M. Hildebrandt, "Trial and 'Fair Trial': From Peer to Subject to Citizen", in A. Duff, L. Farmer, S. Marshall and V. Tadros (eds.), *The Trial on Trial. Judgment and Calling to Account*, Vol. 2 (Oxford and Portland, Oregon: Hart, 2006) 15–37.

5 Towards a Generic Theory of Legal and Technological Norms

Based on the previous sections, a generic definition of normativity would be 'the way humans or non–humans constrain human and non–human interaction'. Interaction between non–humans can be normative if it constrains the actions of, for instance, machines that will eventually constrain the actions of a human person. As we have seen, constraints can be constitutive or regulative of action, both in the case of legal and in the case of technological constraints. A Cartesian mind would probably claim that in the case of technology, we should understand the constitutive as causal, while in the case of law the legal consequence is 'all in the mind'. This would imply that while technology provides causes for action, law provides reasons for action, meaning that technology can thus enforce action in ways the law cannot hope to achieve. Such a division of tasks may suggest the superiority of law in allowing people a choice to obey or disobey, leaving a sense of freedom incompatible with technological normativity.

However, this presumes a rather strict division of tasks between (mental) reasons and (material) causes. It reminds one of the distinction between a subject capable of intentional action and an object that is passive and mainly acted upon. As discussed above, this distinction is not fertile when it comes to increasing our understanding of the implications of non–human action.[41] If I decide to fasten my seatbelt in a car that will not start unless I am fastened in my seat, must we presume that I would not have fastened it in a less proactive car? Is it a fact that my behaviour is caused instead of willed? Perhaps technologies can force me to make a choice I should have made anyway and on this basis one could make a case for technological enforcement of mandatory law. Even if we believe that doing things for the right reason is at least as important as doing them at all, only Kantian purists would prefer deliberate violation of the norm to automatic compliance. Perhaps the problem with the Kantian position is that most of our actions are performed automatically anyway, being a matter of habit rather than conscious reflection. One could even claim they are *caused* by social rather than material pressure, seldom the result of deliberate intention or explicit reasoning. In that case we are fooling ourselves with the illusion that legal normativity provides a type of freedom that technological normativity would annihilate. Still, the normative impact of code should not be mistaken for legal consequence.

Instead of seeking the difference between legal and technological normativity in the traditional opposition of causes and reasons, we should accept the fact that – like legal norms – technological norms do constrain us in regulative and constitutive ways, whereby the capacity of technologies to enforce compliance (ruling out

---

41 In fact the term 'cause' is related to 'case' and often used to indicate motivation or contestation: a 'cause célèbre', a 'cause' of action. The famous dispute on the meaning of the Latin *ius in causa positam* indicates that even the Latin roots of the term refer not only to both ground and cause but also to 'case': something that is contested. See B. Latour, "From Realpolitik to Dingpolitik – or How to Make Things Public", in B. Latour and P. Weibel (eds.), *Making Things Public – Atmospheres of Democracy* (Cambridge, Mass.: The MIT Press, 2005).

non–compliance and thus becoming constitutive for a certain type of behaviour) extends beyond what legal norms can accomplish. The reason for this difference may well be located in the fact that modern law has entangled itself with a specific technology – written text – which has a limited capacity to constrain human interaction. Referring to the shift from an oral to a written tradition, described in the previous section, one could say that constitutive legal norms in fact depend on the creation of a world by means of a series of interrelated legal texts (such as legislation, judgments, doctrine). The materialisation of legal norms in written text has disclosed a world beyond the local context, allowing ever larger communities of people and things to live together in a shared jurisdiction. However, for the law to survive a world in which the 'Internet of Things' constitutes our environment, we may need to find new technologies to embody legal norms.[42]

6 The End of Law?

6.1 Two Types of Limits

As stated in the beginning of this chapter we may reach the end of law in two distinct ways. Firstly, if we categorically refuse to use new technologies to support or enforce legal norms this could mean the end of the effectiveness of law to an extent that such 'law' no longer counts as law. Secondly, if we do choose to use new technologies to support or enforce legal norms this can be done in different ways, some of which may still signify the end of law.

6.2 The 'Internet of Things' and the End of Law

The reason for taking so much space to explain the possible emergence of an 'Internet of Things' is that this may change the way we perceive the world, the way we are present in the world, and the way we live together with other humans and non–humans. This will most certainly affect the legal constitution of our societies. We have described how our offline world may be put online, connecting everything everywhere by means of ubiquitous computing, and how profiling technologies can construct knowledge out of the proliferating data. This allows new mechanisms for inclusion and exclusion to take over, explaining how these developments impact on some of the central tenets of constitutional democracy, such as privacy, equality, fairness, and due process.

---

[42] To assess the potential implications of a shift from written language use to ICT we may draw on P. Lévy, *l.c.*, though he discusses computer simulation rather than profiling and his analysis does not regard the law. See S. Gutwirth, *Waarheidsaanspraken in recht en wetenschap* (Brussels: VUBPRESS, 1993) 498–508.

Since the beginnings of modernity, law has increased its dependence on the written word. Modern law as text, is, if anything, dependent on the bureaucratic State for its enactment and implementation. To follow a text takes time, one reads from beginning to end, taking into account both the semantic reference between text and world and the syntactic connections between different textual elements. The study of written law has thus become a long–term affair, depending on the accumulation of systematic knowledge derived from a proliferation of interconnected texts. The age of ubiquitous computing in a tagged environment that is dynamically interconnected via online databases commits us to a different literacy. Profiling – the technology on which 'Ambient Intelligence' feeds – is based on the detection of relevant and significant patterns or correlations. Autonomic profiling is a dynamic real–time process that includes customised decision–making; continuously adjusting the knowledge the environment has of its inhabitants to the latest input. Whoever tries to 'read' her profilers to assess what she is in for, will need more than access to the existing databases which have collected her data. Reading the way the environment may read us – a precondition for privacy, equality, fairness and due process – will depend on a new type of transparency which cannot be secured by legal protection in the form of written or unwritten text. We may have a right to know which data are being collected, for what purpose, how long they are stored, how they are being processed, and to whom they are being sold. But if we do not have the technological means actually to look into these databases, these rights are moral rather than legal. In fact, quite apart from the need to know about the storage of personal data, citizens will have to find ways to detect which knowledge can be constructed out of these data, because this knowledge (rather than mere data) will impact on their life. We must conclude that the technology which has served law for the last 500 years – written text – will have to be complemented with new technologies in order to achieve the objective of the law: adequate anticipation of the grounds on which we are judged, included, or excluded. To reach this point, transparency enhancing technologies will have to be developed that move beyond history management of one's personal data to, for instance, forms of counter–profiling.

6.3 Technologically Embodied Law

In law and legal theory we can detect three different types of conceptions of law.[43] The first are instrumentalist conceptions, in which law is a tool of government, just like other tools which are designed and used to implement government policies. Such conceptions correspond to the rule *by* law, instead of rule *of* law. Law is regarded as a neutral instrument to achieve certain goals. In a way these conceptions of law coincide with instrumentalist conceptions of technology, which view

---

43 This subsection builds on R. Foqué and A.C. 't Hart, *Instrumentaliteit en rechtsbescherming* (Arnhem/Antwerpen: Gouda Quint Kluwer Rechtswetenschappen, 1990), and on Verbeek, *l.c.*

technology as a neutral tool that is only judged bad if it is used for a purpose that is considered bad. In this view the function of criminal law is to prevent and repress crime, by whichever means best suited to the objective. An instrumentalist position, often based on a utilitarian ethic, also implies that it does not matter which instrument one chooses to achieve one's goal. Legal and technological instruments are exchangeable, so the only criterion is relative effectiveness and/or efficiency. Secondly, we have critical conceptions of law, in which law is a tool to protect citizens against the government. The law is seen as separated from the administrative functions of the government which are presumed as given. Government authority is considered as something that does not depend on the law, but needs to be checked by the law, which is thought to have an intrinsic value. In this view the function of criminal law is not to fight crime but to police the police. One could compare these conceptions with substantivist conceptions of technology insofar as they attribute an intrinsic value to Technology – whether good or bad. Their adherents often believe that Technology follows its own autonomous development. In their view the good or evil of Technology does not depend on the use to which it is put, but is part and parcel of its internal logic. Thirdly, we have relational conceptions of law, in which law is seen from the perspective of a constitutional democracy. From this perspective an effective and legitimate law is always both instrumental and protective, both constitutive and regulative for government authority, creating competences while at the same time limiting them. A denial of the intrinsic value of the law would make law exchangeable with any other tool of administration, but a denial of the instrumental function of the law would turn it into a lame instrument of protection. Instead of separating factual administration from legal protection, a relational conception of law aims to conceive of the law as the specific means to constitute the competence to govern in a way that is both legitimate and effective. One could compare this conception with the pluralist conception of technology in as much as this denies the neutrality of technology but does not consider Technology either bad or good. As discussed above, such a conception acknowledges the normative implications of technology and its multi–stability, which means that the moral evaluation does not only depend on its abuse (as would be the case in an instrumentalist conception), but also on its design and on the way humans and non–humans attach to it and interact with it.

Lawyers or technologists who adhere to an instrumentalist conception of law or technology should have no problem with a technologically embodied law, if it allows government authority to enforce its regulations in a more effective way. Since neither law nor technology has an intrinsic value the point can only be to make a rational choice as to which instrument better enhances compliance and/or reduces the cost of control. The fact that specific technologies may achieve compliance to an extent which cannot be reached by existing legal means would easily provide good reason to choose such technological means to implement the relevant legal norms. In fact, it may even be preferable to choose technological instruments instead of legal regulation. Within an instrumentalist conception we have no arguments to prefer law or a specific technological embodiment of law, except if one is more effective and/or efficient than the other.

Lawyers or technologists who adhere to a critical conception of law, or to a substantive conception of technology, will have a very different attitude to technologically embodied law. Those who believe that law is only an instrument of protection against factual operations of those in power will be suspicious of any government use of technologies to enforce government policies, because they will probably see the technological tools as extensions of a governmental exercise of power. By embedding legal norms in technological devices the government may try to sidestep the checks and balances supposedly inherent in legal regulation. Those who believe that Technology is inherently good or bad will endorse or reject technologically embodied law, depending on their position as techno–optimists or techno–pessimists. If they believe that Technology is – in the end – always for the better of humankind, they will think that technological embodiment of legal norms will always result in better compliance and a better world. If they believe that Technology leads to the end of civilisation, they will think that any technological embodiment of legal norms will certainly be the end of law, annulling the intrinsic protective values of the law in the process of enforcing compliance. One should not be surprised to find affinity for pessimistic Technology substantivism with those who hold a critical conception of law, though it could be that many techno–pessimists have no faith whatsoever in the capacity of the law to counter the internal logic of Technology.

Lawyers who adhere to a relational conception of law, or to a pluralist conception of technology, will again have a different attitude to technologically embodied law. Since law in a relational conception of law is both instrumental and protective, both constitutive and regulative of social order, law is not a neutral instrument which can be replaced by any other effective instrument. However, law cannot be presumed to be protective. It will have to be technologically embodied and interpreted in ways that safeguard both its effectiveness and its protection. *This also means that in specific circumstances law will need to be embodied into adequate technologies other than writing to be both effective and protective.* One cannot determine in abstract terms whether this is the case, as this will depend on the particular legal norms and the context in which they are to be effective. Also, from the perspective of constitutional democracy, the technological embodiment of legal norms cannot be taken for granted in the sense that such embodiment is a good thing in itself. This will always depend on the specific way in which legal norms are embodied. As soon as technologies are used to enforce legal norms they should also provide the means to contest the validity of the norm and to contest allegations of a breach of the norm. From this standpoint autonomic application of sanctions will always be problematic and should at the very least be complemented by the means to contest these sanctions. Those who adhere to a pluralist conception of technology acknowledge the fact that technologies are multi–stable, meaning that depending on their design and the way they are integrated into the social fabric their normative impact will differ. The non–neutrality thesis implies a normative impact, which can be used to stimulate compliance with legal norms. Again this does not mean that any technology can be used to serve the implementation of legal norms. This will always depend on the congruence of the values inherent in the legal norms to be applied with the normativity of the specific technology. In the case of anticipated adverse effects of a particular technology, or technological infrastructure, technologically embodied law may be the only way to counter these effects.

7 Conclusion

Let us end this chapter with a remarkable conclusion: modern law has always been a technologically embodied law. The mnemonic devices of the oral traditions have been replaced by the technologies of the script. Paul Ricœur has convincingly demonstrated the far–reaching implications of the move from spoken to written language for human communication and his analysis has inspired a phenomenology of the differences between written and unwritten law. We are now moving into a new age, creating new classes of scribes, demanding a new literacy among ordinary citizens. To abstain from technological embodiment of legal norms in the emerging technologies that will constitute and regulate our world, would mean the end of the rule of law, paving the way for an instrumentalist rule by means of legal and technological instruments. Lawyers need to develop urgently a hermeneutic of profiling technologies, supplementing their understanding of written text. Only if such a hermeneutic is in place can we prevent a type of technologically embodiment of legal norms that in fact eradicates the sensitive *mélange* of instrumental and protective aspects that is crucial for the rule of law.

Chapter 24 – Darknets and the Future of Freedom of Expression in the Information Society

Hans Graux[1]

1 Introduction

There is no denying the profound impact the advent of the information society has had and continues to have on the way we exchange and perceive information. Each new connection to the internet adds a new participant to the medium, who is not only capable of freely receiving information, but also to disseminate it in a manner which is as amateurish or as professional as the individual's capabilities and desires permit.

In effect, the internet has given all of us the power to broadcast information in a manner and on a scale that has never before been witnessed, and our society is confronted with the consequences of this evolution on a daily basis. We have the capability to publish any information we see fit on the worldwide web without any prior control, to make free phone calls, to send files of any kind to destinations known or unknown across the globe, or to impose hundreds of thousands of e–mails per day on willing or unwilling recipients, asking for their money, their passwords, or simply their attention.

While each country is free in principle to attempt to create its own set of rules to apply to any or all of the aforementioned phenomena, to a large extent these activities have thus far escaped effective and suitable regulation. Even when international initiatives[2] attempt to bridge the cross–border pitfall that is so very inherent in the information society, such initiatives have inevitably failed to assume control over their subject matter, either because of an inability to define an appropriate rule set, a lack of consensus regarding the goals to be achieved, or the Gordian knot of international private law. In the information age, forum shopping and rule evasion has never been easier or more effective for those with time, resources, and above all, knowledge to spare.

---

1 The opinions expressed in this chapter are those of the author alone, and do not necessarily reflect a position supported by any organisation in which the author participates or to which he contributes.

2 Typical examples include *e.g.* the Council of Europe's Cybercrime Convention (see http://conventions.coe.int/Treaty/en/Treaties/Html/185.htm), UNCITRAL E–Commerce initiatives (see www.uncitral.org/), or the European E–Directives (*e.g.*, the E–Commerce Directive 2000/31/EC, the E–Signatures Directive 1999/93/EC, and the E–Invoicing Directive 2001/115/EC).

However, this lack of effective and enforceable legislation and the resulting 'free–for–all' mentality has not been all bad. One might in fact argue with some merit that this basic characteristic has fostered a sense of new entrepreneurship that has been a vital factor for growth for the information society. The old adage 'Knowledge is Power' seems to have proven its worth as a basic truism and as a building block of modern societies worldwide, with the perceived value of information growing day by day.

As the supposed reflection of societies' needs and values, evolutions in the law mirror this trend: record numbers of patent applications are filed and granted each year; incumbents struggle to make sure that their copyrights are protected as thoroughly as possible, and society as a whole has increasingly become aware of the value of its personal data. This evolution has resulted in ever more extensive and complicated legislation, and regulation in all shapes and sizes.

The list of measures which have been taken to ensure the protection of the value of information is as staggering as it is telling. In the information society, intangible assets are regarded as the most valuable component of almost any modern company, and people are only considered to exist if they can present the data to prove it. Information is invaluable, and the law strives to ensure that no value can drain from the system. After all, a society can ill afford to gamble with its basic building blocks.

While the increasing regulatory focus on information control is certainly radical and far–reaching, Western societies have undergone a much more fundamental socio–cultural paradigm shift in their treatment of information in the last centuries, and even more so in the last few decades.

In pre–industrial societies, the cost and effort involved in merely (re)creating physical information carriers could be quite significant, rivalling the cost of collection and processing of information itself. After all, while writing a book may take many months in itself, the need (or desire) to have such a book hand–reproduced through meticulous labour in monastery manufactures effectively meant that easy dissemination of data was out of the question.

Gutenberg's invention of the printing press around 1448 and the gradual improvement of the printing process altered this equation somewhat. As the cost of information reproduction fell to a value that was insignificant compared to investment related to the creation process, an economic need was born to provide creators with an incentive to continue to produce new works, despite the risk of parasitical competition from printing houses with the technical means to profit from another person's creativity. And hence, around the beginnings of the 18th century[3] copyright was created as a (partial) solution to the shortcomings of the systems of patronage that preceded it.

---

3 The exact date is of course debatable, given the wide diversity of possible legal protection mechanisms against copyright infringement. However, in the Western world, the British 1709 'Statute of Anne', also referred to as the 1709 Copyright Act, is often cited as the beginning of duration–limited copyright regulation as has now become the rule.

However, the increasing ease with which information could be disseminated gave rise to concerns of principle in addition to the mainly[4] economic origins of copyright. It is no coincidence that the same period which gave rise to copyright regulation also saw the birth of the first structured legal debates concerning privacy. While a certain *desire* to be left alone seems to be innate to the human condition and prevalent in most societies, the debate regarding the *right* to be left alone seems to have its origins in the late 19th century, being remarked on for the first time in a legal context in the US in an 1879 publication by Thomas Cooley.

Where early legal systems mainly limited their information regulations to the protection of personal reputation through claims such as libel, slander, and defamation, the increasing importance that was attached to information resulted in a gradual extension of this framework to include issues such as intellectual property, data protection, free speech regulations, broadcast licensing, and to what can broadly be referred to as telecommunications law.

The rapid development of communications technology, the birth of mass media, of entertainment industries, and the increasing prevalence and importance of information channels resulted in the birth of a new paradigm: the fundamental conviction that information is vitally important to the economic development of societies and to the personal well–being of individuals, and thus that data ownership is a key economic issue. Information has a value which is quantifiable (either positively[5] or negatively[6]) and can be monetised. As a result, since the beginning of the post–industrial age and the birth of mass media society, the possession, control, and use of information have gradually become the pillars of Western information regulation.

This is an apt solution model in a society where public communication is governed by a number of basic principles, most notably:

- The principle that the power of communication is essentially tiered, in the sense that there are a small number of mass media information broadcasters who produce and distribute information, and a large number of information consumers whose production and distribution capabilities are much more limited, either technically, geographically, or economically. This distinction is important, as it allows a society to control the vast majority of influential information exchanges by focusing on the smaller number of broadcasters, rather than on the larger number of consumers.
- The principle that it is possible to regulate information flows, that a sufficient consensus can be established in a democratic society regarding the scope and application of such a regulatory framework, specifically taking into account

4 The origins of copyright should not be uniformly attributed to economic concerns. Indeed, in a continental European perspective, copyright also entails moral rights, such as the right to integrity of a protected work or the right to claim paternity thereof, which may also have an economic component, but which also seem to constitute an attempt to satisfy the human need for recognition and respect of their innate creative abilities.

5 Such as the licensing value of a created work.

6 Such as the damage resulting from spreading slanderous messages.

socio–cultural sensitivities, dominant economical paradigms, and the basic human right of free speech.

- The principle that both data disseminators and consumers can be identified in case of breach of information regulation. Without the possibility of identifying the participants in a data exchange, enforcement of information regulation by the public authorities becomes impossible, and the rules lose much of their value.

In the author's opinion, all three of the aforementioned principles have become threatened through the aforementioned technological evolutions. Furthermore, it seems unlikely at this point that this evolution could be reversed, even if this would be found to be desirable. Finally, it is not inconceivable that the continuance of this evolution could strongly impact the validity of the Western information regulation model.

As indicated previously, the internet has upset the first principle mentioned above with regard to tiered communication structures. The division between information broadcasters and information consumers is fading, since the entry barrier to joining the information broadcasting market has become quite low. It does not take a great deal of money, effort, or know–how to make one's voice be heard across the globe.

The phenomenon of blogging[7] is an interesting example[8]: while the ability to create a personal news site is anything but new, the availability of widely accessible blogging service providers allows even the most technically inept to gain a forum to spread their personal opinions, however incorrect or insignificant they may be, to a worldwide audience. While most blogs are unable to actually attract a substantial fan base, others have risen in prominence to the ranks of pseudo–news agencies in their own right.

This can lead to legal difficulties, such as occurred in *Apple v Think Secret*, where news regarding several new Apple products was disclosed on Think Secret, a blog[9] dedicated to Apple products and services, before Apple had officially announced their products. Claiming violation of trade secrets, Apple sued the owners of Think Secret who argued that they were protected against the lawsuit through the Californian reporter's shield law, which accords reporters the right to refuse revealing their sources. The California Court of Appeal[10] eventually sided with

---

7 'Blogging', a contraction of 'web–logging', can be defined as a website on which one or more contributors frequently post news messages, which can either be original, or refer to other existing news sources on the internet. They usually focus on a more or less narrowly defined topic, and often include the blog owner's personal views, rather than aspiring to neutrality. For this reason, they are often more reminiscent of an on–line diary, rather than an actual news source.

8 Other interesting examples include certain popular social networking sites, including MySpace (www.myspace.com), Facebook (www.facebook.com) and YouTube (www.youtube.com).

9 See www.thinksecret.com/ (last visited on 28 August 2006).

10 Court of Appeal California, Sixth Appellate District, 26 May 2006; see http://wiredblogs.tripod.com/27BStroke6/AppleRuling.pdf.

Think Secret, while refusing to answer the question of whether bloggers can be considered journalists, stating:

> We decline the implicit invitation to embroil ourselves in questions of what constitutes 'legitimate journalis[m].' The shield law is intended to protect the gathering and dissemination of news, and that is what petitioners did here.

The second principle regarding the possibility of information regulation is equally problematic on the internet, where information is by definition offered on a global scale, and where the ease with which it can be moved around makes it increasingly difficult to answer the questions of applicable law and competent forum in any dispute.

This issue was already demonstrated in possibly the best–known internet law case, *Yahoo! v LICRA*, where Yahoo! Inc., a US–based company, was sued before the French courts by the International League against Racism and Anti–Semitism (LICRA) because auctions on Yahoo! allowed French citizens to purchase Nazi memorabilia. Such auctions would appear to be legal under US law, but not in France. The Paris *Tribunal de Grande Instance* eventually[11] issued an injunction requiring Yahoo! Inc. to take all appropriate measures to prevent access to auctions of Nazi memorabilia on its site by French residents. Thus, the courts chose to apply French law on a service provider from the US to a worldwide audience.[12]

Similar cases have since been brought before a number of courts worldwide, showing one common element: the IPR questions related to the application of national law in an electronic worldwide context have not been uniformly settled.

Yet, this chapter will not focus on the question of determining the applicable law on the internet. Rather, it aims to examine the difficulties resulting from the infrastructural choices that were made when the internet was first formed, as indicated in the third principle above, regarding the need to identify participants in information exchanges.

2 Darknets and the Appeal of Unlimited Freedom of Expression

At its very core, the internet is nothing more than a series of platform neutral information exchange protocols, which allow any form of bits and bytes to be moved from one system to the next, inherently oblivious to the content it is carry-

---

11 TGI Paris, 20 November 2000; see http://www.eff.org/legal/Jurisdiction_and_sovereignty/LICRA_v_Yahoo/20001120_fr_int_ruling.en.pdf.

12 It should be noted that the matter was subsequently presented before US courts, with the United States Court of Appeals for the Ninth Circuit deciding on 23 August 2004 to largely uphold the decision (see www.eff.org/legal/Jurisdiction_and_sovereignty/LICRA_v_Yahoo/20040823_yahoo_v_licra-9th.pdf), after the US District Court for the Northern District of California had first refused to uphold it due to conflict with US free speech principles (see http://www.eff.org/legal/Jurisdiction_and_sovereignty/LICRA_v_Yahoo/20011107_us_distct_decision.pdf).

ing, and even to a certain extent unaware of its own vastness. From a technical perspective, there is no real difference between useful information and background noise.

This key attribute has been its primary strength. The fact that the internet neither favours nor discriminates against any form of message has allowed countless services to be developed 'on top' of the available infrastructure. This is the reason why surfing uses essentially the same substructure as e–mails, internet phone calls, video broadcasts, or peer–to–peer file exchanges. Yet this attribute also poses a very fundamental threat to law enforcement.

2.1 Information Crimes, Freedom of Expression and Enforceability

This chapter was initially inspired by the so–called 'Darknet paper', which was released in November 2002 by a number of Microsoft network engineers.[13] In that paper, they predicted the advent of so–called 'darknets' over the years following its publication. Darknets may be provisionally defined as information exchange networks built on top of the internet (much like the worldwide web, e–mail, or any other application), but which specifically focus on obfuscating the source and destination of any information stored in them or transferred between their members.[14]

The authors of the Darknet paper predicted that information flows on these Darknets could be continuously optimised and offer ever more guarantees with respect to the anonymity of its contributors, using certain techniques summarily described below. As a consequence, such participants would be able to disseminate any information they please, in effect creating a type of 'information free–zone' where any legal restrictions would become unenforceable, and therefore meaningless. In short, an efficient Darknet would directly overthrow all three pillars of information regulation outlined above.

If such a Darknet could become sufficiently efficient, pervasive, and user–friendly, the result would be a virtual forum with an unlimited freedom of on–line expression, both in a positive sense (no *a priori* censorship of any kind, scientific research freedom, freedom of speech, and so on) and in a negative sense (rampant copyright violations, illegal pornography, racism, and such like).

---

13 P. Biddle, P. England, M. Peinado and B. Willman, "The Darknet and the Future of Content Distribution", 2001, http://msl1.mit.edu/ESD10/docs/darknet5.pdf#search=%22The%20Darknet%20and%20the%20Future%20of%20Content%20Distribution%22 (last visited on 28 August 2006).

14 This is a definition derived from the somewhat more complicated descriptions in the Darknet Paper. The notion of Darknets is also more and more frequently used to described a specific sub–category of the Darknets described above; namely information exchange networks which not only attempt to hide the origin and destination of any given message, but also the identity of the members of the network itself.

In this chapter, the feasibility of such Darknets will be described (section 2), along with existing responses from a legal perspective, and potential future developments (section 3).

2.2 Darknets: Theoretical Constructs or a Looming Reality?

Contrary to what one might think, Darknets are not an innovation of the last few years. In fact, they have been under development for quite some time, depending on how a Darknet is defined. Typically (as in the Darknet paper) the origins of modern day Darknets are said to mirror the developments of peer–to–peer file sharing systems in which the end–users connect directly to one another using a common client program, for the purposes of exchanging information without the explicit intervention of a service provider in the transfer itself. We will provide a summary overview of this development below, in order to demarcate more clearly the concept of Darknets.

One of the first peer–to–peer applications to reach a large enough audience to catch the public's attention was undoubtedly Napster. Designed as a tool to share music files through the internet, its operation was simple: users connected to a centralised server[15] using the Napster client and notified this server which files they were sharing. When searching for a specific file, the client would query the central server, which would then return the IP addresses[16] where files matching the query could be retrieved. In essence, Napster functioned as a phone book for on–line music: using the search function of the centralised server (the phone book), users would retrieve IP addresses (phone numbers) of songs (people) they were looking for. After finding the address sought, users could exchange data directly without further intervention from the server.

As such, Napster can of course not be considered a Darknet in any form. Users clearly communicated their identity to the central server along with the content they were offering. Thus no anonymity of any kind was built into the system. Furthermore, the system was very vulnerable to attacks: take away the central server, and no queries were possible (in other words, remove the phone book, and no phone numbers would be found). Eventually, under legal pressure, Napster temporarily disappeared.[17]

---

15 Or rather, one of a series of centralised servers, chosen by the client when the programme was started.

16 IP addresses (Internet Protocol addresses) are the unique numbers used by the Internet Protocol to identify individual systems, allowing computers to address one another. Under the current IPv4 standard, they take the form of a series of four numbers, ranging from 0 to 255, and separated by a dot, *e.g.* 207.142.131.248.

17 On 5 March 2001, Napster was enjoined by order of the US Ninth Circuit to prevent the trading of copyrighted music by its users. As no reliable technologies exist to comply with such an order, the service was shut down completely in July 2001. After a settlement, Napster resumed operations in 2005, this time as an undisputed legal music sales service, under new ownership.

However, even as Napster collapsed, new competitors arose under such names as Kazaa, Grokster, Limewire, and Bearshare. Learning from Napster's vulnerability and eventual demise, these new peer–to–peer services refrained from using a centralised server that would be susceptible to takedown. Rather, these systems relied on a distributed network of nodes[18] which would have either the status of a common node (a normal user) or a so–called 'supernode', also referred to as a 'superpeer' on some systems. While common nodes merely use the system, supernodes help in searching for files, thus assuming the role of centralised servers without the risk of being in the hands of a single entity. While individual supernodes can be taken down, any user has the possibility[19] of declaring himself a supernode. Thus, the network can never truly be stopped.

And yet, this too cannot be considered a Darknet. After all, while search methods are distributed and no centralised system is thus necessary to keep the network operational, the final result is the same: the IP address of the sharer or searcher of a specific file is revealed to both parties. Thus, content cannot be shared anonymously, and no Darknet exists.

Currently, a third generation of peer–to–peer networks which remedies this final shortcoming is slowly on the rise. They are based on so–called 'small world theory', popularised as the notion of 'six degrees of separation'. The latter expression is based on the observation made by psychologist Stanley Milgram that, on average, every person in the US could be connected to any other by a chain of six acquaintances. In other words: to get a message from one person to an entirely random other person within the US, a message only needed to be passed six times to an acquaintance, each time getting closer to its destination, before eventually reaching it.

In peer–to–peer networks, a similar system can be described in a simplified form as follows. Each user connects to as large a number of other users as desirable. Now, when searching for a given piece of information, he sends out a request containing a description of the information he is looking for, and his IP address. If the users he is connected to have the file, they send a positive response back. If they don't, they forward the request to the users they are connected to, this time communicating their own IP address along with the search description. If one of the nodes receiving the request after this second stage has the wanted information, they obviously cannot contact the original user (they do not know his IP address, nor can they uncover it), but will simply send their reply back the way it came: through the party from whom they received the request. The search continues onwards, the original message being forwarded each time, but each time replacing the identifying information of the original requester with the identity of the most recent forwarder, usually until a specified number of nodes has been passed through.

---

18 In computer science, 'nodes' are defined as entities in a network, in this case computers running the required client software.

19 Whether this is wise is a factual question, as supernodes obviously have to send and receive more data, so that supernodes tend to be used only on systems with higher bandwidth connections.

Using this type of infrastructure (or one of the many variations thereupon) has two principal consequences:

- When receiving a request for information, it is impossible to determine with certainty whether the node sending the request is the original requester, or simply a messenger passing the request onwards. Thus, the original source of the request is obscured.
- Secondly (and similarly), when a node receives information with the request to pass it on to another node, it is impossible to determine if the sender actually knowingly held the information to begin with, or if he was merely passing it on. Thus, the original source of the information is also obscured.

And the system can be further optimised for anonymity. Rather than sending entire files, information can be split up into small pieces, each of which are encrypted and bear a common signature identifying them as a part of a larger file. Requests for this information can then be made much less transparent: requests would not be made for an obvious keyword or description (*e.g.* 'Madonna – Like A Virgin.mp3'), but for an incomprehensible signature code (*e.g.* all pieces of the file CHK@V~eOY–QVTDexy5Yyt9Xpyf–dwF8SAwI,KMUx3JU2o7dvXJkvTv Am8[20]). Finally, these split parts of a file can be distributed over multiple nodes in the Darknet, so that no single node will contain the entire file, except by chance or if the user has downloaded the complete file.

The final result is as simple as it is effective:

- A search cannot be easily traced back to the original sender;
- Information sent through the network cannot be easily traced back to the original source;
- Information can be encrypted and spread throughout the network so that it cannot be decrypted without the original key, which is only known to the person who originally inserted the content and to any persons to whom this key is communicated;
- Even node owners are ignorant of the information stored on their own node, unless they have all segments of a file and the key to decrypt it.

Expanding the network into a usable form is relatively simple: all one needs is a program running on top of this Darknet and communicating through it, in which users can announce the availability of files (to resume the example above: a message could state that 'Madonna – Like A Virgin.mp3' would be available as file CHK@V~eOY–QVTDexy5Yyt9Xpyf–dwF8SAwI,KMUx3JU2o7dvX). This announcement could not be traced back to source, since its receivers would only know which node passed it on directly to them, but not who preceded that node (if

---

20 The example is a so–called Content Hash Key (CHK) of the type used by the Freenet project, copied in a slightly modified version from the website http://www.freenethelp.org. As it was edited manually, it is unlikely that the key corresponds to any content presently available in the Freenet network.

anyone) in the distribution chain. Anyone could then look for the file using the key mentioned above, again without being traceable for the same reasons.

And finally, even when checking a user's files on his local system (on his physical computer), no liability for copyright infringement could be established: the file 'Madonna – Like A Virgin.mp3' will not be found, but rather a series of data blocks signed by the common key CHK@V~eOY–QVTDexy5Yyt9Xpyf–dwF8SAwI,KMUx3JU2o7dvX. There is no way to know if the node carrying this information was even aware of its contents, since the storer need not necessarily know the correct key to decrypt the file.

In short, senders and receivers cannot be identified, and even the contents of information itself are indecipherable to anyone who does not possess the right key. Information being passed on might be a private mail message, a news article, pirated software, or instructions for building and using explosive devices. There is no way to know, except to the person who has inserted it and to the person who has successfully retrieved it.

2.3 Darknets and the Limits of the Law

In short, such Darknets would be a clear example of a social reality that escapes any attempts of efficient regulation, merely because the participants to a specific information exchange would become unidentifiable, and because information on a node can not be readily deciphered. Even if the computer system of a user undergoes careful scrutiny, it cannot be determined with certainty what information (if any) is present on his node, and whether or not the user was aware of this. Such Darknets are not purely theoretical constructs.

In fact, many research projects have been attempting to develop Darknets for several years now, and many have been successfully deployed. Common examples include the Freenet project[21], Entropy[22], ANts P2P[23], I2P[24] and Tor.[25] While the implementation and characteristics of each of these projects vary widely, all serve the purposes described above, and are in active use. Nonetheless, use of these networks is far from prevalent at this time, at least not when compared to the staggering usage numbers claimed by earlier and less anonymous peer to peer systems. Darknet usage thus remains a niche activity at this time.

One of the main reasons is that anonymous networks such as the ones above are very inefficient when compared to earlier generations of peer–to–peer networks: data must be carried from node to node, rather than directly to its destination, and searching for data is typically much more cumbersome. The average peer–to–peer software user will therefore often prefer the perceived anonymity of

21 See http://freenetproject.org/ (last visited on 24 August 2006).

22 See http://entropy.stop1984.com/en/home.html (last visited on 24 August 2006).

23 See http://antsp2p.sourceforge.net/ (last visited on 24 August 2006).

24 See http://www.i2p.net/ (last visited on 24 August 2006).

25 See http://tor.eff.org/ (last visited on 24 August 2006).

being one of 20 million[26] Kazaa users – despite the fact that Kazaa has no real anonymity features – rather than one of 10 000[27] Freenet users, which has been designed to anonymity specifications. It goes without saying that the selection of on–line content is also more abundant and diversified when the number of users increases, further diminishing the appeal of higher anonymity networks.

Another significant reason for this limited uptake is simply the lack of any need for anonymous communication to the public at large. Darknets have been designed to mask the identities of its nodes, but a price is paid in efficiency and user–friendliness. Thus, the potential uptake of Darknets is inherently restricted, since its appeal will be mostly recognisable to users who engage in activities that are in conflict with applicable laws (*e.g.* copyright violations) or that they otherwise feel necessary to hide (*e.g.*, life–styles which are legal but frowned upon by the user's environment, such as sadomasochism), and to idealistic participants (such as free speech advocates or political anarchists). This portion of the population will likely remain a clear minority.

And finally, even this third generation of peer–to–peer networks does not offer full anonymity. In most cases, it would still be possible to identify the sender or receiver of information but only through disproportionate effort. For example, if all communication of each node in the network was continuously and fully logged, it would obviously be possible for law enforcement agencies to follow the chain of information transfers back to its source, or forward to its destination. However, most identification methods are either unrealistically burdensome, or will yield no absolute certainty regarding the source or destination of a transfer. For this reason, users of such networks are often said to enjoy so–called 'plausible deniability' regarding their activities, rather than real anonymity.

In the following sections, we will examine possible legal strategies that could be used to combat illegal information exchanges on such networks, and attempt to assess the likely efficacy of such measures. This may prove to be an incentive to interested readers to evaluate the extent to which they value freedom of expression (both from a personal and from a community perspective), at which point sacrifices made to maintain information regulations become disproportionate, and even to question the value that our legal system attaches to information itself.

---

[26] Rather, Kazaa itself claims that 20 million copies of its software have been downloaded through its website. The FastTrack protocol used by Kazaa and a multitude of other peer to peer programmes registers around 2.5 million simultaneous users at any given time. See http://en.wikipedia.org/wiki/Fasttrack.

[27] The number of ten thousand users is a general estimate by Freenet users themselves. However, there is no objective manner to accurately assess their number.

3 Technology, Code and Conflict: How to Get the Darknet Back into the Bottle

The Darknet paper has an outspoken and controversial opinion about the future of Darknets. In its conclusions, it states:

> There seem to be no technical impediments to Darknet–based peer–to–peer file sharing technologies growing in convenience, aggregate bandwidth and efficiency. The legal future of Darknet–technologies is less certain, but we believe that, at least for some classes of user, and possibly for the population at large, efficient Darknets will exist.

Its abstract is even less compromising:

> We speculate that there will be short–term impediments to the effectiveness of the Darknet as a distribution mechanism, but ultimately the Darknet–genie will not be put back into the bottle.

As the legal aspects of Darknets are only cursorily examined in the Darknet paper, this is the exact issue that we will attempt to examine more closely in this section.

3.1 Regulations and Code

The central question from a legal and policy perspective examined in this chapter is a fairly simple paradox: how can regulatory initiatives hope to bring any kind of answer in a problematic virtual environment that has been created by the fact that regulations are fundamentally impotent in it?

While this overview is most certainly not complete, four possible approaches to the dilemma will be outlined:

- a legalistic approach, focusing on a regulatory solution to the problem of enforceability;
- a technological approach, attempting to resolve a technical problem of untraceability through technical means;
- a combined approach, modifying the state of the game through a combination of legal and technical solutions;
- and finally, a philosophical approach, which stresses the possibility of society adapting to the problem, rather than adapting the problem to society.

It is important to clarify from the outset that the first three approaches all have a legal and a technical component. However, the classifications are based on the component that can be considered to be dominant, namely the component which entails the basic principle of that approach.

3.2 The Legalistic Approach: Eliminating Anonymous Electronic Communication

The simplest approach to resolve this particular problem from a legal perspective is obvious: by requiring all electronic data exchanges to be monitored at all times, no circumvention would be possible. After all, as indicated above, in this case each communication in a Darknet could be traced step by step to the originator and to the destination, thus removing the threat presented by anonymity. Yet, this notion is a fallacy for a number of reasons.

First of all, the creation of such a legal framework is virtually impossible. In a global network such as the internet, over which these Darknets function, all countries would have to implement similar regulations. After all, if even a single node is located in a country that has not implemented the required regulation, the information chain is broken as soon as data passes through this node. Given the wide diversity in philosophical approaches to freedom of expression, and the widely differing technological capabilities of societies across the globe, it seems impossible to create such a harmonised framework.

Secondly, even if such a framework could be drafted, it is likely to clash violently with the basic principles of freedom of expression and privacy protection. These principles have been enshrined in various international treaties and declarations, including Articles 12 and 19 of the Universal Declaration of Human Rights[28], Articles 17 through 19 of the International Covenant on Civil and Political Rights[29], and Articles 8 through 10 of the European Convention on Human Rights.[30] It goes without saying that in an international context, a multitude of other legal provisions, including (if not specifically) national constitutional free speech provisions, may also contradict a universal obligation to log all electronic communication.

While Western legal doctrine accepts fairly universally that the aforementioned rights are not absolute, exceptions are subject to strict criteria, the most well-known of which is the requirement that the restriction must be necessary in a democratic society. This requires a cumulative test of legality, legitimacy, and proportionality to be applied to any restrictive measures. Since the goal of such a regulatory initiative would be to log all electronic communications, universally and without discrimination, and regardless of any prior suspicions of unlawful activity, it is extremely doubtful whether the tests of legitimacy and proportionality could be overcome. After all, any interpretation to the contrary would imply that there is quite simply no such thing as an *a priori* right to privacy in relation to law enforcement, which would have the right to monitor and log any exchange, at any time, without having to justify this in any way.

---

28 See http://www.unhchr.ch/udhr/.

29 See http://www.ohchr.org/english/law/ccpr.htm.

30 See http://conventions.coe.int/treaty/en/Treaties/Html/005.htm.

Despite these numerous legal objections, the so–called Data Retention Directive[31] was approved on 15 March 2006. This Directive requires Member States to implement the necessary legal framework to log certain information required to identify the source and destination of all electronic telecommunications, regardless of their contents or of any suspicion of unlawful conduct, at the latest by 15 September 2007. However, the Directive allows Member States to postpone the fulfilment of this obligation until 15 March 2009. Sixteen Member States have immediately taken this option, although the chosen periods of delay vary.

It should also be noted what consensus was achieved during the drafting of the Directive on the precise data to be stored, the entities responsible for this obligation, the measures to be taken to ensure the reliability and confidentiality of the data, or who would be required to bear the costs. Given that these essential elements are left in the hands of the Member States, it remains to be seen how the Member States can fulfil their obligations without violating the right to privacy, and if any kind of harmonisation can be expected.

Thirdly, such a system is likely to fail on technical grounds, even in the unlikely event that the legal web could be successfully untangled, especially keeping into account the goal of collecting usable information for law enforcement purposes. After all, the regulation would also require massive data storage as every contact between every node on the internet would need to be permanently logged. With internet applications becoming ever more ubiquitous – including IP telephony, IP television, and soon even connected household appliances – the growth of the already gigantic information torrent on the internet can be expected to be staggering. It is unclear how this obligation can be met from a practical perspective.

Attempting to distinguish between useful content and irrelevant data exchanges may prove to be a futile and even counterproductive[32] exercise, so that the amount of information to be stored would be prohibitively high. Offloading the burden (and cost) of storage on ISPs (as is often proposed) merely means that the telecommunications costs of the end–users will increase correspondingly, thus harming the growth of the on–line economy. And finally, one might ask the question if indiscriminate logging would not simply result in more information being made available to law enforcement agencies, rather than more useful information.

To summarise, a regulatory approach intended to eliminate anonymous communications (which is at least partially followed by the Data Retention Directive) seems destined to fail, both on legal, technical, and practical grounds. A healthy degree of scepticism with regard to such initiatives thus seems to be in order.

---

[31] Directive 2006/24/EC of the European Parliament and of the Council of 15 March 2006 on the retention of data generated or processed in connection with the provision of publicly available electronic communications services or of public communications networks and amending Directive 2002/58/EC, O.J. L 105/54, 13.04.2006.

[32] After all, if one type of communication is excluded from logging, this only encourages would–be anonymous projects to attempt to route around restrictions by attempting to mask their traffic as an exempted traffic flow.

3.3 The Technological Approach: A Next–Generation Internet

Since the regulatory approach seems unlikely to yield any significant results, a second possibility might offer more promise: recreate the technical framework from the ground up.

As noted above, the internet as it currently exists is essentially an open and content–neutral information exchange platform. New systems can be connected almost at will and without limit[33], and users are free to switch ISPs at will. They are only registered with their current ISP, and there is no way to trace their steps without involving the ISP's records. Of course, alternative technical approaches exist.

For instance, a relatively simple modification to the current infrastructure could take the form of a closed network. Every participant receives a unique identifier, which is presented in every step of each communication. Existing technical protocols would need to be rewritten to ensure that every communication is electronically signed by the sender, and that every information transfer is authenticated in every step of the way. This new internet would essentially be a worldwide private network, which new participants can only join after providing reliable and verified credentials.

This system would carry countless benefits in comparison to the current framework. For one, information security would improve greatly: by authenticating the source of any communication, it would become a great deal more complicated to engage in hacking, denial of service attacks, defacements of websites, or any number of cyber–crime incidents. E–commerce would certainly benefit as well, since one of the current disincentives to e–commerce is the fear of being defrauded, both by potential sellers and buyers. Nonetheless, and despite these clear benefits, a number of reasons exist why this is no solution to the problems presented by Darknets.

First of all, it should be noted that this solution model may start from a different and more positive approach than the first (i.e. by offering a second network with full authentication services as an added value feature, rather than forbidding unlogged electronic communication services), but that the eventual result is largely the same: a network in which all communications can be traced back to their source. The legal issues are thus similar: eliminating the possibility of anonymous communication could be considered a disproportionate invasion of privacy.

However, legal issues are unlikely to be a real barrier to this solution, since the existence of this modified internet does not preclude the existence of other and possibly anonymous networks, and still allows citizens the possibility of commu-

---

33 Technically, the number of available IP addresses is finite, and this could be construed as a technological limit. However, workarounds to this issue exist, and with the expected gradual transition from IPv4 to IPv6, which will increase the number of available IP addresses from roughly 4 billion to roughly 50 octillion (i.e. a 5 followed by 28 zeroes). This makes expansion essentially limitless, especially when considering that further upgrades are conceptually possible.

nication in another fashion. After all, there is no legal reason why this second internet could not impose such requirements on its users, when other closed private networks have done the same in, for example, the finance or public services sectors. Rather than legal issues, it is the technical and conceptual flaws in this approach that could prove to make it unworkable.

From a conceptual perspective, the main issue is that this approach does not solve any perceived problems in the technical framework behind the existing internet, but rather that it simply adds a secondary worldwide network. The risk is then obviously that any party with a vested interest in anonymous communication would be very unlikely to switch to a network where the most beneficial trait of the internet from their perspective would be eliminated. The new and more secured internet could prove to be a hard sell to this group, and without mandatory switching to this network (which would essentially bring us back to the legalistic approach criticised above) it seems unlikely that the existing internet would 'fade away' naturally.

Even if a fully authenticated internet would be generally hailed as an improvement and even if users would flock to this network virtually without exception, significant challenges remain to its actual realisation. Without going into such details as extend beyond the scope of this chapter, the main issue would be the creation of an internationally accepted, fully uniform authentication method that would allow users to authenticate themselves before entering the network. The creation of such an identity management system is certainly non–trivial, and risks being a disproportionate burden.

Furthermore, the network's security would need to be improved significantly in comparison to the present internet. Wireless home networks are becoming increasingly commonplace while knowledge of network security has not kept pace. As a result, unprotected wireless networks (typically WiFi–based) are quite common, allowing anyone to (ab)use the internet connection of an unsuspecting target. Currently, this is a nuisance and an average scale security risk. In a fully authenticated network, such abuses should be made impossible, or its entire purpose would be defeated.

Thus, legal, technical and conceptual weaknesses make this approach unlikely to succeed.

3.4 Patching the Laws through Extensive Privatisation of Data Control

An interesting approach has surfaced in recent years, where technical methods are combined with new legal provisions to create a more global solution. Specifically, the threat presented to copyright holders by new technologies (including peer–to–peer software, but also the relative cheapness of exchangeable mass storage devices such as external hard disks or (re)writable CDs and DVDs) has given rise to so–called Digital Rights Management (DRM) technologies.

DRM is a catch–all denomination for any kind of technology that allows the rights–holder in any given information to limit the ways in which that information can be used. Common examples include anti–copying technologies that stop consumers from copying their audio CDs; the use of region codes which stops consumers from playing DVDs purchased outside of the geographical region to which they were designated, and the playback restrictions on songs purchased through the Apple iTunes store, which prevent consumers from playing the music they purchased on mp3 players that were not produced by Apple.

While the technology is currently aimed specifically at restricting the use of copyright protected information, there is no reason why it could not be used on any electronic information that the original creator would wish to keep under tight control. Essentially, all electronic information could be made subject to a licensing scheme in which the rights–holder decides which uses are legitimate and which are not.

With regard to copyright protected content this idea has received some legal backing through the European Copyright Directive of 2001[34], which included a number of provisions in its Chapter III regarding the "protection of technological measures and rights management information". Specifically, Member States were required to halt the circumvention of "effective technological measures", a complicated notion that encompasses virtually all conceivable DRM schemes. Furthermore, even the production or distribution of devices, products or services (including software) that should be considered as "primarily designed" for this purpose should be banned in the Member States.

While the scope of these provisions is vague and their application is problematic in practice, it is clear that the European law–maker saw some merit in this approach, that effectively gives the rights–holders the right to control the use of their information through technological enforcement. Nonetheless, this approach is also problematic for a number of reasons.

First of all, the success rate of existing DRM schemes can be described as disappointing at best. Thus far, no DRM solution has been able to withstand attacks from piracy communities, and all examples mentioned above have been circumvented in short order. This is significant, because it is obvious that even once a single unprotected copy of originally restricted content has been created, there is no further barrier to distributing this copy across the globe. Therefore, even a single breach of a DRM method will invalidate the entire scheme, merely as a consequence of the ease of propagation of unprotected content.

Secondly, the introduction of DRM regulations has given rise to new legal issues, including concerns regarding the maintaining of a proper balance between the interests of rights–holders on the one hand, and of consumers on the other. For instance, it is not entirely clear why DVDs should be protected against any form of copying, while VHS recordings of the exact same subject can be legally recorded for personal use in most European jurisdictions. Consumers have also oc-

---

34 Directive 2001/29/EC of the European Parliament and of the Council of 22 May 2001 on the harmonisation of certain aspects of copyright and related rights in the information society, O.J. L 167/10, 22.06.2001.

casionally experienced difficulties in simply making normal use of their lawfully purchased content, such as listening to copy–protected CDs in their car CD players. Even in these cases, Belgian copyright law does not allow them to circumvent the DRM scheme to obtain a usable copy of the disc.

The underlying issues with DRM technologies are also related to a matter of principle. Through legally enforced technological measures, information owners essentially write their own laws: they determine what is lawful and what is not, and the role of the law is presently limited to stating that no other party has the right to challenge these rules. Thus, DRM mechanisms essentially result in a privatisation of data control laws, in which any information owner gains international exclusive jurisdiction without regard to other concerns such as consumer protection or even the common good of society. This seems questionable from a legal–philosophical viewpoint, as private actors gain the right to overturn rules established by societies to regulate certain aspects of human interaction.

An interesting example of the potentially perverse side–effects of such rules was observed in a recent incident regarding a DRM scheme employed by Sony.[35] Dubbed 'XCP–Aurora', this DRM scheme essentially installed hidden software on the computer system of any user when inserting a protected audio disc, after the user confirmed his consent to a license agreement and provided that the system was running a version of Microsoft Windows. The XCP–Aurora scheme would then ensure that the songs could not be easily copied. Unfortunately, the cloaking techniques used by XCP–Aurora to hide its presence (in an attempt to prevent being removed) could be very easily abused by viruses to hide themselves in exactly the same manner. Thus, consumers who had agreed to installing XCP–Aurora saw the security of their systems impaired.

As noted above, it is illegal to circumvent DRM schemes such as XCP–Aurora, as is the production of removal software. Thus, despite the clear risk involved in keeping the software installed, it seems that users were not legally allowed to repair their systems by removing XCP–Aurora. Thankfully, following public outrage, Sony authorised the removal of XCP–Aurora and even released software to remove it directly. One might wonder if copyright regulations have not been stretched too far when rights–holders have been given the legal right to insist on keeping dangerous software on lawful consumers' systems.

It should also be noted that, despite XCP–Aurora's best efforts, there was no noticeable slowdown before the protected music appeared on peer–to–peer networks. Thus, even the most optimistic provisional assessment can only be that DRM technology is unproven in the market.

---

[35] See inter alia http://en.wikipedia.org/wiki/XCP-Aurora for an account of this incident (last visited on 28 August 2007).

3.5 Philosophical Adaptations in a Post–Modern Society: A Reappraisal of the Inherent Value of Information

Given that the first three approaches outlined above seem likely to fail for the reasons indicated in their respective subsections, we examine a fourth possibility in this final subsection: rather than attempting to eliminate a new and problematic situation in a virtual environment, an alternative approach might be for society itself to adapt its perception of information to the new state of the game.

As noted in the introduction, information regulation is not a universal and eternal quality of the human condition. It is to a large extent a recent development, created by man to meet the requirements of a society in which the value of information gradually appreciated, but in which only a small number of actors retained extensive control. Information protection is thus a human construct that has since been elevated to the ranks of dogma, as witnessed by the universally accepted truth expressed in the saying 'Knowledge is Power'. Perhaps the simplest concept for a solution to the issue of Darknets is reassessing the principles of this statement. Should information as such be protected? And at what cost?

Reappraising the value of information is a fundamental philosophical change that is unlikely to be welcomed by any *modern* society that has embraced the dogma above, not the least because of its far–reaching moral and economical implications described summarily below. Nonetheless, the change might be inevitable in the *information* society that allows no feasible means of opposing it, and which may not be as fundamentally unacceptable in a *postmodern* society in which a sufficient framework of common norms and ideals seems to be becoming increasingly unrealistic.

Perhaps the rise of Darknets – should they ever come to fruition and common prevalence, which is far from certain – also offers an opportunity to rethink the modern perception of electronic information. Ultimately, it is a data stream consisting of ones and zeroes and nothing more. The information contained therein is often useful, harmful and/or valuable, but what should a society be willing to give up to be able to contain that stream?

This last solution model entails the recognition that current regulations as they apply to information in a digital environment have been drafted from a perspective that is no longer accurate. Society has changed fundamentally, and yet the regulatory framework seems currently more focused on maintaining a cross–medium status quo, rather than recognising that drastic changes may be in order in a virtual environment where such attempts at control stand relatively little chance of succeeding. In effect, in an electronic environment our laws tend to be ineffective because the socio–cultural perspective underpinning these rules has not evolved to keep tune with technological developments. While the existence of Darknets could have a profound impact on society, the consequences might not be as dire as they would appear at first glance.

With regard to copyright, legal protection was in all likelihood necessary in an early mass media society, where the production, promotion, and distribution of music involved massive costs. But these cards seem to have been reshuffled to some extent, as argued above. The digital era has given rise to alternative business models, so that a relaxation of the application of copyright law to electronic content may not have the detrimental effect that is often projected by representatives of the entertainment industries. Furthermore, since art predates copyright, it would appear that creativity does not require copyright, and indeed that creativity is simply a fundamental aspect of the human condition.

For opinion crimes, including slander, libel, and racist/revisionist contents, perhaps Darknets could be considered a valid stimulus to developing an increased sense of criticism against anonymously expressed opinions. While the early mass media society initially resulted in public confidence in content broadcasters, the ease with which information can now be disseminated should give rise to more critical thought in a healthily sceptical society.

More fundamentally, it should be recalled that only anonymous communications are within the scope of this chapter, and that such communications should not *a priori* be accorded a great deal of credibility. While the victims of anonymous hate speech may feel hurt, could this not be considered a consequence of an irrational tendency to take any widespread information at more than its face value, perhaps as an unnecessary and outdated legacy from the traditional faith in information broadcasters, often unwarranted in an anonymous environment? Perhaps the main conclusion should be that any collective entity identifying itself as the 'information society' should worry less about controlling information, and more about accurately and critically assessing its worth.

Finally, with regard to the most painful issue of crimes against public order, morals or decency (such as torture/abuse imagery, child pornography, snuff movies, or any material that offends the sensitivities of almost any human being), it should be noted that, while almost any society across the world will agree that virtually all of this material is undesirable and harmful, there is rarely a consensus on how far regulations should go. Thus, in the international context, enforcing regulations in this regard is extremely difficult even without factoring in the element of anonymity.

One should also realise that anonymous distribution of such materials, however reprehensible it may be to the reasonable observer, has one redeeming feature: it destroys any market value that this material may have. Why pay for commercial abusive materials when they are freely available on an anonymous network? In the longer term, fully anonymous information exchange would all but completely eradicate the commercial trade in abuse materials. Furthermore, it would allow enforcement agencies to focus their efforts where they are most needed: to ensuring right at the start that crimes resulting in such information do not occur.

This latest solution model contradicts the most basic principle of the information society: that knowledge equals money, and that information is – by far – the most important factor in any modern business undertaking. But perhaps this perception has ultimately become flawed in the third millennium. Perhaps information itself should not be considered to be valuable, but rather the application of this information. Not the bits and bytes as such, but the way in which they are manipulated and presented offers value to end–users.

Examples of this are becoming increasingly prevalent, from open source software development where large and often complicated software packages can be offered for free under certain licenses, to community supported projects such as Wikipedia[36] where an on–line encyclopaedia was created based on an open input model, or a variety of social networking sites that allow individuals easier access to a target audience.[37] In all of these cases, value is created not by tightly controlling information flows under exclusive possession, but by ensuring that the information can be utilised / monetised by the largest possible number of people.

After all, is information in itself really valuable if it is only being offered 'as is', without a more concrete application attached to it? What is the value of an intellectual creation as such when the marginal costs of distribution approach zero? Are opinions valuable if they are expressed anonymously without observable real–life consequences? And what should a society be willing to give up in order to ensure that the answer to all of these questions remains exactly the same as it was throughout the 20th century?

4 Conclusion: Can the Turn of the Tide Be Stopped?

What response will free and democratic societies[38] choose for emerging Darknets (if indeed, they ever were to emerge beyond the fringe communities that presently seem enamoured with them), and for the accompanying threats through unfettered freedom of expression? I do not believe that there is anyone who can answer the question at this point. Ultimately however, I believe that we have passed the point where we as a society would have been able to make a conscious and meaningful choice, if indeed such a point has ever existed in our increasingly internationalised and informaticised society.

Quite possibly, the most insightful comment on this question was made by an anonymous poster on an internet news website: "If technology is a river, and everything else is a dam, the river will always overflow." Technological innovations have had a defining influence on human capabilities since the evolutionary development of the opposable thumb allowed us to manipulate basic matter. It has always dictated the limits of what we can do, and has at the same time pushed our borders back, time and time again. But never in history have we been able to turn back the clock, and decide that we should be able – not allowed, but able – to do less tomorrow than we could today.

---

36 See www.wikipedia.org.

37 See *e.g.*, the recent commercial success of the Arctic Monkeys, a UK–based rock band who credit a large part of their success to their on–line presence on the MySpace social networking site (see www.myspace.com), and to the enthusiasm of their fans who freely exchanged their songs on the internet even before they could be made commercially available.

38 The author consciously limits the question to 'free and democratic societies'. It is after all perfectly possible from a technical point of view to require any electronic information exchange to be registered and logged for later scrutiny. For the reasons outlined above, the author does not consider this to be viable, legal, or morally acceptable.

I would happily credit the source of the quote above, but alas, the author decided to keep his identity hidden.[39] However, I do not think he would object to me reusing it. It is, after all, only information. Much like any other part of this chapter, the reader is entirely free to treat it for what it's worth.

[39] The comment was posted as a comment under the pseudonym 'Precision Blogger' on the following page: http://www.techdirt.com/articles/20050518/1455210_F.shtml. The poster's own website can be found at http://precision-blogging.blogspot.com, where the poster's claimed identity can be uncovered.

Chapter 25 – Facing the Limits of the Law (Conclusion)

Erik Claes and Bert Keirsbilck

1 Introduction

All contributors to *Facing the Limits of the Law* explored the limits of a specific legal field. In their capacity of legal scholars, criminologists, social scientists, or philosophers, they identified issues that challenged these fields of knowledge in their effectiveness and legitimacy. They opened new routes for fresh research in a diversity of branches ranging from private law, social law, economic law, criminal law, through European and international law, constitutional law, to human rights law and law and technology. The reader may perhaps feel a bit overwhelmed by such a plurality of voices and perspectives. Let us recall briefly these perspectives.

Legal experts in private, social, and economic law, analysed the potentials and limits of open textured concepts or principles. Starting from the observation that judicial rulings increasingly appeal to principles and policies (besides formal legal sources), *Marc Loth* suggested a 'law in context' approach which may result in a 'de–freezing' of legal dogmatics through an interdisciplinary study of the law (Chapter 2). *Kurt Willems* examined to what extent the law is able to regulate, or at least structure, morality without disordering the internal dynamics of morality, by using open–textured norms such as 'good faith' and 'natural obligation' (Chapter 3). *Mathieu van Putten* explored the limits of labour law by showing how the legal status of collective labour agreements has been contested from a private law perspective, and, subsequently, both from a constitutional law and a competition law perspective (Chapter 4). *Bert Keirsbilck* mapped the limits of EC general clauses in a system of decentralised enforcement, and paid particular attention to the EC general clauses prohibiting unfair, misleading, and aggressive commercial practices (Chapter 5).

Criminal law specialists examined the limitations of key concepts in their discipline. *Erik Claes and Michal Krolikowski* examined to what extent the erosion of the principle of legality can be imputed to the characteristics and classic conceptions of the criminal law itself. They also identified a strategy to respond appropriately to the limits of criminal legality (Chapter 6). *Mark Fenwick* investigated to what extent concepts such as 'moral fault', 'criminal wrong', 'harm', and 'criminal sanction' can be successfully applied to corporate wrongdoing (Chapter 7). Criminologists also explored the limits of the law. *Luc Robert* addressed the limits to the regulatory ambitions of legal rules in the unusual social setting of a prison (Chapter 8). *Tom Daems* explored the limits of a new kind of victim–oriented consequentialism according to which we should strive towards 'healing victims' as a desired end (Chapter 9). *Johan Deklerck* explored the potentials and limits of the traditional criminal justice system and restorative justice (Chapter 10). *Martha Valiñas* examined the limited capacity of formal justice to rebuilding trust within society in the aftermath of mass atrocities (Chapter 11).

In the field of European law expertise, *Stefanie Dierckxsens* explained why the European Union is confronted with a growing loss of legitimacy in the eyes of the public, even though the legal legitimacy of the European construction has increased considerably throughout several Treaty reviews (Chapter 12). *René Foqué and Jacques Steenbergen* sketched the broader economic, political, and sociological background against which legitimacy issues revolving around European law and European institutions could be further explained (Chapter 13).

Legal scholars in international law assessed the limits of law when confronted with the play of political power in international relations. *Cedric Ryngaert* examined extraterritorial jurisdiction and harmonisation of substantive economic law in their limited ability to equally assure the rights of States and transnational economic actors (Chapter 14). *Tom Ruys* examined to what extent international law acts as a restraint on States' decisions to resort to the use of force against other States. To this end, he identified several rationalistic and reflective factors inducing compliance with international law and then applied those factors to the use of force among States (Chapter 15).

Constitutional lawyers, legal historians, human rights specialists, and legal anthropologists pointed to the fragilities of fundamental and human rights instruments. *David Haljan* examined whether the rule of law is a limit to popular sovereignty (Chapter 16). *Bram Delbecke* explained how young Nation–States are urged to restrict civil liberties and to limit their protective function, in order to protect their fragile identity and self–understanding, and he related this difficult relationship between the symbolic and the protective functions of the law to the open texture of the law (Chapter 17). *Aagje Ieven* showed how the open texture of privacy rights as human rights, and the element of judicial interpretation by the European Court of Human Rights (ECtHR) necessitated by the former, can compromise the protective role of human rights (Chapter 18). *Willem Verrijdt* argued that the ever growing backlog at the ECtHR also undermines protective legality (Chapter 19). *Wouter Vandenhole* explored the limits of human rights law in a development context and contended that acknowledgement by human rights lawyers of these limits may determine and circumscribe as a whole the development potential of human rights law (Chapter 20). *Stijn Deklerck et al.* addressed the frailness of human rights law when faced with indigenous cultures, with religious legal sub–systems, or even with broader political transformations such as regionalism in Europe (Chapter 21).

Finally, experts in law and technology also addressed the limits of the law. *Geertrui Van Overwalle and Esther van Zimmeren* showed how technological innovations uncover the limitations of legal instruments such as patents and licensing agreements (Chapter 22). *Mireille Hildebrandt* argued that the articulation of certain legal norms in new technological devices and infrastructures (for example, the so–called 'Internet of Things', or 'Ambient Intelligent environment') is important for otherwise we may run up against the end of the law. In addition, she argued that such technological articulation should be constrained by the central tenets of a constitutional democracy, lest we reach the end of the rule of law (Chapter 23). *Hans Graux* explained how the advent of true anonymous communication techniques ('darknets') could result in the creation of an 'information free–zone', in which the regulatory and pacificatory functions of the law are utterly lost. Additionally, he examined legal, technological, and philosophical approaches to dealing with the problems created by this development (Chapter 24).

Over and above the sheer range of these topics, the authors also engaged in a common enterprise that lies at the foundation of this book: the ambition to revisit the law, in all its varieties, through the lens of its limits. The purpose of this concluding chapter, "Facing the Limits of the Law", is to take stock of the many fruitful insights revealed in the contributions to *Facing the Limits of the Law.* These insights all contribute to answering the three research questions set out in "The Limits of the Law (Introduction)".

The first research question asked, what types of limits of the law could be mapped throughout a variety of legal disciplines. "The Limits of the Law (Introduction)" offered a conceptual 'umbrella' and a common frame of reference from which the contributors could borrow their concepts and methodology. This programmatic outline aimed primarily at facilitating 'limits of the law' research by the different contributors. All authors mapped (types of) limits of the law through an analysis of the law's functions and characteristics. Many authors, however, did much more than just illustrating the editors' conceptual framework and considerably refined and fine–tuned this framework. In doing so, they not only detected new types of limits of the law in their respective disciplines, but also improved the conceptual scheme against which the law's limits can be mapped in other legal fields (see sections 3 through 5 below).

The second research question set out in the "The Limits of the Law (Introduction)" read, "What are the important social and cultural transformation responsible for our sensibility of the limits of the law?" Many authors contributed substantially to getting a more comprehensive picture of evolving social and cultural transformations which are responsible for bringing the limits of the law to the fore in the shape of a collective experience shared by many lawyers and citizens in distinct legal fields and disciplines (see section 2 below).

The third research question was how we can deal with the limits of the law in a justifiable way. Most of the contributors designed strategies to deal with the limits of the law identified through an analysis of the law's functions and characteristics. To this end, they most often exploited the ideals and aspirations that underpin the law's function of protective legality and reconsidered some of the law's most essential characteristics, such as the interaction of law and different societal spheres or the open texture of law (see section 6 below).

2 Late–Modernity and the Limits of the Law

A basic intuition underlying *Facing the Limits of the Law* goes back to what Charles Taylor famously called the 'malaises of modernity', or to what others captured as 'late–modernity'. These are "features of our contemporary culture and society that people experience as a loss or a decline, even as our civilization 'develops'".[1] The ideals of the Enlightenment, such as individual freedom, scientific progress, and welfare, tend to produce immense social costs when pursued in a globalised, highly technological, consumerist environment: mass unemployment, ecological imbalances, an ever growing gap between the wealthy and the poor, religious fundamentalism, and terrorism. From its inception, *Facing the Limits of the Law* embraced the idea that the strange combination of a belief in modernity's achievements and of growing awareness of its darker side tends to reproduce itself in contemporary law and legal self–understanding. Throughout a number of chapters, the intuition that evolving social and cultural transformations are responsible for making our awareness of the limits of the law more prominent, has been reaffirmed. The list of transformations explained in these chapters is impressive: individualism, consumerism, erosion of the public sphere, technological progress, globalisation, decline of the Nation–State, regionalism, convergence of legal cultures, cultural pluralism, a growing gap between the wealthy and the poor, and so on. In what follows we will briefly revisit some of these developments, recalling their relevance in specific areas of the law.

It is important to note that several authors, when engaging in an analysis of the late–modern context from a external point of view, actually did more than just reaffirming, articulating, and explaining a basic intuition underlying their experience of the limits of the law. They broadened their reach by using sociological concepts and explanations in their attempts to reflect critically on the limits of their own legal discipline, and so to find new ways of dealing with these limits. In fact, "there is no other way to make knowledge meaningful except by transcending it."[2] When reading the foregoing chapters, it can be observed that the better the authors got to grips with the fragility of modern ideals such as individualism, technological progress, globalisation, and pluralism, the better they were able to give expression to, and assess the vulnerability of, law in its variety of shapes and practices. Likewise in this concluding chapter, we will actually do more than just summarising the late–modern context responsible for our growing awareness of limits of the law. We will at the same time ask ourselves how our 'knowledge' of the late–modern context helps sharpening the focus of the 'limits of the law' lens, with a view to

---

1 C. Taylor, *The Ethics of Authenticity* (Cambridge, Mass. and London: Harvard University Press, 1991) 1.

2 See on the relation between 'knowledge' and 'understanding': H. Arendt, "Understanding and Politics", in *Essays in Understanding 1930–1954* (New York: Schocken Books, 2005, edited and with an introduction by Jerome Kohn) 311.

reaching a 'true understanding' of late–modern law and its limits.[3] In this way, the external, sociological account of the law's late–modern context might contribute to a more sophisticated analysis of the limits of the law from a participant's perspective.

2.1 Individualism

According to Taylor one of the perplexing sources of worries in contemporary societies is individualism. This trend "... names what many people consider the finest achievement of modern civilisation. We live in a world where people have a right to choose for themselves their own patterns of life, to decide in conscience what convictions to espouse." However, Taylor adds that "... many of us are also ambivalent."[4] Taylor refers to the massive loss of meaning generated by the collapse of traditions, religions, and older moral horizons. As a result, individual lives tend to become flat and untextured, with narcissism and obsessive self–centredness tending to prevail at the cost of neglecting a serious commitment to others. These troubling ambivalencies become even more apparent in our contemporary world where media and market, steered by neo–liberalist thinking, seduce consumers with an ideal of incessant individual self–realisation through a variety of products, goods, and life–styles. In addition, contemporary consumerism simultaneously conveys a whole set of less explicit expectations to consumers, such as that human identity should be taken as an individual task (not as a 'given'), but also that it is up to each individual alone to lead a flourishing life, fed by happy moments, as well as unforgettable kicks and feelings. Individualism and the ideal of unlimited freedom from constraints pairs then with strongly held ideas of individual responsibility. In the end, it comes down only to the individual to account for the degree of success in his life.[5] This existential weight paradoxically throws each individual upon his own limitations and vulnerabilities. He becomes extremely focused on the many sources (illness, unemployment, unsafety) that may negatively affect the conditions of his well–being (health, income, trust, and safety). In short, most of the energy of contemporary consumers is drained in finding new strategies to maximise positive sentiments in the search for self–realisation and to minimise unhappiness, thus to finding remedies for the ever lurking danger of human frailness and suffering. The individual preoccupation with individual well–being, together with extreme fear and sensibility for individual frailness echoes in different areas of contemporary law. *Facing the Limits of*

---

3 See R. Dworkin, *Law's Empire* (London: Fontana Press, 1986) 14: "Both perspectives on law, the external and the internal, are essential, and each must embrace or take into account of the other."

4 C. Taylor, *The Ethics of Authenticity* (Cambridge, Mass. and London: Harvard University Press, 1991) 2–3.

5 See Z. Bauman, *Liquid Modernity* (Oxford: Polity Press, 2000) 30–31.

the Law offers a number of examples where the ambivalences of individualism is responsible for a perception of, and even a construction of, law as a limited practice.

In "Legitimacy in the European Union and the Limits of the Law" (Chapter 12), Dierckxsens traces an interesting link with individualism and the European legitimacy deficit. In order to clarify the European legitimacy crisis, she provides a sociological and anthropological diagnosis of late–modern European societies which puts the legitimacy crisis in a broader perspective. Particular attention is paid to the assault of 'neo–liberalist' thinking on normative legitimacy. The obsessions with individual consumption and with the risk of private suffering seriously diminish the capacity of citizens to invest in a broader, common political project.[6] In our late–modern societies many individuals have stretched their 'consumer' behaviour and instrumental rationality into the realm of national and supranational politics. The dominance of instrumental rationality reduces a preoccupation with the common good into a preoccupation with general welfare. Instrumental reasoning transforms State administrators into managers and social engineers. It changes citizens into consumers. These 'consumer citizens' tend to regard European law and institutions as a legal structure which could serve or hinder their own private interests. The legitimacy of these institutions becomes then unstable, since it can easily become affected by 'consumer dissatisfaction'. Dissatisfied consumers cannot be pacified by pointing out the constitutional principles which discipline the struggle between competing interests. The necessary will to act and deliberate publicly, in the interest of all, is too weak to establish a solid basis of democratic legitimacy on grounds of which European citizens could reasonably accept the legitimacy of European institutions, their decisions, and the resulting legal norms. European citizens are unable to see themselves as both authors and addressees of European law.

In "Criminal Law, Victims, and the Limits of Therapeutic Consequentialism" (Chapter 9), Daems observes that 'victim–oriented consequentialism' originated at a time when people and institutions were increasingly preoccupied with mental health problems and emotional well–being. Daems highlights how the metaphor of 'healing victims' has now stopped being a metaphor: 'healing victims' comes to play a role in what is expected from penal practices. From the perspective of therapeutic consequentialism, the existing system of criminal law is perceived to be inadequate. Arguments are now being put forward that formal reactions to crime *should* adequately respond to these needs – an objective they never had. That is, the limits of criminal law extend to new, formerly unimaginable, domains.

---

6 See also H. Arendt, "On Humanity in Dark Times", in *Men in Dark Times* (New York: Harcourt, 1968) 4–5: "More and more people in the countries of the Western world, which since the decline of the ancient world has regarded freedom from politics as one of the basic freedoms, make use of this freedom and has retreated from the world and their obligation within it. ... But with each such retreat an almost demonstrable loss to the world takes place; what is lost is the specific and usually irreplaceable in–between which should have formed between this individual and his fellow men."

According to Daems, therapeutic consequentialism and, accordingly, redesigning criminal justice in terms of 'healing victims', reflects new cultural attitudes and perceptions. The assumption is made that people who are going through stressful or painful moments are deeply traumatised and scarred for life. People appear as emotionally inadequate, vulnerable, helpless, with low self–esteem. Daems appears wary' about this shift towards victim–oriented consequentialism, which is witnessed in restorative justice programmes as well as in new justifications for the death penalty. This shift risks obscuring the inherent problematic nature of the State's power to punish and risks eroding legal guarantees for the offender. All these dangers confront us with the vulnerability of changing perceptions and reform ambitions in the criminal law. Victim–oriented consequentialism and an all too strong preoccupation in contemporary culture with emotional well–being, might lead to changing dynamics in criminal justice *that produce new limits and limitations*. Or, to put it more radically for the purpose of this volume: by critically exploring the ways in which reformers have launched their attacks on the limits of criminal law, Daems seems to warn us more generally that a 'limits of the law' approach is not an innocent enterprise.

2.2 Technological Progress

Reading "Functions and Limits of Patent Law", "Technology and the End of Law", and "Darknets and the Future of Freedom of Expression in the Information Society", the reader quickly becomes convinced of the fact that the ambivalencies of technological progress – its capacity to extend the space of freedom as well as its ability to create immense social perils – unmistakably feed a strong feeling of malaise regarding the regulatory and protective qualities of the law.

"Functions and Limits of Patent Law" (Chapter 22) considers the intimate connection between technology, the economy, and law. Van Overwalle and van Zimmeren observe that progress in ICT and biotechnologies have created an enormous potential for profit–making with inventors and companies by expanding patentability and licensing practices to new products and materials. The steady increase in patent activity has led to a widespread concern relating to the quality of patents. Instead of holding the optimistic general presupposition that patent law and its benefits stimulate new technological innovation, Van Overwalle and van Zimmeren remark how the expansion of patentability had led to an unfortunate increase of patents and 'patent thickets', the dense webs of overlapping patents which a researcher or company must hack through in order actually to develop and commercialise a new product. In other words, technological progress and the promise of money–making through patent law in our late–modern world have created a socio–economic environment in which the patent system becomes an obstacle to its own objective, that is, stimulating human creativity and technological innovation. Patent law appears to be largely inapt to fulfilling its regulatory function with respect to both the vertical (patent authorities – patent applicants) and the horizontal (patent holders – potential licensees, general public, patients) relationships.

"Technology and the End of Law" (Chapter 23) concentrates on the potential emergence of the 'Internet of Things', a world in which all our gestures are registered by tagged objects in our environment. Since this web of things is linked to complex database–systems and complex data–profiling programmes, all of which store these data and process them as predictable patterns of behaviour, objects in our environment will be able to act upon the behaviour of each human being. These things will serve our wishes at the appropriate moment and at the appropriate place according an appropriate knowledge of behavioural patterns and personality traits. Like the impact of so many contemporary inventions, the creation of an Internet of Things promises ambivalent social consequences. Hildebrandt warns against the worrisome consequences which could put at peril basic democratic values, such as the right to privacy and due process. The Internet of Things would create an immense knowledge asymmetry between the persons being profiled and those who could access all this profiled information in order to pursue certain objectives, be it of a commercial or of a political kind. This asymmetry strongly diminishes the citizens' "capacity to anticipate the grounds on which they are judged, included, or excluded". Hildebrandt shows how awareness of this limited ability of written law to constrain efficiently and effectively human behaviour surfaces prominently in a world where the Internet of Things constitutes our environment. Imagining such a world and its social consequences prompts the conclusion that the absence of a shift from a written legal tradition to a technologically embodied legal practice might lead to the annulment of law's regulatory and protective power. However, the consequences of an Internet to Things announce themselves as beneficial in that they promise to change radically man's relation to the world. Human beings would no longer encounter things as part of an unknown, hostile, unpredictable reality full of obstacles and unhappy surprises, but as a continuous ally in the realisation of their wishes and desires. From an Internet of Things emerges an unseen regulatory power in that it does more than discourage undesirable behaviour: it makes such behaviour simply impossible, for it annuls the conditions of the possibility of autonomous action. When imagining the ambiguities relating to this Internet of Things, our malaise with contemporary law gradually becomes tangible. Imagining an Internet of Things points out to the fragility of our rule of law principles through the knowledge asymmetry and normative impact such an intelligent environment entails. Classic legal instruments such as written prohibitions will then prove inadequate for effectively enforcing the protection of privacy and due process values in a highly technological environment.

"Darknets and the Future of Freedom of Expression in the Information Society" (Chapter 24) addresses the regulation of new ICT technologies. Graux observes that the internet has given all of us the power to broadcast information in a manner and on a scale that has never before been witnessed. It is important to note that this freedom of gathering and spreading information has an enormous empowering impact on human relations. According to Graux, the three basic principles of modern information regulation have been threatened by the newly emerging technologies in our late–modern societies. In an electronic environment, our laws tend to be ineffective because the socio–cultural perspective underpinning these rules has not evolved to keep tune with technological developments. Graux focuses in particular on darknets (information exchange networks built on top of the internet, but which specifically focus on obfuscating the source and destination of any information stored in them or transferred between their members). Participants to darknets would be able to disseminate any information they please, in effect creating a type of 'information free–zone' where any legal restrictions would be come unenforceable and therefore meaningless. Darknets would be a clear example of a social reality that annuls the regulatory potentials of law, merely because the participants to a specific information exchange would become unidentifiable, and because information on a node can not be readily deciphered. Put differently, darknets would reveal the constitutive condition of information regulation. By rendering this constitutive condition ineffective, they would make environments of communication immune to regulation through law.

These three illustrations clearly show how thinking about technology and the environments it creates reveal the fragility of legal instruments as well as the fragile constitutive conditions on which the legal enterprise rests. We will see below how these illustrations prove also fruitful for refining the conceptual tools of a 'limits of the law' approach. The marginal utility of legal instruments in stimulating technology, the possibility of violation of written legal norms, dependence of law upon constitutive preconditions (such as the identifiabiltity of human agents), all call for a more refined analysis of the features of the law to which several limits of the law can be imputed.

2.3 Globalisation

The term 'globalisation' has acquired considerable emotive force. Whereas economic globalisation and the gradual liberalisation of the markets initially were thought to favour political and social integration and to be a key element in political stability and social cohesion, it is now more often considered as the source of political impotence and major societal problems such as mass unemployment, increasing inequality, undermined living standards, security threats (such as terrorism, organised crime, migration issues), and the like.

In "Functions and Limits of Patent Law" (Chapter 22), Van Overwalle and van Zimmeren take globalisation as one of the important trends which help revealing the limits of patent law. The authors associate globalisation with multi–level and multi–institutional decision–making and with the rise of experts. In a globalised world, the decision–making process of patent law issues has shifted from the national to the global level. International organisations such as the World Intellectual Property Organisation and the World Trade Organisation have become central actors in decision–making instead of national authorities. This shift involves a considerable shadow side: the underrating of national and local aspirations, a lack of transparency, a competition among the institutions involved, the divergence of national interests, and the power imbalance between the rich developed and the poor developing States. As to the lack of transparency, the authors also point to the emergence of the so–called 'epistemic communities'. The growing importance of these epistemic communities raises serious concerns of democratic legitimacy. Highly important choices which potentially affect a large group of people tend to be obscured by framing these choices as purely technical. Paying attention to this globalised level of decision–making and to the problems such decision–making raises, pushes legal scholars to become aware of the limits of patent law. According to Van Overwalle and van Zimmeren, the current globalisation trend illustrates patent law's failure to achieve its symbolic function. As the forum of decision–making has gradually shifted from the local to the global level, the scope of protection of patent law is increasingly subjected to multi–level and multi–institutional governance. Patent law appears to be less able to represent national values and to guarantee national public interests as expressed by developing countries, and fails to reflect adequately a coherent set of values that symbolically knits these actors together as political members of one group. In addition, because of the process of expert reliance, patent law struggles with effectively providing political accountability for the decisions and resulting provisions made on a global level. In this way, patent law does not seem to be adequately equipped to guarantee access to and participation in the legal and the political decision–making process.

In "The Limits of Substantive International Economic Law: In Support of Reasonable Extraterritorial Jurisdiction" (Chapter 14), Reyngaert argues that the shift towards 'substantivism', that is, the shift towards internationally standardised substantive rules and procedures, may fail to deliver all the benefits ascribed to it because of the dubious process in which substantive international law may come into being. In this way, Reyngaert traces the limits of an approach that intends to supplant procedural international law based on delimiting States' spheres of competence (the law of jurisdiction), with substantive international law (an international *jus commune* of substantive rules and procedures). In particular, he argues that the weaker members of the international community may, on balance, sometimes be better off with a rule–based framework of international jurisdiction than with common substantive rules and procedures saturated with the interests of the powerful. In practice, the glorification of the benefits of substantivism has obscured the reality that international consultations, or the emphasis put on them, may at times produce outcomes which barely serve the interests of justice and equity. Harmonisation is not achieved nor does cooperation take place in a power–free environment. Parties to international agreements may be only formally equal. In the real world, the more powerful parties will usually weigh heavily on the substantive outcome of a negotiating process. This might produce a regime that favours the interests of the powerful to the detriment of the weaker. Accordingly, in terms of their results, extraterritorial jurisdiction and substantive solutions may not differ that much. Both may coax weaker States into adapting their laws in ways desired by powerful States.

The phenomenon of globalisation also appears as an explanatory scene for other analyses of the limits of the law, in particular in the field of European law. In "The Limits of the Law and the Development of the EU" (Chapter 13), Foqué and Steenbergen explain how the above–mentioned shift in meaning to globalisation is partly responsible for the legitimacy crisis of EU institutions. Since any institution aiming at the free movement of persons and goods tends to be seen as a potential source of social and security risks, European law and its institutions face a considerable deficit of political legitimacy. In other words, shifting perceptions revolving around globalisation and a higher awareness of its drawbacks tend to result in an ever stronger perception that European law and its institutions fail in assuring their citizens "a reasonable degree of control over their destiny".

It would, of course, be too simple to export these insights relating globalisation and the limits of the law to other areas of the law, but they can nevertheless serve as an interesting device to search for new limits in fields such as economic law, criminal law, or international law. One of the research questions might be then to ask to what extent the shifting perceptions regarding globalisation render fragile the political legitimacy of institutions and legal instruments designed to facilitate a global economy. Another question might be to what extent growing scepticism about globalisation and the perceived loss of control cripple the political legitimacy of institutions on which all too high expectations are projected regarding their ability to restrain and remedy the costs of globalisation.

These research questions also invite us to embrace a suggestion which has already been made in "Criminal Law, Victims, and the Limits of Therapeutic Consequentialism" (Chapter 9). Just as contemporary preoccupations with emotional turmoil of vulnerable individuals can easily "'construct' limits of the criminal law", changing perceptions of globalisation can distort our representation of the limits of European law. Excessive fears of globalisation tend to be projected on European institutions, while blinding us to the many potentials it could offer in light of a regulatory, protective, or peace–making perspective. Put more generally, a better insight into the broader framework of our late–modern societies prompts us to recognise fully that lawyers', citizens', and politicians' awareness of the types of limits of the law, is not just the result of neutral observation. Understanding this awareness and mapping the limits of the law does not take place in a social vacuum, and can easily be distorted by the broader cultural and socio–economic developments from which this awareness has emerged. If a 'limits of law' approach aspires still to gain true understanding, then it should also contain a self–critical stance towards its own presuppositions. Such a self–critical attitude could be also fostered by addressing the issue of how pervasive these limits of the law are, compared with the possibilities offered by the legal discipline in question and its legal instruments.

2.4 Pluralism

Many contributors tend to become aware of the law's limits against a background of cultural and legal pluralism. In a globalised world where different cultures meet, mesh, and meld, legal instruments, whether designed by Nation–States or supranational institutions, are limited in their ability to regulate effectively and legitimately the various and diverging cultural attitudes and to resolve cultural conflicts. Whether designed as an instrument of regulating multicultural societies, as a tool for regulating whole regions, or as a lever for global governance, law inevitably encounters tensions among different cultural groups and also among different legal systems which borrow their distinctness from these cultures.

In "The Limits of Legality in the Criminal Law" (Chapter 6), Claes and Krolikowski show that tensions, and even struggles, between different legal traditions might be responsible for the erosion of basic concepts and principles in domestic legal orders. They argue that the principle of legality and its role of legal protection are considerably weakened in many countries sharing the civil law tradition. Claes and Krolikowski examine to what extent the impact of common law traditions (characterised by pragmatism and a strong emphasis on judge–made law) on civil law traditions, affect the idea of legal certainty and the separation of powers which underpin the principle of legality. Claes' and Krolikowski's awareness of the limited ability of that principle to offer legal protection has been sharpened by representing the tension between civil and common law traditions in terms of a dialogue as well as a potential power struggle. The contingent outcome of this struggle seems to determine whether legality may (or may not) effectively protect citizens against the risk of arbitrary judicial discretion.

Finally, the impact of a variety of (legal) cultures on regulation through law, strongly surfaces in the domain of human rights law. In "The Limits of Human Rights Protection from the Perspective of Legal Anthropology" (Chapter 21), Deklerck *et al.* illustrate how the regulatory impact of human rights law should not be overestimated when implemented in or enforced upon indigenous, religious, or subcultural groups. The authors convincingly show that religious or cultural groups shape their own legal norms and institutions according to their own values and beliefs, which may strongly conflict with human rights standards such as gender equality or fair distribution of social and economic rights. Legal anthropologists invite us not to expect too much regulatory effect of human rights standards on such occasions. They also call upon human rights activists to question the legitimacy of their regulatory ambitions, since the legal sub–systems of these cultural groups witness a strong internal legitimacy, expressive of a shared cultural identity. Another important insight offered by legal anthropology is that cultural groups internalise human rights standards differently according to their own convictions and values. They create their own versions of human rights law which may clash with the official versions, or with the interpretations from other cultures. Human rights standards easily become fragmented. They collapse into different and often conflicting habits and representations, which considerably weaken their regulatory impact.

3 Revisiting the Functions of the Law

3.1 Four Functions of the Law?

When composing "The Limits of the Law (Introduction)", we were acutely conscious of the incompleteness of our account of the functions and characteristics of the law. We sketched four functions of the law: the *regulatory function*, the *symbolic function*, the *dispute resolution function*, and the function of *protective legality*. It came as no surprise that, in many chapters, suggestions were made to improve this conceptual framework. The contributors moulded this conceptual framework according to the particularity of their own research areas and conceptually refined the analysis of the law's functions. For example, whereas "The Limits of the Law (Introduction)" analysed different aspects of protective legality under one and the same heading, Foqué and Steenbergen, in "The Limits of the Law and the Development of the EU" (Chapter 13), found it more appropriate to qualify the protection of negative freedom on the one hand, and of positive freedom on the other, as two separate and independent functions of the law: the law as an instrument to organise and regulate the exercise of power by public authorities in order to offer legal protection to citizens, and secondly the law as an instrument to organise the participation of citizens in the process of political will formation. In addition, they distinguished more explicitly between "the law as an instrument to register and consolidate relations and institutions" (including the law as a medium for shaping and giving voice to collective meanings) and "the law as an instrument to change relations and to create institutions or govern their development". In contrast, "The Limits of the Law (Introduction)" implicitly included the law as an instrument for change under the heading of the regulatory function of the law and considered the symbolic capacity of the law as constituting a separate function of the law.

3.2 Alliances and Rivalry between the Functions of the Law

Even more importantly, many contributors disentangled the complex relation between the functions of the law. Whereas "The Limits of the Law (Introduction)" discussed the four functions of the law separately, many authors made efforts to uncover alliances among these functions. For example, Dierckxsens pointed to the intertwining of the symbolic function and the function of legal protection. In "Legitimacy in the European Union and the Limits of the Law" (Chapter 12), she argues that the limited ability of European institutions to serve as a medium for shaping and giving voice to the shared value–orientations of a European polity tracks closely their limited ability to provide legal mechanisms that allow for citizens to deliberate collectively on a common future for Europe and to see themselves as authors of the rules, decisions, and institutions which govern them. The symbolic deficit of European institutions is then intrinsically linked with the difficulties of the European Union to reflect an autonomous society, a society of autonomous citizens capable of deliberating on and of making laws that are intersubjectively valid.

Likewise, in "Rebuilding Trust in the Former Yugoslavia: Overcoming the Limits of the Formal Justice System" (Chapter 11), Valiñas gives an interpretative status to the functional approach of "The Limits of the Law (Introduction)". In order to understand better the potentials and limits of the law in delivering basic social trust among citizens, she combines the symbolic and protective functions with the function of dispute resolution. Through the lens of these three functions, Valiñas explains that rebuilding social trust in the aftermath of mass atrocities committed among ethnic groups requires institutional mechanisms of dispute resolution and peace–making. Basic social trust also requires instruments and institutions by means of which violations of basic rights are acknowledged and respect for these rights are reaffirmed and guaranteed for the future (legal protection). And finally, rebuilding basic social trust requires institutions and mechanisms that express the will to continue to live together as well as the recognition of basic rights in such a way that such trust can be shared by all members of the society experiencing a post–conflict situation (symbolic function).

A number of authors elaborated on the rivalry between different functions of the law. In "Constitutional Ideals, National Identity and the Limits of the Law" (Chapter 17), Delbecke examines the difficult relationship between the symbolic and the protective functions of the law in the context of young Nation–States, illustrated with an historical analysis of freedom of the press in 19th century Belgium. Delbecke shows that an instrumentalisation of fundamental rights and freedoms (facilitated by the open texture of these legal norms) tends to erode the guarantees offered by these rights and freedoms. Interestingly, he argues that this rivalry between the symbolic and the protective capacities of the law seems to show up whenever a young Nation–State needs to affirm its identity before the world. In their quest for a liberal national identity, young Nation–States always somehow seem to try to limit the freedoms and liberties used to construct and maintain these identities.

At the end of "Regulating Prison Life: A Case Study of the Inmate Disciplinary Study" (Chapter 8), Robert points at potential rivalry between the regulative and the protective functions of the law. He observes that if law was a singularly sufficient tool for the regulation of prisons in Canada, the volume of prison–related jurisprudence generated both before and since the introduction of Canadian legislation governing the actions of prison officials would not exist. It is not uncommon that such jurisprudence follows from cases related to tensions between the legal protection of prisoners and the regulatory objectives of the prison.

4 Revisiting the Characteristics of the Law

In *Justice in Robes*, Dworkin notes important shifts in contemporary legal philosophy and legal theory. Classic theoretical issues such as the role of morality in legal reasoning, the problem of judicial discretion, or the nature of legal norms, are no longer debated and explored merely on an academic scene dominated by legal philosophers. The discussion of these topics have migrated to the heart of the legal disciplines themselves.

> Some of the most philosophically sensitive and valuable work in legal theory has been done by academic lawyers who classify themselves not as legal philosophers but as constitutional lawyers or experts in contract or tort or environmental or some other branches of private or public law.[7]

Their insights are often the fruit of interdisciplinary dialogue with economists, political philosophers, experts in ethics, and even in the literary sciences. *Facing the Limits of the Law* tried to contribute to this shift, by easing theoretical insights and concepts away from their classic theoretical spheres, offering them to academic lawyers and legal experts for further exploration.

4.1 Revisiting Law as a Societal Sphere

"The Limits of the Law (Introduction)" did not offer a clear view of the complex interactions between different societal spheres, but only advanced two working hypotheses. According to the first hypothesis, law is limited in its functional abilities for the more fundamental reason that its practices are to a large extent dependent upon the broader dynamic generated by other societal spheres. According to the second hypothesis, law falls short of accomplishing its functions to the extent that it is shown to be structurally inadequate to permeate and guide other societal spheres. Law is therefore often limited in its ability to serve its basic societal functions. The contributors to *Facing the Limits of the Law* were invited to fuel their legal expertise with imaginative and interdisciplinary skills and to assess and qualify these two rather pessimistic working hypotheses. In "The Limits of the Law of Obligations" (Chapter 3), Willems examined the private law concept of 'natural obligation' and the role of this and other open–textured concepts in the relationship with morality. In "Private Law and the Limits of Legal Dogmatics" (Chapter 2), Loth explored the relationship between private law and morality and also focused on the role of open–textured concepts and principles.

In contrast to the first somewhat gloomy hypothesis that the impact of morality, or of any other societal sphere, could be an obstacle to the fulfilment of the law's functions, Loth and Willems present a far more optimistic account. Loth argues

---

7 R. Dworkin, *Justice in Robes* (Cambridge, Mass.: Harvard University Press, 2006) 34.

that the fact that private law is informed by moral norms ("moralisation of private law") should be regarded as a blessing. A connection is kept between law and morality which should reduce the alienation between citizens and their legislation, therefore enhancing its regulatory and pacifying functions, as well as its symbolic function. In addition, morality reinforces the law's ability to answer the values of the rule of law. By offering itself as a guideline for judges, morality helps visualise the dangers of arbitrary State power and, thus, contributes to obtaining legal certainty. Thus, the imprint of morality helps law fulfil its basic functions. Likewise, Willems argues that the disturbing effects of morality on law should not be exaggerated. On the contrary, common values and shared understandings can provide a solid basis for judges to ground and justify decisions based on discretion. In particular, open–textured borderline concepts such as 'natural obligation' which may apply even when a legal obligation is lacking, may serve as a kind of bridge, allowing judges to ground their appreciation in the firm soil of shared moral values and convictions. Willems even suggests that all core concepts of private law (such as 'good faith', '*bonus pater familias*', 'equity', and so on) have an open texture and refer to an underlying moral rule or concept, which has to be used as a guideline when applying and interpreting private law. In this way, the imprint of morality channelled through open–textured concepts helps law in fulfilling its basic functions. It can "comfort citizens that the law will not be an unworldly abstraction, but will lean very much towards the social feeling of what is 'right' and 'wrong' in a given situation".

It is important to note that both Loth and Willems acknowledge, however, that morality does not always reinforce the functional abilities of the law. Other, less comforting scenarios might occur. For example, in cases of abortion, wrongful life, euthanasia, and so on, strong diverging views on morality may tend to weaken law's functional abilities instead of strengthen them. The lesson to be learned from these chapters for a 'limits of the law' approach is this: just as we should avoid unconditionally glorifying the beneficial effects of morality on law, we should avoid the categorical stance that law fails to serve its societal functions, because of the negative impact of morality on law. We should assess in each specific context the potentials as well as the limiting role of moral values and sensibilities regarding the law. The advantage of such a more contextualised strategy is that mapping the limits of the law also prepares a way for managing these limits appropriately.

Loth and Willems also temper the second working hypothesis (law falls short of accomplishing its functions to the extent that it is shown to be structurally inadequate to permeate and guide other societal spheres). Without denying the differences between private law and morality, the authors argue that these differences must not be overrated. On the basis of their analyses, they acknowledge that at least private law practice is not totally ill–equipped for interfering in the sphere of morality. Loth argues that open–textured concepts and principles of private law function as a bridge to the sphere of ethics. More and more social relationships are brought under the influence of private law, such as those between teacher and student, parents and children, and doctors and patients ("legalisation of morality").

Willems also offers reasons to believe that law has "many subtle ways" to penetrate into the sphere of morality, without abolishing the latter's informal, spontaneous, trust–based character, thereby "responding to any situation in the most appropriate manner". In particular, the concept of 'natural obligation' is a handy instrument for gradually and prudently preparing expansion of law into the domain of morality, without blindly and wildly applying the whole machinery of the law on a moral context thereby replacing morality's rule of reason. In this way, Loth and Willems invite us to examine how, in other fields of law, similar intermediary roles can be accorded to other legal concepts and to enquire which legal concepts actually, or at least potentially, mediate between law and still other social spheres, such as politics.

In "When Law Meet Power: The Limits of Public International Law and the Recourse to Military Force" (Chapter 15), Ruys addresses the perennial issue of to what extent international law is able to act as a restraint on governmental decisions in foreign policy matters. The chapter starts from the foregoing working hypotheses. Applied to the context of foreign politics and rephrased in the language of 'realism', these hypotheses come down to two simple and admittedly attractive ideas. First, public international law is governed and instrumentalised by the power politics of States, and therefore, falls short of serving some of its basic societal functions. Second, public international law does not affect the behaviour of States. Ruys' arguments show striking similarities with those of Loth and Willems. By critically addressing the realist school and revisiting different theories of public international law, Ruys reconsiders the two working hypotheses set out in "The Limits of the Law (Introduction)". Ruys proposes a fine–grained conceptual scheme that claims a better description of the role of law in States' policy decisions.

In contrast to the first working hypothesis, Ruys argues that State behaviour in international relations is not steered exclusively by predefined interests and, therefore, does not *per se* hamper the protective function of international law. States' identities and interests are the product of social interaction. Participation in institutional regimes, and thus in public international law, influence States' values, self–understanding, and understanding of other States. When focusing on the deliberative and reflective qualities of international law, Ruys recognises the relative autonomy of international legal regimes. Instead of reflecting individual choices of the powerful States, international legal norms are processed through a deliberative discourse in which beliefs and expectations mark out standards of behaviour, which in their turn carry precedential value for the future assessment of State conduct.

In addition, Ruys considerably tempers the idea that public international law bears no impact on the behaviour of States and that international relations are finally ruled by 'managed anarchy'. Ruys seems to favour a reflective International Relations theory. According to this theory, international legal rules are part of the non–material elements which make up the international social structure. International legal rules are believed to shape States' identities and interests, and to impact on the sphere of political power play through three mechanisms: imagination, communication, and constraint. In turning to the factors inducing compliance, Ruys distinguishes between 'rationalistic' or 'functional' factors and 'reflective' or 'normative' mainsprings. The former category concerns a cost–benefit calculus of the 'sticks' and 'carrots' of compliance when weighed against the possible benefits of a contemplated violation. On the 'reflective' side, Ruys distinguishes between the justificatory discourse process on the one hand, and the process of internalisation at the domestic level on the other. Ruys also observes that the susceptibility of States to these factors and the limits of public international law in serving its basic functions vary greatly depending on the position of the violator as well as the nature of the rule that is violated. For a 'limits of the law' analysis, the clue is not beginning with a crude statement that international law is ill–suited to rule the sphere of politics, but more proceeding to analyse the factors that weaken the inevitable constraining force of international law on State behaviour.

4.2 Revisiting Law as Social Practice: The Open Texture of Law

One of the theoretical concepts which "The Limits of the Law (Introduction)" brought to the attention of the contributors was Hart's famous concept of 'open texture'. Legal norms are the written expression of a social practice which resists complete articulation. The meaning of a legal norm reveals itself in the way the norm is followed, applied, and so on. Its meaning can never be fixed. In "The Limits of the Law (Introduction)", it was assumed that the law's open texture, while surely producing many important social benefits, might simultaneously be responsible for limiting the functional abilities of the law in various ways and throughout different fields of legal practice. The open texture of law bears upon the regulatory, symbolic, dispute resolution, and protective roles of contemporary law, because of difficulties of interiorisation, the inevitable emergence of hard cases, massive loss of meaning, and relative unpredictability of application and enforcement. Many contributors deepened the diagnostic qualities of the 'open texture' of the law with a view to identifying limits of the law.

In a number of chapters, legal experts critically discuss the frequently used legislative technique of open norms in late–modern societies. This technique crosses the borders of private law (*e.g.* 'natural obligation', EC consumer contract law), economic law (*e.g.* EC unfair trade law, EC competition law, and so forth), criminal law, human rights law, and many other branches of the law. In "The Limits of Consumer Law in Europe" (Chapter 5), Keirsbilck placed the open texture of the recent EC directive concerning unfair commercial practices in the context of late–modern regulatory ambivalencies: the need to regulate economic life and to protect internal market participants against unfair commercial practices on the one hand, and the concern to maintain innovation and progressive dynamics of European society and markets, on the other hand. As late–modern citizens, we are not willing to give up the belief in progress and innovation, but at the same time we feel tremendously insecure as to the growing risks that accompany economic and technological growth. On the one hand, the technique of open norms is meant as a cure. They serve as an answer to these complex regulatory needs, and, thereby, embody the belief that we can pursue the path of innovation, and push back its negative effects. On the other hand, regulating societies and their markets on the basis of open and flexible rules throws the law back onto its own fragility. They can poison law's capacity to serve basic social functions, because open norms are a token of law's open texture itself. Keirsbilck takes these fragilities into his analysis of the general clauses prohibiting unfair, misleading, and aggressive commercial practices, and accordingly maps limits of European consumer law.

Some authors further sharpen the diagnostic qualities of the open texture of law by contending that the open texture of the law can easily bring the law to its limits, when the gap between a legal norm and its application or enforcement (inherent to the open texture of the law) also reveals an institutional gap or the absence of an adequate system of fair distribution between institutional competences. This insight underlies various topics and analyses in this book, ranging from the open texture of human rights law, through criminal law, to consumer law. In "Privacy as Human Rights: No Limits?" (Chapter 18), Ieven shows that the vagueness of Article 8 European Convention of Human Rights (ECHR) amounts to considerable uncertainty as to a just and fair application in concrete cases when there is no adequate and principled system of fair distribution between the institutional role of national authorities in assuring respect for the right to privacy on the one hand, and the institutional competences of the ECtHR on the other. Without such a principled system, the protective role of the right to privacy risks being seriously impaired.

Likewise, in "The Limits of Legality in the Criminal Law" (Chapter 6), Claes and Krolikowski argue that the turbulent effect of the criminal law's open texture on the principle of legality and its role to protect citizens against an arbitrary display of State power is all the more pressing when there are no adequate principles governing the inevitable delegation of law–making power from the legislator to the judge. As long as a legal system does not come up with such principles, legality will be utterly vulnerable to erosion and limited in fulfilling properly its function of legal protection.

In "The Limits of Consumer Law in Europe" (Chapter 5), Keirsbilck explains how the European *Flucht in Generalklauseln* is particularly problematic within the current institutional set–up showing a gap between the upper, supranational level of rule–making and the lower, national level of enforcement. This institutional gap increases the danger of unpredictable and incoherent application of the general clauses prohibiting unfair, misleading, and aggressive commercial practices. But it also hampers interiorisation by consumers and business, and, consequently, considerably diminishes the regulatory potentials of these general clauses.

4.3 Revisiting Law as a 'Scientific' Enterprise

Many chapters of *Facing the Limits of the Law* illustrated how the scientific aspirations of contemporary legal practice may limit the ability of the law to serve its most basic functions. Significantly, some authors linked up the 'scientific' character of the law with a particular conception of the law, notably legal positivism. This should not come as a surprise. We have long considered legal dogmatics as a kind of scientific knowledge. Even today, we are inclined to understand the law *more geometrico*, in terms of a transparent, coherent, and rational model. Especially continental legal practitioners have been taught to understand their law as a hierarchical, linear system of clear–cut rules, and clear–cut distinctions. In "Private Law and the Limits of Legal Dogmatics" (Chapter 2), Loth explains how this conception of law as a scientific enterprise rests on the characteristic positivist separation of means and ends, facts and values, 'law as it is' and 'law as it ought to be', the domain of the lawyer and legal scholar and the domain of the politician or the moralist. Many authors in this volume have taken a similar route. By focusing on the failures of legal positivism, they sharpened the 'limits of the law' lens.

In the first part of "Labour Law and the Limits of Dogmatic Legal Thinking" (Chapter 4), van Putten showed how 19th century dogmatic legal thinking was unable to stretch the limits of the Napoleonic civil law concepts, rules and principles, which in fact were never devised for remedying asymmetric power relations, in order to accept the binding force of the normative part of collective labour agreements. Van Putten explains that, eventually, the legal institutionalisation of the collective labour argument overcame this limit of the law: the legislator endorsed the concept of collective labour agreement developed by legal practice; subsequently, this concept was used and refined in legal practice; and, from then onwards, it was no longer unthinkable from a private law perspective to qualify a collective labour agreement as a contract with regulatory effects.

In "Privacy Rights as Human Right: No Limits?" (Chapter 18), Ieven shows how the ECtHR seems to embrace a legal positivist stance, to the extent that it tries to push to the margin considerations of a political or moral nature. Once these considerations are made by the States, they should not be overdone in judicial application of human rights law. It is primarily the States' political responsibility to decide the concrete weight of human rights provisions.

In "The Limits of Legality in the Criminal Law" (Chapter 6), Claes and Krolikowski show that the limited ability of the principle of legality to guarantee legal protection may be partly due to legal positivism. The limited ability of legality to protect citizens against arbitrary State interventions seems to stem from the incapacity of a positivistic conception of law to constrain processes of conceptual erosion. In this way, contemporary law is running up against the limits of its rationalistic self–understanding.

4.4 Revisiting Law as an Institutionalised Practice

"The Limits of the Law (Introduction)" also focused on the law as a complex institutionalised practice consisting of both primary and secondary rules. In a legal tradition governed by the rule of law, complex institutional structures are needed in order to create and ensure a system of checks and balances between different powers, which would also allow citizens to call public officials to account for their actions and decisions. Processes of institutionalisation and processes of empowerment of citizens are two sides of the same coin. Interestingly, several authors intuitively link up the institutionalised character of the law with a State–based conception of law, and trace limits of the law back to a State–based conception of law. This conception is, roughly speaking, comprised of two propositions. Firstly, it entails the idea that law is a system of written rules enacted by State authorities and is enforced by a centralised bureaucratic administration on a fixed national territory. Secondly, a State–based conception of law comprises the conviction that States are the primary and relevant actors in the creation of international norms and standards. Naïve and *passé* as these propositions may seem in a globalised world, they continue to bear influence in many branches of the law. Several chapters witness this impact and contend that it is partly responsible for the limited ability of the law to play its role of protective legality appropriately.

In "Privacy Rights as Human Right: No Limits?" (Chapter 18), Ieven argues that the reticence of the ECtHR to give full weight in hard cases to the protective qualities of the right to privacy (Article 8 ECHR) can partly be traced back to a State–based division of labour between the national States on the one hand and the ECtHR on the other. For Ieven, the ECtHR's conviction that the balancing of privacy interests and State–interests belongs in first instance to the competence of the States is still expressive of the idea that States are the most important actors in giving content to international human rights law. According to Ieven, this State–based conception of human rights law is highly problematic from a limits–perspective, for it brings us to the paradoxical observation. Human rights are typically accorded to individuals, but their validity rests upon agreements between States. "This makes States at once the most important protectors and the most likely violators of human rights."

In "Labour Law and the Limits of Dogmatic Legal Thinking" (Chapter 4), van Putten argues that a State–based conception of law still prevents legal scholars from fully recognising collective labour agreements as a valid, fully fledged source of law. This lack of recognition considerably impairs the law's fulfilment of protective legality, since collective labour agreements have grown as important legal tools in striking balances in the power relations between employers and employees. The lack of recognition may be due to a State–based, 'monistic' perspective. It is only by realising that one and the same collective agreement can be looked upon differently from the State legal order and from a non–State legal order that the nature of the CLA can be understood.

4.5 Revisiting Law as an Argumentative Practice

Many contributions paid particular attention to the argumentative character of legal practice. Most prominently, in "Private Law and the Limits of Legal Dogmatics" (Chapter 2), Loth argues that interpretation is intrinsically interwoven with the argumentation of different positions. In day–to–day legal practice, lawyers must be capable of analysing the problem in its different aspects, addressing them on their own merits and integrating them in one legal judgment. Legal scholars must understand law in its context and "broaden the study of the law from within", not being restricted to legal dogmatics in the strict sense, but including and integrating history, literature, anthropology, and so on. All kinds of arguments, belonging to all kinds of societal spheres, are allowed in legal practice and discourse, to the extent that they can be translated or understood as legal arguments, that is, to the extent that they can be integrated into legal practice (we should not exceed the 'outer limits' of the law and rely on moral principles and pragmatic arguments *per se*). In this way, Loth seems to dramatise the limits analysis set out in "The Limits of the Law (Introduction)". If the theatre of debate is to be enlarged so as to include not only dogmatical legal arguments but all moral or political arguments which can be presented as legal arguments, the deliberative and argumentative nature of the law seems to pose even greater limits to the law.

In "When Law Meets Power: The Limits of Public International Law and the Recourse to Force" (Chapter 15), Ruys elaborates on the argumentative character of international legal practice. According to the reflective International Law approach (elaborating on the ideas of the constructivist school in International Relations theory), public international law induces compliance by means of a communicative process of claims and counter–claims. In this process of 'justificatory discourse', legal arguments are used to explain, defend, justify, and persuade. In this regard, public international law offers a regular, public, and highly articulated procedure for the assertion and evaluation of concrete claims. The justificatory discourse brings together beliefs and expectations and marks out standards of behaviour. It has precedential value in that the outcome will affect future appraisals of State conduct. By doing so, it not only determines the arguments States will invoke to justify their acts. It also affects what they do, since States are less likely to imagine or resort to certain conduct when they know that it will be denounced by the interpretive community. By arguing that public international law like any other part of the law has an argumentative character – not an uncontroversial statement – Ruys invites us to examine to what extent the tension between argumentative debate and authorative decision–making, and the limits this tension engenders, also applies in the field of international law.

4.6 Revisiting Law as an Interplay of Legal Rules, Legal Principles, and Fundamental Rights

In "The Limits of the Law (Introduction)", the editors explained that, within the tradition of the rule of law, legal systems are to be understood in terms of a complex interplay of legal rules, legal principles, and fundamental rights. It has been argued that this complex interaction between legal principles and fundamental rights often brings legal practitioners and citizens to the limits of their legal system. The term 'limits of the law' stands then for the limits of legal reasoning or legal rationality, revealing in the law and legal decisions zones of inescapable arbitrariness. A number of authors illustrated this kind of limit of the law by elaborating on a particular hard case. In doing so, they refined the 'limits of the law' lens.

In the third part of "Labour Law and the Limits of Dogmatic Legal Thinking" (Chapter 4), van Putten elaborates on an interesting hard case: the legality of collective labour agreements which aim to improve conditions of work and employment from a competition law perspective. According to van Putten, the principle of free and unrestricted competition and the principle of the binding legal force of collective labour agreements point to two different directions, but they are "not irreconcilable at all" since "they both serve the purpose of limiting the negative effects of power on a just distribution of freedom". However, van Putten eventually concedes that, although these principles of labour law and competition law may pursue the same collective policy objectives, the exercise of balancing these conflicting principles shows itself to be extremely difficult, resulting in a perception that no ultimate, reasonable measure exists such as to create an equilibrium in one fashion or another. Given these two fundamentally different and necessary accents on power relations, it appears that there is "no conceptual reason for subsuming collective labour law agreements under competition law principles or vice–versa."

As mentioned, in "Private Law and the Limits of Legal Dogmatics" (Chapter 2), Loth stresses the argumentative character of legal practice. Starting from the *Baby Kelly* case, Loth argues that legal reasoning is always defeasible and can always be annulled by adding new information. As a domain of practical reason, law lacks comfortable certainty, leaving its practitioners to find their way in daily practice with no other means than experience and practical wisdom. According to Loth, lawyers have to try to review hard cases from different perspectives, alternatively taking the moral, financial, psychological, and legal aspects into account, and attempt to integrate these different kinds of expertise in a coherent understanding of the case. Lawyers may fail in doing so.

5 The Human Condition and Limits of the Law

5.1 Law Mirrors the Human Condition

As contemporary lawyers we are still inclined to believe that we can control and change the world into the image of our desires and that law is an important tool for this. As explained in "The Limits of the Law (Introduction)" and illustrated abundantly in the subsequent chapters, these beliefs encounter increasing resistance and counter–evidence. Many chapters show that legal instruments often fall short in adequately serving the social functions they are designed for. Open–textured prohibitions of unfair commercial practices fail to provide effective consumer protection; legality proves to be an ineffective instrument in protecting citizens against arbitrary State power; current techniques of corporate criminal liability fail to generate effective regulation of corporate behaviour; a regime of strict enforcement of prison rules appears ineffective, generating ever more discretion for prison officers; formal criminal justice proves to be partly ineffective in restoring basic trust between citizens in the aftermath of mass atrocities; efforts made to increase the legal legitimacy of EU institutions fail to create sufficient social legitimacy; the international petition right for individuals encounters a number of obstacles which hamper effective legal protection; patent law is no more an infallible instrument to increase technological innovation; the implementation of human rights standards meets many hurdles in empowering indigenous cultures or in creating a lever for development in third world countries, and so on.

While some contributors made suggestions to improve law's effectiveness, others appeared sceptical that the limits of the law could be overcome. This scepticism extends over our daily experience, since the lives we live and the societies we take part in inform us on a daily basis that we do not have things under control. Our desire for control often generates unforeseeable and undesirable effects. In this way, the bottom line to these 'sceptical' contributions comes down to a simple message: legal fields such as human rights, criminal law, patent law, and so on all *inevitably* fall short in supplying the means to mould the world according to particular designs, because they reflect the *limits of our ability of control.*

This brings us to a more general intuition that was also hinted at in "The Limits of the Law (Introduction)" and one which remained 'beneath the surface' in several chapters: all social practices, including law, unavoidably echo the human condition, including all its potentialities and fragilities. Human beings are endowed with reason, but also bear the marks of inescapable finitude. We obviously all carry in ourselves our own mortality; we all face the limits of our bodily nature and its basic needs; we all experience the unforeseeability of our actions, encounters and events; we all have to reckon with the frailness of our values and deepest commitments; we all know we are dependent on the confrontation with and assessment of others. All these phenomena, which make up the human condition, are well–known, but we tend to forget that quite naturally they are also mirrored in our social practices: in politics, ethics, aesthetics, religion, and, not in the least, in the law.[8] What does it mean then to understand law as expressive of our frail human condition? And how does such understanding of law bear on a 'limits of the law' approach?

In "Labour Law and the Limits of Dogmatic Legal Thinking (Chapter 4), van Putten explicitly addressed the intimate relationship of law as a human enterprise and law as a limited enterprise. Dependence on others, scarcity of resources, inevitable shortcomings in practical knowledge of the world and in conveyance of this knowledge, human opportunism – all these elements constantly hamper the law in its ambition to distribute freedom and opportunities for personal development in a just and equal way. According to van Putten, preoccupation with the limits of the law often issues from an acute awareness of the boundaries of human existence. In fact, these boundaries can generate many obstacles for the law to guarantee the equal distribution of each person's ability to exercise his freedom. The limits we experience are *inescapable limits of the law*, emerging in a social context in which the boundaries of human existence are acutely felt. Van Putten suggests on several occasions that the limited ability of law to serve its basic societal functions comes most acutely to the surface when these boundaries have been neglected all too long in the daily application of the law. We risk proecting much too demanding expectations onto the law and create an acute awareness of law's limits if we refuse to accept that our legal concepts are often too simple to structure the complex chaos of human life. Alternatively, we risk overstretching the regulatory potential of the law if we ignore that enforcement of law is never fully possible, due to scarcity of resources or the opportunism of those enforcing the law.

The argument that legal concepts and legal instruments link up with various aspects of the human condition, and therefore reveal *inescapable limits*, can be refined by indicating what particular aspects of the human condition may produce what particular kind of limits. In what follows a few illustrations will be given, derived from different chapters linking up types of limits with different dimensions of the human condition: human interdependence, the limited capacity of human understanding, the scarcity of resources and, finally, the embodied nature of human existence.

---

8 It is one of the many merits of contemporary philosophy to have spelled out the boundaries of the human condition, and to examine how they affect our ethical and political practices. See for example H. Arendt, *The Human Condition* (Chicago: Chicago University Press, 1958); Martha Nussbaum, *The Fragility of Goodness, Luck and Ethics in Greek Tragedy and Philosophy* (Cambridge: Cambridge University Press, 1995); B. Williams, *Moral Luck* (Cambridge: Cambridge University Press, 1997).

5.2 Human Interdependence and the Limits of the Law

In "Regulating Prison Life: A Case Study of the Inmate Disciplinary Study" (Chapter 8), Robert shows that we should not overrate the regulatory qualities of a detailed, top–down disciplinary system of prison rules which anticipates strict enforcement and full application by correctional officers ("100 % compliance with 100 % of the policies 100 % of the time"). According to Robert, the prison as a 'total institution' is a unique social setting, where circumstances and situations, unlike those in open society, encounter social dynamics that are likewise unusual. Unlike other actors charged with enforcement in other areas of law, correctional officers are permanently controlling prisoners in one closed space during a considerable length of time. In such a setting, the roles and authorities of the correctional officers vary with the specific social relationships in which the prison and its officers are engaged. This specific social setting tells us a good deal about *human interdependence* as one of basic features of our human condition. It fosters an extremely visible manifestation that identities of human persons and their social roles are constructed through the responses and assessments of others. Data on the inmate disciplinary system in Mission Institution further supports the presence of what Robert calls "'the human factor' in the use of inmate discipline". Management at Mission Institution actively encouraged line staff to use their social skills as a means to regulate and control the prison. This was known as "dynamic security" which is exerted through "ongoing interaction, beyond observation, between correctional officers and inmates, working with and speaking with inmates, making suggestions, providing information, and, in general, being proactive". Robert shows that a process of constantly reinventing social roles and identities (which implies a large degree of discretion in the enforcement of prison rulings on behalf of prison officers) sits ill with a top–down approach of strict compliance with a complex set of disciplinary rules. In discretionary rule–enforcement, the power relationships between staff and prisoners are weakened ("cracks in the monolith") *so as to* maintain order and regulate the prison. Hence, there might be other bases of power than law on which prison officers can draw. While discretion allows some COs to under–enforce the rules, the "legitimate authority" of any staff member remains present, as if a kind of substrate of power on which one can draw when other resources tend to fail. Robert's analysis also illustrates how the blindness in top–down regulation to human interdependence eventually generates an even greater gap between 'the rule–book' and social realities. Policy and law, then grow incrementally, until the prison officers' threshold of policy knowledge are surpassed by the increasing volume and changes in correctional policy. "The use of discretion by prison officers in regulating social life of prison seems even more inevitable."

5.3 The Limited Capacity of Human Understanding and the Limits of the Law

Another important aspect of the human condition is the limited capacity of human understanding, especially in relation to the unpredictability and innovative power of human action. These aspects of the human condition were already hinted at in the "The Limits of the Law (Introduction)", when stating that new circumstances and new events can challenge our familiar categories of understanding, even up to a point of the explosion of these categories. A large number of contributors showed how emerging social phenomena reveal conceptual limits of legal categories and instruments.

For example, in "Corporate Wrongdoing and the Limits of the Criminal Law" (Chapter 7), Fenwick shows how a recent wave of corporate scandals confronted criminal lawyers with the limits of traditional criminal law concepts (criminal wrong, criminal legality, criminal responsibility, criminal punishment). Fenwick observes that one of the basic moral intuitions underlying the criminal law is that punishment without fault or, alternatively, punishment which is disproportionate to the degree of fault, is regarded as inappropriate and unjust. Establishing the existence and degree of moral fault is an essential precondition to the application of criminal sanctions if the law is to retain its normative legitimacy. Understandings of corporate wrongdoing, however, are pervaded by various moral ambiguities. In the context of corporate crime it is often difficult to identify in an analytically precise manner whether sufficient fault exists to justify criminalising the conduct, and, perhaps more frequently, what degree of fault exists and what sanction should be applied. As result, lawyers find that cases of corporate criminal liability cannot be subsumed as such under traditional criminal law concepts. Applying the traditional concepts of the criminal law to corporate crime encounters resistance from our moral intuitions involved in using these concepts and in the practice of criminalising human behaviour. It is as if the emergence of corporate scandal on a massive scale urges lawyers and policy–makers to invent new legal instruments. The wave of corporate scandals prompted policy–makers around the world into a systematic reevaluation of regulatory strategies which, in many cases, has resulted in a significantly expanded role for the criminal law in regulating the organisation, financing, and activities of corporations. Fenwick also reviews existing theories for making sense of corporate criminal liability, and suggests it is highly problematic both on conceptual and pragmatic grounds. In the end, techniques of corporate criminal liability (vicarious liability, identification doctrine, aggregation doctrine, risk management mode) fail to make familiar moral intuitions underlying the criminal law operational. Moreover, there are a number of arguments advanced suggesting that such liability does not add anything extra to existing liability strategies, notably corporate civil liability, and that even if a satisfactory doctrinal basis for such liability could be established, it is simply unnecessary.

A second illustration that mirrors the limits of human understanding relates to the implementation of human rights standards and the limited elasticity of its underlying concepts. Where in some contexts (such as in privacy issues) there could be legitimate reasons for further exploring the open texture of human rights standards, issues ranging from the fight against racism, through the respect for indigenous cultures, over to the fight against poverty in third world countries show how straining human rights standards might prove counterproductive, to a degree that it is "even liable to snap right in your face". In "The Limits of Human Rights Protection from the Perspective of Legal Anthropology" (Chapter 21), Deklerck *et al.* remind us how the strong individualistic dimension underpinning human rights standards impose limits on efforts to transpose human rights standards (notably, property rights) on indigenous cultures (and their cosmological beliefs regarding their territories and natural resources). These inescapable conceptual shortcomings urge us to address the issue to what extent human rights might serve as a fruitful framework to improve the position of indigenous cultures.

A similar conceptual difficulty with human rights surfaces in "The Limits of Human Rights Law in Human Development" (Chapter 20). Vandenhole distinguishes several limits of human rights law in the context of human development which can not be easily overcome by conceptual innovation, because of more fundamental limits. One of these fundamental limits comes down to the fact that applying a human rights view in order to address the issue of human development in countries of the Southern Hemisphere implies projecting a basically individualistic approach on fundamentally structural problems. From this incongruity follows that the conceptual language of human rights law cannot be stretched endlessly without becoming self–defeating. Vandenhole makes this point clear by revisiting Social Action Litigation (SAL) of the Indian Supreme Court, a strategy for judicial enforcement of human rights for the Indian poor. This strategy entails a set of techniques of procedural relaxations, involving, amongst others, far–reaching remedial measures which sometimes extend beyond concrete cases "to the whole class of persons on whose behalf the claim was made". In order to be effective, SAL requires a full recognition of judicial activism, which raises issues of legitimacy because it blurs the lines of competence between the judiciary and the legislator. Put in more general terms, before embracing innovative conceptualisations in the judicial enforcement of human rights, one should ask how far judicial activism can be stretched without compromising 'rule of law' values which are conceptually interwoven with a human rights approach.

5.4 Scarcity of Resources and the Limits of the Law

Scarcity of resources is yet another obvious but often silenced determinator of law's fragilities. For example, the limits of human rights become more sharply apparent from the moment we acknowledge that underdeveloped countries lack sufficient resources or a sufficiently equal distribution thereof to create the conditions of possibility for safeguarding socio–economic rights. In "The Limits of the International Petition Right for Individuals: A Case Study of the ECtHR" (Chapter 19), Verrijdt argues that the limited operational capacity of the ECtHR is partly responsible for the limited ability of legal instruments, such as the universal petition right, for effective legal protection. However, increasing the number of judges will in the end only confirm the scarcity of human resources, because more magistrates will inevitably attract more cases. The example of the limits of the international petition right also shows that not only a scarcity of resources but also legal instruments have a diminishing marginal utility. The protective or regulative potentials of legal instruments are in themselves limited, and legal instruments in themselves create limits which surface from an all too abundant use.

This mechanism of marginal utility is evidenced in the universal petition right, but it also remarked upon by other authors in other areas of law. In the criminal law, the limits of the protective potentials of written criminal legislation are revealed by an inflation of criminal offences, diminishing legal certainty instead of creating it. In patent law, the proliferation of patents and licences, driven by consideration of stimulating technological innovation, tends to hamper innovative research. Various scholars warn of the risk that a "dense web of overlapping patents" discourages researchers or companies from developing and commercialising new products.

5.5 The Limits of the Law as a Materially Embodied Practice

It is an undeniable merit of contemporary philosophy to have rediscovered how much our understanding of the world, of others, and ourselves, depends on our being physically involved in the world. Our contingent physical existence determines the perspective from which we look upon the world and act in it, but at the same time, it defines the limitations of our access to the world. This undeniable fact of our human existence reproduces itself in our social practices, including the law. Just as political practices require architectural spaces, buildings, and representations, so too does contemporary law require verbal infrastructures, such as the existence of institutions, and the production and storage of texts. All these different forms and shapes in which these practices find their expression are constitutive for the potential as well as the limits of these practices. Not that we are always aware of these potentials and limits, but they can sharply surface in new historical circumstances, or through new events or technologies which call for new modes of embodiment.

In "Technology and the End of Law" (Chapter 23), Hildebrandt argues that newly emerging technologies prompt us to realise the contingent embodiment of contemporary law, as well as to imagine a new environment for law. As already explained above, the author points to the possible emergence of an Internet of Things, a world where your environment permanently knows where you are, what you do, what you want, and satisfies your needs, life–styles, and specific preferences at the right place and at the right time. This world can be made technologically possible through the interconnectedness of all things. Ubiquitous computing, online databases, and advanced profiling technologies designed to discover relevant patterns of behaviour: all these technological structures would transform the world of things into a complex interactive intelligent environment.

Against the background of this changing technological environment, Hildebrandt shows us how modern law and its regulatory potentials are still conditioned and limited to a great deal by its embedment in a written tradition. Just as the interconnectedness of written texts was constitutive for the shape of modern law, we should now likewise see this Internet of Things as the coming environment of contemporary law, announcing a new embodiment through which the law might acquire new forms and new regulatory potentials. Imagining such a world and its social consequences brings the author to conclude that the absence of a shift from a written legal tradition to a legal practice which is supported by and embodied in the new technologies can possibly lead to the annulment of law's regulatory power, and also its protective one. Written law as such does not provide us anymore with an adequate technological embodiment in order to serve one of the law's most important functions: adequate anticipation of the grounds on which we are judged, included, or excluded.

6 How to Deal Responsibly with the Limits of the Law?

6.1 The Importance of Retrieving the Normative Sources of the Rule of Law

Revisiting the law from a 'limits' perspective requires critical distance, imagination, and careful judgment, but it also calls for a more practical approach. Indeed, the central endeavour behind *Facing the Limits of the Law* not only pertains to the issue of mapping limits, it equally revolves around the issue of managing responsibly these limits. Whereas the "The Limits of the Law (Introduction)" provided a robust conceptual framework for addressing the first issue, almost no tangible tools were offered for the second.

As to this second challenge, numerous authors invented various strategies to address the different types of limits they encountered in their respective legal fields. To that end, they drew inspiration from one of the basic intuitions of this volume: facing the limits of the law necessarily involves a reflexion on our intuitive grasp of the rule of law and of the values and aspirations they embody. In this respect, "The Limits of the Law (Introduction)" offered substantial background in the section entitled "Protective Legality", where some minimum requirements and some ideas and ideals of the rule of law were sketched out. Many elements of this robust account of rule of law (and democracy) can be traced back throughout *Facing the Limits of the Law*. Interestingly, in most of the chapters these elements are not stated bluntly or rehearsed blindly. Instead, the normative sources of the rule of law are patiently retrieved in a diversity of concrete issues, ranging from the legitimacy deficit of the EU to issues of law and technology. The reader also immediately grasps the importance of these efforts of articulation, because they are part of the authors' ambitions to map, assess, and overcome the law's limits. Finally, by taking effort in spelling out their preunderstanding of the rule of law in a specific context, many authors also discovered surprising links between different dimensions of the rule of law. As a result of this, the different chapters offer a plenitude of interesting insights which may sharpen our 'limits of the law' lens.

In her first novel *The Lying Days*, Nadine Gordimer draws the sensual and intellectual emergence of a young girl into womanhood. The story unfolds against the background of South Africa's beginning period of Apartheid and narrates how the events of Gordimer's main character brought her into a new kind of consciousness. They steadily opened her eyes to structural injustice and issues of race in her own society and designed her deepest moral and political commitments regarding democracy, equality, and the rule of law. The novel gives us a clear idea of how it must feel, deep inside ourselves, to be subject to a political regime embodying the denial of the above–mentioned values. A passage at the end of the book beautifully paints this troubling experience. Involved in an emotional discussion with one of her friends, who still believes that political action against the nationalists' regime makes sense, Gordimer's main character lucidely responds:

> Oh politically, yes, I grant that politically we're protesting madly. Even in ordinary private talk we're protesting. But you know that wasn't what I was talking about. It's inside. Inside ourselves in the – what's the word I want – the non–political, the individual consciousness of ourselves in possession of our personal destiny: it's that which we've put aside, laid away, in the lavender; postponed.[9]

The idea that institutional settings to relating democracy and the rule of law also have an inner counterpart that appeals to autonomy and control over our destiny, strongly echoes throughout *Facing the Limits of the Law*. While mapping the limits of European law and the process of European integration, Foqué and Steenbergen understand autonomy as the capability of citizens "to have a reasonable degree of control over their destiny, or at least the comfort that they can identify the forces that are in control." In her search to improve the protective function of the right to privacy, Ieven developed a procedure to reconstruct human rights according to "our moral nature as potentially autonomous human beings". "Human rights are what we owe to each other if this capacity for autonomy is to be realised." In his search to assess the limits of legal dogmatics in labour law, van Putten came to a similar version, when defining autonomy as the human need to be able to determine freely how to act in private and public spheres. Individual freedom is considered to be a *conditio sine qua non* for developing an individual into a human person capable of expressing his uniqueness in the presence of intimate or distant others. Law should then be identified as the mechanism designed for ensuring equal distribution of the capability of each to exercise this individual freedom.

As to the more concrete content of autonomy, some authors discovered a strong link between autonomy and personal identity. Assessing the limits of the criminal law and mapping the complementary merits of restorative justice practices, De-

---

9 N. Gordimer, *The Lying Days* (Jonathan Cape: London, 1953) 291.

klerck defines freedom and autonomy as the capacity, existing in different degrees of intensity, to develop one's future, to integrate a variety of experiences into one's own life–story and to make sense of one's own identity. Hildebrandt adds a more relational dimension to it, when conceiving autonomy as the equal ability of every person to construct one's own identity in continuing confrontation with others. Their gaze is constitutive for our sense of self. But, as marvellously illustrated by Gordimer's novel, equal ability to make sense of our selves and our destinies is not a natural given. It can be gravely distorted, through political regimes and unjust institutions. Essential to the ability of construing one's own identity is the equal and mutual ability of citizens to freely assess and check the expectations of others regarding themselves. Therefore, they should be able to understand and anticipate the expectations of others regarding one self. Being in possession of our personal destiny, to paraphrase Gordimer, requires equal access and control on to the grounds on which we are judged.

Seen from this relational perspective, personal autonomy is dependent on political institutions that are governed by the rule of law, that is, by a coherent set of principles and rights which makes all of us capable of anticipating and assessing the normative standards of those who claim competence in creating these standards. In this respect, privacy rights, due process values, legality, all these cherished rights and principles should be interpreted in order mutually to reinforce each other. This aspiration of the *Rechtsstaat* or rule of law becomes tremendously precious in a changing technological environment. According to Hildebrandt, in such an environment in which human actors are constantly profiled, remedying law's limits implies assessing in each context how law will need to be embodied in adequate technologies in order to guarantee equal access to "the knowledge that informs the decision–making process of those in power".

Many authors remind us that autonomy as one of major sources of the rule of law and of democracy also has an undeniable public dimension. To Hildebrandt, forging our personal identity and, consequently, assessing the grounds on which we are judged strongly connects with the equal ability to speak up freely for one's interests. In the same vain, Dierickxsens, in her search for improving the legitimacy deficit of European institutions, strongly stresses the idea of autonomous citizenship: the mutual capacity to deliberate on the grounds of common action, to express publicly claims of public reason for one's own preferences and to deliver them for assessment of others. If, to paraphrase Gordimer's words, European citizens really want to be "in possession of their personal destinies", then European political institutions should improve their potentials of deliberate citizenship.

6.2 Strategies of Managing Responsibly the Limits of the Law

Retracing the normative sources of democracy and the rule of law and constructing important dimensions of autonomy is an important step in finding responsible ways to deal with limits of the law. But a 'limits of the law' approach also requires the elaboration of a set of strategies to respond to these limitations. Throughout *Facing the Limits of the Law*, at least four strategies can be distinguished around which the separate contributions could be grouped. Coming to the end of our concluding chapter we will flesh these strategies out in the following subsections.

6.2.1 Dedramatising Law's Limits

Several contributors to *Facing the Limits of the Law* suggest not arriving at an all too quick conclusion on the existence of inescapable limits of the law. Just as they came to a more fine–grained typology of law's limits through a careful analysis of some salient features of the law, they reexamined these features in order to assess the seriousness of these limits. They were guided by the intuition that these characteristics, when properly reconsidered, prompt them to dedramatise law's limits in their legal field.

For example, in "Is The Rule of Law a Limit on Popular Sovereignty?" (Chapter 16), Haljan starts from the antinomy between the rule of law and popular sovereignty. In constitutional law, this issue often emerges in discussions around the role of constitutional courts. Haljan tries to deflate this discussion, by bringing it to a deeper level, for the tension between the rule of law and popular sovereignty mirrors a friction between the world of law and the world of political power. Haljan's argument, and thereby his strategy of dedramatising law's limits, is complex. An essential part of his message is that we should not overestimate the difference between the world of law and the world of popular sovereign power, and that, consequently, we should not exaggerate the limited ability of the law to govern popular will. In contrast with the above–mentioned working hypotheses set out in "The Limits of the Law (Introduction)", Haljan argues that, in a tradition of democracy and the rule of law, law and politics are not so different in nature; that clear boundaries are not easily demarcated; and that law is not always ill–suited to regulating the sphere of politics. Instead, these spheres are made of the same conceptual fabric. Through a careful analysis of the concepts of the rule of law, Haljan shows that on a conceptual level the neat boundaries with popular sovereignty are effaced. From the perspective of the addressee, the binding force of the law depends not only on law's formal characteristics, but also on recognition of authority within a power relationship and within a broader social context. This context – Haljan uses the term 'social normativity' – gives shape to this relationship according to certain ideas of justice and fairness, and generates claims of legitimacy regarding this power relationship. According to Haljan, the best claim of legitimacy for the binding force of the law, is that it has been authored by those who are themselves subject to those laws and that it fully honours the capacity of citizens to deliberate in concert on the content of the law. "Normativity resides in popular sovereignty."

The second illustration relates to the open texture of law. Notwithstanding the undeniable fact that law's open texture in many respects reflects the boundaries of human existence and points out to the intrinsic vulnerability of law, a number of authors reexamined this feature of the law in order to dedramatise law's limits. Willems and Loth, for example, consider the open texture of legal concepts and principles in private law as an opportunity to integrate ethical arguments into the adjudicative process, and, consequently, to temper an unjust situation due to gaps in the law or to correct unjust effects resulting from strict application of the law. Ieven and Keirsbilck dedramatise the open texture of human rights provisions or EC general clauses, provided a principled division of labour between institutions can be found regarding creation, interpretation and enforcement of these provisions or clauses.

The third example of dedramatising the law's limits pertains to the 'scientific' nature of the law. Whereas doctrinal concepts and principles, such as 'legality', 'equality', 'proportionality', 'separation of powers', and so on, can easily be seen as too general, abstract, and vague in nature so as to reflect shared common values and meanings, one should, however, not overestimate the dramatic quality of the limits of law's scientific nature. This feature of the law should not necessarily be seen as detrimental to legal protection and the symbolic function, insofar we understand legal concepts as temporary expressions of an "unfolding political narrative"[10], which tries to represent the plurality of common values and shared understandings in the best–balanced and most coherent way. These suggestions, however, require lawyers to incorporate their technical skills in a broader responsibility to elucidate and communicate the normative point of the principles and values underlying these concepts and principles. Legal practitioners then have an important communicative–pedagogical role to be taken seriously.

6.2.2 Constructivism

The most common strategy to manage law's limits responsibly consists of translating these limits in conceptual shortcomings which, in a further step, can be remedied through conceptual refinement. We will term this strategy 'constructivism', referring thereby to an important strand in contemporary political and legal philosophy which seeks within a specific public political and legal culture, and even within the context of a specific case, to provide for the best articulation of the *normative* point of the concepts of law, justice, democracy, and rights, involved in our existing legal and political practices. Constructivism seeks the conception of these concepts that fits best with and gives the best justification for these practices. To quote R. Dworkin, "It points out to the right direction for continuing and developing that practice".[11] Constructivism comprises also an explicit *discursive* dimension. It sets the stage for debate in which different conceptions of law, justice, democracy, and so on compete for the best argued account of these values and practices. The explicitly normative dimension of this strategy and its dependence

---

10 R. Dworkin (1986), *l.c.*, 225.

11 R. Dworkin (1986), *l.c.*, 116.

on an existing political and legal culture explains why many of these contributors made such serious efforts to retrieve the normative sources of the rule of law and democracy, in order to repair specific conceptual shortcomings. The discursive character of constructivism explains why they oppose competing models and visions.

Given the broad reach of this strategy, constructivism has taken many shapes throughout *Facing the Limits of the Law.* Authors like van Putten, Haljan, Ieven, and Loth have chosen to exchange grand old theories of law for better conceptions of law as a strategy to remedy the limits in their legal fields. Van Putten sought a conception of law that allowed for legal pluralism in order to remedy the problematic legal status of collective labour agreements. Haljan discarded legal positivism in order to solve the antinomy between the rule of law and popular sovereignty. Ieven searched for an alternative between legal positivism and a natural law theory in order to improve the power–critical role of human rights, and more particularly the right to privacy. Foqué and Steenbergen archeologically retrieved the implicit political philosophies behind a State–based conception of law, in order to find new paths for a conception of law which fits and justifies the current processes of European integration. And, finally, Loth argued that the 'law in context' approach offers the best possible theory, both in terms of fit and in terms of justification of current legal practice. In this conception of law, the law's limits are fluid and constantly changing depending on context and perspective. Loth contends that we must not stay within the 'inner limits' of legal discourse constituted by traditional legal sources. In their day–to–day work, lawyers and legal scholars (should) deal with hard cases by changing perspectives – from legal dogmatics to economics, ethics, sociology, psychology, or history of law. 'Law in context' advises them not to end up becoming a psychologist, or economist, but to integrate these disciplines in their own legal discourse.

Most of the authors who engaged in a constructivist approach took effort in refining, or unfolding, the normative point of specific concepts, rights, and principles. Hildebrandt focussed on the deeper normative ground of the right to privacy in a changing technological environment. Claes and Krolikowski tried to improve conceptually the principle of legality by adjusting it to the complex nature of adjudication and by better grounding it in human dignity as one of the central values of the rule of law. Keirsbilck and Loth made suggestions for reformulating the ideal of law as integrity: the former purported to bring this ideal in accord with multi–levelled governance within a European constellation; the latter tried to make law as integrity more receptive for an inter–disciplinary approach of law. Van Overwalle and van Zimmeren reexamined the idea of democracy and the prospects of nodal governance in order to improve 'protective legality' in current patent law. Ieven concentrated on the doctrine of the free margin of appreciation as applied in the case–law of the ECtHR regarding the right to privacy. She attempted to tailor a better conception of this doctrine in accordance with a Rawlsian version of constructivism.

One of the attractive features of this constructivist approach is that it is not only confined to legal scholars, but appeals virtually to all legal practitioners, to law–

abiding citizens, and to politicians. In the end, every member of a political community must ask himself what justice requires in particular circumstances according to the values of his political and legal culture. The discursive character of constructivism suggests that, in democracies, all citizens should be able and feel responsible to engage in the political and legal debate around concrete issues according to the best conception of law, justice, and democracy. Take for example the limited capacity of the right to privacy to ensure full legal protection through the case–law of the ECtHR. What makes Ieven's constructivism, as a strategy of remedying these limits, so attractive, is that it also invites the parties in conflict and citizens to discuss the reach of the right of privacy in a particular case, through a 'theatre of public debate' around the principles of justice according to which competence in rights protection should be distributed between domestic legal orders and supra–national jurisdictions.[12]

6.2.3 Striking the Right Balance between the Functions of the Law

The previous strategies seem to suggest that all types of law are in principle reparable, as long as we gather all our reflexive forces to dedramatise these limitations, or to remedy them through conceptual craftship and a sharp sense for the normative sources of our public political and legal culture. But do these Herculian efforts suffice? In the foregoing paragraphs, we have shown how many authors fully acknowledged the fact that law's limits reflect the boundaries of our human existence and, in this way, are somehow inevitable. Reference was made to human interdependence, the limits of human understanding, the limits of our resources and instruments, as well as the physical embodiment of our human practices. How to manage these types of limits? In what follows we will propose a few strategies. Some of them are implicitly present in the contributions, others pop up more frequently throughout the book.

The first, implicit strategy to manage responsibly law's inescapable limits pertains to the institutionalised quality of the law. As already argued in the "The Limits of the Law (Introduction)", and abundantly exemplified in numerous contributions, processes of institutionalisation are often indispensable in order to build up a system of effective legal protection. In order to realise our democratic aspirations, we need a complex system of political checks. In order to protect human rights, we need a complex arsenal of judicial institutions, with a fair division of labour between national and supranational courts. In order to enforce legal norms over citizens and States according to our ideals of the rule of law, we generally do need complex enforcement mechanisms and legal procedures. Institutional complexity results from a range of diverging societal interests (centralisation and de-

12 Compare R. Dworkin (1986), *l.c.* His version of constructivism is closely connected with his ideal of law as integrity, which brings us to interpret constructivism also as a public attitude or civic virtue.

centralisation, homogeneity and diversity) in connection with a far–reaching ambition of regulation in accordance with the rule of law.

What we do need in all this is to recognise fully that institutional settings, just as any other legal instruments, are subject to an economic logic. The institutions' capacity to serve the function of legal protection can encounter a point of saturation, after which new institutional reforms become counterproductive. One possible strategy to remedy this inescapable limit is then to restrain further reform.

Another inescapable limit related to the institutionalised character of law is that complex institutions can easily become a battlefield for the competing societal functions which the law is supposed to serve. As already explained in the "The Limits of the Law (Introduction)", extreme institutional complexity of law, as processed by protective legality, can easily clash with law's function of dispute resolution. Complex institutionalisation can also hamper the symbolic function of law.

Here, the strategy might be to strike the right balance among different functions of law, between the functional need for regulation and protective legality on the one hand, and maintaining the peace–making and symbolic functions on the other. Institutional complexity is justified, if necessary, in virtue of the law's ability to balance a plurality of interests originating from different singular perspectives on the design of the public interest. Institutional restraints should be built in, whenever an increase of institutional complexity proves disproportionate to the legitimate interests underlying law's symbolic function and its function of dispute resolution. Abolishing or unifying different levels of governance is necessary to the extent that the marginal costs of institutional plurality with regard to the aforementioned functions exceeds marginal benefits. We should avoid that too many institutions and too many perspectives render the law unable to represent collective meanings, such that the design of the public interest risks being paralysed. We should also avoid that poorly defined responsibilities of various regulators and supervisors at numerous levels make law unable to serve its function of dispute resolution. In the end, a lack of clarity in the core functions of the institutions is detrimental to both efficiency and legitimacy.

6.2.4 Seeking for Complementarity

Another, more explicitly used strategy strongly pairs with an attitude of modesty relating to the potential of law to serve important functions in society (regulation, symbolisation, dispute resolution and peace–making, protective legality). Vandenhole takes this stance when he pleads for disciplinary modesty in the context of human rights law and human development. In "The Limits of Human Rights Law in Human Development" (Chapter 20), Vandenhole reminds us of the limits of constructivism regarding human rights, because "every attempt at conceptual renovation may be confronted by the more fundamental limits, and will be challenged by them." As an alternative for constructivism, Vandenhole suggests another strategy which also resonates in other contributions. Given the fundamental and insurmountable character of some of the limits of human rights law, "resort may have to be taken to other disciplines in order to further explore and understand them." Vandenhole makes us conscious that, in full awareness of the limits human rights law, other disciplines or human rights strategies could be deployed which – in tandem with the law – could generate better results in realising human development.

More generally, one could consider the complementarity between law on the one hand and other disciplines and social practices on the other, as the keyword for an alternative strategy in managing responsibly the limits of the law. The underlying idea of such a strategy is that the realisation of the normative sources of the rule of law and of democracy is not exhausted by our familiar legal practices and instruments. Albeit in different ways, other social and cultural practices are also embodying these sources. The strategy would then consist of clearly examining both the potentials and the limits of the law and of other practices with regard to these normative aspirations and values, and, at a further stage, imagining how these practices could mutually reinforce one another. Both Deklerck and Valiñas engage in such a thought experiment when assessing the complementary role of restorative justice practice in interpersonal conflicts, as well as during the aftermath of mass atrocities. The line of argument appears to be quite similar in "Restorative Justice, Freedom, and the Limits of the Law (Chapter 11)" and "Rebuilding Trust in the Former Yugoslavia: Overcoming the Limits of the Formal Justice System" (Chapter 10). It divides into three stages.

In the first stage, both authors define criminality in light of the values they brought to the fore. Deklerck stresses that delinquency should be primarily understood as an act that often reveals the impaired narrative identity (of the offender) and that always engenders to some degree an impaired narrative of self as an extant cost for the victim. In a similar vein, Valiñas understands mass violence in terms of inflicting serious damage to basic social trust. Whereas for Deklerck an appropriate response to criminality and its aftermath should always entail strategies for restoring narrative selves as essential ingredient of personal autonomy, Valiñas argues that rebuilding social trust among those who were on conflicting sides constitutes one of the "major challenges faced in the wake of mass violence".

In the second stage, Valiñas and Deklerck examine the potentials and limitations of the law regarding the restoration of personal freedom, or the rebuilding of social trust. Deklerck's diagnosis sounds quite sceptical in this regard, because the institutional settings, legal principles, and basic rights on which the criminal law is construed, can only create the preconditions for a restoration of personal autonomy. As part of a complex web of institutions and formal practices, and exhibiting predominantly instrumental reasoning, law in itself is not equipped for triggering processes of enlarging freedom. Valiñas grants a more substantial role to law in rebuilding social trust. She acknowledges that law is a system of rules and principles designed for maintaining the rebuilding conditions to basic trust in a community. Subsequently, she identifies law's capacity "to provide an official and authoritative type of acknowledgment that certain violations took place and that they are wrong." Law, and more particularly the judicial practice of the courts, also serve here as a medium through which fundamental values are reaffirmed, and a commitment is expressed to uphold these values in the future. When examining law's potentials for rebuilding social trust in the context of the International Criminal Tribunal for Yugoslavia, Valiñas, however, encounters several limits to the judicial practice of criminal courts. The distance between officials and the people concerned, the exclusive focus on individual criminal responsibility, and concern for factual truth (which easily attracts controversy), all these elements which are bound up with criminal proceedings risk producing further social division instead of contributing to social trust.

In the third, and last stage, which is presented as a strategy to remedy law's limits, Deklerck as well as Valiñas praise the complementary potentials of restorative justice practices. In such practices victims and offenders enter a process of dialogue to deal with the aftermath of crime. Both parties are offered equal space to tell each other how the facts entered their personal lives. Restorative justice aims here at inclusion, empowerment, and the participation of both parties, who are given full opportunity to be heard in their story of the facts and to deliberate on an appropriate answer to the inflicted injustice. Deklerck sees in this narrative component of mediation an important complementary answer to criminal wrongdoing that remedies the law's limits with regard to restoring personal autonomy. Equally enabling the stakeholders in the conflict to tell their own story is more likely to trigger a process of restoring their capacity to reconstruct their own narrative identities. Valiñas, from her side, values the establishment of narrative truth in restorative dialogue as an essential condition for basic trust. "The very fact that those affected participate in the process … hold a greater promise that the 'truth' that will emerge be more easily accepted and even internalised than as a result of judicial processes."

6.2.5 How to Manage the Tragic Quality of the Law?

Trying to build up joint ventures with other practices still presupposes that there are somewhere out there remedies to overcome law's limits. But how to manage responsibly these limits when no such solutions can be found? Close examination of some basic features of the law in "The Limits of the Law (Introduction)" and the idea that law reflects the boundaries of our human condition, suggest that such possibilities can always arise. In such situations law takes then a 'tragic quality' in the sense that its actors (legal scholars, citizens, judges, politicians) are driven to a position of passivity, and of recognition of their own vulnerability with regard to their roles and responsibilities. At the end of this chapter, two examples will be given which point in the direction of the law's tragic quality. In both cases, the attitudes or strategies displayed, whether it be mild irony or commitment to a specific value, all express a strong awareness of the vulnerability of our assessments, choices, and actions in law.

In "Darknets and the Future of Freedom of Expression in the Information Society" (Chapter 25), Graux ends up with an unresolved puzzle. On the one hand, Graux suggests that rather than attempting to eliminate a new and problematic situation in a virtual environment, an alternative approach to the phenomenon of darknets might be for society itself to adapt its perception of information to the new state of the game. Perhaps information itself should not be considered to be valuable, but rather the application of this information. Not the bits and bytes as such, but the way in which they are manipulated and presented offers value to end–users. But, on the other hand, Graux fully admits the vulnerability of the foregoing suggestion. Reappraising the value of information is a fundamental philosophical change that is unlikely to be welcomed by any modern society, not in the least because of its far–reaching moral and economical implications. Indeed, in a late–modern society a sufficient framework of common norms and ideals seems to be becoming increasingly unrealistic.

The second example, revolves around the limits of legal reasoning. In "The Limits of the Law (Introduction)", it was argued that due to open texture, the argumentative character, and the interplay of principles and fundamental rights, legal practitioners can always be confronted with extremely difficult assessments between concurring legal principles or fundamental rights, where in the end there seems to be as many reasonable arguments in favour of one principle (right) as there are in favour of another concurring principle (right).

Insofar no extra–legal arguments provide any useful help, legal practitioners should avoid in any case that the dynamics of argumentative refinement take unreasonable proportions, *e.g.* when previous decisions are all too frequently reconsidered or when decisions are endlessly postponed. The only real plausible answer to the law's limits for judges and lawyers seems to be to embrace legal modesty and to somehow evoke the vulnerability of the grounds on which the decisions rest. According to Cappelletti,

> [a good judge is] one who is aware of the above limits and weaknesses and sensitive to those many circumstances which might advise restraint in some periods, areas and cases, and boldness in others.[13]

[13] See M. Cappelletti, "The Law–Making Power of the Judge and its Limits: A Comparative Analysis", *Monash University Law Review* 1981–1982, 51.

List of Contributors

Erik Claes (°1968) is Professor of Law at the Faculty of Law, University of Leuven. His main research areas are theory of adjudication, philosophy of criminal law, penal theory, and restorative justice. His Ph.D. thesis in law, defended at the University of Leuven, *Legality and Adjudication in the Criminal Law* (Leuven: Universitaire Pers Leuven, 2003) was awarded the Fernand Collin Prize for Law in 2002. He is contributing editor with R. Foqué and T. Peters of *Punishment, Restorative Justice and the Rule of Law* (Antwerp/Oxford: Intersentia, 2004) and recently with A. Duff and S. Gutwirth of *Privacy and the Criminal Law* (Antwerp/Oxford: Intersentia, 2006).

Tom Daems (°1978) is a postdoctoral researcher of the University of Leuven Research Fund, at the Department of Criminal Law and Criminology. He is co–editor with Ivo Aertsen and Luc Robert of *Institutionalizing Restorative Justice* (Willan Publishing, 2006) and with Luc Robert of *Zygmunt Bauman. De schaduwzijde van de vloeibare moderniteit* (Boom Juridische Uitgevers, 2007), and editor of *FATIK. Tijdschrift voor Strafbeleid en Gevangeniswezen,* a journal on prisons and penal policy, published by the Flemish League of Human Rights.

Bram Delbecke (°1980) studied history and law at the University of Leuven. Since 2003, he is a Ph.D. candidate at the University of Leuven, Campus Kortrijk, working in the field of legal history, specifically Roman law and the history of public law. His research topics are press offences, jury trials, and the magistracy in 19th and 20th century Belgium.

Johan Deklerck (°1959) is Professor of Criminology at the Leuven Institute of Criminology (LINC), Faculty of Law, University of Leuven, and responsible of the Academic Teaching Training Programme Criminological Sciences. He is coordinator of the LINC Research Line 3 (youth, delinquency, prevention). His main research themes are: youth and delinquency, prevention, safety, restorative justice and mediation, fundamental criminological theory. In addition, he is a staff member of the *Master Européen en Médiation,* coordinated by the Institut Universitaire K. Boesch, Sion, Switzerland.

Stijn Deklerck (°1977) is affiliated with the Faculty of Law (Institute for Migration Law and Legal Anthropology) of the University of Leuven, where he currently teaches Modern Chinese Law. His main research areas are Chinese Law and legal culture, human rights in China, and civil society in China.

Ellen Desmet (°1979) studied law and obtained a Master of Cultures and Development Studies at the University of Leuven and Development Cooperation at the University of Ghent. Since 2005, she is preparing a Ph.D. thesis on the relationship between nature conservation and the rights of indigenous peoples and local communities, from a legal anthropological and human rights perspective (Institute for Migration Law and Legal Anthropology). The research is funded by a grant of the Flemish Interuniversity Council (VLIR–UOS).

Wouter Devroe (°1967) is Professor of Law and Vice–Dean Research at the Faculty of Law, University of Leuven, where he teaches public economic law, comparative law, and *ius commune europaeum.* He teaches European competition law at the Law Faculty of the University of Maastricht. He is attorney at the Brussels bar (Allen & Overy LLP). He previously clerked at the European Court of Justice and served as an expert member at the Belgian national competition authority. He studied law in Leuven (University of Leuven, lic. jur. 1990, summa cum laude), Heidelberg (Ruprecht–Karls Universität, 1989–1990, Erasmus) and Chicago (Northwestern University, LLM 1991, Fulbright Scholarship). Publications focus on national, comparative and European economic law.

Stefanie Dierckxsens (°1978) is a Ph.D. candidate at the Centre for Legal Theory and Legal Philosophy, University of Leuven. She studied political science at the Universities of Antwerp and Leuven (lic. 2001, magna cum laude) and applied ethics at the University of Leuven (Masters, 2003, magna cum laude). From 2001 to 2003, she was engaged in the Flemish Community project, "Preparation of the Flemish Viewpoints for the Intergovernmental Conference 2004" under direction of Prof. dr. K. Lenaerts. Her research focuses on the legitimising capacity of parliamentarism and constitutionalism in the European integration process.

Mark Fenwick (°1968) is Associate Professor at the Faculty of Law of Kyushu University (Japan) and part time Lecturer at the Faculty of Law at the Seinan University (Japan). He was awarded a Ph.D. by Cambridge University (Faculty of Law) in 1995 for his thesis, *Knowledge and Passion: A Critical Exploration of the Affective Dimension of the Criminological Field.* He has published numerous articles in the field of youth criminology, cultural criminology, crime control and transitional justice. He wrote a chapter on "Youth Crime and Crime Control in Contemporary Japan", for *The Blackwell's Companion to Criminology*, edited by C. Summer, Oxford: Blackwell (forthcoming).

Marie–Claire Foblets (°1959) Lic.Iur., Lic.Phil., Ph.D. Anthrop. (Leuven, Belgium). She is Professor ordinarius of Law and Anthropology at the Universities of Leuven (Institute for Migration Law and Legal Anthropology), Brussels and Antwerp, member of the Flemish Royal Academy of Sciences and honorary member of the Brussels bar. She received the Francqui Prize 2004 (Human Sciences). She has done extensive research and published widely on issues of immigration, integration and nationality law in Belgium. In the field of anthropology of law, her research focuses on the application of Islamic family laws in Europe, *inter alia*: M.–C. Foblets, *Les familles maghrébines et la justice en Belgique. Anthropologie ju-*

ridique et immigration (Paris: Karthala, 1994); M.–C. Foblets (ed.), *Familles – Islam – Europe. Le droit confronté au changement* (coll. Musulmans d'Europe) (Paris: L'Harmattan, 1996); M.–C. Foblets (ed.), *Femmes marocaines et conflits familiaux en immigration. Quelles solutions juridiques appropriées?* (Antwerp: Maklu, 1998); M.–C. Foblets and J.Y. Carlier, *Le nouveau Code marocain de la famille. Son application en Europe* (Brussels: Bruylant, 2005); M.–C. Foblets, *Culturen voor de rechter* [*Cultures Before the Courts*], Antwerp, Maklu (forthcoming).

René Foqué (°1946) is Professor of Legal Theory and Legal Philosophy at the Law Faculties of the University of Leuven and of the Erasmus University Rotterdam. He is a correspondent member of the Dutch Academy of Sciences. His main publications cover the domains of legal philosophy and of criminal law theory. His recent research interests are in the areas of the foundations of human rights and of international law.

Hans Graux (°1979) is an IT lawyer at the Brussels bar and a partner in the IT law firm time.lex. He is an Associate Researcher at the Interdisciplinary Centre for Law and Information Technology (www.icri.be), University of Leuven. He studied law (Masters in Law, 2002) and obtained a complementary degree in Informatics at the University of Leuven in 2003.

David Haljan (°1968) is a research fellow with the Institute of Constitutional and Administrative Law, University of Utrecht, and with the Institute for Constitutional Law, University of Leuven. A graduate of Osgoode Hall, Toronto (LLB, 1991) and King's College, University of London (LLM, 1995), he specialised in commercial and administrative law litigation. He obtained a Ph.D. (Laws) from the University of Leuven in 2007 based on his thesis, *The Justiciability of Secession? A Theoretical Foundation for Constitutional Association and Disassociation.* He has published a number of articles, notes, and reviews.

Mireille Hildebrandt (°1958) is a senior Lecturer in Law and Legal Theory and Dean of Education for the Research School on Safety and Security at the Erasmus University Rotterdam. She has been seconded as senior researcher to the Institute of Law, Science, Technology, and Society (LSTS) at the Vrije Universiteit Brussels on a GOA project on "Law and Autonomic Computing: Mutual Transformations". She participates in the EU–funded network of excellence on the "Future of Identity in Information Society (FIDIS)" as work–package leader on profiling technologies. Her research interests include criminal law, the relationship between law and technology, legal philosophy, and the philosophy of technology.

Aagje Ieven (°1977) is a Ph.D. candidate at the Centre for the Study of the Foundations of Law, University of Leuven. She is working towards a Ph.D. thesis on privacy rights as human rights. From January to June 2007 she was a Visiting Scholar at the Centre for the Study of Human Rights of Columbia University (New York) on a Fulbright scholarship. She is a member of the editorial board of *Tijdschrift voor Mensenrechten*, a human rights periodical, and of the board of directors of Amnesty International. She studied medicine in Leuven (B.Med., 1998) and philosophy in Leuven and Nijmegen (M.Phil., 2002).

Bert Keirsbilck (°1980) is a Ph.D. candidate at the Faculty of Law of the University of Leuven (under a grant from the Science Research Fund (FWO) – Flanders). He studied law and philosophy at the University of Leuven (lic.iur. 2003; lic.phil. 2004). He is currently preparing a doctoral thesis on the harmonised law of unfair commercial practices and its interaction with competition law after modernisation. His publications focus on European economic law and comparative law.

Michal Krolikowski (°1972) is an Assistant Professor in the Comparative Criminal Law Division of the University of Warsaw (since 2005) and Head of the Office for Research with the Polish Parliament (since 2006). He has completed courses in Jurisprudence, Criminal Justice and Penal Policy at the Centre of Criminology of the University of Sheffield (2001) and a program at the Centre for American Studies of the Florida State University and the University of Warsaw (2000). In 2001 he obtained a M.L.A. in Law at the University of Warsaw and in 2004 a Ph.D. in legal science. During 2005–2006 he was a research fellow at the Cardiff Law School, and the Department of Philosophy of the University of Stirling. Among his recent publications are, *Just Punishment in Liberal Democracies* (C.H. Beck, 2005) and *Principle of Proportionality in European Corpus Iuris* (Warsaw, 2004). He is also editorial secretary of "Ius et Lex" (since 2001).

Joke Kusters (°1978) studied law at the University of Antwerp and Social and Cultural Anthropology at the University of Leuven. Since 2001, she is a Ph.D. candidate at the University of Antwerp, working in the field of legal anthropology. Her main research areas are the Jewish communities of Antwerp and the State legal approach of Romani culture.

Marc A. Loth (°1956) is Dean and full time Professor of Jurisprudence and Legal Theory at the Law School of Erasmus University Rotterdam. His main research areas are the theory of adjudication, professional ethics, legal methodology, the legal professions and the judiciary. After he wrote his Ph.D. thesis on the relevance of analytical theory of action for the theory of liability in law (1988), he switched from the university to the judiciary. He was a judge in The Hague, the Dutch Antilles, and is now still part time judge in The Hague and Amsterdam. Besides, he is a member of the national selection committee for judges in the Netherlands. He has been a member of several advisory commissions (for example on the future of the Bar). He has published on law and language, legal concepts, private law (Dutch and Antillean), legal ethics and legal methodology. He has lectured in the Dutch Antilles, China, Indonesia, the Czech Republic, the United States and France.

Luc Robert (°1977) is a Ph.D. candidate at the Department of Criminal Law and Criminology, University of Leuven. He is co–editor with Ivo Aertsen and Tom Daems of *Institutionalizing Restorative Justice* (Willan Publishing, 2006) and with Tom Daems of *Zygmunt Bauman. De schaduwzijde van de vloeibare moderniteit* (Boom Juridische Uitgevers, 2007). He is also an editor of *FATIK. Tijdschrift voor Strafbeleid en Gevangeniswezen*, a journal on prisons and penal policy, published by the Flemish League of Human Rights, and editorial secretary of *Panopticon. Tijdschrift voor strafrecht, criminologie en forensisch welzijnswerk*, one of the leading journals in Flanders on Criminal Law and Criminology.

Tom Ruys (°1981) is since October 2004 a Ph.D. candidate at the Institute for International Law of the University of Leuven, under a grant from the Research Foundation Flanders (FWO) – Flanders. He studied law and political science at the University of Gent and holds an LLM in Public International Law from the University of Nottingham. His research focuses on international law on the use of force and collective security arrangements. His recent publications include: J. Wouters, F. Hoffmeister, and T. Ruys (eds.), *The United Nations and the European Union: An Ever Stronger Partnership* (TMC Asser Press, 2006).

Cedric Ryngaert (°1978) is a Lecturer in Public International Law at the University of Utrecht. He was a research fellow at the Institute of International Law of the University of Leuven from October 2002 through September 2006. He was a visiting researcher at Harvard Law School in 2005, and an assistant public prosecutor from October 2006 through December 2006.

Jacques Steenbergen (°1949) is Professor of European Competition Law at the Law Faculty of the University of Leuven. He is Director–General in the Belgian Competition Authority since 2007. Before joining the Authority, he was partner at Allen & Overy LLP. He practiced at the Bar of Brussels from 1979–1982 and from 1984 to 2007 where he started as a trainee of Prof. P. van Ommeslaghe. He was from 1982 to 1986 référendaire to the President of the Court of Justice of the European Communities in Luxembourg, Prof. J. Mertens de Wilmars. He is editor in chief of the Dutch–Belgian review on European law *SEW* and member of the Round table working party of the Ministry of Economic Affairs for the evaluation and modernisation of Belgian economic law. His main publications cover the domains of European and competition law. He lectured, gave conferences and seminars or served as member of nomination or Ph.D. examination committees in various universities or academies of science in Austria, Belgium, China, France, Germany, Hungary, Italy, the Netherlands, Spain, the United Kingdom and the United States. He defended his Ph.D. thesis at the K.U. Leuven (on legal remedies and ailing industries, directed by Prof. W. van Gerven) where he obtained his masters degree in law (licentiaat) and his bachelors degrees in law, philosophy and economics at the University of Antwerp.

Marta Valiñas (°1980) holds a graduate degree in Law (2002) from the Faculty of Law, University of Porto (Portugal) and the European Master's Degree in Human Rights and Democratization (2004) during which she wrote her Master's thesis on "The Position of the Victim in Truth and Reconciliation Commissions: The Case of Peru". In October 2004 she was appointed full–time researcher in a four–year research project on "Restorative Justice and Mass Victimization. Case studies in Serbia and Bosnia and Herzegovina", funded by and carried out at the Faculty of Law of the University of Leuven, where she is also a Ph.D. candidate. As part of this project, she has conducted extensive field research in Serbia and Bosnia and Herzegovina. She has also been a member of the COST Action 21 (Restorative Justice Developments in Europe) from February 2006 onwards. Her work has mainly focused on human rights, transitional justice, and restorative justice in diverse contexts such as former Yugoslavia, Peru, Guatemala, and the Democratic Republic of Congo.

Wouter Vandenhole (°1970) holds the UNICEF Chair in Children's Rights at the University of Antwerp. He is also a senior researcher at the Centre for Transboundary Legal Development, University of Tilburg and a research fellow at the University of Leuven. He graduated in law at the University of Leuven, obtained an LLM in Law in Development from the University of Warwick, and holds a Ph.D. from the University of Leuven. He has previously held positions at the University of Leuven and at the European Master's Degree in Human Rights and Democratisation (Venice, Italy). His research interests include human rights, in particular economic, social and cultural rights, and the relationship between human rights law and development. He is the author of *Non–Discrimination and Equality in the View of the UN Human Rights Treaty Bodies* (Antwerp: Intersentia, 2005) and *The Procedures Before the UN Human Rights Treaty Bodies: Divergence or Convergence?* (Antwerp: Intersentia, 2004), and has co–edited *Protocol No. 14 and the Reform of the European Court of Human Rights* (Antwerp: Intersentia, 2005).

Geertrui Van Overwalle (°1958) is Senior Research Fellow at the Centre for Intellectual Property Rights (CIR), University of Leuven. She is Professor of Intellectual Property Law at both the University of Leuven and the Université de Liège. She is also Professor of Law at the University of Brussels, where she teaches plant breeder's rights law. She has been visiting Professor at the United Nations University (2000–2003) and Monash University (2003). She has authored numerous articles and monographs in the field of patent law and patent law in genetics, in a national and international context. At present she is directing a research project on "Gene Patents and Public Health", funded by the Science Research Fund (FWO) – Flanders and the Sixth Framework Programme of the European Union (Eurogentest). This research resulted in a major publication on "Models for Facilitating Access to Patents on Genetic Inventions" (G. Vanoverwalle, E. Van Zimmeren, B. Verbeure, and G. Matthijs, *Nature Review Genetics* 7, 2006, 143–148). She is a member of the Belgian High Council for Intellectual Property, the Belgian High Council for Plant Breeder's Rights and of the Belgian

Council for Bioethics. She is also a member of the European Commission's Expert Group on Biotechnological Inventions.

Mathieu van Putten (°1977) studied law at the University of Leuven. Since 2001, he is a Ph.D. candidate at the Institute for Labour Law, University of Leuven, working in the field of labour and employment law. His research topics are *inter alia* discrimination law and the legal conception of the firm in labour and employment law.

Esther van Zimmeren (°1978) is a Research Fellow at the Centre for Intellectual Property Rights (CIR), University of Leuven since September 2004. For the last two years she has been working on the project "Gene Patents and Public Health". In October 2006, she was awarded a grant from the Science Research Fund (FWO) – Flanders to start her Ph.D. research on the interface between patent and competition law with a focus on public health issues. From September 2002 until August 2004 she clerked with the Dutch judge Mr. A.W.H. Meij at the Court of First Instance of the European Communities in Luxembourg. She studied both European and International law (summa cum laude) and Dutch law (with a specialisation in international private law) at the University of Tilburg (summa cum laude), and received an LL.M. in European and Intellectual Property law (cum laude), from the University of Leuven. Her publications focus on licensing practices and new licensing models in the area of genetics.

Willem Verrijdt (°1981) is a Legal Secretary at the Belgian Constitutional Court and a Ph.D. candidate at the Institute for Constitutional Law at the University of Leuven, where he teaches tutorials and seminars in constitutional law. His Ph.D. research involves the right to petition for individuals and the increasing backlog at the ECtHR. His publications also address the Belgian "Genocide Law", the retroactive entry into force of laws, the right to a judgment within a reasonable delay before the Belgian Courts, and the jurisprudence of the Belgian Constitutional Court and the ECtHR.

Jogchum Vrielink (°1976) is a Ph.D. candidate at the University of Leuven (Institute for Migration Law and Legal Anthropology). His research areas include discrimination law; racism, anti–semitism and homophobia and the law; freedom of speech and hate speech. Amongst other things he co–authored a handbook on discrimination law (Mechelen: Kluwer 2005).

Kurt Willems (°1982) is a Ph.D. candidate with the Faculty of Law, University of Leuven. He studied law at the University of Leuven (Masters in Law, 2005, magna cum laude) and at the University of Sheffield (2003–2004, Erasmus). Currently he is preparing a doctoral thesis on the 'natural obligation' (*obligatio naturalis*). His publications deal mainly with the law of obligations.

GPSR Compliance

The European Union's (EU) General Product Safety Regulation (GPSR) is a set of rules that requires consumer products to be safe and our obligations to ensure this.

If you have any concerns about our products, you can contact us on ProductSafety@springernature.com

In case Publisher is established outside the EU, the EU authorized representative is:

Springer Nature Customer Service Center GmbH
Europaplatz 3
69115 Heidelberg, Germany

Batch number: 10755248

Printed by Printforce, the Netherlands